D0915274

GALILEE

FROM
ALEXANDER THE GREAT
TO
HADRIAN

UNIVERSITY OF NOTRE DAME
CENTER FOR THE STUDY OF
JUDAISM AND CHRISTIANITY
IN ANTIQUITY

Number 5

GALILEE

FROM
ALEXANDER THE GREAT
TO HADRIAN

323 B.C.E. to 135 C.E.

A Study of Second Temple Judaism

By Seán Freyne

Copublished by

Michael Glazier, Inc.

and

University of Notre Dame Press

Carlyle Campbell Library
Meredith College
Raleigh, N. C.

First published in 1980 by

Michael Glazier, Inc.,
1210 King Street,
Wilmington, Delaware 19801

and

University of Notre Dame Press
Notre Dame, Indiana 46556

Copyright © 1980 by Seán Freyne

Library of Congress: 79-57485

ISBN: 0-89453-099-2 (Michael Glazier, Inc.)

ISBN: 0-268-01002-1 (Notre Dame Press)

Printed in the United States of America

TABLE OF CONTENTS

113347

INTRODUCTION

A s this study has been taking shape over the past several years numerous colleagues in the fields of New Testament and related areas have looked at me quizzically on hearing that I was engaged in a study of Galilean Judaism. Yet I have repeatedly found remarks of eminent scholars commenting on the absence of a complete monograph on Galilean Judaism, implying that such a study could shed important light on the origin and development of primitive Christianity. Professor Martin Hengel, the director of the Institutum Judaicum of the University of Tübingen, has written: 'Eine Geschichte Galiläas zwischen Alexander und Bar Kochba wäre ein dringendes Erfordernis, nicht zuletz, um unbegründete Spekulationen über das frühe 'galiläische Christentum' zurechtzurücken.' However, it was not Professor Hengel's written words but his spoken suggestion that prompted me to undertake the present study, while enjoying the luxury of a Forschungsstipendium from the Alexander von Humboldt Stiftung at Tübingen from 1972-4. Professor Hengel's encouragement and helpful criticism during that period and since have for me been a genuine example of that community of learning that is often spoken of but all too rarely experienced. His own monumental studies, *Die Zeloten* (1960) and *Judentum und Hellenismus* (1968) had laid the remote and more immediate groundwork for such an undertaking and those who are familiar with the latter work will readily recognize its influence on the layout and approach of this present study.

A number of other scholars have already dealt with Galilean life and times from one or other perspective. In particular the series of essays by Albrecht Alt, entitled, 'Galiläische Problemen', helped to direct my focus to historical geography as a solid starting point on which to build any hypothesis about the social and religious life of the area. Ernst Lohmeyer's *Galiläa und Jerusalem* (1936) did not stand up to the critical analysis of scholars, yet the question he posed concerning the possibility of a pluralism, even rivalry, between early Christian communities that were geographically distinct, is a very live one today, and had to be addressed eventually in this study also. It seemed a better methodology, however, to first paint the larger picture as sharply and accurately as possible, before later attempting to sketch in the details of Christianity. Among earlier Jewish scholars, the writings of A. Büchler and S. Klein have special relevance for our topic even when today the use of literary and historical criticism calls for a different evaluation of the material they have collected. On the other hand Christian writing on Galilee has often been influenced, either consciously or sub-consciously by the quest for the historical Jesus, and as a result has for the most part adopted a too narrow approach.

Perhaps more significant than previous studies in shaping my approach has been the repeated cataloguing of certain themes, some of them having virtually attained the status of axioms, in regard to Galilean life in all the secondary literature. 'Galilee of the Gentiles', the hot-bed of a revolutionary ideology, hellen-ization as a result of the cities, the Galileans' disregard for Torah - these and other generalities were repeated so frequently that it seemed to be a worthwhile project to test their accuracy and probe their likelihood from several different perspectives.

The political, social and religious aspects of life are normally so interwoven in any community that the isolation of any one of them to the exclusion of the others can easily lead to distortion. This observation may help to explain why our study has a three-tiered structure, beginning with a brief recapitulation of the main geographical features that were likely to shape the manner and method of human settlement in the area (chapter 1). The *political* situation of Galilee was and remained that of an out-lying region rather than an independent state, yet this circum-stance itself raises many questions. Why did Galilee not have any independent political will of its own? Was the rise of the Jewish state in Hasmonaean times welcomed there? What, if any, were the residual loyalties from Israelite times, given the chequered history of the north? (chapter 2). How did Galilee respond to the intervention of Rome and the rise of the Herods? Did the absence of Roman provincial rule - or should I say, misrule - until a relatively late date in the first century bring about a dif-ferent political climate there to that of Judaea proper? What part did Galilee play in the two revolts against Rome? (chapter 3). These were some of the questions that emerged from a reading of the general history of the times focused specifically on this territory, with its own problems and circumstances. It came as quite a revelation to see how that general history was itself illumined by a concentration on one apparently remote area.

The recurrence of certain topics in the literature determined which aspects of the *social life* were most important and likely to shed light on the ethos of the province as a whole. The multifaceted phenomenon of hellenization as a major shift in civilization created new tensions, presented new possibilities and challenged the old order in so many different ways. For Galilee, the rise of the cities in a 'circle' around it, giving new relevance to an old name, was the most obvious indication of the changing times. Did the cities really function as agents of social change in Galilee, and if so how deep-seated was that change likely to have been? If the language became Greek was the pattern of ideas radically altered also, or were there conservative agents operative and likely to act as counters to the new mood? (chapter 4). If the cities were the most obvious sign of the times, the economic realities were likely to be the more far reaching since these touched the heart of rural Galilee also. In this regard the question of land-ownership becomes one of prime importance, not only because of its religious connotation but also because of its relative fertility. Was the peasant class totally wiped out by the increased and more stringent tax system, and did a new middle class emerge as a result of the commercial and technical possibilities? (chapter 5). Hengel's study, *Judentum und Hellenismus*, has shown how the Hellenistic reform had made Palestinian Judaism particularly sensitive to any possible threat to its identity, and the economic and social realities have been frequently represented as the reason for the Zealotism of the province, typified by the founder of the Fourth Philosophy, Judas the Galilean. Yet the political history had indicated that relatively speaking, Galilee had fared rather better than other regions under Roman and Herodian rule. How revolutionary was Galilee? becomes a natural question, therefore (chapter 6). In particular what was the nature of the violence that erupted there from time to time? Did it have an ideological base in the Fourth Philosophy? If not was there any other particular focal point within Galilean life that might have acted as the catalyst that could have ignited the passions of the population at large and embroiled them in a bloody but noble confrontation with

the Imperial power? Or is this a correct interpretation of the
Galilean involvement in the revolt? In attempting to answer
such questions as these, it became obvious that the current opinion about the nature and extent of revolutionary concerns in
Galilee needs to be seriously nuanced, if not modified, in order
to do justice to the probabilities of the situation.

Conceived in the broadest terms as world-view, *religion*
can be the cement which holds together the structure of life in an
area, yet paradoxically is itself shaped by all the human factors
in which it subsists. This reflection became the focal point of
the final section of the study. Did the history of Galilee make it
particularly susceptible to the religious syncretism of the hellenistic age? What was the extent of Galilean attachment to the
temple, the central symbol of Jewish religious life and worship?
Did that symbol and its ritual provide any special support to
the Galileans in their unique, 'fringe' situation, and how did
that situation determine their perception of the meaning of
the temple's symbolism? (chapter 7). Side by side with the temple
and as a replacement for it, after its destruction, Judaism had
been developing what one of its sages was to call 'the other way'
of the *halakhah*, which attempted to extend the holiness of the
temple to the everyday. Galilee's ignorance of and non-concern
for this way was already proverbial in the Talmuds. The obvious
question is why this reluctance, given the loyal attachment to
the Jewish faith? Did the destruction of the temple create new
possibilities and opportunities for the sages and a greater concern
on the part of the Galileans? Or were there still alternative religious options within Judaism that could bring the holiness
of the temple near? (chapter 8). One possible answer to this
question is Christianity, seeing that its founder was a Galilean
Jew, and the region looms large in the documents which expressed the Christian community's memory of Jesus and his
meaning for life. Was the fate of Christianity in Galilee similar
to that of its founder or did the new religion, in one or other of
the varied forms in which it was soon to emerge, succeed in
making a sizable impact within the province? What, if any, effect
did the turmoil of the post-70 situation have on this movement -
in a word could Galilee tolerate Gospel and Mishnah?

Asking the right questions from history can be a rewarding
experience or a futile exercise, depending on how adequate the

sources are to yield up the secrets of the past in the areas under scrutiny. No startlingly new sources are at hand for a study of Galilean life, and some may be justifiably sceptical of the enterprise, however well meaning, for lack of sufficient hard data. However, a number of developments suggest that the difficulties are not insurmountable and that this may be an opportune time for a fresh evaluation of the data already in our posession. In terms of literary sources Josephus' writings and the Gospels are of primary importance, yet the problems of using either as reliable historical documents are well known. In regard to the former it seems legitimate to speak of a renaissance in Josephan studies, at least to the point that the tendentiousness of his various writings is being more clearly recognized and so need not preclude us from using them in historical reconstruction. Critical caution rather than dismissive casting aside seems to be the correct scientific approach, especially where Josephus' own interests are at stake, as in his handling of the Galilean campaign with the two contrasting accounts of *War* and *Life*. The enormous amount of work that has been done on the Gospel traditions over the last fifty years, may still appear to the unintiated to have achieved very little positive result, yet a heightened sensitivity to the history of the tradition and its various layers is a very valuable asset for anyone wishing to use the gospels as historical documents. Besides, the insight that each layer of the tradition, each redaction, can, if properly evaluated, be a useful clue in reconstructing the development of early Christian communities, increases their value for the historian. Mention has already been made of recent approaches to the study of the rabbinic material. The recognition that embedded in these documents and their later concerns are valuable historical traditions of the pre-70 period has convinced many scholars that these must be chiseled out and evaluated by the norms of historical criticism before being used in historical reconstruction. This means that they must be set side by side with the certain pre-70 data we know of from the other sources and judged accordingly. Previous studies have tended to rely too much on one or other of these sources with the resulting loss of perspective, and the danger, not always avoided, of taking the tendency of the source being used as representative of the actual historical realities. By juxtaposing all three literary sources and recognizing the tendencies of each it is hoped to reconstruct various aspects of Galilean life in a more balanced and historically reliable way.

Our explorations in the past are happily not confined to literary testimonies alone. Archaeology, in terms of the material remains of various sites, coins and inscriptions, is also important, and once again Professor Hengel has shown the way in which these can supplement our knowledge of the times. His essay on the social relations reflected in the parable of the wicked husbandmen in the light of the Zenon papyri has direct relevance for our topic. Besides, a more systematic approach to the archaeology of Palestine, exploring remote sites and settlements, such as Tel Anafa and Meron, rather than concentrating on the more recognizable biblical locations like Hazor and Megiddo, is an important advance in the science's contribution to historical reconstruction. Such soundings are likely to be more representative of the general picture than those conducted at the important cultic and administrative centers, and as this approach develops our knowledge of everyday Palestinian life and culture will undoubtedly be greatly enriched. Fortunately, we have at least been able to draw on the first results of such work.

The problem of developing a general picture from the data in our possession, which are often scattered and isolated, is always a difficult one, and of necessity the answers must be hypothetical. It is here that the sciences of sociology and cultural anthropology have an important contribution to make and are being increasingly invoked by ancient social historians in general and by scholars concerned with Christian origins in particular. It has been claimed by some that whereas the social sciences deal with the typical, history is concerned with the unique, and so the former can never really be of assistance in the task of the latter. Yet while the warning is timely it should not be made into an absolute principle. Social history too is concerned with typical patterns - of a particular place and time, to be sure - but nonetheless typical, in that it may be safely presumed that - to take a pertinent example - peasant farmers respond to a threat to their ownership of the land in similar ways, whether they be in first century B.C.E. Galilee or nineteenth century C.E. Connacht. In attempting to put together the scraps of information to be gleaned from the various sources, we have felt free to draw on some general insights of this nature, without necessarily opting for any particular social theory and consistently applying it to the data, as for example Kreissig has done with a Marxist theory of class struggle in his study of the causes of the Jewish revolt against Rome. This has seemed all the more legitimate when an occasional remark from Josephus points in this direction also, as when for example he tells us that the country people of Gischala were more concerned with their crops than with the revolt against Rome.

As well as Professor Hengel other people have contributed to this study, and it is a pleasant duty to gratefully acknowledge their assistance. The Alexander von Humboldt Stiftung made my stay in Tübingen possible with their generous research grant extended for a second term, and the unfailing courtesy and friendship of the Generalsekretär, Dr. Heinrich Pfeiffer and his staff is a very pleasant memory of my *Deutsches Aufenthalt.* The warm and friendly atmosphere of the Institutum Judaicum and its staff is for me typified particularly by Professor Otto Betz, with whom I had many friendly and helpful discussions. My thanks are also due to the two academic institutions with which I have been associated, St. Patrick's College Maynooth, Ireland, and Loyola University, New Orleans, U.S.A. - the former for early sabbatical leave to undertake the research in Germany and the latter for generous help in defraying the typing and other costs of this book. Finally, my wife, Gail, has more than lived up to the biblical ideal, in burning many late-night lamps to ensure that this work might be worthy of the topic with which it deals. It is to her that it is gratefully and lovingly dedicated.

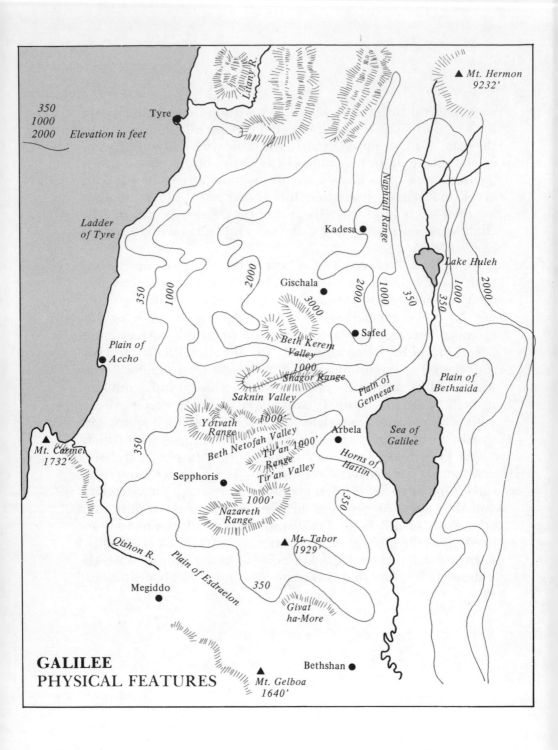

350
1000
2000 *Elevation in feet*

▲ *Mt. Hermon*
9232'

Tyre ●

Litany R.

Ladder of Tyre

Kadesa ●

Naphtali Range

Lake Huleh

Gischala ●

3000

2000

1000

350

Safed ●

Plain of Accho ●

Beth Kerem Valley

1000

Shagor Range

Saknin Valley

Plain of Gennesar

Plain of Bethsaida

Yotvath Range

1000

Arbela ●

Sea of Galilee

▲ *Mt. Carmel*
1732'

350

Beth Netofah Valley

Tir'an *1000'*
Range

Tir'an Valley

Horns of Hattin

Sepphoris ●

1000'

Nazareth Range

350

Qishon R.

Plain of Esdraelon

▲ *Mt. Tabor*
1929'

Megiddo ●

350

Givat ha-More

Bethshan ●

GALILEE
PHYSICAL FEATURES

▲ *Mt. Gelboa*
1640'

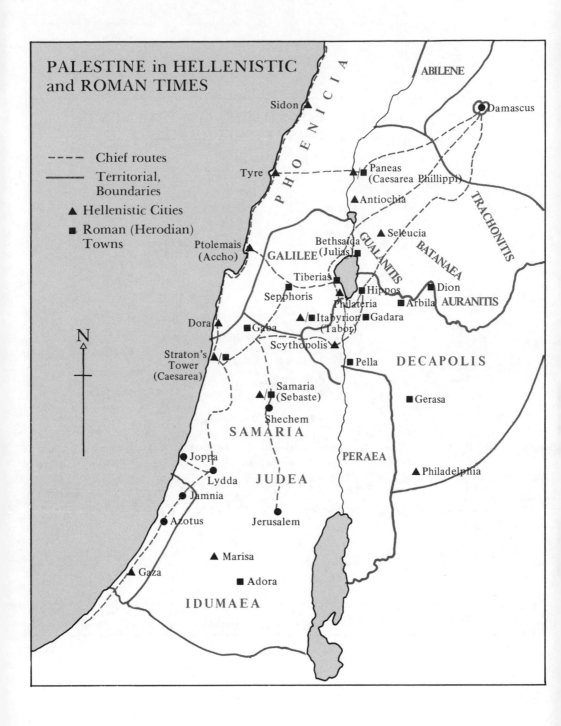

PALESTINE in HELLENISTIC and ROMAN TIMES

---- Chief routes
——— Territorial, Boundaries
▲ Hellenistic Cities
■ Roman (Herodian) Towns

ABILENE

Damascus

PHOENICIA

Sidon ▲

Tyre ▲

Paneas ■ (Caesarea Phillippi)

TRACHONITIS

Antiochia ▲

Seleucia ▲

BATANAEA

Ptolemais (Accho) ▲

GALILEE

Bethsaida (Julias) ■

GAULANITIS

Tiberias ■

Hippos ■ Dion ■

Sepphoris ■

Philateria

Arbila ■ AURANITIS

Itabyrion ▲/■ (Tabor)

Gadara ■

Dora ▲

Gaba ■

Scythopolis ▲

Pella ■

DECAPOLIS

Straton's Tower (Caesarea) ▲/■

Gerasa ■

Samaria ▲/■ (Sebaste)

Shechem ●

SAMARIA

N

Joppa ●

Lydda ●

JUDEA

PERAEA

Philadelphia ▲

Jamnia ●

Azotus ●

Jerusalem ●

Marisa ▲

Gaza ▲

Adora ■

IDUMAEA

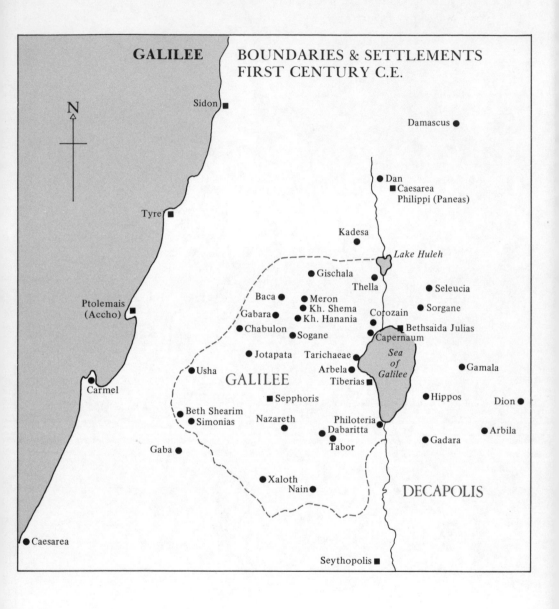

GALILEE BOUNDARIES & SETTLEMENTS
FIRST CENTURY C.E.

N

Sidon ■

Damascus ●

● Dan
■ Caesarea
Philippi (Paneas)

Tyre ■

Kadesa ●

Lake Huleh

● Gischala
Thella
● Seleucia

Baca ● ● Meron
● Sorgane
Gabara ● Kh. Shema
Kh. Hanania
Corozain
● Chabulon ● Sogane
■ Bethsaida Julias
Capernaum

Ptolemais
(Accho) ■

● Jotapata Taricheae ●
Sea
of
Galilee
Arbela ● ●
● Gamala
Usha ● Tiberias ●

GALILEE

Carmel ● ■ Sepphoris
● Hippos
Dion ●

Beth Shearim ● Nazareth Philoteria ●
● Simonias Dabaritta
● Arbila
● Gadara
Gaba ● Tabor ●

Xaloth ●
Nain ●
DECAPOLIS

Caesarea ●

Seythopolis ■

Part One
GEOGRAPHICAL AND HISTORICAL

CHAPTER ONE
THE GEOGRAPHY OF GALILEE AND
ITS HUMAN SETTLEMENT

'**W**ell ours is not a maritime country; neither commerce nor the intercourse which it promotes with the outside world has any attraction for us.' Thus wrote Josephus at the beginning of his defense of Judaism in the *Against Apion* (1:60). Presumably the tragic irony of the remark was not lost on Apion or any other hellenistic reader, for the history of Israel even as it had been described by Josephus himself was the struggle of a people to establish itself within humanly viable limits on that narrow strip of land between sea and desert that linked the outer extremities of the fertile crescent. Our study concerns one segment of that land, Galilee, literally meaning 'the circle' הַגָּלִיל , a name which originally may have had geographic rather than ethnographic connotations. From earliest times however, the name had attracted to itself the qualifier 'of the nations' הַגּוֹיִם , possibly as a reflection of the earliest Israelite experience there—surrounded by other peoples.[1] It is more than a mere coincidence that after centuries of non-use the name reappears as Γαλιλαία ἀλλοφυλῶν in a second century B.C.E. writer (*1 Macc* 5:15), as expressive of Jewish feelings there in his own day. Since our project is to understand Judaism in Galilee in hellenistic and Roman times we must begin by picking up the clue that the name itself suggests—the likely impact of Galilee's physiography on human settlement. Some at least of the subsequent story is anticipated in the ways sea, lake and river, mountain and plain can be expected to shape any people's struggle for identity in the area. This is all the more likely in the case of a people whose conviction it was that this was part of the land that Yahweh, their God, had given them.

From the fairly detailed description of boundaries which Josephus gives us (*War* 3:35-40), and aided by references from rabbinic sources and early Christian writings, historical geographers have been able to reach a general agreement on the area of political Galilee in the first century C.E.[2] However, some scattered references suggest that a larger area was still remembered.[3] We hear that Galilee reached as far as Sidon (*Ant* 8:36—city or

3

territory?); Upper Galilee once stretched to Lebanon and the sources of the Jordan (*Ant* 5:89) and Kedasa which in Josephus' day belonged to Tyre (*War* 2:459; 4:105) once was Galilean (*Ant* 5:63). In the west, Carmel also had belonged to Galilee but was later a possession of Tyre (*War* 3:35), and there is even the suggestion that Ptolemais too was a Galilean city, though apparently Josephus corrects himself in that context (*War* 2:188f). Consequently, before we examine the physical pattern of the interior of Galilee, we must situate the region as a whole within the larger context of the physiography of northern Palestine. Perhaps this will give some clue to the fluctuations in the political history of the area to which these scattered references from Josephus point.

I

THE LOCATION OF POLITICAL GALILEE IN THE LARGER GEOGRAPHIC REGION.

The physical features of northern Palestine are part of a general pattern following a north/south axis, to be found in the whole region, that traditionally came to be known as the land of Israel.[4] This pattern, moving from west to east consists of a coastal plain, a central hill country, the Jordan rift and the highland plateau of Transjordan. There are, however, some important interruptions or modifications in this pattern in the northern region. The coastal plain is narrow and broken by the central hill country jutting out to the sea at two points—the Carmel range in the south and the Ladder of Tyre (Rosh ha Nikrah). The central hill country varies considerably in height from south to north, for whereas in the south no hill exceeds 1,850 feet in the north the peaks are between 2,000 and 4,000 feet as they ascend to the Hermon range. Furthermore, the hills in the south are broken by a series of valleys running in an east/west direction, a feature not found in the Judaean or Samarian hill country. The plain of Esdraelon extending from Carmel to the Jordan valley, is of course the outstanding example of these interruptions, and once its fertility had attracted human habitation it took on a special character that effectively separated north and south. The Jordan valley especially between the lakes of Huleh and Gennesareth is neither so narrow nor so deep as farther south, and extends into the plain of

Bethsaida on the northeastern corner of the lake and that of Gennesareth at its western angle. East of the Jordan the high tablelands of Bashan slope gently from west to east and are covered by a rich alluvial soil from the volcanic nature of the rock. This, coupled with the good year-round rainfall, makes this region extremely fertile pasture and grain-producing land and gives it a very different character from the western side of the rift where the vine and the olive predominate as produce of the sloping, terraced hills.

Perhaps the most important physical feature of the whole region, especially in contrast with the south, is the plentiful supply of water.[5] The amounts of rainfall increase in all regions as one moves from south to north, and the variations are much greater than in countries of comparable size, ranging from as low as 1.2 inches per annum in the desert regions of the south, to 44 inches per annum in the mountains of Upper Galilee.[6] This, coupled with an almost annual snowfall, ensured excellent watering and irrigation possibilities for the many basins, which, we shall see, form an essential part of the landscape, especially in Lower Galilee, and cause a rich vegetation. Yet this can be a mixed blessing, since soil erosion is a constant problem in the upper regions of the hills due to the steep inclines and the sudden, heavy rainfall that is confined to a relatively short period of time in winter and early spring. Furthermore, since the rock in Upper Galilee is mostly a tough limestone variety, under-surface water is not easily discovered, so that year-round storage had to be arranged for animals and humans, in caverns, pits and cisterns (*M. Ta'an* 3:2), making life in the region that much more difficult. While Josephus, wishing to extol the richness and fertility of the province he once governed, would have us believe that nature smiled on Galilee by comparison with other regions (*War* 3:44), this should not obscure the fact that even there life was a constant struggle with rough terrain, lack of natural resources, and seasonal hazards. *M Ta'an* 3:1f reflects the anxiety of Galilean farmers no less than those in other regions of the country: 'So, too, if rain had failed for forty days between rainfall and rainfall, they forthwith sound the *shofar,* since it means the onset of dearth'.

Looking more closely at the outer rim of the circle that is Galilee, we start our tour on the coastal plain. As already mentioned, this Galilean section differs considerably from that farther south, in that the interior hill country comes much closer to the shore, in fact dividing it at two points by the Carmel and Ladder of Tyre promontories. Thus we find three naturally divided areas—the Zebulun valley (Haifa Bay), the Acre plain and the Tyre valley, all equally suited for separate settlements, something that would benefit the quasi-independent city state, with its own territory, of hellenistic times. The Mediterranean coast of Palestine is singularly lacking in navigable ports due to the extensive shelf, but with Acco and Tyre, the Galilean coastline has two notable exceptions. It was inevitable therefore that maritime concerns would always dominate life here, leading to the earlier urbanization and development of strong, stable centers, at once capable of handling the trade from the interior, for which these ports formed a natural outlet, and serving as military strongholds to protect the narrow route from north to south which every military conqueror had of necessity to control. This dual role of these settlements inevitably differentiated them sharply from life in the interior. As Karmon writes: 'The plain did not form the western fringe of the southwest Asiatic region, but the eastern margin of the Mediterranean region.'[7]

The plain itself was not wide enough for any large-scale agricultural pursuits, and this was to be a constant cause of friction as we shall see. It was natural for those who inhabited the interior to want to control its proximate outlets, and once a separate and different way of life had been established on the coast, its inhabitants needed the interior to serve both as a hinterland for agricultural produce and to act as a buffer state in case of reprisals from within. This relatively isolated character of the coastal settlements is echoed by Josephus' description of Ptolemais: 'a maritime town in Galilee, built at the entrance to the Great Plain and encompassed with mountains. To the east at a distance of 60 furlongs is the Galilean range; to the south, 120 furlongs off, lies Carmel; to the north is the highest chain of all, called by the natives 'the Ladder of Tyre', 100 furlongs off' (*War* 2:188). He then goes on to describe one natural resource of the area, vitreous sand, which apparently meant a lively maritime trade there. This further underlined the need for a suitable agricultural hinterland. Farther north the dilemma of Tyre, situated on a reef island was even more acute, for the coastal plain here is even narrower than at

Acre and some encroachment of the hinterland was inevitable not just for adequate supplies, but to ensure that the city itself would not be totally isolated as happened during Alexander's seven month siege.

Turning to the south, Galilee is bordered by the Plain of Esdraelon, with the Qishon and Harod valleys at either end, separating the Galilean hill country from that of Samaria and Judaea. This is potentially an extremely fertile plain, with thick alluvial soil. It is well-watered, the river beds being less steep than in the hill country and so having a steadier and more constant flow, but when badly drained it could be swampy in the wet season.

Besides its agricultural significance, the plain also served as an opening up of the country between east and west, often impeded in the hill country. Apparently one traverse of the so-called *Via Maris* passed through the Beth Shean valley and across the Great Plain possibly along its northern frontier, verging on the Galilean hills.[8] Thus the plain also became an important overland commercial link between east and west, and its control was of extreme importance to anyone who wished to dominate the whole area. The Megiddo pass on its western edge has been one of the most strategic passes in Palestine from the time of Thutmose III (1500 B.C.E.) to the present century, controlling as it does the meeting point of east/west and north/south traffic.[9] Little wonder then, that the area always seems to have been a separate administrative unit, forming part of 'the king's land' all through recorded history.

On its Eastern side the Jordan rift, including the lake, separates political Galilee from Transjordan. There is a marked contrast in the landscape, for instead of series of ridges and valleys, as in the west, the eastern uplands slope away gently, gradually merging with the desert. As already mentioned, the volcanic nature of the rock and the good amount of rainfall has made this area extremely fertile. From antiquity it was a wheat-producing area and later became one of the granaries of the empire. The bulls of Bashan are storied in the Old Testament (*Ps* 22:12; *Amos* 4:11; *Ez* 39:18) and the Talmud also recognizes the distinction between it and Galilee in terms of the type of cattle it produced.[10] This difference in land contour and produce gave a very different character to life in the two regions.[11] Urbanization became much more a feature of

Transjordan than Galilee proper, because of the remoteness and inaccessibility of many of the latter's settlements. Accordingly human contacts between the two regions were not likely to be particularly frequent or important. Each could develop its own life-style, for there was no natural dependence of the one on the other. The only possible common factor was the lake and the industry that it generated, and in fact we do hear of a lively boat traffic there in both Josephus and the New Testament.[12] In this regard the valley of Beth Shean formed a natural link between east and west, below the lake, while north of it the crossing of the river is easier and the natural dividing line between east and west is not the river itself but the Naphtali range running in a north/south direction protecting the Huleh valley on the west. This natural boundary seems to have been observed by the political lines of Trachonitis, as part of Philip's kingdom in New Testament times.[13]

Finally we reach the northern boundaries of Galilee, and it is significant that the physical features here are much more complex and that no outstanding natural boundary suggests itself to mark off the region in any particular direction. Perhaps we should not then be surprised to find that the political boundaries have apparently reflected this confusion of nature. On the western side, the valley of the Litany River could have served as one such natural dividing line, but this would take us well north of Tyre, and we have seen why the narrowness of the coastal plain inevitably caused this city to expand forcibly into the interior. This political pressure proved stronger than Upper Galilee's impetus to extend itself to its natural frontier further north. On the eastern side the natural dividing line was Mount Hermon, and early Israel laid claims to the territory as far north as Dan at the foot of this storied mountain (*Gn* 14:14; *Jdg* 18:7.27). However, these claims were rarely actualized and once again political rather than natural reasons seem to have determined the dividing line along the much less prominent *Wadi 'Oba*, which farther south runs between Kedesh and Gischala.[14] As we shall presently see, north/south movement in this area was difficult due to the natural terrain. Abandoned sites are today silent witnesses of a somewhat indeterminate boundary. This frontier region received little enough support from the central administration, and so those who did survive and retain an ethnic identity were likely to be both independent and resentful of those who might wish to exploit their region's natural or strategic potential for personal reasons.

Our tour of the outer circle of Galilee has isolated a central hill country surrounded by markedly different physical features— a coastal plain linked with harbours, a large inland plain, unusual for Palestine, and a rift comprised of river and lake, the only navigable waterway in inland Palestine. We have suggested that this distinctive physiography suggests rather different possibilities for human occupation and life-style. We must now visit the interior to see whether the natural cohesiveness of its physical features would further support this contention.

II

THE HILL COUNTRY OF GALILEE

Both Josephus and rabbinic literature speak of Upper and Lower Galilee, but whereas the former seems to be more concerned with the political realities of his own day the latter explicitly mentions physical features as determinative of the dividing line— Upper Galilee begins at Kefar Hanania, above which the sycamore does not grow (*M. Sheb* 9:2). Altitude and vegetation determine the division and presumably political administration followed suit. But the Mishnah also recognizes a third division, the Valley, probably the whole basin of the lake and not just the Gennesareth plain on its northwestern corner, which Josephus describes in such glowing terms (*War* 3:516-21).[15] Josephus gives further details that help to locate the boundary line between Upper and Lower Galilee more precisely. Lower Galilee in his day extended in a north/south direction from Xaloth, a village in the Great Plain, to Bersabe. 'At this point Upper Galilee begins, which extends in breadth (i.e. north/south) to the village of Baca' (*War* 3:39). Both Bersabe and Kefar Hanania have been identified as two sites proximate to each other in the Beth ha-Cerem ('House of the Vine') Valley, and in all probability this valley and its continuation to the east in the deep gorge of the Ammud stream separated Upper from Lower Galilee.[16] In fact there are peaks of over 3,000 feet north of this line, Mt. Meron at 3,963 feet being the highest, whereas south from there all are less than 2,000 feet. Since this threefold distinction would appear to be based on physical features, a brief consideration of how these were likely to have affected human occupation seems called for.

(i) *Lower Galilee.*

We may divide the region of Lower Galilee into two parts, based on rock formation on its west and east sides. On the western side the dominant feature is a series of ranges of limestone or related rock, separated by deep basins running in a WSW/ENE direction. These ranges, going from north to south, are Shagor, Yotvath, Tir'an and Nazareth, separating the valleys of Beth Kerem, Sakhnin, Beth Netofah and Tir'an, and south of the Nazareth range the plain of Esdraelon.[16] The Nazareth range has a softer rock formation than the other three and so presents less of a massif form with quite an amount of erosion isolating different sections. To the east one finds a series of plateaus, covered by sheets of basalt, due to volcanic activity in the area, of which the Horns of Hattin is the outstanding reminder. These plateaus ascend from a SW to a NE direction, eventually reaching the escarpment which overlooks the lake. This series begins in the south with Mt. Gilboa and Givat ha More at the NE edge of the Plain of Jezreel; next comes the Yavna'el mountains and valley, and finally, before the lake, the Poriya ridge. Further north there is Hattin and Arbela, all part of the same faulting. Thus the eastern side of Lower Galilee is much more rugged than the western where the valleys between the ranges open out towards Ptolemais and the coast, and so the region was never densely populated.

Looking at the picture just presented, it is not difficult to detect certain features which were likely to affect human life in the area. The valleys on the eastern side are narrow and devious and communication on an east/west axis is not at all as easy as might appear at first sight. In turn this means that the region of the lake is to some degree cut off from the rest of Lower Galilee, a factor that will have to be kept in mind when discussing the likely sphere of influence of Tiberias on the hinterland. The rugged terrain especially in the region of Arbela appears repeatedly in history as a haven for those who were attempting to flee from enemies or invaders. On the other hand the broader valleys of the west side were not so threatening to the invader since the country-side did not lend itself so easily to guerilla-style activity, and the Ptolemais—Sepphoris route was taken more than once by a general who wished to instil fear into the populace of Lower Galilee.[18]

Perhaps even more significant than the strategic effects is the impact of the physical features on everyday life. How was the terrain likely to have shaped life in the area? What degree of cohesiveness and sense of community was likely to be generated by these conditions? At first sight the sheltered valleys of Lower Galilee might appear ideal for human habitation, but in fact this is not entirely true. The streams that water these basins are rapid and seasonal, so that there is too much land erosion and possibility of flooding when the outlets are not able to take the sudden flow of water. As a result most of the settlements are off the floor of the valleys, yet near enough to be able to utilize the fertile basins and avail of the water supply by irrigation and damming. The slopes of the hills, especially the steeper ones, were more suited to the cultivation of the vine and the olive, either by terracing or strip lynchet, the former apparently being the more popular form in Judaea while the latter is characteristic of Galilee.[19] A recent demographic survey of settlement sites in Lower Galilee has discovered an interesting contrast between the three northern spurs on the one hand and the Nazareth range of hills on the other. In the former seventy-one percent of the settlements (that is 22 out of a total of 31 villages) are to be found on the slopes, lower ridges and just off the basins, whereas in the latter the instances of lower sites are far less frequent and many are found right at the top.[20] The reason for this surprising difference is apparently the contrasting rock formations of the hills—those of the Nazareth range being semi-pervious chalk, as we noted, and therefore providing adequate soil coverage and plenty of springs which make agriculture possible even on the top of the range. Thus we have a very striking example of human settlements following the natural potentialities of the country. At the same time the locating of the settlements shows the relative independence of each in relation to its neighbors, but with the possibility of local inter-communication along the basins.

The question of more extensive communication is related to the road system, the situation of which is partly the result of natural conditions and partly man's attempt to adapt this to his own best interests. In the ancient world roads often ran on higher ground avoiding the swampy lower regions and being less open to attack from highway robbers and villagers. The great through roads are likely to take the safest routes, avoiding the more remote and inaccessible regions. While Galilee did have a number of such roads,[21] they were secondary by comparison with that which came from the east via the Beth Shean valley and skirted Lower Galilee on its way to the coast. In a sense the lake formed the ultimate barrier between east and west and the roads from the coast had to turn northward to cross the Jordan at the 'Daughters of Jacob' bridge, but this was in all probability less popular than the other arm further south because of the rugged terrain to be crossed before reaching the lake shore. Similarly the mountain road from Hebron via Jerusalem, apparently did not continue beyond Nazareth, and certainly did not traverse Upper Galilee because of the natural barriers to traveling in a N/S direction which the Galilean terrain presented. This in turn contributed to the sense of remoteness of the northern area from its cultural and cultic center at Jerusalem. What is noteworthy about all these major arteries, even today, is the fact that while they connect the major towns, the villages are all located at some distance from them.[22] No doubt security played a major role in this, but it helps to underline the secluded nature of village life in Galilee and the lack of any permanent contacts with the larger world, except on very special occasions. This is perhaps the outstanding fact that this brief opening look at life in Galilee has to offer for the purposes of the present study, and it will be confirmed in many different ways in subsequent chapters.

(ii) *Upper Galilee.*

As already noted the Mishnah makes a clear distinction between Upper and Lower Galilee on the basis of the geographic features of 'where the sycamore grows'. There are however, other differences between the two regions, for in the north not merely do the mountain ridges go in an east/west direction, but these are crossed by other faults with a SE/NW orientation, making the whole area a maze of valleys, gorges, basins, ridges and isolated peaks. The elevation on the western side is not so great as on the east, but the

agriculture, and there is ample evidence that this was exploited to the full. Besides, as already mentioned it was navigable, and so contacts with the different life-style of Transjordan were possible. Inevitably, the process of urbanization here was hastened by the industries associated with the lake, and the shore is dotted with settlements, some of which at least had a very different atmosphere to the villages of the interior (Philoteria, Tarichaeae, Tiberias). Both Josephus (*War* 3:516-21) and Pliny (*Nat Hist* V,15.70-72) speak of the area in glowing terms, the former in particular praising the hearty wine and fertility of the plain of Gennesareth and the latter mentioning the hot springs in the neighbourhood of Tiberias that must have been a tourist attraction (cf. *Life* 85). Life in the valley then appears more cosmopolitan and mobile than elsewhere in Galilee, where the older more settled form would seem to have a better opportunity to prevail despite various political changes.

(iv) *Some Tentative Conclusions.*

This rapid survey of the physical features of Galilee and their likely impact on human habitation and life in the area has already indicated certain topics of discussion that will have to be explored in greater detail in the pages ahead.

Firstly, the soil and climate of Galilee make it by far the most fertile and productive region of the country, and its location as a hinterland to two thriving ports meant that its produce could be easily transported to lucrative markets. Galilee produced all the important agricultural items that were in demand in the ancient world. Wheat and grain are associated with the plains and the larger tracts of arable land, and it is not surprising to hear of granaries at Beth Shearim in the south (*Life* 118f) and Gischala in the north (*Life* 71).[28] The vine and the olive are also to be found everywhere, but they are more often mentioned in conjunction with sites in the central highlands, where they can be tended even on small plots of ground on the hillsides and mountain slopes. It will be interesting to see how these advantageous conditions affected the quality of life of the inhabitants.[29]

Secondly, we found that the name Galilee, meaning 'circle' is not just an accurate ethnographical description, as is generally assumed, but is also and perhaps originally, a suitable geographic one too. The central hill country, despite the internal differences between north and south, is still quite distinct from the surrounding plains and rift, and historically we know that such distinctions generated a very different culture and life style between the center and the periphery. Inevitably, social and cultural tensions were to emerge between coast and interior, but it should not be assumed that the older way of life had always to be the loser in such circumstances. On the other hand commercial links can co-exist within such cultural diversity provided no attempt is made by the stronger partner to 'take over' or totally dominate the weaker. If this does occur it is likely to be resisted fiercely, and so we find that the geographical diversity of coastal plain and interior gave rise to a fluctuating set of human relations between the two. While conditions in the rift differed considerably from the interior, there was not likely to have been such a sharp cultural clash there, since the narrow rift region could not have supported the population it attracted without the back-up support of the interior's agricultural produce.

Thirdly, we have seen how the physical features in the interior rigidly determined the settlement pattern in the hills and valleys. This strict correlation suggests that many of these settlements were very ancient indeed, undisturbed through the centuries. This must have given a great sense of permanency to life there, and a strong adherence to traditional patterns. Urbanization was never likely to take over the control of life in central Galilee, and in fact never did. Sepphoris, for all its political importance, did not grow out of the confluence of natural and human resources in the way that Beth Shean did, and so it could never hope to dominate life in the villages of Galilee. This means that geophysically the interior of Galilee was particularly suited to a peasant style of life with people living together in close ties of kinship in relatively small and isolated settlements. This tentative conclusion is perhaps the most important of all for the shape of our further enquiries.

III
THE EARLIEST RECORDS OF HUMAN HABITATION IN GALILEE.

Our conclusions naturally have to be rather tentative and we may even be accused of reading into them the known historical data of a later period. We are fortunate therefore in being able to test them in the light of the biblical records of the Israelite occupation of northern Palestine, the earliest written records of human habitation in the area. As is well known, these accounts pose special literary and historical problems which we cannot discuss here. However, the fact that the books of Josua and Judges have two rather different accounts of the settlement of the tribes is in this instance a real bonus, for it has convinced scholars that the later theologians and chroniclers of Israel had available to them older traditions dealing with their ancestors' occupation of the land.[30]

Two major triumphs of the Israelite league over the Canaanites are recorded, the victory of Josua over Jabin, king of Hazor by the waters of Merom (*Jos* 11:1-12) and that of Deborah and Barak over the same king and his general Sisera (*Jdg* 4). Whatever the historical realities underlying these two campaigns it is clear that tradition remembered a bloody conquest of the north, particularly associated with Hazor and its king.[31] This city has now been identified with a strategic site in the upper Jordan valley on the inland road leading north to Syria about halfway between the northern shore of Lake Gennesareth and the southern tip of Huleh, just at the point where the river is most easily crossed. Modern excavations have shown that the city occupied an easily defended mound overlooking the plain of Hazor, just the kind of site we would expect for the city that led the Canaanite league.[32] Presumably then the victory over Jabin gave the Israelite league a foothold in the north, for next we hear of the parceling out of the conquered territory to the various tribes. However, it is generally recognized that the lists of *Jos* 19:10-24 reflect a much later situation and so the account of *Jdg* 1:30-36 is to be preferred.[33] According to this version the Israelites were only partially successful. Zebulun and Naphtali failed to drive out the Canaanites who dwelt among them in the hill country while reducing them to forced labour. Asher was equally unsuccessful on the coastal plain for 'it had to dwell among the Canaanites, the inhabitants of the land'. The tribe of Dan, overrun in the south by the Amorites, migrated north and inhabited the outskirts of the territory of Sidon. Though the inhabitants of Laish lived after the manner of the Sidonians, the Danites succeeded in capturing it 'for the city was far from Sidon' (*Jdg* 18:7.28). One of the chief cities of the coastal plain had pushed inward and to the south as we had projected, yet the relationship between coast and plain is rather loose and the one is seen as removed from the other. There is no mention of Issachar in the account of *Jdg* and the territory ascribed to it in *Jos* 19:17-23 (the plain of Esdraelon as far as the Jordan) is said to have been occupied by Manasseh who initially failed to expel the Canaanites from Beth Shean, Taanach, Megiddo and Dor, and the villages associated with these places. Even later when the Israelites grew stronger they were not able to completely expel the Canaanites from this fertile valley but imposed forced labour on them.

It is possible to fill out this picture of gradual Israelite settlement by occupation or assimilation with references to the northern tribes in the lists of blessings (*Gn* 49 and *Dt* 33) as well as from the canticle of Deborah celebrating the victory over Sisera (*Jdg* 5), all of which are considered to have genuine historical information from an earlier period.[34] Two themes recur—the attraction of the sea and the fertility of the land—both of which had already been suggested by our geographical survey. In the canticle of Deborah, Dan and Asher are both chided for their non-involvement in the campaign: 'And Dan, why did he abide with the ships? Asher sat still at the coast of the sea, settling down by his landings' (*Jdg* 5:17), whereas Naphtali, Issachar and Zebulun are praised for their generosity and daring (*Jdg* 5:15.18). The blessings of Jacob and Moses on the other hand both refer to the fertility of the regions inhabited by the Israelite tribes. Zebulun and Issachar are to rejoice 'for they suck the affluence of the sea and the hidden treasures of the sand' (*Dt* 33:18), and Naphtali is said to be full of the blessing of the Lord because it possesses the south and the lake (*Dt* 33:23). Asher shall dip its foot in oil (*Dt* 33:24), a clear allusion to Galilee's plentiful supply of the olive, reflected in later sources also as we have seen. Subsequent developments in the fortunes of different tribes are also reflected. Thus Zebulun 'shall dwell at the shore of the sea; he shall become a haven for ships' (*Gn* 49: 13), echoing the expansion to the coast, probably around Acco, since farther north Sidon seems to have controlled the plain and the interior. Issachar 'saw that his resting place was good and that the land was pleasant, and so he bowed his shoulder to bear and became a slave at forced labour' (*Gn* 49:15), whereas Asher's 'food will be rich and he shall yield royal dainties' (*Gn* 49:20).

Early Israelite tradition recalled therefore with pride the richness of the land occupied by the northern tribes. At the same time it also recognized the attraction of the sea for some, at least, of those tribes and as a result their questionable support for those struggling to occupy the interior hill country, especially Naphtali and Zebulun. The fact that Israel was not totally successful is acknowledged, and, significantly, those very places where Canaanite presence was believed to have persisted, the coastal plain and the plain of Esdraelon, are the ones where it was felt that geographical considerations might give rise to a different life-style from the interior hill country. Even in the interior there were pockets of resistance also, around Beth Anath and Beth Shemesh in particular (*Jdg* 1:33), and, as we shall see, the former, wherever its precise location, was the centre of a thriving royal domain in hellenistic times. Probably, therefore, the Israelites were most successful in those areas that were less attractive to the older native population, that is, in the central hill country. In this connection it is interesting to note that Sisera, the Canaanite general defeated by Deborah, is said to come from *Harosheth haggoyîm*, but no such city is known to us, and attempts at identifying it have not been very convincing. Besides it is unlikely that the prince of such an obscure place would have taken precedence in the Canaanite league over such well established places as Hazor, Shimron and Megiddo. Accordingly it has been suggested that the name *Harosheth haggoyîm* (literally, 'the wooded hill of the peoples') refers to central Galilee, inhabited by less well-organized tribes.[35] Sisera's victory would mean that the central region would now be predominantly Israelite, and the peoples were to be found in the circle (*galîl*) rather than the center.

The pattern of human occupation of Galilee suggested by its physical geography seems to be substantiated by what we know of one major settlement in the area at an earlier period. Presumably these same factors continued to operate subsequently and play an important part in further developments. In the hellenistic period, the focus of this present study, roles were to be reversed, however, since the older population now inhabited the interior and had remained stable there for centuries, while the newcomers were most interested in the plains that encircled it for strategic and economic reasons. Thus paradoxically, those very regions that were resistant to change earlier now became the areas of greatest mobility. Yet the old struggle between circle and center continued and took on many different forms, which we must now seek to explore.

NOTES FOR CHAPTER 1

[1] For a full discussion of the origin and significance of the expression, but without any reference to its possible geographic connotation, cf. A. Alt, 'Die Herkunft des Namens Galiläa', *Galiläische Probleme*, (hereafter, *G.P.*) 1, 363-374, in *Kleine Schriften zur Geschichte des Volkes Israel*, 3 vols. Munich, 1953-64 (hereafter *Kl. Schr.*), vol. 2 (1959) 363-435. He favors the view that the expression גְּלִיל הַגּוֹיִם is more primitive than the shortened גָּלִיל, originating in pre-Israelite times of the Canaanite leagues mentioned in the Egyptian execration texts. However, he does not rule out the possibility that it may be of Israelite origin, expressing their early experience in the land.

[2] H. Hoehner, *Herod Antipas*, S.N.T.S. Monograph Series, ed. M. Black, 17, Cambridge, Univ. Press, 1972, has a detailed discussion in appendix II, 'The Boundaries of Antipas' Territories', 277-285, with reference to both ancient and modern literature.

[3] W. Oehler, 'Die Ortschaften und Grenzen Galiläas nach Josephus', ZDPV 28 (1905) 1-26 and 49-74, esp. 2 and 65. Cf. also G. Stemberger, 'Galilee, Land of Salvation?', Appendix IV, 409-438, esp. 415-21, in W.D. Davies, *The Gospel and the Land*, Berkeley, Univ. of California Press, 1974.

[4] For the following description I am indebted to these studies: D. Baly, *The Geography of the Bible*, New York, Harper and Row, 1957; G.A. Smith, *The Historical Geography of the Holy Land*, 25 ed., London, 1931; I. Schattner and others, *Israel Pocket Library. Geography.*, Jerusalem, Keter Books, 1973; E. Orni and E. Efrat, *Geography of Israel*, 3rd rev. ed., New York, American Heritage Co., 1971.

[5] V. Schwöbel, 'Galiläa: die Verkehrswege und Ansiedlungen in ihrer Abhängigkeit von den natürlichen Bedingungen', ZDPV 27(1904) 1-151, esp. 112-20 on the water supplies of Galilee.

[6] Baly, *The Geography of Palestine*, 53-66. The figures are those of D. Ashbel, 'Climate', in *Geography*, 98-104.

[7] Y. Karmon, 'Geographical Aspects of the Coastal Plain of Israel', IEJ 6(1956) 33-50, here 36.

[8] The name of this route is apparently not very old, but the route itself is well attested in ancient records according to Z.Meshel, 'Was there a *Via Maris*?' IEJ 23 (1973) 162-66; cf. also Schwöbel, 'Galilaa: die Verkehrswege', 61-85.

[9] Y. Aharoni and M. Avi-Yonah, *The Macmillan Bible Atlas*, New York/London, 1968, 32.

[10] A. Neubauer, *La Géographie du Talmud*, Paris 1868, 180 cf. *T. Men* 8:3.

[11] Baly, *The Geography of Palestine*, 218f.

[12] *Mk* 4:36; 6:53f; *Jn* 6:17; *Life* 165.

[13] M. Avi-Yonah, *The Holy Land from the Persian to the Arab Conquests. A Historical Geography*, Grand Rapids, Baker Books, 1966, (hereafter, *The Holy Land*), 166f.

[14] Hoehner, *Herod Antipas*, 283f; Avi-Yonah, *The Holy Land*, 130.

[15] Neubauer, *Géographie*, 207-25.

[16] Avi-Yonah, *The Holy Land*, 133; Neubauer, *Géographie*, 178.

[17] Baly, *The Geography of Palestine*, 184-90; D.H. Kallmer and E. Rosenau, 'Regions of Palestine', *Geographical Review* 29(1939) 61-80. Orni and Efrat, *Geography of Israel*, 73-9.

[18] The rough terrain of Arbela is mentioned in *Ant* 14:420ff; the approach from Ptolemais to Galilee was used by Caesennius Gallus, *War* 2:510; Placidus, *Life* 214; Vespasian, *War* 3:115. On the strategic importance of this route cf. M. Avi-Yonah, 'The Missing Fortress of Flavius Josephus', IEJ 3(1953) 94-98.

[19] B. Golamb and J. Kedar, 'Ancient Agriculture in the Galilean Mountains', IEJ 21(1971) 136-40.

[20] D.H.K. Amiram, 'Sites and Settlements in the Mountains of Lower Galilee', IEJ 6(1956) 69-77.

[21] Schwöbel, 'Galilaa: die Verkehrswege', 61-88; Smith, *Historical Geography*, 277-81, paints a rather romantic picture that is one-sided.

[22] D.H.K. Amiram, 'The Pattern of Settlement in Palestine', IEJ 3(1953) 65-78, 192-209, 250-59.

[23] Baly, *The Geography of Palestine*, 191f.

[24] W. Prausnitz, 'The First Agricultural Settlements in Galilee', IEJ 9(1959) 166-74, esp. 167f on Khirbet Kharruba in Upper Galilee where a settlement too low down in the valley had to be abandoned.

[25] Its official Roman name in the third century C.E. was Tetracomia, according to Georgius Cyprius 1040, thus emphasizing the continuing pattern of village life in the area.

[26] Y. Karmon, 'The Settlement of the Northern Huleh Valley since 1838', IEJ 3(1953) 4-25.

[27] Baly, *The Geography of Palestine*, 194f.

[28] Wheat is associated with other places also: the plain of Arbela, *p. Peah* 1, 20a, and the Netofah valley, *Nm R* 18:22. There was a wheat market at Tiberias, according to *Gn R* 7:9.

[29] There are a number of recent surveys of the produce of Palestine, including Galilee, in biblical times. The following have been found helpful: Avi-Yonah, *The Holy Land*, 'Economic Geography' 188-211; J. Klausner, 'The Economy of Judea in the Period of the Second Temple', in *The World History of the Jewish People*, First Series: Ancient Times, vol. 7, *The Herodian period*, Jerusalem, Masada Publishing Co., 1975, ed. M. Avi-Yonah and Z. Baras, (hereafter *W.H.Her.P.*), 180-206; S. Applebaum, 'Economic Life in Palestine', in *Compendia Rerum Judaicarum ad Novum Testamentum. Jewish People in the First Century*, 2 vols. ed. M. Stern and S. Saffrai, Van Gorcum, Assen, and Fortress, Philadelphia, 1974-6, (hereafter, *Compendia*) 2, 631-700.

[30] Cf. e.g., M. Noth, *The History of Israel*, 2nd English ed., A. and C. Black, London 1959, 53-84; A. Alt, 'The Settlement of the Israelites in Palestine', in *Essays on Old Testament Religion*, English trans. Oxford, B.A. Blackwell, 1966, 133-70; G. Mendenhall, 'The Hebrew Conquest of Palestine', BA 25(1962) 66-87; M. Weippert, *The Settlement of the Israelite Tribes in Palestine*, SBT 2nd Series, 21, London, S.C.M. Press, 1971; J.M. Miller, 'The Israelite Conquest of Canaan', in *Israelite and Judaean History*, Old Testament Library, Philadelphia, Westminster Press, 1977.

[31] In all probability two independent traditions of victories by the Galilean tribes of Zebulun and Naphtali over Jabin, king of Hazor, and by Deborah and Barak over Sisera, the Canaanite general, have been conflated into the one account of *Jdg* 4, as A.M.H. Mayes, *Israel in the Period of the Judges*, SBT 2nd series, 29, London, S.C.M. Press, 1974, 87-9, argues, on the basis of a literary criticism of the chapter. According to him the later victory should be dated in the eleventh century and represented the first serious incursion of the Israelite tribes into the plains of Palestine, 94ff.

[32] Y. Yadin, *Hazor. The Rediscovery of a Biblical Citadel*, New York, Random Books, 1975.

[33] A. Alt, 'Eine Galiläische Ortsliste in *Jos* 19', ZAW 4(1927) 59-81 and M. Noth, 'Studien zu den historisch-geographischen Dokumenten des Josuabuches; ZDPV 58(1935) 188-255, both agree that this chapter reflects a much later historical situation, while disagreeing on the nature of the sources the author had at his disposal. Alt, 72f and Noth, 216, accept that the account in *Jdg* 1 is much earlier.

[34] Cf. Mayes, *Israel in the Period of the Judges*, esp. 27.84ff. 116, n.49, with reference to the recent secondary literature on these chapters.

[35] This is the suggestion of Aharoni and Avi-Yonah, *Macmillan Bible Atlas*, 47. Alt, 'Herkunft', *G.P.* 1, 372, locates the city at the foot of Carmel, but notes the similarity of the addition with the usual one for Galilee. He suggest that Harosheth could have been the principal place of Galilee, but this is unlikely in view of the silence of the other sources, such as the Egyptian execration texts and city lists. The position adopted here is also that of B. Maisler, 'Beth Shearim, Gaba, Harosheth of the Peoples; HUCA 24(1952) 75-84, who recognizes that the designation suggests a region rather than a town. He accepts the account of *Jdg* 4 that Sisera was the general of Jabin, who harassed the Israelites for 20 years before being lured to the river Kishon, where he suffered a severe defeat, *Jdg* 5:14.18f. (82f).

CHAPTER TWO

GALILEE, THE RISE OF HELLENISM AND THE
JEWISH RESPONSE.

I n 333 B.C.E. Alexander the Great inflicted a crushing defeat
on the armies of the Persian king Darius at Issus in northern
Syria, and opened up a new and very different phase in the history of Palestine and the Jews. Before that they were part of the
Orient, finding themselves now at the fulcrum of the balance of
power between Egypt and Mesopotamia, or again an outlying
province of the Babylonian or Persian Empires. After Alexander
the orientation was to the west, as a new and very different political
and cultural world emerged. Greeks had been to Palestine before
Alexander, but in the wake of his conquests these casual and
individual contacts became enshrined in political and social
institutions that were to survive for centuries. The transition, like
all major changes in civilization, was not easy, for it was to touch
every aspect of life and challenge centuries-old traditions at their
very roots. Perhaps no people of the east were to feel this challenge
more keenly than the Jews, and in the ensuing struggle both
Hellenism and Judaism were changed considerably. Our task in
this chapter is to trace the steps that lead to that struggle and the
Jewish reaction to it, as these were likely to manifest themselves
in Galilee—a name that re-emerges from the shadows of the past
and appears for the first time in its Greek form as Γαλίλα , in a
document that itself reflects perfectly the change of which we
speak.[1]

The likelihood is that Alexander had to delay in Palestine
longer than he had bargained for, with his seven-month siege of
Tyre and two-month siege of Gaza. In all probability these 'delays'
only increased his anxiety to push on, for his objective was not
Palestine or even Egypt but the farthest east. The stories of his
meetings with the Jews are for the most part legendary and
improbable in their present form (*Ant* 11:304-45; *b Yoma* 69a)[2],
but the likelihood seems to be that the Jews did accept him or one
of his generals without demur, and were consequently allowed to
continue with their singular worship at Jerusalem 'according to

their ancestral laws'. By contrast Alexander seems to have encountered some problems in Samaria which necessitated his planting a Macedonian colony there.[3] Galilee it may be safely presumed did not merit his undue attention, yet because of its geographical location it was soon to be at the center of one of the struggles for control of his vast empire.

I

THE SITUATION ON THE EVE OF ALEXANDER'S CONQUEST

In order to appreciate the impact of the rise of Hellenism on life in Palestine it is necessary to glance briefly backwards to see how political changes had worked in the previous centuries. Only then will the radically new reality of Hellenism stand out in its proper perspective and the challenges it posed be understood. Our focus is on Galilee, but this necessarily involves events in Samaria and Judaea as well.

At the time of Alexander's appearance, Palestine was part of the fifth Persian satrapy, known officially as *Eber ha-Nahar*, 'Beyond the River', formed by Darius I (522-485 B.C.E.) in his administrative reorganization of his empire.[4] In the succeeding two centuries of Persian rule certain administrative changes, the details of which need not concern us, had taken place which were to have far-reaching effects on Jewish life in Palestine. The most significant of these was the gradual re-emergence of Judaea as a province separate from Samaria, centered on the temple state which Cyrus had restored.[5] The Samaritan opposition to this development was apparently political, since the religious divisions of later times only emerged towards the very end of the period, hastened indeed by the advent of hellenism to Samaria. There is a growing scholarly consensus that the building of the schismatic temple on Mount Gerizim took place shortly after the Macedonian conquest and probably due to the presence of the Greek colony that was planted in Samaria itself. Dissident priests from the Jerusalem aristocracy took part in this new religious enterprise (*Ant* 11:297ff.307-11), but the final rift between the two communities only took place in Maccabaean times when the

'Sidonians at Shechem' wrote to Antiochus IV disassociating themselves totally from the opposition to his reform in Jerusalem and accepting the worship of Zeus Hellenios (or Zenios) at their shrine (*2 Macc* 6:2f; *Ant* 12:257-64).[6] It would seem then that Hellenism was able to achieve something that Persian administrative changes, despite the inevitable tensions, had not done, namely to drive a lasting wedge between the Samaritan and Jewish communities.

In view of Galilee's previous history as part of the northern kingdom of Israel it might be expected that it too would have followed Samaria and joined in rejecting the authority of the Jerusalem cultic community. As we shall see, subsequent events make it clear that this did not take place and the explanation of the separation of Galilean from Samaritan loyalties must be sought at an even earlier period still. The Assyrian conquest of the north in the eighth century took place in two quite distinct phases, the first concerned the setting up of a separate province of Megiddo and the second led to the downfall and replanting of Samaria. By breaking the alliance of his predecessor Menahen with Tiglathpilesar III, the Israelite king Pekah incurred the wrath of the Assyrian monarch, who advanced on Palestine and removed from the control of Pekah a large part of his kingdom, organizing these territories in three separate provinces. The biblical narrative of these events is brief and uncircumstantial: 'In the days of Pekah, king of Israel, Tiglathpilesar king of Assyria came and captured Ijon, Abelbethmaacah Janoah, Kadesh, Hazor, Gilead and Galilee, all the land of Naphtali, and he carried the people captive to Assyria' (*2 Kgs* 15:29). From the Assyrian annals for the same period we hear of the three new provinces, Gilead in Transjordan, Dor on the coastal plain and Megiddo. The new province of Megiddo certainly included Upper and Lower Galilee, as can be seen from the list of towns in the biblical account from which captives were taken as well as names of places mentioned in other inscriptions of Tiglathpilesar— Gabara, Hinatuma, (cf. *Nm* 8:17), Qana (Cana), Iatbite (Jotapata), Irruna and Marum (Meron), all apparently in Lower Galilee except for the last named.[8] The lament of Isaiah accurately describes these events: 'In the former time he brought into contempt the land of Zebulun and the land of Naphtali, but in the latter time he will make glorious the way of the sea, the land beyond the Jordan, Galilee of the Gentiles' (*Is* 8:23). Despite present humiliation the three newly-formed Assyrian provinces can look for the redemption to come.[9]

The first phase of the Assyrian take-over was largely administrative, though the biblical narrative does speak of captives being taken from the places listed. However, those measures were only directed at the upper levels of society, the possible leaders of any disturbances against the new arrangement.[10] This treatment differed quite substantially from what took place in Samaria itself. At first the truncated kingdom was made a vassal state with a new king, Hosea. But when he revolted, probably in 727 B.C.E. on the death of Tiglathpilesar, he was imprisoned by the next Assyrian king, Shalmaneser, Samaria itself was razed to the ground in 721 B.C.E. after a three year siege (*2 Kgs* 17:4.6) and this territory also was organized as a separate province. Significantly we hear not merely of deportations, but also of replanting of peoples from many other parts of the Assyrian realm (*2 Kgs* 17:24) and the annals of Sargon II bear witness to similar plantations for a slightly later period (716 B.C.E.).[11] The only other significant change to take place in the north was the extension of the province of Megiddo to include Acco after the victories of Esharhaddon in 673 B.C.E., while its capital seems to have been transferred to either Hazor or Acco at that time. This linking of coast and hinterland was not to last for long, however, for the Persians did have a special interest in maritime activity and in return for assistance in this regard the kingdoms of Tyre and Sidon were given control of the coastal plain, so that Galilee became once more a rural, inland province.[12] It is not clear whether or not it was attached to the province of Samaria then. Subsequently in Seleucid times Samaria does appear to include Galilee (*1 Macc* 10:30; *Ant* 12:154), but this need not be taken as decisive for the earlier period also.[13]

From this outline of the administrative history of Palestine, Galilee and Samaria would seem to have been handled rather differently by the successive regimes, ever since they were included in the Assyrian kingdom as separate provinces. Presumably the reason for the rather different handling of affairs in the two regions was originally due to the fact that as the capital, Samaria was seen to be the real center of resistance over against its fertile rural hinterland which would have guaranteed it economic independence. This in turn must have given rise to cultural and social differences, clearly echoed in the Old Testament prophets already, and the planting of foreigners in Samaria can only have exacerbated this situation subsequently (2 Kgs 17:29-31). True, we do hear of the efforts to instruct the new arrivals in the ways of Yahweh (2 Kgs 17:27f), and, as already mentioned, after the restoration in Jerusalem religious differences between the Jews and the Samaritans seem to have surfaced as late as the Greek period. Presumably the efforts of Josiah to extend his reform to the north were motivated by the hope of uniting all who professed Yahwism, old inhabitants and new arrivals alike. Yet ultimately, the estrangement between rural Galilee and Samaria seems to have continued, with the fertile plain of Esdraelon constituting royal domains and acting as a buffer zone between them. It is unfortunate that our sources are so scant for this period, since, as Alt points out, the books of *Tobit* and *Judith* from the Persian and Greek periods simply presume the contacts between the north and Jerusalem, and the setting up of the separate cultic center at Shechem does not seem to have ever seriously threatened that relationship.[14]

What is particularly significant about this situation is the fact that religious and ethnic loyalties transcend administrative and political boundaries. In all the changes of regimes in the previous centuries, Samaria is the only place where we find a change of population, and significantly it is there that we subsequently find Hellenism able to successfully challenge the cult of Yahweh. We shall presently see that as represented by the Ptolemies in particular, this new movement was to introduce into Palestine foreign elements at every level of society. In this it differed radically from the changes that went before. It is our task to examine the effects of this social and cultural upheaval on every aspect of life in the succeeding centuries. Can the old loyalties survive such a challenge? Now that the stage is set we shall begin in the present chapter to lay the foundations for an adequate answer to that question.

II

GALILEE UNDER PTOLEMIES AND SELEUCIDS.

In the troubled years of the Diadochi (321-301 B.C.E.), as Alexander's generals laid rival claims to his empire, Palestine or rather Coele-Syria as it was most frequently called[15], was one of the areas that was likely to be a source of contention since it was the traditional bridge between the east and west ends of the fertile crescent. Little wonder that Josephus can write of those troubled times as follows: 'The result was that continual and prolonged wars arose, and the cities suffered through their struggles and lost many of their inhabitants, so that all of Syria at the hands of Ptolemy, son of Lagus who was then called Soter, suffered the reverse of that which was indicated by his surname' (*Ant* 12:3). For the most part the territory was in the hands of Antigonus, the most powerful of the generals, but Ptolemy who had earlier been made satrap of Egypt made several swift incursions north in 321 and 312, thereby laying a certain claim to the territory[16]. He successfully repulsed first Demetrius, Antigonus' son, and then Antigonus himself at Gaza (312) and Raphia (306). As a result of these successes Ptolemy was granted Coele-Syria in an agreement of 303 but failed to join the others, Seleucus, Lysimachus and Cassander, when Antigonus was finally defeated and killed at the battle of Ipsus in 301. Accordingly the previous agreement was nullified and Coele-Syria was now granted to Seleucus, an arrangement that Ptolemy refused to accept and that Seleucus was not anxious to insist on because the former had befriended him when he was attempting to establish himself in Syria. This impasse gave rise to the Coele-Syrian problem and was to be a central issue in the four Syrian wars that punctuated Seleucid-Ptolemaic relations throughout the next century.[17]

Coele-Syria was an important strategic and economic extension of the Egyptian territory as Diodorus notes (XVIII,6), and it is no coincidence that losing their grip on the area after 217 marks the beginning of the decline of the power of the Ptolemies. The boundary apparently ran along the valley of the Eleutherus River, so that Galilee was at the center of the controversy. On his first

excursions to the north it appears that Ptolemy's policy was to use
the area as a source for labor and other resources and so we hear
of Jews being taken captive and brought to Egypt, presumably
after his victory at Gaza in 312. Yet the fact that Jerusalem and
Gerizim are explicitly mentioned as two focal points of these
forays is indicative of his real ambitions for lasting control of the
territory, since both centers were the strongholds of the cultic
communities of the Jews and Samaritans that had been granted
independence in Persian times.[18] It was not until 286 B.C.E. that
Tyre and Sidon finally fell within his grasp, and this would surely
apply to some of their Galilean hinterland as well. This possibility
receives strong confirmation from the appearance of Antigonus'
son Demetrius, who had control of the Phoenician sea and the
towns of Tyre and Sidon after Ipsus and in 296 B.C.E. was able to
lay waste the city of Samaria.[19]

Even though Coele-Syria was at the center of the dispute between Ptolemies and Seleucids that gave rise to the four Syrian
wars, it was not until the third of these (219-217 B.C.E.) that we
find any large scale activity in Palestine, and then, significantly
as we shall see, in Galilee. Consequently the Ptolemies, especially
Ptolemy Philadelphus (285-246 B.C.E.), were able to include
Palestine in their elaborate administrative arrangement. Our
knowledge of this has been enormously increased through the
Zenon papyri, forty of which reflect the situation in Palestine in
the mid-third century B.C.E., including Zenon's own tour of
inspection there in 259 B.C.E.[20] This system, especially by comparison with that of the Seleucids, was despotic and centralized,
based on the principle that territory won by the sword was king's
land. He was therefore the sole administrator of the country and
in this task he had at his disposal a vast hierarchy of officials to
carry out his decrees and control the use of the land according to
his wishes. To impose such a bureaucracy on the old indigenous
population of Egypt, demanded rigid control by a centralized
government, the effects of which can clearly be seen in Palestine
also. The administrative unit, the hyparchy, is smaller than the
Persian satrapy and was further subdivided into toparchies and
villages. In Palestine it would appear there were four hyparchies:
Judaea, Samaria, Galilee and Idumaea, even though the two
former are not mentioned in the Zenon correspondence and the

latter two only once each. Concerning the inner subdivisions of these units we must rely partly on the picture that we know from Egypt itself, and partly on that which can be gleaned from the Zenon correspondence with which we shall presently deal.[21] For the present it is sufficient to note that it was complex and multiform. In all probability the whole territory did not have an overall governor, such as the Persian satrap of *Eber ha-Nahar* or the Seleucid *stratēgos prōtarches* (*1 Macc* 3:32; 7:8, *Ant* 12:295.393) but was controlled by the central administration in Alexandria. Inevitably such a system of centralized government involved a large network of hellenistic officials scattered throughout the hyparchies at least in the more important centers, as Zenon's journeys testify, though native sheiks could also be employed as in the case of Toubias (*PCZ* 59003) or Jeddua (*PCZ* 59018), even when as in the latter instance such trust was misplaced.[22]

Authoritarian as this system of Ptolemaic administration was in its outward form, its effects were to be felt mainly in the economic and to some extent the military spheres. The Ptolemies did not attempt any large scale cultural or religious reform such as the Seleucids were later to instigate in Palestine. The old, indigenous village population of Egypt would scarcely have tolerated such radical changes, nor in the interests of stable government was it desirable, and *a fortiori* this would apply to the less homogeneous cultural situation of Palestine. In this respect the Ptolemaic policy in regard to the greatest instrument for change in hellenistic times, the *polis*, is particularly interesting. In Ptolemaic Palestine there is no example of a completely new foundation, such as the Seleucids were to create later, but only the upgrading of certain centers which can easily be explained for traditional or strategic reasons. Thus in the Galilean interior only Philoteria (Beth Yerach) at the exit of the Jordan from the lake, and Scythopolis (Beth Shean) can be classified as Ptolemaic. The latter had already achieved prominence much earlier and so presumably the Ptolemies merely recognized this situation. In the case of Philoteria however, it is doubtful if it ever achieved full city status, with its own independent territory, as its subsequent departure from history indicates, though it may well have served as the administrative center of the hyparchy, because of its special location. Naturally, the situation was quite different on the coast for here there was a long history of independence, and important as these ports were to the overall Ptolemaic military and economic policy, some degree of autonomy had to be conceded to them, even though the classical description 'free and autonomous' can only be applied to any hellenistic foundation in a limited sense.[23] The upgrading of Acco with its new dynastic name of Ptolemais was the most important single development in this area, for under Ptolemaic patronage it now finds itself equal in rank with, and therefore the rival of, the old established Tyre and Sidon, both reconstituted as hellenistic cities under Ptolemaic patronage.[24] On the basis of the Zenon papyri Ptolemais became the gateway not just to its own immediate surrounds in the plain of Acco, but to the whole Galilean hinterland. Thus the administrative arrangement of the Ptolemies succeeded in breaking down the natural separation between coastal plain and interior just as in the Assyrian times. The only difference now was that the interior too was organized in such a way that the new influences could work more easily from within, rather than merely touch the periphery of life from the outside.

The first signs that Ptolemaic hold on Palestine was beginning to loosen came during the fourth Syrian war (221) 219-217 B.C.E. when the energetic Seleucid king Antiochus III succeeded in reducing the northern part of Palestine, and was only finally repulsed at Raphia, the very gate of Egypt. Already in 221 B.C.E. Antiochus was turned back at the Biqa' pass between the Lebanon and Antilebanon and had to temporarily abandon his plans on Coele-Syria, because of problems at home (Polybius *Histories* V, 45:10 - 46:6). In 219 B.C.E. he again took the initiative, this time travelling the coastal road. The important (naval and arsenal) bases of Tyre and Ptolemais were handed over to him by Theodotus (V,65:2f), but he failed to capture Dor (V,66:1). Ptolemy IV Philopater suggested discussions which proved fruitless, rehashing the old claim and counter-claim to Coele-Syria already referred to (V,67), and so in the following year (218) Antiochus proceeded to reduce the interior. His itinerary as given by Polybius is of special interest to our study since it took him to the heart of Galilee (V,70f). His first objective was Philoteria and Scythopolis, the two Ptolemaic foundations there. These were captured, thus assuring supplies. His successes appear to have been gained without any great difficulty, and next he attacked Atabyrion (Thabor) where an Egyptian garrison was located. This too was taken and the garrison replaced by a Seleucid one. Having secured Galilee he then crossed the Jordan and eventually reduced a number of important fortresses there, thus gaining the support of the Arab tribes of the region. Returning to Ptolemais, he sent two officers, Ceraeas and Hippolochus, who had both previously defected to him from Ptolemy with five thousand footsoldiers, to the district of Samaria, 'with orders to protect the conquered territory and assure the safety of all the troops he had left in it' (V,71:11). However, final success was not to be his, for in the following year he was decisively beaten by Ptolemy, who had used the interval to gather his forces, with the native Egyptians playing as great a part as the Greek mercenaries. As a result Antiochus had to withdraw from the captured territory and Ptolemy and his sister Arsinoe conducted a highly successful tour of the re-captured territory, re-appointing military commanders in the area and re-establishing order in the towns (Poly.*His.* 87:1-7).

Two features of this whole campaign are worthy of special attention. In the first place it is noteworthy that a number of Ptolemaic officers defected to Antiochus - Theodotus who had previously repulsed him at Biqa' and who seemed to have been in control of the military arsenal at Ptolemais (Poly.*His.* V, 62:2), Ceraeas, the commander of the Atabyrion fortress and the possible hyparch of Galilee, and Hippolochus, a Thessalian commander of a cavalry regiment, as well as some Arab princes. These defections are symptomatic of unrest with the Ptolemaic system at least on the part of its officials. Accordingly Polybius' remark that the peoples of Coele-Syria had always preferred the Ptolemies to the Seleucids (V, 86:10) cannot be accepted as a blanket description of the total situation. Further, we hear later of pro-Seleucid and pro-Ptolemaic elements in Jerusalem, presumably among the aristocracy. It may well be that the ordinary populace found the Ptolemaic rule on the whole acceptable since they were sensitive to the needs of the rural population of their provinces on the basis of their experience with the old village population in Egypt itself. On the other hand, the upper classes, native and foreign alike, may have found their 'benefactors' rigid taskmasters, and hoped instead to benefit more from the less tightly knit administrative system of the Seleucids.[25]

The second point of significance is that Antiochus seems to have met little or no resistance in Galilee, and in fact was able to rely on the territories of Philoteria and Scythopolis to provide him with sufficient provisions for his army. This may be an indication of the close eye Egyptian officialdom had kept on these and other Palestinian cities.[26] It is not clear from Polybius what the position of Ceraeas was, but the assumption must be that he was not merely in charge of Atabyrion but was in fact the military official in charge of Galilee, as can be seen by the fact that Ptolemy IV took care to appoint a new military commander, Andromachus after his victory at Raphia (Poly.*His.* V, 87:6). It is presumed by several commentators that Antiochus reduced Jerusalem and Judaea as well when he sent Ceraeas and Hippolochus 'to the parts of Samaria' ἐπὶ τοὺς κατὰ Σαμαρίαν τοποὺς, but it seems an unlikely assumption. Polybius says they were charged to ensure the safety of the soldiers he had left behind in the places *already* conquered, and it is altogether unlikely that any force less than that under the command of the king himself should be sent to capture Jerusalem. If this interpretation is correct then it is far more likely that Galilee proper, the plain of Jezreel and part of Samaria came easily into the hands of the Seleucids on this occasion.[27]

This understanding of the events is further supported by the course of happenings during the final showdown between Seleucids and Ptolemies eighteen years later. Once again Antiochus occupied Palestine, this time apparently with little or no opposition in 201 B.C.E., and while the Egyptian general Scopas did manage a counter-attack the following winter he was decisively beaten at Paneion in Upper Galilee near the source of the Jordan in 200 (*Ant* 12:132). Josephus' is a fragmentary account of these events—Scopas the Egyptian general was sent against the people of Coele-Syria 'and took many of *their* cities and also our nation, which went over to him after being attacked'; yet after Paneion Antiochus recaptured the cities of Coele-Syria and Samaria, and then the Jews willingly admitted him to their city, assisting him in besieging the Egyptian garrison which was in the citadel at Jerusalem (*Ant* 12:131-3). When this outline is compared with another summary of the same events in Antiochus' decree concerning the Jews, after the final capture of Jerusalem, a similar picture emerges: 'In as much as the Jews *from the very moment* when we entered their country showed their eagerness to help us, and *when we came to their city*, gave us a splendid reception and met us with their senate and furnished an abundance of provisions for our soldiers and elephants, and also helped us to expel the Egyptian garrison in the citadel, we have seen fit on our part to requite them for these acts . . .' (*Ant* 12:138). This sequence of events is further filled out by some citations from Polybius given by Josephus to the effect that Scopas, 'setting out for the upper country during the winter *subdued* the Jewish nation', but 'that after a short time there came over to him those Jews who live near the temple at Jerusalem, as it is called' (*Ant* 12:135). From these scattered remarks then, it seems that Scopas' campaign which took him to Upper Galilee was a forced one, that is, that he could not rely on the Jewish population for support, and further that Antiochus' advance to the south was via Transjordan and Samaria with the population of Jerusalem eventually accepting him.[28] It is surely more than a mere coincidence that there is no mention of any Galilean resistance to the Seleucids. Philoteria, Scythopolis and Atabyrion had come over to his side during the previous campaign and so, it would seem, could now be relied on. It was only in Jerusalem that any Jewish hesitation appears, but eventually the pro-Seleucid party won out there also.[29]

The official Seleucid name of the newly acquired territory was 'Coele-Syria and Phoenicia', and its incorporation into the Seleucid system must have followed their policy elsewhere. Because their kingdom was much more scattered than that of the Ptolemies it was impossible to impose a unified and centralized system of government. Instead, they allowed for local differences within the vast territory and they also encouraged the emergence of cities, always of course with the limited independence that marked hellenistic from classical times in this regard. Thus their primary unit of administration, the eparchy, included several Egyptian hyparchies, but in the fairly short space of time that the Seleucid administration had effective control of Palestine it is doubtful if this new administration could have broken down older territorial unities. In Palestine, there were in all, four Seleucid eparchies on the basis of Strabo's information: Samaria (including Galilee and Judaea), Idumaea; Paralia and Galaaditis. Thus both Galilee and Judaea lost their independent status of hyparchy or province at least until the outbreak of the war in 167 when Judaea was treated separately by the Seleucids because of the military situation there.[30] We hear nothing of the effects of this new administrative set up or the situation in Galilee, and it is unlikely to have changed the pattern of life there, especially since in all probability the smaller secondary units were still retained within the larger eparchy system.

Neither did the Seleucid policy in regard to cities have any radical effects on life in Galilee. The only new foundation there was in the Upper Jordan valley where the names of Seleucia and Antiochia would seem to indicate Seleucid foundations. However, neither ever attained any great prominence either administratively or commercially and consequently can scarcely have been the media of hellenistic culture on any large scale. The Ptolemaic foundation, Scythopolis received the additional name of Nysa, the mythical nurse of Dionysus and also the name of a princess of the Seleucid house in the time of Antiochus IV. These indications suggest that the status of this city improved under the Seleucid regime, something that would be quite in keeping with their overall policy. We hear nothing of Philoteria in the period, but its non-resistance to the advances of Antiochus III in 218 B.C.E. could not have adversely affected it. Its decline would appear to date from a much later period. Ptolemais also had its 'Antiochene' settlers just like Jerusalem (*2 Macc* 4:19) probably from an earlier date, however, in view of its importance for trading as well as serving as a military base during the earlier Seleucid campaigns in Coele-Syria (cf. Poly.*His.* V, 62:2).

There is little evidence, therefore, of any radical change of fortunes for Galilee in the transfer from Ptolemaic to Seleucid control of Palestine. The reasons for the ease with which the north came under the control of the Seleucids is a question which must remain with us, but even at this stage we can state that geographical considerations seem to have gone hand in hand with the actual historical realities. Once the key centers of settlement had been conquered there was no possibility of any resistance from the peasant rural population, and this was already achieved during the campaigns of 218 B.C.E. with the control of the cities like Ptolemais and Tyre on the coast and Philoteria and Scythopolis in the valley. The plain of Jezreel makes a suitably distant geographic boundary to the south for the Seleucids as had the Eleutherus valley in the north for the Ptolemies, and their military efforts in the interior seem to have been concentrated here. Control of this valley meant that they could proceed along the Via Maris to the south, the only possible way for the attack on Egypt itself which was their main objective. Yet the Seleucid administrative system would appear to allow for older differences of tradition or boundaries to re-emerge - something which, we have seen, the Ptolemaic system tended to obliterate.

III
GALILEE AND THE HELLENISTIC REFORM

Under the new Seleucid administration, Galilee as well as Judaea were units within the eparchy of Samaria, which in turn was part of the province ($\sigma\tau\alpha\tau\eta\gamma\acute{\iota}\alpha$) of 'Coele-Syria and Phoenicia'. At the same time the decree of Antiochus III, which Bickerman rightly calls the Seleucid charter for Jerusalem, granted very special privileges to the $\ddot{\epsilon}\theta\nu os\ \tau\hat{\omega}\nu\ '\text{I}ou\delta\acute{\alpha}\iota\omega\nu$, singling out the inhabitants of Jerusalem in particular for partial remission of tribute (*Ant* 12:138-44). While the term $\ddot{\epsilon}\theta\nu os$ is indeed a hellenistic juridical term, as distinct from the city ($\pi\acute{o}\lambda\iota s$) and the king's land ($\beta\alpha\sigma\iota\lambda\iota\kappa\acute{\eta}\ \gamma\grave{\eta}$), referring not just to a particular ethnic group but also to their territory ($\gamma\grave{\eta}\ \dot{\epsilon}\theta\nu\iota\kappa\acute{\eta}$), its use in this decree bears close examination. Clearly Antiochus did not wish to extend the privileges of his decree to all the Jews in his kingdom, since we hear from another decree of a quite separate arrangement for Jews from Babylonia who were to be planted in Lydia and Phrygia (*Ant* 12:147-53), and the question is to whom does the earlier one refer when it says, 'and all the members of the nation shall have a form of government in accordance with the ancestral laws' ($\pi o\lambda\iota\tau\epsilon\upsilon\acute{\epsilon}\sigma\theta\omega\sigma\alpha\nu\ \delta\grave{\epsilon}\ \pi\acute{\alpha}\nu\tau\epsilon s\ o\acute{\iota}\ \dot{\epsilon}\kappa\ \tauo\hat{\upsilon}\ \ddot{\epsilon}\theta\nuo\upsilon s\ \kappa\alpha\tau\grave{\alpha}\ \tauo\grave{\upsilon}s\ \pi\alpha\tau\rho\acute{\iota}o\upsilon s\ \nu\acute{o}\mu o\upsilon s,\ Ant\ 12:142$)? It should be noted in the first place that the decree is not addressed to the Jewish leaders (high priest or $\gamma\epsilon\rho o\upsilon\sigma\acute{\iota}\alpha$), but to Ptolemy, probably the governor of Coele-Syria and Phoenicia at that time.[31] This raises the question of whether other Jews living in that province might not also be included. The actual wording of the decree $\pi\acute{\alpha}\nu\tau\epsilon s\ o\acute{\iota}\ \dot{\epsilon}\kappa\ \tauo\hat{\upsilon}\ \ddot{\epsilon}\theta\nuo\upsilon s$ would seem to support this conclusion, as well as the specification of the separate tax concessions to the inhabitants of Jerusalem and to certain temple officials. The phrase $\kappa\alpha\tau\grave{\alpha}\ \tauo\grave{\upsilon}s$

πατρίους νόμους is a general one found frequently in similar hellenistic documents, whereby the continuance of traditional laws and customs are guaranteed to a city or territory by its new overlord.[32] In this case the right to live according to the Jewish law was confirmed to all the Jews under Ptolemy, and this must have included Galilean Jews also. This conclusion helps us to understand better the background to the reform of Antiochus IV forty years later, which was such a deep trauma for the Jewish people, in that it was not merely an attack on their religion but a revocation of the agreement which the earlier Seleucids had sanctioned in the best hellenistic spirit.

It is generally recognized that the reform itself was the out-growth of social and religious changes that had been taking place within the Jerusalem aristocracy for some time, part polit-ical (pro-Seleucid or Ptolemaic), part social (priestly aristocracy and the lay nobility represented by the Tobiads) and part religious (the hellenisers and the Hasîdîm). Apparently, the intention of the hellenisers was to transform Jerusalem into a hellenistic city with Jason the high priest appointed by Antiochus as chief instigator (2 Macc 4:9-11). What was at first a cultural and social reform was turned into religious persecution when Antiochus, involved in war with Egypt and in need of financial resources, first invaded the temple treasury and then, a second time, ruth-lessly crushed a popular uprising against him and his puppet high priest Menelaus, who had ousted Jason (2 Macc 5:12ff). A colony of Syrian soldiers was established in the area, and appar-ently this move already cemented the forces of resistance under the aegis of the Hasîdîm (1 Macc 2:31ff) or pious upholders of Israel's religious traditions. It was their opposition coupled with the extreme hellenizing policies of Menelaus and his Jewish supporters that led eventually to the actual religious persecution (167 B.C.E.), in which the worship of Yahweh was to be assim-ilated to that of the Zeus Olympius cult in the temple at Jeru-salem, and the practice of distinctive Jewish religious observances outlawed (1 Macc 1:44-51; 2 Macc 6:1-5).[33] This attack was directed at the cities of Judaea as well as at Jerusalem, but apparently it soon moved northward, for the following year we hear of a letter from the Sidonians at Shechem to Antiochus (Ant 12:259-61) in which reference is made to harassment by Apollonius (probably the governor to Coele-Syria and Phoenicia, *1 Macc* 3:10; *2 Macc* 3:5) and Nicanor, an agent of the king working in the area to raise money (*2 Macc* 8:9ff). Reading between the lines we can gather that this group had succeeded in controlling the temple at Gerizim and in having the worship of Zeus accepted there also (*2 Macc* 6:2; *Ant* 12:261).

Even rural Galilee could not hope to escape these pressures, and unfortunately the rather schematic treatment of the topic by the author of *1 Macc* makes it difficult to reconstruct the whole story in its chronological details. Apparently *1 Macc* 5 is a patchwork of different Jewish reactions to the religious reform in which the Maccabaean brothers were engaged. Thus, one literary analysis suggests that vv. 3-8.65-8 refer to a campaign of Judas alone, in the vicinity of Judaea before the rededication of the temple in 164 B.C.E., whereas vv. 1-2.9-64 deal with excursions to Galilee and Gilead after that event.[34] In any case the reference to Galilee is brief and uncircumstantial. Word arrived in Jerusalem that the men of Ptolemais, Tyre and Sidon and all Galilee of the Gentiles had gathered against the Jews to annihilate them (*1 Macc* 5:14f). Simon was deputed to go to their aid with an army of 5,000 men. 'He fought many battles against the gentiles and the gentiles were crushed before him. He pursued them to the gate of Ptolemais and as many as 3,000 of the gentiles fell and he despoiled them. Then he took the Jews of Galilee and Arbatta and their wives and children and all that they possessed, and led them to Judaea with great rejoicing' (*1 Macc* 5:21-23). An uncritical reading of this passage has lead Schürer and after him many other proponents of a gentile Galilee to conclude that at this point in time the Jewish population of Galilee was only a tiny minority living in a hostile environment seeing that Simon was able to transplant them.[35] However, apart from the consciously archaizing style of the author that explains the phrase Γαλιλαία ἀλλοφυλῶν,[36] and the heroic description of 'many battles against the gentiles', concentration on the geography is also called for. The whole operation took place in the western part of Galilee, apparently in the region of Ptolemais, which significantly Simon did not attempt to capture, nor did he push farther north to the other Phoenician cities. Almost two hundred years later we hear of the Jewish population in the neighborhood of the same Syrian cities being harassed and of Jewish reprisals (*War* 2:458f). The M.S.S. evidence for Arbatta is uncertain, and various emendations have been suggested, but it may be inferred that it lies outside Galilee, and was in the same general region as Ptolemais.[37] At all events Simon's activity is localized in the neighborhood of the Greek cities, and presumably the Jewish population of these regions had been under attack because of their resistance to the changes which Antiochus and his officials were imposing. Possibly also, there was resentment on the part of the Greek population because of the special status of the Jews of the area which the decree of Antiochus had granted. For our purposes the most important conclusion is that even at this hour of crisis for Judaism, the old Israelite population of the interior of Galilee was able to survive relatively unscathed, whereas those in trouble turned instinctively to Jerusalem.

In the subsequent struggles of the Maccabaean brothers with the Seleucids we find confirmation of this conclusion. On the one hand, it would seem, the Maccabaeans were genuinely concerned about their co-religionists in Galilee, yet at the same time practical politics did not allow them to conceive of incorporating the area within the territory they were carving out for the ἔθνος τῶν Ἰουδαίων, in relative autonomy from the Seleucid overlords. Gradually, as the spiritual impetus of the movement declined and its secular, political aspects came to the fore, Galilee had to wait for the opportune moment before it could be politically re-united with the territory where its cultic center lay. Josiah had briefly attempted a similar acquisition of the north in the seventh century, but his efforts foundered with his death.[38] Ironically, even though the same religious ideology - the ideal of the land - seems to have been the underlying driving force of the struggle against the Seleucids, for that struggle to succeed the Jewish state had itself to be transformed into that which it sought to overcome - a hellenistic power. Thus the very tension between religion and nationhood which the struggle attempted to resolve continued in a new form, now transferred to the center of Judaism itself, there to fester and erupt at various moments of national or religious crisis. But we must retrace our steps.

The first stage of Jewish liberation was achieved when Antiochus, under pressure because of wars in the east granted an amnesty, allowing the Jews to live in accordance with their own laws (*2 Macc* 11:27-33), thereby restoring the charter of Antiochus III. This was in October of 164 B.C.E. and that winter Judah and his followers captured a part of Jerusalem and rededicated the temple (*1 Macc* 4:36-59). It was after this, and possibly as a result of it, that the persecution of Galilean Jews, already discussed, took place. The death of Antiochus IV and the regency of his governor Lysias meant new troubles for the Jews, as Judah's attempt to remove the Syrian colony from the Acra failed. For a time Judah seemed isolated, even from his own people, but an indiscretion by the high priest Alcimus once more aroused the ire of the *Hasidim* who had previously acquiesced in his appointment (*1 Macc* 7:13f; 9:54f) and the general Nicanor was sent by the current incumbent of the Seleucid throne, Demetrius I, to quieten the trouble. This expedition was to lead to Nicanor's defeat by Judah and death, near Beth Horon, giving rise to the 'day of Nicanor' celebrated in Jewish lore (*2 Macc* 15:35f).

Judah's victory was not for long, for a new and more powerful general, Bacchides was dispatched against him. Significantly, Bacchides did not take the usual coastal route but travelled south through Galilee along the Jordan rift and encamped at Arbela, overlooking the lake of Gennesareth (*1 Macc* 9:1f).[40] Here he began his campaign against the local people, presumably because the Galilean peasants of the region had given some sign of their support for their Judaean brothers, and it would be dangerous to leave such an enclave in his rear. The pattern would repreat itself more than once in the subsequent two centuries. Bacchides was not to make the same mistake as Nicanor, and before returning Judah had been defeated and killed, and Jewish resistance quenched finally, it would seem.

After a lull of several years (160-152 B.C.E.) the second Maccabaean brother Jonathan emerged from the obscurity of a village chieftain to carry on the struggle, availing himself of the dynastic difficulties among the Seleucids that were eventually to be their downfall. Siding first with Demetrius I and then with his rival, the pretender Alexander Balas, Jonathan succeeded in obtaining from the latter the right to occupy the vacated high priesthood and two years later was appointed general and governor of the province of Judaea (*1 Macc* 10:30f.65), a post that had apparently been created to deal with the crisis there after the reform, when Judaea was severed from the eparchy of Samaria (*2 Macc* 14:12). In effect Jonathan became an official of the Seleucid administration and we catch a glimpse of the growing independence of his position in the various tax concessions that the Demetrids were prepared to grant him.[41] Apparently the tribute (φόρος) which was the chief tax paid collectively under the earlier hellenistic monarchies (*2 Macc* 4:8; *Ant* 12:144, the Seleucids; *Ant* 12:154ff, the Ptolemies) had been transformed into a direct land tax during the period of the reform for the obvious reason that the leadership of the Jewish people, on whom collection of the tribute devolved, was so unstable. Now however, Demetrius I, and after him his son, Demetrius II, in return for Jonathan's support were prepared to make sizable concessions in regard to the land taxes, not only of Judaea, but also of the three districts of Samaria and Galilee that had been ceded to him (*1 Macc* 10:30.38; 11:28.34). The basis for both concessions is ostensibly the recognition of the Jewish cultic community (cf. 10:38; 11:34b), and in the case of Demetrius II a tribute of three hundred talents is expected in return. Josephus supplements his source *1 Macc* at this point, for he tells us that later there was an arrear of tribute owed by the Jewish people (*Ant* 13:143; cf. *1 Macc* 13:15). Clearly the political pendulum had begun to swing in Jonathan's favor, and despite outward displays of subservience (cf. *1 Macc* 11:24-7), he was able to adopt an increasingly independent attitude that reached its climax after his death in 142 B.C.E. when, in the words of *1 Macc* 13:41, 'the yoke of the heathen was lifted from Israel'.

The absence of any mention of Galilee in all these arrangements between the later Maccabaeans and the various Seleucids might appear to contradict our earlier contention that the area was essentially Jewish and that its inhabitants enjoyed the rights of Antiochus III's charter. However, it should be remembered that the formal ceding of Jewish territory by the later Seleucids was done from a position of weakness, unlike the situation with Antiochus III. Thus the three districts explicitly mentioned, Aphairema, Lydda and Ramathaim bordered Judaea. Presumably they strongly supported the Maccabaeans, since Modein, their home town, was in the district of Lydda, and this natural enlargement could not be prevented. Galilee on the other hand was geographically separated by Samaria, and administratively linked with it still, for whatever support was shown for Judah in the district of Arbela does not appear to have been serious enough to warrant a separate administrative arrangement.[42]

Despite Jonathan's and Simon's exercise of *Realpolitik* it would seem that they did not forget the older links that bound the north with Jerusalem. Thus we find the former confronting the army of Demetrius II at Hazor in Upper Galilee in 144 B.C.E. and routing the enemy as far as Kadesh (*1 Macc* 11:63-74). Josephus explains that Kedasa lies between the land of Tyre and Galilee, and adds that the Syrians hoped to draw Jonathan off to Galilee, 'as an ally of the latter country, and that he would not allow the Galileans, who were his own people to be attacked by his enemy' (*Ant* 13:154). No doubt there is an echo of his own times as general in Galilee and an idealization of the Maccabaean general in this comment, but subsequently we hear in the same vein from the author of *1 Macc* that Jonathan marched as far as Hamath in Lebanon to forestall an attack of Demetrius from coming into his land (χώραν, *1 Macc* 12:25).[43] At the time of his capture by Trypho he can rely on Galilee for support, as Trypho himself recognizes (*1 Macc* 12:47.49f). Undoubtedly these indications are rather general, but they do suggest that Galilee was certainly considered to be within the area of ancestral Jewish claims (*1 Macc* 13:33), even if these could not be pressed. The fact that Simon was not able to consolidate the north was due to the appearance of the last strong Seleucid, Antiochus Sidetes, and the Maccabaean had to be content with maintaining control of Judaea and consolidating his internal position (*1 Macc* 14:25-49). Even this was lost to his son John Hyrcanus for a time, and so Galilee had to await until the final phase of Hasmonaean expansion before it was eventually reunited politically with its cultural and cultic matrix.

IV
GALILEE AS PART OF THE HASMONAEAN STATE

It was not until relatively late in the long reign of John Hyrcanus, Simon's son, (134-105 B.C.E.) that any effective steps took place to incorporate Galilee into the emerging Jewish state. This in itself is significant, for it means that considerations of strategy made it more important to consolidate the territory already controlled. This in turn highlights the dilemma of Galilee, for it was geographically isolated from its center by the territories of the Greek cities, Straton's Tower on the coast, Samaria in the hill country and Scythopolis in the valley. Besides, the Great Plain was still king's land and strategically important as we have been. Thus, expansion to the north had to be well planned, and practical politics rather than ancient loyalties were to determine the rate of expansion, no matter how much these could be appealed to. Access to the sea and control of the maritime plain had to be an important step in establishing an independently viable Judaea. On the East the King's Highway through Transjordan was secured by the capture of Madaba and Samaga (*Ant* 13:255f). Next we hear of the destruction of the Samaritan temple at Shechem and the enforced circumcision of the Idumaeans (*Ant* 13:256-8), thus indicating that the religious ideology that originally sparked the revolt had not been completely lost sight of despite the hellenistic-style army that Hyrcanus had organized.[44] The Greek cities remained, but they too eventually succumbed. After a one year siege, Samaria fell, probably in 107 B.C.E., being razed to the ground (*Ant* 13:281), and at the same time Scythopolis came into Jewish hands, either by bribery (*Ant* 13:280) or captured by Hyrcanus' sons (*War* 1:66), who are also reported to have ravaged the whole country south of Mt. Carmel, that is, the Great Plain. The conquest of the former was celebrated as a Jewish national holiday according to the *Megillath Ta'anith*, to underline once more 'the holy war' aspect of the campaign, at least in popular imagination. The way to Galilee was at last secure.[45]

The only possible allusion to a Galilean campaign in the sources is in reference to Hyrcanus' son Antigonus returning to Jerusalem in glory during the reign of Aristobulus I (*Ant* 13:304). The parallel account in *War* 1:76 says that he 'procured for himself fine armour and military decoration in Galilee', (παρασκευασκέναι ὅπλα τε αὐτῷ κάλλιστα καὶ πολεμικὸν κόσμον ἐν τῇ Γαλιλαίᾳ). This may refer to a campaign in the province, possibly the destruction of Philoteria which we know suffered the same fate as the other cities at this time[46], but it may also simply mean that Antigonus dwelt in Galilee like his brother Alexander Jannaeus (*Ant* 13:322) and came from there to the feast of Tabernacles with a display of independence that was a threat to his ailing brother Aristobulus. At all events, the silence of our sources can only mean that there was no campaign here similar to that in other regions once the hellenistic cities had been overthrown, nor would we have expected any in the light of what was seen of the situation there after the reform.

Josephus does tell us that Aristobulus made war on the Ituraeans, and on the authority of Timagenes cited by Strabo, declares that he acquired additional territory for the Jews, 'and brought over a portion of the Ituraean nation, whom he joined to them by the bond of circumcision' (*Ant* 13:318f). It is on the basis of this information that Schürer speaks of the judaizing of Galilee, identifying the part of the Ituraean territory conquered by Aristobulus with Galilee, 'or the greatest part of it'.[47] But this conclusion is based on no solid evidence, and does not stand up to close examination. Very little is known of the expansion of the Ituraeans before the first century B.C.E. but apparently they, like the Jews, had availed of the weaknesses of the Seleucids to extend their territory, originally situated in the Massyas valley between Lebanon and Antilebanon.[48] We know that later when that part of their territory that was still intact was transferred to Herod the Great it consisted of Batanaea, Trachonitis and Auranitis in Transjordan and Ulatha and Paneas on the west bank - that is the Upper Jordan valley (*Ant* 15:343.360), and we can certainly allow for an infiltration into Upper Galilee also, given the political vacuum at the turn of the century in that region. Yet, if the tactics of Zenodorus their leader a half century later are any indication, their expansion was not at all likely to have been the kind that would strike deep roots or permanently disrupt an old indigenous population. They engaged in brigandage and had no other means of livelihood according to Josephus (*Ant* 15:346), and while they certainly did harass the surrounding peoples there can be little question of them taking over a whole territory at an earlier period.

Thus, the judaization of Galilee in the sense of converting to Judaism the inhabitants of a large tract of the area which had not previously been associated with the Jewish faith has no real basis and should be abandoned, despite the number of reputable scholars who have repeated Schürer's views uncritically. The earlier Maccabees had pushed as far north as Hamath in their efforts to establish defensible boundaries, and the activity of Alexander Jannaeus in Transjordan later (*Ant* 13:393f; *War* 1:104f) shows a similar expansionist policy in the north. We can therefore accept that those Ituraeans who had infiltrated the Upper Jordan valley were forcibly judaized like the Idumaeans to the south (*Ant* 13:257), but the probability is that these dwelt well outside the area that is known as Upper Galilee at a later time. We have seen that the northern boundary fluctuated considerably, and in Ptolemaic times it ran well to the north of here including the original Ituraean lands of the Lebanon. Perhaps it is legitimate to speak of this whole region as Galilee for this period, though there is little evidence for such a usage in official documents. In that case the population would undoubtedly be mixed and the picture would be considerably changed. It is interesting to note that we never hear of the Galileans being subsequently reproached as half-Jews, unlike the Idumaeans (cf. *Ant* 14:403), even though many other distinctive aspects of their Jewishness are noted or criticized. Only a few years after the reign of Aristobulus during which the alleged judaization of Galilee is supposed to have taken place, Ptolemy Lathyrus, who had come to the aid of Ptolemais, then besieged by Alexander Jannaeus, was able to surprise the city of Asochis (Talmudic Sikhnin) five miles north of Sepphoris (*Life* 207.233.384) because it was the Sabbath (*Ant* 13:337). In other words the Jewishness of Lower Galilee seems secure even at that early stage of its incorporation into the Hasmonaean kingdom. If this had been of such recent vintage the boundaries of Pompey's carve-up of the kingdom makes little sense, for we would expect Galilee like other areas to revert to its former condition. Instead it was included in the ethnarchy of Hyracanus II, presumably because the ἔθνος τῶν Ἰυδαίων could claim it as its own territory, not by right of recent conquest, but rather on the strength of ancient allegiances.

Equally important as the inclusion of Galilee within the Hasmonaean kingdom was the extension of the internal political and social institutions of that kingdom to the province. These would survive the subsequent breakup and shape life within the province for the future. Unfortunately our sources are largely silent about these developments in Galilee and we can only surmise the broad outline from scattered pieces of evidence and inferences from what is in general known of Hasmonaean internal policies.[49]

In all probability the division of the country into the larger units of Judaea, Samaria, Idumaea, Galilee and Peraea, of later times (*War* 3:35-58) goes back to the period of the conquests. In other words, the fact that these different regions of the country were incorporated into the one kingdom did not mean that the older administrative divisions were done away with. This would be inconsistent with the hellenistic tendencies in the policies of the Hasmonaeans. We do not hear of any governor for the whole of Galilee, but such an appointment would not be improbable. We have mentioned that Alexander Jannaeus was brought up there, and also noted his brother Antigonus' military exploits. This could reflect an earlier policy of assigning certain members of the ruling house as military commanders of various districts - John Hyrcanus at Gezer and his brother-in-law Ptolemy at Jericho (*1 Macc* 16:11.19). During the reign of Alexandra when the Pharisees were in the ascendancy, we hear the complaints of the military commanders who ask to be stationed at various garrison outposts to escape the vengeance of their enemies (*Ant* 13:411-15). As Schalit observes these must be considered 'the friends of the king', that is the close associates of the ruler known to us from other hellenistic monarchies.[50] The overtures of this group to Alexandra are an important insight into the way in which internal politics had developed under the Hasmonaeans. A landed aristocracy had emerged who had acted as generals in the wars of conquest and expected special treatment in the running of the kingdom, something that Alexander Jannaeus in particular had granted them. As we shall see later, Sepphoris is one such center of Hasmonaean landed nobility in Galilee, and it comes as no surprise to hear that Ptolemy was unable to capture it on the occasion of his surprise attack on Asochis (*Ant* 13:338).

In all probability the toparchical system of local government inherited from the hellenistic monarchies was combined with the *Mishmaroth* divisions of the country which related to temple worship and had been in existence since the restoration from

Babylon. Of course as the Jewish territory extended the *Mishmar* divisions had also to be revised, and at the time of Alexander Jannaeus these appear to have been settled at 24, corresponding to the 24 toparchies.[51] This is yet another example of that strange accommodation of Jewish religion to the realities of a hellenistic state that is such a constant feature of the Hasmonaean kingdom. In Galilee there were at least five, and possibly eight such divisions, serving as centers of local administration for tax and other purposes, as well as providing the local contributions for the temple (*M. Ta'an* 4:2; *M. Bikk* 3:2; *p. Ta'an* 4,69a).[52] Later we shall have occasion to discuss the tax system in general, but it is apposite to mention in this context that according to an ancient *baraita* one-third of the tithe should be apportioned to the treasury, the other two-thirds being given to priests and Levites and to the poor and scholars who were in Jerusalem (*p. Ma'as Sch* 5,9). Thus we catch a glimpse of how the secular and religious administrative webs were put to the services of the new state and its growing fiscal demands.

Perhaps the most important single internal development of the whole period was the gradual alienation of the religious element within the state from the ruling body, despite the latter's effort to maintain close links between the two spheres of life as we have just seen. Already in the days of Judah the Maccabee the *Hasidim* were prepared to accept a legitimate priest of the house of Aaron and abandon the freedom struggle (*1 Macc* 7:13), and at the very end of the period we find representatives of the people, that is the Pharisees, complaining to Pompey that 'it was the custom of their country to obey the priests of the God who was venerated by them, but that these two (the rival Hasmonaean brothers, Hyrcanus II and Aristobulus II) who were descended from priests, were seeking to change the form of government in order to make them a nation of slaves' (*Ant* 14:41). In the interim this rift which was built into the different aspirations of those who could unite in face of a common enemy had surfaced during the reign of John Hyrcanus. Josephus mentions the three Jewish parties, Pharisees, Sadducees and Essenes for the first time already during the time of Jonathan (*Ant* 13:171-73), but in that version they are philosophical schools debating a theoretic question about free will. However, subsequent events were to show that the first two in particular were an integral part of the social and political life of Judaism. John Hyrcanus rejected their petition that he abandon 'the high priesthood and be content with governing the people' (*Ant* 13:288-300; *b.Qidd* 66a). The political nuance of being a ruler in a theocratic state without controlling the high priesthood was not lost on him and he accordingly aligned himself with the Sadducees.[53] In all probability this statement represents a move in the direction of absolutism on the part of John, for Josephus adds that John 'abrogated the regulations of the Pharisees and imposed penalties on those who observed them' (*Ant* 13:296). In being accepted as high priest for ever by the *Hever ha-Yehudîm*, John's father Simon had entered into a bilateral agreement which recognized the rights of the Jewish assembly to appoint him, a fact that is reflected in his title ἐθνάρχος, 'ruler of the people'. John's behavior apparently was far too independent for those who saw the progressive secularization of Judaism. It may well be that the decision to do away with the confession (in regard to tithes) which *M. Ma'as Sch.* 5:15 attributes to Johanan the priest,[54] especially when seen in conjunction with his other regulation about one-third of the tithe for the treasury, was the occasion for the Pharisees' opposition to John, which the legendary story in Josephus and the Talmud reflects.

John Hyrcanus seems to have been able to ride out the storm but the problem re-emerged under his son Alexander Jannaeus, who showed far less tact than his father in handling this delicate matter which touched the nerve center of Judaism within a Jewish state. Now the title 'king' had also been acquired as a further sign of Hasmonaean independence.[55] His military conquests gave him greater freedom of operation, yet at the same time increased the financial and other burdens he had to place on the people and no doubt this fired the flames of opposition against him, with the Pharisees, the espousers of the popular cause, in the van. While the trouble flared up on the occasion of Jannaeus' celebration of the feast of Tabernacles (*Ant* 13:372-4; cf *M. Sukk* 4:9), the real issue was not one of ritual ceremonial but the question of who was to control the Jewish people. Schalit draws the plausible inference from Jannaeus' arrogation of the title 'king' and the dropping of the phrase *Hever ha-Yehudîm*

from his coins that he had in fact abolished the Jewish assembly
altogether and adopted a dynastic form of government so typical
of hellenistic states.[56] As long as the assembly continued the
Pharisees felt they had some control over the way the affairs of
state were conducted, but with its abolition pure despotism had
taken over, and this is the very charge that was later proferred
by them against Jannaeus' successors before Pompey. This would
explain the ruthlessness of the king's reaction to his enemies
using foreign mercenaries to kill 6,000 Jews on a Jewish feast - as
well as the protracted civil war subsequently, during which
the Pharisees adopted the extreme measure of enlisting the aid
of Demetrius Akairos, the current Seleucid monarch, in an attempt to oust their hated enemy (*Ant* 13:372-83; *War* 1:90-8; cf
b. Sota 47b; *b. Sanh* 107b). The opposition continued, and during
the regency of Alexandra, Jannaeus' wife, the positions are
completely reversed, apparently on the advice of the dying king
(*Ant* 13:400-4). The anti-Hasmonaean propaganda which subsequently received literary expression in the Pharisaic *Psalms
of Solomon* must have had its origins in this period, for one of
the specific charges hurled against them is that they had violated
the promise made to David's seed: 'what thou hadst not promised
to them, they took away (from us) with violence . . . They laid waste
the throne of David in tumultuous arrogance' (*Ps Sol* 17:1-11).[57]
The Sadducaean nobility, 'the friends of the king', complain
bitterly at being ousted from power, and once again a bloody
civil strife developed with the Pharisees having the upper hand
on this occasion (*Ant* 13:408f). The failure to work out a com-
promise meant that soon Rome would have the opportunity to
intervene as would-be resolvers of the tension between the rival
factions supporting one or other of the Hasmonaean claimants
to the crown of Alexandra. For the present the Pharisaic rise to
power meant a much more energetic effort to disseminate their
teachings and knowledge of the Torah to ordinary people. At
the very beginning of her reign 'whatever regulations introduced
by the Pharisees in accordance with the tradition of their fathers
(κατὰ τὴν πατρῴαν παράδοσιν) that had been abolished by her
father-in-law Hyrcanus, these Alexandra again restored'. Exiles
were recalled and captives set free (*Ant* 13:408f). The figure of
Simeon ben Shetah looms very large in Talmudic literature for

this period, and undoubtedly he was a dominant figure in the Pharisaic takeover. In particular the attribution to him of the institution of the *beth sefer* or Jewish school was to have far reaching effects for the future, though it is difficult to assess how widespread it became at this period.[58]

Our sources do not have even as much as one reference to Galilee in regard to all this turmoil at the center of Judaism in this period. We do hear of the various fortresses throughout the countryside Hyrcania, Alexandreion and Machaerus, as well as the lesser ones, but none of these appear to be in Galilee proper, and many apparently were in Transjordan (*Ant* 13:395-7.417f). Undoubtedly there was some Hasmonaean activity in Galilee, and presumably the emergence of such Galilean fortresses as the old castle of Sepphoris, Gush-Halab (Gischala) and old Yodpat (Jotapata), mentioned in the Mishnah (*Arak* 9:6), date from this period of national consolidation. It is doubtful if the Pharisees succeeded in extending their campaign of instructing the people in their own *halakhah* to the north, at least this early, despite Klein's valiant efforts to extend the number of Galilean scribes of an earlier period.[59] In all probability it was much later before the institution of the *beth sefer* reached Galilee, for the Talmud (*b. Bab Bat* 21a) attributes its extension 'to every town and district' to Josua ben Gamala (Gamaliel), who may be the same person as the high priest of that name from 63-65 C.E.[60] Other evidence about Pharisaic influence in Galilee to be discussed later supports that view. Thus we are left with a Jewish Galilee somewhat on the periphery of these major disturbances within Judaism whose ordinary people have no apparent say in the councils of the nation at Jerusalem. At the same time native aristocracy based on Hasmonaean conquests and appropriation of lands belonging to the hellenistic monarchs is beginning to emerge within the province. This agrees with what we know of the situation later, as Gabinius turns to a native aristocracy to run the assembly for the province that he set up at Sepphoris (*Ant* 14:91; *War* 1:169f). Yet as we shall see, this group had neither the will, nor the interest in pushing the independence of Galilee further, and the common people could scarcely be expected to take the initiative.

CONCLUSION

At the end of the first phase of Jewish contact with Hellenism within Palestine, we have discovered the strange paradox that just when Judaism had achieved autonomy after centuries of subjection to foreign overlords, a deep cleavage emerged within it on the question of the nature of that state and the control of power. Rural Galilee seems to have escaped relatively unscathed from the political upheaval that this issue brought about, as well as from the immediate effects of the hellenistic reform and its aftermath. But the effects of hellenization were felt there from the very start, down to the lowest rung of village life, it would seem. Ancient loyalties which had been lived for centuries in relative isolation from their center prevailed, however, and Galilee passed naturally into the emerging Jewish state once the geographical and cultural obstacles, the cities, had been removed. The political reality of the Hasmonaean state was experienced chiefly in the realms of taxes and the rise of a native nobility. The impact of these developments on everyday life within the province will be discussed in subsequent chapters. First, however, we must see what, if any, reactions were produced in Galilee by Judaism's second encounter with Hellenism in terms of the incorporation of the new Jewish state into the structures of the Roman Empire.

NOTES FOR CHAPTER 2

[1] *P Col Zen* 2 col 3, in *Corpus Papyrorum Judaicorum*, ed. Λ. Fuchs and V. Tcherikover, Cambridge Mass. 1957, (hereafter *CPJ*), 1, 124. The papyrus deals with a caravan of camels, trading between Egypt and Palestine, and the name Γαλιλα appears on 1.20. Alt, 'Herkunft', *G.P.* 1, 364, considers this to be a direct transliteration of the Aramaic emphatic form, pre-dating the LXX Γαλιλαία, which he considers to be a *nomen gentilicium*. However, both he and W.L. Westermann, the original editor note that the caravaneers may simply have been using the local pronunciation, since this is not a literary document.

[2] V. Tcherikover, *Hellenistic Civilisation and the Jews*, English trans. Philadelphia, Jewish Publication Co., 1959, 42-50, and *World History of the Jewish People*, First Series, Ancient Times, vol. 6, *The Hellenistic Age*, Jerusalem, Masada Publishing Co. 1972, ed. A. Schalit, (hereafter, *W.H.Hell.A.*), 56-62.

[3] E. Schürer, *Geschichte des Jüdischen Volkes im Zeitalter Jesu Christi*, 3 vols. Reprint Darmstadt, 1970, (hereafter, *Geschichte*) 2, 195, citing Curtius Rufus and Eusebius, *Chronicon*.

[4] Avi-Yonah, *The Holy Land*, 11ff.

[5] This is the view of Alt, 'Die Rolle Samarias bei der Entstehung des Judentums', in *Kl. Schr.* 2, 316-37, on 328f, and also that of E. Bickerman, *From Ezra to the Last of the Maccabees. Foundations of Post-Biblical Judaism*, New York, Shocken Paperback, 1962, 43. However, Avi-Yonah, *The Holy Land*, 13, thinks that it was a separate province from the beginning.

[6] Below, Ch. 7 n.22.

[7] Alt, 'Die Rolle Samarias', *Kl. Schr.* 2, 318f and 'Die Assyrische Provinz Megiddo und ihr Späteres Schicksal', *G.P.* 2, 374-84, esp. 375f.

[8] E. Fohrer, *Die Provinzeinteilung des Assyrischen Reiches*, Leipzig 1920, 56-61; F.M. Abel, *Géographie de la Palestine*, 2 vols., *Etudes Bibliques*, Paris 1933, 2, 104ff.

[9] A. Alt, 'Jesaja 8:23-9:6. Befreiungsnacht und Kronungstag', *Kl. Schr.* 2, 206-25, relates the geography of this oracle of Isaiah to the events of 733, when, according to the Assyrian annals, the three provinces of Duru (Way of the Sea, that is the Coastal Plain), Magidu (Galilee) and Gala'zu (Transjordan) were set up.

[10] Alt, 'Die Umgestaltung Galiläas durch die Hasmonäer', *G.P.* 5, 407-23, esp. 409-11, argues this position convincingly from the Assyrian records concerning the captives, the fact that Galilee had shown no particular resistance and the presence of the new arrivals only at the main centers, especially Samaria, ten years later. He writes: 'Von einer Importation fremder Elemente nach Galiläa fehlt uns jede Kunde'. The same position is adopted by K. Galling, 'Judäa, Galiläa und der Osten im Jahre 163/4 v. Chr.', PJB 36(1940) 43-77, esp. 64, but with no new arguments.

[11] Aharoni and Avi-Yonah, *The Macmillan Bible Atlas*, 96f.

[12] This is the conclusion of Alt, based on the archaeological evidence from Megiddo from the sixth century and thereafter, which suggests a rapid decline in its importance, 'Die Assyrische Provinz', *Kl. Sch.* 2, 378f, n.3. He suggests that it was replaced by Acco as the chief seat of the province, once the Assyrians had conquered the Phoenician coastal cities, at the latest 50 years after the fall of Samaria when Sidon fell to them, 676, B.C.E. There is also the possibility that Hazor served as the administrative center as a result of the Assyro-Persian palace discovered there, according to Avi-Yonah, *The Holy Land*, 25.

[13] Avi-Yonah, *The Holy Land*, 25, agrees with Alt, 'Galiläas Verhältnis zu Samaria und Judäa im hellenistischen Zeitalter', *G.P.* 4, 396-407, esp. 404f. against U. Kahrstedt, *Syrische Territorien in Hellenistischer Zeit*, Göttingen 1926, 65f, who claims that the later Seleucid arrangement for Galilee and Samaria should not be projected back to an earlier period, since Galilee was never treated as a people's land but as a king's land, in contrast to the other areas. However cf. below n. 30 for a critique of Alt's views for the Seleucid times.

113347

[14] Alt, 'Zur Geschichte der Grenze zwischen Judäa und Samaria', *Kl. Schr.* 2, 346-62, esp. 359 and n. 3, argues from the geographical evidence of the Book of Judith, which, he believes, is based on an older account of the campaign of Artaxerxes III, Ochus, through Palestine, around the middle of the fourth century B.C.E. Similarly, O. Eissfeldt, The *Old Testament. An Introduction*, English trans. Oxford, B.A. Blackwell, 1965, 58f.

[15] 'Syria and Phoenicia' is the official name of the province, appearing in such Ptolemaic documents as the Vienna papyrus, *Aegyptus* 16(1936) 258, and the purported decree of Ptolemy II, *Letter of Aristeas*, 22. However, it also occurs in official Seleucid documents, as is clear from the Hefzibah inscriptions, Y.H. Landau, 'A Greek Inscription found near Hefzibah', IEJ 16(1966) 56-70; cf. also, M. Hengel, *Judentum und Hellenismus. Studien zu ihrer Begegnung unter besonderer Berücksichtigung Palästinas bis zur Mitte des 2. Jh. v. Chr.*, W.U.N.T. 10, 2 Auf., Tübingen, J.C.B. Mohr, 1973 (hereafter *Jud. und Hell.*) 10, n. 4, and Avi-Yonah, *The Holy Land*, 44. E. Bickerman, 'La Coele-Syrie. Notes de Géographie Historique', RB 54(1947) 256-68, has traced the usage of Κοίλη Συρία both in popular and official usage in hellenistic and Roman times. He concludes that it was a rather fluid term in popular usage, referring either to the whole of southern Syria (Coele-Syria and Phoenicia was the full designation, cf. *Ant* 11:25) or later to the interior of southern Syria. Antiochus III was the first to give it official currency as applied to the administrative district taken over from the Ptolemies in 198 B.C.E. Cf. *2 Macc* 3:5; 4:4; 8:8. The actual derivation of Κοίλη is uncertain. Schalit thinks it comes from the Hebrew *kol*, and explains the original meaning as 'all Syria'. Strabo, *Geographica*, XVI, 2.21 would appear to support this. However, he also recognizes its local (ἰδίως) usage for the country between Libanus and Antilibanus, and hence it is often taken to mean 'hollow' Syria, originating as a local name for the Beqa' valley.

[16] The exact line of the border between the two kingdoms is discussed by Kahrstedt, *Syrische Territorien*, 24-33; V. Tcherikover, *Palestine Under the Ptolemies. A Contribution to the Study of the Zenon Papyri, Mizraim* IV-V, New York, 1937, (hereafter *Mizraim*), 32-6; Abel, *Géographie*, 2, 129; Avi-Yonah, *The Holy Land*, 32. Whatever the details, the Ptolemaic territory certainly included later Galilee, reaching in all probability as far north as a line running from the Litany river to north of Damascus.

[17] For an account of these and the subsequent struggles they gave rise to cf. W.W. Tarn, *The Cambridge Ancient History*, vol. 7, Cambridge, Univ. Press, 1928, 'The New Hellenistic Kingdoms', 75-109. F.M. Abel, *Histoire de la Palestine*, 2 vols., Paris 1952, esp. 1, 27-50; Tcherikover, *W.H.Hell.A.*; Hengel, *Jud. und Hell.*, 8-21. Polybius, *Histories*, V,67.6-10, dealing with the negotiations that preceded the fourth Syrian war of 219-17 B.C.E., mentions that the rival claims to Coele-Syria were still being discussed. Cf. also XXVIII,20. F.W. Walbank, *A Historical Commentary on Polybius*, 2 vols., Oxford, Univ. Press 1957, 1, 592-7 has an excellent summary of the question.

[18] In his account of these happenings, *Ant* 12:5-10, Josephus has a rather confused report of Jews at the same time having been taken captive and being granted privileged citizenship in Egypt. Both statements are quite plausible provided a sufficient time lapse is allowed, as Josephus himself indicates, *Against Apion*, 1:186f, where he relates that many Jews went willingly to Egypt after the battle of Gaza in 312 B.C.E., on hearing of Ptolemy's kindness. Probably only influential Jews who were likely to have been dissidents were forcibly taken earlier, especially from the cultic centers of Jerusalem and Samaria. The former is described by Agatharcides of Cnidus, one of the sources of the passage in *Ant*, as a strong fortress, *Against Apion*, 1:205. Cf. Markus' notes in the *Loeb Josephus*, VII, 3-9.

[19] The situation regarding Tyre and Sidon may be inferred from the coins of both cities, Abel, *Histoire*, 1, 52, and for Samaria from a remark in Eusebius' *Chronicon* concerning a campaign of Antigonus' son after Ipsus: 'Samaritarum urbem vastat'. Cf. Hengel, *Jud. und Hell.*, 9, n.2.

[20]Tcherikover, *Mizraim*, is fundamental and more recently *W.H.Hell.A.* Also cf. M. Hengel, *Jud. und Hell.*, 38ff; 571f and *passim*, and his 'Das Gleichnis von den Weingärtnern, Mc 12:1-12, im Lichte der Zenonpapyri und der rabbinischen Gleichnisse', ZNW 59(1968) 1-39; L.H. Vincent, 'La Palestine dans les Papyrus Ptolémaiques', RB 29 (1920) 161-202; F.M. Abel, 'La liste géographique du Papyrus 71 de Zénon', RB 32(1923) 409-15; G. McLean Harper jnr., 'A Study in the Commercial Relations between Egypt and Syria in the Third Century B.C.' AJPH 49(1928) 1-35; J.D. Herz, 'Grossgrundbesitz in Palästina im Zeitalter Jesu', PJB 24(1928) 98-113, esp. 105-9.

[21] Avi-Yonah, *The Holy Land*, 32-41; Kahrstedt, *Syrische Territorien*, 42-4, suggests that the towns where separate minting of coins took place must have all been administrative centers, though not necessarily of the same rank. Tcherikover, *Mizraim*, 82, n. 64, doubts that there would have been so many, eleven in all on Karhstedt's reckoning. He discusses the relevant evidence from the papyri, 38ff.

[22] *Mizraim*, 51f.

[23] On the cities of Palestine in hellenistic times, cf. below in detail, ch.4. If we accept the suggestion of A.M.H. Jones, *The Cities of the Eastern Roman Provinces*, 2ed., Oxford, 1971, 241, that the ending -*itis* is indicative of a Ptolemaic district, it is noteworthy that in contrast with Palestine proper, there were more new foundations east of the Jordan, serving as fortresses against the Arabians and Nabataeans. The fact that we hear of an ἄρχων at Sidon,*P Mich Zen*3, is no indication of absolute autonomy, since officialdom of the central government kept a strict watch on local affairs, as we learn from *PCZ* 59341 for Kalydna in Caria. The story of the Tobiad Joseph being appointed controller of taxes for Syria and Phoenicia, *Ant* 12:169.175. 180, is indicative of the general situation of the cities under the Ptolemies.

[24] Hengel, *Jud. und Hell.*, 36f, n. 118 and Abel, *Histoire*, 1, 53f. It is mentioned 11 times in all in the Zenon correspondence, more than any other city of Palestine.

[25] Hengel, *Jud. und Hell.*, 12. Polybius' remarks may stem from his anti-Seleucid tendencies as a friend of the Romans. *Qoh* 8:2ff; 10:20, indicates a rather uneasy situation among the aristocracy of the time, probably under the Ptolemies, Hengel, *op. cit.* 212f, n. 57.

[26] As an example of this, *Ant* 12:180-3 mentions that Joseph, the taxman, who had won the favour of Ptolemy, arrived in Palestine accompanied by an army, and was able to wreak vengeance on the people of Askalon and Scythopolis because of their unwillingness to pay their taxes to him.

[27] Hengel, *Jud. und Hell.*, 12; Abel, *Histoire*, 1, 77 and 79,n. 1; M. Stern, *Greek and Latin Authors on Jews and Judaism*, vol 1, Jerusalem, 1976, 112, who notes that Polybius' silence is not decisive, since he also fails to mention the capture of the coastal line from Dor to Gaza. On the other hand Sidon must have held out for the Ptolemies for it is not mentioned with Tyre and Ptolemais as having been handed over by Theodotus, and in the following year Antiochus decided to bypass it because of its supplies, the size of its population and the forces that had taken refuge there, Polybius. *Histories*, V,62.2 and 70.1f.

[28] Abel, *Histoire*, 1, 523f. Stern, *Greek and Latin Authors*, 114, with detailed notes on Josephus' citations from Polybius; Walbank, *A Historical Commentary*, 1, 523f. The order of events seems to have been as follows: (i). 201 B.C.E. capture of Gaza by Seleucids (ii). Winter, 201/200: counter-offensive of Ptolemaic forces led by Scopas, the Egyptian general; (iii). 200: battle of Paneion and conquest of Batanaea etc. It was only in 198 that the last vestiges of Ptolemaic resistance were wiped out, when Sidon, where Scopas had taken refuge, was captured. Cf. Polybius, *Histories*, XVI, 18-19,39; Jerome, *In Dan* 11:15f; Abel, *Histoire*, 86. On the authenticity and significance of the decree of Antiochus concerning Jerusalem, cf. E. Bickerman, 'La Charte Séleucide de Jerusalem', REJ 100(1935) 4-35 and R. Marcus, *Loeb Josephus*, VII, appendix D, 743-66, esp. 751-61.

[29] Jerome, *In Dan* 11:14: 'Scopas cepitque Judaeam et optimates Ptolemaei partium secum abducens, in Aegyptum reversus est' (Migne*PL* XXV, 562). Hengel, *Jud. und Hell.*, 14, n. 25.

[30] Avi-Yonah, *The Holy Land*, 44f; Alt, 'Galiläas Verhältnis', *G.P.* 4, 404, n.3, feels that Galilee was never joined with Samaria, even under the Seleucids, claiming that *1 Macc* 10:30 (which mentions Samaria and Galilee as one territory, seemingly) when compared with *1 Macc* 10:38; 11:28.34 (where Galilee is not mentioned), does not support such a view. However, Alt, in trying to prove that Galilee was juridically a different kind of region to Samaria and Judaea, may have pressed the evidence too far, especially since the lesser units were preserved within the larger eparchic system, as Avi-Yonah notes, *op. cit.* 48.

[31] Bickerman, 'La Charte Séleucide', 22, n.1, referring to an inscription dated between 197 and 188 B.C.E., no. 20 of W. Dittenberg, *Orientis Graeci Inscriptiones Selectae*, 2 vols. Leipzig 1903-5, (hereafter OGIS), 1, 376. Ptolemy is called 'high priest and governor (στρατηγὸς) of Cole-Syria; also Landau, 'A Greek Inscription', where the same title is used more than once for Ptolemy on the Hefzibah inscriptions. We hear of another Ptolemy as governor of Coele-Syria under Antiochus IV, *2 Macc* 8:8.

[32] Bickerman, 'La Charte Séleucide', 25, n.4. Cf. *Ant* 13:245; *1 Macc* 14:38.

[33] Below, ch. 7; Tcherikover, *Hellenistic Civilisation*, ch. 3; *W.H.Hell.A.* 115-44; Hengel, *Jud.und Hell.*, 486-555, esp. 513f; E. Bickerman, *Der Gott der Makkabäer*, Berlin 1937, 120ff.

[34] Galling, 'Galiläa, Judäa und der Osten', esp. 44-7.

[35] *Geschichte*, 1, 185f and 2, 9f; W. Bauer, 'Jesus der Galiläer', in *Festgabe für Adolf Jülicher*, Tübingen, 1927, 16-34, esp. 18; W. Bertram, 'Der Hellenismus in der Urheimat des Evangeliums', ARW 32(1935) 265-81; Avi-Yonah, *The Holy Land*, 61, cautiously; B. Reicke, *New Testament Era*, English trans. A. and C. Black, London, 1968, 68f.

[36] Alt, 'Die Umgestaltung Galiläas', *G.P.* 5, 407-23, esp. 414; Galling, 'Judäa, Galiläa und der Osten', 64, who considers the expression in *1 Macc* 5:15 to have been borrowed from *Is* 8:23.

[37] S. Klein, *Galiläa vor der Makkabäerzeit bis 67*, Berlin, 1928, (hereafter *Galiläa*), 1-5 discusses the exact location of the places listed in *1 Macc* 5 and believes that v.23 should read ἐν Νάρβαττοις a place known to us from *War* 2:291.509, north east of Caesarea on the coast. This would mean that the emigrée Jewish families would all have been from the neighborhood of the gentile cities of the coastal plain. Alt, 'Zur Geschichte der Grenze', *Kl. Schr.*, 2, 349f and 352f, reads Arbatta and locates it on the northern boundary of the territory of Samaria, arguing that it is one of the four districts ceded to Judaea in 145 B.C.E., the other three being known to us already from *1 Macc* 11:34; cf. vv.28.57. In the MSS the following variations are found: 'Αρβανοις, 'Αρβαττοις, 'Ακραβαττοις, 'Αρβακτοις.

[38] *2 Kgs* 23:15.19f; *2 Chron* 34:6f. Cf. A.C. Welsh, 'The Death of Josiah', ZAW 2(1925) 255-62, who argues that Josiah's campaign was based on his refusal to have the Yahweh cult linked with the syncretistic Bethel cult of the Assyrians. This does not, of course, exclude other motives for the campaign to the north. Cf. e.g. W.E. Claiburn, 'The Fiscal Basis for Josiah's Reform', JBL 92(1973) 11-22.

[39] In *1 Macc* 15:33 Simon appeals directly to the Jewish claim to the land and at 3:36 we hear of the threat to settle aliens in their lands. Nevertheless, as Davies, *The Gospel and the Land*, 90-4, points out, the idea is more implicit than explicit in both the Maccabaean and Zealot revolts, since in both the concentration seems rather to be on temple and torah. This does not mean that the notion of the purity of the land was not a powerful motivating factor, especially for the Zealots, as Hengel has argued, *Die Zeloten. Untersuchungen zur jüdishen Freiheitsbewegung in der Zeit von Herodes I bis 70 n. Chr.*, AGJU 1, Leiden, Brill, 2ed. 1976, 201-4.

[40] Josephus, *Ant* 12:421, has read into the account some of the geographic realities of his own day, in particular identifying Galgala of *1 Macc* with Galilee, which he apparently identifies with Judaea, as at *War* 1:309. However, he does not change the actual location of the event, which took place in Galilee according to both versions. Cf. Marcus, *Loeb Josephus* VII, 220f.

[41] Below, ch. 5, II, iii, for a detailed discussion.

[42] Above, nn. 13 and 30.

[43] Again Josephus introduces 'Ιουδαία into the text of *1 Macc* at *Ant* 13:174, but clearly referring to the whole of Palestine. Cf. n. 40 above.

[44] Hengel, *Jud. und Hell.* 21-32, deals with the influence of hellenistic war techniques in Palestine in general. *Ant* 13:374.409 mentions foreign troops in the armies of Jannaeus and Alexandra slightly later.

[45] H. Lichtenstein, 'Die Fastenrolle', HUCA 8/9(1931/2) 257-351.

[46] Avi-Yonah, *The Holy Land*, 37, n.29, identifies this city with Beth Yerach, and locates it just east of the Jordan's exit from the lake, and so outside Galilee. He also attributes its destruction to Alexander Jannaeus, following Syncellus, *op. cit.* 70, n. 109.

[47] *Geschichte*, 1, 275f;2, 9-12. Klein, *Galiläa*, 17-21, righty criticizes Schürer, after presenting the evidence for a Jewish Galilee from an earlier period. Even though one suspects that some of this evidence is made to carry too much weight, he rightly stresses that nowhere in Tannaitic literature are the Galileans chided for being half-Jews, or of Ituraean extraction. Alt, 'Die Umgestaltung Galiläas' *G.P.* 5, 414-6, has opposed the idea of a gentile Galilee, judaized by the Hasmonaeans, based on a position that he has argued in a number of articles, which holds that an old Israelite population with cultic loyalties to Jerusalem continued on in the region over the centuries of foreign domination. Stern, *Greek and Latin Authors*, 225f, summarizes the arguments against Schürer's view, 'at least in its extreme formulation'. He rightly rejects E. Meyer's suggestion that 'Ituraean' is a mistake for 'Idumaean' in Josephus' source already, *Ursprung und Anfänge des Christentums*, 3 vols., Reprint Darmstadt, 1962, 2, 274, n. 4.

[48] A.M.H. Jones, 'The Urbanization of the Ituraean Principality', JRS 21(1931) 265-75.

[49] A. Schalit in *W.H.Hell.A.*, ch.XI, 225-97, 'Domestic Politics and Political Institutions', is an excellent treatment of this neglected topic, based on his earlier study, *König Herodes*, Berlin 1969.

[50] Schalit, 'Domestic Politics', *W.H.Hell.A.*, 283f.

[51] This is the conclusion of Schalit, *Herodes*, 205f and 'Domestic Politics' 265f. Avi-Yonah, *The Holy Land*, 97f, agrees that the two systems must have been closely identified and 'developed piecemeal during the Hasmonaean period'. However, he doubts if the process was completed by the time of Jannaeus.

[52] Both Schalit, *Herodes*, 205ff, 'Domestic Politics', *W.H.Hell.A.* 265, and Avi-Yonah *The Holy Land*, 97, agree on five toparchies for Galilee, based on data gleaned from Josephus, *War* 2:252.629, and the Mishnah, *Shabb* 16:7. However, changes must have occurred in the course of time. Before the founding of Tiberias, e.g., Arbela may have been such a center. Klein, *Galiläa*, 44-7, holds for eight toparchies in Galilee, based on the recipients of letters from the Jerusalem sages at a later time, below, ch. 7, n. 73. By reconstructing what he considers to be a corrupt text, he opts for the following toparchic capitals: Sepphoris, Tarichaea, (Magdala), Tiberias (Arbela), Arab and Upper Galilee, in addition to Simonias, Mahlol and Dobrat (reconstructed). In the absence of any other positive evidence, however, this seems unwarranted.

[53] Tcherikover, *Hellenistic Civilization*, ch.7. Schalit's treatment of this episode, *W.H.Hell.A.*, 272-4, fails to bring out this essential aspect of the struggle, but agrees that Josephus is correct in dating the incident to the reign of Hyrcanus rather than Yannai, as in the Talmudic tradition.

[54] Cf. below ch.7, n.80 for the identity of the John in question.

[55] Following Schalit, *Herodes*, 743f and *W.H.Hell.A.*, 343, n. 63, against Schürer, *Geschichte*, 1, 274, n.5, who follows Josephus, *Ant* 13:301, that Aristobulus was the first Hasmonaean to adopt the title 'king'. Schalit's argument is based on the coins which do have 'king' for Alexander, but only 'priest' for Aristobulus. Cf. A. Reifenberg, *Ancient Jewish Coins*, London, 1948. Strabo, *Geographica*, XVI,2.40, also says that Alexander was the first Jewish king.

[56] Schalit, *W.H.Hell.A.*, 277-8, esp., 285 and 8.

[57] R. Meyer, *Tradition und Neuschöpfung im Antiken Judentum. Dargestellt an der Geschichte des Pharisäismus*, Sitzungsbericht der Sächsischen Akademie der Wissenschaften zu Leipzig; Philologisch-historische Klasse, Bd. 110, 2, Berlin 1965, 44f, points to the anti-Hasmonaean polemic of the *Tar Ps-Jon*, to *Dt* 33:11, as well as that of the Qumran literature, which he dates to the same period.

[58] According to *p.Keth* 8,32c, Simon, as head of the Sanhedrin in the time of Alexander Jannaeus, was responsible for the setting up of the Jewish school. Another tradition, *b. Bab Bat* 21a, attributes it to Josua ben Gamala, a high priest, shortly before the fall of the temple. S. Safrai, 'Education and the Study of the Torah', ch. 19 of *Compendia*, 2, 945-70, esp. 947f, attributes a certain credibility to both traditions.

[59] Klein, *Galiläa*, 38-44. His attempt to make a case for many teachers of torah in Galilee at an early period is not very successful. Cf. below, ch.8, n.78.

[60] Schürer, *Geschichte*, 2, 494, takes the notice of *b.Bab Bat* 21a seriously. It states that under Josua ben Gamala, highpriest from 63-5 C.E., the children of six and seven years had to be brought to the teachers 'in every province and in every city.'

CHAPTER THREE
GALILEE UNDER THE ROMANS
63 B.C.E. - 135 C.E.

It is idle to speculate how the Jewish state might have survived the crisis of the Hasmonaean brothers' struggle for power if Rome had not been waiting in the wings, ready to include it within the borders of its growing eastern territories. With the decline of the Seleucid empire Hellenism as a political power had been on the wane for quite some time, and independent monarchies or principalities like the Ituraeans, Nabataeans and Hasmonaeans had emerged in the vacuum. Matters could conceivably have righted themselves in Palestine, for the subsequent history will show a deep-seated desire for self-government at the center of the Jewish state, a desire which was ultimately to lead to its downfall. At an earlier stage of its history Rome had accepted the newly established Jewish state as its friend and ally and presumably it was in that role that Pompey was approached also (*Ant* 14:34-45). It soon became apparent that Rome had much more serious designs than simply coming to the aid of an ally at a moment of internal crisis.[1] Thus the final chapter of Judaism had begun to be written in terms of its relations with Rome. From then on, every aspect of Jewish life was dominated by the new overlords, and Judaism had to brace itself for financial domination, political subjection and a new aggressive hellenization.

That struggle would last for almost 200 years, until the political will of the Jews was eventually crushed, and a nonpolitical Judaism emerged, built on torah and book rather than temple and land. In this chapter we wish to retrace the stages of Rome's political take-over in Palestine, paying special attention to its impact on Galilee.

(i) From Pompey to Caesar, 63-44 B.C.E.

The intention of Pompey's initial settlement of the Jewish question seems obvious. The axiom *'divide et impera'* is at work as the Hasmonaean kingdom is carved up.[2] Many of the hellenistic cities conquered by the earlier Hasmonaeans were restored

57

with their territories to their former inhabitants within the newly formed province of Syria. A partial list is given by Josephus: Gadara, Hippos, Scythopolis, Pella, Dium, Samaria, as well as Marisa, Azotus, Jamnia and Arethusa, and on the coast Gaza, Joppa, Dora and Straton's Tower (*War* 1:156f; *Ant* 14: 75f; cf. 13:395).[3] Jerusalem was made a tributary city and so the Jews, confined within their own borders (ἐντὸς τῶν ἰδίων ὅρων), received *autonomia* or self-government in accordance with the Roman principle of *libertas*, as was customary for a *civitas stipendaria*.[4] In effect the old temple state was re-established, except that now Galilee, Idumaea and Peraea were included as part of the Jewish territory, with the former suitably isolated from its Judaean center.[5] Even in this limited area the authority of Hyrcanus covered inner-Jewish affairs only. The legate in Syria had a right to intervene when he thought fit, a right that Sextus Caesar availed of in coming to the aid of the young Herod, who was on trial before the Sanhedrin for the murder of Hezekiah, the Galilean brigand chief. It is noteworthy that Hyrcanus was forced to bend the law to meet the legate's requests on that occasion (*Ant* 14:170; *War* 1:211).[6]

On what basis did the Romans decide which territory should belong to the Jews and which should be cut off? Josephus' statement, 'the entire nation, which before had raised itself so high, he confined within its own borders' (*Ant* 14:74), is rather vague, and raises the further question of what criterion was used for deciding that certain territories were Jewish. If the sole purpose was to undo the military conquests of the Hasmonaeans, then Galilee too would be excluded, since as we have seen, Jewish claims to it were not automatically granted by the Seleucids. Nor is it sufficient to assume, as many commentators appear to do, that the judaization of certain regions was so complete that they could not be detached from Jewish jurisdiction. Such an argument could hardly apply to Idumaea and yet it is to be included in the Jewish territory of Hyrcanus according to most commentators.[7] No explanation is given however as to why this supposed judaization policy was so effective in some areas. Obviously, it is not itself sufficient reason for such a far-reaching political decision by the Romans, especially in view of their treatment

of the cities, which presumably had attracted a considerable
Jewish population also. In truth Pompey's arrangement which
was simply further developed by Gabinius, suited both the general Roman policy *and* the existing political realities of Palestine.[8] It would have served no useful purpose to attempt any
new, far-reaching divisions, when old established ones could be
resurrected which also respected the special wishes of the predominant population in various areas. Thus Galilee with its
Jewish loyalties rooted in its Israelite past, was in no danger of
being annexed to the new Roman province of Syria, yet it found
itself once more geographically isolated from its cultic and
cultural center.

Such a settlement of the Jewish question was not likely to be
accepted without a struggle and resistance crystalized around
the ousted Aristobulus and his sons, Antigonus and Alexander.
Matters came to a head when Gabinius, Pompey's general returned as governor of Syria (57 - 54 B.C.E.). Alexander began to
rebuild various fortresses, Alexandrium, Hyrcania and Machaerus, and even the walls of Jerusalem itself which Pompey had
broken down. This was an indication that the Romans would
have to adopt tougher measures if they were to succeed with their
plans. While laying siege to Alexandrium, Gabinius pursued the
reconstitution of Greek cities with energy, in line with Pompey's
policy, 'colonists gladly flocking to them' (*Ant* 14:82-88; *War*
1:162-6).[9] Eventually Alexander was defeated and the fortresses
destroyed, but Gabinius went even further by dividing the Jewish
territory into five councils (συνέδρια *Ant* 14:91; συνόδοι *War*
1:170), one of which was for Galilee and situated at Sepphoris.[10]
The form of government was aristocratic, and in this way Gabinius hoped to overcome whatever natural opposition the Jews
were likely to feel towards this further division of their territory.
Apparently reactions were mixed, for even though Josephus says
that 'the Jews welcomed their release from the rule of an individual' (*War* 1:170) subsequent support for Aristobulus and his
sons would seem to indicate the contrary. Clearly Josephus is
speaking of those who stood to gain from the new arrangement,
but even their personal interests were threatened in the ensuing
developments, as Antipater and his sons climbed the ladder of

Roman patronage and ousted those Jewish aristocrats who may have been tempted to avail of the new situation for their own interests.

The first test for Gabinius' settlement came when Aristobulus, escaping from Rome with his younger son Antigonus, attempted to win support for his cause among the Jewish populace. He seems to have had some initial success, even to the point of gaining the support of one of the newly established Jerusalem aristocracy (ὑποστράτηγος), Peitholaus. However, the resistance presented no real threat and Aristobulus was once more captured and sent to Rome. On that occasion his support seems to have been based in the south, for he resorted to the fortress of Machaerus in southern Peraea for his final stand (*Ant* 14:92-7; *War* 1:170-4). Moreover, while Gabinius was occupied in Egypt with the active support of Antipater and Hyrcanus, Alexander, the other son of Aristobulus, conducted a second campaign, only to be finally defeated at Thabor, with very substantial losses to his forces (*Ant* 14:101f; *War* 1:175-8).[11] The site of this final encounter might indicate that this revolt was based in Galilee, but nothing in Josephus' remarks indicates that since he explicitly states that Alexander was engaged in a wholesale slaughter of Romans in the country (κατὰ τὴν χώραν). What is significant about both engagements is the support for Aristobulus in the country and Antipater's (and Hyrcanus') support for Rome despite the fact that the setting-up of the five councils must have meant a diminution of status for them. A second attempt on behalf of Aristobulus took place after the defeat of Gabinius' successor Crassus, the triumvir, at Carrhae (53 B.C.E.). Presumably Peitholaus considered this a suitable time to strike for independence, but he was defeated by Cassius Longinus, Crassus' successor, at Tarichaea in Galilee and 30,000 men were reputedly sold into slavery and Peitholaus put to death at the instigation of Antipater (*Ant* 14:119f; *War* 1:180). It is tempting to suggest as Alt does, that on this evidence, Galilee was a staunch supporter of Antigonus and his royal claims.[12] However, before drawing sweeping conclusions, either about massive Galilean support for the Hasmonaean kingship or concerning the anti-Roman stance of the inhabitants, it should be remembered that the followers of Antigonus were forced to find a power base other than

Jerusalem, since Antipater had succeeded in having affairs arranged in Jerusalem to suit himself as a reward for his support both for Gabinius and Cassius (*Ant* 14:103.121; *War* 1:178).[13] This is not to suggest that there was not real support for Aristobulus in Galilee, as the subsequent history of his son Antigonus makes clear. It does however, pose the question of the political motives for such support and its likely base within the province. Herod's activities there later may offer a solution to the problem, as we shall presently see.

The next phase of Roman intervention in Palestine is connected with Caesar's reorganization of the province of Syria after the defeat of Pompey at Pharsalis in 48 B.C.E. Antipater had once again succeeded in reading the political signs correctly, and as a result of his aid to Caesar in Egypt (*Ant* 14:127-33; *War* 1:195-9), he and Hyrcanus could naturally expect their rewards. They were not to be disappointed, as the decrees of Caesar which Josephus has preserved for us (*Ant* 14:190-216) make clear, even though in renewing (ἀνανεοῦσθαι) the treaty between Rome and the Jews, Caesar changed it into a *foedus inaequum* which meant that the Jews had to pay tribute, something we shall discuss in the next section of our study.[14] Without going into the question of the exact dating of the various decrees we can list the relevant decisions for our study.[15] The whole Jewish territory was once again administratively reunited, with Hyrcanus as ethnarch and high priest and Antipater as his procurator (*Ant* 14:192-5.199).[16] Furthermore, the Jewish territory was to be enlarged by the return of certain villages in the Great Plain which had presumably been part of the private possessions of the Hasmonaeans;[17] the port of Joppe (and Lydda) were also returned, thus providing access to the sea; finally, 'the places, lands and farms, the fruits of which the Kings of Syria and Phoenicia, as allies of the Romans, were permitted to enjoy by their gift (κατὰ δωρεάν), these the Senate decrees that the ethnarch Hyrcanus shall have' (*Ant* 14:205-10).[18]

This final statement is part of a *senatus consultus* confirming, presumably, a decree of Caesar, reference to which may be contained in the earlier general statement: 'his children shall rule over the Jewish nation and enjoy the fruits of the places given them' (*Ant* 14:196). The impression one gets from these statements is that Caesar took positive steps to prevent encroachment of Jewish territory, and this may explain why a copy of the earliest decree was sent to the Sidonians informing them of Caesar's arrangement for Judaea (*Ant* 14:190-5). In this the billeting of troops or the demanding of money from the Jews is also expressly forbidden (§ 195). Furthermore a bronze tablet containing the decrees was to be set up at Sidon, Tyre and Ascalon, engraved in Latin and Greek, and they were to be communicated to the quaestors and magistrates of the various cities (*Ant* 14:197f). The singling out of the kings of Syria and Phoenicia, and the publication of the decrees at Tyre and Sidon give rise to the suspicion that such encroachments were most likely in Galilee, and Caesar is clearly recognizing it as a Jewish land that was to share in all the rights and privileges of Judaea proper. This suspicion is confirmed by the course of events after Caesar's death in 44 B.C.E. Cassius who, we have seen, was already involved in events in Galilee after the defeat at Carrhae, now returned to Syria against Antony's wishes. He supported Marion, one of the petty princes whom he had previously established at Tyre, in his invasion of Galilee in support of Antigonus; but Herod, who had been governor of the province since 47 B.C.E. (*Ant* 14:158), succeeded in dislodging him from three strongholds (*Ant* 14:271.297f). However, Herod's success must not have been complete, for soon we find delegates of Hyrcanus meeting with Antony at Ephesus, and he promised to restore the occupied sites to the Jews. He communicated his decision to the Tyrians as follows: 'If they hold any places which belonged to Hyrcanus, the ethnarch of the Jews as recently as one day before Gaius Cassius, waging an unlawful war, invaded our province, you shall return them to him' (*Ant* 14:313.317.320). Furthermore, he wrote to Sidon, Antioch and Aradus in the same vein (*Ant* 14:323). In others words Antony restores the Jewish territory to the same position it had prior to the Tyrian invasion, thereby confirming Caesar's arrangements.

From this survey of the first period of Rome's involvement in the affairs of the Jews, it is clear that Galilee could claim to be Jewish, both in fact and by tradition, and such claims were recognized and embodied in legal enactments by the Roman authorities. For a brief period the arrangement of Gabinius had made it possible for Galilean Judaism to organize itself politically as an independent entity, had it the desire to do so.[19] But the subsequent events make it clear that no such will existed there.

Already a new period was under way in which Roman rule was mediated to Galilee in particular for almost a hundred years through Herod and his successors, Antipas and Agrippa I. Their impact on life in the province had far-reaching social, economic and cultural effects. First however, we must concentrate on the political and administrative changes that took place in that period.

(ii) Herod and Galilee, 47-4 B.C.E.

We have noted more than once that Antipater had been able to stay in control of the political situation under Hyrcanus because of his ability to read the changing Roman political scene. The appointment of his sons to subordinate positions, Phasael in Jerusalem and the surrounding regions and Herod in Galilee, is a sign of his determination to control Palestinian politics, while all the time remaining himself in the background. However, his son Herod showed no such reticence, displaying energy, ambition and ruthlessness from an early age.

Herod's early period as governor in Galilee is marked by three incidents: his destruction of the robber chief, Hezekiah and his band; the collection of his share of the special tribute imposed by Cassius for 'his illegal war', and the routing of Marion already referred to. Of the three, the first is by far the most significant since it sets the tone for subsequent events. In all probability it caused the Hasmonaean aristocracy that was prepared to go along with Roman rule to join Antigonus rather than Hyrcanus,[20] whose total dependence on Rome was painfully exposed in the whole incident. Despite Joscphus' branding him as an 'arch-brigand' (ἀρχιλήστης - *Ant* 14:159; *War* 1:204) Hezekiah was no outlaw, whatever tactics he may have been forced to adopt. He was, in all probability, one of the Hasmonaean nobles of Galilee who opposed both Roman and Herodian domination and may have been forced into an extreme position after Cassius' defeat of Peitholaus at Tarichaea, already mentioned.[21]

Hyrcanus' behavior in the whole affair is ambivalent, and Josephus' accounts have a number of inconsistencies. If our identification of Hezekiah is correct, in all probability the flouting of his own position as ethnarch and chief priest would have gone unnoticed, were it not for the pressures that were put on him by the members of the sanhedrin, who saw the whole affair as a threat to the newly established order of things in Judaea. The intervention of Sextus Caesar, the governor of Syria, only increased Hyrcanus' dilemma, since Sextus made it clear that he wanted Herod acquitted and subsequently showed his further trust in him by appointing him governor ($\sigma\tau\rho\alpha\tau\eta\gamma\grave{o}\varsigma$) of Syria and Coele-Syria, an honor which made Herod more independent than ever of the Jewish arisocracy. His way forward in achieving his ambtion was through active support of Rome, and in this Herod showed himself a good pupil of his mentor, Antipater. Having energetically collected his own share of the tribute imposed by Cassius, 100 talents for Galilee (*Ant* 14:274; *War* 1:221), and being rewarded with the office of procurator of all Syria (*War* 1:225), or more probably, confirmed as governor of Coele-Syria (*Ant* 14:280),[22] he was still able to convince Antony, Cassius' deadly enemy, of his loyalty, to the point that he and his brother were appointed tetrarchs (*Ant* 14:326; *War* 1:244).

Herod's steady rise to power in the service of the Romans had not gone unnoticed by the Jewish aristocracy, and it probably led to Antipater's death, arranged by one of them, Malichus. However, this did not bring relief from the Idumaeans but merely thrust Herod into the position of prominence he was so eager to fill. His energetic support of Cassius had made him unpopular with the masses of the Jewish people, for whom the extra burden of tribute must have been very severe, and many of them were sold into slavery (*Ant* 14:275). At the same time Herod's continued favor from the Romans, even to the point of being supplied with ships and cavalry and the promise of kingship by Cassius if he succeeded in defeating Antony (*Ant* 14:280), must have been a real threat to the aristocracy. His appointment by Antony as tetrarch, after the victory of Philippi (42 B.C.E.), without removing the ethnarch, Hyrcanus, meant that the latter's sphere of influence was of steadily diminishing importance in Roman eyes. There was then, a genuine sense of rejoicing on all sides when the Parthians eventually invaded Palestine as part of their long-planned campaign agabnt Rome's dominance in the East, and were everywhere received as liberators, most of all in Galilee, which had experienced Herod's ambitions and tactics at first hand.

Roman domination of Asia was seriously challenged, not only because of the Parthians' desire to invade Palestine, but also because of the repeated civil wars and the drain on its economy of several competing generals and their armies. Antigonus, then in exile at Chalcis in the Lebanon, negotiated with them, agreeing that he would be king under their protection. The Parthian advance was by the familiar coastal route, and both Sidon and Ptolemais admitted them, though Tyre resisted. An intermediate camp was set up near Carmel, at a place called the Grove, but the ultimate goal was Jerusalem (*Ant* 14:334f), as it was the feast of Tabernacles and Antigonus could rely on popular support from the country. Eventually Herod's brother, Phasael, and Hyrcanus were lured into going on a peace mission to the Parthian general, Barzaphranes, in Galilee. They were eventually arrested and Herod, realizing that his worst fears had eventuated, fled Jerusalem and went finally to Rome, where he was declared king 'and friend of the Roman people' by the Senate with Antony's and Octavian's support.[23] Meanwhile in Judaea, Antigonus had also established himself as king with popular support. A deadly confrontation was inevitable.

Here we need only relate Galilee's role in the subsequent struggles between Antigonus and Herod from 40-37 B.C.E., not an easy task as Josephus' account seems to lack inner consistency. Herod returned from Rome in 39, disembarked at Ptolemais and collected a mercenary army as well as natives, and marched thrugh Gailee - obviously good strategy before making the assault on Jerusalem, which any aspirant to kingship had to capture (*Ant* 14:394). Meanwhile, the Parthians, having been defeated by the Romans in Syria, had withdrawn, and Antigonus, lacking the drive of Herod, seems to have let events pass him by in Jerusalem. Herod established a base in the north and was hampered in taking Jerusalem only by the sluggishness of the Roman general who apparently had been bribed by Antigonus. We hear that 'all Galilee, except for a few of its inhabitants, came over to his side' (*Ant* 14:395; *War* 1:291), and so he marched south to liberate his family, incarcerated at Masada, and make an assault on Jerusalem. Winter had arrived and the Roman troops needed proper billeting, so Herod had to abandon the siege, but occupied himself with another attack on Galilee, as *War* puts it, 'to reduce

the remaining strongholds and expel the garrisons (τὰς φρουρὰς)
of Antigonus.' (*War* 1:303; *Ant* 14:413). Sepphoris fell to him
without a struggle as Antigonus' garrison had fled, and this
provided him with ample supplies, and the opportunity to
attack 'the brigands' living in caves in the neighborhood of Arbela
in western lower Galilee (*War* 1:304-7; *Ant* 14:415-17). The *War*
account says that Herod slaughtered many of them as they fled,
though both versions agree that Herod's army was on the retreat
under severe pressure from 'the enemy' for a time. Again we hear
that all Galilee, 'was brought to his side (προσάγεται) except for
those living in the caves' (*Ant* 14:417), whereas the statement in
the *War* (1:307) that 'thus Galilee was purged of its terrors save
for the remnant still lurking in the caves', while introducing
greater consistency with the narrative has a very distinctive ring
of later Josephan polemic. The following spring Herod is back
again in the same region, this time using special equipment in
an attempt to dislodge the cave-dwellers, where he encountered
a Maccabaean-style act of defiance from one of them with his wife
and seven children (*Ant* 14:421-30; *War* 1:310-15). With this
engagement Herod seemed to have rooted out the last of Antigonus' supporters, and he appointed Ptolemy as general
(στρατηγὸς) of that region. Very soon afterwards we hear that 'the
men who formerly disturbed Galilee' ('those whose custom it
was to create disturbance in Galilee', *War*) once more rose up
and killed Ptolemy, but Herod returned, slaying some of the
rebels, besieging those who had taken refuge in fortified places,
and exacting a tribute of 100 talents from the cities (*Ant* 14:433;
War 1:316). Not even these measures succeeded in destroying all
opposition in the province, however. The following year while
Herod was away at Samosata seeking adequate Roman aid from
Antony to finally reduce Jerusalem, his brother Joseph got
drawn into an engagement with Antigonus near Jericho, and was
killed. Encouraged by this, the partisans of Antigonus ('the
Galileans', *Ant*) rebelled against the supporters of Herod ('the
nobles of their country', τῶν παρὰ σφίσι δυνατῶν, *Ant*) and threw
them into the lake. Herod, returning to Palestine with adequate
Roman reinforcements, marched against them, once more
through Galilee. The enemy met him but they were defeated in
battle and shut in their fortress (unnamed). A second Roman
legion came to Herod's aid, and his opponents fled by night,

alarmed at the size of the army lined up against them (*Ant* 14:452f; *War* 1:330).

This is the end of recorded Galilean resistance to Herod, but we may be sure that it did not end there. In all probability, some of the Hasmonaean nobles whom Herod assassinated after the final defeat of Antigonus had Galilean connections (*Ant* 15:5f) and the founding of Gaba on the borders of Galilee, with allotments of land for his cavalry veterans (*Ant* 15:294.), may well have had a strategic intent also, a function it served a century later (*War* 3:36; *Life* 115).[24] Certainly, the disturbances at Sepphoris under Judas son of Hezekiah (*Ant* 17:271f.288), to be examined later, show that Hasmonaean opposition to Herod in Galilee was not totally eradicated, no matter how much it had to go underground or swallow its pride during his long reign.[25] It has even been suggested that Herod himself retained the governorship of the recalcitrant province, as one of the five larger districts into which his kingdom was divided.[26]

From this survey of Herod's dealings with the province certain conclusions may be drawn concerning the inner political thrust of the people there. There is little doubt that a certain segment of the population was decidedly pro-Hasmonaean and anti-Herodian, but the impression is that this group is rather localized - around Sepphoris and in the caves of Arbela in the west. It seems pretty clear also that once we recognize Josephus' or his source's polemical attitudes against this group, they are not to be identified with robbers or outlaws. Whatever the social reasons for Hezekiah's raids on Syrian territory, possibly, we suggested, reprisals for the enslavement of people after Peitholaus' defeat by Cassius, those Galileans who continued his struggle seem to have been firmly established. They have fortresses and a not inconsiderable army, and even though Herod appears to quell dissent, it erupts again at the first signs of Hasmonaean success. It must therefore have had some popular support, even though its leaders, Hezekiah and the others, were aristocrats who, whatever their feelings about an independent Galilee, were certainly not in favor of either Roman or Idumaean control of their affairs. Of the Hasmonaeans, Aristobulus' family emerged as by far the more suitable contender for their support, since the weak Hyrcanus showed no signs of independence and his vacillation over the Hezekiah affair made him totally untrustworthy in the eyes of would-be Hasmonaean defenders. Herod undoubtedly added to his own problems in the province with his vigorous pursuit of the special tribute for Cassius, and subsequently by imposing a similar fine on the cities of the province as a penalty for the murder of Ptolemy. This may have led to a more broadly based attack on Herod's supporters, who presumably were engaged in raising the levy. But when all this evidence is sifted, it seems legitimate to suggest that there was no widespread involvement of the whole population in the events on either side. This explains why Josephus could repeatedly say that all Galilee was on the side of Herod, only to appear to contradict himself immediately by reporting a new outbreak of hostilities. This conclusion is of great significance for our further consideration of events in the province.

(iii) Galilee under Antipas, 4 B.C.E. - 39 C.E.

While the sons of Herod were debating their respective points of view in Rome before Augustus, trouble broke out at various centers in Palestine, sparked off originally it would seem by Archelaus' brutal treatment of the Jewish people who had presented certain demands to him during the feast of Passover (*Ant* 17:200-218; *War* 2:1-13). For the present we may pass over the revolt in Galilee under Judas son of Hezekiah (*Ant* 17:272; *War* 2:56) since, whatever the purpose of Judas and his philosophy, the revolt was unceremoniously snuffed out by the army of the legate from Syria, Varus. Sepphoris was destroyed and its inhabitants sold into slavery (*Ant* 17:289; *War* 2:68). Apparently the effects of this experience were to determine the subsequent political stance of Sepphoris. What is particularly significant in this context is that it seems to have removed any rebellious elements from the territory, which now fell to Antipas as tetrarch. We shall have to discuss later whether this opposition was driven underground there to fester and sprout again, or whether the last vestiges of Hasmonaean support in the province were finally removed. At all events everything we know of Antipas' long reign suggests that whatever other criticisms could be made of it, it was not punctuated by outbreaks of strife and internal dissension.

In attempting to determine the effects of this period of stability for political life in Galilee we have unfortunately precious little hard evidence. Whereas Herod the Great never attempted to build any cities within Galilee itself, this was perhaps politically the most significant action of Antipas. In the next section of our study we shall discuss the cultural and social impact of Sepphoris and Tiberias on the life of the province. What should be under-lined here is that neither was intended for nor aspired to autonomy within the realm of Antipas.[27] From the purely polit-ical point of view therefore these cities were intended as inte-grative rather than disruptive forces. Probably, Gabara, Tari-chaeae and Gischala (Upper Galilee) functioned as toparchical centers together with Sepphoris and Tiberias, but first the former and then the latter functioned as the center for the royal court, and thereby achieved greater prominence than the merely top-archical centers. In this way Antipas appears to have achieved an integrated administrative system for Galilee—and presumably a similar one was established in Peraea, which also appears to have had its own toparchic divisions.[28]

One highly significant aspect of Antipas' reign is the fact that its stability meant that there was no need for direct Roman in-tervention in the internal life of the province. In view of the military, financial and social upheavals of the previous period this was indeed a great blessing for the ordinary people, and stands in sharp contrast to the situation in Judaea, where the insensitivity and brutality of the Roman procurators make a sorry story of mismanagement, and is generally accepted as one of the major immediate causes for the revolt of 66 C.E. Apparently, Antipas was present at Rome in 6 C.E. when his brother Arch-elaus was deposed, possibly even in the role of his brother's accuser.[29] Presumably it was at this time that the dynastic name Herod was given. Undoubtedly this increased his international stature as the representative of a famous line, even if it did not mean any real increase in rank or territory.[30] Nor did he receive the territory of his brother Philip on the latter's death in 34 C.E., which was instead annexed to the province of Syria (*Ant* 18:108). Recognition was given him by the Romans towards the end of his life when Tiberius asked him to act as intermediary between Rome and the Parthians, for long a source of real trouble for Rome's foreign relations. Antipas seized the opportunity with typical Herodian style, had a special bridge built over the Eu-phrates where the Syrian legate Vitellius and the Parthian king

Artabanus signed a treaty and a special reception was arranged by Antipas (*Ant* 18:101-5; Suetonius, *Caligula* 14,3). In his desire to ingratiate himself further with Tiberius, Antipas hastened to send a full report to the emperor but only succeeded in arousing the animosity of Vitellius, who felt he had been upstaged in the whole event. As a result Vitellius was in no haste to come to Antipas' aid in his difficulties with the Nabataean king Aretas, with whom relations were particularly strained since the insult to his daughter by the divorce involving Herodias. Antipas' army suffered a heavy defeat on the borders of Peraea, and Claudius ordered Vitellius to go to Antipas' aid. However, before any effective action had been taken Claudius had died, Gaius Caligula was the new emperor and Antipas' career was on the wane.

This brief survey of the main foreign involvements of Antipas makes clear that Galilee had not to contend with external pressures during his long reign. It is more difficult to assess the internal political relations with the other parts of Palestine. Peraea, the other half of Antipas' own territory, was organized independently of Galilee it would seem, since it was geographically separated from it by the territories of Scythopolis, Pella and Gadara, and presumably it was this that necessitated it having its own capital at the second Gadara.[31] One could make too much of the divisions that this kind of isolation might create, since all these territories were part of the larger Roman network. While borders were definitely recognized for customs and other duties, this did not prevent mobility between the different regions, as the Gospels, despite all the problems of their geography, make clear. Apparently also, the population of Peraea was Jewish as distinct from the majority Greek population of the Dekapolis cities. Thus we can assume that Antipas' territory was able to achieve some kind of homogeneity of political life, which may be reflected in the scene described at *Mk*. 6:21, where the Galilean village leaders, the Herodian court nobles and the military commanders are all gathered to celebrate his birthday. How did such a unity reflect on the relations with Jerusalem, which was now under direct Roman control? The high priesthood and the Sanhedrin had lost most, if not all of their political power within Judaism during the long reign of Herod the Great.[32] Their revival subsequently as effective political instruments for dealing with the administration of Jewish affairs to Rome's satisfaction was only gradual and partial, and accordingly the Herodian princes played an important middle role in Rome's view. However, Antipas was apparently not involved in Jewish affairs to the degree that he would have liked, and he does not seem to have been given any powers over the selection of the high priest, a right enjoyed and exercised by the later Herodian princes (*Ant* 20:15f). His respect for the sensitivities of his Jewish subjects can be seen by the lack of images on his coins and his frequent visits to Jerusalem on the occasion of feasts (*Lk* 23:7; *Ant* 18:122). He might have expected therefore to be entrusted by Rome with greater control of Jewish affairs. As bearer of the dynastic name 'Herod' his hopes of being 'king' remained with him to the end, it would seem (*Ant* 18:240ff). We have already seen his desire to upstage Roman officials with the Emperor, and presumably it was this very attitude that created the animosity between himself and Pilate to which Luke refers (23:12). In these circumstances, and with such hopes, it is unlikely that Antipas would have ever attempted to turn his territory into a Jewish counter-center to Jerusalem - the capital had too much attraction both for him and his subjects, but for very different reasons. The ability to handle awkward situations to suit Roman policy was, he recognized, his only way to advancement, and so, astute character that he was, he decided on that course even if eventually it led to his downfall.[33]

Antipas' reign had far-reaching consequences for Galilean Judaism in that it offered the possibility for it to develop a political identity of its own without in any way tampering with its religious affiliations to Jerusalem. In this the circumstances had changed considerably from Gabinius' day, when, we saw, Galilee showed no great desire to go its own way. Now with Judaean public life on the decline a new kind of Galilean Jew emerges, who is at once a man of the hellenistic world *and* a Jew. This development was to create another tension of a social nature, which we shall have to explore further at a later stage.

(iv) From Antipas to the Great Revolt, 39-66 C.E.

Antipas was eventually banished into exile for his ambitions -prompted and fired by Herodias- to be king like his nephew and brother-in-law Agrippa. Gaius Caligula had conferred that honor on his friend Agrippa in 37 C.E., giving him the territory of Philip the tetrarch who had died in 34 C.E. The fact that Antipas had befriended Agrippa in his days of penury, appointing him 'supervisor of the market' (ἀγορανόμος) at Tiberias, only added to the irony of the relationship between the two men. The territory of the deposed Antipas now passed to Agrippa also (*Ant* 18:252), but in view of his general attitudes towards Judaism, life in Galilee was not likely to have been affected very much by this change. With the death of Gaius and the accession of Claudius, the procuratorship of Judaea also passed to Agrippa (41 C.E.), so that now he ruled over practically the same Jewish territory as his grandfather, Herod the Great (*Ant* 19:275). Unfortunately his death in 44 C.E. put an end to the experiment, and the whole of Palestine, Galilee included, once more became part of the Roman province of Judaea.

It is difficult to assess the impact of Agrippa's short reign on the political life of Palestine. It could be argued that since the north was the starting point for his career as king its separateness might be further accentuated, and on two important occasions Tiberias rather than Jerusalem was the center of action. The peasant people of the countryside flocked to the Syrian legate Petronius there, protesting about the statue which Caligula had proposed to set up in the temple (*Ant* 18:270ff; *War* 2:193); and the council of the subject kings which Agrippa convened, much to the annoyance of the Roman legate in Syria, Vibius Marsus, also met at Tiberias (*Ant* 19:338-42). Undoubtedly, the Herodian lay nobility that emerged under Antipas continued to thrive under Agrippa also (cf. *Ant* 19:317-25). However, Agrippa was also deeply involved in Jerusalem's political affairs, especially concerning the high priesthood (*Ant* 19:297.313-16.342). Thus while he definitely sought to win the favor of the Pharisees as a conscious part of his policy, he apparently also courted the Sadducaean aristocracy. The fact that his Hasmonaean ancestry was still remembered – Mariamne was his grandmother (Philo *Legatio* 278) - certainly meant that his appeal to Jewish loyalties was all the greater, and this is apparent both in Josephus' comparison of him with his grandfather (*Ant* 19:328-31) and the Rabbinic traditions concerning his piety (*M.Sot.* 7:8; *M.Bikk.* 3:4).[34]

Agrippa's familiarity with and involvement in Roman imperial policies was of great significance for the larger Jewish population of the Empire as the universal decree of Claudius on behalf of the Jews makes clear (*Ant* 19:286-291). His intervention in the affair of the statue of Gaius helped to avert what would have certainly been a major confrontation between Rome and the Jews. While Petronius, the legate in Syria, who had also resisted the Emperor on the issue of the statue, remained in office, all went harmoniously. However, later in his reign Agrippa seems to have adopted a more independent line, as the affair over the council of the kings and his attempt to rebuild the walls of Jerusalem without permission make clear (*Ant* 19:338-42; 326-8). It could be argued that such independence might have eventually led to an earlier showdown with Rome, had he survived long enough. Certainly the immediate effect of his death was to open up a very different chapter of Jewish/Roman relations as the whole of Palestine came under direct Roman rule once more, the youthfulnes of Agrippa's son, Agrippa II, being offered as the pretext for Claudius' decision.[35]

For Galilee this introduced a new political situation - its first immediate contact with direct Roman rule. Cuspius Fadus, Josephus tells us, was appointed procurator of Judaea *and of the whole kingdom* (*Ant* 19:363; cf. *War* 2:223). As is well known, the period as a whole is marked by deteriorating relations between Rome and the Jews, climaxing in the procuratorship of Gessius Florus (64-66 C.E.), whom Josephus explicitly blames for the outbreak of the first revolt (*Ant* 20:257; *War* 2:283). There are many different facets to the decline - the insensitivity of successive procurators to Jewish religious concerns (e.g. *Ant* 20:105-12; *War* 2:224-7.229.289.328-31) and the ruthless handling of Jewish revolutionary leaders with messianic pretentions such as Theudas (*Ant* 20:97f; *Ac* 5:36 - Cuspius Fadus), Jacob and Simeon, the sons of Judas the Galilean (*Ant* 20:102 - Tiberius Alexander), the Egyptian prophet (*Ant* 20:169-72; *War* 2:261-3; *Ac* 21:38 - Felix), the prophet in the desert (*Ant* 20:188 - Festus). Josephus also accuses several of the procurators with venality and corruption, climaxing in Florus' appropriation of 17 talents from the temple treasury (*War* 2:293f; cf. *War* 2:273-6 - Albinius). There was also the worsening of relations between the Jews and their

Syrian neighbors, especially in Caesarea, which the procurators tolerated, indeed openly encouraged (*War* 2:266-70.284-92). All this led to a general breakdown of law and order as the country became a prey to brigandage (*War* 2:238; *Ant* 20:124), which the Romans either ignored or handled very ineffectively (*War* 2:254. 271; *Ant* 20:165). In particular we hear of the rise of the *sicarii* during the procuratorship of Felix (52-60 C.E.), operating apparently both in the city and countryside alike, creating social havoc and political unrest (*War* 2:254-6; *Ant* 20:185-7; 208-10).

Our concern is to decide the impact of this deterioration of social and political life in Palestine on Galilee, and evaluate the special factors that might have been at work in the province, now that it was in a very different administrative situation. The only episode involving Galileans directly that is mentioned in our sources occurred in the reign of Cumanus (48-52 C.E.). There are three accounts, for Tacitus (*Ann.* XII, 54) as well as Josephus (*War* 2:232-46; *Ant* 20:118-36) mentions the affair, if only in passing. The broad outlines are clear even though different *Tendenzen* may be detected in all three versions. The incident took place as Galilean pilgrims were on their way to Jerusalem, and one of them ('a multitude' according to *Ant*) was killed, sparking off a violent confrontation. The leaders of the Galileans appealed to Cumanus but he ignored them because he had been bribed by the Samaritans (*Ant*) or because of more urgent business (*War*). When news of the incident reached the city, the Galileans (who presumably had arrived before their fellow-countrymen) incited the crowds, who engaged the aid of a brigand chief Eleazar ben Deinaeus and sacked Samaritan villages. The Jewish leaders had attempted to restrain the crowd but were unsuccessful, and eventually Cumanus intervened on the side of the Samaritans. Still not satisfied, they appealed to Ummidius Quadratus, the governor of Syria, and he executed some of the leaders on both sides, and sent the rest including the Jewish high priest and the temple captain as well as Cumanus to Rome to explain the whole affair to Nero.

We shall have occasion to examine the incident later for possible traces of a Galilean revolutionary spirit. Significant for our discussion at this stage is the fact that as procurator of Judaea, Cumanus appears to be under the immediate jurisdiction of the Roman legate in Syria. This is an important insight into Roman policy towards Palestine. Technically Judaea was an imperial province but of equestrian rank, whereas Syria was governed by a man of senatorial rank, which meant that Roman legions could be stationed there, whereas only auxiliaries were stationed in Judaea. Besides, the governor of Syria had special military responsibility for the East, presumably because of the constant threat of the Parthians.[36] It was a serious matter for a governor of Syria to intervene in Judaean affairs and usually involved some very emphatic statement of Roman presence. At the time of the disturbances after Herod's death, for example, Varus had made his intentions clear to the people of Sepphoris. It is highly significant therefore that on this occasion Jerusalem and Samaria rather than Galilee became the center of Ummidius' concerns, and it was Jerusalem authorities, not the οἱ πρῶτοι τῶν Γαλιλαίων who were also active in the incident (*Ant* 20:119), that were sent to Rome in chains. In Roman eyes then, the official spokesmen for Judaism are still the Judaean religious authorities, and if there was a special administrative situation recognized for Galilee, this is not regarded as directly answerable for the events.

This conclusion is all the more important because of Tactitus' reference to the affair. Apparently he believes that Felix as well as Cumanus held some official post in Palestine at this time, for in describing the events in the most general terms he writes that Felix had for a while past held the governorship of Judaea *iam pridem Judaeae impositus.* Yet for him this does not exclude the official presence of Cumanus also, for he says that the province was so divided that Cumanus was in charge of Galilee and Felix over the Samaritans (*aemulo ad deterrima Ventidio Cumano, cui pars provinciae habebatur, ita divisio, ut huic Galilaeorum natio, Felici Samaritae parerent*). Several different suggestions have been made for reconciling this with the statements of Josephus who declares that Felix was 'sent' (ἐκπέμπει, *War* 2:247; *Ant* 20:137) to Palestine by Claudius to replace the banished Cumanus, but none of them are completely satisfactory.[37] It certainly is not inconceivable that Rome would have appointed somebody to take special charge of Galilee. Such an official position existed earlier under the triumvirs when Herod was governor there, and in all probability he retained the office during his long reign. Subsequently it would have been embodied in the tetrarchy of Antipas and the Kingdom of Agrippa, only to surface again as part of the Roman provincial structure of Palestine. Josephus does in fact hint at such a Roman administrative set-up also, for in describing the appointment of Felix in *War* he says that he was sent out as procurator of Judaea, Samaria, Galilee and Peraea (*War* 2:247). Such an enumeration of the divisions of the kingdom is unusual, and suggests at least that Cumanus, whom Felix was replacing, was not in charge of all Palestine. But that still does not reconcile the two accounts since Tacitus presumes that Felix was in charge of Samaria and Cumanus Galilee, whereas Josephus certainly presumes that Cumanus and the Samaritans were in collaboration over the whole affair.

Whatever the final solution be, it seems clear that such an arrangement of appointing regular Roman officials in charge of various sections of the country was not established Roman policy at the period of the first revolt. At that time Sepphoris was the capital of Roman Galilee (*Life* 37ff) and everything we know about its situation then suggests that it did not have an official Roman presence, no matter how Romanophile its tendencies were. In fact we hear of the people of Sepphoris appealing to Cestius Gallus, the governor of Syria, for help (*Life* 30.346.373.). This was only granted after some delay (*Life* 394) and finally Vespasian granted them a permanent garrison (*Life* 411; cf. *War* 2:510-12; 3:30-34). In fact the impression one gets from Josephus is that at the time that he took over as governor of Galilee for the revolutionary government, Roman interest in the north was represented by Agrippa II, who had gradually climbed the ladder of favor since he was considered too young by Claudius to inherit the kingdom of his father.

Even though Agrippa, the Younger, did not receive his father's kingdom in 44 C.E. he was still able to play a prominent part in Jewish politics at Rome, until he was eventually rewarded on the death of his uncle Herod, with his own territory of Chalcis in 49 C.E. Even before that he had successfully intervened with the Emperor on behalf of the Jews over their right to keep the high priestly vestments, which the procurator Fadus wanted to usurp (*Ant* 20:6-9). As king of Chalcis he also inherited the right of selection of the high priest - a right he subsequently exercised (*Ant* 20:179.213). His intervention in the affair over Cumanus was also decisive in having the Jewish point of view vindicated (*Ant* 20:135; *War* 2:245). About that time Claudius had given him the tetrarchy of Philip in exchange for the kingdom of Chalcis, thereby installing him in the nucleus of his father's previous kingdom (*Ant* 20:138). The final addition to his kingdom came with the grant by Nero of Tiberias, Tarichaeae, Julias and Abila with their territories probably in 54/55 C.E. (*Ant* 20:159; *War* 2:252).[38] Thus, by a gradual process Agrippa II had been inserted more and more into the political life of Palestine, presumably because his acceptability to both Jews and Romans was recognized by the latter.

Agrippa II formĕd an important bridge between the pre- and post-war years as far as Galilean life was concerned. The granting of Tiberias and Tarichaeae with their territories may have upset the existing social life in the province as can be seen from Justus' remarks (*Life* 37ff), yet it saved that section of Galilee at least from the worst ravages of the victorious Romans in 67 C.E. There seems to be no good reason why the whole of Galilee was not granted to Agrippa, since he was and remained a loyal supporter of imperial policy, even to the point of having to abandon Jerusalem in his attempt to avert the revolt (*War* 2:345-407), and further attempts to intervene from outside proved equally futile (*War* 2:421.523-6).[39] Thus the concession of this one piece of Jewish territory may have been a personal gift from Nero and not a part of any larger-scale Roman strategy for the province. As already mentioned we do not find an explicit Roman presence in the remaining section of the province when Josephus took over command in 66. It would seem therefore that up to that point at least Galilee had not proved particularly troublesome to the Roman administration or that any special measures were called for in dealing with its administration. As will presently emerge, Agrippa's control of the two Galilean centers was tenuous, even if for rather different reasons, and the provisional government of 66 C.E. took no cognizance of this changed situation in Galilee in their appointment of Josephus to the province or in their subsequent instructions to him. Indeed the inclusion of Gamala in his commission indicates that they may have had in view a larger territory than political Galilee of the immediate past - possibly even recalling ancient Israelite territory.

While the period from 44-66 C.E. was a particularly turbulent one for Jewish/Roman relations our sources have very little to offer on the overall effects of this changed situation in Galilee. The one serious episode dealing with Galileans took place outside the area and seems to have had greater repercussions in Jerusalem than Galilee. The impression one gets is that the province emerged relatively unscathed from the period, however we may wish to understand Tacitus' indication of the turbulence there and the apparently temporary division of the territory under two procurators. Subsequent events will test the accuracy of that impression.

(v)Galilee from 66-135 C.E.

The silence of our sources about Galilee for the period of the procurators comes to an abrupt end with the appointment of Josephus to the province and the subsequent accounts both of his difficulties there with the various factions and of the Galilean campaign itself. Complicated though the task is because of the apologetic nature of both the *Life* and the *War*, it should still be possible to draw some conclusions concerning various aspects of life in the province in this turbulent period from the two works, and also estimate the accuracy of our judgement concerning the previous period.[40]

Even before Josephus' appointment to Galilee after the takeover by the provisional government in Jerusalem, the province had begun to feel the mounting tension of the later procuratorial period - at least on its borders. Almost contemporaneous with the Zealot takeover of the temple in Jerusalem, trouble broke out also at Caesarea between the wealthier Jewish inhabitants and the more numerous gentile population who were supported by the Syrian troops stationed there. A wholesale massacre of Jews naturally led to reprisals 'as the whole nation was infuriated' (*War* 2:458). Josephus gives a list of cities where Jewish reprisals took place, most probably in the surrounding villages rather than in the cities themselves, and they include the outer circle of Galilee: Philadelphia, Heshbon, Gerasa, Pella, Scythopolis, Gadara,

Hippos and Gaulanitis - all in Transjordan or the Dekapolis, Kedasa on the Tyrian borders, Ptolemais, Gaba and Caesarea, Sebaste, Ascalon, Anthedon and Gaza, moving south along the coast (*War* 2:458-60). The Jewish population in the cities suffered a similar fate to their brothers at Caesarea - with the exception of Sidon, Apamaea, Antioch and Gerasa, though Alexandrine Jews were not so fortunate (*War* 2:477-80.487-98; cf. *Life* 24-27).

These disturbances also reached Galilee proper and their repercussions were still being felt within the province on Josephus' arrival there as governor. The Babylonian Jews of Batanaea were lured to Caesarea Philippi by Agrippa's viceroy Varus (Noarus, according to *War*) in league with the gentile population of the city, only to be slaughtered together with the Jewish leaders of the city who had been duped in the whole affair (*Life* 54-61). Gischala in Upper Galilee also suffered at the hands of marauders from Gadara, Gabara, Sogane and Tyre, even though the leading townsman John had advocated peace with Rome (*Life* 43-5).[41] The mention of Sogane and Gabara in this list of places hostile to Gischala is surprising, since later John is able to win over the latter to his side (*Life* 122f) and the former is listed as one of the places fortified by Josephus, so that presumably both were predominantly Jewish.[42]

Justus of Tiberias also attacked Gadara and Hippos (*Life* 42), and later the minority Greek population in the city was killed on the occasion of the implementation of the Jerusalem authority's decision concerning Herod's palace (*Life* 67). We also hear of disturbances between the Galilean countrypeople and Tiberias (*Life* 392) but we are not in a position to determine more precisely the nature of this episode of inner Galilean politics.[43] It is difficult to imagine this large scale civil strife being part of an organized plan, since the places mentioned are so widely scattered, and local conditions varied enormously. Yet it is equally difficult to think of it as a fortuitous concurrence of similar events, for apart from Caesarea we do not hear of a build up of hostilities of that proportion between Jewish and Gentile inhabitants in the earlier period.

Planned or spontaneous, Rome could not turn a blind eye to these disturbances, and Cestius Gallus began his effort to restore peace to Jewish territory that was to eventually founder at Beth Horon, with such disastrous consequences for the Jews, at least in Josephus' eyes. The antipathy of his Syrian auxiliaries for the Jews is explicitly mentioned (*War* 2:502). He began his offensive at Chabulon, a border town of Galilee, described as a πόλις κάρτερη by Josephus, yet deserted by its inhabitants, who had all fled to the hills. Even though he admired its Phoenician-style architecture, he destroyed the city, presumably as a sign of his intentions, and he also sacked the surrounding villages. While the Jews succeeded in waylaying Cestius' returning army and killing about 2000 of his men, Cestius apparently did not feel it incumbent on him to advance further on Galilee at this point, but headed south from Ptolemais to Joppa. This decision of Cestius suggests that the attack on Chabulon was more precautionary than demanded by the situation. This is borne out by a similar attack on the district of Narbatene, bordering Caesarea. Cestius subsequently sent Caesennius Gallus, the commander of the 12th legion to Galilee 'with such forces as he considered necessary for the reduction of that province'. Once Sepphoris received him with open arms the other cities also remained quiet, and Caesennius' only engagement was against 'all the rebels and brigands' (τὸ δὲ στασιῶδες καὶ ληστρικὸν πᾶν) who had fled to an unidentified mountain near Sepphoris called Asamon, and more than 2000 of these perished. The account of this excursion of Roman troops into Galilee concludes: 'Gallus, seeing no further signs of revolt in Galilee returned with his troops to Caesarea' and Cestius was able to continue his march on Jerusalem (*War* 2:510-13).[44]

In assessing the situation in Galilee up to this point, therefore, one can only be struck by the relative passivity of the area. At least the indications are that it did not cause the Romans any undue anxiety. Strategically, it was unlikely that Cestius would march south, and more especially on Jerusalem itself without making his presence felt in Galilee also, since as we have seen, it was always the first objective of armies invading from the north.[45] Even after Cestius' defeat and withdrawal there does not appear to be any immediate worsening of the situation, for Josephus recounts his own involvement with another of Cestius' generals, Placidus, again in the region of Chabulon, who had been sent 'with two cohorts of infantry and a squadron of horse to burn the Galilean villages in the neighborhood of Ptolemais'. However, both sides seem to be prepared to play a 'wait-and-see' game, and the impression one gets is that Josephus is more concerned about his Jewish enemies than his Roman foes (*Life* 213-15).

In attempting to understand Josephus' mission and his conduct within the province we immediately run into the differing perspectives of *War* and *Life* and the way the narrative of each is colored. Josephus was the emissary of what has come to be called the provisional government which controlled Jewish affairs after the defeat of Cestius Gallus. It is often assumed that this government was 'moderate', that is, not in favor of war with Rome but eventually forced to that position by actual circumstances (*War* 2:562), and that is the way in which Josephus wishes to portray himself also in *Life* (28f.175f).[46] On the other hand in the *War* version he sets out for Galilee to organize men and provisions for the coming conflict (*War* 2:577-82), and the subsequent narrative highlights his capabilities as a general, fighting a legitimate war. Which, if either, of these two positions is more likely, or is it possible to reconcile them?

Despite Josephus' protestation of pacifism in *Life* there is little doubt that a militarist undercurrent can be detected in that work also.[47] Thus we get a list of fortified places, similar to, if not identical with the list in *War* (*Life* 186-8; *War* 2:573-5). While the list in *Life* stands in a certain tension with the peace-keeping policy of Josephus, he attempts to soften the impact by suggesting that this action was due to his πρόνοια or foresight: 'these places I stocked with ample supplies of corn and arms for their future security', while in *War* his action fits in perfectly with the picture of the ideal general, since he foresaw 'that Galilee would bear the brunt of the Roman assault'. Though different, these are not irreconcilable reasons, the former that of the humanitarian caring for his people, and the latter that of the general planning military strategy. But in fact there are difficulties with both lists, at least as fortresses. Elsewhere Josephus admits that he did not fortify all these places. John fortified his native Gischala (*Life* 71.189; *War* 2:575.590); Sepphoris was allowed or encouraged to build its own walls (*War* 2:574) even though Josephus tries to claim credit for them later (*War* 3:61); at the time of the affair of the highwaymen from Dabaritta the walls of Tarichaeae and Tiberias were not built (*Life* 142-4; *War* 2:606.9). The blatant exaggeration about the size of the fortifications at Itabyrion (*War* 4:54-61) makes one suspicious that Josephus' lists represent a situation he might have wished for rather than actually realized.[48] Elsewhere he recognizes the natural remoteness of places like Jotapata and Japha (*War* 3:158-60.290) and undoubtedly these and other places became centers for refugees from the countryside fleeing from the Roman scorched earth policy, as well as hideouts for would-be revolutionaries.

What then are we to make of Josephus' army? Once again an underlying concurrence between *War* and *Life* suggests that there is some substance to his reports, though on a vastly diluted scale. The discussion in *War* 2:577-82 about the recuiting and training of his Galilean troops is patently obvious as a piece of self-glorification by the general turned historian. The figures are highly exaggerated, 100,000 persons at *War* 2:576, reduced to 60,000 persons at *War* 2:583, is already indicative, and attempts to harmonize the two figures are rather unconvincing. Yet, turning to *Life* we do find a regular army of much smaller proportions independent of the Galilean reserves who can be summoned for special engagements of a shorter period when a special danger threatens (*Life* 98.102.213.305). In all probability the permanent force was made up of non-Jewish mercenaries, for we hear that they are dismissed on a sabbath at Tarichaeae, not to disturb the populace (*Life* 159). Their numbers are never very large. He engages Aebutius, Agrippa's decurion with an army of 2,000 infantry (*Life* 116f), and similarly he has only a small force when he attempts to prevent the Romans coming to the aid of Sepphoris (*Life* 394-7), but he claims to have 10,000 men for his attack on Tiberias without any mention of Galilean reinforcements (*Life* 321.327.331). He sends James with 200 men to guard the routes to Galilee from Gabara, and Jeremiah with 600 to watch the roads leading to Jerusalem in an attempt to cut off the delegation. He can supply an escort for his counter-embassy (*Life* 240f) and a soldier for each of the 30 Galilean notables whom he sends to discuss with the Jerusalem embassy (*Life* 228). From these figures it is obvious that Josephus' army was of rather modest proportions, and little wonder that he had only a limited success in his various engagements with those places which he attempted to reduce even before the Romans arrived. The various strategies he employs to avoid taking or destroying such places as Sepphoris and Tiberias are rather thinly veiled excuses for his own inability to impose a strong will on all the various dissidents, especially the larger towns (*Life* 104-11; 155-73; 246-65; 373-80; 394-6).[49]

If then Josephus was no general of outstanding bravery, foresight and moderation, as he would have us believe, neither was he a pro-Roman peacemaker. In accepting a position under the provisional government he had already thrown in his lot with the revolutionary party, whatever his earlier feelings.[50] That this government thought of itself as being in permanent control is clear from the fact that it struck its own silver coins for the first year of the revolt, even though it had nothing to offer politically other than the restoration of the old theocracy.[51] Thus Josephus was infringing directly on Roman rights. Significantly he speaks of his appointment to the two Galilees, Upper and Lower, without any recognition of the recent grant of Tarichaeae and Tiberias to Agrippa, and the inclusion of Gamala in his jurisdiction was a further infringement of the king's rights (*War* 2:568). He saw his role not merely in military but also in administrative terms, and so we find him setting up a provincial juridical system with himself as the final arbitrer (*Life* 79; *War* 2:570f). He appointed a governor ($\sigma\tau\rho\alpha\tau\eta\gamma\grave{o}s$), Silas, over Tiberias (*Life* 89.272) even though the city had its own administration of a $\beta o\upsilon\lambda\acute{\eta}, \check{\alpha}\rho\chi\omega\nu$ and $\delta\eta\mu\grave{o}s$. A council of Galilean nobles may also have been established as a way of marshalling broad-based support throughout the whole province (*Life* 78f.310f), and this was to prove effective against the counter-claims of such local aspirants to power as John of Gischala (*Life* 73) and Justus of Tiberias (*Life* 42.392). Inevitably the preparation for the war had to be a large part of his strategy since it must have been plain to all that Rome would eventually take full revenge for the humiliation of her eagles,[52] and previous experience ensured that there would be very little discrimination between promoters of the revolution and the ordinary populace. One did not have to be a Zealot to be aware of the need to be prepared for the onslaught at the close of 66 C.E. in Palestine, and this was precisely Josephus' position in Galilee.

Turning now to the Galilean campaign of 67 C.E. we can evaluate the success or otherwise of Josephus' attempts to reconstitute Jewish Galilee since his appointment to the province. He would like us to believe that it was a glorious, if ill-fated, campaign, 'providing the Romans with a strenuous training for the impending Jerusalem campaign' (*War* 4:120). Once again however, fact and literary fiction have to be distinguished as we are alerted to the fact that this is both apology for himself and encomium of his opposing general, Vespasian, who is the literary patron of the work. Not even Josephus is able to disguise fully the real dimensions of the campaign which for convenience may be divided into three phases: a) the initial onslaught of Placidus and Vespasian; b) the assistance to Agrippa in reducing those places in his territory which had revolted - Tiberias, Tarichaeae and Gamala; c) a final mopping up operation in which such 'border' places as Thabor and Gischala are reduced. We shall briefly examine each phase.

Vespasian recognized that Sepphoris afforded an excellent springboard from which he could control the whole of Lower Galilee (*War* 3:30.34), and so the tribune Placidus is stationed there with 1,000 cavalry and 6,000 infantry as reinforcement for the garrison already sent by Cestius (*Life* 394; cf. *War* 2:510). This force was adequate to overrun the surrounding countryside. Josephus' 'army' was not able to take the city which he himself had so strongly fortified as to render it practically impregnable! The Romans adopted a scorched earth policy: 'they never ceased, night or day, to devastate the plains and to pillage the property of the country folk, killing those who might be able to carry arms, and reducing the weak to slavery' (*War* 3:59-63.110f). This seems an altogether likely tactic if Galilee was as thickly populated as Josephus reports. He prides himself on the fortresses he had provided as the only source of refuge for the country folk, and while we have already voiced certain misgivings about the list, undoubtedly there must have been great numbers of refugees leaving the villages and attempting to dig themselves in in the more easily defended centers. Vespasian's first arrival in Galilee is told as though it were a triumphal journey already. As he proceeded from Ptolemais to the borders of Galilee, Josephus' army deserted before even catching sight of the enemy. They fled from the camp at Garis near Sepphoris, willing to capitulate, and Josephus himself retired to Tiberias with a few loyal supporters (*War* 3:127-31). Vespasian was not about to expose his troops to possible attacks in the open country after Cestius' defeat, so instead he turned north-west to Gabara (one of the three largest cities in Galilee), and though there was no resistance there he slaughtered all the inhabitants of age, and burned all the small towns and villages in the neighborhood, finding some completely deserted and reducing the inhabitants of others to slavery (*War* 3:132-4). The rest of the first phase of the campaign was taken up with the siege of Jotapata, and Josephus devotes a long section of book III of *War* (141-339) to describing both his own military prowess and that of the Romans. There is a brief interlude in which the siege and capture of Japha, 'a neighboring village' is described - 'a disaster that befell the Galileans' in July of 67 C.E. In recognizing the literary exaggeration of this narrative it would be hyper-critical to suggest that the whole affair was the invention of Josephus, but it should also be realized that the account does serve the additional purpose of filling out the report of the Galilean campaign, in the absence of any other engagements.[53] We hear of such Galileans as Eleazar son of Sameas, a native of Saba, and Netiras and Philip, brothers from the village of Ruma who distinguished themselves in the fighting (*War* 3:230-3), and no doubt there were others from the lower Galilean countryside who made the center their last refuge from the Romans. However, Josephus' explanation of his proposed flight as an attempt to muster the Galileans from the countryside to create a diversion (*War* 3:199) is indicative of the scale of operations for Galilee as a whole. This is no last ditch stand of a province geared for war with Rome, but rather a fairly isolated outpost of desperate refugees from the countryside who realize what their ultimate fate in the hands of Rome is likely to be.

Once Jotapata had surrendered Vespasian did not feel it incumbent to press on to Upper Galilee or towards the lake, but withdrew his troops to Caesarea and billeted others at Scythopolis (*War* 3:409-13). It is only sometime afterwards while on a visit to Agrippa at Caesarea Philippi that he becomes involved in the revolt within the king's territory. First Tiberias and then Tarichaeae had revolted at the instigation of Jesus son of Sapphias, and Vespasian 'wishing to repay his hospitality' decided to restore both cities to their allegiance to the king (σωφρονίσων αὐτῷ τὰς πόλεις). In other words, Vespasian did not consider these

cities his personal responsibility, and obviously he does not
regard the disturbances in either as the continuation of the struggle that he had completed at Jotapata. Once Jesus and his followers left Tiberias the peace party there quickly prevailed and
there were no undue reprisals on the part of the Romans (*War*
3:453-61). At Tarichaeae matters were slightly different. It had
accepted Josephus' position in the earlier period, and stood
solidly behind him in his dealings with Tiberias - possibly because of jealousy towards its more prominent neighbor (*Life*
158f.174.276.304.404). It seems that the city was an accepted
refugee center (φιλοξενώτατος) for people from the countryside
despite the obvious exaggeration of *Life* 142, which speaks of
vast numbers having come there to throw in their lot with Josephus. Presumably, these earlier refugees were from Agrippa's
territory or from the Syrian cities in the Dekapolis (*War* 3:541f),
but these would now be joined by people from Galilee, who were
on good terms with the city and its inhabitants (cf. *Life* 98f.
304-6). In view of the earlier attitudes it seems a little surprising to
hear that after a preliminary skirmish 'the native population,
intent on their property and their city, had from the first dis-
approved of the war, and were now more opposed to it than ever'
(*War* 3:492f). Yet there is nothing inconceivable about such a
change in the light of the Roman presence and apparently they
recognize the difference in their handling of the affair, by separating the aliens and selling them into slavery while the natives
were left unmolested (*War* 3:532-42). The long description of
Gamala and its siege at the beginning of Book IV of *War* (4-83)
corresponds to the description of Jotapata in Book III, and once
more it affords Josephus the opportunity to extol his Roman
patrons - their bravery, skill and foresight. In this instance the
drama of the siege is interrupted by an attack on Thabor (*War*
4:54-61). The interest in Gamala and Philip ben Jacimus, especially in *Life*, has baffled many commentators, and we need
not enter those discussions here.[55] No doubt the prominence of
the siege at this point in the *War* narrative is related to Josephus'
own association with the place, for it was explicitly mentioned
as being part of his command (*War* 2:568) and he now draws

attention to his fortifying the place, making the obvious comparison with Jotapata (*War* 4:9f). Whatever the scale of the operation - and we can well believe that it was considerable - its reduction meant that Agrippa's territory was now completely subdued and the Romans were able to turn their attention to the serious business ahead.

One final phase of the Galilean campaign remained, the reduction of various 'strongholds' throughout the country. Most of them 'surrendered' as soon as Jotapata had fallen, Josephus admits (*War* 4:1); only Gischala and Itabyrion remained and the narration of these events allows him to honor Titus, Vespian's son who reduced Gischala. It is difficult to estimate the proper extent of either operation, given the highly anti-John polemic of the *War* account, and the fact that the description of the size and quality of the Itabyrion fortress is blatant exaggeration, presumably to extol his own achievements.[56] It is noteworthy that John did not appear at any of the lower Galilean centers to aid his fellow countrymen in their hour of need. Of course, his absence may be explained by the antipathy that had grown up between himself and Josephus and the failure of the Jerusalem delegation to unseat his great rival. Even so, it is unlikely that John would have openly revolted after the treatment meted out to Lower Galilee by the Romans. John would be known to them as a potential threat to peace in the north, since his attack on the imperial granaries (*Life* 71), and so it was decided to bring him to heel before turning all the attention to the south. The sequel paints John as a traitor to his fellow townsmen fleeing by night to Jerusalem with some followers, whereas Titus, sated with bloodshed, spared the masses with typical Flavian sympathy (*War* 4:92-120). The probabilities are that capture of John rather than the rebelliousness of the people (cf. *War* 4:102) was the real purpose of Titus' mission, and therefore no drastic measures were taken. Itabyrion, which bordered on the Great Plain, might well have been a center of some resistance, for it was in this very neighborhood that the highwaymen of Dabaritta had waylaid Herod's steward's wife early in Josephus' command (*Life* 126; *War* 2:595ff). However, as noted, the area of the enclosed rampart is impossible, and this reduces the vast multitude considerably. Presumably some did escape to Jerusalem, there to join (?) John and the 2,000 Tiberians who are also supposed to have fled to the capital (*Life* 354). However, their numbers must have been small since 600 calvary had been sent against them by the Romans, and again the natives were left unmolested as at Tarichaeae and Gischala.

Reviewing the events of 66-67 C.E. as they can be reconstructed from Josephus' accounts we can recognize the many weaknesses of the Jewish handling of affairs in the province. A Jerusalemite was given control of the province and this was the first cause of friction, since it alienated local leadership to the point that when a common front and special tactics were called for in face of the Roman onslaught there was no planned strategy or mutual assistance. At first the Romans handled matters without any discrimination, until eventually a more moderate approach was adopted when the lack of any real threat was recognized.

This inner-Galilean weakness is most clearly illustrated in the tensions between town and country that emerged in the crisis. The bitter rivalry between Tiberias and Sepphoris meant that the upper classes were divided, and the latter's aristocratic pro-Roman stance isolated it from those to whom it should have offered some leadership. Josephus never succeeded in breaking down these barriers, and so he found himself with no real power-base within the province. As a Herodian prince, Agrippa II might be expected to have had some influence on Galilean Jews, but he does not seem to have been able to control those parts of Galilee that had been granted to him, and after his rebuff at Jerusalem he showed no desire to meddle further in Jewish or Galilean affairs.

Though Josephus had been appointed by the Jerusalem council and was ultimately responsible to them, events at the center moved so rapidly that it became impossible to remove him, despite the desire of a newly constituted council to do so (*Life* 196; *War* 2:627). We shall return to the circumstances of this attempt later, but for now we wish to underline how quickly events went out of the control of the provisional government, as each part of the country was left to its own devices. Josephus appealed for help to Jerusalem on the arrival of Vespasian, but none was either likely or forthcoming (*War* 3:138-40). If this report is correct, was he now hoping for a wholesale surrender from Jerusalem, so that he too could have resigned with dignity? Thus in its hour of need Galilee was left to its own devices, and these proved totally inadequate, if indeed the people as a whole had ever seriously contemplated opposing the might of Rome. It could be argued that had Josephus never been sent to the province the country people would have fared much better. His presence there gave the illusion of a province in revolt and ready for war. Of course, Josephus did nothing to destroy that illusion for Roman readers of *War*. Later in the *Life* account he transformed his own role from that of rebel general to peacekeeper and moderate. In all probability his true position lay somewhere in between. He was vain enough to think of himself as a great general and aspired to the honors that came with his office as governor of Galilee. Yet he was sufficiently astute to try to ride out the storm once he foresaw the inevitable defeat. The fact is that while allowing his vanity to challenge Rome and fail, his astuteness made it possible for him to survive when all the other revolutionary leaders perished.

How did the province that he hoped to govern fare in the Roman settlement? Presumably no permanent arrangement was made while the war in Judaea continued, and unfortunately our sources are almost silent about Galilee when it does come to the final decision. But this silence may itself be significant, in that the Romans felt that no drastic measures had to be taken to control the province. Of course the order of Vespasian (*War* 7:216) to have the land of the Jews leased (πᾶσαν γῆν ἀποδόσθαι τῶν Ἰυδαίων) did include Galilee, and we shall discuss the social implications of this decree later.[57] It did not itself mean a new political arrangement, even though we know that a larger province of Judaea of senatorial rank was reconstituted, that is, of the same status as the province of Syria, with a Roman legion (*Decima Fretensis*) posted on the ruins of Jerusalem (*War* 7:17). This new province included not merely the strictly Jewish territory of the pre-revolt province, but also some gentile cities of the coast from Raphia to Caesarea as well as Samaria.[58] Within this new arrangement the city territories that had proved so loyal to Rome had their status increased as administrative municipalities, whereas the country areas were managed by the central Roman authority. Gradually however, the cities began to encroach more and more, so that by the third century almost the whole of the province was directly controlled by cities within the provincial framework.[59] The transformation of the half shekel offering for the temple into the *fiscus Judaicus* to the Capitoline Jupiter was a further blow to Jewish pride, in that it challenged the distinctiveness of the ἔθνος τῶν Ἰουδαίων, without however removing its legal status completely within the Roman Empire. The general recognition by the Romans of the title הנשיא (Greek πατριάρχης) as designating the official head of the Jewish people probably only came in the time of Rabbi Judah I around 170 C.E., yet long before that in the Jamnia period, particularly under Rabban Gamaliel II's leadership, the court of Jamnia began to take responsibility for Jewish affairs within the Empire and was recognized by the Imperial authorities. While this arrangement suffered a serious setback in the aftermath of the Bar Cochba revolt, it gradually re-emerged, and under the Antonine Emperors Rabbi Judah (170-220 C.E.) put Jewish self-rule on a firm footing once more within the imperiod constitution.[60]

Naturally these developments had serious repercussions in Galilee. Numismatic evidence indicates that already in 68 C.E. Sepphoris as a reward for its faithfulness was allowed to strike its own coins with the inscriptions NEPΩNIAC and EIPENOPOΛIC 'City of Peace', thus confirming the evidence of *Life* concerning the attitude of the city from the start.[61] This concession may have meant a very early addition to its territory, and no doubt it was further increased under Hadrian when it received the added name, Diocaesarea.[62] Tiberias, however was not so fortunate. It had to wait until the death of Agrippa II before its status was restored, and even then there may have been some hesitation due to its more dubious record during the revolt.[63] Eventually all of Lower Galilee was divided between the territories of these two cities but Upper Galilee apparently continued as the separate district of Tetracomia. This is best explained by the strong persistence of Jewish village life in the area which had not been disturbed by the revolt.[64] The question of Galilee's involvement in the Bar Cochba revolt is not absolutely certain, but on the generally accepted assumption that it was not,[65] we have testimony of how effective this Roman settlement of the province really was after the first revolt. We shall have to return to this question in the next section.

CONCLUSION

This outline of Galilean history under Roman domination from Pompey to Hadrian shows that, relatively speaking, Galilee fared better than Judaea under Roman rule. This is only as we might expect, since Jerusalem was both the political and ideological center of Judaism where opposition to Rome was most keenly felt and expressed. Galilee had no individual political will of its own apart from the center. Having been politically dominated for so long, Galilean Judaism had come to live with Gentile neighbors and overlords. This is not to suggest that the region did not have its own identity as we shall see. Rather it underlines the fact that both its geographical features and its historical conditioning had made it a region rather than a country, a province rather than an aspiring state. Gabinius' experiment or Josephus' efforts could not change the course of history. Under Herod Antipas it acquired a certain identity and stability, but only at the price of social tensions that were to emerge so very clearly at the time of crisis.

NOTES FOR CHAPTER 3

[1] Josephus highlights the effects of the feud in terms of loss of territory, tribute to be paid and the transfer of kingship from high priests to commoners, *Ant* 14:77f. On Roman expansionist policy in general cf. E. Badian, 'Patron -State and Client-State', reprinted from *Roman Imperialism in the Late Republic*, Oxford, B. Blackwell, 1968, in *Imperialism in the Roman Republic*, ed. E.S. Gruen, New York, Holt, Rinehart and Winston, 1970, 102-10; also, M. Avi-Yonah, 'The Rise of Rome', *W.H.Her.P.*, 3-25. E. Bammel, 'Die Neuordnung des Pompeius und das römisch-jüdische Bündnis' ZDPV 75(1959) 76-88, discusses the legal implication of Pompey's action and concludes that the earlier treaty between Rome and the Jews, dating to Maccabaean times, was not abolished but temporarily put in abeyance. External circumstances were to help the Jews subsequently yet Pompey's action was the beginning of the transformation of the old treaty into a *foedus inaequuum*.

[2] Alt, 'Die Vorstufen zur Eingliederung Galiläas in das Römische Reich', *G.P.* 6, 423-35, esp. 427.

[3] Schürer, *Geschichte*, 1, 299f, n. 25, on the basis of those cities whose coins have the Pompeian era, especially in the Dekapolis, argues for other cities also. Cf. H. Bietenhard , 'Die Dekapolis von Pompeius bis Traian. Ein Kapitel aus der neutestamentlichen Zeitgeschichte', ZDPV 79(1963) 24-58, esp. 33-7.

[4] Schalit, 'The Fall of the Hasmonaean Dynasty and the Roman Conquest', *W.H. Her.P.*, 26-43, esp. 36, based on *Ant* 20:244 and Cicero, *Ad Atticum* VI,2.4.

[5] Avi-Yonah, *The Holy Land*, 79; however, Alt, 'Die Vorstufen', *G.P.6*, 426, n.3., doubts about Idumaea because it had not previously belonged to the cultic community, but had been forcibly judaized. Cf. n.7.

[6] Schalit, 'The Fall', *W.H.Her.P.*, 36, thinks that Pompey's measures were only temporary, since he hoped to eventually subjugate the Jews totally. However, Bammel, 'Die Neuordnung', points to the abnormality of the situation in purely legal terms, and hence the Senate's reluctance to ratify it, (79, n. 23). Nor is it likely that the subsequent arrangement of Gabinius was ever ratified, if indeed he had not himself begun to dismantle it after his return from Egypt (80f). Cf. further, E. Bammel, 'The Organization of Palestine by Gabinius', JJS 4(1959) 159-62.

[7] Thus Alt, 'Vorstufen', *G.P.6*, 426, n.3. Schürer, *Geschichte*, 1, 339, n.5; Schalit, 'The Fall', *W.H.Her.P.*, 65f; Avi-Yonah, *The Holy Land*, 79; Reicke, *New Testament Era*, 83, all assume that Idumaea was part of Judaea because it had been judaized. Yet this may be questioned on the basis of *Ant* 15:253f, where we hear of Herod's appointee, Costobar, attempting to establish its independence because of its different religious tradition. B. Kanael, 'The Partition of Judaea by Gabinius', IEJ 7(1957) 98-106, recognizes the problem but suggests that the resistance to Judaism in Idumaea was not likely to have been as great as in Samaria, and so he feels free to include the greater part of the territory with Judaea (excluding Marisa), and to locate Gabinius' fifth district there.

[8] Alt, 'Vorstufen', *G.P.6*, 427f.

[9] The list of cities restored by Gabinius is not identical with that given earlier for Pompey, *Ant* 14:75f; *War* 1:155f. Alt suggests that this may have been due to the speed of the restoration in some cases, 'Vorstufen', *G.P.6*, 424, n.2.

[10] The others were Jerusalem, Jericho, Amathus (in Peraea) and Gadara (or Gadora, MS,P). However there is doubt about this latter, since the Greek city of that name is impossible, and Gazara (Gezer) in NW Judaea is suggested by Marcus, *Loeb Josephus*, VII, 494, n.d. Avi-Yonah, *The Holy Land*, 84, seems to favor Kanael's position, 'The Partition', 98f, that Adorais should be read and the fifth council located in eastern Idumaea.

[11] Thabor (Itabyrion) had been a military fortress since the time of the Ptolemies, and the Jewish insurgents used it as a center of refuge during the first revolt. It is possible that the Romans had a garrison there.

[12] 'Vorstufen', *G.P.* 6, 429.

[13] Both accounts stress that the arrangement was in accord with Antipater's wishes. The exact nature of the appointment is not clear. Bammel, 'The Organization of Palestine', 161f, suggests that he was made financial supervisor of the partitioned Jerusalem in 55 B.C.E. A. Momigliano, *Guidea Romana. Ricerche sull' Organizzazione della Guidea sotto il Dominio Romano* (63 a.C-70 d.C) Reprint Amsterdam, 1967, (hereafter *Ricerche*), 8f, also argues that already in 55 C.E. Gabinius had dealt his own reorganization a severe blow by replacing Peitholaus as head of the Jerusalem synod with Hyrcanus.

[14] A. Büchler, 'The Priestly Dues and the Roman Taxes in the Edicts of Caesar in *Studies in Jewish History*, ed J. Brodie and J. Rabbinowitz, Oxford, Univ. Press, 1956, 1-23, esp. 20ff.

[15] Momigliano, *Richerche*, 7-19, and Schalit, *Herodes*, 754-9 and 777-81, for a full discussion.

[16] Josephus describes Antipater as τῆς 'Ιουδαίας ἐπιμελητής at *Ant* 14:139 whereas he calls him ἐπίτροπος at 14:143. As already indicated (above, n.13) he may have held the former office since 55, whereas the latter was apparently conferred on him in 47, after Caesar's return from Egypt. From *War* 1:225 compared with *Ant* 14:280 (with reference to Herod) the former could mean 'governor'; cf. Marcus, *Loeb Josephus* VII, 514f, n.d. Momigliano opts for the role of financial controller, or overseer for the Romans of the synodal districts, if he had the title already in 55. Later his role must have been similar to that of the procurators of imperial times.

[17] Alt, 'Hellenistische Städte und Domänen in Galiläa', *G.P.* 3, 384-95, esp. 388f shows that the territory of the Megiddo plain belonged to the different ruling houses in an unbroken line from the Ptolemies down to Roman Imperial times. Cf. also Schürer, *Geschichte*, 1, 345ff, and Büchler, 'Priestly Dues', 18f, who, however, argues that the villages of the Great Plain, but not Scythopolis or its territory, were returned to Hyrcanus because of their predominantly Jewish population. This may be true, but the real reason would seem to be that as King's land these territories had been the private possession of the Hasmonaeans, as the decrees of Caesar seem to explicitly affirm: 'the villages . . . . which Hyrcanus and his ancestors before him possessed' (*Ant* 14:207).

[18] There is no explicit record of any such gift of Jewish territory, as Schürer, *Geschichte*, 1, 347f, n. 25; Marcus, *Loeb Josephus*, VII, 559, n. e; Büchler, 'Priestly Dues', 20ff all observe. Schürer speaks of a possible gift by Pompey to Syrian dynasts, but does not further specify what Jewish territory could be in question. As the argument of the following paragraph suggests, this could only have been in Galilee, tentatively suggested also by Büchler, art. cit. 22. He had pointed out earlier that Tyre, Askalon and Sidon were *civitates foederatae*, and Rome would not normally interfere in their internal affairs, yet the decrees of Caesar concerning the Jews were to be published in those places. Another reason may have been as a warning against further encroachment, and thus related to the present *senatus consultus*.

[19] Alt, 'Vorstufen', *G.P.* 6, 428 makes this point forcibly.

[20] Peitholaus and Malichus are good examples of this situation. The former fought against Alexander, *Ant* 14:84, but for Antigonus, *Ant* 14:120. The latter remained loyal to Hyrcanus but was fiercely anti-Herodian, *Ant* 14:84.277.293.

[21] Both accounts agree that it was the Syrians, not the Galileans, who were relieved at his death. The indignation felt in Jerusalem at Herod's peremptory action in putting him to death without a Sanhedrin trial, *Ant* 14:167; *War* 1:209, suggests that the Hasmonaean aristocracy could sense their own fate.

[22] Marcus, *Loeb Josephus*, VII, 599, n. d, thinks that *Ant* is a correction of *War*, against Momigliano, *Ricerche*, 37f, who regards it as quite probable that Herod held both posts at different times.

[23] Schalit, 'The End of the Hasmonaean Dynasty and the Rise of Herod', *W.H. Her.P.*, 44-70, esp. 63, regards the story of Herod's surprise at being appointed king a fabrication to justify his taking the throne from the Hasmonaeans.

[24] Cf. below, ch. 4, II, (iii) on the significance of this foundation.

[25] Cf. below, ch. 6, II, on the significance of Judas' rising.

²⁶ We know that Herod's kingdom was divided into various regions and that trusted individuals called μεριδαρχής (cf. *Ant* 15:216) were put in charge of these, like his brother-in-law Costobar in Idumaea. Since we do not hear of any such appointment for Galilee it is a fair assumption that he retained his special charge of the province which he had held on his way to power. Cf. M. Stern, 'The Reign of Herod and the Herodian Dynasty', in *Compendia*, 1. 216-307, esp. 272, for Herod's subsequent relations with Galilee.

²⁷ Cf. the detailed discussion of the foundation of both places in ch. 4, II, (i) and (ii).

²⁸ Avi-Yonah, *The Holy Land*, 96.

²⁹ Hoehner, *Antipas*, 103-5, attempts to reconcile the conflicting accounts of Josephus (*Ant* 17:342-4; *War* 2:111), Strabo (*Geographica*, XVI,2.46) and Dio Cassius (*History*, LV,27.6) concerning the circumstances of Archelaus' deposition. According to Dio it was Antipas and Philip who proferred the charges, whereas Strabo says that all three brothers were summoned to answer charges, and Josephus claims that it was the Jews and Samaritans who accused Archelaus, with no mention of Antipas.

³⁰ Hoehner, *Antipas*, 105-9, giving the text of two inscriptions (OGIS 1, 416-7) which apparently refer to Antipas (the only Herodian with the title tetrarch) and use the name Ἡρῷδου. Josephus attributes it to him after the deposition of Archelaus, *War* 2:167: Ἡρῷδης ὁ κληθείς Ἀντίπας.

³¹ Mentioned in *War* 4:413 and not to be confused with the city of that name in the Dekapolis. For a discussion of its location cf. Hoehner, *Antipas*, 289f.

³² Schürer, *Geschichte*, 2, 244; A.M.H. Jones, *The Herods of Judaea*, Oxford, the Clarendon Press, 2nd print. 1967, 8-3; E.M. Smallwood, 'High Priests and Politics in Roman Palestine', JTS 13(1962) 17-37; Momigliano, *Ricerche*, 64-72; H. Mantel, 'The High Priesthood and the Sanhedrin in the Time of the Second Temple', *W.H.Her.P.*, 264-73.

³³ According to *Ant* 18:251f, Agrippa accused Antipas of having equipment for 70,000 foot-soldiers, and the latter admitted to the charge. While the number is unlikely there is nothing improbable about Antipas having a private army in view of the war with the Nabataeans.

³⁴ Thus Stern, *Compendia*, 1, 294f. His courting of the Sadducees may be seen in his appointments to the High Priesthood: after first appointing a Boethusian, Simon Cantheras, to the office, his next two appointments were from the influential house of Ananus.

³⁵ Momigliano, *Ricerche*, 80, suggests that the real reason was Agrippa I's mismanagement of financial affairs, as indicated by *Ant* 18:242.

³⁶ There are several examples of direct oversight by the governor of Syria in Judaean affairs, even though the latter ranked as a province, Tacitus, *Ann.* II,42.5; Josephus *War* 2:117. We hear of Varus (*Ant* 17:89); Quirinius (*Ant* 17:355); Vitellius (*Ant* 18:89); Petronius (*Ant* 18:261-3; *War* 2:185ff); Quadratus (*Ant* 20:125-30); Cestius Gallus (*War* 2:280-3; *Life* 23f), all intervening in Judaean affairs even though there was a Roman procurator at hand in all but the case of Varus.

³⁷ For a brief but good discussion of the issues and a relevant recent bibliography, cf. Stern, *Compendia*, 1, 374-6: 'The Conflict between the Samaritans and the Jews under Cumanus according to Josephus and Tacitus', Appendix II.

³⁸ On the date of this transfer cf. below, ch. 4, n.69.

³⁹ Rome may not have seen him as an impeccable ally for he does not seem to have been involved in the war after the question concerning his viceroy, Philip, had necessitated the latter being sent to Rome, *Life* 407-9.

⁴⁰ In attempting to unravel the relationship between *War* and *Life*, I have found the study of S. Cohen, *Josephus in Galilee and Rome: His Vita and Development as a Historian*, Columbia University, Ph.D. 1975, published by University Microfilms, Ann Arbor, Mich., 1976 very helpful. I gratefully acknowledge Dr. Cohen's permission to use this study before its publication. In ch. 2, 33-72, he has a clear statement of the issue and a helpful survey of the various solutions that have been offered. Cf. also, A. Schalit, 'Josephus und Justus: Studien zur *Vita* des Josephus', Klio 26(1933) 67-95.

[41] In *War* John is the aggressor and a brigand, whereas here he is the concerned aristocrat who counter-attacks only after his native place has been sacked. For a discussion of John's revolutionary stance cf. below, ch. 6, III.

[42] The MS evidence at *Life* 44 is uncertain and the emendation of Thackeray, *Loeb Josephus*, I, 18, to Γαβαρηνοί and Σωγαναῖοι is not very helpful, as Cohen, *Josephus in Galilee*, 36, n.6, points out. There were two Soganes, one in Gaulan which is unlikely, and the other in Galilee which was Jewish. Besides, it is difficult to imagine the Gadarenes attacking Gischala, a border town of Upper Galilee.

[43] Part of the reason was undoubtedly social and cultural, as will emerge in later chapters. Cf. *Life* 375.384 where Galilean hatred of Tiberias is emphatically stated and not unlikely, even if it fits in well with Josephan polemic. *Life* 177 tells of an episode concerning Justus' brother, who was punished by the Galileans for forging letters, but it is not possible to determine the details of the incident further.

[44] In view of Sepphoris' subsequent attitude it is worth noting *Life* 31, where we hear of some of its citizens being kept hostage by the Romans at Dor.

[45] This can be substantiated by the campaigns of Antiochus III, Scopas, Herod, Antigonus, Varus and Placidus.

[46] Schürer, *Geschichte*, 1, 607 and 617, and many others following him. Cohen, *Josephus in Galilee*, 334f, n.16 has a list of those who espouse this position. D.M. Rhoads, *Israel in Revolution, 6-74 C.E., A Political History based on the Writings of Josephus*, Philadelphia, Fortress Press, 1976, is a recent attempt to reexamine this position, suggesting various reasons why it might be misleading to describe the Sadducean aristocracy as moderate, 'that is, those who remained in Jerusalem, preparing to defend against the Romans, but who would have been willing to accept the right kind of terms, were they offered'' (150-3). Cohen's approach is more radical, denying that the leaders of the revolutionary government were ever moderate, including Josephus. In discussing such terms as 'peace party', 'moderate', 'war party' (328f), he rightly emphasizes that these must be understood as very fluid terms, because of the mixed motives that must have been at work in all sectors of the people. S. Zeitlin, 'A Survey of Jewish Historiography: From the Biblical Books to the *Sefer ha-Kabbalah*, with special Emphasis on Josephus', JQR 59(1968) 171-214 and 60 (1969) 37-68, espouses the view that Josephus, like the provisional government, was inwardly for peace but outwardly adopted a war stance to placate the Zealots. Hence, he regards *Life* as giving the true historical picture of Josephus' attitudes in Galilee.

[47] Cf. below, n.50.

[48] The approach of M. Avi-Yonah, 'The Missing Fortress of Flavius Josephus; IEJ 3(1953) 94-8 and M. Har-El, 'The Zealot Fortresses in Galilee', IEJ 22(1972) 123-30, does not query the reliability of Josephus' account but concerns itself only with the location of the fortresses and the possibility of strategic communication between them (Har-El). However, there is no evidence of any such strategic planning either before or during the Galilean campaign, and we can be sure that Josephus would not have missed the opportunity to stress the point, especially in *War*, had such ideas been operative.

[49] Cf. *War* 2:646, where the revolt of Sepphoris is mentioned almost as an afterthought in conjunction with that of Tiberias. Josephus would have us believe that he allowed his soldiers to take spoils and then insisted that they return them in order to let the inhabitants know at once his authority and his magnanimity.

[50] Cf. below, ch. 6, III, for a full discussion of Josephus' 'revolutionary' tendencies, which Cohen accepts to be genuine, *Josephus in Galilee*, esp. 372-7. He argues that Josephus' main army, as distinct from the militia, which were part-time, was made up of λῃσταί, with whom he made a deal, *Life* 77. He also finds further evidence of this in Josephus' address to his troops, exhorting them to refrain from pillage, *War* 2:581f.

[51] C. Roth, 'The Historical Implications of the Jewish coinage of the First Revolt', IEJ 12(1962) 33-46, has made this point, drawing attention to the fact that the coins

of the first year were silver, clearly designed on the model of the Tyrian half-shekel, with the inscription שקל ישראל חצי השקל and on the obverse ירושלים הקדושה. These indicate that it was an urban mint, and that the country was subordinated to the city, in striking contrast to the Maccabees, whose coins show that they identified with the Jewish people as such.

⁵² Suetonius, *Lives: Vespasian*, 4,5, says that an eagle was captured in the defeat of Cestius Gallus, who apparently died that winter, 'fato aut taedio occidit', as Tacitus, *Histories* V,10 puts it. *Life* 30, mentions the apprehensions of the people of Sepphoris in 66, and their overtures of loyalty to Rome.

⁵³ Cohen, *Josephus in Galilee*, 187-9, has shown that the various strategems, six in all, used by Josephus to repulse the Romans, can be documented from Greco-Roman literature. Thus the whole account is likely to have been a free composition to glorify the general's ingenuity. However, he also recognizes that while Josephus often exaggerates, he rarely invents totally fictitious narratives (362, n.44). We do hear of the siege elsewhere, *Life* 350, and apparently the site was a strategic one as far back as Assyrian times, since it appears on the list of places conquered by Tiglathpilesar.

⁵⁴ A section of the wall was broken down, not to let the army enter (*War* 3:460), but to indicate subjugation (cf. *War* 4:117f). On the attitude of Tiberias throughout the whole campaign, cf. below, ch. 4, II, (ii).

⁵⁵ Cohen, *Josephus in Galilee*, 292-307, has a detailed discussion of the material dealing with both Gamala and Philip in *War* and *Life*. He adopts a modified version of the proposal of R. Laqueur, *Der Jüsische Historiker, Flavius Josephus*, Giessen 1920, to the effect that Josephus had written a history of Gamala or of Agrippa II's kingdom, which he now draws on to refute certain charges of Justus. Schalit, 'Josephus und Justus', esp. 80-91, also sees the treatment of Philip in *Life* as an answer to charges made by Justus, accusing Josephus of being the real cause of the trouble in Gamala, leading to the death of some of Justus' kinsmen, *Life* 177f,186.

⁵⁶ Thackeray, *Loeb Josephus*, III,19, n.c, notes that the height of Thabor is 1312 ft. and the length of its table-land is 3000 ft., not 30 and 26 stadia respectively as suggested by Josephus.

⁵⁷ Momigliano, *Ricerche*, 85, against Schürer, *Geschichte* 1, 650, who points out that the expression τῶν Ἰουδαίων should not be interpreted of Judaea in the narrow sense, but of all Jewish land, including Galilee and Peraea but excluding that of the restored cities.

⁵⁸ Avi-Yonah, *The Holy Land* 110-12.

⁵⁹ A.M.H. Jones, 'The Urbanization of Palestine', JRS 21(1931) 78-85.

⁶⁰ S. Safrai, 'Jewish Self-Government', *Compendia*, I, 377-419, esp. 404-12, has a good summary of the overall situation in the Jamnia period, with special emphasis on the Rabbinic literature. The title נשיא was in all probability first translated by ἐθνάρχης, according to Origen, (*Ep. ad Africanus*, 14,P.G. 11, 84f), to describe an office that extended back to Maccabaean times, *1 Macc* 14:47; 15:1. However, Origen also indicates that the title πατριάρχης was in use in his day to describe the official head of Judaism (*Sel. in Ps.*, Ad Ps. 89,1 PG 12:1056). According to Hengel it emphasized more the spiritual qualities of the *nasi'* for hellenistic Judaism, clear evidence for which is now to be found in the Stobi inscription; cf. M. Hengel, 'Die Synagogeninschrift von Stobi', ZNW 57(1966), 145-83, esp. 152-5 and notes. On the reorganization of Judaism after 70 C.E. cf. further, Meyer, *Tradition und Neuschöpfung*, 71-5.

⁶¹ Cohen, *Josephus in Galilee*, 7-12, gives a summary of the debate concerning the correct reading and interpretation of the coins in question, following H. Seyrig, *Numismatic Chronicle* 10(1950) 284-98. He explains the possible reference to revolutionary tendencies in Sepphoris, *War* 2:574; 3:61; *Life* 31, as part of Josephan polemic and/or self-defense, and concludes that the city may indeed have fortified itself, but only as a protection to hostile Galileans, and not as a preparation for war against Rome.

[62] Jones. 'The Urbanization of Palestine', 82.

[63] Below in detail, ch. 4, II, (ii).

[64] S. Klein, *Neue Beiträge zur Geschichte und Geographie Galiläas*, Vienna 1923, argues from silence in the Jewish sources concerning settlements in Upper Galilee until after 135 C.E. to the conclusion that the Romans had devastated that area during the first revolt. However, the administrative arrangement after 70 as well as the course of the war, as outlined by Josephus, would appear to make this highly improbable.

[65] Already A. Büchler, 'Die Schauplatz des Bar Kochba-Krieges', JQR 16(1904) 192-205 had argued against A. Schlatter that no case could be made for Galilean involvement in the second revolt on the basis of such rabbinic texts as *p. Ta'an* 4: 69a and *Qoh R* 1:1, which refer to Galilean loyalty to the temple and which Schlatter had sought to interpret in relation to an alleged attempt to rebuild the temple under Hadrian. More recent discoveries in the Judaean desert have not given any clearer evidence of Galilean involvement, *pace* H. Mantel, 'The Causes of the Bar Coqba Revolt', JQR 58(1968) 224-42 and 274-96, who applies the statement of *p.Peah* 7, 20a to Galilee also: 'Olive trees were few, tor Hadrian the wicked came and destroyed the whole land' (294). Galileans are referred to in one of the letters trom the Judaean desert related to the revolt, *Mur* 43, but there is no agreement about the meaning of the reference. The letter from Simon ben Kosiba himself, is addressed to Yesua ben Galgulah, who apparently was in charge of a rebel camp, whose location is unknown. A solemn warning is given: 'if any of the Galileans who are with you is mistreated I shall put irons on your feet'. Unfortunately the reading of the Hebrew word, here translated as 'mistreated' is uncertain, and other translations have been suggested like 'guard well' or 'is missing'. The Galileans could either be Jews or Jewish Christians (Milik), and so it is not clear whether they had been engaged in the struggle or had been taken captive. For a discussion cf. J.T. Milik, 'Une lettre de Simeon Bar Kokeba' RB 60(1953) 276-94 and later, *Discoveries in the Judaean Desert*, II, ed. P. Benoit, J.T. Milik and R. de Vaux, Oxford 1961, 160ff. J.J. Rabbinowitz, 'Note sur le lettre de Bar Kokbha', RB 61(1954) 191f; S.A. Birnbaum, 'Bar Kokhba and Akiba', PEQ 86(1954) 23-33; J. Fitzmyer, 'The Bar Cochba Period', in *Essays on the Semitic Background to the New Testament*, London 1971, 305-51, esp. 339. This article was first published in 1962.

Part Two
SOCIAL AND CULTURAL

CHAPTER FOUR

THE CITIES AND THE HELLENISTIC ETHOS OF GALILEE

Much of the earlier discussion of Hellenism in Galilee has been conducted on the assumption that Hellenism and Judaism were two mutually opposed, even hostile cultural forces that could not and did not tolerate each other. Accordingly, many of the signs of Greek influence in the province have been taken to prove that the population there was non-Jewish and the ethos thoroughly pagan. This state of affairs continued, it is argued, until the judaization of Galilee - to use Schürer's phrase - under Aristobolus and Alexander Jannaeus, and was merely the continuation of conditions that reached back to the fall of the northern kingdom, or even possibly to the Israelite occupation of the north. In this view, it is seen as no coincidence that Isaiah in the eighth century B.C.E. and the author of *1 Macc* in the second can speak of 'Galilee of the Gentiles' (*Is* 8:23; *1 Macc* 5:23), since the expression aptly described ethnic and social conditions there throughout this whole period. However, we have already seen that Schürer's theory about judaization is not very solidly based on the evidence of the time nor on the earlier historical probabilities.[1] Furthermore, Martin Hengel's monumental study of Judaism and Hellenism has shown definitively that all of Palestinian Judaism was thoroughly hellenized by the second century B.C.E. Consequently the question of Greek influences on Jewish life and practice has to be posed in a new way, since obviously there were within Judaism different reactions to this encounter with the larger cultural world, ranging from total abandonment of Jewish life and practice to extreme opposition to all that Hellenism stood for.[2]

One of the problems of dealing with the extent of Hellenism's influence on Galilean Judaism is the absence of any first-hand literary sources, at least for the earlier period. Accordingly, we must try to evaluate the significance of the various indications of active hellenistic influence there, conscious that even when we do find Judaism in direct and immediate contact with outside influences in various spheres of life, the immediate result was not always total collapse of the older way of life. If, as we have argued, Israelite religion survived the various external forces of the great powers from the Assyrian to the Persian periods, what new factors could Hellenism draw on that might appreciably alter the Jewish response? One immediately thinks of the cities as the most likely new agents for far reaching social and cultural change, and it is on these that we shall focus our attention in this chapter, conscious that the cities alone do not tell the whole story of Galilee's meeting with the new culture. This procedure recommends itself particularly for Galilee, since, it was precisely in the surrounding circle that Israelite and later Jewish believers experienced the threat of the outsider, as the expression הגוים גליל, Γαλιλαία ἀλλοφυλῶν suggests. It is no accident that it was in this very circle, that is, the outer perimeter of Galilee, that we find all the major hellenistic foundations.[3] Naturally, the immediate sphere of influence of each was confined to its own territory, but inevitably wider contacts were set up between the different cities and their populations primarily, but also with the larger rural hinterland insofar as this served as the source of necessary supplies or required outlets for produce from the interior. However, it is only possible to judge the likely effect of these relations on the older population when the character of each foundation has been thoroughly examined and its military, commercial and administrative links with the whole of Galilee probed in detail.

In the hellenistic period the institution of the *polis* had been modified considerably from that of classical times to meet the demands of Alexander's and his successors' political ambitions.[4] Instead of being absolutely free and autonomous the city became part of a network designed to spread the Greek way of life in the conquered territories. New foundations sprang up and older oriental cities changed their character considerably with the influx of population and the replacement of the older political order by the democratic Greek one. Yet urbanization in the sense of a radically new life-style and ethos is not just dependent on the number of new or changed cities in the area. The manner of their foundation and their wider relations with the surrounding countryside are all important factors.[5] In hellenistic times some at least of the new foundations were initially intended as colonies of Greek veterans whose presence in an area insured its loyalty and the stability of political life for the central administration. Sometimes too a number of villages were fused together in what was technically known as a synoecism, thereby replacing the more ancient clan pattern of life with one based on citizenship but without any necessary displacement of the native population.[6] Not all foundations enjoyed even the modified status of a *polis* of the hellenistic epoch so that the dividing line between city and village is not easy to determine.[7] All these considerations are important in deciding the orthogenetic as distinct from the heterogenetic function of each individual foundation. Any city or large foundation will function more easily as an agent for social change in a wider area if it arises out of local needs and is not imposed from the outside, thus being seen by the natives as a symbol of alien domination and oppression.

As the following detailed survey will show all of these factors were operative in varying degrees in the foundations of Galilee. Of the earlier foundations Scythopolis and Philoteria in the interior were hellenized versions of older centers, Beth Shean and Beth Yerach, while the same applies to Ptolemais/Accho on the coast. Other foundations such as Antiochia and Seleucia seem to be new foundations, of lesser status however. In the second (Jewish) phase of urbanization Tiberias and Gaba were totally new (Herodian) foundations whereas Bethsaida Julias, Caesarea Philippi and Tarichaeae had older semitic antecedents. Sepphoris too would appear to have undergone some change of character and population at least after the revolt of 70 and possibly much earlier under Antipas. Apart from these places Josephus gives the impression of a fairly densely populated and urbanized province; 'there were 204 cities and villages in Galilee' (*Life* 235). But his distinction between city and village does not seem to be too sharply drawn, for on another occasion we hear that Sepphoris was one of the *three* chief cities of Galilee - Tiberias and Gabara being the others (*Life* 123) - suggesting by implication, at least, that Galilean life was mainly organized on village lines. Yet we read elsewhere: 'The cities (πόλεις) lie very thick and the very many villages (κώμας) that are here are everywhere so full of people by the richness of their soil, that the very least of them contained about 15,000 inhabitants' (*War* 3:43).

Even allowing for notorious exaggeration of population figures, it seems likely that quite a few Galilean settlements were anything but villages by the modern use of that term, and clearly some criterion other than that of population is operative in his thinking.[8] Walled fortifications can also be described as villages as is clear from the list given in *Life* 187f where all the fortified places of Upper Galilee are so designated, so that the distinction cannot be based on the root meaning of the word *polis*.[9] Perhaps, the distinction is based on the character - Greek or Jewish - of the various foundations, though Sherwin-White's proposal, based on *War* 2:252; *Ant* 20:159, that the chief town of a toparchy was called a city, seems the most convincing explanation, if consistency is to be sought at all.[10] This theory would fit the gospel evidence also, at least that of Mark, who seems better acquainted with Palestinian geography than either Matthew or Luke.[11] Setting aside this terminological problem, we shall do well to focus our attention on the known centers, as indicated by Josephus himself as well as other sources, in our search for possible centers of Hellenism in Galilee.

I
THE FIRST PHASE IN THE URBANIZATION OF GALILEE

Historically, it is possible to distinguish two phases in the urbanization of Galilee. The earlier one took place under the Ptolemies and Seleucids but suffered a set-back under the Hasmonaeans, who saw the Greek cities as the opponents to their territorial aggrandizement. Yet that did not mean an anti-hellenizing campaign in general as we have already seen in discussing their overall achievement in setting up a Jewish state. The second phase took place under the Herodians, especially Antipas, and differed in character from the earlier one in that now the new element is itself a Jewish population. The character of the various centers changed considerably throughout their history, as will emerge from our survey, and this needs to be carefully noted in our assessment of their contribution to the hellenizing process.

(i) *Ptolemais/Accho*

According to *Ps Aristeas* 115 Ptolemais was founded by King Ptolemy II Philadelphus, and this information coupled with the coins suggests that the year 261 B.C.E. was the date for the re-naming of the city.[12] However its Greek contacts had been established long before that, as already in the fourth century B.C.E. we hear of Athenian businessmen there and its coins carry both the name of Alexander in Greek and the old name Ako in Phoenician script.[13] In dealing with the geography of Galilee we have already drawn attention to the natural outlet that the port of Ptolemais/Accho afforded for the interior of Lower Galilee, and it is no surprise to find that in the Zenon Papyri Ptolemais is mentioned in all eleven times, more than any other city of Palestine.[14] In an unguarded moment when geography rather than political history is foremost in his mind, Josephus can simply write 'Ptolemais is a maritime town of Galilee built at the entrance to the Great Plain' (*War* 2:188). He goes on to describe the natural hinterland provided by the plain of Accho amid the surrounding mountains - Carmel 120 furlongs to the south, the ladder of Tyre 100 furlongs to the north and the Galilean range 60 furlongs to the east. This information corresponds with what he tells us elsewhere, namely, that Chabul was a border town between Galilee and the territory of Ptolemais about 60 stadia from the city (*Life* 213-215). Clearly the border between political Galilee of Josephus' day and the territory of Ptolemais ran along the line of the Galilean hills, following the natural boundary, and it is unlikely that there would have been any major fluctuations in this line over the centuries. This means that the Jewish territory of Galilee lay close to the actual city itself and helps to explain the frequent hostilities between hellenistic city and Jewish hinterland, not just during Roman times (e.g. *War* 2:67 (Varus); 503ff (Cestius); *Life* 213f (Placidus) and *War* 2:458 for Jewish reprisals), but already under the Seleucids (*1 Macc* 5:15.22; 12:48).

From the very beginning the position of Ptolemais represented two different aspects of Hellenism's incursion into Palestine. On the one hand the Zenon Papyri give ample evidence of the commercial links with the interior, since the list of produce which we know entered the Egyptian markets from Syria - grain, olive oil, smoked fish, cheese, meat, dried figs, fruit, honey, dates, etc. - represents most if not all the produce of Galilee as listed in the Talmuds and Josephus. A large amount of this produce must have come from the fertile Galilean estates as the Papyri themselves testify. Zenon's journey, according to *PCZ* 59004, took him from Straton's Tower (later Caesarea) to Transjordan, returning via Galilee to Ptolemais. Presumably this was the obvious outlet for produce from Galilee, since the places visited, Beth Anath and Kedasa, were both in the province and these were the last stops on Zenon's journey before his arrival at Ptolemais.[15] This commercial link between port and hinterland must have brought about a lively movement of people in both directions, with the inevitable contacts that such day to day business would establish between Egyptian customs officials, merchants, caravaneers and at least some levels of the native population. While the fragmentary evidence from Zenon's correspondence would suggest that even these contacts were not always amicable, they should I feel be distinguished carefully from another type of contact which followed from the second aspect of Ptolemais' function for the early hellenistic monarchs, namely its role as a military garrison.

To support their tight control of the commercial situation, the Ptolemies also established in Palestine and Syria a vast network of police and military officials who appear in the Papyri as soldiers ($\sigma\tau\rho\alpha\tau\iota\hat{\omega}\tau\alpha\iota$), cavalry generals ($\iota\pi\pi\acute{\alpha}\rho\chi\eta\varsigma$), military officers ($\dot{\eta}\gamma\epsilon\mu\acute{\omega}\nu$), garrison commanders ($\dot{\alpha}\kappa\rho\circ\phi\acute{\upsilon}\lambda\alpha\xi$), chiefs of police ($\dot{\epsilon}\pi\iota\sigma\tau\acute{\alpha}\tau\eta\varsigma$ $\tau\dot{\eta}\varsigma$ $\pi\acute{o}\lambda\epsilon\omega\varsigma$), etc.[16] We know that already Alexander established military settlements of a more permanent kind at Samaria and Gaza and it is only natural that the Ptolemies would have continued this policy also, given the disputed nature of their control of Palestine. Hengel goes so far as to suggest that all Ptolemaic foundations were in fact military settlements, and certainly the evidence as well as the political probabilities would seem to support this view.[17] However, it does seem that the military aspect is more accentuated in some settlements. There is little doubt, for example that the settlement of Toubias at Birta in Transjordan with its mixture of Greek, Jewish and Persian *Kleruchs* had the character of a strong military fortification.[18] Likewise, the evidence of Polybius is illustrative in this regard. Whereas Philoteria and Scythopolis fell rather easily to Antiochus III during the fourth Syrian war, it called for real military strategy to take Atabyrion (Thabor) where an Egyptian garrison was located (Polybius *Hist* V, 70f). Perhaps the distinction is merely technical: the former are settlements where the *Kleruchoi* are

given lots in reward for services rendered and can act as a reserve
force in time of war, the latter represent a genuine military stronghold where a company of active army units is strategically located.

Ptolemais is also strategically well-placed on the direct road
between the conflicting contenders for Palestine and so fits the
latter category of a military stronghold. Once Theodotus handed
over the military arsenal there to Antiochus III in 219 B.C.E.
Ptolemais seems to have served as the center for Seleucid presence
in Palestine, so that the city had a certain military character, as the
expression Ἀντιοχεῖς οἱ ἐν Πτολεμαίδι sometimes with the addition
ἱερα ἄσυλος on its coins, makes clear. Successive Seleucid kings
operated from there in their frequent incursions into Palestine
during the second century B.C.E.: *1 Macc* 10:56-60; 11:22.24; 12:49;
13:12. It is interesting that Ptolemais was able to resist Alexander
Jannaeus in his attempt to control the whole of mainland Galilee
(*Ant* 13:324 ff), and later it withstood Ptolemy Lathyrus, the
deposed king of Egypt (*Ant* 13:333.336). Subsequently it never
became part of the Hasmonaean kingdom and seems to have
retained its pro-Syrian loyalties (*Ant* 13:419f). Under the Romans,
Ptolemais continued to be an important military center, even
though geographical location (closer to Jerusalem) gave Caesarea
a new-found importance on the coast. Thus we hear of Herod
using Ptolemais as a base for incursions into Galilee against his
Hasmonaean rival Antigonus (*Ant* 14:394.452). The Emperor
Claudius settled a colony of Roman soldiers there and thereafter
it was known as *Colonia Ptolemais*.[20] As already mentioned, it
became the base for Roman attacks on Galilee in the period prior
to the war of 66 C.E., as successive Roman generals over a period
of 70 years launched their attacks on Galilee from there.

In the light of this survey it would seem that Ptolemais is unlikely to have exercised any great cultural influence on the interior
beyond the borders of its own territory, either during the first wave
of hellenization or throughout the subsequent history. We do find
occasional traces of influence, the inevitable outcome of gradual
processes of assimilation on the basis of close proximity. Thus an
anecdote reported by Josephus is indicative of what may have
been the level of such day to day contacts. He tells us that in the
year 66 C.E. Cestius Gallus found the fortified town of Chabulon
deserted of its Jewish population, and after allowing his soldiers

to pillage the goods of the natives, he set fire to the town 'even though he admired its beauty with its houses built in the style of those at Tyre, Sidon and Berytus' (*War* 2:504).

However, the dominant atmosphere seems to have been one of hostility to the Jewish population, hostility that stemmed from the days of Antiochus Epiphanes and beyond (*1 Macc* 5:15). While Demetrius I was apparently prepared to cede Ptolemais and its territory (*1 Macc* 10:39f) for the support of the temple at Jerusalem after the fashion of temple lands elsewhere in the Seleucid kingdom, this does not prove the Jewishness of the area, as we may infer from its subsequent resistance to Alexander Jannaeus. It is not surprising then to find the populace at Ptolemais sharing in the anti-Jewish riots of 66 C.E. after militant Jews had pillaged the villages of several Syrian cities, Ptolemais included, and murdered their inhabitants (*War* 2:460-477). Thus the commercial contacts between Ptolemais and the interior were not sufficiently powerful to counter-balance the alien and heterogenetic cultural influences of the city as one of the most important coastal military centers of what, for the Jew, was an unfriendly and hostile presence.[21] Our judgment in the light of the evidence must be that despite the close physical proximity Ptolemais had little or no effect on the hellenization process among Galilean Jews. If anything, such a threatening center so close to them may have operated in reverse, tending to create an atmosphere of mutual distrust if not downright animosity, which was likely to erupt into violence at the first opportunity. Villages lying close to the border inevitably bore the brunt of repeated incursions and Jewish counterattacks, and it is not surprising that by the time of the war of 66 C.E. we find a Jewish brigand chief (ἀρχιλῄστης) Jesus, operating in this no-man's land on the borders of Ptolemais (*Life* 105). His presence there with a force of eight hundred men may not be so much a reflection of a general breakdown of law and order in the area as a symptom of the deprivation and social unrest of the Jewish community which had built up over a long period. This is not the atmosphere for everyday cultural exchange between city and country.

(ii) *Scythopolis/Beth Shean.*

Moving inland from the coast, an equally important Ptolemaic foundation was Scythopolis, that formerly as Beth Shean had achieved prominence in Israelite times due to its location in the heart of a fertile valley on the route between east and west. The actual significance of the name Scythopolis had given rise to a lively debate of how the city could be linked to a nomadic people of the seventh century who are supposed to have settled here according to Herodotus (1,105). The most likely theory, favoured by Avi-Yonah, Hengel and others is that the name comes from the fact that the Ptolemies settled a colony of Scythian soldiers here, as was their wont elsewhere.[22] On this understanding the place would represent the presence of a non-Jewish element similar to Ptolemais on the southern boundaries of Galilee. However, whatever the character of this military colony attributed to Ptolemy Philadelphus for the year 254 B.C.E.,[23] Scythopolis does not seem to have adopted a very militant position subsequently, since together with its neighboring sister foundation Philoteria it surrendered freely (κάθ' ὁμολογίαν) to Antiochus in 219 B.C.E. This may have been due to the influence of the Ptolemaic general Theodotus who, we have seen, surrendered the armory at Ptolemais to Antiochus also. The recently discovered inscriptions at Hefzibah in the region of Scythopolis show that there was a real desire, not merely on the part of Ptolemaios, the *strategos* of Coele-Syria,[24] but also of the villagers themselves to be free of military presence in the area. The picture one gets from this set of ordinances dealing with billeting of soldiers and movement of goods within the villages is essentially a peaceful one, where commercial rather than military interests are most important. The acquisition of the further name Nysa, probably in the Seleucid period, can scarcely have meant a radical change of character for Scythopolis. Rather it then became a center for Dionysus worship, which was particularly cultivated by the Seleucid monarchs, and no doubt meant greater prosperity for the town.[25] Archaeological remains and ancient testimony give evidence of a thriving industrial center, the former suggesting a pottery-making industry for Rhodian jars, presumably for the wine industry, and a coin mint, while the latter attests that Scythopolis was famous for linen.[26]

Together with this picture of hellenistic Scythopolis as a peaceful and thriving center is a further related one of peaceful Jewish co-existence in the area, in striking contrast to their relations with Ptolemais. There is some evidence that the city was a *synoecism* since Malalus speaks of *trikomia,* suggesting the coming together of a number of villages rather than a totally new foundation.[27] This would correspond well with the prominence of the place from Israelite times, which had not been diminished during the intervening centuries, and it does not preclude the upgrading of the status of the town subsequently by the Ptolemies and the settling of a military colony there. This may also help to explain the persistence of the old name Beth Shean *side by side* with the Greek name (cf. *Ant* 5:83; 6:374; 12:348; 13:188) and its presence also in the Mishnah (*Ab Zar* 1:4;; 4:12), both references incidentally reflecting a situation of Jew and Gentile exchange there. This picture can be filled out by a brief survey of the Jews in Scythopolis. During the Maccabaean uprisings the Jewish inhabitants of Scythopolis are not harassed as were their co-religionists on the coast and at Ptolemais (*2 Macc* 12:29-31), a picture that is confirmed by Judas' being able to return unmolested to Jerusalem 'through the large plain before Beth Shean' after his mission in Gilead (*1 Macc* 5:52). Furthermore, Jonathan is not afraid to meet Trypho there for battle, but instead is tricked into accompanying him to Ptolemais where he and his men meet real hostility (*1 Macc* 12:39-48; *Ant* 13:192 says that Trypho had ordered the people of Ptolemais to shut their gates with Jonathan and his men inside— a detail missing in *1 Macc*). Scythopolis came within the net of the Jewish territorial aggrandizement of the Hasmonaeans, and fell to them towards the end of the reign of John Hyrcanus, between 111 and 107 B.C.E., either by a bribe (*Ant* 13:280) or by attack (*War* 1:66), and with it the whole country south of Mount Carmel, that is, presumably, the plain of Esdraelon which would have been king's land and in the hands of Syrian owners. Shortly after this Samaria also fell to the Hasmonaeans, and both events are recorded as days of rejoicing in the *Megillat Ta'anit.*[28] However, the fate of Scythopolis seems to have been less dramatic, for its Greek inhabitants are exiled only and return again in the reign of Jannaeus according to *Ant* 13:355, whereas Samaria was razed to the ground. According to Strabo (16,2.40 it contained treasures of the Jews when Pompey captured it (*Ant.* 14:75) while Gabinius restored its city status (*Ant* 14:88). This presumably means that its Gentile population was considerably increased (*War* 1:166), since *War* 1:156 suggests that it had not been wholly razed.

Despite this upset to Jewish-Gentile relations in Scythopolis and its surroundings, the older pattern of peaceful co-existence seems to have been re-established, for by the time of the Jewish War 100 years later Jew and Greek appear to be living in harmony. However, in the general upheaval following the massacre of Jews in Caesarea in 66 C.E., Scythopolis did not escape. The troubles there were started by Jews from elsewhere who went on a general rampage through all the Syrian towns, but the native Jews of Scythopolis decided to fight against their co-religionists, 'regarding their own security as more important than the ties of blood' (*War* 2:466). Even though the outcome of this loyalty to their city was only met by callous, wholesale slaughter of more than 13,000 Jews by the citizens of Scythopolis, such an outcome should not obscure the fact that the Jews did feel impelled to act against their fellow Jews on that occasion, and the reasons that lay behind that decision. While Josephus may present this incident as part of Jewish revolutionary propaganda elsewhere (*War* 7:364), or explain the Jewish behaviour as being due to fate, one suspects he knows the real reasons and may even have identified with their decision. Thus he tells us that not only were they slaughtered but that their possessions were also confiscated (*War* 2:468). It may well be that the Jews of Scythopolis were by this time prosperous and thriving and like many others throughout the nation did not wish to risk their position, if they could avoid being embroiled in war with Rome. Whatever the reasons for this savage outburst it did not preclude Jews returning to Scythopolis in great numbers in the period after 70 C.E., as the references from the Mishnah already mentioned indicate.

This survey of Judaism in Scythopolis presents quite a different picture to that at Ptolemais. Situated inland in the center of a fertile valley, Scythopolis and its region had a natural self-sufficiency which was not true of the cities of the coastal plain that were dependent on passing trade and commerce, as well as being at the mercy of invading armies. This stability of life based on natural resources created a very different atmosphere in which Jew and Gentile could co-exist without being a threat to each other, with the one notable exception of 66 C.E. Presumably the 'semitic' if not the explicitly 'Israelitic' character of the Beth Shean valley had continued through the centuries, even if the hellenistic age introduced new elements that were assimilated rather than received with hostile acquiescence by the native population.[29] The Dionysiac cult for example might well have been seen as a revival of old Canaanite nature religion. As a market center with a natural demand for the produce of Galilee, especially wine and flax, it is legitimate to speculate on the possible influences that it was likely to have had on the neighbouring countryside. While the region of Scythopolis was used by Pompey as a base of operations on Judea (*Ant.* 14:49), and by Vespasian (*War* 3:412. 446. 487), there is no suggestion of continued and renewed hostilities between Galilee and the territory of the city. We do hear of a certain Neopolitanus with a squadron of horse ravaging the territory of Tiberias from the region of Scythopolis in 66 C.E. However, once Josephus routs him, there is no further mention of his presence, and he certainly was not representative of any large-scale designs against Galilee that would build up resentment and hostility.

Such isolated incidents were not likely to disrupt the more established pattern of life that was based on natural and economic factors, and it is these that over a period of time built up mutual confidence and contacts. The fact that Scythopolis was a member of the Dekapolis (*War* 3:446; Pliny, *Nat. Hist.* V, 18.74) gave it an easterly orientation also. Its territory on the west bordered on that of Philoteria first and later Tiberias, both foundations of reigning monarchs, and so it was not likely to have adopted aggressive or hostile attitudes towards the interior. As an example of this Josephus tells us that Agrippa II exercised jurisdiction over the area at the time of the Jewish War of 66 C.E.[30]

For all these reasons then we can assume that Scythopolis had some contacts with those parts of Lower Galilee close to its territory (*War* 3:37), but it is not easy to assess the impact of such contacts on the peasants there. Presumably they were not of the kind that would change the character of life appreciably. The peasants' visits would be confined to times of market or festival, and these would be relatively infrequent, even though one of the possible ways to Jerusalem, the eastern route, passed through the territory of the city. From the Hefzibah inscriptions we see that the contacts even between villages were restricted for commercial reasons, at least in the earlier period. Given the fact that the greater part of the plain of Esdraelon was divided into larger estates, the tenants had leased lots or worked as hired laborers and so had little reason for going to the city, unless it had other attractions for them. Thus, even though the character of the relationship between Scythopolis and the interior was very different to that of Ptolemais, there seems to be no compelling reason to suggest that it ever exercised any great influence outside its own territory. True it did attract some Jews to take part in the busy commercial life, but the vast majority of Galilean peasants would not have been greatly affected by its presence close to their borders. At least no existing evidence points in that direction, and the probabilities are that it did not.

(iii) *Philoteria, Antiochia and Seleucia*

I have grouped these three centers together, even though the former is a Ptolemaic and the latter two are Seleucid foundations, because together they represent the hellenistic presence on the eastern borders of Galilee, that was later continued by the Dekapolis.

It is generally recognized that Philoteria was a foundation of Ptolemy II, Philadelphus, since it was named after his sister. There is some doubt about its actual location, since Polybius' account points to its being a city of Galilee, but recent archaeological evidence concerning Beth Yerach, the older foundation with which it is associated places it east of the Jordan close to where the river leaves the Lake of Gennesareth.[31] At all events it does not seem to have been restored after being destroyed by Alexander Jannaeus during the Jewish conquest of the north, and this has led some commentators to suggest that it never was a city proper. Nevertheless, the evidence of Polybius cannot be taken lightly and it seems certain that at the time of Antiochus III's takeover of Palestine it was a thriving center with its own territory.[32] Archaeological evidence at Beth Yerach suggests a similarity to Scythopolis as a market center, and the later prosperity of Tiberias in that region suggests a natural center at the southern end of the lake to serve the surrounding fertile region, just as Beth Shean had done farther south in the valley.[33] In that event we are justified in assuming a similar pattern of life between older population and new arrivals to that of Scythopolis, but with no widespread influence outside its own immediate territory.

Antiochia and Seleucia were Seleucid settlements as is clear from their names . However, our knowledge of the circumstances of either foundation or the extent of their territories is extremely scant, and can really only be determined on the basis of much later evidence. Alt argues convincingly that both places are to be seen as principal towns of royal domains with the character of military outposts rather than independent city states.[34] By the time of Herod the Great, the whole northern region of Trachonitis, Batanaea and Auranitis east of the Jordan, as well as Ulatha and Paneas in the northern Huleh basin, had become king's land (*Ant.* 15:346f. 360f.) and settlements there are totally dependent on the rulers' graciousness (*Ant.* 17:24f, Herod; 18:28, Philip). Accordingly, neither Antiochia nor Seleucia are likely to have exercised any great cultural influences on the territory we are describing as Galilee, or on the life of the older population there. Geographically, Antiochia appears to have been situated in the Huleh basin near Paneas (*Ant.* 17:24) and its orientation was towards the south, something indicated by Josephus' phrase 'the valley of Antiochia' (*Ant* 13:394; *War* 1:105).

Seleucia on the other hand lay in the Gaulan across the Jordan (*Ant.* 13:393), and the fact that by Josephus' day it is a village (*Life* 187), having been superseded both by the nearby Bethsaida, upgraded by Philip and given the name Julias (*Ant.* 18:28), and by the fortress of Gamala (*Life* 398), indicates that its sphere of influence was never very wide. In view of other contacts between the regions, it would have been the more likely of the two to have affected Galilean country life, but from the later evidence it does not seem to have done so.

(iv) *Tyre*

Returning once more to the coast our attention has already been drawn to the geophysical features which gave rise to a real tension between coastal settlements and the hinterland. This was nowhere more apparent than at Tyre which had the benefit of only a narrow strip of plain before the beginning of the interior mountainous region, with its own very different physical features and consequent pattern of human habitation. We must now examine the extent of Tyrian 'incursions' into the interior, and see how these were likely to have affected Jewish life and culture in Galilee.

Alexander's seven months' siege of Tyre shows how important the reduction of this independent and commercially important city was to his plans. It is not certain when exactly we are to date the founding of the hellenistic city, but Tcherikover makes a good case for attributing it already to the Ptolemies.[35] It is unlikely that this act of refounding the city brought about any large-scale change of population. Undoubtedly the Greek element would have been increased there in terms of customs officials and other administrative personnel, as the Zenon papyri illustrate.[36] However, Greek had long before mingled with eastern in this commercial city and the new arrivals cannot have drastically altered its character, even though the monarchical system of government appears to have been dropped about the year 259 B.C.E. In this regard Bickerman has shown how the hellenization process operated both here and at nearby Sidon. While this latter city is thoroughly hellenized to the point where its citizens can participate in the Olympic games—the true hallmark of the Hellene—nevertheless it retained its own oriental form of government with δικάσται in control (cf. *Contra Apionem* 1:158).[37] The same applies to Tyre where the Olympic games were held in the year 172 B.C.E. (*2 Macc.* 4:18) and we find inhabitants of the city taking part in the games at Delos about 100 years earlier. Yet, side by side with this picture of thoroughgoing hellenization and adoption of the Greek way of life, the evidence of the inscriptions shows that Phoenician as well as Greek continued to be spoken as late as the first century B.C.E.[38] Yet the system of government was still oligarchic rather than democratic as was characteristic of the Greek city proper. It is evident then that in discussing the possibility of Tyre's cultural impact on its Galilean hinterland we are dealing with a developing situation where the character of the agent for change is itself undergoing transformation with the passage of time, but without losing its older identity.

There was one area of life where Tyrian influence on the interior was not likely to have changed very much over the centuries, namely its commercial relations—something that is testified to by two biblical writers as far apart as Ezechiel in the 6th century B.C.E. and Luke in the 1st century C.E. The former in ch. 27 paints a vivid picture of the lively commercial life of this busy and

rich metropolis, 'merchants of the peoples on many coastlands.'
That the Jews also took part in this exchange is made clear in
v. 17: 'Judah and the land of Israel traded with you; they exchanged
for your merchandise wheat, olives and early figs, honey, oil and
balm.' It is not surprising to find this exchange to be the interior's
(especially Galilee's) agricultural produce for Tyre's merchandise. This process was likely to have been accentuated in the
hellenistic period with the development of new markets for agricultural produce on the one hand, and the improved agricultural
techniques introduced by the Ptolemies in particular. Little seems
to have changed in this regard when Luke could write as follows
for the end of the 1st century C.E.: 'Now Herod (Agrippa I, 40-44
C.E.) was angry with the people of Tyre and Sidon; and they came
to him in a body, and having persuaded Blastus, the king's cham-
berlain, they asked for peace, because their country depended on
the king's country for food' (*Acts* 12:20). That this trade between
Tyre and its Jewish hinterland continued through the centuries is
also evidenced by other literary as well as archaeological evidence.
We hear of donkey caravans bringing corn to Tyre from the
interior (*T. Dem* 1:10). At Tyre there was a huge trading market
and this too is mentioned in the Talmud (*p. Ab Zar* 4,39d). As a
result of these commercial connections we know of a Jewish
community at Tyre and hear of rabbis visiting it, and a Christian
community seems to have established itself there fairly early
(*Ac* 21:3-7). This presence would have meant particular demands
on Jewish wine and oil products as we know from *Life* 74 where
John of Gischala was able to establish an oil monopoly in dealing
with Syrian Jews. The presence of so many Tyrian shekels in
Palestine as distinct from other coins is not just to be explained
by the yearly half shekel offerings that every male Jew made to
the temple in Tyrian coinage, but must also be attributed in part
to the commercial traffic between the city and the interior.[39]

Inevitably these relations were not always likely to remain
on a purely amicable basis. Precisely because the produce of the
interior was so vital to Tyre's trade and life they were not likely
to leave it dependent on good relations alone. Some kind of
political consolidation was called for, and this is precisely what
can be seen developing over the centuries. Already Solomon
exchanged with Hiram king of Tyre twenty cities of Galilee for

the timber and gold he needed for Jerusalem (*1 Kgs* 9:14-20),[40] but territorial aggrandizement does not normally take place on that grand scale and the passage cited from *Acts* shows that in the days of Agrippa I there were still disputes between the two sets of interests.

In describing the boundaries of Galilee, Josephus mentions for the north only the territory of Tyre (*War* 3:39); yet there is no final agreement among political geographers on the actual location of this boundary or its extent. The most likely view is that it ran along the Wadi' Oba, thus passing between Kedasa and Gischala.[41] As early as the Persian period the territory of Tyre had been increased considerably towards the interior according to Alt, but this may have been reduced subsequently during the Ptolemaic period, for as we have seen, they insisted on having their own officials there, in line with their policy of only limited freedom to the cities.[42] At all events it is for a much later period that we have the best evidence for this encroachment by the Tyrians, but presumably this is only one example of a constant feature of the relations between the two territories, depending on the way the political pendulum was swinging. Thus during the disturbed times of the Roman civil wars (49-45 B.C.E), with the Herodian and Hasmonaean involvement in these, we hear of a fairly serious encroachment of Jewish territory by Marion 'the tyrant of Tyre' (*Ant.* 14:297; *War* 1:238), who invaded Galilee and captured three strongholds. Herod is reported to have immediately dislodged him, but in the light of the subsequent events he must not have been altogether successful, for later Antony promises the delegates of the Jewish ethnarch Hyrcanus that he would restore those places they had lost, forbidding the Tyrians to use violence against them (*Ant.* 14:313). He then writes to the people of Tyre commanding them to return to Hyrcanus all those places which belonged to him before Marion's invasion, which had been undertaken at the instigation of Cassius, Antony's enemy. They are further ordered to make this decree public, written in Greek and Latin (*Ant.* 14:317.319). This arrangement by Antony corresponds to an earlier enactment by Julius Caesar which shows a similar concern for the rights of the Jews along the coastal plain, especially in relations with Tyre, Sidon and Ascalon (*Ant.* 14:197), since the decrees in question are to be published in these cities. From these it emerges that the Jews 'are to enjoy the fruits of the places given to them' (*Ant.* 14:196). Further, and this seems to be specifically directed at Tyre, 'as for the places, lands and farms, the fruits of which the kings of Syria and Phoenicia, as allies of the Romans, were permitted to enjoy by their gift (κατὰ δωρεὰν), these the senate decrees that the Jews shall have' (*Ant.* 14:209). There is no actual record of such a gift of Jewish territory by the Romans, but it may be inferred that what is in mind here is territory which had been under Hasmonaean control, but which Pompey had bequeathed to the various cities and rulers when he liberated the hellenistic cities of Palestine. On this understanding Caesar's arrangement did not reverse that of Pompey but merely curtailed the rights of the various cities over the surrounding territory, particularly it would seem Galilee, since it was there that rights to the fruits of their land were likely to be violated, at least by Tyre and Sidon.[43]

Herod the Great appears to have established good relations with the Tyrians, but these were based on his hellenistic tendencies rather than on any coming to terms with 'the Galilean question.' Thus we hear that Herod endowed this city as well as Berytus 'with walls, porticoes, temples, and market places' (*War* 1:422). He was actually present in the city when Jewish delegates who had come to protest to Antony about his being appointed tetrarch are slaughtered by Antony's troops (*War* 1:242-47). The governor of Tyre supported him fully, just as later he can rely on their support in his attempts to liberate his brother Phasael from the Parthians (*War* 1:275). Yet the indications are that throughout the next century relations were not always so good. The reference from *Acts* (12:20) already cited, indicates hostility at the time of Agrippa I, and when again our sources begin to cover the area at the outbreak of the war, nothing seems to have changed. In the disturbances of the year 66 C.E. Kedasa a Tyrian village, is mentioned as one of the places destroyed by the Jews (*War* 2:459) and in the sequel we hear that 'the Tyrians dispatched a considerable number, but imprisoned the majority in chains' (*War* 2:478) — on the whole a milder fate than that of the Jews elsewhere, especialy at Scythopolis. As already mentioned Gischala seems to have been situated close to the Tyrian borders and its relationship with the neighboring territory seems to be typical of such isolated outposts — economic necessities do not allow a total break in relations, but rarely do these blossom into co-operation and mutual trust. Thus we hear of John drawing on Tyrian (mercenaries?) to ravage Galilee (*War* 2:589) and later he has still 1,500 men from the Tyrian metropolis in his ranks (*Life* 372), despite the fact that Gischala had been sacked in the interim by people from, among other places, Tyre (*Life* 44). Typical of similar relations on the Tyrian side is the village of Kedasa. It is said to be situated 'between the land of Tyre and Galilee,' according to *Ant* 13:154, called a Tyrian village (*War* 2:459) and described as 'a strong inland village of the Tyrians, always at feud and strife with *the Galileans,* having its large population and stout defenses as resources behind it in its quarrel with *the nation*' (*War* 4:105). It is from there that Titus launches his attack on Gischala just as Demetrius II had done two centuries before against Jonathan (*1 Macc.* 2:67; *Ant.* 13:162).

In attempting to sum up the possible cultural influences of Tyre on Jewish life in Galilee, two important aspects of the history just outlined are to be noted. In the first place one must recognize the changing circumstances of Tyre itself. Already established as a commercial and industrial center before Alexander's attack, it quickly recovered in the Hellenistic period, despite the fact that it had to buy its independence from the Seleucids and was probably restricted by the Ptolemies.[44] The heyday of its position within our overall period probably came between the years 126-25 B.C.E. and 56-57 C.E. when as a free city it struck its own coins which were recognized throughout the whole world for the excellence of their quality and their real worth, which had not been diminished despite a major inflationary situation that was being experienced in Parthia, Egypt and Syria.[45] On being incorporated into the Roman province of Syria by Pompey, Tyre's fortunes seem to have survived better than many other Syrian cities, but there is little doubt that it paid a price for this.[46] It may be no accident of history then that it is in this period that we hear of its encroachment on the interior as this is reflected in Caesar's decrees. The more external pressures came to bear on the buoyant economic life of the city, the more it had to draw on the resources of its own hinterland nearer home.

Secondly, we can contrast this relationship of need for an adequate hinterland at Tyre with the situation at Scythopolis and Ptolemais already described, both having their own natural territories without any need for encroachment. This did not necessarily mean that Ptolemais was any more tolerant of its Galilean neighbors however, and we have noted how persistently it was the source of attack against the interior. However, it should be noted that these attacks were by outside rulers, Seleucids, Ptolemies or Romans — there is no evidence of actual encroachment by Ptolemais itself. Scythopolis, we have argued, had on the whole peaceful relations with its northern neighbors, partly perhaps because these were like itself, city territories — Philoteria and later Tiberias — and partly because of its own self-sufficiency. Tyre, however, has a history of personal encroachment into Galilean territory from the days of Solomon to Caesar. Thus it poses the threat not of the invader but of the permanent aggrandizer. It needed the interior for supplies of food and raw materials and to insure a safe passage for the many traders who frequented its markets, probably explaining the fact that Kedasa, a border town, was so stoutly fortified. As such it posed a different and more subtle threat to the way of life of the people of the interior.

The economic attractions of having such a lively market for one's produce close at hand inevitably helped the Galilean peasant overcome the sense of loss of identity with his own community and heritage, isolated as he was geographically from its center. The process had to be one of slow absorption rather than violent takeover, and when this does take place it arouses resentment and reawakens older differences that have been gradually eroded through contact. In the case of Tyre and the Galilean hinterland this relationship did not begin with the hellenistic age, but had pre-dated it by several centuries at least, as Ezechiel testifies. It was accelerated certainly by the increased productivity of hellenistic times. One thinks of the evidence for Greek influences in architecture, pottery, language and the glass industry unearthed at Tel Anafa in the Huleh basin for the 2nd century B.C.E.[47] While the preponderance of Tyrian coins among the finds there does not definitively prove the direct contacts— since the coins had a wide circulation — the presence of the glass industry in both centers probably insured frequent and stable contacts.[48] Undoubtedly this is but one example that has come to light of a process of cultural adaptation through economic and social contacts on a much wider scale. The hostile attitudes towards their neighbors displayed both at Gischala and Kedasa does not disprove this hypothesis. Both are border towns, each outposts of two very different cultures, Jerusalem and Tyre, and therefore likely to be aggressively assertive of their different traditions and hostile to the other. It only calls for an ambitious man, as John undoubtedly was, to exploit on one side or the other the latent loyalties of the peasant people. Yet even in the very act of doing so he can still avail himself of the greater possibilities that contact with the enemy offers, without seeing the apparent contradiction. To this consideration must be added the amount of social unrest that came from loss of lands on the Galilean side, which explains some at least of the brigandage so frequently mentioned by Josephus. In these circumstances it is easy to understand Kedasa's constant state of feud with Galilean Jews. Its function was to protect the caravans of eastern traders which were one source of Tyre's prosperity.[49] Such wealth passing on its borders was a constant temptation for the deprived Galilean to engage in brigandage, as can be shown for other border areas (*Life* 126ff. for the Great Plain and *Ant* 15:346f. for Batanaea).

CONCLUSION

Our discussion of the first phase of Galilee's contact with Hellenization in terms of the emergence of the Greek cities surrounding it has led to no overall conclusions. Our call for carefully distinguishing the influence of different cities has, we believe, been substantiated by the evidence. Different political, geographical and economic factors operate both in the emergence of these cities themselves and in the extent and nature of their contacts with the interior. On the whole the evidence weighs against those who see the cities as the agents for large-scale cultural change in Galilee, at least in the earlier period.

II
THE SECOND PHASE OF URBANIZATION:
THE ROMAN PERIOD

While the first phase of urbanization touched the outskirts of the political area that was Galilee, the second phase reached the very heart of the province. However, the difference is not just a matter of the geographical siting of cities, since this by itself is no guarantee of cultural change. The difference between this second phase and the earlier one we have discussed is that the two cities of most interest - Sepphoris and Tiberias - are the outgrowth of cultural and political developments within Judaism itself and are therefore Jewish cities, not, primarily at least, the introduction of aliens by foreign powers. As we shall see, this difference is of vital importance in assessing their impact on Galilean Judaism and in particular on the peasants whose situation we have yet to discuss.

(i) *Sepphoris*

Archaeological investigation has confirmed the written testimony of the Mishnah that Sepphoris was a strong fortress (*M. Arak* 9:6), and it is probably for this reason that it emerged as the most important center in Galilee, despite the lack of any older Israelite roots. Its strategic location, lying in the heart of fertile Galilee is not lost on Josephus who describes it as 'the strongest city of Galilee,' with a mountain fortress facing it in difficult terrain 'in the heart of Galilee' (*War* 2:510f.). Once fortified it was impregnable, in his estimation, even from the Romans (*Life* 346), and should the lower city be occupied the people were able to take refuge in the citadel (ἀκρόπολιν ; *Life* 376). Vespasian too was well aware of its strategic position for the campaign against Galilee (*War* 3:34). In all probability this was why both Antigonus (*Ant.* 14:413f.; *War* 1:304) and Herod (*Ant.* 17:271) had earlier used it as a stronghold from which to establish themselves in the province.

However, the real importance of Sepphoris stems from the fact that Gabinius made it the seat of one of the five councils (συνόδοι) into which he divided the Jewish nation in 57 B.C.E. (*War* 1:170; *Ant.* 14:91, συνέδρια), the only one for Galilee. It retained this position of pre-eminence in the surrounding countryside for several centuries, except for a period of thirty years or so when Antipas made Tiberias his capital. However, when this city was transferred to the territory of Agrippa II in 54 C.E. Sepphoris was restored to its former position with the royal bank and the archives, a fact that caused chagrin to Justus of Tiberias (*Life* 38; cf. *War* 2:252f.). While never enjoying the full rights of a Greek city, given the bureaucratic form of both Jewish and Roman government that operated throughout its history, in all probability it was endowed with some land at least on being rebuilt by Antipas (*Ant.* 18:27).[50] Comparing it with Tiberias at the outbreak of the war in 66 C.E. Josephus writes: 'Now Sepphoris, situated in the heart of Galilee, surrounded by numerous villages, and in a position, without any difficulty had she been so inclined, to make a bold stance against the Romans, nevertheless decided to remain loyal to her masters' (*Life* 346). From this passage at least it would seem that having surrounding villages gave it a better chance of withstanding the Romans, had it so desired, presumably because this ensured it adequate supplies (cf. *Ant.* 14:418, *War* 1:304).

For our purposes it is this pro-Roman stance of Sepphoris during the first Jewish revolt that is of particular importance in attempting to assess its sphere of influence on the surrounding area.[51] In itself the attitude is most surprising given the general anti-Roman approach of Galilee and the Galileans as a whole. Besides, at an earlier period of its history it was the scene of Judas' (the son of Hezechiah) act of defiance in assembling a considerable body of followers and invading the royal arsenal on the death of Herod in 4 B.C.E. (*War* 2:56; *Ant.* 17:271f.). However this show of independence by some at least of the people of Sepphoris and its neighborhood drew a quick and severe response from the Romans, for the governor of Syria, Varus, and his army destroyed the city and reduced the citizens to slavery (*War* 2:68; *Ant* 17:288). It was this that led to the rebuilding by Herod Antipas already referred to, making it 'the ornament of all Galilee' (*Ant* 18:27), a description which undoubtedly should be understood in the light of his hellenistic style of art and architectural embellishment of Tiberias.

To what then are we to attribute Sepphoris' refusal to engage in the revolt? There is no question that the population was Jewish, for Josephus sees its pacifism as a rejection of kinsmen (ὁμοφύλοι *War* 3:32) and declares that 'when the temple that is common to us all was in danger of falling into the enemy's hands' they refused to send help (*Life* 348). Almost 150 years earlier in fact Ptolemy Lathyrus attempted to surprise the city and nearby Asochis on the sabbath, an indication that even then its population was Jewish (*Ant.* 13:337f.). Several explanations of this cautious if unpopular stance have been given. The archaeological evidence shows, it is suggested, that there was no internal water supply in the city, elevated as it was, but in fact an elaborate system had been built along Roman lines to the east, replacing an older storage system within the walls. This situation would have made it extremely vulnerable in the event of a siege.[52] Josephus suggests that their overtures to Vespasian on his arrival at Ptolemais were with an eye to their own security and conscious of the power of the Romans (*War* 3:30f). This would support Hoehner's opinion that the experience of the previous rebellion had taught them a salutary if bitter lesson.[53]

Both suggestions seem inadequate to me. Sepphoris' strength as a fortress is reiterated by friend and foe alike. Besides, it is not at all clear that the people of Sepphoris themselves engaged in the previous revolt under Judas, even if Varus subsequently made them pay the price for it.[54] In fact a closer reading of Josephus shows that the theme of Sepphoris' pacifism is matched by the (country) Galileans' animosity towards it. We suspect that a consideration of both these themes may help to give a better appreciation of the place of Sepphoris within the life of Galilee, since tensions existing for a long time suddenly came into bold relief at a moment of crisis.

The pro-Roman stance of Sepphoris is a constant thread running through Josephus' *Life*: 30. 38. 104. 124. 232. 345-48. 373. 394f., but it is mentioned in *War* also where the people of Sepphoris greet Vespasian at Ptolemais and ask for his help, something he gladly grants, since he is aware of its strategic position in the heart of enemy country, and so he sends Placidus his general to the area and lodged troops in the town (*War* 3:30. 34. 59. 61.).[55] Nowhere do we get a hint of who are the leaders of public opinion at Sepphoris, a striking contrast with Tiberias where Josephus goes into great detail about the various factions (*Life* 34ff.). Only in one instance is there a suggestion of anything less than full support for the policy (*Life* 346f.), where Josephus declares that Sepphoris excluded him from the city and forbade any of her citizens 'from taking service with the Jews.' Thus we see a well organized and on the whole united city. Apparently it was wealthy enough to rebuild its own walls (*War* 2:574) and had some influence on the surrounding towns also, at least at the beginning of hostilities (*War* 2:510f.). It should not be forgotten that at the time of the first revolt Sepphoris was the Roman administrative center of that part of Galilee which did not belong to the territory of Agrippa II (*Life* 38). Apparently this brought the city commercial benefits which Justus of Tiberias bemoans, and no doubt it was the controlling voice of public opinion there that stood to gain most from this position.[56] Little wonder that it had already made its position clear to Cestius Gallus, the governor of Syria, before Josephus' arrival in the province in 66 C.E. Presumably such loyalty was well repaid in the post-war period, as is clear from the fact that already in the year 68 C.E. it was allowed to strike its own coins.[57]

Equally emphatic appears to be the Galileans' hatred of Sepphoris and their desire to destroy it. Indeed Josephus clearly distinguishes between them and the people of Sepphoris, even though the latter is described as one of the three largest cities of Galilee (*Life* 123). Clearly by his day attitudes had hardened to the point that this very specialized use of the term 'Galilean' was justified without taking account of its purely geographic associations. It is in the *Life* that the polemic is most pointedly articulated. Before Josephus' arrival in the province the Galileans had already decided to sack the town, but he was able to use his influence with the crowds and so avert the danger (*Life* 301). A large body of Galileans under arms accompany him to Sepphoris when he uncovers a plot there against himself involving the archbrigand Jesus, but there are no reprisals against the town's people (*Life* 104-10). However, Josephus was not so successful in restraining his Galilean supporters on a later occasion, and he had to resort to spreading a false alarm about the arrival of the Romans to put an end to the pillaging which the Galileans were engaged in, having seized the opportunity 'to vent their hatred on this city which they detested' (*Life* 373-80). However much this theme may be part of the apologetic of the *Life* it is at least echoed in the *War* also, where we hear of 'Sepphoris abandoning the Galilean cause' (*War* 3:61), and of its being plundered, if not specifically by the Galileans, at least by Josephus' soldiers (*War* 2:646).[58]

This introduces a further anomaly in the attitude of Sepphoris, namely its relationship with Josephus. For a time he seems to have had his headquarters there (*Life* 64. 103) and saved it from the ire of the Galileans (*Life* 31), yet the people of Sepphoris mistrusted him and attempted to plot against him with Jesus, the archbrigand from the district of Ptolemais (*Life* 104-10). Their hostility to Josephus can be seen in their attitude towards his rivals from Jerusalem who had been sent to remove him from office at the instigation of John of Gischala. In the summary account of this episode in the *War* (2:626-31) we hear of Sepphoris, Gabara, Gischala and Tiberias joining his opponents on their arrival (ἀπέστησαν), but that Josephus was able to win them back without violence. In *Life* these same towns (Gischala is naturally omitted in the context) are said to have been ordered to support John (*Life* 203). Yet later the delegates after making an unsuccessful tour of villages in an attempt to stir up animosity against Josephus repaired to Sepphoris, where they were received by the inhabitants, rather coldly, one suspects, for they moved on to other villages and finally to Gabara (*Life* 232).[59]

From this evidence, highly personal though it is, one gathers that the Sepphorites' pro-Roman stance, their attitude towards Josephus as well as the antipathy existing between themselves and the Galileans are not due to a disregard for Judaism as such, but rather show a refusal to become involved in the political turmoil that was developing. Fortunately we are in a postion to fill out this picture of Sepphoris from rabbinic sources, both prior to and after 70 C.E. From these it is apparent that in the period before 70 C.E. Sepphoris was one of the few priestly towns in Galilee.[60] The evidence of Rabbi Jose ben Halaphta who lived in Sepphoris in the second half of the second century C.E. is of particular significance, given his own genuine historical interest in the past of his people, and the fact that his father was head of the community in Sepphoris shortly after 70 C.E. Jose mentions that a priest from Sepphoris, Jose ben Illem took the place of the high priest on the day of atonement. We are able to date this event more precisely from Josephus, who tells that it was the place of his cousin Matthias who had rendered himself unclean the previous night. This occurred towards the end of the reign of Herod the Great (*Ant* 17:166), long after his purge of the Hasmonaean nobility.[61] We are safe in assuming that this family at least survived both Herod's purges and the attack on the Galilean nobles who remained faithful to him (*Ant* 14:450) and that Sepphoris was their home, even though Matthias is described by Josephus as being from Jerusalem (*Ant* 17:78). We hear also of Arsela from Sepphoris, 'an Israelite' (i.e. a lay noble) who was given an active role in regard to the scapegoat rite on the day of atonement usually reserved for a priest (*M. Yoma* 6:3), and Rabbi Jose also informs us that old registers were kept in this city indicating who were Israelites of pure blood, equal to those whose ancestors were priests, levites, or members of the Sanhedrin (*M. Kidd* 4:5).[62] A priest from Sepphoris who was given the doubtful name of בן דהאכין because of his greed also occurs (*T. Sota* 13:8; *p. Yoma* 6, 43c), and the women of Sepphoris are mentioned as being particularly dutiful in attending the temple (*p. Ma'as Sch.* 5,56a).

As well as this picture of dutiful attachment to the temple in Jerusalem, we also find another picture of Sepphoris emerging from the rabbinic sources, namely that of wealthy Jewish land-owners dwelling there in the 2nd century C.E. These 'great ones' or 'heads' were the recognized leaders of the Jewish community and acted as judges in their law courts, as well as representing them in the city council which was part-Jewish, part-Gentile, at least after the Bar Cochba revolt and the re-naming of the city as Diocaesarea.[63] The picture which rabbinic sources paint of these great ones and their oppression of their poorer Jewish brothers is not very complimentary, giving rise to the bitter disputes with the Jewish teachers who transferred there after 135 C.E. Presumably this Jewish landed aristocracy can be dated back to the period immediately after the first revolt when, as we have seen, many, especially of the upper classes, fled Jerusalem for safer places like Agrippa's kingdom, and presumably also Sepphoris, which was spared the ravages of the war due to the presence of the Roman garrison which Vespasian had granted them. The social picture that emerges here is rather similar to that which we shall discover many centuries earlier in Galilee for Ptolemaic times, and which can be traced through the centuries in regard to the ownership of the land. Now however the owners are Jewish aristocracy, owning the land at the good pleasure of the Romans, and paying for it in terms of heavy taxes which, as always, the weakest in the community must carry.

It seems valid to suggest that the attitudes of Sepphoris which we have seen from Josephus' writings for the 1st century C.E. are best explained in the light of its character as this emerges from the rabbinic materials just discussed. From the start it was a Jewish aristocratic city in the heart of fertile Galilee, given its position of prominence by the Romans originally and aware that this was dependent on their continued good pleasure. This explains the striking uniformity and consistency of its attitudes throughout the revolt, but it also helps to explain the Galileans' detestation of it, despite their sharing similar religious loyalties. This Jewish aristocracy who controlled the situation at Sepphoris were equally suspicious of their Galilean neighbors and of anyone who appeared to make common cause with them, even if these were priestly and upper class like Josephus or those sent to replace him. Some at least of their ruling class survived the purges of Herod, even though originally they may have been Hasmonaean rather than Herodian in their basic loyalties, as appears from Antigonus' use of the city as his base of operation against Herod (*Ant.* 14:413f).[64] Such people can shift their basic loyalties for the sake of political expediency much more easily than peasants, whose lot is not likely to change very much no matter who is in control. Those who did suffer losses for their loyalties were replaced by others who were prepared to accept Herod, and that was not likely to make them any more popular with the Galilean peasants. We shall have occasion later to discuss the religious loyalties of both groups; for the moment it is sufficient to stress their social differences and the unlikelihood of any great exchange between them. During the long and apparently peaceful reign of Antipas the lot of the peasant must have improved somewhat and peaceful co-existence was possible. Once the war with Rome became inevitable, the tensions that had existed between the peasant and the townsman and were built into the social structures of townsman/landowner and country/serf could not remain beneath the surface any longer. After the catastrophe of 70, and with their numbers augmented by relatives and people of a similar class from Jerusalem, both priestly and lay, the position of this group at Sepphoris must have improved while that of the Galilean peasant—or at least those who survived the purges—can only have deteriorated still further. It is thus that the picture which emerges clearly in the 2nd century C.E. is of a piece with that which was already there in the first.

(ii) *Tiberias*

If Sepphoris could not lay claim to any Israelite roots, much less could Tiberias its great rival, founded by Antipas about the year 13 C.E.[65] Its very name is indicative of its spirit, dedicated as it was to the Roman Emperor of that name. The character of the city can already be discerned from Josephus' account of its foundation (*Ant.* 18:36-38).[66] Geographically it was ideally situated, on the Lake and in the most fertile region of Galilee, with hot springs nearby; it was intended to benefit from the fish trade of the lake, the agriculture of the surrounding region and the tourist attraction of the springs (see *Life* 85; *War* 2:614). The population was mixed, but at the head of the list Josephus mentions Galileans, some of whom were people in authority (τινὲς δὲ καὶ τῶν ἐν τέλει). The fact that the Galileans were initially coerced may be the result of the city being founded on tombs in violation of Jewish law, a fact mentioned both by Josephus and recalled in rabbinic sources, but it may also be due to the Galileans' preference for village life, as Jones suggests.[67] Apart from this contingent from his own territories, Perea as well as Galilee may also be included in the phrase ὅσοι μὲν ἐκ τῆς ὑπ᾽ αὐτῷ γῆς, Antipas also accepted poor people from everywhere (πανταχόθεν), some of them freedmen (with the restriction of not leaving the city), building houses for them and giving lots of land, which explains why it had its own χώρα to defend at the outbreak of the war (*Life* 155). In Josephus' day, we know that it had a stadium (στάδιον; *Life* 92) and a prayer house (προσευχῆς; *Life* 277), but if Antipas had actually given it walls these were certainly in need of repair (*Life* 144; *War* 2:573). Besides there was a royal palace with animal decorations (*Life* 65) and Greek-styled furniture (*Life* 68). Its administration too seems to have been on the lines of a Greek *polis*, since we hear of an ἄρχων (*Life* 271.278.294), ten leading men (πρῶτοι; *War* 2:639), a βουλή of 600 citizens (*War* 2:641) and an assembly of the citizens (*War* 2:618, the δῆμος of the classical *polis*). However, even though the coins of Herod Antipas were minted there, Tiberias does not seem to have issued its own coins until the time of Trajan, or possibly for a time under Claudius.[68] Further signs of restriction on its freedom emerge from Josephus' appointment of superior

officers (ὑπάρχης ; War 2:615, called στρατηγὸς at Life 89.272) and
Agrippa's as an'αγορανομὸs or financial controller (Ant 18:149).
Justus laments the fact that it lost its position of pre-eminence as
capital of Galilee to Sepphoris through being transferred to the
territory of Agrippa II by Nero, probably at the beginning of his
reign (War 2:252f; Ant 20:159; Life 34.38f).[69] Specifically he mentions the transfer of τὰ ἀρχαῖα and the βασιλικὴ τράπεζα as a loss
to the city, apparently because of the financial control of the
whole area that these gave the city and the commercial advantages
accruing to its leading citizens.[70] Nevertheless, Tiberias seems to
have retained a large degree of autonomy under Agrippa as its
stance during the course of the war indicates.

In attempting to assess the sphere of influence of Tiberias we
must be careful to recognize the polemical nature of Josephus'
remarks regarding its attitude to the revolt as part of his desire
to discredit Justus. Nevertheless, something of its overall character and relations with the rest of Galilee may be gleaned from the
events of the revolt years, however difficult it is to piece them together coherently. Prior to the outbreak of hostilities we hear of
some rift between the Galileans and Justus' brother, leading to
the latter's hand being cut off for forging of letters (Life 177f).
Nothing more is told us of this episode, but it seems likely that it
was related in some way to Justus' attempt to control Galilee
which had led to bitter resentment on the part of the Galileans
(Life 392).[71] Nor was Justus very successful in firing his fellow
Tiberians with ambition to join the Galileans against Sepphoris,
even though his and their motives for such an attack were not the
same as the Galileans, the former being envious of Sepphoris'
status as capital of the province (Life 38).[72] Justus was said by
Josephus to be the leader of a third party separate from those of the
leading men and the destitute classes (Life 36). If that were the
case, then Justus' relations with Galilee could not be regarded as
typical for Tiberias. However, the likelihood is that the only
thing that separated him and his family from the upper class
party, headed by Julius Capellus, was his personal ambition, and
elsewhere we find him a member of the city council, presumed to
be a pro-Roman, like its other members (Life 175-7), for, according
to Life 32, this party of respectable citizens was from the outset in
favor of loyalty to Rome and the King (Agrippa II). It is little

surprise to find that two of them have the family name Herod—
the sons of Miasus and Gamalus—and the brother of Julius
Capellus, Crispus, had been prefect (ἐπαρχὸς) of the city in the
days of Agrippa I, but was at this time absent at his private estates
across the Jordan (*Life* 32-34). Insofar as these are representative
of Tiberias it is obvious that it is a dominantly aristocratic
town, whose character would have little appeal to rural Jewish
peasants.[73] Socially and culturally, its inhabitants represented a
new and different type of Jew, and expression of similar religious
beliefs at certain festivals was not likely to bridge the gap between
them.

Yet despite this influential group in Tiberias the facts are that
the city did revolt eventually, and paid a certain price for its behavior. The (minority) Greek population was massacred and
Herod's palace burned down, and in these actions Jesus, son of
Sapphias, the leader of the revolutionary party, had been joined by
some (τίνες) Galileans (*Life* 66f). Significantly, this party is said
to be comprised of sailors and the destitute classes, so that part at
least of the motivation for these revolutionary actions must be
attributed to their social status, something we shall explore in
greater detail in subsequent chapters. Jesus was certainly a man
of some influence. We find him at Tarichaeae, brandishing a copy
of the law of Moses before the populace and denouncing Josephus
as a traitor (*Life* 134f). Even more important was his role in the
internal affairs of Tiberias and his association with the Galileans.
As regards the former, the attitude of Tiberias to revolt was to say
the least ambivalent, and it seems that the war party did not
control the city council all the time during the year of 66 for twice
we hear of overtures to Agrippa for help (*Life* 155; 381-9; *War* 2 :
632-46). This can also be seen from Josephus' lack of popularity
there, despite his own statements to the contrary (Compare *Life*
96.300f.327-31 with 279.298-303). The open declaration of war
only came after the fall of Jotapata (*War* 3:343ff), and after an
initial skirmish with Vespasian Jesus and his fellow-revolution-
aries, 2,000 strong, fled to Jerusalem. Apparently the affair was
not treated with the same seriousness by the Romans as elsewhere
and the city was reduced as an act of friendship for Agrippa—
an indication that some at least of the turmoil there was inspired
not by the revolutionary war against Rome but by the tensions

regarding the city's independence in the pre-war days. Through the mediation of the elders the Romans were received by the people at large as saviors, and Vespasian forbade any looting by his soldiers, merely destroying one section of the wall (*War* 3:445-61). The fact that Tiberias did not fare as well as Sepphoris in the immediate post-70 period may be deduced from its coins, the former issuing some only in the reign of Trajan, with further increase of status under Hadrian.[74] Undoubtedly its ambivalent attitude towards being part of Agrippa's kingdom was as much responsible for this as was its revolutionary character, something that Josephus' account glosses over in his desire to discredit Justus before the Roman readers.[75]

For our present purposes the relations between Jesus, the Galileans and Tiberias are particularly significant, since we are exploring the sphere of influence of this city on the Galilean hinterland. We have already suggested that there was likely to have been little sympathy or understanding between the country peasants and Tiberias' upper class. This is easily documented from Josephus, who says that the Galileans hated Tiberias as much as they had Sepphoris and that he had to restrain them from destroying the city on hearing of its defection to Agrippa (*Life* 381-9). In the destruction of Herod's palace 'some' Galileans are involved—a qualification that must be taken seriously in view of Josephus' usual designation οἱ Γαλιλαῖοι simply. The actual population of Tiberias was from the start made up of country people, some moved against their wills (*Ant.* 18:37). No doubt those who were not of the magistrate class (οἱ ἐν τέλει) were brought there for the menial tasks and so their links with the countryside would not have been severed because they had never become integrated into the urban life of this metropolis. We shall return to the point below but here it is sufficient to note that these links emerging at the time of the revolt were not typical of the day to day relations throughout the whole century and cannot be seen as indicating a wide sphere of influence for Tiberias in the rural hinterland of Galilee.

By way of corroboration Tarichaeae provides an interesting contrast, both in regard to its attitude towards Josephus and its acceptability to the Galileans. Apart from one incident which outsiders had instigated (*Life* 132.152) Josephus seems to have been well-received there and used it as his base (*War* 2:602; *Life* 127.152.162f. 304.404). Apparently it became a refugee center for the surrounding countryside (*War* 3:532.42; *Life* 141f), a fact that its own inhabitants, thinking of their possessions were rightly concerned about as the Romans advanced (*War* 3:492). Significantly its native population was treated well and only the refugees were sold into slavery (*War* 3:532-42). We find Galilean leaders meeting with Josephus there to plan strategy against Tiberias (*Life* 304), and there is every likelihood that a certain local rivalry operated between these two toparchic capitals, both of which had been transferred to Agrippa's territory by Nero (*War* 2:252). Though it had a hippodrome (*War* 2:598; *Life* 132.8) and had been walled (which it could not afford of itself, *Life* 142; *War* 2:606), it could never aspire to the same prominence as its near neighbor along the lake, Tiberias. In all probability it was a fishing village at the south end of the lake whose change of name from Magdala to Tarichaeae was due to the increase in this industry in hellenistic times,[76] but it did not have any great significance as a cultural center. Apparently country Jews felt more at home at Tarichaeae than in the more cosmopolitan Herodian center nearby, and flocked there, more in fear than in hope on hearing of Rome's policy of scorched earth in the countryside.

Yet Tiberias was a Jewish city, *pace* Schürer, but its character and ethos were shaped by factors that tended to isolate it from the rest of Galilee.[77] Its geographic situation was an important factor, since it bordered the Dekapolis, and was withdrawn from the center of Galilean country life, unlike Sepphoris, a fact that Josephus drives home, when contrasting the war attitudes of the rival cities (*Life* 346.349). It was built initially because Herod Antipas did not feel comfortable in an old Jewish city, even an aristocratic one, and the character given it then was likely to remain with it subsequently, producing a type of Jew that differed both from the older priestly aristocracy and the peasant people alike. This new kind of Jew, Herodian and upper class, was a direct product of urbanization's effects on Palestinian Judaism. We shall return to discuss his type in our final evaluation of the cities' impact on Galilean life. It is sufficient for our purposes now to conclude that on the basis of Tiberias' relations with the countryside at the time of the first revolt the city was not likely to be a great attraction for the countrypeople. It was only in the second century that it became a thriving center of Jewish ortho- doxy and it is to these changing circumstances that we are to attribute the story of its cleansing by R. Simon ben Yohai in the period of Usha.[78]

(iii) *The Dekapolis and Other Greco-Roman Towns.*

In dealing with the other towns that could be considered as agents for cultural change in Galilee, one thinks first of all of the Dekapolis. Both the New Testament and Josephus give ample testimony to the constant traffic between Galilee and the whole area of Transjordan, at least for Roman times. We hear of crowds from the Dekapolis listening to Jesus (*Mt* 4:23-25), and he himself ministered there according to *Mk* 5:1-20; 7:31. Whether such geographical references are based on genuine historical recollec- tion or reflect the spread of the church to these areas later is immaterial, since in either case the accounts presuppose move- ment between the two areas.[79] The links of Tiberias with the Dekapolis were noted by Josephus in the passage already cited (*Life* 349) and the fact that Scythopolis is numbered among these cities is itself a guarantee of such ties, part commercial, part cultural, between both east and west sides of the river. The terri- tories of Hippos and Gadara as well as Gaulanitis are also men- tioned as eastern borders of Galilee (*War* 3:37). so that presumably these lands reached to the eastern shore of the lake with the possi- bilities of lake traffic to the western side. Contacts with the interior of Galilee would therefore be indirect—through Tiberias and Scythopolis.

The Dekapolis is of course a generic name for those cities and their territories that formed a loose confederation, at least since the time of Pompey, and served as a buffer zone between the Arabian steppelands and the Roman Empire.[80] The extent of their autonomy varied at different periods of Roman provincial policy, for whereas Pompey seems to have intended the organiza- tion as part of his *"divide et impera"* policy, Augustus seems rather to have included them in his vassal king policy and so we find them subject to Herod (*Ant.* 15:217). Later they are regarded as part of the Roman province of Syria (*Ant.* 17:320), and later still they experienced a period of real development under Trajan and Hadrian when they are fully incorporated into the Roman provincial system and benefited by the Imperial conquests of Parthia. Independently of these political fluctuations the area as a whole and the cities that dotted it in particular were essentially hellenistic in their organization and outlook. Hippos calls itself σόφη, 'wise,' and fancies itself as a city of learning, whereas an inscription from Gadara describes it as χρηστομουσία, that is, cultivator of the arts.[81] This is confirmed by Strabo (16,759) who mentions as citizens of Gadara 'the Epicureans, Philodemus and Meleager, Menippus the author of Satires, and Theodoros the orator who lives to our own time,' this latter being the instructor of the emperor Tiberius. Yet this factor did not inhibit a thriving Jewish population in the area. Both Gadara and Hippos are listed among the towns attacked by Jewish insurgents following the defeat of Cestius Gallus (*War* 2:459) and naturally there were counter-reprisals in both, but without any wholesale massacre as at Scythopolis (*War* 2:477ff.). People from Trachonitis, Gaulanitis, Hippos and Gadara figure among the Jews captured by Vespasian at Tarichaeae but probably Josephus' rather disparaging dismissal of them as troublemakers in unfair (*War* 3:542), since some at least were fugitives from a hostile situation.

In striking contrast to these essentially Greco-Roman towns of the Dekapolis having Jewish minorities is the fortress of Gamala (cf. *War* 4:4-8; *M. Arak* 9:6) which seems to have special links with Galilee. Josephus' assignment from the revolutionary government included Gamala as well as the two Galilees according to *War* 2:568, the only place in Transjordan under his control in fact. In compliance with this command it figures together with the lesser fortresses of Sogane and Seleucia in both lists of places fortified by Josephus (*War* 2:574; *Life* 186f.). The presumption must be that Gamala was primarily Jewish, and so the revolutionary government claimed a *de facto* control of it, despite its belonging to the territory of Agrippa II (*War* 3:56). It is natural to attribute the reasons for these claims to the Babylonian Jews planted in the neighborhood by Herod the Great, over a century earlier, and who apparently were able to preserve their identity in this outpost of Jewish territory despite all the surrounding hellenistic influences, no doubt because they were rural peasants living in villages rather than townspeople (*Life* 58). However, the matter is not so simple since we hear of Philip ben Jacimus, his kinsman Chares, and this latter's brother Jesus, brother-in-law of Justus of Tiberias, all Herodians and presumably loyal to Rome, associated with the place (*Life* 46-61. 177f. 183.).[82] Apparently, however, more nationalist-minded youths took over, and compelled or coerced the magistrates of the city to join the pro-war faction (*Life* 185f.). Later Gamala put up a very stout resistance to Vespasian, but was eventually captured with huge loss of life (*War* 4:11-54. 62-83.). What is not easily explained is the apparent turnabout of the city from being Herodian to becoming a staunch revolutionary city. Schalit has pointed out that of all the cities of Jewish resistance Gamala alone does not seem to have had any anti-war party.[83] This presentation of the situation may be due to Josephus' self-defense against charges by Justus that it was he who caused the troubles there, but it may also result from the fact that the Babylonian Jews had already left the city and returned to their village life before the Roman arrival as Agrippa had requested (*Life* 183).[84] At all events we hear no more of their leader Philip, and Gamala thus became the last outpost of all who were fleeing the Romans and who wished to revolt from Agrippa. No doubt some Galilean country people had also made Gamala their last refuge in attempting to escape the fury of the Roman scorched earth policy, for *Life* 398 indicates that supplies were passed to the beleaguered fortress from the Galilean Jewish peasants.

Three other foundations must be mentioned in this survey of places which might conceivably have served as agents for social change in Galilee, Bethsaida Julias and Caesarea Philippi, and the earlier Herodian foundation of Gaba in the Great Plain. Apparently Caesarea was by far the more significant, and potentially at least more culturally heterogenetic for Galilean Judaism. The hellenistic roots of this city go back at least to Ptolemaic times, for under the name Paneas it is mentioned by Polybius as the place ot Antiochus' defeat of the Egyptian general Scopas and so captured Palestine in 198 B.C.E. (Polybius, *History* 16,18; 28,1). Herod the Great built a temple to Augustus there after the territory of Zenodorus had been given to him, including

Ulatha (Huleh) and Paneas (*Ant.* 15:360-64; *War* 1:404-06).
Probably this very temple is represented later on the coins of
Herod's son Philip the tetrarch. It was he who upgraded Paneas
further, giving it the new name of Caesarea (*Ant.* 18:28; *War*
2:168), and presumably also the status of a (limited) city, for we
hear elsewhere of the villages in its territory (*Mk.* 8:26f.). Under
Agrippa II it may have lost some of this independence since he
had a viceroy, Modius in the city (*Life* 74), but this did not mean
a change in its character for he named it after his patron Nero,
enlarged it further (*Ant.* 20:211) and entertained Vespasian and
his troops there at the end of the Galilean campaign (*War* 3:444f.).
The continued associations with the god Pan, a rural deity in both
Greek and Roman dress, as well as the temple to the Emperor
ensured the heathen character of this city and its territory. However, some Jews resided there, though obviously in the minority
and severely restricted, and the journey of Jesus in that region
indicates some contact with Galilee proper.[85] However, as Alt
points out, this journey need not have included the city itself, but
only the southern villages which had retained their essentially
Israelite population through the centuries. Politically then the
city belonged to a region other than Galilee, bordering Tyre and
Batanaea. Given the stringent toll controls between the various
regions, we cannot assume that too much traffic across the borders
was feasible for Galilean peasants. On the other hand Bethsaida
Julias situated on the lake did allow for much more frequent
contacts, especially with the Galilean villages and settlements
along the lakefront such as Caphernaum and Corozain, but its
threat to an essentially Jewish way of life seems to have been much
less. Despite Philip's renaming it after Augustus' daughter Julia,
in all probability it never enjoyed full city status. The extra
population that Philip attracted there (*Ant.* 18:28), probably
some lesser officials for the most part, was not likely to have
appreciably changed its character from that of fishing village
to hellenistic city.

Finally there is Gaba, the πόλις ἱππέων, 'city of cavalry' founded
by Herod the Great (*Ant.* 15:294; *War* 3:36). Josephus mentions
the place in conjunction with Herod's foundation of other
fortresses throughout the country, and so presumably it had the
character of a *kleruchia* of earlier times, for we hear that lots of

land were assigned to the soldiers. There is some question about
its actual location, since the earliest reference, *Ant* 15:294, seems
to distinguish between Gaba in Galilee and a site for picked
cavalry in the plain.[86] Elsewhere we hear that it is near Carmel
(*War* 3:36) and from *Life* 115ff we glean the additional information
that it was located 60 stades (about 11 kms.) from Simonias, a
border town of Galilee, and 20 stades (about 3.7 kms.) from
Besara, and these data alone ensure that if it was not within the
borders of political Galilee it was close enough to have had a real
impact on life there, if such was its character. There are, however,
a number of signs which suggest that it was never likely to blend
with the rural, Jewish countryside of the north.[87] For one thing
it apparently retained its military character, for we hear that in
Josephus' day it was the seat of a Roman decurion, Aebutius, who
had been entrusted with control of the Great Plain. Presumably
then it was pro-Roman and no more acceptable to Galilean Jews
than was Sepphoris within the province. Furthermore its orientation was toward the Great Plain where the allotments of the
veterans were located within the king's land. Most significant
of all is the fact that Gaba may well have been a hellenistic city,
even prior to Herod, if as Alt contends, we should read Γάβα instead of the variants Γαβάλα and Γάζα in the list of Greek cities
rebuilt by Gabinius (*War* 1:166; *Ant* 14:88).[88] In that event Gaba
was no more likely to have had influence on the Galilean Jewish
countryside than was any of the other Greek cities of the circle.
It is also significant that it was the nearby Besara (Beth Shearim)
that was to become the thriving Jewish center later. Our conclusion then must be that the foundation did not greatly impinge
on the life of the surrounding area, and it is no surprise to hear
of it in the list of places attacked by the Jews in 66 C.E. (*War* 2:459).

III
GALILEE OF THE GENTILES — FACT OR FICTION?

We have focused on the rise of the cities as the most tangible
sign of change in Galilee and the possible catalyst for a hellenistic ethos there. Yet our survey has shown that the cities had only
a limited sphere of influence and no one of them seems to have
dominated the cultural life in either phase of urbanization. Sepphoris is the most obvious case in point. It can hardly be said to
have been a threat to the basic beliefs and value system of the

Jewish inhabitants of the province, yet it never became the natural center despite its geographic location and its administrative role.[89] Other foundations seem equally isolated and the violence that erupted between Jew and Gentile in 66 C.E. (*War* 2:457-86) is also symptomatic of the tensions between town and country. Part of the reason for this was the fact that as the cultic center, Jerusalem was also the real cultural center for Galilean Jewish loyalties, a relationship which the various pilgrimages had developed and fostered. Nevertheless, we do find Jews, presumably Galilean Jews, living in all the northern urban centers of the circle, no doubt because these had emerged from social, economic and administrative concerns of a wider nature embracing the whole of life in the area and inevitably attracting some of the surrounding population. Consequently, the question must still be posed concerning their influence on rural life in Galilee. The economic changes wrought by Hellenism, and the consequent social stratification call for special treatment in the next chapter, but now other aspects, especially those associated with the urban way of life, can be evaluated in light of our treatment of the cities.

Language may be seen as one way of measuring other changes, for without this basic means of communication no real contacts are possible. There is general agreement that Greek was widely spoken in Palestine as a whole, even in Jerusalem and among nationalistic circles in New Testament times - a conclusion based on epigraphic, archaeological and literary evidence that need not be summarized here.[90] Undoubtedly the beginnings of this language change took place in the Greek cities and among the new administrative and business personnel that entered Palestinian life already in Ptolemaic times.[91] As we shall see in the next chapter these were not confined to the cities but were distributed throughout the villages and estates in charge of the affairs of the government. The frequent journeys of these officials, some of higher, others of lesser rank, ensured a network of communication that tied village life to the various cities and touched everybody from the poorest peasant to the various village officials. Many country people were either attracted or forced to these larger centers, often in menial roles, and while the Zenon correspondence suggests heavy traffic in slaves from among the native population it can be presumed that others moved freely to the cities while at the same time preserving contact with those left behind on the land.[92] Inevitably such mobility was bound to bring about some change in language patterns for the native population, at least to the point of being able to understand basic terms related to everyday life.[93] Some amount of intermarriage took place and was undoubtedly encouraged by the Ptolemaic regime, but insofar as this occurred in isolated rural areas, the older language would be likely to prevail.[94] One might also point to the official decrees such as that of the Hefzibah inscription, whose contents are to be discussed later, which were written in Greek and to be erected for publication. What knowledge of Greek did these presuppose for the ordinary people whose lives were determined by them?[95] Presumably, periods of more intense hellenization such as that of Antiochus IV or Herod the Great saw an increase in the official use of Greek and it has been suggested that a similar policy took place under the Romans after 70 C.E.[96] Yet at the same time we have no evidence of any compulsory language policies, and the counter movement of extreme nationalists suggested by the coins of the two revolts as well as the regulations in the Mishnah, do not appear to have been very effective even in their own circles.[97]

It has sometimes been suggested that Greek was the language of the upper classes and the educated, whereas Aramaic continued to be spoken by the unlettered especially in the country areas.[98] However, this assumption has been seriously challenged by recent evidence and is based on a too intellectualist understanding of the whole hellenization process in Palestine. The Greek documents from Waddis Murabbat, Habra and Seiyal are those of country people,[99] and many ossuary inscriptions, both by the quality of the Greek and their craftsmanship, have no particular signs of sophistication or education.[100] The large number of these inscriptions from Beth Shearim in Galilee from the second to the fourth centuries C.E. is particularly suggestive, provided we could be sure that they come from the inhabitants of Galilee, and that similar language patterns existed for an earlier period also. Sevenster, in particular has argued this latter point, basing himself on the fact that in the Murabbat documents a number of contracts written in Greek are summarized in Aramaic (Nabataean) for the benefit of those who did not feel comfortable with the Greek original.[101]

This evidence for Greek being known by some Jews and functioning as a *lingua franca* in a border district is seen by Sevenster as typical of other areas of Palestine. It might certainly apply to Galilean conditions given the fact that Greek was so widely spoken from an early period in all the surrounding cities there.[102] More recently however, Eric Meyers has called for greater attention to regionalism within Galilee and suggests that on the basis of language patterns as well as other factors a sharp distinction can be drawn between Upper and Lower Galilee.[103] While such an approach agrees in general with the assumption of this study it seems doubtful if the available evidence allows for distinguishing the cultural patterns so absolutely, at least on current evidence. It may be that Lower Galilee had more cosmopolitan connections, but our study of the cities has not indicated any greater empathy between the Galilean countryside of the south and the surrounding cities. Significantly the data on which Meyers bases his conclusions - epigraphic material from seventeen sites - all come from 'the western shore of the lake and the southern half of Lower Galilee', and this would cause no surprise in the light of our survey of the various foundations.[104] The question to be answered is whether this widespread change of language patterns, even among country people, is a real indicator of deep changes within their thinking and attitudes. Given the fact that the administrative and commercial life of the country was conducted in Greek from a very early stage, it is only natural that ordinary people would have some acquaintance with it, even use it, so long as no particular hostile overtones were associated with this. From being a *lingua franca* it could become a first language for many, even unlettered people, but without thereby necessarily indicating a radical break with older traditions.

The obvious way to test this conclusion is to look for other more far-reaching and corroborative expressions of hellenistic civilization in Galilee. Unfortunately lack of material evidence on a sufficiently broad basis leaves any general conclusion tentative. Justus of Tiberias is the only Galilean writer known to us and his writing in its outer form at least was in the tradition of hellenistic historiography. Even his arch-enemy Josephus, writing to discredit him with the Roman leadership has to admit that he was not unfamiliar with hellenistic culture (*Life* 40), and presumably this had been acquired at his native Tiberias, whose thoroughly hellenized political structure and architecture we have seen. Besides, the presence of a stadion there suggests that the Greek passion for sport was cultivated there also. Unfortunately, Josephus did not cite from Justus' work and any attempt to reconstruct either its contents or overall inspiration has to be extremely tentative. Presumably however, it fitted into the general category of Palestinian-Jewish historiography as described by Hengel; a highly hellenized external form in terms of style and language yet thoroughly Jewish in its inspiration, viewing the history of the war as the sphere of divine action and judgment.[105] This would mean that Justus has to be seen as a Jew, who if unacceptable to certain elements of his own people, especially the country people, (Galileans, *Life* 177.391f) was equally not integrated into the completely hellenized world of the Dekapolis. This fact had lead to a confrontation between Justus and these cities, prior to Josephus' arrival, something attested to both by the latter's charge and the *Commentaries* of Vespasian (*Life* 42.341f).

It is difficult to say how typical Justus was of Tiberians, for he was certainly more ambitious, and had personal aspirations of his own which almost proved his undoing, yet clearly he did not share the zealotic tendencies of Jesus and his followers who had been responsible for the massacre of the Greek inhabitants of the city. If we abstract from the war period and the radical elements that emerged then, we might have expected that in Tiberias, if anywhere in Galilee, Judaism would have succumbed to the wider culture, yet in Justus and his type we discover a new hellenized Jew that had emerged in Herodian times within the hellenistic environment, at once sufficiently Jewish in his basic attitudes not to be able to identify with his pagan neighbors, yet so different that the uneducated rural Jew found him unacceptable also. Later, we find Rabban Gamaliel at Tiberias reading the book of Job in Greek and being gently reprimanded by Rabbi Halaphta (*b. Shab* 115a; *T. Shab* 13:2), and in its later development the city was able to combine a very obvious Hellenism in coins, inscriptions and architecture with a strong Judaism.[106]

These observations about the character of the hellenistic ethos in Tiberias are all the more significant in view of the fact that a natural cultural matrix was available in the bordering territory of the Dekapolis, especially at Gadara, where we have found real signs of Greek intellectual and literary activity from an early date. Meleager, the first century B.C.E. poet remembered his native city with affection, though educated at Tyre.[107] This shows the cultural relations between all the Greek cities of the northern region. Yet according to a rabbinic anecdote attributed to another inhabitant of Gadara 200 years later, Oinomaos, a Cynic philosopher and friend of R. Meir, the Jews had been able to resist the influence of the gentiles because of their schools and synagogues where the children had continued to learn the torah.[108] Proximity, even close contact with the various expressions of the new way of life did not always pose the threat to basic Jewish attitudes that one might suppose. No doubt the religious persecution of Antiochus IV and the successful Jewish resistance had a lot to do with this state of affairs, and one can postulate a similar situation for Roman Galilee of later times in the wake of the two revolts. It is understandable, if ironic, that many of the architectural features of Herod's palace in Tiberias which extreme Jewish piety had found so offensive in 66 C.E. were two centuries later to be found on the Galilean synagogues of the basilica style, without any complaints being raised.[109] It cannot just have been a matter of the two defeats by Rome but rather a changed political climate in which assimilation of this kind was not seen as symptomatic of a deeper threat. Much earlier, as already noted, there is evidence of a similar situation obtaining on the western borders of Galilee. Chabulon was a Galilean town bordering the territory of Ptolemais (*Life* 213), and we hear that Cestius Gallus destroyed it in 66 C.E. despite the fact that he admired its houses built in the style of those of Tyre, Sidon and Berytus, and even though its inhabitants had fled the place (*War* 2:504). The plain inference is that architectural style alone is no indication of rejection of Jewish ways, as Cestius was quick to recognize.

Another indication of the cultural tenor of Galilee is the Herodian policy in regard to coins. The acceptance of the Tyrian half-shekel with its representation of the god Melkart under the form of Zeus' son Heracles on one side and the Ptolemaic eagle known as 'the bird of Zeus' on the obverse, as 'the coin of the sanctuary', is just one anomaly of the Jewish resistance to paganism.[110] Given this situation it is significant that the coins of Herod Antipas, minted for the most part at Tiberias, avoided human representation of any kind, but do have a wreath and palm branch, symbols of the god *Nike*, which were not offensive to the Jews yet clearly flattered the Roman overlords of Palestine, whose names (those of Tiberius and Claudius) appear on the few extant coins of the period. This is in striking contrast to Antipas' brother Philip, who in the pagan Trachonitis and Batanaea had no scruple in having both his own and the emperor's image on his coins. Likewise Agrippa II was clearly more concerned to celebrate his Flavian overlords than to placate his Jewish subjects, since images of both Vespasian and Titus together with the symbol of victory occur on his coins as early as the year 74 C.E.[111] This numismatic evidence from the different Herodian princes is an indication that at least during Antipas' reign, and probably until the revolt of 66-67 had been put down, it was necessary to proceed cautiously in openly displaying the signs of hellenism. Significantly the two coins of Sepphoris for the year 68 C.E. have a Greek legend but no human representation. This can only mean that the total ethos, as distinct from certain centers, was still thoroughly Jewish, even if architectural designs and pottery styles taken in isolation could suggest the opposite.[112]

As a final confirmation of this situation it is necessary to return to the language patterns in the province. While Greek was certainly widely used even among the lower, uneducated classes, we have allowed, there seems little doubt that Aramaic remained the most commonly spoken language of the vast majority of the inhabitants of Galilee throughout the whole period of this survey. There is a growing consensus that Mishnaic Hebrew too was spoken in first century C.E. Palestine, and in fact had developed from spoken Hebrew of earlier times that had never been totally replaced. Given the close affinity of Hebrew and Aramaic it is quite possible that a situation of *diglossia* existed, namely Aramaic as the ordinary language for everyday speech and Hebrew for formal occasions, especially the cult.[113] At least that would be the most likely situation in Galilee. Apart from the usual evidence for a spoken Aramaic - words preserved by Josephus and the gospels, ossuary inscriptions and most recently the aramaic paraphrases of documents from Wadi Habra[114] - reference may be made to Galilean speaking habits as these are related in *b. Erub* 56a. It is possible to dismiss this evidence as purely ficititous and related to Babylonian speech habits of the third century C.E. where the gutturals seem to have disappeared entirely. However, a small body of direct evidence especially from poetic texts does suggest its authenticity, especially the weakening of *'ayin* and *he*. Kutscher dates this to the second and third centuries C.E. and suggests that it may have taken place under Greek influence, with the local semitic-speaking natives imitating the hellenized artistocracy.[115] At all events the discussion is suggestive in regard to Galilean speech patterns of a later period and shows that Greek never totally replaced Aramaic as the spoken language of the people.

Before concluding that this was due to a positive resistance, to the whole cultural phenomenon that the Greek language represented, we must consider that Aramaic itself had also entered Galilee as the language of the conqueror in the eighth century B.C.E., aided no doubt by the introduction of the Assyrian aristocracy at various centers. Our contention has been that this social change in the north did not radically upset the old Israelite way of life then, and we may now add that this was the case despite the changing language patterns of the period. Thus Aramaic did not have the same cultural overtones for the Jew of a later period as did Hebrew,[116] a fact recognized by R. Judah ha-Nasi: 'Why use the Syriac (i.e. Aramaic) language in Palestine? Either the holy tongue (Hebrew) or Greek'. (*b. Bab. Kam.* 82b; *b. Sota* 49b). If, therefore, Aramaic did not represent deeply felt traditional cultural and religious loyalties for the Jew, its continued use yet gradual erosion through an increasing number of Greek and Latin loan words or its replacement by Greek in certain circles must be seen as an indication that a considerable percentage of the population had not been unduly disturbed by the hellenization process in our period. In the light of the evidence of this chapter this would have to be true of those areas that were outside the range of the (Greek-speaking) cities and showed no affinity with them, both in Upper and Lower Galilee. This tentative conclusion may be tested, or modified in the light of other aspects of life, yet for the present the conclusion must stand that the cities were not the agents for change that some would claim when discussing the total ethos of Galilee in Greco-Roman times.

NOTES FOR CHAPTER 4

[1] Above, ch.2, I and IV.

[2] *Jud. und Hell.* 193, he writes: '*Das gesamte Judentum* ab etwa der Mitte des 3.Jh.s v.Chr. müsste im Strengem Sinne als '*hellenistische Judentum*' bezeichnet werden.'

[3] Tcherikover, *Hellenistic Civilisation*, 90-116, with a brief history of each. Schürer, *Geschichte*, 2, 94-222, has a wealth of detailed information about the cities.

[4] For a full discussion of the rights of the cities in the hellenistic age cf. C. Préaux, 'Les Villes Hellenistiques, Principalment en Orient: Leur Institutions Administratif et Judiciaires', in *La Ville. Receuils de la Societé Jean Bodin*, 3 vols. Brussels 1954-7, 1, 67-134.

[5] R. Redfield and M. Stringer, 'The Cultural Role of Cities', in *Economic Development and Social Change*, 3, 57-73, is extremely helpful on the theoretic aspect of this question.

[6] M. Launey, *Recherches sur les armées hellénistiques*, Bibliothèque des Écoles françaises d'Athène et de Rome, 169, 2 vols., Paris, 149/50, 2, 699-712 on the general institution of σταθμός, the military settlement, based mainly on the Egyptian material, which offers the closest parallel to Palestine. Cf. also, Hengel, *Jud. und Hell.*, 24-7 and M. Rostovtzeff, *Social and Economic History of the Hellenistic World*, 3 vols. Reprint Oxford, Univ. Press, 1959, (hereafter *SEHHW*), 1, 472-502 and 3, 1437f, n. 268. V. Tcherikover, *Die Hellenistischen Städtegründungen von Alexander dem Grossen bis auf die Römerzeit*, *Philologus* Suppl., vol. 19,1, Leipzig 1927, 112-37, on the various ways in which a hellenistic foundation was established.

[7] G. McLean Harper, 'Village Administration in the Roman Province of Syria', Yale Cl St 1 (1928) 105-68, esp. 105-9, on the question of city and village.

[8] A. Byatt, 'Josephus and Population Numbers in First Century Palestine', *PEQ* 105(1973) 51-60, makes a valiant effort to vindicate Josephus' figures, yet even he admits that a village of 15,000 inhabitants 'remains outstandingly inconsistent'. M. Broshi, 'La Population de l'ancienne Jérusalem', *RB* 82(1975) 5-17, is rightly critical of Byatt's eclecticism and discusses possible methodologies for checking ancient figures.

[9] W. Strathman, πόλις, in *TDNT*, 10 vols. English trans., Grand Rapids, Wm. Eerdmans, 1964-76, 6, 516-22, deals with the lexicography and use of the term in Greek literature.

[10] A. N. Sherwin-White, *Roman Society and Roman Law in the New Testament*, Oxford, Univ. Press, 1963, 130. In War 2:252 Josephus writes: 'the four cities (πόλεις) with their districts'(σὺν ταῖς τοπαρχίαις),and at *Ant* 20:159: 'Julias (in Peraea) and the fourteen villages that go with it'.

[11] Mark uses the word κωμοπόλεις for the Galilean settlements that Jesus visits (*Mk* 1:38) and speaks of the villages of Caesarea Philippi κῶμαι *Mk* 8:26; cf. 6:56: 'wherever he visited their villages (κώμας cities πόλεις or fields (ἀγροὺς).However, he calls Bethsaida a κώμη rather than a πόλις (*Mk* 8:23; cf. *Mt* 11:20; *Lk* 9:10). where it is called a πόλις, even though Josephus says that Philip raised it from a village to a city (*Ant* 18:28). Luke calls Naim a πόλις (*Lk* 7:11), but for Josephus it was a village, *Life* 86. All three Synoptists agree in calling Caphernaum a πόλις (*Mk* 1:21.33; *Mt* 4:13; 9:1; *Lk* 4:31) and again according to Josephus, it was a village of Galilee, *Life* 403; *War* 3:519. The phrase κατὰ πόλεις καὶ κώμας is also found in *Mt* and *Lk*, without any clear distinction between the two terms: *Mt* 9:35; 10:11; *Lk* 13:22. At Lk 10:1 we read: εἰς πᾶσαν πόλιν καὶ τόπον which may be an echo of Josephus' designation of a πόλις as the capital of a toparchy.

[12] Schürer, *Geschichte*, 2, 141-50, has collected all the relevant data from ancient sources.

[13] Hengel, *Jud. und Hell.*, 61-7, on early Greek trading between Palestine and the Greek world.

[14] Cited by Hengel, *Jud. und Hell.*, 36f, n. 118.

¹⁵ Abel, 'La liste géographique du Papyrus 71 de Zenon', locates Beth Anath in Upper Galilee, but subsequently, *Géographie de la Palestine*, 2, 265, opts for a site in Lower Galilee, 19 kms. east of Ptolemais. For a full discussion cf. Tcherikover, *Mizraim*, 84, n. 80, who is also uncertain, opting for either Ainita in Upper Galilee or el-Eb'eneh, northeast of Nazareth.

¹⁶ Tcherikover, *Mizraim*, 36-8.

¹⁷ *Jud. und Hell.*, 24-7.

¹⁸ *PCZ* 59003 speaks of τῶν Τουβίου ἱππέων κληρούχο   Text in *C.P.J.*, 1, 119.

¹⁹ Schürer, *Geschichte*, 2, 145.

²⁰ Pliny, *Nat. Hist.*, V,17.75 writes: 'colonia Claudii Caesaris Ptolemais quae quondam Acce'. Cf. Schürer, *Geschichte*, 2, 148, n.213.

²¹ While not making too much of Josephus' figures (cf. n. 8, above), it is worth noting that in the riots of 66 C.E. we hear of 13,000 Jews being killed in Scythopolis and only 2,000 in Ptolemais (*War* 2:468.477). Apparently, the latter city had attracted very few Jewish inhabitants despite its advantageous commercial position.

²² Avi-Yohan, *The Holy Land*, 36; A.M.H. Jones, *The Cities of the Eastern Roman Provinces*, 242; Hengel, *Jud. und Hell.*, 25, against Schürer, *Geschichte*, 2, 171, who derives the name from the Scythians, who are said to have settled there in the seventh century B.C.E.

²³ This is the date suggested by M. Avi-Yonah, 'Scythopolis', IEJ 12(1962) 123-34, esp. 127.

²⁴ Landau, 'A Greek Inscription', lines 14f, 23-5.

²⁵ Avi-Yonah, *The Holy Land*, 51; Hengel, *Jud. und Hell.*, 474 and 521.

²⁶ Hengel, *Jud. und Hell.*, 86f; Avi-Yonah, *The Holy Land*, 202-4, who notes that the flax which grew in Galilee had a natural market in Scythopolis.

²⁷ Tcherikover, *Hellenistischen Städtegrundungen*, 71f.

²⁸ 'On the 15th and 16th of Siwan the people of Beth Shean and its valley went into exile', Lichtenstein, 'Die Fastenrolle', 288.

²⁹ The city is not mentioned in the list of places from which captives were taken by Tiglathpilesar III in 733 B.C.E. However, some traces of Samaritanism have been detected in this valley according to I. Ben-Zevi, in the report of the annual convention of the Israel Exploration Society, 'The Beth Shean Valley', IEJ 11(1961) 198-202.

³⁰ *Life* 349. Schürer, *Geschichte*, 2, 173, points out that this can only mean that it was on the side of Agrippa, since it is not mentioned as part of his territory elsewhere.

³¹ Avi-Yonah, *The Holy Land*, 70, n. 109, with reference to the archaeological evidence from the excavations of the Oriental Institute of the Univ. of Chicago, 1952.

³² Polybius seems to make no distinction between Philoteria and Scythopolis on the basis of the territory belonging to each.

³³ B. Maisler and others, 'The Excavations at Beth Yerach (Khirbet el Kerach) IEJ 2(1952) 165-73 and 218-29.

³⁴ Alt, 'Hellenistische Städte und Domänen', G.P. 5, 392f.

³⁵ *Hellenistischen Städtegründungen*, 68, noting that according to Diodorus, (XVIII. 37, 3-4) it was a fortress again in 321 B.C.E.

³⁶ *PCZ* 59093 tells of the effort of a certain Apollophanes to evade customs duties by exporting slaves illegally from Tyre, with the aid of the customs official of the city, Menekles. For a discussion of the papyrus in question, cf. Tcherikover, *Mizraim*, 68ff.

³⁷ 'Sur une Inscription Grecque de Sidon', *Mélanges Syriens offerts à M.R. Dussaud*, 2 vols. Bibliothéque Archaéologique et Historique, 30, Paris 1939, 1, 91-9.

³⁸ *Ant* 8:144, speaks of Tyrian records written in Phoenician script, that had to be translated into Greek.

³⁹ A. Ben David, *Jerusalem und Tyros. Ein Beitrag zur Palästinensischen Münz- und Wirtschaftsgeschichte* (126 a.C.-57 p.C.), Tübingen, J.C.B. Mohr, esp. 19-24. A steady supply of Tyrian coins at Khirbet Shema' in Upper Galilee from the second century B.C.E. to the third C.E. indicates continued commercial links with Tyre according to R.S. Hanson and M.L. Bates, 'Numismatic Report' in E. Meyers, A.T.

Kraabel, J.F. Strange, *Ancient Synagogue Excavations at Khirbet Shema', Upper Galilee, Israel, 1970-72*, AASOR, vol. XLII, Duke Univ. Press, 1976, 146-69, esp. 148-50 and 168.

[40] E. Bickerman, 'Les Priviléges juifs', in *Mélanges Isidore Levy*, eds., H. Gregoire, J. Moreau and P. Orgels, Brussels, 1955, 11-34, comments on the documents preserved in the Tyrian archives relating to the transfer of Galilean territory by Solomon to Hiram, *Ant* 8:55. Clearly these documents do not date to the period of Solomon, but rather represent some later situation in which the same area was in dispute between the two peoples. Cf. *War* 4:105 on the dispute between Galilee and Kedasa.

[41] Above, ch. 1, n. 14.   Also Alt, 'Hellenistische Städte und Domänen', *G.P.*, 4, 392, n.3.

[42] Above, notes 4 and 36. Tcherikover, *Mizraim*, 43f.49, is cautious on the question of the autonomy of the Greek cities of Palestine under the Ptolemies and their encroachment on the king's land. Hengel, *Jud. und Hell.*, 43, n.149 is more positive on the 'freedom' of Scythopolis and the Phoenician coastal cities. In New Testament times it would appear from *Mk* 7:31 that the territory of Sidon had encroached between that of Tyre and the lake, but the geography of this verse is very difficult as the many conjectures, cited by V. Taylor, *The Gospel according to St. Mark*, London, 1963, 352f, make abundantly clear.

[43] Above, ch. 3, I, and n.18 for a discussion based on the decrees of Caesar.

[44] Rostovtzeff, *SEHHW*, 2, 846f and 3, 1534, n. 126.

[45] Ben-David, *Jerusalem und Tyros*, 8f and 16f.

[46] Rostovtzeff, *SEHHW*, 2, 980ff and 3, 1573, n. 72.

[47] S.S. Weinberg, 'Tel Anafa', IEJ 19(1969) 250-2 and 'Tel Anafa: the Hellenistic Town', IEJ 21(1971) 86-109.

[48] Rostovtzeff, *SEHHW*, 2, 861 and 3, 1538f, n. 146. Gladys Davidson Weinberg, 'Hellenistic Glass from Tel Anafa in Upper Galilee', *Journal of Glass Studies* 12(1970) 17-27. The glass industry was also found in the region of Ptolemais, as Josephus, *War* 2:190f and archaeological findings make clear.

[49] Cf. Rostovtzeff, *SEHHW*, 1, 461f on the need to protect the caravan routes from the east. Josephus' agreement with the brigands from Upper Galilee to confine their activities to the border area, *Life* 77, is an example of this situation and of the way officialdom regarded it.

[50] The uncertainty of the MSS evidence makes it difficult to interpret the phrase ἠγόρυεν αὐτὴν Αὐτοκρατορίδα, and several different emendations have been suggested for ἠγόρυεν; cf. *Loeb Josephus*, IX, 24. The actual significance of the title Αὐτοκρατορίδα, is also uncertain. As Feldman, *loc. cit.*, n. b remarks the term is the Greek equivalent of Imperator and so the name probably honors Augustus. It can hardly mean that it was made autonomous, though Schürer's observation that Galilee was subordinated to it is probably true, *Geschichte*, 2, 211, n. 496.

[51] Cf. above, ch. 3, n. 44.

[52] This is the suggestion of S. Yeivin, 'Historical Notes', in *Preliminary Report of the University of Michigan Excavations at Sepphoris, Palestine in 1931*, ed. L. Waterman, Ann Arbor, 1937, 23ff. The remains of an aqueduct linking the city with a spring to the east and a reservoir to the SE have been described by N.E. Manasseth in the same report, 1-16. There is no evidence of the Galileans having ever attacked this water system, which, given their animosity, was an obvious strategy. This suggests that the system may have been a later installation.

[53] Hoehner, *Antipas*, 87; cf. *Ant* 17:271f.288.

[54] Neither the *Ant* nor *War* accounts say that the people of Sepphoris were involved in this attack, and the phrase in *Ant* 17:271, περὶ Σέπφωριν, might suggest that they were not. Though of Hasmonaean aristocratic background presumably, he must have been able to escape the purges of Herod, by remaining concealed among the peasantry.

[55] Cf. above ch. 3, notes 44 and 61 for possible suggestions of anti-Roman attitudes at Sepphoris.

[56] *War* 2:338 says that the men of property in Jerusalem were desiring peace because of their possessions.

[57] Above, ch. 3, V and n.61.n. 61.

[58] The mention of Sepphoris in this passage seems an afterthought, cf. above, ch. 3, n. 49. Possibly the same incident as *Life* 373ff is intended, where the looting of Sepphoris is explicitly mentioned. In the *War* account it serves to underline further the image of the far-seeing and clever general.

[59] There is nothing improbable about Sepphoris' support for the Jerusalem delegation sent to unseat Josephus and this in no way conflicts with its pro-Roman stance. Its Pharisaic composition may have led them to presume that it stood for peace. However, it is noteworthy that it was at Tiberias, not Sepphoris, that it made its center of operation in Lower Galilee, *Life* 271-308, and we hear of no further contacts with the latter city.

[60] The rabbinic evidence for this has been discussed by S. Klein, *Beiträge zur Geographie und Geschichte Galiläas*, Leipzig, 1909, 26-45, esp. 38-41, and by A. Büchler, 'Die Schauplätze des Bar Kochba-Krieges' 198f. The former rightly criticizes the latter for his claims concerning Galilean priests in the pre-70 period.

[61] The following Rabbinic texts mention that Jose came from Sepphoris: *p. Yoma* 1, 38d; *Hor* 3,47d; *Meg* 1, 72a; *b. Yoma* 12a; *Meg* 9b; *Hor* 12b. We agree with Stern, 'Herod and the Herodian Dynasty', *Compendia*, 1, 272, n. 2, in dating the incident to the reign of Herod, against Büchler, 'Schauplätze', 198, who wishes to assign it to the time of Agrippa II, immediately prior to the revolt.

[62] For a discussion of this difficult saying of R. Jose, cf. Schürer, *Geschichte*, 2, 211, n. 495 and A. Buchler, *Die Priester und der Cultus im letzten Jahrzent des Jerusalemischen Tempels*, Vienna, 1895, 198f. Whatever the exact meaning of the expression בארכי הישנה it may safely be concluded that there were at Sepphoris during the second temple period Israelites of pure stock who could legitimately marry their daughters to priests. Cf. J. Jeremias, *Jerusalem at the Time of Jesus*, English trans., London, S.C.M. Press, 1969, 297f.

[63] Avi-Yonah, *The Holy Land*, 111, n. 18, dates the new name to the time of Hadrian, even though there is no numismatic evidence for it before the time of Antonius Pius. The rabbinic material dealing with life in Sepphoris in the second century has been presented by A. Büchler, *The Political and Social Leaders of the Jewish Community of Sepphoris in the Second and Third Centuries*, Jews' College Publication, London. M. *Kidd* 4:5, speaking of the old archives at Sepphoris, seems to indicate a mixed population there at the time of R. Jose.

[64] Alt, 'Die Vorstufen zur Eingliederung Galiläas in das Römische Reich', *G.P.* 6, 430ff, notes that we cannot interpret the silence of our sources as though no measures had been taken by Herod against the Jewish aristocracy of Galilee also.

[65] This is the date suggested by M. Avi-Yonah, 'The Foundation of Tiberias' IEJ 1(1950) 160-9, based on the earlier coins. Hoehner, *Antipas*, 93-5, suggests 23 C.E., but he does not seem to be aware of the more recent numismatic evidence presented by Y. Meshorer, *Jewish Coins of the Second Temple Period*, English trans., I.H. Levine, Tel Aviv, 1967, indicating that coins of Herod Antipas of his regnal year 24 (i.e. 19/20 C.E.) have the name Tiberias on the obverse side.

[66] By a comparison of *Ant* 18:37f with *War* 2:168, Cohen, *Josephus in Galilee* 261, concludes that the former text reflects an anti-Tiberian bias of Josephus at the time of writing *Ant* and *Life*. However, the fact that some at least of the details are also to be found in rabbinic sources cautions us not to disregard the account entirely as Josephan polemic. Is it legitimate to transfer to *Ant* the polemic of its appendix *Life* dealing with Justus and Tiberias, especially when his history was written after the publication of *Ant*? Cf. *Ant* 20:267 and *Life* 369f.430 Cohen (309) anticipates this by claiming that *Ant* 18:36-8 belongs to the 2nd ed. of the work, but without proof.

[67] The rabbinic material dealing with the impurity of Tiberias has been collected by A. Kaminka, *Studien zur Geschichte Galiläas*, Berlin 1889, 9-29.

However, his theory that the lifting of the ban by R. Simon ben Yohai, was really the lifting of a ban on the whole of Galilee, imposed by the Jerusalem Sanhedrin and known to R. Simon, is unconvincing.

[68] *Life* 68 ἄσημον ἀργύριον. On the coins of Tiberias cf. F.W. Madden, *History of Jewish Coinage*, London, 1861, 97f; G. Hill, *Catalogue of Greek Coins of Palestine in the British Museum*, London, 1914, xiiif and 229f; A. Kindler, *The Coins of Tiberias*, Tiberias 1961; Meshorer, *Jewish Coins of the Second Temple*, 74f; A. Wirgen, 'A Note on the Reed of Tiberias', IEJ 18(1968) 248f; Hoehner, *Antipas*, 99, n. 2; T. Rajak, 'Justus of Tiberias', CQ 23(1973) 345-68, esp. 349, considers that the inscription κλανδιωπολίτων is a retrojection from later times emphasizing the city's loss of status under his successor Nero, but Cohen, *Josephus in Galilee*, 258, n. 133, disagrees, following Kindler.

[69] This is the date accepted by Avi-Yonah, *The Holy Land*, 106, and Stern, *Compendia*, 1, 301, n. 3, based on the evidence from the coins of Agrippa II, as interpreted by H. Seyrig, 'Les Eres d'Agrippa II', *Revue Numismatique*, 6th series, 1964, 55-65. Schürer, *Geschichte*, 1, 588, n. 7 and J. Meyshan, 'A New Cointype of Herod Agrippa II and its Meaning', IEJ 11(1961) 181-3, prefer the year 61 C.E., but this seems unlikely.

[70] The story of the *epitropos* of King Agrippa consulting about his fulfillment of certain rabbinic regulations because he owned property in both Sepphoris and Tiberias (*b. Sukk* 27a), is an interesting example of exchange between the two places at that social level.

[71] Schalit, 'Josephus und Justus', 78, surmises that it must have involved political activity of some kind. Josephus punishes one of his soldiers for attempted treason with a similar measure, *Life* 171-3, *War* 2:642f. J. M. Derrett, 'Law in the New Testament:Si scandalizaverit te manus tua abscide illum', RIDA 20(1973) 11-41, notes that the right hand was used in legal transactions (Cf. *Sir* 21:9)

[72] Cohen, *Josephus in Galilee*, 248-50, thinks that this speech is bogus, yet accepts the rivalry of the two places as genuine, after the manner of many similar rivalries between neighboring cities.

[73] *Life* 69 suggests that Julius Capella shared in the booty from the destruction of Herod's palace, but this does not take from the overall conclusion. Agrippa II was never as popular with the Jews as his father, who had planned a meeting of the four kings for Tiberias, (*Ant* 19:238f), and he never made Tiberias his headquarters.

[74] On the question of the coins cf. above notes 65 and 68.

[75] Cohen, *Josephus in Galilee*, 258-60, conjectures that after the death of Agrippa II, normally dated 92/3 C.E., Rome was reluctant to grant Tiberias full city rights because of its record in the Jewish revolt almost 30 years earlier, and that this occasioned Justus' history as an act of loyalty to his native city. The absence of any hard evidence for this, coupled with the fact that there are indications of city status so soon afterwards for the reign of Trajan makes it a rather unlikely hypothesis. Cf. Rajak, 'Justus of Tiberias', 349f, for the subsequent city status.

[76] Avi-Yonah, *The Holy Land*, 105.

[77] Schürer, *Geschichte*, 2. 218. A.M.H. Jones, *The Herods of Judaea*, 178, describes it as 'a Greek city built for Jews'.

[78] Above, n. 67. The Zealot presence there at the time of the revolt would seem to make it problematic for the first century. Perhaps the story serves as a legitimization for the setting up of the Sanhedrin there in the days of R. Judah.

[79] G. Schille, 'Die Topographie des Markusevangeliums, ihre Hintergrund und ihre Einordnung', ZDPV 73(1957) 133-66. For a full discussion cf. below, ch. 9.

[80] Bietenhard , 'Die Dekapolis von Pompeius bis Traian', is a thorough collection of all the evidence.

[81] Schürer, *Geschichte* 2, 157-61.

[82] Philip had been sent to Jerusalem by Agrippa in order to help the peace party, according to *War* 2:421, and barely escaped with his life. *War* 2:556; *Life* 46f. However the fact that he was later sent to Rome to defend himself before Nero concerning the rumors of his revolutionary activity in Gamala, *Life* 180-2; 407-9, at least raises the question of where his true loyalties lay. Cf. above, ch.3, n. 55.

[83]'Josephus und Justus' 80-91. He contends that in *Life* 177 Josephus is answering the charge of Justus, and that in reality Chares, an aristocrat, and Joseph, the mid-wife's son, fought together in defense of Gamala (*War* 4:18). Justus had charged that the troubles in Gamala were the direct result of Josephus' intervention and, it is argued, he countered that they had taken place already before his arrival. This still does not explain why the aristocracy would have made common cause with the revolutionaries. It is possible that they were more opposed to Agrippa than to Rome (cf. above n. 73), and hoped that by causing trouble in his territory Rome might depose him.

[84]They had fled there originally for protection because of the threats of Varus, Agrippa's viceroy and aspirant to the throne (*Life* 54-8), and Agrippa seems to have been uncertain about their loyalties (*Life* 114f. 179f).

[85]'Die Städten des Wirkens Jesu in Galiläa, territorialgeschichtlich betrachtet', *Kl. Schr.* II, 436-55, esp. 454f.

[86]Schürer, *Geschichte*, 2, 199, n. 429, believes that the text should be emended to make the two identical, but Maisler, 'Beth Shearim, Gaba and Harosheth of the Peoples', 77, thinks that Josephus wanted to distinguish carefully between Gaba and camps in the Plain of Esdraelon. However, the fact that he calls it Γάβα ἱππέων at *War* 3:36 would seem to preclude this. As regards the exact location, Maisler had argued for el-Harithiyye, a site inside Galilee and near Carmel, rather than Alt's Jalamet el-Mansûra, which is located not *near* Carmel, but on its very slopes, 'Die Reitestadt Gaba', ZDPV 62 (1939) 3-21, 8ff.

[87]For the nature and function of such Herodian foundations cf. *Ant* 17:23-30, dealing with the Babylonian Jews of Trachonitis. Also, G.M. Cohen, 'The Hellenistic Military Colony: A Herodian Example', TAPA 103(1972) 83-95 and Launey, *Recherches sur les Armées hellenistiques*, esp. ch. XII, 'les Armées et la population', 1, 690-715.

[88]Alt, 'Reiterstadt', 8. He cites in support of this some coins of the Pompeian era with Γαβηνῶν on the obverse side. Cf. also, Jones, 'The Urbanization of Palestine', 79, n.18.

[89]The evidence for Greek influences in first century C.E. Sepphoris is rather limited. The coins of 68 had a Greek inscription as one might expect, cf. above, ch.3, n. 61. According to W.F. Albright, it is doubtful if the theatre is Herodian, contrary to the views of Manasseh, in his article, 'Architecture and Topography', in *Preliminary Report*, 1-16. (*Classical Weekly* 21 1938 148, in a review). Roman presence there increased after 70, and with it came a changed character: Büchler, *The Political and Social Leaders*, esp. 39-43.

[90] J.N. Sevenster, *Do You Know Greek? How Much Greek Could the First Century Jewish Christians Have Known?* Supplements to *Nov. Test.*, vol. 19, Leiden, E.J. Brill, 1969; J.A. Fitzmyer, 'The Languages of Palestine in the First Century', CBQ 32(1970) 501-31; G. Mussies, 'Greek in Palestine and the Diaspora', in *Compendia*, 2, 1040-65, with bibliography, are recent comprehensive surveys of the evidence, all agreeing about the widespread use of Greek at all levels of society in first century Palestine.

[91] The Zenon papyri offer the clearest evidence for this from the earliest period, as Tcherikover's studies have shown. Cf. also, Hengel, *Jud. und Hell.*, 108-20 and 193f, noting in particular the early appearance of Greek names in Palestine (114-20).

[92] Tcherikover, *W.H.Hell.A.*, 87-95, with reference to *PCZ* 59093 (slave trade); *PSI* 406 (prostitution); *PCZ* 59004 (Zenon's journey).

[93] Hengel, *Jud. und Hell.*, 109f, notes that knowledge of Greek would have been important for any native who wished to rise in the foreign administration, as e.g. the son of the Tobiad, Joseph, *Ant* 12:191.196f. (Cf. *Letter of Aristeas* 121 on the translators of the LXX). The letters of Toubias to Ptolemy, *PCZ* 59075 and 6 (= *C.P.J.* nos. 4 and 5) are written in excellent Greek, but this is probably due to a Greek secretary, as Tcherikover notes, *W.H.Hell.A.* 97f. However, he is doubtful about the extent to which Greek had made inroads in the villages, on the basis of evidence from the Egyptian papyri, where the recurring expression is found: 'so-and-so wrote for so-and-so, since the latter cannot read or write', *W.H.Hell.A.*, 46 and 308, n.34.

[94] The Vienna papyrus with some decrees of Ptolemy II, Philadelphus, seems to explicitly encourage intermarriage between natives and foreigners, by declaring that wives of such marriages were to be regarded as free women. Thus Tcherikover, *W.H.Hell.A.*, 89, and more cautiously Rostovtzeff, *SEHHW*,1,344. Cf. 11. Liebesny 'Ein Erlass des Königs Ptolemaios II, Philadelphus über die Deklaration von Vieh und Sklaven in Syrien und Phönikien', *Aegyptus* 16(1936) 257ff.

[95]Landau, 'A Hellenistic Inscription'; even more pertinent for our purposes is the so-called Froehner inscription, dealing with respect for the tombs of the dead, found near Nazareth in the last century. It is probable that it belonged to Galilee and is usually dated to the age of Claudius, or at least to the first half of the first century C.E. Sevenster, *Do You Know Greek?*, 117-21, has a full discussion of the problems relating to the inscription and its implications for language patterns in Galilee.

[96] Sevenster, *Do You Know Greek?*, 178f, but without any positive evidence.

[97]On the coins cf. A. Reifenberg, *Ancient Jewish Coins*, 2ed. Jerusalem 1947, 28-38; Hill, *Catalogue of the Greek Coins of Palestine*, and esp. L. Kadman, *The Coins of the Jewish War*, Jerusalem 1960. Cf. also Roth, 'Historical Implications', above ch.3, n. 51. *M. Sot* 9:14 (Cambridge text) as well as the 18 halakhôt (below ch. 8,) prohibited the teaching of Greek. Sevenster, *Do You Know Greek?*, 47f, claims that this was a general decree, against S. Lieberman, *Hellenism in Jewish Palestine, Jewish Theological Seminary Texts and Studies*, vol. XVIII, New York, 1950, 100-14, esp. 102, who attempts to distinguish between private study (allowed) and public study (prohibited). The language patterns of the Bar Cochba period are also illuminating in this regard. One letter from Waddi Habra concludes: διὰ τ[ὸ ὁρ]μὰν μὴ εὑρηθ[ῆ]ναι 'Εβραεστὶ γράψασθαι,'because a desire was not found to write in Hebrew', and is signed by a certain Συμαιος, whom B. Lifshitz, 'Papyrus grecs du Désert de Juda', *Aegyptus* 42(1962) 240-56, has identified with Simeon bar Cochba; also Fitzmyer, 'Languages', 514f, with text; Sevenster, *Do You Know Greek?*, 171, n.1, doubts this but admits that it must have been somebody close to him. As Fitzmyer notes, the spelling leaves much to be desired and the handwriting is far from elegant, so that it is unlikely that a scribe was employed.

[98]Thus M. Black, *An Aramaic Approach to the Gospels and Acts*, 3ed. Oxford, Clarendon Press, 1963, 15f and 47-9; Schürer, *Geschichte*, 2, 84ff. Josephus, *Ant* 20:263-5, condescendingly declares that knowledge of Greek diction and style was common for freedmen and slaves, yet admits that he himself had found it difficult to master Greek pronunciation. The impression is that Greek was pretty widely used among all classes, but not very accurately. Thus, Fitzmyer, 'Language 511, and Sevenster, *Do You Know Greek?*, 65-71.

[99]*DJD* II, 209-69; Sevenster, *Do You Know Greek?*, 154-75 and 186; Fitzmyer, 'The Bar Cochba Period', in *Essays*, 305-54, esp. 324-40, on the contents of some of the letters; Y. Yadin, *Bar-Kokhba*, New York, Random House, 1971, esp. 124-39 and 222-54.

[100]B. Lifshitz, 'L'hellenisation des Juifs de Palestine A propos des inscription de Besara (Beth Shearim)', RB 72(1965) 520-38, esp. 523. However, he seems too ready to make generalizations for earlier times from later evidence. Beth Shearim became an important center for Jewish burials only in the late second and third centuries C.E., and even then not all those buried there were from Palestine, even though the names of two Galilean villages, Araba and Baka, do occur, as Sevenster, *Do You Know Greek?*, 135, notes.

[101]*Do You Know Greek?* 165; Fitzmyer, 'Languages', 522f, also notes the bilingualism of the Babatha documents but comments on the absence of any evidence for Greek influence on first century Palestinian Aramaic, which might have been expected.

[102]It is significant, though not unexpected that most of the Greek inscriptions from the Galilean region come from the circle of the Greek cities: Ptolemais, Tyre, Carmel, Scythopolis, Tel Anafa (graffiti). However, some Greek inscriptions from synagogues occur, but for the 2nd to the 4th centuries; cf. B. Lifshitz, *Donateurs et Fondateurs dans les Synagogues Juives*, Cahier de la RB 7, Paris, Gabalda, 1967, esp.

59-70, where the following Galilean places are listed: Caphernaum (=*C.I.J.* 2, 983);
Tiberias (=*C.I.J.* 2, 984.5.6); Kasjun, Upper Galilee, honoring Septimius Severus
(=*C.I.J.* 2, 973). Cf. Schürer, *Geschichte*, 3, 93. On the whole question, Sevenster,
Do You Know Greek?, 126-37 and W. Schrage, συναγωγή *TDNT*, 7, 798-841, esp. 813
who notes that archaeological remains suggest that there were two synagogues at
such Galilean centers as Gischala, Nabratein, and Kefr Bir'im. Presumably this
would have been for language reasons, as at Jerusalem.

[103]E. Meyers, 'Galilean Regionalism as a Factor in Historical Reconstruction',
BASOR 221(1976) 93-101, esp. 97 for language patterns.

[104] I have not been able to consult the paper of James Strange, 'New Evidence for the
Language of Galilee/Golan: 1st to 5th Centuries', which was read to the National
(American) Association of Professors of Hebrew cited by Meyers.

[105] On hellenistic-Jewish historiography in general, cf. Hengel, *Jud. und Hell.*,
183-6. Unfortunately no explicit citation from Justus' *History* or from his other
alleged work, *The Chronicle of the Kings*, has been preserved. Nevertheless various
attempts have been made to reconstruct the former, at least in outline. Cf. H. Luther,
*Josephus und Justus von Tiberias, Ein Beitrag zur Geschichte des jüdischen
Aufstandes*, Halle, 1910, esp. 65-82; F. Jakoby, 'Justus' (5) in *PW* 10/2(1919) 1341-6;
H. Drexler, 'Untersuchungen zu Josephus und zur Geschichte des jüdischen
Aufstandes, 66-70', *Klio* 19(1925) 277-312; Schalit, 'Josephus und Justus', maintaining that the whole of *Life* and not just certain inserts into a previously composed
document is directed against Justus; Rajak, 'Justus of Tiberias', dealing with the
evidence for other alleged literary projects; Cohen, *Josephus in Galilee*, esp. 217-66,
who believes that the history was written after the death of Agrippa II and as an
attempt to defend his native place's record during the revolt, before the Romans.

[106] Cf. above, n.77, and notes 65 and 68 on literature dealing with the coins of
Tiberias.

[107] Above, n.81. Due caution has been observed in discussing the hellenization
process in any eastern city, as Bickerman pointed out, 'Sur une inscription grecque
de Sidon', esp. 99, since, on an inscription celebrating the deeds of one of the citizens
in the Olympic games in a thoroughly Greek spirit, one finds clear evidence of the
city's older political structure about the year 200 B.C.E.

[108] A. Schlatter, *Geschichte Israels von Alexander dem Grossen bis Hadrian*,
Reprint, Darmstadt, 1972, 369, with reference to *Ruth R.* 1:8.

[109] E. Meyers, art, 'Synagogue Architecture', *IDB*, Suppl. vol., 842-4, who notes that
given the variety of recent archaeological data it is not possible to classify certain
types to a fixed time-period, since local conditions must have played an important
role. At Khirbet Shema' near Meiron e.g., a site recently excavated by Meyers and
others, a broad-house type synagogue has been found which has adapted the basilical
style to local conditions, and differs considerably from the broad-house style in vogue
at other centers in the south, *Ancient Synagogue Excavations at Khirbet Shema'*, 57,
n. 26 and 259. Cf. also, R. Meyer, 'Die Figurendarstellung in der Kunst der späthellenistischen Zeit', *Judaica* 5(1949) 1-40, esp. 15-25, on the rabbinic material dealing
with art forms in the synagogue, indicating a coming to terms with the problem on
the part of the rabbis of the 2nd and 3rd centuries. Cf. also J. Neusner, 'Jewish use of
Pagan Symbols after 70 C.E.', JR 43(1963) 285-94, who suggests that tolerance of
many of the symbols was based on the more internal and mystical elements of Jewish
piety after 70, which had brought it more into line with hellenistic piety. For archaeological evidence of synagogue mosaics, cf. H. Kohl and C. Watzinger, *Antike
Synagogen in Galiläa*, Leipzig, 1919, esp. 184-203, and more recently, M. Avi-Yonah,
'Mosaic Pavements in Palestine', QDAP 2(1933) 136ff and 3(1934) 26ff, as well as his
introduction to *Israel: Ancient Mosaics*, U.N.E.S.C.O. World Art Series, 14, Paris,
1960. Meyers, 'Galilean Regionalism', 99, calls for greater attention to differing
regional attitudes and suggests a more conservative approach to the question in
Upper Galilee.

[110] E. von Schroetter, *Wörterbuch der Münzkunde*, Berlin-Leipzig, 1930, 7.

[111] J. Meyshan, 'A New Coin Type of Agrippa II and its Meaning', IEJ 11 (1961) 181-3. For the coins of Antipas cf. Reifenberg, *Ancient Jewish Coins*, 44f, and for those of Philip, A. Kindler, 'A Coin of Herod Philip the Earliest Portrait of a Herodian Ruler', IEJ 21(1971) 161-3.

[112] Davidson Weinberg, 'Hellenistic Glass from Tel Anafa', describes the extraordinary amount of glass finds from the early hellenistic period for one site. Cf. also, Meyers et al., *Ancient Synagogue Excavations at Khirbet Shema'*, 170-241 and 243-56, on the ceramics and other artifacts at the site for a much later period; also S. Loffreda, *Cafarnao II, La Ceramica*, Jerusalem 1974, who suggest a northern or Galilean-type bowl also found at a number of sites in Transjordan, thus supporting the view of Meyers, 'Galilean Regionalism', 98f, concerning close links between Upper Galilee and the Golan.

[113] Ch. Rabin, 'Hebrew and Aramaic in the First Century', in *Compendia*, 2, 1007-39, esp. 1008f, has a discussion of *diglossia*, which he describes as the same community using two different languages in its inner-community activity, within certain social conditions, e.g., cult as opposed to the everyday. This situation is to be distinguished from that of a *lingua franca*, which obtains when people with different home languages, but living within the same area, use one language for inter-communication. This may be one of the native languages or an outside one, sometimes called *pidgin*, which comes into being precisely with a view to inter-community contacts.

[114] The question has been much debated in relation to the language of Jesus, for which an extensive bibliography is to be found in *Compendia*, 2, 1037-9, but with the surprising omission of Fitzmyer's 'Languages'. He deals with the Aramaic question in first century C.E. Palestine, 518-28, with special emphasis on the Wadi Habra bi- and tri-lingual texts and their paraphrases and summaries, 522f.

[115] E.Y. Kutscher, *Studies in Galilean Aramaic*, English trans., Bar Ilan Univ. Jerusalem, 1976, 67-96.

[116] This point is well made by Rabin, *Compendia*, 2, 1032.

CHAPTER FIVE
ECONOMIC REALITIES AND SOCIAL STRATIFICATION

The rise of the cities was only one sign of the change that was going on in the territory throughout the whole period. Indeed there were other more far-reaching changes that had caused the cities to emerge and prosper originally. Hengel has convincingly shown that Palestine's first encounter with Hellenism was as a secular, political and economic power, and not, as is sometimes assumed, in terms of intellectual or spiritual influence.[1] Our aim in this chapter is to explore this insight further with special reference to Galilee by describing the changed economic situation there and attempting to evaluate its impact on the social life of the province. These wider changes we associate with hellenization did not just affect the cities but were felt in the countryside also, and so our investigation in this chapter should take us to the heart of life in Galilee.

In attempting to trace these social changes our attention will focus particularly on changing patterns of wealth and prosperity. Later we shall see that other factors also are reflective of, if not contributory to this changing social order. For now we wish to explore the economic factors, since historically it was in this area that Galilee first experienced the changing times, and fortunately we have some first hand information in the form of the Zenon papyri which break the silence for us concerning the introduction of hellenistic civilization to life in the country.[2] Since Galilee was and remained an essentially rural province it is obvious that landownership was of primary importance in determining class distinctions.[3] Wealth derived from commerce and trading was by comparison more precarious and less significant. Consequently, we may carry out our survey of classes in Galilee on the basis of property owners and other business enterprises. We shall then attempt to apply the findings under these two headings to the wider social relations.

I
LAND OWNERSHIP IN GALILEE

To understand the situation in Galilee outside the city territories it is necessary to decide how far the principle of δορίκτητος
χώρα —land won by the spear—applied to Palestine.[4] This
principle was certainly invoked by the Ptolemies in Egypt, and
while it did not entirely exclude private ownership of land there,
it certainly curtailed it considerably and meant that the trend was
towards large holdings of lands belonging to the royal house, to
be given as γῆ ἐν δώρεα —bequests of land—to worthy clients or
parceled out to the soldiers in lots.[5] Furthermore the use of this
land had to be in conformity with the overall agricultural policy.
Given the political uncertainties concerning Coele-Syria for
almost all of the 3rd century B.C.E. it is extremely unlikely that
the Ptolemies attempted to uproot the native peasants of Palestine.
Certainly, native sheiks like Toubias in Transjordan were incorporated into the overall system, as the net of administrative
bureaucracy was cast over the countryside. To attempt to uproot
all of the native people or claim total proprietorial rights over
their holdings would probably have been possible only at a price
in terms of policing and manpower that the Ptolemies were not
prepared to pay. Far better to integrate the locals into a larger
system, and in that way control them and their production as the
native fellaheen were handled in Egypt.[6]

The Zenon papyri make it clear that there was *some* royal land
in Palestine, and in all probability the estate at Beth Anath in
Lower Galilee,which seems to have been the private possession of
Apollonius, the royal financier, was γῆ ἐν δώρεα.[7] Tcherikover
makes the plausible conjecture that a number of other places
mentioned in *PCZ* 59004 which were visited by an official inspection party sent by Apollonius belong to royal lands, inherited
by the Ptolemies from the Persian kings.[8] Of these places apart
from Beth Anath, Kedasa is also in Upper Galilee. In the south,
other lands were either confiscated or acquired in some other way,
so that in all probability a good portion of Palestine, north and
south, was in the hands of the king or his agents.[9] In other instances
older property rights may have been confirmed, as presumably
was the case with Toubias in Transjordan. No doubt there were
such native princes in Galilee though not on the same scale, but
we know nothing about them, unless we identify the highly

independent village chief, Jeddua, of *PCZ* 59018, as a Galilean. He was certainly Jewish, and we can at least regard him as typical of whatever local chiefs may have been left in Galilee.[10]

Unfortunately there is no way of deciding what percentage of the land remained in the hands of small private owners. Certainly, on the basis of Egypt not all the royal gifts of land were of the same size as Apollonius' estates. In fact the κλῆροι of the veterans ranged considerably in size depending on rank, and in the territory of Toubias we find both natives and κληροῦχοι mixed, presumably on fairly equal distributions of land.[11] Normally these lands were leased, with the possibility of acquisition over a period of time, even though ownership did not free one from the burdens of land taxes.[12]

A closer look at the situation at Beth Anath[13] can help to clarify the matter further, even though the evidence is admittedly rather fragmentary. The manager of the estate is Melas who has the title of κωμομισθώτης, an official title known to us also from the Vienna papyrus.[14] His duties seem to be chiefly concerned with the collection of rents and other taxes, though no doubt they varied considerably on the basis of local conditions, and it would be hazardous to build a theory of land ownership on the fact that this title is used for the resident official of Apollonius in this instance. Indeed the transaction between Melas and the villagers does suggest a more complex legal situation than simply land-lord's agent and tenants. A quarrel had arisen because of wheat which apparently the tenants had not delivered, and whereas Melas bases his claim on his official position, they refer to a formal petition which they had made to the king (ἐντεῦξις). Damage to the papyrus does not allow us to determine the out-come, but we do hear of another dispute concerning raisins (στέμφυλα) which the villagers had to provide, but failed to do so because of shortage of water. Melas seems to have 'recovered' the debt from the tenants' own supply and justifies his action by the fact that many of the villagers owned their own vineyards, and that in the case of those who did not he had made good their losses from his own share. At the same time they counter that he took too large a portion of their figs (συκῶν).[15] While the letter is important testimony to the fact that there were royal estates in Ptolemaic Palestine, it is interesting that even there some of the villagers appear to own—not just lease—their own property.[16]

Perhaps this is an indication of older native peasants side by side with the foreign κληροῦχοι. If such a surmise is warranted, it would be an interesting example of class structure rather than cultural background as the more important social factor in this situation, something we shall return to later in this chapter. Perhaps it was this mixture which led to the official protest (ἐντεῦξις) to the king, rather than the kind of outburst that occurred in the all-Jewish (presumably) village of Jeddua, who expelled the messengers of Zenon's agent and refused to pay the money he owed (*PCZ* 59018).[17] Of course in real terms there is very little distinction between the two. In Egyptian eyes both are equally controlled by the overall economic policy, but for the older, native tenant some recognition of ownership had important psychological and religious significance.

If this line of argumentation is correct, perhaps we are justified in at least looking for further signs of small landowners in Palestine, no matter how much the move towards large domains, owned or leased by the royal houses, was the trend, as has been emphasized particularly by Alt and Tcherikover.[18] In our subsequent investigations we shall at least have to consider the possibility that small traditional landowners did co-exist with the larger estates. A number of general considerations point in that direction. For one thing Jewish law fashioned in the Roman period recognized the existence of such rights for much later times without any evidence that there had been a radical change in the situation of land ownership in the intervening centuries.[19] Secondly while Rome did in general continue the land policies of the hellenistic monarchs, it is worth noting that their policies varied in different parts of the Empire. Thus e.g. the policy of centuriation—a gridded system of land partition that was used extensively in Africa—does not appear at all in the East, where advanced social and cultural patterns with their roots in the past could not easily be disrupted.[20] Often the Roman allotments that were given were quite small—sufficient for subsistence farming, but not likely to create a wealthy or independent peasantry.[21] The very areas which are mentioned in the Zenon papyri and which we have assumed to be royal estates—Beth Anath and Kedasa—recur again at the end of our period as areas where Imperial granaries were located (*Life* 71.119). This is not to suggest that these were the only places in Galilee where royal estates were to be found, but simply to underline the fact that we cannot conclude from the existence of some large estates that the whole territory was so divided, to the exclusion of smaller landowners.

Given the previous history of Israelite occupation of the land, it is unlikely that a radical upheaval of land ownership could have been carried through without leaving some indication in our historical sources. Yet there are none. While there are traces of communal property and possibly also a system of fiefs in early Israel, family property seems to have been the normal system. The story of Naboth's vineyard shows how attached the small owner was to his ancestral property (*1 Kgs* 21), and the system whereby a גאל had to buy the land which his near relations had to abandon, was intended to preserve for one's kinsfolk the family property (*Lev* 25:25; *Jer* 32:6-9; *Dt* 4:9).[22] The natural expansion of the wealthy landowner was already a fact of life however as the antimonarchic tradition of *1 Sm* 8:12-14 had warned.[23] The strict legal prescriptions concerning the removal of boundaries (*Dt.* 19: 14; 27:17) as well as the prophetic condemnations of those 'who covet fields and seize them' (*Mic* 2:2; *Is* 5:8) make it clear that the social ideal of every man 'living under his own vineyard' (1 *Kgs* 5:5; *Mic* 4:4; *Zech* 3:10) was not always realized in practice. Furthermore the gleanings for the poor (*Lev* 19:9-10; 23:22; *Dt* 24:19-21) and the tithe for the poor man indicate a genuine concern for poverty in an essentially rural society. Thus it would seem that the picture which has emerged for Ptolemaic times is an accurate reflection of existing land ownership relations of a much earlier period. Our conclusion in the historical section that there was no great uprooting of Galileans in the transfer from Israelite to Assyrian control in the 8th century would strengthen this conclusion, and so we are faced with a fairly stable, centuries-long situation, which was not totally disrupted through Galilee's initial contact with hellenistic monarchies. Was this situation likely to continue in the succeeding centuries?

Earlier when dealing with the history of the transfer from Ptolemaic to Seleucid control of Palestine, we argued that the north, including Galilee, accepted the change without any great resistance, once the key centers, such as Scythopolis, Tyre, Ptolemais and Philoteria had capitulated. These represented the more thriving centers and the defection of key Ptolemaic officials probably reflects the tight rein that was held on local ambition by the central Ptolemaic bureaucracy. Qoheleth, himself a member

of the upper classes presumably (cf. 7:12 e.g.), would seem to
reflect the social situation under the Ptolemies as felt by the
upper classes: 'If you see oppression of the poor and violation of
rights and justice in the realm do not be shocked by the fact, for
the high official has another higher than he watching him, and
above these are others higher still' (Qoh 5:7). Yet while the upper
classes feel the pressure of the hierarchy of power, the fact that the
king is concerned about the arable land (ἀγροῦ) is considered a
blessing in every respect in the very next verse.[24] Presumably, this
would explain Polybius' statement that the people of Coele-Syria,
meaning the peasants, preferred the Ptolemies to the Seleucids
(V, 86. 10), since the former had a greater understanding of the
needs of the peasants due to their experience with the native
fellaheen at home.

However, this contrast between the two hellenistic monarchies,
no matter how it is to be explained, does not necessarily mean
that the trend towards large estates was accelerated by the Seleucid
takeover of Palestine. The little information we can glean about
their land policies would suggest the contrary. The recognition of
the Jews as an *ethnos* by Antiochus III in his famous decree of
197 B.C.E. (Ant. 12:145-47) even if it extended religious recognition to the Jews of Galilee was unlikely to have affected land
ownership there very much. Thus Galilee would still belong to
the χώρα βασιλική, and the land there was likely to have been
treated similarly to other parts of the Seleucid empire.[25] The
discovery of the Hefzibah inscriptions for the neighborhood of
Scythopolis may not be quite so dramatic as the Zenon papyri for
the Ptolemaic period, but it does give some concrete comparable
evidence with developments elsewhere.[26] Thus we learn that
Ptolemaios, the military strategos of Syria and Phoenicia was the
owner (ἐγκτήσει) of certain villages in the neighborhood, possibly from his time as a Ptolemaic official, and that others had
been leased to him on a hereditary basis, possibly after his change
of side.[27] It is interesting to note that even such a high official as
the στρατηγὸς could not regulate certain matters concerning the
sale of goods outside the territory (11.13ff.) nor prohibit the
billeting of soldiers in his villages (11. 24ff.). The same direct
control by the monarch through his διοικήται is attested from other
inscriptions for other areas also, and shows that the Seleucid
organization of the royal lands was not as loose as is sometimes

suggested, even when these lands are transferred to a city territory, sold, or given as bequests, as presumably was the case at Hefzibah.[28]

This raises the important question of the status of the λαοί or inhabitants of the villages in question. A number of influential scholars including Rostovtzeff and Welles have argued that these natives are 'bound to the soil' so that ownership of the land in question means ownership of its inhabitants, and thus their position is best described in feudal terminology as 'bondsmen.' [29] If this were true then it would raise serious doubts about the likelihood of small landowners existing in Seleucid Palestine, even if Welles' suggestion be accepted that there was a humanitarian aspect to the Seleucid alienation of crown lands to cities, thereby allowing the status of the λαοί to be raised to that of κατοῖκοι of the city to which they were attached.[30] However, the position that the λαοί or bondsmen were tied to the soil has been challenged by, among others, Bickerman, and thoroughly discussed most recently by Briant, taking account of all the relevant material.[31] In the Hefzibah inscription Ptolemy asks that the soldiers should not have the right to expel the λαοί (1. 26) and the king instructs the officials in the area to ensure that this does not happen and that they be punished tenfold if any damages do take place. In other words, it is the administration rather than Ptolemy that is in charge, and there is no question of a sale either of the land or its inhabitants. 'Ce que vend ou donne le roi, c'est ni la terre ni le paysans: c'est le produit de la première que permet le travail des seconds.'[32] The continued existence of independent village life in Seleucid Syria, which is amply attested by literary and inscriptional evidence[33] is a further sign of the freedom of the inhabitants in relation to the owner of the estate, and their position is to be judged in relation to the king rather than the owner of the village. The λαοί are free but dependent, and their condition can deteriorate with the changing economic or agricultural situation which makes it impossible for them to meet the demands of the φόρος or royal tribute. In Strabo's words they are 'poor and slaves' (XII, 2. 9) in that their inability to overcome the prevailing economic conditions makes them equivalent to slaves. This very pattern will re-emerge for Galilee at a much later period.

There is then no reason to believe that the land ownership situation in Galilee which we have found in Ptolemaic times was disrupted by the Seleucid take-over.[34] Neither their policy of urbanization nor their administration of the king's land as we can reconstruct this was likely to affect the existing situation in Galilee. The extra villages which Ptolemaios received, as witnessed by the Hefzibah documents, is only what we might have expected both in that area of the country—the Great Plain—and to such a personage.[35] His ownership of extra estates was presumably a gift for services rendered, and is similar to Appollonius' estates at Beth Anath under the Ptolemies. Even there however, the villagers were certainly free and may even have owned, or at least permanently leased, their own lots, so that the owner of the village was rather a mediator between the villagers and the royal administration, and 'the rent' which was paid to him was their share of the φόρος to the central bureaucracy.[36]

The subsequent history of Palestine as well as concrete evidence from different regimes show no radical break with the pattern already established under the Ptolemies and Seleucids, something Alt in particular has underlined with his method of *territorialsge-schichtliche* studies. One might have expected changes, even to the point of the abolition of the large estates, as the Hasmonaeans pushed northwards and included the whole of Palestine within the one cultic community on the basis of the Deuteronomic ideal of the land.[37] This is all the more probable in view of the fact that Antiochus had given orders 'to settle aliens in all their borders and to divide their land into allotments' (1 *Macc* 3:36). Yet there is no mention of action regarding the land in the sources. According to Davies this silence is to be explained by the inner connection between temple and land, so that the religious significance of the latter was implicitly yet deeply expressed in the zeal for the former.[38] At all events, the willingness of harassed Galileans to migrate to Judaea is indicative of how the harsh realities of life had to take precedence over ideas based on Israel's past. Presumably, these were peasants in the region of Ptolemais whose lands had been confiscated for allotments as Antiochus had ordered, but, if our previous reading of the situation is correct, this upheaval was not general in Galilee but localized in the one area where the country-people were most defenseless and open to attack from the neighboring territory.

In the campaigns of the later Hasmonaeans, the only mention of activity in the countryside is Alexander's capture of villages in the region of Scythopolis (*Ant.* 13:280). Significantly, Caesar's decrees renewing (ἀνανεούμενοι) the old treaties between Rome and the Jews, which presumably had been broken by Pompey's arrangement, without proper ratification of the senate,[39] mention this very area and recognize that traditionally these lands have belonged to the Hasmonaean family. 'As for the villages in the Great Plain which Hyrcanus and his forefathers before him possessed, it is the pleasure of the Senate that Hyrcanus and the Jews shall retain them, with the same rights that they formerly had' (*Ant.* 14:207). It seems that this decree should be carefully distinguished from the other more general ones relating to the high priesthood and the Jewish nation as a whole in accordance with their laws.[40] Scythopolis itself is not restored but sections of its territory are left in Jewish hands. Presumably these lands passed from Hasmonaean to Herodian hands, since we hear that in 66 C.E. Berenice, the sister of Agrippa, II owned villages in the Great Plain near Besara on the borders of Ptolemais (*Life* 118), and at the same time Agrippa also had estates in the same region (*Life* 126). At an earlier period Herod had settled veterans at Gaba in the Great Plain, giving them allotments of land (*Ant* 15:294), and on the basis of *War* 3:36 this must have been in the same region as Berenice's estates later. It would seem then that the Great Plain was one area of Palestine where we can locate large private holdings passing from one ruling house to another—the Hellenistic monarchies, the Hasmonaeans and the Herodians. Thus a definite pattern of land ownership appears to be established through the differing regimes, and presumably this would have held true for other areas also—with certain obvious modifications, of course.

It is to the long reign of Herod that we must look for any large-scale change in the position of land-ownership. At the beginning of his reign forty-five of the most prominent supporters of Antigonus were killed (*Ant* 15:5f.). Undoubtedly these were Hasmonaean nobles living in the country—some of them based in Sepphoris, we have argued, and their lands were now at the king's disposal to sell or lease in order to offset the huge financial burdens of his various philanthropic and building programs. On rebuilding Samaria as Sebaste he settled six thousand veterans in its vicinity, apportioning to them the nearby lands, which were the best in the country (*Ant.* 15:296; *War* 1:403). Presumably his adviser, Ptolemy was one of those who received these lands, for later we hear of him owning an estate (κτῆμα) in the vicinity of Samaria where the Roman army of Varus could billet (*Ant.* 17: 289). Another estate of his son Antipater in the same region was said to produce two hundred talents annually (*Ant.* 16:250), certainly an exaggeration in the light of a later reference to fifty talents, but even so no little income from private lands. Augustus put Herod in charge of the lands of the deposed Zenodorus in Transjordan-Trachonitis, Batanaea and Auranitis (*Ant* 15:342f. 360f.), and subsequently he was able to settle Babylonian Jews there on his own terms, a clear sign that Herod owned rather than simply administered the territory (*Ant.* 17:24f.). At his death besides the income guaranteed to his three sons as ethnarchs large private estates were assigned to his sister Salome (*Ant.* 17:321).

We have no direct information of Herod's handling of the land situation in Galilee, but we can presume that the pattern was similar to other parts of the country—the best lands became part of the royal possessions, either through confiscation or because their owners could not meet the heavy taxes which Herod exacted from the country people. We can presume that some at least of the Hasmonaean nobles whom Herod executed owned lands in Galilee since, as we have seen, it was the center of support for Antigonus, and probably these lands had been in their families since the incorporation of the north into the Hasmonaean kingdom. Whether or not Herod retained direct control of the province as one of the *meridarchai* who administered the various districts of his kingdom, as Momigliano suggests,[41] we do find traces of a pro-Herodian nobility there despite the general hostility. Certain notables (δύνατοι) in the province who supported Herod suffered for their loyalty at the hands of the Galileans by being drowned in the Sea of Gennesareth (*Ant* 14:450; cf. 415ff. 432ff.). We can only assume that they had either been confirmed in their lands by Herod as the price of loyalty or had been put there by him on lands which he had taken over during his time as governor when Hezekiah and his followers were killed. Does the manner of their death suggest that they lived in the fertile region of Gennesareth? At all events Herod's son Antipas must have owned private estates in that region with which to endow his new city,

Tiberias (*Ant.* 18:37). Likewise, we can surmise that there were estates in the region of Sepphoris, which he had earlier made the ornament of all Galilee (*Ant.* 18:27). One possible example of such landed gentry in Galilee for Herodian times is Joseph ben Illem who in an emergency functioned as high priest for his cousin Matthias (*Ant* 17:166), and who, according to Talmudic sources was a native of Sepphoris in Galilee.[42]

These scattered indications suggest that Galilee did not escape the advancing aggrandizement of the Herodian dynasty as more and more of the best lands of Palestine fell into their hands and were subsequently donated by them to suitable beneficiaries. Sherwin-White has observed that behind the parables of Jesus are to be found two classes only, the wealthy landowner and the impoverished peasant constantly beset by debts.[43] There is the rich man and his steward and the poor man owing one hundred measures of oil and wheat (*Lk.* 16:1-6); we hear of a king with his debtor owing a huge sum, while he in turn is owed a mere hundred denarii (*Mt.* 18:23-34; *Lk.* 7:41); and the vineyard owner and his lessees (*Mt.* 21:33-41 and parallels) is known to us from the time of Zenon on;[44] the rich fool feels he can enlarge his granaries because of a good harvest yield (*Lk.* 12:13-21); the servants who show their managerial ability with investments can be entrusted with ten or five villages respectively (*Lk.* 14:11-27); the vineyard owner goes in search of hired labor even though he has a bailiff (*Mt.* 20:1-16); the faithful servant makes sure to dispense proper rations of grain to the slaves even when the master is absent (*Lk.* 12:42-46; *Mt.* 24:45-57). It would be hazardous to generalize from these stories to an overall theory of land ownership in Galilee, yet the picture does recur with such frequency that it must have been the dominant one. True one also finds traces of family farms— the father of the prodigal son has to share the inheritance (*Lk.* 15: 11-31); the father needs the help of his sons in the family vineyard (*Mt.* 21:28-32); Zebedee has hired servants as well as his sons engaged in the fish industry (*Mk.* 1:20).[45] These pictures suggest peasant economic conditions rather than those of large land owners, and presumably we can allow for the presence of both systems, despite developments in the Herodian period. The retention of small landowners would have been in line with Roman land policies elsewhere in the early Empire. A peasant

class was an important social stabilizer, and the expropriation of
peasant farmers did not lead inevitably to the absorption of their
farms into large holdings. Thus the large *latefundia* manned by
slaves working under the supervision of a slave bailiff is not necessarily the typical unit. Indeed outside Italy and Sicily agricultural slavery does not seem to have been widely practised in the
Empire.[46]

Looking at the picture that emerges from Josephus' *Life,* the
most dominant single group is 'the Galileans,' who seem to be
found all over the province, just as we might expect (cf. *Life* 99.
102.206f.383). They are usually associated with the land ($\chi\omega\rho\alpha$)
and dwell in villages (*Life* 142.207.242-44). Thus they are carefully distinguished from the inhabitants of the cities, especially
Tiberias, Sepphoris and Gabara. On several occasions they arrive
with provisions to assist Josephus, and in the corresponding *War*
account we read that various towns were easily able to provision
the auxiliary troops each sent to assist Josephus, since half of the
levy imposed on each place stayed at home to arrange for provi-
sioning of supplies ($\sigma\upsilon\nu\pi\omicron\rho\iota\sigma\mu\grave{o}\varsigma\ \tau\hat{\omega}\nu\ \grave{\epsilon}\pi\iota\tau\eta\delta\epsilon\acute{\iota}\omega\nu$) while the other
half were under arms ($\grave{\epsilon}\iota\varsigma\ \grave{o}\pi\lambda\alpha$, *War* 2:583f.). There is nothing
here that directly sheds light on our question of ownership of the
land, but the unmistakable impression is that these country
people are in charge of their own agricultural affairs, and the
assumption must be that not all are simply tenant farmers, even
if, as we shall see, all have to pay taxes. At Gischala many of the
people were not interested in war with Rome because it was time
for sowing (*War* 4:84). Earlier in the same century the country
people (of Galilee, presumably) threatened not to till the ground
because of their objection to Gaius' statue, and Josephus tells us
that Petronius feared 'there would be a harvest of banditry because
the requirements of tribute ($\phi\acute{o}\rho\omicron\varsigma$) could not be met' (*Ant.* 18:274;
War 2:200). These incidents would seem to confirm the sugges-
tion that the Galileans were indeed free landowners, however
small their plots. Owners of large estates or bailiffs do not intrude
themselves into the picture, presumably because for certain areas
at least no such existed —especially, one suspects, in Upper
Galilee.[47]

Absence of direct sources hampers our estimation of how much
Roman resettlement of the land affected Galilee after the year

70 C.E. Quite an amount of land must have become vacant there, due to the hazards of the war, refugees and forced enslavement, according to Josephus more than thirty thousand after the capture of Tarichaeae, though not all were Galileans (*War* 3:540-42). Theoretically both Vespasian and Titus claimed ownership of the whole land. The former gave orders 'to farm out (ἀποδόσθαι) the whole Jewish territory' (*War* 7:216f.)[48] and Titus pointedly reminded the Jews that the Romans had left the land in their possession, allowed them to gather taxes and bring gifts for divine service; yet 'you armed yourselves with *our* money' (*War* 6:333-36). The only settling of foreigners that we hear of is the eight hundred veterans at Emmaus (*War* 7:216f.), so presumably Galilee did fare better than Judaea in this respect. It is not until the reign of Hadrian that Sepphoris and Tiberias had their territories extended to include all Lower Galilee,[49] but we can be sure that the process of parceling out Jewish territory to those who had proved their loyalty during the first revolt had already begun immediately after the reduction of the province. Jews who had been previously befriended by Rome had proved their loyalty in the course of the uprising, as the instance of Sepphoris shows, or even belatedly as in the case of Josephus (*Life* 422). We know that many moderate Jews fled Jerusalem probably to the territory of Agrippa after the failure of his plea to avert the war (*War* 2:418-21.536), and no doubt were subsequently well rewarded for their non-involvement. In all probability those prominent men of Galilee who had acted like the citizens of Tiberias and Sepphoris in refusing to be engaged in the war (*Life* 386) did so in order to preserve their lands. These δοκιμώτατοι would correspond to the wealthy Jewish landowners in Judaea attested by rabbinic sources for the period between 70 and 135 C.E. who had either been left in possession of their lands or had been allowed to lease vacant ones, provided they took responsibility for the taxes.[50]

It is in the period after 70 C.E. that such commentators as Klein and Büchler locate the *'annasîn* and *mesîqîn* (or *mesîqîn*) known to us from rabbinic sources.[51] It seems clear that these people are Jews as well as Gentiles since their selfish tactics against fellow Jews are lamented in several rabbinic texts (*Sifra Lv* 26:17; *Midrash Tannaim, Dt* 32:13; p.198:15-17). It has been

suggested that the terms *'annasîn* and *mesîqîn* indicate the
violent tactics used by these oppressors against their fellow
Jews,[52] but more recently Gil has attempted to explain the terms
in relation to the institutions of *annona*, an oppressive Roman
tax in kind imposed on farmers, and *mēsitēs* (Latin *sequester*) an
officer in charge of the confiscation of mortgaged properties,
who in later times had control of procedures dealing with the
ceding of goods.[53] This would explain the hostility towards them
which is found in the Jewish sources. If this derivation of their
description is correct they would be collaborationists who stood
to profit from the gradual take over of the Jewish land by the
foreigners, either by imposing exorbitant taxes which caused
the owners to cede their lands, or by acquiring legal rights to
mortgaged lands. Furthermore it was due to pressure from Imperial realities that Jewish law eventually yielded in the direction
of recognizing use rather than absolute ownership in its regulations about *hazāqā*. This was an attempt to meet the real circumstances where ownership rights could not be pressed against
superior authority and was the Jewish equivalent of the Greek
and Roman distinction between *usucapio* and *possessio* (κτῆμα
and κρῆσις).[54] While these developments are most easily documented for the second and third centuries, one must place their
origins in the period after the revolt of 70 C.E. when Rome's
dominium of the land had actually been won by the sword,
something that was only further emphasized in the aftermath
of the Bar Cochba revolt.[55]

The law of *siqarikon* seems to presuppose a similar social
situation where less than full rights of ownership of the 'usurping occupant' are reflected in a number of rabbinic regulations.
They do not have to bring the *bikkurim*, or 'first-fruits', since
the law in question speaks of the first fruits of *your land* (*Ex.*
23:19) and they are not recognized as owners of the land (*M. Bikk*
1:2). On the other hand the law of heave offering and second
tithe does apply to them, and in this they are equiparated with
lessees and robbers (*M. Bikk* 2:3). Most commentators of these
particular provisions see in the *siqarikon* law a reflection of the
political situation, and some even attempt to link it with the
actual *sicarii* of the war period.[56] However, these associations

are not very convincing and more promising is Gil's effort to understand the provisions in question in the light of socio-economic conditions in which lands that had been ceded through debt or loan could be acquired in Roman courts.[57] According to *M. Gitt* 5:6 the sale of lands which had been acquired by *siqarikon* in Judaea was not recognized until after the Bar Cochba war, but thereafter a more compromising attitude emerged whereby the sale was regarded as valid, but the original owner was partially compensated. The actual mention of Judaea in this context is particularly significant seeing that in an admittedly much later tradition Galilee is said to be particularly harassed by 'the usurping occupant' גלל לעלם ישומשום סיקריקיקן ; *p.Gitt*5, 47b). Does this mean that Judaean courts attempted to ignore the new situation and to insist on ownership rights until after the second revolt, whereas Galilee was always under pressure to recognize them? This might explain why Judaea rather than Galilee was the center of the second revolt, which had definite social causes. It is impossible to press these texts too far but they do fit admirably the social and economic situation that the first revolt already created in Galilee, and we can see reflected in them further confirmation of the worsening condition of the Galilean peasant between the two revolts, even if the actual traditions themselves stem from a later period. It is interesting to note that a later third century Amora, Ulla, attributes to Johanan ben Zakkai, the famous dictum that because of its ignorance of Torah, Galilee was the particular prey of the *mesiqin (p. Shabb* 16,15d). While the reasons for the statement reflect later controversies, the projection of the social condition back to the pre-70 days corresponds with our own sketch of land relations in the province insofar as we have been able to determine them.[58]

When one looks at this, admittedly fragmentary, survey of land ownership patterns in Palestine as these applied to Galilee, no very definite conclusions can be drawn. Nevertheless it does seem safe to suggest that at least in certain areas private ownership on a small scale did somehow survive side by side with the trend in the direction of the large holding with its tenant farmers.[59] In view of the heavy rate of taxation to be discussed in the next section the distinction may be somewhat theoretic, as in the

days of the Ptolemies. Nevertheless, ownership of the land had a
deeper significance for the Jew than the purely financial consideration. Large holdings are more likely to be in Lower Galilee
where the urban centers of Sepphoris and Tiberias became the
places of residence of wealthy Jewish landowners in the second
century.[60] To what extent this tentative conclusion can allow
us to speak of Galilee having a predominantly peasant culture
will have to be further explored in the remaining sections of
this chapter.

II
COMMERCE AND DISTRIBUTION OF WEALTH

In the previous section we have concentrated on the question
of land ownership in Galilee because agriculture remained the
single most important occupation of the province despite all
the technical advances of the hellenistic age. The older standard
works on Palestinian life such as Neubauer, Heichelheim,
Krauss and Klausner all emphasize the fertility of Galilee, and in
this they are merely reflecting ancient witnesses such as Josephus,
Pliny and the Talmuds, as was already pointed out in the opening
chapter.[61] There can be little doubt that such generalizations
are on the whole accurate — Galilee was and remains the relatively more fertile area of Palestine due to natural and climatic
factors already discussed. Yet, it was also pointed out that even
there conditions varied considerably from one district to another.
The fertile plain of Gennesareth was singled out by Josephus for
special mention (*War* 3:515-21), and the valleys of Lower Galilee,
with their more gentle, undulating terrain were also suited to
intensive farming. Our task here is not to repeat the catalogue
of produce for the various regions, but rather to discuss the developing economic and commercial life of the area in the light
of the changing political situation, paying special attention to
the distribution of any increased wealth or new resources in the
area.

(i) *The Rise of Agro- and Other Industries*

While the hellenistic age witnessed an increase of industry
and commerce with the development and diffusion of technical
skills, it still remained true that agriculture was the backbone of
economic life. Naturally, the new situation brought about

changes even in this ancient occupation of farming, and if Galilee were to profit from the improved conditions it too had to avail of the new techniques and skills now being employed.[62]

Fortunately we can document such developments in agriculture for Ptolemaic Egypt with a fair amount of detail, and these reflect similar developments in Palestine. As portrayed in the Zenon correspondence we find that the state monopolies and controls are operative there also. This emerges in particular from Zenon's journey, which has all the appearances of an official tour of inspection even though private business was also apparently conducted. Apart from the slave trade, the chief Egyptian imports mentioned are grain (especially wheat) and oil, and presumably also wine. However the export of these goods from Palestine and their import into Egypt were under the strictest state control, and in order to profit from the enterprise one needed to be a highly placed official such as the διοικήτης Apollonius or an immediate official of his like Zenon.[63] What is really taking place is the transformation of Palestinian agriculture into agrobusiness, controlled and monopolized by outside agencies, to whom there was no recourse, unlike the days of social injustice under Nehemiah and the Persians (*Neh* 5:1-13). Then at least the state religion could be invoked in an attempt to prevent small landowners having to barter their lands and even their children to meet tax demands and high rates of interest from fellow Jews. Now however no such sacral sanctions could be invoked, and all that remained for the peasants was to accept whatever crumbs their foreign overlords were willing to grant them, such as better living conditions at Beth Anath or royal philanthropy in a hard year (*PSI* 554). Occasionally under a native chief such as Jeddua (*PCZ* 59018) they could give a fleeting display of independence, only to be crushed or appeased, but without any greater possibility of improving their economic situation by sharing in the increased productivity and output of the land.[64]

Increased productivity and diversification certainly appear to have been Ptolemaic agricultural policy in Galilee, and no doubt elsewhere in Palestine also. In the year 257 B.C.E., only two years after Zenon's visit, a report by Glaukias, another agent of Apollonius, relates that the wine of Beth Anath is comparable to that from the island of Chios — presumably because techniques of viticulture as well as new strains of vine had been introduced there by Apollonius.[65] Hengel surmises that this attempt to improve the native wine was Apollonius'way of competing with the import of their own native wines, preferred by the Greek officials, which is amply demonstrated by the many Greek jars found in the material remains of hellenistic Palestine.[66] Glaukias' report mentions 80,000 vine in the estate which gives some indication of the intensity of the farming.[67] We also hear of a large well being sunk at the estate, presumably to meet water shortage during a drought, and also to counter the complaints of tenants that they could not meet their lease agreements due to failure of the fig crop through lack of water.[68] In all probability this estate also produced grain, and we know for certain that grain was transported from Galilee to Sidon (*PCZ 2*, col III), presumably from the royal estates, since the official procedures for its export to Egypt were strictly controlled and the merchants dealing in the grain appear simply as middlemen between the local officials of the government and the agents in Egypt.[69] In such circumstances private profits would be minimal and it is little wonder that various individuals engaged in underhand slave trade in order to increase their earnings.[70] Finally, we hear of oil being exported from Palestine to Egypt — again with rigid state controls both at points of export and import, due to the Egyptian oil monopoly.[71]

The diversification of Galilean agricultural produce in hellenistic times is further illustrated from other papyri. Among various lists of imports to Egypt from Syria we read of dried figs, cheese, salted fish, sea fish, all sorts of meat, honey, pomegranate seeds and mushrooms. Not all come from Galilee, or only from there, yet the unmistakable impression is that the province which served as the natural hinterland for the ports of Tyre, Sidon and Ptolemais produced many of the goods listed in these export catalogues.[72] A rich variety of vegetables, fodder, herbs and other plants are found in the later Talmudic literature — a much more varied assortment than one finds in the Old Testament, and one is justified in accepting Hengel's suggestion, following Heichelheim, that the beginnings of such expansion in farming and gardening must date from hellenistic times.[73] In particular Strabo mentions that the rare balsam tree was found in the

Gennesareth plain, which thus shared with Jericho and Engeddi
in the almost total monopoly of this highly treasured commodity
in the ancient world.[74] No doubt this diversification and exploitation of the natural resources of Galilee was due not only to the
influx of outside population in hellenistic times, but also to better
techniques of farming and irrigation, as well as the more sophisticated knowledge of plants and climate which the hellenistic
monarchies fostered for their own financial gain.

Rostovtzeff asks a very pertinent question concerning the
extent of the influence of this technical knowledge on the native
peasants in their small holdings, as distinct from the crown
lands and larger estates.[75] Unfortunately there is very little hard
evidence on which one could build any hypothesis. One can only
conjecture that while Apollonius and his agents were concerned
to make the country as economically productive as possible, they
concentrated mainly on those estates in which they had personal
interest. At least, that is the impression one gets, which makes
it difficult to decide at times whether or not they are acting in
an official or private capacity. In short, one does not meet a
general policy of improvement for all, comparable to a modern
socialization program from a central government. If, as seems
likely, the larger tenant farmers of the royal estates were at first
foreigners rather than natives,[76] the process of dissemination of
new ideas from the large estates to the smaller holdings must
have been slower and would ultimately be dependent on the
assimilation of foreign and native populations through intermarriage over several generations. As Rostovtzeff writes, 'The
general impression left on the student is that the estates managed
in the Greek manner remained scattered islands in the oriental
sea of small peasant holdings and larger estates, whose native
owners had their own traditional methods of exploitation and
cultivation.'[77] The parable of the sower with his oriental method
of scattering the seed may be a small piece of evidence to sub-
stantiate that conclusion for two centuries later.[78]

Turning from agriculture to other aspects of industrial development, there seems to be little evidence for any large-scale
impact on life in Galilee. The fish industry is one possible exception. Mention of salted fish occurred in the Zenon papyri as an
export from Syria,[79] and the changing of the name of Magdala

to Tarichaea is generally associated with this development in Ptolemaic times.[80] Of course both Josephus and the New Testament give ample witness to the continued importance of this industry along the shores of the Sea of Galilee (*War* 3:508. 520; *Life* 165ff.; *Mk.* 1:16-20; *Mt.* 17:27; *Lk* 5:1-11; *Jn* 21). However, as Rostovtzeff points out, fishing techniques were highly developed already in classical times, as is evidenced by the various treatises on the matter from Aristotle and others, and the rise of the hellenistic monarchies was not likely to bring about any large-scale changes. What was new however, was the methods of preservation and marketing, and we have positive evidence from Egypt of how this was controlled by a large-scale enterprise, either a royal concern or one managed by the holder of a gift estate. According to the document in question (*P. Teb* 701) we see that the king or holder of the estate made a large amount of profit, whereas the fishermen made very little. According to another system mentioned in the same document the fishing rights were farmed out at a very high rate of between thirty and forty per cent of the total catch, which shows once more the tight state control of all aspects of the Egyptian economy.[81] Presumably similar conditions obtained in Palestine also. In fact Josephus mentions one species of fish found in the Sea of Galilee, the *coracin*, which was primarily known from the Nile in Egypt and the lakes around Alexandria (*War* 3:520).[82] This slight indication may be a pointer that in fact the waters of the lake were re-stocked as part of a government fisheries' policy. At all events, given this overall state of affairs related to the fish industry, it is unlikely that small Galilean fishermen would profit from the new markets and better techniques of preservation, even if these were carried out on such a scale that one of the older settlements along the lake front, Magdala, received a Greek name from the new industry.

Another industrial development which appears to have taken place in Galilee in hellenistic times is the emergence of a glass-making industry. Pliny (*Nat. Hist.* 36,191) attributes the development of the art of glass blowing to the Phoenicians in the 1st century B.C.E., thereby replacing older forms of the art such as use of moulds or hewing out of solid blocks of cast glass in imitation of metalware, methods that had been used in Egypt for centuries. However, even before the discovery of the new techniques, Egyptian glassware showed distinct signs of new vitality in the hellenistic age, especially in terms of gold ornamentation.[83] What is of special interest is that the plain of Acco on the borders of Galilee provided the raw material for this industry, with its vitreous sand mentioned by both Strabo and Josephus (*Geographica* XVI, 2, 25. 35; *War* 2:190f.), in this connection it is interesting to note that recent excavations at Tel Anafa in Upper Galilee have unearthed large quantities of glassware — pieces of 80 vessels in all — dating from the middle of the 2nd century B.C.E. Such a quantity of remains for a period before the invention of glass-blowing is a rare discovery, since normally only a few pieces are found on hellenistic sites for the earlier period. After the year 50 B.C.E. the market was flooded with blown glass and Talmudic evidence shows that it was relatively frequent in Palestine at a later period also. Yet, there is not a single trace of blown glass at Tel Anafa![84] The only feasible conclusion would seem to be that it was as a center of the glass industry at an earlier period, probably under the influence of Phoenician and Egyptian craftsmen, but that subsequently the town declined for other reasons, and did not continue into Hasmonaean and Roman times as the thriving metropolis it had been.[85] Nevertheless, the presence of such an industrial center in this fairly remote part of Upper Galilee during Ptolemaic times is indicative of how widespread and diversified hellenistic influences were on this relatively rural outpost of Egyptian territory.

These are the only examples of early hellenistic industrialization to be found in Galilee in the literary records or material remains. While this in itself does not allow us to draw firm conclusions, it can be seen that on the whole it was peripheral to the lives of the countrypeople and was likely to have remained so. The development of such a natural resource as the lake and its fish might have been expected to bring advantages to a sizable part of the population, but from what we know of the controls that were exercised on the fish industry elsewhere and the farming out of fishing rights to middlemen at high rates, it was clear that any advantages accruing from better marketing facilities would be beyong the reach of the average Galilean. It is in this area of the lake front that we are likely to find the most thriving commercial life and the greatest concentration of outsiders. For the peasants of the interior the impact on their lives of the more intensive and commercialized farming was of greater significance. No doubt the familial arts and crafts such as spinning and weaving for which the Galilean women are praised in the Talmud are the survival of local, indigenous non-commercial industry, as part of the everyday life of rural people.[86]

(ii) The Distribution of Wealth

On surveying these various economic developments in Galilee in hellenistic times one important fact emerges — the increased possibilities were clearly to the advantage of the few rather than the many. It is true of course that peasant economies are always slow to reflect wider economic growth precisely because the peasant runs his farm on considerations other than financial — considerations such as family loyalty and faithfulness to ancestral ways.[87] A lack of interest in the purely commercial aspects of running a farm tends to make him oblivious to changing economic and industrial patterns. Adherence to old ways rather than experimentation or adaptation becomes the hallmark of the peasant's existence in every aspect of life. In surveying the question of land ownership in Galilee we have argued that small landowners somehow managed to survive the various social and economic changes that occurred there throughout the period of our survey. Insofar as this is an accurate assessment of the situation it is only reasonable to expect the general outline of peasant economics to be verified there also. Sherwin-White has astutely remarked that there is one obvious difference between the social world of the Gospels on the one hand and Acts of the Apostles on the other. This difference concerns the absence of any middle-class in the gospels' background as distinct from the picture in Acts where we meet the traders, craftsmen and other officials of the hellenistic cities.[88] Such an observation based on the world of Galilee as reflected in the Gospels agrees rather well with the larger picture we are able to reconstruct from other sources. We must briefly examine those factors which controlled the distribution of wealth there before attempting to outline the resulting social stratification within the area.

For the earlier period of Ptolemaic and Seleucid domination it is obvious that the real sources of productive wealth were in the hands of foreigners and the increased prosperity of Galilee inevitably fell into the hands of the few. The state monopolies and control of the exports of all essential produce such as wheat, wine, oil and fish ensured that there was very little room for the enterprising native who might try his hand in exploiting the larger markets. The undercover activity in the slave trade of Heracletus the coachman of *PSI* 406 and his colleagues is indicative of the lack of real commercial possibilties that the whole new situation offered for all but those controlling the royal monopolies and their immediate agents.[89] The rise of indigenous aristocracy under Hasmonaean and later Herodian control did not lead to any grater democratization of the native resources of wealth. True, John of Gischala fits the category of opportunistic entrepreneur rather than aristocratic landowner. But he may well have been the exception who was able to exploit the proximity of his native area to the large commercial center of Tyre, all his pietistic protestations notwithstanding. Certainly the situation reflected at Tiberias does not disprove this contention, since the Herodian aristocracy of that town owed their wealth to their land rather than to commercial or other business occupation (cf. *Life* 33). All this is not meant to completely exclude small, but successful businesses, especially in the towns along the lake shore, and at the larger centers inland; the need for services other than agricultural labor must have existed, even when the means of production were in the hands of the few. In such situations those members of the peasantry who could find local employment either in relation to the fish industry or as skilled artisans of one kind or another would still be under enormous pressure to retain their peasant associations. We shall have occasion to return to this rural proletariat later. Here we want to stress that at no time in Galilee's history do we find traces of the outside political agents who might have been instrumental in initiating widespread economic reform or change in the social fabric of life there.[90] Qoheleth's observation about the aristocracy of his own day continued to ring true. No matter what step of the ladder one had reached there was always someone higher, a situation which made life essentially unstable, if not precarious. Even Antipas could be deprived of his possessions, and benevolence to the deprived does not dominate in such a situation.

Other factors also determined the economic realities of Galilean life for the period under discussion. Lack of any long-term planning left the peasant farmer open to the vagaries of the seasons and the uncertainties of the markets.[91] Josephus records a number of instances when one bad harvest created great physical hardship and economic disaster for the people (*Ant.* 14:28; 15:299f. 365; 16:64; 18:8; 20:101). Talmudic evidence confirms the picture for situations after 70 C.E. (*b. Ta'an* 24b; *b. Ketub* 97; *b. Ta'an* 19bf.; cf. *Ac* 11:27-30). In such circumstances towns-people were liable to be even worse off than those in the country, but for either, relief from the ruling authority was only temporary and the essentially unstable situation was likely to reassert itself at any time. Josephus paints a particularly gruesome picture of people even being deprived of clothing because of the failure of flocks and without the seeds for the next year's planting (*Ant.* 15:310. 302f.). Herod, for all his brutality in other spheres, seems to have been sensitive to the needs of his subjects in such circum-stances, even allowing for the pro-Herodian source of Josephus and Herod's own desire to ingratiate himself with his alienated subjects. In particular the tax-relief of 20 B.C.E. in which he remitted one third of the taxes of the people of his kingdom 'under pretext of letting them recover from a period of lack of crops' (*Ant* 15:365), seems to have been prompted by attitudes of dissent among both country and townspeople, which may be inferred from the other harsh measures outlined in that context. Such concessions only serve to underline the basic problems of the peasant, as can be illustrated for a later period when the Jewish leaders appeal to Petronius in the case of the statue of Gaius Caligula to be erected in the temple at Jerusalem. Their fear was that the agricultural strike of the (Galilean?) peasants would lead to a harvest of banditry 'because the requirements of tribute could not be met' (*Ant.* 18:274). In other words, a large part of the fruits of the peasants' labor went to others and any disruption of this only served to make his position still more precarious.[92] Alternatively, the smaller peasant was not able to make the most of the economic possibilities of a good year, since the market was over-supplied and prices fluctuated considerably to the advantage of the more wealthy landowners whose margin of profit did not need to be so great.[93]

Besides the natural hazards of climate and the resulting fluctuation of the market, the Galilean peasant had to contend with the more serious problem of constant wars with all the resulting evils for the native inhabitants. As has already emerged from our survey of the history of Galilee the area was a battlefield throughout the whole of our period, with a few notable exceptions, e.g. during the reign of Antipas and again at the end of our period after the war of 67 C.E. This was not necessarily due to the fact that the Galileans were any more rebellious or militant than the inhabitants of other areas — a fact we shall examine in greater detail later — but rather because it did represent a homogenous and to some degree independent area at one of the major crossroads beween east and west. The effects of this crisscrossing of Galilee by opposing armies from the days of Antiochus III to Vespasian was to make further demands on the already overextended resources of the country people of the province, to the point where many of them were forced into slavery. The Zenon papyri already testify to a thriving slave trade between Palestine and Egypt, some legitimate and some counterfeit. No doubt Galileans figure among the captives, seeing that Ptolemaic officials included the area in their tour of inspection of royal estates. Later we hear of Philoteria and Scythopolis providing Antiochus with adequate supplies for his army in the campaigns of the fourth and fifth Syrian Wars. The Hefzibah inscriptions from the neighborhood of Scythopolis show that the billeting of soldiers among the villages was a constant threat for the countrypeople of that area. Much later the decrees of Caesar offer respite from this dreaded burden (*Ant.* 14:202).[94] At least some Galileans chose to abandon their posessions rather than suffer harassment from their neighbors in the Syrian towns of the coast after the reform of Antiochus IV (*1 Macc.* 5:15), yet the interior of Galilee continued to be the battleground for the emerging Hasmonaeans and successive Syrian pretenders throughout the 2nd century B.C.E. The respite was short-lived, since the Hasmonaean Aristobulus II and later his son Antigonus made Galilee the base of operation in their attempts to recapture their kingdom. Thirty thousand men from Tarichaeae were sold into slavery by Cassius after Crassus' defeat at Carrhae in 53 B.C.E. In Herod's struggles against

Antigonus we hear of Galilee (as well as other parts) supplying his army with provisions and winter quarters for the Roman troops (*Ant.* 14:411.414; cf. 408). On the death of Herod the disturbances at Sepphoris caused the enslavement of many of its inhabitants (*Ant.* 17:289). On several occasions we hear of Josephus' orders to the Galileans to assemble under arms *with provisions* (*Life* 212.242), thus indicating that the Galilean peasant even at that late period, stood to lose a lot of his hard-earned food supplies if he became embroiled in military action. Elsewhere Josephus intimates that in organizing the rather free-flowing army of Galilean regulars, half the male force of each area was engaged in supplying provisions while the other half made ready for the impending struggle (*War* 2:584). Little wonder that the farming stock from the Gischala neighborhood were anything but anxious for action, being much more concerned for their crops (*War* 4:84). The Roman reduction of the province during the revolt of 66-67 C.E. was ruthless and undiscriminating. A scorched earth policy terrified the countrypeople and those resisting were sold in slavery to work at Corinth after the final reduction of Tarichaeae. When one adds to this catalogue the hazards from banditry in border areas[95] from the days of Herod to the Jewish Revolt, it becomes apparent that the economic position of the Galilean peasant was anything but secure. The country area between Ptolemais and Sepphoris was particularly vulnerable, it would appear, but all alike must have lived in constant danger of having their possessions seized, their homes destroyed and their liberty taken from them, caught as they were between opposing political forces from outside over which they had no control.

It is generally recognized that the introduction of money enormously increased the possibilties for trade in the ancient world. Surpluses could be exported and achieve a better margin of profit for their producers, and they in turn were capable of much more flexibility in commercial enterprises, since the barter system necessitated dealing at a fairly local level and over a limited range of goods. However, it is doubtful if the more extensive use of money as a medium of exchange in hellenistic and Roman times brought any real advantages to the Galilean peasant. From the Zenon papyri we see that money rather than barter was more usual, but the fact that the state had such a tight monopoly on the essential produce of Galilee — wheat, wine, and oil — meant that the traders had no direct access to the producers, and the peasants, rather than attempting to bargain for better prices, would have had to relinquish their surplus in taxes or tribute to the government, as we see happening at Beth Anath. The fact that the Hasmonaean Simon was allowed to strike his own coinage was seen as a great step forward in the thrust towards an independent state, and might have been expected to eventually increase the economic opportunities for all who were part of the new state (*1 Macc.* 15:6). However, economic and social realities usually outweigh national and religious loyalties. The expense of maintaining a full-scale army for John Hyrcanus' and Alexander Jannaeus' wars of expansion meant that money, not just tithes, was required to keep mercenaries happy and this must have put a severe strain on the resources of the people, town and country alike. Throughout the whole period of our investigation Tyrian coinage remained by far the most popular currency in Palestine and this indicates that financial rather than national interests prevailed. The new native and hellenized aristocracy of the Hasmonaean state did not allow religious affiliations to control their lives to the point that a stable and highly respected international currency would be abandoned for a native one that could not command the same confidence and was subject to fluctuation as a result of factors outside their control. Indeed, so powerful was this consideration that, as is well known, Tyrian coinage became the 'money of the sanctuary' to the end of the Temple period, despite the sensitivity of Jews concerning their own coinage at the periods of the two revolts against Rome.[96]

There would seem then to be little likelihood of the poorer countrypeople being able to break out of their deprived condition through the possibilities that the wider use of money created. Whatever limited amount they might earn as laborers or obtain through trading at local markets was quickly eaten up with little chance for investment or expansion. The mention of an *agoranomos* at Tiberias controlling the market, and *trapezai* and *archeai* at Sepphoris for the money changers and lenders are mere passing indications of the harsh realities of peasant economics in Galilee. Toll fees had to be paid for the transportation of goods from one district to another — Levi of Caphernaum is a reminder of that fact for Galilee (*Mt.* 9:9) — so that there was little incentive for 'the small man' to go in search of better markets.[97] No doubt Jewish communities in such centers as Tyre or Caesarea Philippi (cf. *Life* 74f.) would have preferred and even sought out goods that were produced in Eretz Israel, but even then it was such opportunists and middlemen as John of Gischala who stood to make the real profit, not the native producer (*War* 2:591f.). According to *Mt.* 20:2.9.13 a denarius is the usual day's wages for a hired laborer at the time of Jesus and this represented the cost of one *sea'* of wheat in a good season according to *b. Ta'an* 19b , but this price varied considerably apparently, since the same amount could cost four to eight denarii according to *M. Ma'as Sch.* 4:6.[98] The fact that Justus of Tiberias bemoans the transfer of the *trapezai* and *archeai*[99] of the money lenders to Sepphoris shows that these could be a source of great revenue for a city (*Life* 38). No doubt the chief victims were countrypeople who had fallen behind with taxes or rent or needed the money to buy seeds for planting in a bad season. The gospel story of the dishonest manager (*Lk.* 16:1-7) fits this situation perfectly, where debts were paid in kind in order not to violate the prescriptions of the Jewish laws about usury. In this case the dishonest manager forewent his own profits — an accepted reality of life apparently — and simply asked the debtors to pay the amount owed to the owner of the estate, thereby ingratiating himself with them for the future.[100] The lot of those who failed to pay such debts is graphically portrayed in such parables as the unjust steward (*Mt.* 18:25-34) and the talents (*Mt.* 25:14-30), though there could also be exceptions (*Lk.* 7:41f.).

The fluctuations of the political and economic pendula were naturally felt most keenly at the bottom of the social scale. As can be imagined, conditions were particularly difficult after the Jewish wars and these are reflected in many passages in the rabbinic literature, where we find regulations against speculators who raise the price of essential foodstuff at times of national crisis.[101] Devaluation of money, which took place by lowering the percentage of silver in the coins seems to have had an immediate impact on prices, though apparently Palestine fared somewhat better than elsewhere in the empire under this heading.[102] Earlier we have argued that Galilee's relations with Tyre were ambivalent, as the latter both posed the threat of territorial aggrandizer and offered possibilities for commercial and economic relations, for the city desperately needed the foodstuff of the interior. It may be that it was these very possibilities which made it possible for Galilean peasants — especially in Upper Galilee — to survive all the social changes of the centuries despite all the pressures of brigandage, agrobusiness and state monopolies.

(iii) *The Burden of Taxation*

It was the tax system which was particularly burdensome to the peasants' economic situation. As Grant has pointed out, two quite independent systems operated - one religious and the other secular - and each pressed its full demands without taking any account of the exigencies of the other.[103] Later we shall see that the Galileans took their tithe offerings seriously right through our period. The majority of the Jewish population of the province would have been producers from the land, no matter how small their plots, and it was this produce that was subject to the tithing laws. By itself this system would have put a severe strain on the resources of the smaller landowners and tenant farmers, but it is the secular tax system that was a particular problem, since there was little or no redress, and the ordinary people were at the mercy of the financial needs of the rulers, foreign and native alike. And these were many. Constant wars with the inevitable disruption of life and devastation of the country, the need to maintain an adequate permanent army, and in peace times the elaborate building and other projects of the Herods coupled with their extravagant life style — all made heavy demands on the central treasury.

Already we can see the subsequent pattern set in the tax-net of Ptolemaic times which was modelled on the Greek system. Melas is the κωμομισθωτὴς of Beth Anath and his responsibilities covered the contracts of tenants and native farmers alike. His role can best be seen as a government official in charge of the leasing of land and gathering of taxes at the village level.[104] Presumably a hierarchy of such officials operated from the village to the hyparchy, all under the direct control of the royal finance minister (ὁικονομὸς) in Egypt. Side by side with, or possibly linked to this official bureaucratic control was the farming out of the taxes of particular villages, city territories or larger units, as we can gather from Josephus, who mentions that 'the prominent men (of Palestine) purchased the right to farm the taxes in their several provinces, and collecting the sum fixed, paid it to the royal couple,' whose dowry it was to be (*Ant.* 12:155). This passage seems to presuppose local magistrates operating as tax-farmers being acceptable to the state, and whatever be the historical facts behind the legend of the energetic Tobiad Joseph, it seems certain that his initiative in suggesting one tax-farmer for the whole area won favor in the Ptolemaic court, because it presumably involved greater revenue (*Ant.* 12:169.175ff.).[105] The effects of such a policy can be seen in his confrontation with the people of Askalon and Scythopolis subsequently (*Ant.* 12:180-85) — those without defense were at the mercy of ruthless and self-seeking power climbers. Clearly Jews are prepared to be part of this system, since the tax-farmers were originally local magistrates, and Joseph's success is due to his being more ambitious and so more courageous than the others. The possibilities of effective resistance for the peasants were slim despite their protests of unfair treatment or seasonal hardships, as we see at Beth Anath. The net was cast too widely and the central control too rigid, except for the rare exception of Jeddua and his villagers, whose independence we have already discussed, or such occasional temporary exemptions as the Vienna papyrus indicates.[106]

The letter of Antiochus III (*Ant.* 12:138-44) written sometime after 198 B.C.E. might appear at first sight to have brought considerable tax relief to all the Jewish population of Palestine, since it is addressed to Ptolemy, the governor of Coele-Syria, and could conceivably include all the Jews under his jurisdiction. However, on closer inspection one can recognize the validity of Bickerman's description, 'the Seleucid charter for Jerusalem,' since tax relief was aimed primarily at the restoration of Jerusalem and for the benefit of its cultic officials. In § 142 we hear that 'all the members of this nation (πάντες οἱ ἐκ τοῦ ἔθνοῦς) shall have a form of government in accordance with the laws of their country,' but the actual remission of taxes is granted 'to the senate, the priests, the scribes of the temple and the temple-singers,' while the reduction of the tribute is only for Jerusalem itself. Undoubtedly, *ethnos* in this context does not mean the whole Jewish nation wherever they may be, and as noted, it is only the religious aspects of the concessions that extended outside Judaea of Persian times.[107] Be that as it may, the important fact for our present discussion is that the reduction of taxes, both personal and communal is strictly circumscribed — the remission of personal taxes (ὧν ὑπὲρ τῆς κεφαλῆς τελοῦσιν), including salt and crown taxes, is granted only to the aristocracy and certain temple officials, and the reduction of the tribute (φόρος) is confined to Jerusalem itself. This is apparently the only clear reference to a head or poll tax in Seleucid times, and the tone of the expression ὧν . . . . τελοῦσιν is taken by Schürer and Bickerman to refer to a general head tax that may have varied considerably in degree but was personal in nature as distinct from the tribute or φόρος to be paid collectively by the whole community.[108] We have no direct evidence of a head tax for Ptolemaic Palestine, but this partial remission by the first Seleucids suggests that one was in fact imposed in Palestine (Phoenicia and Coele-Syria) as distinct from Egypt. In all probability the Ptolemies were not content with the annual tribute alone, but gradually introduced a number of royal taxes in addition, designed to reach every member of the population, city and country person alike.[109] The letter of Antiochus III indicates the partial remission of these, but since Galilee cannot arguably be included in the area to which the concessions were granted, we catch a glimpse of the burden the peasant there had to bear.

Developments of the later Seleucids help to underline and expand this fact further. In *1 Macc* we have two letters, one from Demetrius I (152 B.C.E.) and the other from his son Demetrius II ten years later, both addressed to the Jewish leader Jonathan offering certain tax remissions to Judaea, and these enable us to see how tightly the screw has been turned in the interim (*1 Macc.* 10:29-35; 11:32-37; cf. *Ant.* 13:48-57). What emerges from these letters is the fact that an exorbitant land tax (one third of the produce of land and one half of the produce of the trees) is now being remitted to the people of Judaea and the three districts of

Samaria and Galilee being ceded to it. The origin and extent of this tax is not absolutely clear. Bickerman and Rostovtzeff see it as an extra tax beside the tribute for which the temple state of Judaea was collectively responsible, but disagree as to its origins, the former assuming it to be the result of disturbances in Maccabaean times whereas the latter considers it to have originated already under the Ptolemies.[110] For him the only innovation of the Seleucids was the collecting of the taxes directly 'in addition to and not as part of the tribute.' However, there are serious arguments in favor of the suggestion that the land tax was a new tax introduced in place of the tribute when Antiochus IV abrogated the ethnic privileges of Judaea and Jerusalem after the revolt of Jason in 168 B.C.E.[111] The payment of the tribute by a formal vassal state was no longer feasible or admissible and instead a severe land tax was imposed on the former cultic community to be directly collected by the Seleucid officials at the local levels. Thus, Judaea and Samaria were temporarily reduced from the status of the territory of an *ethnos* to that of kingsland, which had been the status of Galilee all along, as Alt has convincingly argued.[112] Presumably this meant that taxes which had previously been operative in kingsland elsewhere were now imposed in Judaea and Samaria also. If this line of argumentation is correct there can be little doubt that Galilean land taxes were exorbitantly high, and may have been so since Ptolemaic times, since the figure mentioned in *1 Macc*. 10:41 corresponds to those of the land taxes of Egypt.[113] If in addition one takes account of the religious dues and the provision of seeds for the following season, at best mere subsistence farming was all that was possible.

The emergence of the Hasmonaean state could only have improved the financial lot of the ordinary people, as we see happening in the concessions Demetrius I is prepared to grant them. In actual fact Jonathan refused the offer of Demetrius since he backed his rival Alexander Balas in the Syrian power struggle. As a result he may have had to pay him tribute, for according to Josephus, Alexander's successor, Demetrius II, expected the annual payment of tribute 'which the Jewish nation was required to pay since the time of the first kings' (*Ant.* 13:143), even though he had previously recognized the tax concessions offered

earlier by his father (*1 Macc.* 11:28). The matter obviously remained a delicate one subsequently (cf. *1 Macc.* 13:15), and even
though no formal lifting of the tribute is actually recorded or
likely to have been granted, a *de facto* situation gradually emerged
where the Syrians were no longer able to enforce their claims,
nor were the Jews willing to pay. As *1 Macc.* 13:41 puts it: 'In the
170th year (i.e., 140 B.C.E.) the yoke of the Gentiles was lifted
from Israel.' However, it was not until the reign of Aristobulus I
(104 B.C.E.) that all Galilee was formally included in the Hasmonaean state, and by then a new tax net must have begun to be
cast, as the finances of the militantly expanding state became
more complex and demanding. Schalit sees the beginnings of a
national tax under John Hyrcanus reflected in an ancient *baraita*
which suggests that the tithe was divided into three parts: 'one-
third was given to priests and Levites known (to the donor), one-
third went to the treasury and one-third went to the poor and
scholars who were in Jerusalem' (*p. Ma'as Sch.* 5,9; *p. Sota* 9,24a),
thus recognizing both the religious and political power of the
king.[114] The many wars and internal strife of Alexander Jannaeus' reign may be reflected by the author of the *Psalms of
Solomon*, claiming that the Messiah King 'would not multiply
gold and silver for war' (*Ps. Sol.* 17:33). The dissatisfaction with
the house of Hasmon which the Pharisaic faction expressed to
Pompey, 'that they (Hyrcanus and Aristobulus) were seeking
to change the form of government in order that they might become a nation of slaves' (*Ant.* 14:41), presumably had an economic as well as a religious point. Later Caesar in his decree in
favor of Hyrcanus stressed the obligation to pay the tithes to him
as they had done previously, no doubt because there had been
some resistance to it on the part of ordinary people (*Ant.* 14:202).

Meanwhile a new and decisive force had entered Palestinian
economic life with Pompey's, and later, Gabinius' carving up
of the Hasmonaean state, and the parceling out of its revenues
for interests other than the good of the native population. This
in turn opened up possibilities for others like Antipater, and in
particular Herod to ingratiate themselves with the foreign power.
There was no surer sign of support for Roman policy than by
providing the different Roman generals with financial and other

aid, the burden of which was carried ultimately by the people. We shall now examine the way in which Galilean economic life was affected by these new factors.

As part of the Jewish territory which Pompey recognised, Galilee had to pay its share of the tribute imposed on the Jerusalem community (*Ant.* 14:74; *War* 1:154), the collection of which would normally be the responsibility of the Jewish high priest, as the recognized ethnarch of the Jewish community. However, the fact that Josephus mentions a total sum of ten thousand talents exacted in a short space of time — presumably between Pompey's settlement and Gabinius' subsequent arrangement of 57-55 B.C.E. — suggests that a more ruthless method was introduced by Pompey, in the form of the Roman *societas publicanorum*, who followed the Roman armies, cashing in on their victories in various ways. This is Momigliano's contention, basing himself on some remarks of Cicero as well as Dion.[115] In that event Gabinius' subsequent fivefold division of Palestine must be regarded as an improvement from a Jewish point of view, but only for those who could avail of the opportunities which the aristocratic form of government of Gabinius had to offer (*War* 1:169f.; *Ant.* 14:91). Whether or not the division was intended to be rigidly enforced, as had been done by Lucius Aemilius Paulus in Macedonia with disastrous economic results, is not absolutely clear,[116] but at all events the frequent disturbances of the next few years must have suggested to the Romans that no such policy could be imposed on the Jewish nation. This was clearly recognized by Caesar, for he restored Hyrcanus as ethnarch of the Jews and appointed Antipater as his financial overseer in 47 B.C.E. (*Ant.* 14:143).[117] In gratitude for the military aid he had received, Caesar also made tax concessions of a substantial nature to the Jews, including Galilee which was now properly regarded as Jewish territory and included in the ethnarchy of Hyrcanus. The exact extent of these tax alleviations depends on an interpretation of the decrees of Caesar as reported by Josephus (*Ant.* 14:190-216), who apparently has abridged official documents, and various scholars have attempted to reconstruct their originals in the light of their overall understanding of the Roman tax system in Palestine.[118]

It is certainly clear that Josephus intends these decrees to be understood as an act of friendship on the part of Caesar towards the Jewish people, and by comparison with Pompey's arrangement their situation had improved.[119] The Jews have now to pay one-fourth of the produce of the land (τὸ τέταρτον τῶν σπειρομένων) "in the second year" (τῷ δευτέρῳ ἔτει) at Sidon, excepting the seventh or sabbatical year. Two questions arise from this difficult passage. Firstly does τῷ δευτέρῳ ἔτει mean every second year, as Momigliano and Heichelheim suppose, or alternatively does it refer to the second year of the lease cycle, on the basis of *Ant.* 14:201 where a later decree of 44 B.C.E. states that in the second year of the rent term (ἐν τῷ δευτέρῳ τῆς μισθώσεως ἔτει) the Jews should deduct one *cor* from their taxes?[120] Related to this question is a second one concerning the nature of the tax in question. Clearly it is a land tax, but is it the total Jewish tribute or simply a supplementary tax (to be paid every second year or on the second year of the cycle)[121] on top of an annual poll tax?[122] Momigliano argues strongly for the former position claiming that our sources have no evidence of a poll tax paid by the Jews to the Romans before 70 C.E.[123] but others, especially Rostovtzeff and Büchler,[124] seem to presuppose it, and regard the payment at Sidon as a supplementary land tax, considerably reduced from Seleucid times, when the annual percentage was one third (grain) and one half (trees), whereas now the bi-annual is one quarter. On the evidence available it seems impossible to decide these questions finally. We have argued, against Rostovtzeff, that the Seleucid tribute had been turned into a land-tax, and in that event the force of his argument would be considerably weakened, since it seems correct to assume that the decrees of Caesar in 47 B.C.E. resurrected the tax structure of Seleucid times, but with the reduction in the percentage of agricultural produce to be paid. On that understanding the Jewish peasants should have fared considerably better than in the previous century. The formal recognition by Rome of the sabbatical year was also a bonus, but on the other hand it is clear that all Jews had to pay a tax for the city of Jerusalem (presumably for its restoration after Pompey's attack and to reimburse the treasury after Crassus' appropriation of Jewish money), as well as the religious dues to Hyrcanus.

It is a fairly widespread assumption that the long reign of
Herod the Great was a particularly difficult time financially for
the inhabitants of Palestine. Certainly the expenditure was
lavish, and we hear of his subjects being in bad financial straits
more than once (*Ant.* 15:365; 17:308; *War* 2:85f.). Besides, after
Caesar's death in 44 B.C.E. Herod had demonstrated his ability
to raise extra tribute — one hundred talents in Galilee (*Ant.*
14:273; *War* 1:221) — and was rewarded by Cassius with control
of financial matters (ἐπιμελήτης) in the whole of Coele-Syria.[125]
He himself imposed a heavy fine (one hundred talents also) on
the Galilean towns for their insubordination (*Ant.* 14:433; *War*
1:316), and this may have caused further social unrest and un-
popularity for Herod with the masses (*Ant.* 14:450). We have
already noted the increase in crown land in Herod's reign, attributable in part at least, to the confiscation of private holdings.
However, it seems likely that the main victims were the larger
rather than the smaller owners of the better land, in the Great
Plain e.g., or in Trachonitis and Batanaea, for the complaints
of the Jewish delegation at Rome after his death have the definite
air of the more wealthy elements in Jewish society, who of course
had stood to lose more if they dared to oppose Herod (*Ant.* 17:304-
10). Despite his self-centered ruthlessness Herod was also a shrewd
administrator and businessman. His treatment of the people
during the famine of 25 B.C.E. — provision of grain, clothing,
etc. — is indicative of his control of the overall financial situation, and his recognition that a prosperous kingdom called for
skillful exploitation of its resources. Another example of this
far-sightedness is his granting of lands, tax-free, to the Babylonian Jews in Trachonitis and Batanaea. Their presence there as a
military colony served the twofold purpose of protecting the
kingdom from marauding robbers and of developing the rich
agricultural lands of Transjordan (*Ant.* 17:23-31). The success
of this venture may be judged by the fact that almost a hundred
years later Philip ben Jacimus, the grandson of Zamaris, the first
leader of the colony, was a loyal supporter of Agrippa II, and
the people in his territory were prosperous and well to do (*Life*
46-58). Herod's tax system was at least as hard for townspeople,
for we hear of sales taxes in Jerusalem about which the people

complained to Archelaus (*Ant.* 17:205) and which were subsequently partly removed by Vitellius (*Ant.* 18:90). Taxes on fruits are explicitly mentioned as being remitted, and of course these would have been a greater burden for the poorer townspeople than for their country equals, who could at least produce the necessities of life on their own plots.

This sketchy summary of Herod's economic policy as this was likely to have affected Galilean countrypeople is not intended to minimize the real hardships of his reign. Rather it suggests that the picture was not all bleak, and in fact some stabilization of life seems to have come about for those who were prepared to accept Herod and pose no particular threat, real or imagined, to his plans. The fact that Herod's early conflicts with Antigonus took place in Galilee might give rise to the opinion that he was particularly severe on the Galilean peasants later, but such an assumption is not well-founded as we shall see in a subsequent chapter. In fact we have no definite figures for the income of Herod's kingdom or the amount of tribute he had to pay to Rome; some have suggested that he paid no yearly tribute after 30 B.C.E. — the year in which he gave eight hundred talents as a gift to Augustus. However, the argument from silence is in favor of an annual tribute, as Hoehner points out, and it was only lavish gifts like the one mentioned that drained the state coffers and imposed extra hardship for the natives.[126] Momigliano has in fact computed that the annual income which Herod received from his territory remained constant throughout his reign and was less than that of Agrippa I forty years later, even though Herod's public expenditure on the temple and other building projects was much greater.[127]

The long and peaceful reign of Herod's son Antipas, had a further stabilizing effect on the economy of Galilee, it would seem. His private income from both parts of his territory, Galilee and Peraea, was fixed at two hundred talents by Augustus (*Ant.* 17:318; *War* 2:95). This considerable amount of money was presumably raised in part through land taxes both from his own leased estates and from private holdings, and in part from the tolls and other customs taxes that operated at the various markets and border posts between the different territories (cf. e.g., *Mt*

9:10f.; *Mk* 2:15f.; *Lk* 5:29f.; 19:2, cf. *Mk* 12:17). In all probability
there was the Roman tribute too, which would have equalled
the amount of private revenue, though we have no direct information on the matter. Neither is the method of collecting these
taxes very clear. The system of Roman *publicani* had been abandoned either by Gabinius or Caesar, but Herod sent his own
slaves and officials to collect the taxes, something that often
resulted in further harassment of the countrypeople (*Ant.* 17:205.
308).[128] Presumably this method also obtained in Antipas' realm,
though the existence of imperial granaries in Upper Galilee
suggests central depots where the corn was delivered by the people
(*Life* 71f.)[129] The gospels occasionally mention the presence
of tax-collectors in Galilee during the ministry of Jesus, but
there seems to be fairly widespread agreement that these correspond to *môkesîm* rather than the *gabbāîm* of rabbinic literature, that is to the toll rather than the tax collectors, who were
hated not because they were foreigners or Roman collaborationists, but because of the presumed dishonesty they practised in
discharge of their duties (cf. *Lk.* 3:13).[130] Of course in Judaea as
distinct from Galilee, the office could have the further overtones of collaborationism, since toll collectors were in the direct
employment of the Roman procurators, and may themselves have
been Romans. Certainly Antipas does not seem to have been
lacking in financial resources, as the foundation and endowment
of Tiberias testifies. At the same time, neither the gospels nor
Josephus indicate severe social unrest in the province despite
the obvious distinctions between poor and rich. It must be presumed that for the ordinary people the advantages of a peaceful
reign outweighed the disadvantages of having to support a
hellenistic-style monarch, since heavy taxes on the produce of
the land had been a fact of life for a very long time. Besides, Antipas' nickname 'the fox' (*Lk.* 13:32) presumably referred to his
cunning nature, which was able to manipulate the situation to
his own ends rather than arouse passions, since utlimately his
position was not based on power but the good will of the Romans.
Had social unrest been widespread in his province Antipas
would presumably have suffered a similar fate to his brother
Archelaus in Judaea. His eventual deposition was not due to
such disturbances, but rather to his losing favor with Caligula,
who gave his kingdom to another Herodian, Agrippa I.

The story of the subsequent fluctuations of the financial conditions of Galilee may be told briefly. No change seems to have taken place under Agrippa — failure to sow the crops by the Galilean peasants would mean no tribute and consequent danger of banidtry, as already mentioned (*Ant.* 18:274; *War* 2:200). This was because the Emperor would insist on its being paid, and with the country lacking the resources there would be a breakdown of law and order with the weaker suffering the consequences. This suggests that merely subsistence farming continued to obtain, with very little margin for error. Whatever the final judgment about the political situation, it seems that after the death of Agrippa I Galilee came under the direct control of Roman provincial administration of some kind. Yet what is remarkable is that there is no clear mention of a census, or popular outrage as was the case in Judaea half a century earlier.[131] True, Justus of Tiberias laments the fact that the royal tables and the archives had been restored to Sepphoris, presumably indicating that it had become the center of Roman administration of Galilee. The *archaia* in question were official records of debts, presumably both private and public, yet strangely enough we hear nothing of the Galileans' desire to destroy these records despite their hatred of Sepphoris, rather unlike the revolutionaries in Jerusalem, one of whose first acts was to destroy all such records (*War* 2:427; 6:354; 7:61). The only mention of poverty as a contributory factor in the events leading up to revolt was significantly enough in the urban center of Tiberias, where the destitute class are singled out as one definite element in the troubles there (*Life* 66). The Jewish refusal to pay the tribute to the Romans may have extended itself to Galilee, but if so it is strange that Josephus missed the opportunity to stress his own role in such action, nor does it appear to have been on the list of charges which Justus leveled against him.[132] There is no suggestion that Josephus' capture of the grain from Queen Berenice's estates was due to any shortage in Galilee, and the affair of the highwaymen of Dabaritta was apparently a relatively isolated incident directed at the wealthy (*Life* 119.126). As already mentioned the social conditions of the rural people of Galilee who supported Josephus is not one of penury since they can provision themselves, and each community makes it contribution of fighting men and supplies. There was no objection on the part of the Galileans to pay their tithes, and Josephus' colleagues are said to have amassed a great amount of money (*Life* 63). It is impossible to say whether this relative affluence, or at least self-sufficiency, was due to their withholding the Roman taxes. The probabilities are that such a boycott did not take place in Galilee and so the resulting picture is one in which the country-people of the province were in a more stable position economically than those of other areas of the country, even though the economic hardships of brigandage were always with them (*Life* 77. 206; *War* 2:581). The aftermath of the Roman campaign did bring serious hardships as we have seen with its scorched earth policy, mass enslavement of people, and failure to differentiate between innocent and guilty alike (cf. *War* 3:59-63. 110f.). Yet there was no exorbitant tax burden imposed on those who did somehow survive.[133] The temple tax of all Jews now became payable to Jupiter Capitolinus (*War* 7:218) and, however objectionable this might be on religious or national grounds, it did not impose a heavier financial burden on the people, nor do we hear of any additional taxes imposed as a punitive measure.[134] Presumably the Romans' scorched earth policy had made it impossible for them to exact any more from the people, and indeed total submission rather than increased revenue must have been the primary aim of their settlement policy.

III
SOCIAL STRATIFICATION IN GALILEE

The examination of ownership of the land and the distribution of wealth has certainly enabled us to recognize the various classes within society in Galilee. It has also given us a criterion for isolating the underlying factors that separated people, both socially and culturally, even to the point of uncovering the tensions and animosities that existed between the various groups. It remains to spell out these distinctions more clearly by describing the social classes that emerged within the province for the period covered by this study. Our discussion up to this point has made it clear that these relations did not remain static throughout the whole period. Galilean life was directly affected by the changes in the broader political world, and these in turn had repercussions on every aspect of internal social life.

One class which survived the many vicissitudes was what we have been calling the Galilean peasant. In attempting to identify these more clearly we do not consider it necessary to draw a sharp distinction between those who may have owned their own plots and those who were tenant farmers of the larger estates.[135] As we have just seen, the tax burden was spread over all alike in terms of a definite percentage of the produce of their land. This meant that financially both groups were under the same pressures. Indeed many tenants may have originally been owners of their own plots, but in a bad year had had to barter their land in order to pay tribute or buy grain for the following season and even feed their families. Once that had happened there was never any possibility of their retrieving the situation, and they were fortunate indeed if they could survive as tenants on what was formerly their own land.

What was really distinctive about their class was their non-involvement in the larger commercial life of the area. Their farming of the land was not a business but a duty to ancestral loyalties that were deeply embedded and thus resistant to change. Not that they are to be thought of as a ghetto, since life in the country does not give rise to the kind of social isolationism which could be regarded as typical of the city ghetto. Rather their life style and occupation did not bring them into any kind of meaningful contact with the real agents for social change. When work or market did involve such interaction it was a purely formal affair that was not likely to alter peoples' lives to any great extent. The older value system of the folk tradition that had resided in the villages remained intact, and the various seasonal or annual festivals, often of a religious nature, cemented these and acted as a powerful antidote to change. For the most part the peasant's life was lived within the village, where kinship, real or imagined, and loyalty were the dominant attitudes. Horizons were limited because the rhythm of life was determined by the seasons, and so there was no sense of unrest or frustration. Undoubtedly there was some movement away from the land to the surrounding cities,[136] but if Josephus' figure of 204 settlements in Galilee has any degree of accuracy, we still get a picture of a large rural population even at that late stage when the lure of the cities had existed for quite some time.

At Beth Anath we got some hint of what was likely to occur when peasants of older Israelite stock came into contact with foreigners of their own class. A common position at the same level of the economic scale was more influential in uniting them, than was their diverse cultural background in keeping them apart. Outsiders who are introduced into another society at that level are not culturally very aware, and the likelihood is that they will merge with those natives of the same class, and gradually become indistinguishable from them in terms of the prevalent older culture. This is certainly what took place in Egypt and no doubt the Ptolemies offered the same encouragement for inter-marriage with the natives in Palestine also.[137] This means that the older peasantry did come into contact with the new civiliza-tion, but in a culturally non-threatening way, as new skills and techniques were absorbed and the overall quality of life improved, always within the framework of the older world view. Our judg-ment must be that the Galilean peasantry did profit from this initial introduction of hellenistic civilization into Palestine. Indeed in contrast with their Judaean brothers the change was likely to find them less threatened and more receptive, since for them the political change at the top was merely a change of foreign overlord and not the loss of autonomy, and this was something for which centuries of political turmoil had them well prepared.

Closely associated with and forming the same class as the peasants was the so-called 'rural proletariat'. Under this heading we include the day laborers, the traveling craftsmen, even the less organized type of brigands, all of whom seem to be on the increase as time progresses. Presumably this was due to the fact that economic hardship increased with the wars and the heavy taxes, even though, as we shall see in the next chapter, social unrest to the point of violent subversive revolution was more typical of the Judaean than the Galilean countryside. A rural proletariat has its roots deep in peasant origins. Scarcity of land and natural increase give rise to a surplus rural population, who have no great desire to break ties with their own class. Economically less stable, they remain a 'concealed' factor within peasantry be-cause very often they share the same roots as their landed fellows and render services within the community that tend not to isolate them into a separate class existing for itself. The underlying social world of the gospels indicates that there was a large element of this kind within Galilean peasantry. We hear of day laborers (*Mt.* 20:1-16), hired servants (*Mk.* 1:20) and deposed stewards faced with manual labor or beggary (*Lk.* 16:1-6), and their lot seems to differ very little from the tenants who work the vineyard (*Mk.* 12:1-10) or the fishermen who labored all night to no avail (*Lk.* 5:1-11).[138] It is subsistence living in both cases.

Nevertheless, the rural proletariat does introduce a new element into the peasantry, in that they obviously have less to lose than those who are tied to a plot, either leased or their own. Lack of access to the sources of production can cause not just poverty, but an awareness that that condition 'is not merely a matter of *poor* times but of *evil* times.' [139] Such a breakthrough of consciousness in which the legitimacy of the existing authority is challenged and the right not to be oppressed asserted, seems, *a priori* at least, to be more likely among those who have absolutely nothing to lose. Links with the established land-owning or leasing peasantry and the compensation of being accepted as part of it, may inhibit such an awareness emerging on its own initiative, but under the stimulus of larger social questioning, the rural proletariat is more likely to make common cause with the agents for change. The more conservative peasants are torn between their desire to preserve what they have in trust from the past and the real deprivation they are experiencing. This insight will call for further exploration in the next chapter.

Peasantry has its own structures for coping with the various patterns of life within the village. We have seen in the previous chapter that the cities introduced new 'types' into Galilean life, and in all probability this reflected itself in the reorganization of rural life also. Since the basic structure of life in Palestine for hellenistic times was fashioned by the Ptolemies, we can expect that they respected the existing patterns insofar as these could be made to fit in with their own overall policies. Toubias and Jeddua, both natives whom we meet in the Zenon correspondence, are warrants for this claim. True, we meet Greek offices such as the κωμομισθωτὴς, but this need not necessarily mean that the position had always to be filled by a non-native. No doubt experiences such as that of Zenon with Jeddua slowed down the process of intergrating local chiefs into the new administrative system, and at Beth Anath Melas is certainly a Greek. Gradually, one may suspect, natives rose in the service of the foreigners from being service people to local officials, and this must certainly have created its own tensions within Galilean peasantry. By the first century C.E. village life in Galilee seems to be organized on thoroughly Jewish lines — a process that no doubt had been accelerated by the Hasmonaean conquests and the Judaizing of the aristocracy of the province. Thus Josephus can appoint local judges at various centers to handle the lesser cases and seventy elders of mature years as the magistrates for all Galilee (*War* 2:571), for the administration of justice in accordance with Jewish legal practice.[140] Josephus has several different expressions relating to the social structures of the country Galileans and while none of them help us in defining more precisely their exact social status and function within the local community, it seems natural to identify them with village leaders and local magistrates. These mediated between the country people and the ruling political bosses, and so must retain favor with both groups, but often no doubt lost the confidence of the one side or the other.[141]

Another type of lesser official that the Galilean peasant had to deal with was the steward of the absentee landlord. This character appears in our sources from the third century B.C.E. (Zenon's correspondence) to the first century C.E. The gospels speak of the good steward as a cautious man, constantly expecting that his master will come unexpectedly (*Lk.* 12:42-46; *Mt.* 24:45f.), yet dishonesty, exploitation of the tenants, and personal greed seem to have been the order of the day (*Mt.* 18:24-35; *Lk.* 16:1-6). In such a social structure it is usually those at the bottom that suffer most, since they are the most vulnerable, and it is interesting to find that already at Beth Anath, native peasant and lease-holder had shown a solid front to Melas the estate-manager of Apollonius. Such relations are inevitably tense however. The agent depends on the successful conducting of the master's affairs, and this makes him less likely to be tolerant of the servants' demands, easily mishandling awkward situations.

Reference has been made more than once to Sherwin-White's observation that one finds no real middle class in the gospels, unlike the urban background of much of Acts of the Apostles.[142] John of Gischala was the exception whose wealth came from his proximity to Tyre and its affluent markets, not just from Galilean conditions. The emergence of a Jewish aristocracy within the province is associated with the rise of Sepphoris and Tiberias, the only two real urban centers of Galilee. In time this was to create a further anomaly in the social relations there. In the earlier period there is no native Galilean chief of the stature of Toubias, even though there may have been lesser village leaders recognized by the Ptolemies and Seleucids. The Hasmonaean re-allotment of royal lands eventually gave rise to a native aristocracy, but without disrupting the social structure already established. This cleavage was further accentuated when Gabinius used the aristocracy in his council for the rule of Galilee. They are now clearly seen as supporters and officials of the foreign overlord for their own advantage (*Ant* 14:91). Galilean support for Antigonus the last of the Hasmonaeans was centered on Sepphoris, but insofar as this was popularly based it must be seen as an expression of Israelite loyalties against the Idumaean half-Jew, Herod, rather than the result of widespread support for social reforms which the successors of the Maccabees had introduced. The outrage in Jerusalem's aristocratic circles over Herod's slaughter of Hezekiah and his robber band was, we saw, an indication of how the class of Hasmonaean nobles despised the opportunistic rise of Antipater and his sons. Thus the Galilean Jewish peasant found himself in the rather strange position that those very people to whom he felt bound by ties of national and religious loyalty, the priestly aristocracy, were in fact his social oppressors.

Herod eventually triumphed and so the Hasmonaean nobles were replaced by a new nobility centered on the court of Antipas, first at Sepphoris and later at Tiberias. In all probability these are the Herodians of the gospels (*Mk.* 3:6; 12:13; *Mt.* 22:16), men of substance and influence whose outlook was friendly to Roman rule as the basis for their own positions. Some of them we know by name from Agrippa II's time — Julius Capellus, Herod son of Miarus, Herod son of Gamalus, Compsus son of Compsus and his brother Crispus, as well as Philip son of Jacimus from Gamala. Probably Justus of Tiberias and his family should also be included in the list, despite Josephus' attempts to blacken him (*Life* 32-42). In Antipas' reign they were called simply οἱ ἐν τέλει (*Ant.* 18:37) or οἱ μεγιστάνες or χιλίαρχοι(military description, *Mk.* 6:21).[143] On that occasion the οἱ πρῶτοι τῆς Γαλιλαίας are also present, a term which Josephus uses for the leaders of the Galileans who supported himself (*Life* 220. 266. 305). Perhaps on state occasions such as the king's birthday they took part in the royal festivities, showing the social gulf that had emerged between them and the peasants whom they represented.[144]

Indeed social attitudes seem to have hardened considerably in the one hundred years since Antigonus could count on support in Galilee. We have already dealt with the hatred of the Galileans towards Sepphoris in the previous chapter. This was to be explained, we argued, not primarily in terms of the pro-Roman stance of Sepphoris, but rather becaue of the social gulf between country peasant and city aristocrat, who now presumably was also supporting Roman officialdom in running that part of the province that did not belong to Agrippa II. At least this is what happened in the second century, and its origins can be traced back to the first already. True, Galilean country people were included in the population of Tiberias from the start but there were no real links maintained with the broader hinterland, except presumably for that minority of the population that never integrated with the urban society and remained socially deprived, a hidden rural proletariat forming an urban ghetto. The sailors, presumably fishermen and ferry boat operators on the lake, are included in the same bracket with the destitute class in 66 C.E. (*Life* 66). But for the bulk of the Galilean peasantry Tarichaeae rather than Tiberias was more inviting as they fled from the Roman attack. They could expect little sympathy or protection from the Herodian aristocracy that was much more concerned with its own affairs than with revolt from Rome or the flight of the peasants (cf. *Life* 33).

NOTES FOR CHAPTER 5

[1] *Jud. und Hell.* Cf. the *Zusammenfassung* to ch. 1, 105f.

[2] Thus R. McMullen, *Roman Social Relations,* New Haven, Yale Univ. Press, 48.

[3] Tcherikover, *W.H.Hell.A.* 310, n. 4, gives a complete list of publications to which that of T.C. Skeat, *Zenon Papyri in the British Museum,* Cambridge, 1975, should now be added.

[4] On Ptolemaic land policies in general, cf. Rostovtzeff, *SEHHW,* 1, 267-91, esp. 277ff where he distinguishes royal, sacred, kleruchic and private lands. Apparently, the Jerusalem temple did not own any lands.

[5] Launey, *Recherches sur les Armées hellénistiques,* 713-15; Tcherikover, *W.H. Hell.A.,* 45-50.

[6] An example of such policy can be seen in the Vienna papyrus. Cf. above ch. 4, n. 94.

[7] Above, ch. 4, n. 15, for the location of this site. The place is mentioned in the following papyri: *PCZ* 59011, 59004, *PSI* 594. Even though *PSI* 554 does not actually mention Beth Anath, Tcherikover, *Mizraim,* 45f and *W.H.Hell.A.,* 316, n. 5, rightly assumes that it deals with the estate there.

[8] Tcherikover, *Mizraim,* 48 and 86, n. 87, relates them to the *paradeisoi* comprising forests, vineyards and orchards, of Persian times, mentioned by Xenophon, *Anab* 1,4.9 and Strabo, *Geographica,* 16,756. Cf. also S. Applebaum, 'Economic Life in Palestine', *Compendia,* 2, 631-70, esp. 641-6, who notes that the root meaning of the rabbinic עיר was a rural settlement or an isolated farm, and suggests that archaeological evidence from the Shepelah region of Judaea points to a pattern of such settlements there, similar to the Roman villa of later times. By contrast, in the Judaean and Samarian hills there are traces of nucleated villages and single farms dating from early Roman times. Presumably this pattern would have been true of Galilee also, with the larger estates being located in the plains. Cf. above ch. 1.

[9] Thus Tcherikover, *Mizraim,* 48, who however is more cautious in *W.H.Hell.A.,* 94. The problem is complicated because our sources do not distinguish between crown land and private estates of the royal household, and in times of peace especially the distinction can be easily blurred. Cf. B. Levick, *Roman Colonies in Southern Asia Minor,* Oxford, Univ. Press, 1967, Appendix 6, 'Client Kings, Royal Domains and Imperial Estates', 215-26.

[10] Tcherikover, *Mizraim,* 51, and *W.H.Hell.A.,* 95, with text of this letter.

[11] *PCZ* 59003: τῶν Τουβίου ἱππέων κληροῦχοι, numbered a Macedonian, a Greek and a Jew. Text in *C.P.J.* no. 1.

[12] C.B. Welles, *Royal Correspondence in the Hellenistic Age,* New Haven, 1934, esp. 205-9, deals with a letter from an Attalid king to cleruchs which distinguishes between leased lots and those to which they have absolute title, even in the absence of offspring.

[13] Tcherikover, *Mizraim,* 45ff; Hengel 'Das Gleichnis von den Weingärtnern' esp. 11-16.

[14] This office may have included some of the duties of the κωμογαμματεύς known to us from other sources, including the Vienna papyrus. Cf. *Ant* 16:203, for the office in Herodian times, and Tcherikover, *Mizraim,* 46, and McLean Harper, 'Village Administration', 121f, dealing with the Roman period. Rostovtzeff, *SEHHW,* 1, 345 and 3, 1403, n. 149, disagrees with Tcherikover about the status of the Beth Anath estate, which he considers to be a private holding (κτῆμα) and not part of the βασιλικὴ χώρα. Consequently, he considers the κωμομισθωτής to be a village tax-collector, not a royal financial official, as in the Vienna papyrus. Hengel, 'Das Gleichnis von den Weingärtnern', 14, notes 51 and 54 thinks that the term κτῆμα applied to the estate does not exclude the estate from being part of the kingsland and suggests that κωμομισθωτής may be a 'zwischenpächter' between the government and the villagers, 15.

[15] This reconstruction of the contents of the letter is based on Tcherikover, *W.H.Hell.A.*, 94. In *Mizraim* however, he had treated the letter as coming from a travelling agent of Apollonius and not from Melas, the manager of the estate, who was different from the κωμομισθωτής.

[16] Thus Tcherikover. Rabbinic sources have a threefold distinction, corresponding more or less to Greco-Roman categories: there was the אריס (Greek, μέτοχος; Latin, *partiarius*), who received part of the produce as a wage; the שוכר (Greek, μισθωτής) who paid a fixed amount in rent, and the שטלה ה (Greek, γεωργοί, Latin, *coloni*), who developed an estate and received part of it in return for their labor. For a detailed discussion cf. S. Krauss, *Talmudische Archäologie*, 3 vols, Reprint Darmstadt, 1966, 2, 105-11; F. Heichelheim, *Roman Syria*, in T. Frank, ed., *An Economic Survey of Ancient Rome*, Baltimore, 1938, vol. IV, 121-257, esp. 147f; Applebaum, 'Economic Survey', *Compendia*, 2, 656-60.

[17] Hengel, 'Das Gleichnis von den Weingärtnern', 26f; Tcherikover,*Mizraim*, 26f.

[18] Alt, 'Hellenistische Städte und Domänen', *G.P.* 3, 384-95; Tcherikover, *Mizraim*, 46-50 and *W.H.Hell.A.*, 94f; cf. however, Rostovtzeff's criticism of the latter, *SEHHW*, 3, 1403, n. 149.

[19] M. Gil, 'Land Ownership in Palestine under Roman Rule', *RIDA* 17(1970) 11-53.

[20] P. Garnsey, 'Peasants in Ancient Roman Society', *JPS* 2(1975) 222-35, esp. 230.

[21] McMullen, *Roman Social Relations*, esp. 15, and Garnsey, 'Peasants', 233, n. 6, based on an inscription from Veleia near Parma for Trajan's reign.

[22] R. de Vaux, *Ancient Israel. Its Life and Institutions*, English trans., London, Darton, Longman and Todd, 1965, 164-7.

[23] de Vaux, *Ancient Israel*, 124f, on the royal estates.

[24] Hengel, *Jud. und Hell.*, 98f and 212f, n. 57.

[25] Bickerman, 'La Charte séleucide', 26. Alt has argued that Galilee never belonged to the ἔθνος τῶν Ἰουδαίων, but was always treated as χώρα βασιλική, 'Galiläas Verhältnis zu Samaria und Judäa', *G.P.* 4, esp. 404-6.

[26] Landau, 'A Greek Inscription'.

[27] This is Landau's interpretation of these difficult and partially obscured lines, 'A Greek Inscription', 64 and 67, n. 14, based on the suggestion of A.G. Woodhead.

[28] P. Briant, 'Laoi et Esclaves Ruraux', in *Actes du Colloque 1972 sur l'esclavage, Annales littéraires de l'Université de Besançon* 140 and 163, Paris, 1974, 93-133, has collected and collated the available evidence from epigraphic and literary sources.

[29] Rostovtzeff, *SEHHW*, 1, 503 and 2, 1103; Welles, *Royal Correspondence*, 96.

[30] *Royal Correspondence*, 96f.

[31] Bickerman, *Institutions des Séleucides*, Paris, 1938, 176ff; Briant, 'Laoi et Esclaves Ruraux', esp. 96-106, with charts, 95f.

[32] Briant, 'Laoi et Esclaves Ruraux', 105.

[33] *Ant* 12:147-53 for a decree of Antiochus III, transferring 2,000 Jewish families from Babylon to Phrygia and giving them their own plots of land for building and cultivation. Cf. also, *OGIS* 488 for a second century C.E. inscription, and McLean Harper, 'Village Administration', esp. 151ff, on public land, and 160ff on private ownership of villages in Roman Syria.

[34] This is not to deny a strong social component to the hellenistic reform in the plans of Antiochus IV; cf. *1 Macc* 9:23ff and Hengel, *Jud. und Hell.* 529f. However, this change was only likely to have touched Galilee in those areas where Jewish refugees abandoned their homes and left for Jerusalem.

[35] κώμη can refer to the land that goes with a cluster of dwellings as well as to the dwellings themselves.

[36] As Briant notes, 'Laoi et Esclaves Ruraux', 117f, the φόρος or tribute is itself to be seen as a debt that the vanquished 'owed' to the conqueror, thereby making the villagers dependent on the royal fiscal administration.

[37] Alt, 'Die Umgestaltung Galiläas durch die Hasmonäer', *G.P.*5, 407-23 presumes this to be the ideological base for the expansion. However, Davies, *The Gospel and the Land*, 90-104, notes the absence of any direct appeal to the land as a religious symbol in the sources of the time.

[38]*The Gospel and the Land*, 98f.

[39]Above, ch. 3, n. 6.

[40]Momigliano, *Ricerche*. 10-27, esp. 14f.

[41]It is unlikely that Herod would have been able to deal with Galilean land in the same way as he did with those he was granted in Batanaea, despite Alt's suggestion to this effect, 'Die Vorstufen zur Eingliederung Galiläas', *G.P.6*, 431. Momigliano's suggestion occurs in *Ricerche*, 41.

[42]M. Stern, *Compendia*, 1, 272, n.2, Cf. above, ch. 4, n.61.

[43]*Roman Society and Roman Law*, 139f.

[44]Hengel, 'Das Gleichnis von den Weingärtnern', and Herz, 'Grossgrundbesitz'.

[45]Rabbinic sources also suggest family holdings as Gil, 'Land Ownership', 27, notes.

[46]Thus Garnsey, 'Peasants', 226f and literature cited by him 233, n.8.

[47]Cf. *War* 3:62.110.132 for the Roman scorched earth policy in the Galilean countryside, presuming an independent peasantry rather than a subservient aristocracy.

[48]Schürer, *Geschichte*. 1, 640, n. 141, emphasizes that the correct translation of ἀποδόσθαι is 'to lease', not 'to sell'. Cf. also Momigliano, *Ricerche*, 86f, for the legal situation, and A. Büchler, *The Economic Conditions of Judaea after the Destruction of the Second Temple*, London, Jews' College Publication, 4, London, 1912, esp. 29-33. He points out that the new land policy caused great hardship for countrypeople, according to rabbinic sources, yet notes the many examples of Jews continuing to own land up to the Bar Cochba revolt.

[49]Above, ch. 3, V.

[50]Büchler, *Economic Conditions*, 37-41, and Yadin, *Bar-Kokhba*, esp. 233-53 on the land contracts of Babata.

[51]Klein, *Neue Beiträge*, 10-18, and A. Büchler, *Der Galiläische Am Ha-'Ares des zweiten Jahrhunderts*, Reprint Darmstadt, 1968, 32-36.

[52]Klein, *Neue Beiträge*, 13, n. 7, argues that *mesiq* is the more original on the basis of *Is* 29:7; 51:13, and notes that the letters sâde (שׂ) and samech (ס) are often confused in the Mishnah MSS. Gil, 'Landownership', regards *mesiqin* as the more difficult reading and suggests an underlying Greek term.

[53]'Landownership', 40-4.

[54]'Landownership', 14-20, where he points out that the Roman distinction underlies the lack of dominion, whereas the Jewish position stresses that there is little point to ownership without actual use.

[55]Büchler, *Der Galiläische Am Ha-'Ares*,187f, in line with his general thesis, to be discussed below, ch. 8, places most of these developments in the post-135 C.E. period. Yet this seems to ignore the historical and social realities of the situation after 70, already.

[56]Thus, e.g. J. Klausner, *Jesus von Nazareth*, Berlin 1930, 229, n.30. Gil, 'Landownership', 47f, n.40, gives a history of this line of understanding. Hengel, *Die Zeloten*, 53f, prefers Klein's interpretation above notes 51 and 2, linking the term with the new landowners introduced by the Romans.

[57]'Land Ownership', 45-53, where he also suggests an etymological link with the συνκεκώρηκα formula of hellenistic papyri contracts.

[58]J. Neusner, *Development of a Legend. Studies in the Traditions concerning Yohanan ben Zakkai*, Leiden, E.J. Brill, 1970, 138f, notes that the saying is probably pseudepigraphic, since it is in Aramaic, whereas all the other sayings of Johanan are in good Mishnaic Hebrew.

[59]Herz, 'Grossgrundbesitz', 112, notes the need to distinguish between the various regions of the country when dealing with the large estates, and locates the small farmers in the hill country of Judaea, Samaria and Galilee. Cf. above, n.8.

[60]S. Krauss, *Talmudische Archäologie*, 2, 110 and 502, n. 755 gives references to *latefundia* in rabbinic literature, presumably reflecting the later Galilean situation; also Büchler, *The Political and Social Leaders of Sepphoris*, esp. 34-49, who points out that the basic source of wealth still continued to be land.

[61]Above, ch. 1, n.29.

[62]McMullen, *Roman Social Relations*, 48.

[63]Tcherikover, *Mizraim*, 20-3 on the state control of the grain and oil trades by the Ptolemies.

[64]Th. Shanin, 'Nature and Logic of Peasant Economics', JPS 1(1974) 186-204, esp. 192-5, points out that in peasant societies change usually takes place as a result of outside agencies, though much depends on the local situation and the historical background for the effectiveness of such agencies.

[65]*P. London* 1948 (=*Inv.* 2661), now published by Skeat, *Zenon Papyri*; cf. Hengel, 'Das Gleichnis von den Weingärtnern', 12f, and *Jud. und Hell.*, 76f. Rostovtzeff, *SEHHW*, 1, 364, suggests that Zenon himself may have known one of the many treatises on viticulture, on the basis of *PSI* 624.

[66]*Jud. und Hell.*, 85f and n. 332, with a list of places where such jar handles with Greek inscriptions have been found.

[67]Hengel, 'Das Gleichnis von den Weingärtnern', discusses its dimensions and suggests that by modern standards 80,000 vines would require seventeen hectares, and at least 25 workers for the vineyard alone, which would amount to the population of a small village.

[68]*P. London 1948* mentions that Melas had provided the villagers with a well (φρέαρ). The papyrus is dated about a year after *PSI* 554 where the complaints of the tenants are mentioned.

[69]*PSI* 324 and 5; Tcherikover, *Mizraim*, 20f and *W.H.Hell.A.*, 91.

[70]*PCZ* 59093 and *PSI* 406; Tcherikover, *Mizraim* 16-20 and *W.H.Hell.A.*, 91f.

[71]*Mizraim*, 22f.

[72]*Mizraim*, 24. The fact that *P Col Zen* 2, col III, mentions grain being brought into Galilee from Sidon, according to the emendations of the editors of *C.P.J.* 1, need not surprise us, since it could well be seed grain for planting.

[73] *Jud. und Hell.*, 86, n. 333, following Heichelheim, *Roman Syria*, 130ff.

[74] *Geographica*, 16,2.16. Stern, *Greek and Latin Authors*, 289, suggests however that Strabo may have confused lake Meron (Huleh) with the Sea of Tiberias, since his description fits the northern lake better.

[75] *SEHHW*, 2, 1198.

[76] This was certainly the case at Philadelphia, Apollonius' large estate in Egypt, about which we are best informed.

[77] *SEHHW*, 2, 1196.

[78]Jeremias, *The Parables of Jesus*, 12. The evidence adduced by Krauss, *Talmudische Archäologie*, 2, 160ff, is certainly later, though irrigation techniques do seem to have been in use at a much earlier period.

[79] *PCZ* 59004 and 6. Cf. *Mizraim*, appendix 1, 57ff.

[80] Hengel, *Jud. und Hell.*, 91.

[81] *SEHHW*, 1, 297 on *P Teb* 701; 2, 1177-9 and 3, 1387, n. 101 on the Egyptian fish industry in general.

[82] Thackeray, *Loeb Josephus*, 2, 723, n. b, cites Martial, *Ep* XVIII, 85: 'princeps Niliaci macelli'.

[83] *SEHHW*, 1, 370f.

[84] S.S. Weinberg, 'Tel Anafa', 95ff.

[85] Davidson Weinberg, 'Hellenistic Glass from Tel Anafa', esp. 27.

[86] *M. Bab Kam* 10:9; cf. Heichelheim, *Roman Syria*, 191-3; Krauss, *Talmudische Archäologie*, 1, 137.

[87] Shanin, 'Nature and Logic of Peasant Economics', esp. 67-72.

[88] *Roman Society and Roman Law*, 139f.

[89] Above, n. 70.

[90] Above, n. 64.

[91]Applebaum, 'Economic Life in Palestine', 662f, criticizes H. Kreissig, *Die Sozialen Zusammenhänge des Judaischen Krieges*, Berlin 1970, 36-51, for his theory about control of the markets by the wealthy, on the basis that such a theory presupposes a countrywide price structure which did not in fact obtain. Rather the different towns depended on their local hinterlands because of the problems and costs of transporting goods. Yet this fact does not still remove the disadvantages of the small farmer in competition with the large landowners.

⁹²Tactitus, *Ann* 2:42 writes: 'Provinciae Syria atque Judaea, fessae oneribus, diminutionem tributi orabunt', referring to the time of Tiberius.

⁹³Kreissig, *Die Sozialen Zusammenhänge*, 37f; F.C. Grant, *The Economic Background of the Gospels*, Oxford, 1926, 65.

⁹⁴According to *Ant* 12:299 slave dealers followed conquering armies in order to benefit from the increased supply of slaves from the vanquished. *Ant* 14:408-13 illustrates the problems of countrypeople, including Galileans, as rival armies looked for supplies. On the problem in general, Launey, *Recherches sur les Armées hellénistiques*, 690-715.

⁹⁵Hengel, *Die Zeloten*, 26-35, deals with the question of banditry in the ancient world and in Palestine in particular. *Ant* 18:274; 20:256 illustrate the social effects for countrypeople - emigration or impoverishment.

⁹⁶Heichelheim, *Roman Syria*, 211-13, and Ben David, *Jerusalem und Tyros*, 5-9, deal with the question of Syrian currency.

⁹⁷*PCZ* 59093 and 4 indicate the presence of τελῶναι, that is, toll collectors, at Tyre and Gaza for a much earlier period. Cf. also *Lk* 19:2.

⁹⁸Ben David, *Jerusalem und Tyros*, 17; Grant, *Economic Background*, 64-71.

⁹⁹The Jewish rebels of 66 C.E. burned the ἀρχεαῖ as their first act of revolt, *War* 2:427, so that debts could not be collected, thereby showing that they were financial records. According to Büchler, *Der Galiläische Am Ha-'Ares*, 244f, n. 3, the Roman authorities kept such financial records and so it is not surprising to hear of their transfer to Sepphoris. Cf. also *War* 6:354 and 7:61 for a similar usage, though in the former instance the building that housed the records may be intended.

¹⁰⁰This interpretation of the legal background of the parable is that suggested by J.M. Derrett, 'Fresh Light on St. Luke XVI,1. The Parable of the Unjust Steward', NTS 7(1960/1) 198-219. It presupposes that v.8a is part of the story. *Ant* 18:157 gives an example of usurious lending, which however comes from the urban setting of Ptolemais, not the rural context of the Lukan story.

¹⁰¹*T.Ab Zar* 4:1; *b. Bab Bath* 90b, which forbade the storing up of essentials—wine, oil and meal, except during the Sabbath year and the year that preceded it, presumably because this would have increased the prices in an ordinary year. Büchler, *Der Galiläische Am Ha-'Ares*, 241-3, sees these prescriptions as applying particularly to Galilee.

¹⁰²Ben David, *Jerusalem und Tyros*, 16-8, who attributes this to the relatively intensive production of the necessities by the small farmers of Palestine.

¹⁰³*The Economic Background of the Gospels*, 89.

¹⁰⁴Above, n.14.

¹⁰⁵O. Michel, art. τελῶνης, *TDNT*, 8, 88-105, esp. 91f, for the tax-farming in Egypt, based on evidence from the papyri.

¹⁰⁶Rostovtzeff, *SEHHW*, 1, 344, who translates cols. 17-20 as follows: 'those who have leased the villages and the *komarchs* shall register at the same time the cattle in the villages liable to tax and exempt from it'. (ὑποτελὴ καὶ ἀτελὴ)

¹⁰⁷Above, ch. 2, III.

¹⁰⁸*Geschichte*, 1, 229, n. 14. Bickerman, 'La Charte Séleucide',17f, and *Institutions des Séleucids*, 111.

¹⁰⁹This is the conclusion of Rostovtzeff, *SEHHW*, 1, 349 and 469-71, on the basis that the decree of Antiochus is a concession from a previously existing ordinance.

¹¹⁰Bickerman, *Institutions des Séleucids*, 131f, and Rostovtzeff, *SEHHW* 1, 467f. Cf. also, Hengel, *Jud. und Hell.*, 52.

¹¹¹This is the conclusion of a well argued article by A. Mittwoch, 'Tribute and Land-tax in Seleucid Judaea', *Biblica* 36(1955) 352-61, esp. 356f, where he suggests that the ἄρχων φορολογίας of *1 Macc* 1:29 and the μυσαρχὴς of *2 Macc* 5:24, sent by Antiochus to Jerusalem, should be understood as a special royal appointee in charge of taxes, now that the high priest, the official administrative head of the Jewish state in charge of the collection of the tribute, was no longer recognized. The old order of a tribute for the whole of Judaea reappears in the preferred concessions of the later Seleucid kings: *1 Macc* 11:28; 13:15.41; *Ant* 13:143.

¹¹²Galiläas Verhältnis zu Samaria und Judäa', *G.P.* 4, 406.

[113]C. Préaux, *L'Economie royale des Lagides*, Brussels, 1939, 134.

[114]*W.H.Hell.A.*, ch. XI, 'Domestic Politics and Political Institutions', esp. 265-9.

[115]*Ricerche*, 19f. He thinks, however, that the system only continued until Gabinius, for Cicero writes of him: 'Iam vero publicanos miseros . . . . . tradidit in servitutem Iudaeis et Syris' (*De Prov. Consul.*, V,10). Cf. also, Schalit, *Herodes*, 35, based on Josephus' remark, οἱ ἐνθαῦτα (Jerusalem) 'Ρωμαῖοι,whom he considers were Roman *negotiatores*.

[116]Thus Schalit, *W.H.Her.P.*, ch. 1, 'The Fall of the Hasmonaean Dynasty and the Roman Conquest', 26-43, esp. 41f. However, Momigliano claims that his was never the policy of Rome in Judaea, *Richerche*, 6.

[117]Antipater is styled ἐπιμελητής at *Ant* 14:127.139, apparently an official designation, elsewhere used for a procurator, whose role, at least initially had a strong financial aspect, *War* 1:225; *Ant* 17:6. It seems then that he enjoyed an official position even before Caesar made him ἐπιτροπόςin 47 B.C.E. Marcus, *Loeb Josephus*, VII, 514f, n.d., suggests that Josephus may have been anticipating in the earlier notice, but Momigliano, *Ricerche*, 25, considers that they were two distinct offices, that of ἐπιμελητής having to do with religious dues even when the five sanhedria were in existence.

[118]Momigliano, *Ricerche*, 10-30; Rostovtzeff, *SEHHW*, 1, 467f; 2,999-1001 3, 1578, n. 104; Heichelheim, *Roman Syria*, 231-45; Schürer, *Geschichte*, 1, 511-13; Büchler, 'The Edicts of Caesar', 13-18.

[119]There was no intention of restoring total independence to the Jews, however, as Büchler, 'The Edicts of Caesar', 2-5, points out, from the general tenor of the decrees.

[120]Momigliano, *Ricerche*, 21, and Heichelheim, *Roman Syria*, 231 and 5; Büchler, 'The Edicts of Caesar', 17. Schalit, *Herodes*, 760, interprets 'the year following the sabbath year'.

[121]Büchler, 'The Edicts of Caesar', 17, thinks that the second year tax was an *annona militaris*, a supplement in that year to the *annona horrea* or land tax. The fact that one *kor* was deducted from the latter 'in the second year of the lease', *Ant* 14:201, presumably by way of relief, would seem to support this view. However, his idea about a separate lease cycle, independent of the sabbath year cycle seems unlikely, since the latter was recognized by the Romans, *Ant* 14:202.

[122]Schürer, *Geschichte*, 1, 511-13, gives details of the poll tax. The text from Appian: *Syr.* referring to a φόρος τῶν σωμάτων is not clear, and at all events deals with a later time.

[123]*Ricerche*, 28f, based on the text of Appian (cf. n. 122). However, the census of Quirinius, *Lk* 2:1, would seem to argue against this position: Sherwin-White, *Roman Society and Roman Law*, 167; H. Braunert 'Der Römische Provinzialcensus und der Schätzungsbericht des Lukas-Evangeliums', *Historia* 6(1957) 192-214.

[124]*SEHHW*, 2, 1000f and 3, 1578, n. 104, but with some hesitation. Büchler, 'The Edicts of Caesar', 13-16, argues on the basis of the annual tax Joppe had to pay and reconstructs the text accordingly.

[125]This is the title given him at *War* 1:225, whereas the parallel in *Ant* 14:280, describes him as στρατηγός, governor. Marcus, *Loeb Josephus*, 599, n.d., thinks that *Ant* is a correction of *War*, whereas Momigliano, *Ricerche*, 37f, seeks to retain both titles for different times. Cf. above, n.117.

[126]In *Herod Antipas*, Appendix IV, 298-300, Hoehner discusses the question of the tribute and concludes that in all probability the Herods had to pay a tribute, but did not have to give financial support for auxiliary troops.

[127]*Ricerche*, 48f.

[128]J.R. Donahue, 'Tax Collectors and Sinners. An Attempt at an Identification', CBQ 33(1971) 39-61, esp. 45-9, underlines the need to clearly distinguish between Galilee and Judaea and between the period before and after 44 C.E. before deciding the role of tax collectors in first century Palestine. For Antipas' Galilee he concludes that the toll collectors (τελῶναι) were despised, not because they were seen as collaborationists of Rome, but because they engaged in a despised occupation.

[129]M. Rostovtzeff, *SEHRE*, 2, 664, n.32, considers that the granaries of Upper Galilee belonged to Imperial estates and were not central depots. On the basis of *PCZ* 59004 we can presume a royal estate for Kedasa, and at *Life*, 118f we hear of corn from the royal estates of Queen Berenice.

[130]Donahue, 'Tax Collectors and Sinners', 50-3; Michel, art., τελῶνης, 101-3; Kreissig, *Die Sozialen Zusammenhänge*, 73. Cf. *War* 2:4: and *Ant* 17:205.

[131]*War* 6:422-4 does speak of a census of all Jews taking part in the Passover celebrations, conducted by Cestius Gallus in 66 C.E. However, even if this actually took place it is noteworthy that the computation was done on the basis of the number of lambs slain for the festival, rather than by enrollment procedures for the participants.

[132]According to *War* 2:404-6 the Jerusalem magistrates were responsible for the collection of the tribute. The arrears of only 40 talents suggests that Galilee was not involved, but presumably a similar arrangement obtained in that part that was under direct Roman rule.

[133]Tithes were still expected to be paid according to rabbinic regulation, as is dealt with in detail, below, ch. 8. Cf. also, Büchler, *Economic Conditions*, 33-6.

[134]Heichelheim, *Roman Syria*, 145f, speaks of official registration of lands and points to Eusebius' account, taken from Hegesippus, *Eccles. Hist.* 3,20, about the land that was owned by the brothers of the Lord in the reign of Domitian, and had been valued (διατίμησις) at thirty nine plethora of ground on which they had to pay taxes.

[135]Cf. above. n. 16 on the different types of tenant according to rabbinic sources.

[136]One notes the Jewish population to be found in all the gentile cities of Palestine on the occasion of the riots of 66 C.E.

[137]The Vienna papyrus, above ch. 4, n. 94, gave official encouragement to intermarriage between Greeks and natives.

[138] Krauss,*Talmudische Archäologie*, 2, 105f gives a long list of such occupations.

[139] S. Mintz, 'The Rural Proletariat and the Problem of Rural Proletarian Consciousness', JPS 1(1974) 291-325, esp. 315.

[140] This is the picture one gets from the gospels: a local judge with jurisdiction over inheritance and punishments (*Lk* 12:14.58; *Mt* 5:25); the synagogue with judicial authority even in a matter of life and death (*Lk* 4:29); the local synagogue ruler is an influential person (*Mk* 5:22); arguments should be settled by local synagogue councils (*Mt* 5:22); it has power of corporal punishment for specific crimes (*Lk* 12:11; *Mt* 10:17; 23:24); there is no clear distinction between treason and blasphemy (*Mk* 2:7; 3:22: *Lk* 13:31). Cf. Sherwin-White, *Roman Society and Roman Law*, 133-43, and Safrai, 'Jewish Self-Government', *Compendia*, 1, 413f, for the later, post-70 period.

[141] Cf. R. Redfield, *The Little Community and Peasant Society and Culture*, Chicago, Univ. Press, 1960, esp. *Peasant Society*, 36-8, where he underlines the important social function of such 'hinge-men', whose lives are 'in part in the local community and in part—at least mentally—in more urban circles'.

[142] Above, n.43.

[143] Hoehner, *Herod Antipas*, 102, n.3, discusses the significance of the different titles, concluding that the former may have been head of toparchies, since it often occurs for the leading men of a group, whereas the latter seems to suggest rather a social class, 'l'aristocratie du pays', as M.J. Lagrange, *Évangile selon Marc*, Paris, 1926, 160, calls them.

CHAPTER SIX

HOW REVOLUTIONARY WAS GALILEE?

As we traced the political history of Galilee, especially in relation to Rome, in the first section of this study, the view gradually emerged that the province suffered less at the hands of the foreign overlord than did Judaea proper, the most obvious comparative example for our purpose. Even at the time of the first revolt, while certain parts of Galilee felt the full weight of the Roman conquest, we contended that there was no serious widespread revolt throughout the whole province, and that eventually Rome came to recognize this also. Have we then answered in advance the question posed for this chapter? Apparently not, or at least not fully, for there is a very widespread body of opinion in contemporary scholarship that speaks of the revolutionary ethos of Galilee, especially as the backdrop to the ministry of Jesus, and we must examine both the evidence and rationale for these assumptions. Our aim will not be to repeat the argumentation of the historical section, but rather to attempt to break new ground, by asking the question: what were the likely revolutionary elements within Galilean life and where were these located? Then we shall be better able to discuss the possible extent of their influence, given the network of social relations we discussed in the previous chapter.

First however, we must attempt to give some precision to the word 'revolutionary', since even within the political arena it is capable of many different shades of meaning and it has been further diluted by contemporary popular idiom and usage. As generally applied to first century Palestine the term 'revolutionary' is synonomous with membership of the Zealot party, whose ideology is identified with that of the Fourth Philosophy described by Josephus: 'as for the fourth of the philosophies, Judas the Galilean set himself up as leader of it. This school agrees in all other respects with the opinions of the Pharisees, except that they have a passion for liberty that is unconquerable, since they are convinced that God alone is their leader and master. They think little of submitting to death in unusual forms and permitting vengeance to fall on kinsmen and friends if only they may avoid calling any man master'. On these terms a first century C.E. revolutionary in Palestine would refuse to submit to Roman rule and from religious convictions be actively engaged in its overthrow. The assumption is that these convictions are so deeply felt that violence is an integral part of the Zealot make-up, to the point that they can endure great physical suffering themselves and inflict it on those who disagree, foreigners and natives alike. In his monumental study *Die Zeloten*, (Leiden 1961) Martin Hengel has underlined in particular the religious, even the messianic and eschatological orientation of the movement, as zeal for temple and torah fired them to engage in a holy war for the restoration of Israel and the establishment of God's kingly rule.

Not everybody accepts the view that all Jewish resistance to the rule of Rome in the first century C.E. is to be identified with the Zealot party.[1] Indeed some go so far as to suggest that the Fourth Philosophy, at least as formulated by Josephus, is a retrojective apologetic device on his part and that in reality the Zealot party only emerged during the great revolt, a mixture of Judaean peasantry fleeing from Vespasian in the winter of 67 C.E. and Jerusalem priests of lower rank who had sown the seeds of revolt in the city before the arrival of Gessius Florus in 66 by terminating the twice-daily sacrifices for the Emperor (*War* 2:409-10; 4:130-4).[2] Though the point is disputed, Josephus, it is maintained, reserves the word ζηλωτής as a party name for this group, never actually designating the Fourth Philosophy in that way in the earlier period.[3] In fact the number of revolutionary groups that Josephus mentions during the later stages of the revolt suggests a very complex picture (*War* 7:262-70), and we are faced with adopting one of two alternatives. Either there never was a single unified Jewish revolutionary party, or that party became so badly splintered in the immediate pre-war period that it is scarcely recognizable as the Fourth Philosophy by the time Vespasian begins the siege.[4]

A complex situation becomes even more complicated when it is recognized that not everybody who eventually became embroiled in the war, did so because they found the Roman rule intolerable. Some Jews abandoned Jerusalem entirely (*War* 2:556)

or refused to become involved (Sepphoris), while others hoping
for peace, attempted to contain the situation, only to find themselves involved in a war they did not really want. Others saw the
revolt as an opportunity for personal advancement - never stop-
ping to think of the ultimate consequences. It does not serve
Josephus' best interests to relate the whole range of Jewish views
about the war, but this should not obscure the fact that many
such views must have existed, from those who were prepared to
die in blaze of glory to those who wanted peace at all costs.[5]

Faced with these difficulties, the question, 'how revolutionary
was Galilee?' focuses on a very specific group, small though
influential, who, it is alleged, originated in and continued to
have strong support in Galilee. Hopefully other views along the
spectrum from revolutionary to peace party will come into clearer
perspective by a particular concentration on these radicals. The
enquiry seems all the more urgent since 'the Galileans' both in
ancient and modern writings have been branded with certain
characteristics which make the identification between first
century Galilean and revolutionary almost absolute.[6] It suited
Josephus' own interests to describe the unruly characteristics of
the provincials he had to weld into an army as follows: 'With this
limited area, and although surrounded on all sides by such
powerful foreign nations, the two Galilees have always resisted
any hostile invasion, for the inhabitants are from infancy inured
to war, and have at all times been numerous; never did the men
lack courage or the country, men' (*War* 3:41f). The fact that Judas
the founder of the Fourth Philosophy is constantly described as
'the Galilean' (*War* 2:118.433; *Ant* 18:23; 20:102; *Ac* 5:37), though
in one instance he is said to come from Gamala in the Gaulan
(*Ant* 18:4), has given further warranty to the claim for a revolutionary Galilee. Thus the tendency has been to see a long tradition
of revolution in the area, starting with Hezekiah, the ἀρχιλῄστης
put to death by Herod, and climaxing in the revolt of 66 C.E.
Rabbinic and early Christian sources seem to confirm the picture.
The former speak of such Galilean characteristics as preferring
honor to money (*p Ket* 4,29b) and of their being quarrelsome and
aggressive among themselves (*M Ned* 5:5; *b Ned* 48a). Besides, we
hear of a Galilean heretic who reproaches the Pharisaic scribe
for including the name of the emperor on a bill of divorce (*M Yad*
4:8). Justin Martyr (*Dialogue with Trypho* 80.2) and Hegesippus
(Eusebius *Hist. Eccl.* 4,22.7) list Galileans among various Jewish

sects. It is merely the continuation of that tradition when a modern writer claims: 'I venture to say that the term 'Galileans' in the *Vita* does not have a geographical connotation, but is an appellative name given to the revolutionaries against Rome and the rulers of Judaea appointed by Rome'.[7]

Naturally the period of the revolt against Rome has to be our special concern, not just because our information for the period is more detailed than for any other moment of Galilee's history, but also because it was then, if ever, that a revolutionary Galilee should come clearly into view. However, such movements are never mushroom growths, and so we must retrace the earlier history for evidence of Galilean revolutionary activity or situations that might have caused it to emerge. Such an historical perspective is all the more necessary since our discussion in previous chapters has made it clear that Galilee was part of an evolving and changing social and cultural situation. Urbanization in its earlier or later phases had not destroyed the essentially rural and peasant society of the province, and the indications are that social, economic and cultural divisions more or less corresponded with the primary distinction between town and country. Examining this many-sided social situation might suggest that all the elements for the classic revolution by modern standards were to be found amongst the peasant population there.[8] Galilee, it could be argued was particularly vulnerable: absentee landlordism, centuries of being deprived of the best produce of a fertile country, aristocracy and their ways, a heavy burden of taxes both secular and religious, a sense of inferiority vis à vis their Judaean brethren, yet with a great attachment to the ancestral religion and its cultic center - these and other factors in the Galilean peasants' life might be regarded as creating a deep-seated feeling of dissent that only needed to be ignited in order to erupt into violent and bloody revolution against oppressors, native and foreign alike. Does this picture correspond with the facts?

I
THE NATURE OF GALILEAN RESISTANCE TO HEROD THE GREAT

In our historical survey of Herod the Great's relations with Galilee we argued that Hezekiah, the archbrigand whom he executed was no ordinary highwayman, but rather a Hasmonaean supporter, who may indeed have been forced to adopt robber tactics due to the defeat of Peitholaus. We noted that relief at his removal was felt not in Galilee but in Syria, and the reactions show that the incident was much more serious in Jewish eyes than Josephus or his pro-Herodian source would have us believe.[9] Thus the labeling of Hezekiah ἀρχιλήστης is itself no proof that he was a forerunner of the Fourth Philosophy whom Josephus repeatedly describes in similar terms. While readily admitting the possibility that such tactics are quite conceivable in the border area (cf. *Ant* 17:26; *War* 4:105), the likelihood is that it is intended as a term of opprobrium for Hezekiah, either stemming from Nicholas, who in turn would have been influenced by Roman propaganda writers, or from Josephus' own polemical concerns about the revolutionaries of his day.[10]

What of Herod's subsequent problems in Galilee? We have also argued in the historical section that while the province was the center of Hasmonaean resistance to Herod, this was localized and to some extent socially restricted. The Parthian presence rather than the Galilean populace was the decisive factor in the resistance of those Hasmonaean supporters who had continued Hezekiah's struggle. Of course Antigonus was not slow to point to his own ancestry in an attempt to win widespread support and establish his and his family's claims. His address to Silo, the Roman commander (*Ant* 14:403-5) surely echoes Hasmonaean thinking, whatever the source of this passage.[11] Herod was an Idumaean and a commoner (ἰδιώτῃ τε ὄντι), and as a half-Jew he should not receive the kingship; whereas his family had the tradition of kingship and were priests. This same emphasis underlies the recollection that Aristobulus I was the first Hasmonaean to accept the title of king '48 years and 3 months after the time the people were released from Babylon' (*Ant* 13:301), an implicit claim to the restoration of the Davidic kingship, apparently.[12] It is difficult to say how successful such appeals were, but we do hear of support for the Hasmonaean in Jericho and, surprisingly, in Idumaea also (*Ant* 14:410.413).

Mention has already been made of the heroism of the old man of Arbela who, rather than surrender to Herod, sacrificed his wife and seven sons and then hurled himself over the cliff 'thus submitting to death rather than slavery' (*Ant* 14:429f). This recalls both the Maccabean martyrs and the later slogans of the Fourth Philosophy, and we must recognize the possibility that there was an underlying ideological link between the Maccabees and the defenders of Masada, as W.R. Farmer in particular has argued.[13] Nevertheless, caution is called for, not just because of Josephus' well-known literary and apologetic device of such retrojections,[14] but also because of the nature of the old man's protest. In fact he upbraids Herod, not for assuming kingship but for his 'meaness of spirit' or more probably (Thackeray), 'lowly origins' (ἐις ταπεινότητα , *Ant* 14:430; *War* 1:313).

Was the issue of kingship - Herod's or the Hasmonaeans' - likely to have been a vital one among the Galilean populace? Seeing that Roman rule had put an end to the Hasmonaean kingship and Hyrcanus was given the title 'ethnarch' (*Ant* 14:194)[15], it might seem that this would be the case. Certainly the *Psalms of Solomon,* especially Ps.17, generally recognized to be a response to the crisis of Pompey's takeover[16], points in that direction, with its longing for the messianic king of David's line: 'Behold O Lord, and raise up unto them their king, the son of David, at the time in which thou seest, O God, that they may reign over Israel thy ser-vant' (v.23). Yet one detects in this psalm (cf. also 8:5-14) not merely a critique of the Roman sinners who have defiled the sanctuary, but also of the Hamonaean kings.[17] Thus we read: 'They set up a (worldly) monarchy (βασιλεῖον) in place of (that which was) their excellency (ἀντὶ ὕψους αὐτῶν). They laid waste the throne of David in tumultuous arrogance' (v.6), but the Davidic king to come 'shall be righteous and taught by God . . . For he shall not put his trust in horse or rider and bow, nor shall he multiply for himself gold and silver for war. Nor shall he gather confidence from a multitude for the day of battle' (vv.32f).[18] This Pharisaic criticism of the existing Hasmonean kingship had already appeared during the reign of Alexander Jannaeus and at the time of the deposition of Hyrcanus, when Josephus says that the people (ἔθνος) were against both Hyrcanus and Aristobu-lus and asked not to be ruled by a king, 'saying that it was the custom of their country to obey the priests of the God who was venerated by them, but that these two who were descended from priests were seeking to change the form of government in order that they might become a nation of slaves' (*Ant* 14:41). Similar

sentiments were expressed again on the death of Herod the Great
when Jewish envoys speaking on behalf of the people asked for
the dissolution of kingship and declared their readiness to be
integrated into the Roman provincial system (*Ant* 17:299f.304.
314).[19]

There was then a consistent critique of existing kingship both
Hasmonaean and Herodian throughout the first century B.C.E.
in Palestine, without the outright rejection of the idea itself in
terms of the ideal messianic king of David's line. But since these
ideas are to be identified with Pharisaic circles in particular it
seems unlikely that they would have been very current in Galilean
peasant circles, at least at that stage.[20] This should be kept in mind
in evaluating the impact of the revolt of Judas son of Hezekiah in
4 B.C.E. at Sepphoris in Galilee.

Josephus links this particular disturbance with a general revolt
all over Palestine that occurred while Archelaus and Antipas
were in Rome defending their respective claims to the throne
before Augustus. The trouble began during the feast of Pentecost
when pilgrims from Galilee, Idumaea, Jericho and Transjordan,
as well as Judaea displayed their anger with the Roman general
Sabinius who had offended their sensitibilities by raiding the
royal treasury within the temple precincts. The Judaeans are
particularly singled out for their aggressiveness on that occasion
(*Ant* 17:254; *War* 2:43). The ensuing pitched battle saw many
Jews killed, and presumably this gave rise to disturbances all over
the country. After briefly mentioning a revolt of some 2,000 of
Herod's former troops, Josephus lists the revolts of Judas in
Galilee, Simon, a royal slave, in Jericho and Athronges in Judaea.
There is a schematic quality about this enumeration, and the
impression is that Josephus wishes to elaborate further on his
earlier statements that people from the various geographic
regions were involved in the disturbances at Jerusalem (254)
and that subsequently 'new tumults filled Judaea and in many
quarters many men rose in arms either in the hope of personal
gain or out of hatred for the Jews' (269; cf. *War* 2:55). There is no
indication that the three examples given in more detail, Judas,
Simon and Athronges, were part of any united front, indeed they
are rival royal aspirants and *War* 2:55 suggests that many others
aspired to the sovereignty (βασιλείαν; *Ant* 17:285). This is

obviously an exaggeration and raises the question of how seriously we are to take the royal pretensions of any of the contenders, or more importantly, how seriously their claims were taken by people in general. The *Antiquities* account of Judas' revolt says 'that he was zealous for kingly power' (καὶ ζηλώσει βασιλείου τιμῆς), and having armed his men from the royal arsenal at Sepphoris engaged in plundering, whereas in *War* we hear that he attacked the other aspirants for power (τοῖς τὴν δυναστείαν ζηλοῦσιν).

Both Hengel and Farmer seek to emphasize the messianic quality of this uprising, thus seeing it as part of the apocalyptic-messianic background of the later Zealot party. According to Hengel, Josephus does not present it in that light because, as apologist of his people to the Romans, he tends to ignore the future hope that was an integral part of Jewish theology.[21] Yet this should not obscure the fact that within Jewish Apocalyptic expectation no sharp distinction should be drawn between an earthly-political and transcendental, other-world figure, as the imagery of much of this literature makes clear.[22] One can readily accept that the deepest well-springs of Jewish religious belief would be used in order to gain wide popular support for royal claims that any messianic pretender might have wished to make. Yet the question of legitimacy was an important one, and in realistic terms Judas son of Hezekiah would have had to represent himself as carrying forward some recognizable tradition of kingship - Hasmonaean or Herodian.[23] Naturally, because of his father, he would have been deadly opposed to Herod and his line, and besides in the light of our previous discussion about Hezekiah, it would have been natural for him to have claimed Hasmonaean lineage.[24] To have escaped the purges of Herod meant that he was not in the direct line and may have been able to hide his real loyalties during that period only to re-emerge as the leader of those remnants of Galilean Hasmonaean aristocracy that had survived at Sepphoris and its neighborhood.[25] The possibility of Judas gaining wide popular support for his claims by appealing to their messianic expectations would appear to be limited, however. True there is evidence of messianic qualities being attributed to John Hyrcanus, but not to any of the other Hasmonaeans. On the other hand, if Rudolf Meyer's conjecture that the

Hezekiah of rabbinic literature with whom certain end-time expectations were linked, is to be identified with the Hezekiah whom Herod executed, it may be that Judas was able to appeal to legendary beliefs about his father and draw on some popular assumptions about a warlike Messiah as a way to bolster his campaign.[26] We shall have occasion to return to these suggestions in the final section of our study in an examination of the religious, or more specifically the apocalyptic climate of Galilee. For now, however, the conclusion from our earlier historical section must stand, namely that the main support for Hasmonaean royal claims in Galilee came from the upper levels of society rather then the populace at large. The effort to whip up popular support by making appeal to the religious sentiment of the people seems to have failed since Varus or his delegate(s) had only to subdue Sepphoris, in a rather ruthless fashion admittedly (*Ant* 17:295; *War* 2:75), to put an end to the uprising, and we hear nothing further of Judas son of Hezekiah. Our conclusion must be that the disturbances in Galilee at the beginning and the end of Herod's reign do not warrant the assumption that Galilee as a whole was a hot-bed of revolutionary apocalyptic messianism from that early date, no matter how much the attempt was made to exploit such ideas among the common people. Insofar as these events betray the attitudes of the masses, the Galileans included, it is the violation of the temple in Jerusalem rather than would-be messianic or royal claimants that aroused their passions. Does this suggest a separation between kingship and temple that is at least unexpected, even unlikely, given the Davidic background of both hopes?

II
JUDAS THE GALILEAN AND JESUS OF NAZARETH AS FOCAL POINTS FOR GALILEAN REVOLUTIONARY IDEOLOGY?

A distinguished Jewish Rabbi, Gamaliel I, compared the fate of Jesus of Nazareth with, among others, that of Judas the Galilean (*Ac* 5:37) For our discussion the comparison is particularly suggestive in that Jesus' ministry was in Galilee and Judas apparently came from there, it being generally agreed that the epithet 'Galilean' was given to him after he had actually left the province.[27] Even more intriguing is the fact that whereas Judas proclaimed the kingship of God alone, and this eventually led to his own downfall and that of his family, Jesus was put to death on a charge of, amongst other things, seeking to destroy the temple. In the light of the question just posed – temple or kingship as the focus of the Galilean populace's revolutionary concerns – perhaps an examination of the impact of these charismatic figures on life in the province may point towards a possible answer.

Judas the Galilean is mentioned for the first time by Josephus in connection with a census of the territory of the deposed Archelaus which was being incorporated into the Roman provincial system (*War* 2:118; *Ant* 18:23).[28] Since it was only Judaea in the strict sense that was involved, it is generally recognized that Judas' call to 'his kinsmen' (τοὺς ἐπιχωρίους) was addressed to Judaeans rather than Galileans. Nevertheless, there is a general assumption by many scholars, presumably because of the epithet 'Galilean', that this Judas is to be identified with Judas son of Hezekiah whose revolt in Sepphoris we have just discussed. Since Josephus speaks of sons of Judas the Galilean being actively engaged in subsequent resistance to Rome in Judaea, down to the fall of Masada in 73 C.E. a dynasty of Galilean revolutionaries is established ranging from Hezekiah to Eleazar of Masada.[29] There is nothing inherently improbable about such an identification, yet a consideration of other possibilities will at least suggest caution in building up any elaborate theories about the revolutionary spirit of Galilee on the basis of this family having deep roots there. It will also serve to underline the very different character of the events of 6 C.E. from those of ten years earlier in Galilee.

Even though there are obvious discrepancies between the two accounts, the basic outline of the Fourth Philosophy emerges from both *War* and *Antiquities*.[30] Judas is described as a 'sophist' who together with a Pharisee named Saddok issued a call to freedom by refusing to pay tribute to the Romans or accepting any man as master, but only God alone (*Ant* 18:6-10.23-25; *War* 2:118). The most significant difference between this program and the aim of Judas son of Hezekiah is that the latter sought the kingship for himself whereas Judas the Galilean's platform as described by Hengel is, 'a radicalization of the first command-ment' and a refusal to accept any form of human kingship.[31] Of

course it can be argued that this difference is more apparent than
real. Once it is admitted that the Judas of 4 B.C.E. saw himself as a
messianic pretender and the Judas of 6 C.E. was opposed to
illegitimate human overlordship, the two positions would have
a common meeting place in the royal messianic traditions of
Judaism.[32] However, we have seen that there are strong reasons
for suspecting that Judas son of Hezekiah was laying claim to the
Hasmonaean traditions of kingship and so would have a
Sadducaean base, whereas in all probability Judas the Galilean's
position was rooted in Pharisaism (*Ant* 18:23), despite the attempt
to isolate him and his philosophy from all the other sects in *War*
2:118.[33] There had always been a certain reserve in Israel with
regard to human kingship, dating from the anti-monarchic
traditions of *I Sm* 8-12, and the Pharisees had carried on this
tradition in their opposition to the Hasmonaean kingship, as
already discussed. It would seem then that Judas the Galilean
must be regarded as having made a definite theological and
social shift in the intervening ten years if he is to be identified
with Judas son of Hezekiah. Of course such a change is not
totally improbable, as the example of Josephus a half century
later makes clear (*Life* 11f). Several perfectly good reasons can be
suggested. He may have become disillusioned with the lack of
support from the Sadducaean aristocracy who saw better times
ahead now that the rule of the Herods was over; or the popular
appeal of Pharisaism may have attracted him on his transfer to
Jerusalem from Galilee; or he may not be the same person!
Fortunately we do not have to pass judgment on any of these
conjectures once it is recognized that Judas' radical call is Judaean
and Jerusalem-based, not Galilean. In other words Judas' revolutionary spirit had been fostered not in his homeland but at the
ideological center of Judaism and under the influence of the
party whose program it was to extend the theocratic ideal to the
daily lives of all Jews.[34]

We hear nothing from Josephus about the outcome of Judas'
call to revolt, and are dependent on the brief notice at *Ac* 5:37 for
the information that he perished and his followers were scattered.
This raises the question of what became of the Fourth Philosophy
and its ideals from the death of Judas to the time when it emerges
again under a different though recognizable guise in the

immediate pre-revolt period. Judas is described as a powerful teacher (σοφιστὴς δεινόνατος, *War* 2:433) and presumably his opinions were carried forward, no matter how difficult it was to take positive steps to implement them. Certainly the silence of our sources is in this case no evidence that such a movement did not continue to exist, even flourish, given the harsh realities of political life in procuratorial Judaea.[35] The differing scholarly opinions about the existence of the Zealot party between 6 C.E. and 66 C.E., already referred to, may to some extent be a difference of emphasis, since Hengel (as the classic representative of the view that it was a unified movement which later splintered), Smith and Rhoads (spokesmen for a disparate and multifaceted situation) would all agree that Judas' action did have a continued relevance up to and including the period of the revolt.[36] Our concern is to see how far that influence moved from the center to Galilee, since we know that more orthodox Pharisaism was attempting to move in a similar direction in the same period.[37]

Before turning to the ministry of Jesus of Nazareth for a more adequate view of the situation in the province, there are two brief notices concerning the Galileans worthy of consideration. The first is the tantalizingly vague reference to 'those Galileans whose blood Pilate mingled with their sacrifices' at *Lk* 13:1-4 and the second concerns Galilean attitudes on the occasion of the border incident with the Samaritans (*Ant* 20:120). There seems to be no possibility of identifying the former episode with any of the reported acts of cruelty of Pilate, especially if we insist with Blintzler that the phrase ὧν τὸ αἷμα Πίλατος ἐμίξεν μετὰ τῶν θυσίων refers to the actual act of sacrificing in the temple area rather than loosely describing the general occasion of a pilgrimage to the temple, when the episode could have taken place.[38] Unfortunately Luke's often acclaimed historical interest is not matched by his carefulness in checking his facts[39] and to attempt to bring this incident into close relationship with the so-called 'revolt in the desert' (cf *Jn* 6:14f) is a rather hazardous, if tempting undertaking.[40] For our purposes it is sufficient to note that the incident involving Galilean pilgrims took place within the jurisdiction of Pilate, who handled the affair with his usual tactless brutality.

The other incident with the Samaritans is more circumstantially reported, but as already noted there are important lacunae. In particular we should like to know more about the Roman administrative take-over of Galilee on the death of Agrippa I in 44 C.E. and whether there had been any disturbances in the province comparable to those of 6 C.E. in Galilee, but in the absence of any positive information we have no right to assume that there was. In fact the attitude of the Jews, presumably Galilean Jews, at Tiberias who resorted to a peaceful agricultural strike rather than violent resistance in the affair with Petronius over Gaius' statue, would seem to point to a rather different atmosphere in the province (*Ant* 18:274.284). However, Josephus does attribute Zealot-type tendencies to the Galileans in the border incident with the Samaritans. The *Ant* account implicates them much more than *War,* for it asserts that once the appeal of the leaders (οἱ πρῶτοι) to Cumanus had fallen on deaf ears for whatever reason, the Galileans, indignant at this, urged the Jewish masses to resort to arms and to assert their liberty, (ἐλευθερία) for, they said, slavery was in itself bitter, but when it involved insolent treatment it was quite intolerable' (*Ant* 20:120).[41] It could be argued that the placing of this slogan on the Galileans' lips was Josephus' way of branding the whole population of the area with the attitudes of their fellow countryman, Judas (*Ant* 18:23) and in line with his own self-defense as a peace-keeping moderate in the province later – the theme of *Life* which is the appendix to *Ant.* If that was his intention then he was particularly successful, since the picture of the Galileans he wished to portray is still the accepted one. Nevertheless, we must be open to the idea that genuine revolutionary ideas were actually current in the province then, while noting once again that it is on the occasion of national festivals in Jerusalem that these manifest themselves. As a significant footnote to the whole affair it should also be noted that when the governor of Syria, Ummidius Quadratus eventually intervened, chastising the culprits and sending those responsible to Rome, he turned his attention to Jerusalem, not Galilee, there to find that all was peaceful as the people celebrated a feast (*Ant* 20:133; *War* 2:244).

Turning from Judas to his younger contemporary Jesus, takes us back from Jerusalem to Galilee. Immediately we encounter the problem of how legitimate it is to use the Gospels as sources to reconstruct pre-Easter Galilean situations given their clearly kerygmatic and theological concerns. We cannot here delay to elaborate any overall theory about the historical nature of the gospels, but simply declare our conviction that it is possible to reconstruct from the tradtions embedded in them certain patterns of life in Galilee and Jesus' response to his own socio-political situation, provided we proceed with critical caution. Such caution is all the more necessary in view of the very differing assumptions that underlie many of the contemporary views of Jesus, even among scholars supposedly engaged in scientific study. S.F.G. Brandon, for example, brings a wealth of scholarly information and a keen historical sense to show that Jesus, if not a member of the Zealot party at least aligned himself very closely with their philosophy, with only a difference of emphasis. He was more concerned 'to attack the Jewish sacerdotal aristocracy than to embroil himself with the Romans'.[42] At the other end of the spectrum, Heinz Kreissig, arguing from a self-consciously Marxist position, maintains 'that Jesus and his followers were a group of counter-agitators operating against the Judas-Saddok group. This is all the more likely since Jesus spent such a long time in Galilee'.[43] More recently, Geza Vermes has attempted to recover Jesus for pietistic Judaism by locating him within the context of the Galilean *Hasîd* tradition.[44] What is significant about these three samples is not the fact that all three have been less than enthusiastically received in the scholarly world, but rather the different emphasis that different presuppositions can find in the same material. We have no intention of competing by offering a fourth version. Our aim is simply to ask the question whether the main thrust of Jesus' ministry presupposes a Galilean revolutionary ethos, as all three books just mentioned, and many of their critics alike, presuppose.[45]

By general agreement central to the preaching of Jesus was the notion of the kingdom of God, whose advent he proclaimed to the Galilean crowds.[46] In view of our previous discussion about kingship in Judaism, the possibility must have been very real that Jesus' audience would have understood his message and the symbols he used to express it in political terms. Further, Jesus' association with the Baptist and his movement, attested in various ways by all the gospels, should have made him suspect in Herodian eyes, especially if we accept the Josephan rather than the gospel version of John's death as the more historically probable.[47] The Baptist's preaching as recorded by Luke (3:10-14) would have been interpreted as a serious criticism of the court and its officials and likely to make him popular with those who suffered social or economic oppression. Little wonder that Antipas wanted to be rid of John as a social agitator (*Ant* 18:118) and was apparently also concerned about Jesus and his doings (*Mk* 6:14-16; *Lk* 13:31-33). If Galilee was the center of Jewish revolutionary ideas at the time, one would expect that both hypotheses would be verified, namely an excited acceptance of the liberator Messiah by the populace and a hostile, decisive movement against him on the part of the defenders of the political status quo. Does this picture fit well with the recoverable facts and what stance did Jesus adopt in this allegedly revolutionary environment?

Even allowing maximum historical reliability to all the passages that relate to Jesus and Antipas, one has to be struck by how little the Herodian monarch intrudes himself into the gospel story. True, Mark does suggest that the Herodians joined forces with the Pharisees in seeking to destroy Jesus, both in Galilee (3:6) and Jerusalem (12:13), but the combination is, to say the least, very unlikely historically in either place and in fact is dropped by Luke altogether and retained by Matthew only in the Jerusalem pericope (22:16). This also raises problems about the warning concerning the leaven of the Pharisees and the leaven of Herod (or Herodians according to WΘ Φ Sa), whatever the original import of the saying (*Mk* 8:15), and once again both Matthew and Luke omit the reference to Herod or the Herodians altogether (*Mt* 16:6; *Lk* 12:1).[48] The frequent withdrawals of Jesus might be interpreted as indicative of his need for constant vigilance before the threat of Herod, especially since there seems to be a conscious avoidance of the Herodian towns of Sepphoris and Tiberias (cf *Mk* 6:31f; 6:45; 6:53; 7:31; 8:10; 8:22; 8:27; 9:2; 9:30. 33; 10:1). Even Hoehner's historicizing treatment of these incidents admits that some at least had religious rather than political intent, and thus the warning of *Lk* 13:31 and Jesus' independent attitude on hearing of Herod's threats stand in isolation.[49] The appearance of Antipas in the trial of Jesus (*Lk* 23:6-12) raises as many questions as it answers, but at least it does make it clear that there was no open animosity between the prophet and the king - whatever the motives of Pilate - or Luke? - for introducing the latter.[50] This backstage role of Herod in the whole ministry of Jesus may have been part of early Christian apologetic in which the ministry of Jesus was depoliticized. Yet on the available evidence all we can say is that, though Jesus may have aroused the curiosity, even the suspicions of Antipas and his court, no drastic action was taken, and the course of his ministry in Galilee was not unduly impeded, quite a contrast to the fate of the Baptist.

What of the Galilean crowds and Jesus' relations with them? Does their overall reaction to him suggest large-scale revolutionary or zealotic concerns, and how did he conduct himself in the context of such attitudes? There is no necessity to refute in detail here Brandon's theory of a zealotic Jesus since there is large-scale agreement that it is far too one-sided, hypothetical and based on unfounded assumptions.[51] Nevertheless it does help to focus on certain aspects of the ministry and sayings of Jesus that call for discussion in this context. The fact that one of Jesus' close followers is called Simon, 'the Cananaean' (*Mt* 10:4; *Mk* 3:18) which Luke translates 'the Zealot' (ὁ ζηλώτης, *Lk* 6:15; *Ac* 1:13) is perhaps the one single piece of information from the gospels that most clearly suggests a revolutionary situation in Galilee and of course it played a large role in Brandon's argument. Hengel, at least in his more recent publication, is more cautious, since clearly Simon would have to be regarded as an ex-Zealot, especially since the same group contained a tax-collector, one of the most hated symbols of Roman control.[51] Still others argue with some justification that since ὁ Καναναῖος of *Mt* and *Mk* is clearly more original than Luke's ὁ ζηλώτης, Simon was one of that class of Jews known from rabbinic sources as the *qannaim*, those specially zealous for the law and its observance who later formed a party of zealous defenders of the temple.[52]

Turning to the actual teaching of Jesus we can begin with the parables since it is generally recognized that they, more than any other section of the gospels, reflect the social situation of Galilee in the first century C.E. It is noteworthy that of all the parables of Jesus - forty in all according to Jeremias' count - only two have been understood as reflecting a possible Zealot situation. The first of these is the parable of the patient husbandman, *Mk* 4:26-29. The point of contrast in this parable clearly lies in its stressing the passivity of man and his powerlessness to bring about the kingdom prematurely once the sowing has taken place (ἀυτομάτη, of itself). In attempting to attribute to the parable a *Sitz im Leben Jesu,* it would be generally accepted that the story is addressed to those who were impatient with the approach and success rate of Jesus' ministry. However, there is nothing in the story itself to suggest that this impatience springs from adherence to the tenets of the Fourth Philosophy. In cautiously making that suggestion Jeremias introduces the extraneous information that two ex-Zealots were to be found in the intimate circle of Jesus' followers, Simon, and Judas Iscariot presumably.[53] The second parable, that of the king who went to a far country to obtain kingly power and then return, has been interpreted to refer to Archelaus who in 4 B.C.E. went to Rome to obtain formal ratification from Augustus as his father's successor.[54] If this is the actual historical referent of the original parable, now conflated with that of the talents in Luke (19:11-27 cf. vv. 12b.14-15a.27), it is noteworthy that the story does not seem to have supported the zealot ideal, even though elsewhere Jesus has rejected such displays of power from the kings of the gentiles as unworthy of his disciples (*Mk* 10:42). Rather in this case the king's authoritative relationship with his subjects is underlined, for he has the rebellious servants 'who did not want him to rule over them' slain before him (v.27). Thus Jesus used what could have been a sensitive example in terms of his hearers' attitudes as illustrative of his own message, without affirming or challenging the values of either the subjects or the king. True the example came from Judaean rather than Galilean political life, but the question remains whether this kind of illustration was likely to have been chosen had his hearers been infected with Zealot ideals.

Examination of the other pertinent sayings of Jesus would appear to confirm this first impression, namely that Jesus was not overly concerned with zealotism, and did not regard it as the dominant ideological competitor for his audience's attention. The enigmatic saying about violent men forcing their way into the kingdom (*Mt* 11:12; *Lk* 16:16) may indeed reflect an increase in zealotism 'since the days of John the Baptist until now', but it is not at all a dominant note, and it certainly cannot be taken as a call for radical action by Jesus to his own followers.[55] Perhaps more telling is his emphatic renunciation of violence in the Q sayings preserved in *Mt* 5:38-48; *Lk* 6:27-36, behind some of which at least lies a very definite social and political situation of law courts, usury and legal constraint.[56] While it is possible to recognize in these sayings a situation of injustice, inequality and even violence, it would be limiting their original application unduly to suggest that they were addressed solely or even primarily to the dangers of zealotism infecting the circle of Jesus' disciples. In our chapter dealing with the social relations in Galilee we have touched on the widespread injustice in the province and the economic pressures on the 'small man' in town or country with increased taxation, ambitious rulers and ruthless foreign exploiters. All these were endemic to the social fabric of the ancient world and in this respect Galilee was no different from other areas with good agricultural potential. But before we can identify all such evils as indicators of the widespread acceptance of the ideology of Judas the Galilean, we would have to be able to show that resistance, even violent resistance, was motivated by religious as well as social ideals. We shall be in a better position to discuss this point when we come to examine the conditions obtaining at the outbreak of the first revolt, since the sources do reflect a combination of social and religious concerns at that time. For the present we must avoid retrojecting this combination of motives to an earlier period if there is no clear evidence to support it.

A strong component in the recorded teaching of Jesus is his admonitions on the dangers of riches and his radical call for detachment by his disciples (*Mt* 5:3; 19:16-30; *Lk* 6:20-21; 12:22-34; 16:10-14; *Mk* 10:17-30).[57] Yet this theme does not dominate the parables with the two exceptions of the rich fool (*Lk* 12:16-20) and the rich man and Lazarus (*Lk* 16:19-31), even though so many of them reflect the social conditions of his own day, as we saw in the last chapter. Once it is accepted that Jesus had no desire to align himself with political action against Rome (*Mk* 12:17),[58] we are faced with the same dilemma as earlier – Jesus felt free to draw on the world of experience of his hearers for his images and meta-phors without passing any moral judgment on that social situa-tion.[59] If social issues and political activism had been so inextricably bound together as Kreissig, for example, would have us believe, surely greater caution would have been called for and a much more hostile reception experienced. The silence of the gospel tradition concerning the Zealots, especially when one considers the condemnations of Pharisees and Sadducees, cannot be used to argue for a deep-seated agreement between Jesus and the Fourth Philosophy, as Brandon maintains, in view of the other ideological differences to which we have already alluded.[60]

Neither is Yoder's explanation of the non-appearance of the Zealots in the gospels being due to the later disappearance of the group, very convincing.[61] The Zealots were, after all, a very powerful force in Palestine in the period of the formation of the gospel tradition, and after 70 C.E. a Jesus-figure totally opposed to the Zealot ideal would have made excellent propaganda material in the Roman world, as the line of argument in Josephus' *Life* indicates. It may be then, that the gospels do not reflect zealotic ideals, or avoid issues that might be deemed sensitive to Zealots because these were not dominant issues in Galilee at the time of Jesus.

This tentative conclusion has, however, to be balanced by the fact that Jesus was put to death by Romans on charges of 'perverting our nation . . . from Galilee to this place', as Luke puts the charge (*Lk* 23:3-5; cf *Jn* 11:48; 19:12; *Mk* 15:2.26).[62] We must avoid what Yoder calls 'over-spiritualizing exegesis' and recog-nize that his ministry and his movement were seen as a threat to Roman good order in Palestine.[63] Nor can we confine this 'political' aspect of Jesus' life to the Jerusalem phase where confrontation with Jewish religious authorities in the temple inevitably left him open to the charge of being a disturber of the peace. For our purposes the so called 'revolt in the desert' (*Jn* 6:14f; cf. *Mk* 6:45) is more significant since it involved Galilean crowds, and the desert had apparently become an evocative loca-tion for religio-political revolutionaries (*Ant* 20:168; *Ac* 21:38). The incident in question is closely related to the first feeding miracle, but even if we prescind from this story with its theologi-cal and mythological traits, we are still left with a 'framework', to use Dodd's term, the historical value of which cannot be dismissed so lightly.[64] As already noted, Blintzler has suggested bringing the incident into relation with the episode of the Galileans and Pilate to which Luke alludes (13:1), as well as with Jesus' reluctance 'to go up openly to the feast' (*Jn* 7:2).[65] While such conflations are not likely to gain very wide acceptance, his following is reported to have sought forcibly (ἁρπάζειν) to install Jesus as king.

The incident is merely suggested by Mark's language - Jesus 'compelled' the disciples to enter the boat while he himself 'dismissed' the crowd, whereas John states explicitly: 'when the people (οἱ ἀνθρώποι) saw the sign(s) which he had done, they said, 'This is indeed the prophet who is to come into the world!' Perceiving that they were about to come and take him by force and make him king, Jesus withdrew again to the hills by himself' (*Jn* 6.14f). How are we to judge the historical reliability of this report? *Pace* Dodd, Brown and Glasson[66] for example, a good case can be made out for the view that *Jn* 6:14f fits extremely well into the larger theological scheme of the author. The titles 'prophet' and 'king' are brought together here as applicable to Jesus, only to be rejected in favor of a deeper understanding of both - the prophet who not merely does signs but speaks of God, and the king whose kingship is not 'from here', but is based on his bearing witness to the truth (*Jn* 18:36-38).[67] As is frequently the case in John, however, theology is grounded in history,[68] and the fact that the Markan narrative reflects the same incident, though apparently there is no literary relationship between the two[69], points to tradition older than either gospel. Josephus (*Ant* 20:168f) shows that there is no historical improbability about the crowds' reactions to the sign-performing prophet. Therefore, Dodd's suggestion that there was a *prima facie* political aspect to the claims made for Jesus, fragments of which are still to be found in our gospels and which reflect the earliest unformed traditions in Palestine, is worthy of serious consideration,[70] These elements would have become largely submerged later as the political scene changed or because it was no longer expedient to retain them. Yet the recognition of this fact hardly allows us to build up a theory such as that of Montefiore who sees in the Markan account the elements of a genuine revolt of 5,000 men in the desert.[71] The Baptist's fate on being suspected of initiating an insurrection

would seem to preclude that Jesus' revolt was of similar proportions. We are thus faced with the possibility that the Galilean
crowds did in fact respond politically to Jesus' ministry among
them, but we are largely in the dark about the exact magnitude or
nature of their involvement. That Jesus utterly rejected such
expectations is clear from the whole understanding of his
message as well as his reaction to individual disciples' expectations (*Mk* 8:33; 10:38f; *Lk* 24:21; *Ac* 1:6), yet the movement and
expectation was sufficient to serve as the basis for a later charge
against him before the Roman authorities. Once again Jerusalem
rather than Galilee was the scene of the final authoritative
reaction.

Summing up this discussion of Galilean revolutionary attitudes as these crystalized around Judas the Galilean and Jesus of
Nazareth, we can say that Jerusalem rather than Galilee was the
focal point of resistance – even for Galileans. This helps to underline the religious aspect of all resistance to Rome in the first
century, as Hengel so rightly stresses. Galilee and Galileans were
not so isolated from attitudes elsewhere to have been unaffected by
strong nationalistic feelings, at least on the occasion of the great
feasts and the pilgrimages, and as we suggested, there must have
been many shades of opinion as to how these feelings could best
be implemented. One suspects that countrypeople were likely to
react spasmodically and in a disorganized way, if only because
they were cut off from each other in the isolation of village communities. A wandering prophet-like figure such as Jesus, was
likely to draw together many such disparate strands, and the
religious-apocalyptic tone of his language could easily have been
interpreted in political terms by those with such hopes and
expectations. To use the terminology recently adopted by
Norman Perrin,[72] the tensive symbol, 'kingdom of God', would
easily have been turned into a steno symbol with a purely political
referent by those who were looking for a catalyst who could draw
together such varied hopes and expectations. However, this was
only one aspect of the fascination of Jesus for the Galilean crowds,
for, we shall see, interest in his thaumaturgic healing powers,
displaying a personal rather than a national concern, was an
equally attractive aspect for many, at least on the basis of the
gospel portrait.[73] This false understanding of his person and

mission was, for him, as dangerous as the politicization of his message in terms of the Zealot's ideals. Once it is recognized that viewed sociologically, 'charisma is a social relationship rather than an attribute of individual personality or a mystical quality', it is clear that Jesus, with his explicit rejection of the Zealot ideology could never have functioned as the charismatic prophet that a revolutionary Galilee would have required.[74] The essential correspondence between popular expectation and prophetic intuition would have been lacking. Our argument has been that in fact no such revolutionary ethos comes clearly into focus in the ministry of Jesus, despite occasional pockets here and there. This explains the apparent indifference of Jesus to the concerns of the revolutionaries, both in the images he chose to illustrate his message and the choice and constitution of his intimate band of followers. Specifically as the Twelve, his followers, if not himself, might have been seen as standing for the restoration of national unity, in terms of the twelve tribes, yet no such movement crystalized around them in Galilee.[75] Rather, their thaumaturgic powers are likewise stressed. We must now consider whether the situation had materially changed at the outbreak of the first revolt, since, one suspects, it is on the basis of the alleged revolutionary spirit then in the province that many commentators assume a previously similar situation.

III
GALILEAN REVOLUTIONARY ASPIRATIONS AND THE REVOLT AGAINST ROME

We have already discussed the situation in Galilee immediately prior to the great revolt and noted that Cestius Gallus does not appear to have been unduly disturbed by developments in the province except for the border territory with Ptolemais around Chabulon and the neighborhood of Sepphoris (*War* 2:502.10-13). Perhaps we have minimized this situation since Josephus does admit that even after pillaging the countryside around Chabulon the Jews were able to reassemble and surprise 2,000 of the Roman auxiliaries from the Syrian towns. Furthermore the rebels and brigands of the Sepphoris area, τὸ δὲ στασιῶδες καὶ λῃστρικὸν πᾶν, resisted the advances of Cestius' general, Caesennius Gallus for some time, even though only 2,000 plus in number. There is then armed resistance to Rome in Galilee even before Josephus' arrival in the province, and perhaps we, or Cestius Gallus, were deceived in assuming that it was not of more serious proportions.

This suggestion might appear to receive further support from the Galilean hostility to the pro-Roman town of Sepphoris (*Life* 30.39.373-80) and the Herodian city of Tiberias (*Life* 98-100.381-9) but our discussions in previous chapters concerning the relations of these cities with their hinterlands and the social stratification of Galilee suggest caution at this point. When we examine the full range of antipathy between town and country in Galilee the division is not just between pro-Roman centers and an anti-Roman populace, even though this was no doubt one aspect of the pattern. Gabara and Gischala were also unpopular with the Galileans, if we are to trust Josephus, even though both were unquestionably Jewish towns. (*Life* 102f.368, Gischala, and 124f. 263-5, Gabara). To further complicate the issue Gabara is listed as one of those places the inhabitants of which engaged in the sacking of Gischala (*Life* 44).[76] Tarichaeae, on the other hand might be expected to be on the list of pro-Roman centers, since it had an amphitheatre, one of the sure signs of the Greek way of life, and was in Herodian territory, yet it retained excellent relations with the countrypeople apparently (*Life* 98f.304-6). Thus we are faced with a complex situation of loyalties and tensions. Thus not all violence or hostility is directly attributable to the Fourth Philosophy's ideology for it had social and cultural roots as well that may have existed independently of the struggle with Rome.

Before inquiring further about possible revolutionary characteristics of these inner-Galilean tensions it is well to compare it, however briefly with the situation in the Judaean countryside at the same time. The signal for revolt against Rome was given by Eleazar ben Ananias, the temple captain and some lesser priests, who took control of the temple and its worship, outlawing sacrifices for the Romans (*War* 2:409f). That this revolt had a strong religious motivation is made clear by the fact that the chief priests and the leading Pharisees attempted to dissuade the revolutionaries by an appeal to tradition, declaring that this 'was a strange innovation into their religion' and priestly experts were found who declared that 'all their ancestors had accepted the sacrifice of aliens' (*War* 2:414.417).[77] Despite all the subsequent faction fighting and civil strife, this essentially religious aspect of the struggle for freedom was never totally obscured, no matter how distorted it became. The temple, and what it represented remained the rallying point for the different groups that emerged, and not just for strategic reasons. The *sicarii* entered Jerusalem and the temple on the feast of wood-carrying, and their leader,Menahem, went up to the temple 'in state to pay his devotions, arrayed in royal robes and attended by his suite of armed fanatics' ($\kappa\alpha\grave{\iota}$ $\tau o\grave{\upsilon}s$ $\zeta\eta\lambda\acute{\omega}\tau\alpha s$), (*War* 2:425f.444). The Zealots, abandoned the idea of an hereditary high priesthood and elected a country priest from Aphthia as an apparent attempt to evoke ancient loyalties among the populace (*War* 4:151-7). Even John of Gischala, despite all the impiety of which Josephus accuses him, is reported to have had a religious motivation for his actions, declaring 'that those who fought for the temple should be supported by it' (*War* 5:564; cf. 6:99). The Idumaeans too initially had a religious motivation for coming to the aid of the city torn by civil strife, for their intention was 'to preserve God's house and fight to defend our country from both her foes, the invaders from without and the enemies from within' (*War* 4:281). And while Simon bar Giora is never actually stated to have taken on himself messianic claims, there are strong reasons for recognizing a religious undercurrent to his activity and bearing.[78] There were of course other motivating factors behind each of these groups, in particular a strong social dimension to the activities of the Zealots and Simon, yet Hengel is surely correct in insisting that only powerful religious convictions can explain all the aspects of Jewish resistance that come to the fore in 66 C.E.[79]

What was the response of the Judaean countryside to the call of Jerusalem and its holiness? The *sicarii* were prevalent in the villages of Judaea from the procuratorship of Festus (*Ant* 20:185-7 208-10; *War* 2:254f locates them in the city of Jerusalem rather than the countryside), where they appear as similar to, if not an offshoot of Eleazar ben Dinai and his bandits, who had aided the Galileans and Judaeans against Samaritans at the time of the border incident (*Ant* 20:165). They entered Jerusalem in force on the feast of wood-carrying in 66 C.E. to aid Eleazar ben Ananias and his revolt, a clear indication of their country base, despite the fact that their name was apparently derived from their tactics with the *sica* or short lance in urban conditions.[80] Their leader Menahem, who was the (grand?) son of Judas the Galilean soon joined them, having invaded the Roman arsenal at Masada and obtained a supply of arms and 'returned to Jerusalem like a veritable king', becoming the leader of the revolution. However, after the murder of Menahen the *sicarii* withdrew to Masada and took no further part in the fighting in Jerusalem.

The next activity we hear of in Judaea is during the advance of Cestius Gallus on Jerusalem, and later during his disastrous retreat at Beth Horon (*War* 2:523-55). One gets the impression that there is a real unity of purpose and organization between the rebels in the city and the people in the countryside, and twice Josephus mentions that the surrounding mountains were swarming with Jews (*War* 2:523.545). Subsequently after Vespasian had successfully conquered Galilee we hear of a new movement of Jews from the countryside entering Jerusalem, there to join the rebel group whose leader now was another Eleazar, ben Simon, who had come to the fore in the defeat of Cestius, and may have been a Judaean, even though he was a priest (*War* 2:564f; 4:225). These rebels from the country were the ones who elected the new high priest by lot, and this fact combined with the vehemence of Josephus' attack on them (*War* 4:135-57) makes it almost certain that there was a real link between them and the city rebels, and that they both shared a deep distrust of the priestly aristocracy of the city.[81] This was further accentuated by the social gulf between the two groups, since we hear of the slaves of the high priests being sent to the (country) threshing floors to receive tithes, so that the priests starved to death (*Ant* 20:180f. 205-7).[82] The Idumaean countrypeople also came to the support of Jerusalem under four of their generals, on hearing that it was about to be handed over to the Romans by the moderates (*War* 4:228. 272-81). Perhaps this support was due to the efforts of Eleazar ben Ananias who had been sent as general there by the moderate government (*War* 2:566). Even though some returned home after experiencing the atrocities of the rebels (*War* 4:353), others stayed to fight, first under John of Gischala and then under Simon bar Giora in defense of the mother city (*War* 4:566f.571-6). Simon, coming from the Judaean countryside with his army of ex-slaves, promised freedom to the underprivileged and harassed the wealthy collaborationists (*War* 2:652). For a time he based himself in Masada with the *sicarii*, but on hearing of the death of Ananus, the deposed high priest, he embarked on a more ambitious campaign 'by proclaiming liberty for slaves and rewards for the free' (*War* 4:507f). He succeeded in establishing himself in the hill country of the South and about Idumaea and was even joined by 2,000 young aristocrats whom the Zealots had imprisoned at Jerusalem, thus giving him even greater illusions, and eventually he entered Jerusalem being hailed as 'savior and protector' by the people (*War* 4:353.510.574f).

The unifying principle for all these various 'invasions' of Jerusalem from the countryside was the religious, even eschatological hopes that fired them. The social aspect of the revolt is certainly stressed by Josephus, and it may have been this that lead to the splintering of loyalties and faction fighting, as the different personalities sought to control the sources of wealth. Yet all this should not detract from the central attraction of Jerusalem and the ideological base it provided for the Judaean countryside. The fact that many of the lesser priests lived in Judaea rather than Jerusalem was probably a contributory factor to the close links that existed between city and country, since presumably village life in Judaea was structured on the priestly divisions, thus providing a network of relations with the central sanctuary that had roots deep in the past.[83] For those who recognize the ideological links between the Maccabaeans and the later revolts the prevalence of such support for the revolt of 66 C.E. in the Judaean countryside will come as no surprise.[84] The temple-state may have disappeared as a political reality, but it still continued to shape the lives and loyalties of the rural people, it would seem. That Vespasian was well aware of these loyalties and was not about to make the same mistake as Cestius Gallus is clear from the careful preparations he made in each place as he advanced. He installed garrisons everywhere, 'posting decurions in the villages and centurions in the towns' (*War* 4:442). He thus succeeded in encircling the outer rim of Judaea from Idumaea to Jericho and Antipatris and enclosed Jerusalem completely (*War* 4:443.446.486).

With this general picture of the situation in the southern countryside it is time to return to Galilee and attempt to isolate comparable revolutionary elements there. In the absence of a central sanctuary such as Jerusalem within the territory and with the abstention, if not the defection of Sepphoris, it is obvious that what zealotism in Galilee needed most was a strong central figure that could draw together the disaffected elements there and capitalize on the tensions within the province already discussed.[85] Several such characters attempted to insert themselves into the Galilean situation and by examining the reactions to each we should be better able to measure the revolutionary spirit of the people.

(i)   *Jesus of Tiberias.*

The most obvious act of zealotism to take place in Galilee was the burning of Herod's palace at Tiberias with its animal representations.[86] Josephus claims that as he was cautiously moving to implement instructions from the revolutionary government in Jerusalem the palace was burned by Jesus son of Sapphias, the ringleader of the party of the sailors and the destitute classes. Subsequently all the Greeks in the city were massacred (*Life* 66f). Apparently, Jesus was prompted by religious zeal which included hatred of foreigners and had a strong social component, for he was a member of the destitute classes, which were also mentioned earlier in the classification of the various factions at Tiberias (*Life* 35). Josephus attempts to exonerate himself completely from this affair, but the fact that he was able to get his hands on the booty and leave it in the safekeeping of the ten chief men of the city suggests that initially he may even have used Jesus and subsequently refused to give him his share of the spoils, since the latter later accused Josephus of double dealing (*Life* 295-8).[87] It should be noted that 'some Galileans' assisted Jesus in this revolutionary venture. Despite his lowly origin, Jesus is described as ἄρχων of the city (*Life* 134.271.295), but it is not clear that he retained this position throughout since the council of Tiberias adopted several different stances, at one time apparently supporting John of Gischala and being for war (*Life* 87), again seeking assistance from Agrippa (*Life* 155.381.9; *War* 2:632-46), and yet again supporting the Jerusalem delegation (*Life* 271). It may well be that Jesus did not confine his efforts to

Tiberias for on one occasion we meet him at Tarichaeae accusing Josephus of treachery in the affair of the highwaymen of Dabaritta who had seized personal effects of Ptolemy, Agrippa's viceroy, which Josephus wanted restored (*Life* 132-5). Again Jesus is represented as adopting a religious pose, for he brandished a copy of the law of Moses and accused Josephus their commander-in-chief of being about to betray them. Though Josephus succeeded in defending himself to the satisfaction of the crowd, the Galileans and Tiberians were still dissatisfied (*Life* 143f; *War* 2:608 has τοῖς ἄλλοις instead of Γαλιλαῖοι). He promised to aid those places in need of fortifications, only to have a further attack made on his life by 'the brigands and the promoters of disturbance' (οἱ λῃσταὶ καὶ τῆς στάσεως αἴτιοι) who feared they would be brought to trial for the earlier revolt, but their numbers were not very great (600, *Life*, or 2,000, *War*). Nevertheless the question of treason combined with lack of fidelity to the Jewish law remained a sensitive issue, for shortly afterwards Josephus' refusal to have the Herodian noblemen, who had thrown in their lot with the Jews, circumcised (*Life* 112f), was used by certain people, (τίνες), to arouse the suspicion of the crowd (ὄχλος) that there was collusion with the enemy; the nobles were reputed to be sorcerers' 'who made it impossible to defeat the Romans' (*Life* 149).

We must therefore allow for a pocket of zealotism in Tiberias and its region, surprising as this might appear. Yet a little reflection in the light of earlier discussions will indicate that it is not so strange after all. Their number does not appear very great, but presumably because of the firebrand quality of their leader, Jesus, and possibly because of the vacillation of Justus they succeeded in controlling the city council of Tiberias for at least part of the crucial year 66/67 C.E. These Jews may have had their origins in rural Galilee, but their faith had been radicalized in the urban and semi-hostile environment of this Herodian city, and possibly also because of contacts with the center of the movement in Jerusalem. Certainly the fact that 2,000 Tiberians eventually arrived in the mother city, there to take part in the final struggle with Rome (*Life* 354) would indicate that there had been such previous direct exchange. Nor should the presence of 'some Galileans' cause any particular problems in this context, even though we argued earlier that Tiberias' range of influence

on the hinterland was likely to have been limited. Those Galilean Jews who had been forced to inhabit Tiberias originally,
especially the poorer element (*Ant* 18:36f) were not likely to have
broken all ties with their rural origins. Presumably they had not
become socially mobile and so had not availed themselves of the
opportunities of the hellenistic city environment. As the lowest
rung of the social ladder they would have felt themselves isolated
and some links with their rural past would have continued. In
dealing with the social situation among the peasantry we argued
that 'the rural proletariat', was more likely to give vent to feelings
of repression and resentment than were those who, no matter how
economically deprived, could still cling to an ancestral plot of
ground.[88] In all probability those Galileans who joined in the
sacking of Herod's palace or saw Josephus' behavior as trea-
sonous belonged to the former class. On their own they would
only have been able to perpetrate the occasional act of violence,
like the robbery by the young men of Dabaritta (*Life* 126ff), or
the tenants who thought that killing the heir would leave them
owners of the vineyard (*Mk* 12:7) - isolated outbursts of resentment against the nearest symbol of repression, but lacking any
long-term plans or proper appreciation of the total situation.
It was such a vision that Jesus presumably succeeded in giving - at
least to a limited degree - by appealing to ancestral laws and
spreading the rumor that Josephus 'was about to hand over
their country ($\chi\acute{\omega}\rho\alpha\nu$) to the Romans' (*Life* 132). One can only
presume that this appeal to the laws was based on the Penta-
teuchal gift of the land, a right that Rome had implicitly rejected
by claiming its full share of the fruits in tribute.

(ii) *Justus of Tiberias.*

The sequel to the revolt in Tiberias makes it clear that Jesus
had only partial success. He could not bridge the social gap
between himself and the Herodian nobility, who might have
been tempted to participate if proper motivation and suitable
prospects could be offered to them. Perhaps Justus of Tiberias
could have played such a role? We have already noted the impact
of Justus' *History* on Josephus' later literary productions,[89]
especially *Life*. It is remarkable that somebody to whom such

revolutionary attitudes are attributed in the later work is not mentioned *at all* in the *War* account. This fact should make us cautious if not downright skeptical of the characterization of Justus that Josephus gives as a way of discrediting the claims of his work. Josephus would have us believe that Justus was the leader of a third party at Tiberias; 'Justus, son of Pistus, the ringleader of the third party, while feigning hesitation on the subject of hostilities, was really eager for revolution, reckoning that a change of government would bring him into power' (*Life* 36). As an expression of this mentality we are given a speech of Justus' resenting the fact that Tiberias had lost its position of prominence to Sepphoris, and calling for a revolt, 'joining hands with the Galileans', but the sequel to this harangue is an attack by the citizens of Tiberias on Hippos and Gadara, two towns of the Dekapolis (*Life* 37-42).[90] There is nothing inherently improbable about the sentiments expressed by Justus, since the inclusion of the city into the territory of Agrippa II must have been a blow to its pride, and a diminution of status for its aristocracy. But the sentiments were surely not held by Justus alone, and they scarcely prove that he had his own revolutionary party. However we explain the attack on Hippos and Gadara, it does not warrant such a claim, given the confusion of the times.

In fact the only direct confrontation reported between Justus and Josephus presumes that Justus is not one of the brigands but a Romanophile (*Life* 175-8), and Justus' eventual flight to Agrippa II would seem to put the matter beyond discussion (*Life* 390.393). Undoubtedly Josephus would like to paint Justus as a revolutionary, presumably to defend himself by claiming that it was Justus not Josephus who caused Tiberias to revolt (*Life* 340-4) and he never misses the opportunity to implicate him in the seditious events in the city (*Life* 65.88.279). Yet when all this invective is sifted there is little hard evidence beyond the fact that Justus was initially jealous of the position of Sepphoris, and may have attempted to seize the confusion after the defeat of Cestius to make the break with Agrippa, only to realize that he could expect little Galilean support.[91] The attempt may have embroiled him unwillingly in the Jewish-pagan strife of the period and almost cost him dearly (*Life* 410), but in the end the Herodian court rather than an independent Galilee was clearly more to his liking.[92]

(iii)   *John of Gischala.*

Another contender for the role of revolutionary leader in
Galilee is John of Gischala, especially in view of the subsequent exploits in Jerusalem. But once again we must proceed
with caution, given the very different treatments of John's character in *War* and *Life*.[93] In the former account John is portrayed
not simply as a revolutionary but as a brigand and tyrant, but the
stock quality of much of this language makes the whole picture
highly suspect (*War* 2:585-9; 4:85-127; 389-91; 7:263f). One thing
it does indicate is that Josephus and John became deadly enemies
in the course of the former's sojourn in Galilee, and a careful
reading of the *Life* gives us some indication of the complexity
of the relationship between the two men. Initially, John may have
hoped to avoid confrontation, but gradually one detects where his
true interests lay, as he strove to unseat Josephus and obtain
command himself. John's initial caution may have been related
to his business instincts and a shrewd assessment of the likely
outcome of any revolt. Besides, if he was the eparch of Upper
Galilee, as suggested by *Life* 73 (ἐν τῇ αὐτοῦ ἐπαρχία), he had
accepted a position in the Roman administration of the district,
though this is never explicitly stated.[94] In view of his associations with Jerusalem, especially with Simon ben Gamaliel, John
may well have expected, or at least been prepared to accept governorship of Galilee as a price for his support of the revolt, and
this rather than any deep-seated ideological difference explains
the eventual antagonism between him and Josephus. Indeed the
Jerusalem delegation had hoped to achieve a reconciliation
between them at first (*Life* 217f).

At what point did John abandon his caution? *Life* 43-5 is
generally understood to reflect the turning point in his career
from being against the war to becoming a revolutionary (Hengel;
Kingdon) or a 'moderate' (Rhoads).[95] However, the episode needs
to be further clarified. He had hoped to restrain his fellow citizens, 'who were highly elated by the revolt from Rome' (Thackeray), urging them to maintain their allegiance (πίστις) - to John
or to Rome or to both, if John was in the service of Rome. However, his entreaties fell on deaf ears, and the explanation for this
failure puts the blame not on the inhabitants of Gischala as we
might have expected from the logic of the argument, but on the

neighboring cities who sacked the town. It is highly unlikely that John was able to defeat these surrounding peoples in the manner suggested. Undoubtedly the episode had to do with the anti-Jewish riots in the Syrian cities and the Jewish reprisals in the surrounding villages, which *War* (2:457-65) suggests took place before the defeat of Cestius, but which *Life* (24f), probably more accurately, locates after that event. It would seem that John had hoped to ride out this storm and avoid losing his own position, and that he looked for the allegiance of his townsmen to himself when others were seeking revenge. Eventually he had to take the field or relinquish his position of leadership in the area, and once he had taken that plunge he had thrown down the gauntlet to Rome and had no other option but to continue along the path of revolt.

In these circumstances one can imagine the resentment of John at the arrival of Josephus as governor of the whole province. His Jerusalem contacts might have been presumed to support him for the position and he was not about to relinquish the leadership role. The second mention of John in *Life* describes him as 'eager for revolution and ambitious of obtaining command', and this rather general description is illustrated by his desire to seize the Imperial granaries, to which Josephus also aspired (*Life* 71-73). Despite the blatant self-defense of the passage,[96] Josephus was not able to prevent John taking charge of all of the grain of the province (or 'district', ἐπαρχία), and this act clearly demonstrates at once John's rejection of Roman claims and his own push for control, at least in Upper Galilee. Subsequently, we hear of his attempting to oust Josephus in the important centers of Lower Galilee also - Tiberias (*Life* 84.96.101; *War* 2:614-21), Sepphoris and Gabara (*Life* 122-5). He appears to have had some success except at Sepphoris (cf. *Life* 124.237), even possibly resorting to violence in the process (*War* 2:588f), though this last passage may be part of the blackening of his character which is so much a theme of *War*. When all else failed John turned to the Jerusalem authority that had appointed Josephus, now that his own Pharisaic friends were in control (*Life* 189-93).[97] However, he was no more successful in this effort, for it appears that there was never any likelihood of John being given command, even if Josephus was to be replaced (*Life* 267.271.

278.287). Once he perceived this John was less than wholehearted
in his support of the delegation, being eventually confined to
his own territory of Upper Galilee (*Life* 372; *War* 2:632).

All this jockeying for position between Josephus, John and the
delegation might obscure the fact that they are squabbling over
control of a territory that is officially part of the Roman province
or belongs to king Agrippa. Therefore all are revolutionaries in
Roman eyes. While the faction-fighting never reached the same
proportions as in Jerusalem, nor apparently the same violence,
the elements were similar - a provincial Jew, whose affiliation
with the religious aspects of Judaism may not have been as tenuous
as Josephus would have us believe (e.g. *Life* 74-76; *War* 2:590-2;
5:36f.100-2; 562-5; 7:263f), was not prepared to relinquish leadership to a Jerusalemite who had no ties with the province, once
circumstances had pushed him into the situation of revolt. Nevertheless, one cannot avoid the impression that John's zealotism
was opportunistic, and there probably are good grounds for
accepting his avarice as genuine. In particular his refusal to 'bury
the hatchet' and come to the aid of his fellow Galileans at Jotapata, when this might have won him the prize he so eagerly
sought, shows how disorganized and episodic the whole Galilean
campaign was. Even more despicable was the abandoning of his
native place, seeing that some at least of the inhabitants did not
want the revolt there in the first place (*War* 4:84). It is difficult
to estimate John's real strength. Josephus talks of him having
a small army of mercenaries - 400, according to *War* 2:588 increased to 1,500 at *Life* 371 - but elsewhere we hear of an army
of 3,000 (*Life* 233) and later he had an army of 6,000 in Jerusalem,
though not all were Galileans (*War* 5:249). Presumably these
figures mean that John did have limited support among the
Jewish population of his area, even if one should query the figure
of 9,000 fugitives who were prepared to flee Gischala with him.[98]
The peasant stock were distrustful of his manoeuvres and did not
wish to become involved so that in all probability he relied on
mercenary troops rather than popular support (cf. *War* 4:97).
John's subsequent behavior in Jerusalem, if we can credit Josephus' account at all, shows once more his opportunism, first
aligning himself with Ananus, the high priest (*War* 4:213), and
later with the Zealots (*War* 5:528). It would seem then that John's

motivating concerns were personal rather than ideological, no matter how much he drew on Zealot ideals for support later. This is exactly what we might expect from his social status as an opportunistic 'new man' - one of the rare genuine middle class we meet in Galilee, for whom pragmatism rather than idealism was the overriding concern. He was not the type to fire the Galilean peasantry with ancient loyalties, and their rejection of him (*Life* 103.304ff.368) has all the appearance of being authentic, even if it also fits in with the apologetic of Josephus.

(iv) *Josephus*

Finally there is Josephus, whose position in Galilee we have discussed in an earlier chapter. It is necessary to raise the question of his role in this context also, especially because of Galilean loyalty, real or imagined, to him. Certainly the likely native Galilean leaders had only very limited local support, and if we are to discover any broadly-based Galilean attitudes towards the revolt, we must look to Josephus, who did manage to retain his governorship of the province despite all attempts to unseat him, presumably because he reflected in some way the feelings of the masses there.

Recent scholarly opinion seems prepared to accept Josephus' own position in *Life* that he was the representative of a moderate government that attempted to contain the revolutionary situation in Palestine, while at the same time placating the extreme radicals under the guise of preparing for war.[99] Our earlier discussion has made it clear that we regard this position as oversimplistic, even if we were to accept the statement that a general council of official Judaism took control of the war effort, and so gave it a specious legitimacy (*War* 2:562-8).[100] In Roman eyes the whole of Palestine was in a revolutionary situation and those who took part in any capacity must have been aware of the implications of their actions. The provision of an army and fortifications, even if the proportions are exaggerated, and his attempts to make Sepphoris abandon its pro-Roman stance (*Life* 104.111.378-80.394-6), all make it clear that Josephus actively pursued war with Rome, and these actions cannot be explained on any other grounds. The question we wish to pursue here is how far such militancy was based on or drew its inspiration from the ideals of the Zealots. In short was Josephus fired by the ideals of the Jerusalem Zealots, and is this the basis of Galilean support for him?

Unfortunately we are totally dependent on his own accounts for an explanation of his motivation, and as far as can be ascertained he had no previous association with the province. While his Pharisaism may well be questioned there seems little reason to doubt his priestly, if not Hasmonaean, background, and his aristocratic status.[101] The fact that he owned lands near Jerusalem and was later granted other land in exchange on the plain (*Life* 422) would seem to confirm this. Cohen,[102] who has made the most compelling case for Josephus' zealotism points to the fact that he had gone to Rome to plead for imprisoned Jewish priests, during the procuratorship of Felix, but so did Philo, Agrippa and other prominent Jews. The episode seems to point to his aristocratic contacts rather than his revolutionary spirit, even if the tone of the report is tendentiously pious (*Life* 13-16). Nor does the fact that he fled to the temple from Menahem necessarily align him with the revolt of Eleazar ben Ananias (*Life* 20f), though it should be remembered that he too was from an aristocratic priestly family. Subsequently, despite the many charges hurled at him both personal and political, the only clear instance of a charge of zealotism occurs in his response to Justus, namely that he was responsible for the revolt of Tiberias (*Life* 340-54). Yet the seriousness of this charge has to be judged in the light of Justus' own polemical concerns, the presence of a known Zealot, Jesus ben Sapphias in the city, and the fact that Justus can apparently also charge him with *not* causing Sepphoris to revolt! Cohen is surely right in insisting that those who subsequently took charge of the revolt, including Ananus the high priest and the aristocracy, must have been more involved in the events leading up to it than Josephus would have us believe, but it is difficult to imagine that even then their reasons were free of all personal interest and motivated solely by pure religious concerns. It seems more consistent to suppose that the Josephus who subsequently was happy to enjoy the favor of Rome was, even prior to his involvement more concerned about his own personal position than apocalyptic-style revolutions in favor of the socially oppressed. His vanity is certainly a factor in judging his motives and involvements, and after his abyssmal failure he can discover supernatural reasons to explain both his remaining in office to fight the Romans (*Life* 208f), and his acceptance of the security of the enemy camp after his defeat (*War* 3:400).

What then are we to make of the Galilean allegiance to Josephus? Certainly their loyalty to him is one of the major threads of *Life*, so much so that several commentators have dismissed it as contrived.[103] They are distinguished from the inhabitants of Sepphoris, Tiberias and Gabara, the three largest towns of Galilee for whom they have nothing but hostility (*Life* 30.39.373-80, Sepphoris; 98-100.381-9, Tiberias; 263-5, Gabara), and they come from the villages and the country (*Life* 242-4). In short they are synonymous with those country-people who accepted Josephus' governorship and remained loyal to him (*C.Ap* 1:48). They are more concerned for his safety than for their own and their families' fate (*Life* 84.125.250.252), and the Jerusalem delegation is asked to ascertain the source of this loyalty (*Life* 198). The Galileans answer his call to arms repeatedly (*Life* 100.103.108.242) and their anger is directed against John (*Life* 102.386), Justus (*Life* 392) and the Jerusalem delegation alike (*Life* 211.230.260.262). Josephus can rely on them to testify in his favor (*Life* 228.258), and John is not able to alienate them from him (*Life* 237). Their leaders dine with him (*Life* 220), or he can call them to a general meeting (*Life* 305.310f, σύνοδος) to discuss his position within the province. The overall impression is that the Galileans behave like a chorus to be introduced at suitable moments as a support to Josephus' personal and moral qualities and proof of his responsible handling of affairs in the province. In their words he is 'the savior of their country' (*Life* 244).

It is difficult to resist the impression that we are dealing with Josephan apologetic, all the more so since in a few places we can pick up hints of a rather different attitude. Thus Josephus has to send soldiers to accompany the Galilean leaders lest they double-deal with the Jerusalem embassy (*Life* 228). Their real concern is for their own safety, 'influenced, I imagine as much by alarm for themselves as by affection for me' (*Life* 206f cf. 84). Of the two accounts of the Galilean judicial system he established (*War* 2:570f; *Life* 79) that of *Life* is more realistic—he made seventy of their leaders his constant companions, 'under guise of friendship', but in reality as hostages for the loyalty of the district. These indications suggest a slightly less flattering picture. The Galilean countrypeople and most of their leaders preferred Josephus to any of the possible local contenders, except for the minority whom we saw were attracted to the zealotism of Jesus, or those from Upper Galilee who supported John. But it was a marriage of convenience rather than love on both sides. *War* 2:589 perhaps captures best the overall mood of the Galilean peasants at the period: they were 'distracted' (μετεώρους ὄντας) rather than revolutionary (νεώτερους) or seditious (στασιώδες) at the coming war, well aware of their vulnerable situation.

The presence of brigands in their midst was a further problem, since under the guise of protecting the province these opportunists whom we meet on the different borders (*Life* 105, Ptolemais; 77-79, Gischala) were able to demand provisions and support from the defenseless country people.[104] As the representative of outside authority located at the nation's center, Jerusalem, Josephus could expect to draw on peasant loyalties, all the more so if he could convince them of his ability to remove their anxieties. His arrangement with the brigands, as well as the preparations for war that he initiated, may have added to the impression that he was to be their 'savior', without suggesting any religious over-tones to the word. In such an atmosphere rumor and hearsay are rife and one can readily recognize the passions of threatened people when word was passed around by his enemies that Josephus was about to betray the country to Rome (*War* 2:595.602; *Life* 129.132.149). We have already discussed the arming of the Galileans and the obvious exaggeration in view of their dis-appearance at the very beginning of trouble. Nevertheless, there is nothing improbable about a local militia from different regions, supported by their fellow villagers, coming to Josephus' aid in times of crisis (*War* 2:584). The very spasmodic nature of their appearance makes it clear that they are not prepared for or capable of conducting a long campaign, even of a guerilla-type, such as the supporters of Antigonus had conducted against Herod in the same area. If the general was no firebrand revolutionary, these peasant people were not likely to push him into that position.

Our survey of the impact of the various possible revolutionary leaders of Galilee has suggested negative results for the most part.

We have not found a single trace of a messianic-style leader there, who at the moment of great crisis and opportunity might have steeled the people to a genuine revolutionary struggle, drawing on ancient loyalties to land and temple—a striking contrast to events in Judaea. Insofar as we can penetrate behind the, admittedly, highly-colored sources, no such attempt was made and no genuine resistance to Rome (as distinct from her agents like Agrippa or supporters like Sepphoris) was ever consciously fostered. One gets the impression that the whole campaign did more to bring to the surface social animosities and tensions long existing within Galilean life than it achieved in spreading the radical ideology of zealotism within the province. Perhaps most telling of all is the fact that we find no traces of the Fourth Philosophy's ideology there, and least of all at Sepphoris, where it was reputedly rooted. Subsequent events would seem to confirm this picture, for it is generally recognized that the Bar Cochba revolt, which carried forward the ideology of the first one, had little or no impact on Galilee. This is all the more surprising in view of the fact that social unrest in the countryside was apparently a contributory factor.[105] The transfer of the Beth Din to Usha in Lower Galilee after 135 C.E. merely confirms our conclusion that Galilean Judaism, at least of the peasant variety, was never so revolutionary or violent as many authorities seem to assume.

GENERAL CONCLUSION

Focusing on the revolutionary ethos of Galilee has opened up for us another vista on life in the province and helped to confirm the impressions of previous chapters in this part of our study. It has also pointed the way forward to the final section on the religion of Galilee. It has emerged that in asking the question 'how revolutionary was Galilee?' we have ultimately raised a religious rather than a purely social question. Here it is opportune to draw together some of the more important lines of our discussions in this chapter.

Galilee was certainly not so isolated that it could remain untouched by the general discontent with Roman rule in Palestine that had been building up for over a century. Yet the contrast with Judaea proved illuminating. There, social unrest allied to an apocalyptic-style fervor seemed to be a constant fact of life, but very little of this intense feeling came to the fore in Galilee, with the one notable exception of the destitute classes of Tiberias in 66 C.E. This could mean that despite all the social injustices already described, the Galilean peasant fared better than his Judaean counterpart. It might also indicate that Judaism as a religious way of life was not overly threatened by the everyday experience of Galilean Jews, even if the general ethos of the province had been deeply affected by Hellenism for a long time, as we have seen. Hengel has concluded that one of the results of Judaism's violent clash with the new culture under Antiochus IV was to make the former extremely sensitive to any outside forces that were likely to threaten its distinctive way of life.[106] Certainly this can be perceived in the response to the various threats to the temple subsequently. Galilean Jews seem to have been as highly motivated as any others on such occasions, especially during pilgrimages to Jerusalem. Yet apparently this threat was not felt with the same intensity in the home province on a day-to-day basis. This may have been due to the fact that the effects of the reform did not have the opportunity to reach Galilean peasants, with the exception of those living near Ptolemais, and accordingly their pilgrimage religion was not unduly disturbed. Or it may have resulted from the fact that the realities of life had long since forced Galilean Jews to work out a *modus vivendi* with the new way of life of Hellenism, even the new language, without seeing its every advance as a death blow to the Jewish religion. These are questions that must still be addressed in our final chapters.

Thus our theory of a predominantly peasant ethos for Galilee appears to be further substantiated. The individual and unsustained outbursts of violence against Sepphoris, Tiberias or Agrippa have all the appearances of unplanned and unthinking displays of feeling that lacked a proper framework. In general, part of the problem is to convince peasants that the whole world and not just their own village or lot can be changed. As Hobsbawn puts it, it is an error to label every incident of force a 'rising' or an 'insurrection'. It is only when peasants can be convinced about universal or cosmic change that one can expect the abandonment of hard political assessment for hope of an apocalyptic nature.[107] The reaction of the men of Gischala, desirous of peace because the crops were engaging all their attention (*War* 4:82), illustrates very well the problems that faced any would-be revolutionary leader in Galilee. Centuries of political isolation had made those who were able to maintain any kind of stable links with the land cautious about any large-scale movement that drew its inspiration from the religious and urban conditions of Jerusalem. It was necessary to work out a much more careful approach to the problem of preserving ancestral loyalties with foreign overlords. The emergence of a Jewish aristocracy did not arouse any great hopes, given the compromises which they sought to work out with the new *Zeitgeist*, nor any assurance that their lot would be appreciably improved by throwing off the yoke of Rome. This is not to deny the presence of some idealism and theoretical aspirations in Galilee, even among the countrypeople, but it underlines that such aspirations need the proper political and social environment in which to flourish. Apparently the scattered Galilean hamlets did not provide that kind of atmosphere.

NOTES FOR CHAPTER 6

[1]M. Smith, 'Zealots and *Sicarii*. Their Origin and Relation', HTR 64(1971) 1-19, is the most trenchant critic of the prevailing position concerning the identity of the Zealots and the Fourth Philosophy of Josephus. It is also usual to identify Zealots and *Sicarii* on the basis of *War* 2:444, where Menahen the leader of the latter group is said to have entered the temple, taking with him τοὺς ζηλωτάς. Smith's most critical remarks are reserved for Hengel's massive study, *Die Zeloten, art. cit.*, 10-15, to which the latter has answered in his usual scholarly fashion in 'Zeloten und Sikarier.'Zur Frage nach der Einheit und Vielfalt der jüdischen Freiheitsbewegung, 6-70 nach Christus' in *Josephus-Studien, Festschrift für Otto Michel*, eds. O. Betz, M. Hengel, K. Haacker, Göttingen, Vandenhoeck und Reprecht, 1974, 175-96, also reprinted in *Die Zeloten*, 2nd ed. 1976, 387-412. D.M. Rhoads, *Israel in Revolution, 6-74 C.E.*, Philadelphia, Fortress Press, 1976, is a more developed treatment of Smith's position concerning the origin of the Zealots during the actual Revolt period, argued essentially from Josephus. Cf. esp. 97-110, where he characterizes the differing factions of the war period, and their varied background and leadership.

[2]Rhoads, *Israel in Revolution*, 97-110. Smith, 'Zealots and *Sicarii*', 15f, who regards *War* 4:129-61 as vital for understanding the origin of the Zealots.

[3]Thus Smith, 'Zealots and *Sicarii*', 7f, who follow Thackeray's translation of τοὺς ζηλωτάς at *War* 2:444: 'his suite of armed fanatics' (*Loeb Josephus* 2, 496f) that is, not as a party name, citing in support of this the Latin version and Hegesippus. In this Smith is following K. Lake in F. Jackson and K. Lake. *The Beginnings of Christianity, Part One: The Acts of the Apostles*. Vol. I, *Prolegomena*, London, 1920, Appendix 1, 'The Zealots', 421-5, who had argued that the party name 'the Zealots' occurred for the first time only at *War* 4:160f, and that accordingly earlier uses had to be understood in a general sense of 'admirer' or 'fanatical follower' or of individual zealots. Hengel has countered this position in 'Zeloten und Sikarier', 182-5, recalling his arguments of *Die Zeloten*, 61ff, overlooked by Smith, in relation to *War* 2:444. 564. 651, all three passages in his view using ζηλωταί as a party name. In particular he notes that the absolute οἱ ζηλωταί does not occur in Greek literature up to the 2nd century C.E., whereas in Josephus on the other hand there are 53 (from a total of 55) absolute uses, including *War* 2:444.

[4]Hengel, 'Zeloten und Sikarier', 195f, is aware of these two possible interpretations of the facts, yet concludes that the view that links the Zealots with the Fourth Philosophy founded by Judas the Galilean, in 6 C.E., best explains the strong religious component of the revolt as well as the fanatical attitudes of the participants.

[5]Cohen, *Josephus in Galilee*, 327f, and Rhoads, *Israel in Revolution*, 2f, discuss the various possibilities and the different nuances such words as 'moderate', 'revolutionary', 'peace party' can have. Cf. above ch. 3, n. 46.

[6]Hengel, *Die Zeloten*, 57-61, 322, assumes that the Galileans were rebellious ever since the days of Herod the Great at least, and so such references as *M. Yad* 4:8 (the Galilean heretic who attacks the Pharisee for including the name of the ruler on the bill of divorce); Justin, *Dial. with Trypho*, 80,2; Hegesippus in Eusebius, *Eccles. Hist.*, 4,22.7 and Epictetus in Arrian, *Dissert.*, 4,7.6 should all be taken to refer to the followers of Judas. Many other contemporary scholars adopt the same position, e.g. G. Vermes, *Jesus the Jew*, London, Collins, 1973, 46-8; S. Brandon, *Jesus and the Zealots*, Manchester, Univ. Press, 1967, 54; Reicke, *The New Testament Era*, 69, 118, 136f. Cf. my article, 'The Galileans in the light of Josephus' *Vita*', forthcoming in NTS.

[7]S. Zeitlin, 'Who were the Galileans? New light on Josephus' activities in Galilee' JQR 64(1973/4) 189-203.

[8]Hengel is his more recent article emphasizes this aspect more so than in his earlier study, while maintaining that similar conditions prevailed elsewhere in the eastern empire, but without the same dire consequences, 'Zeloten und Sikarier', 181f. *War* 2:427f notes that the rebels burned the moneylenders bonds with the explicit intention of cancelling all debts and starting a social uprising of the poor against the rich.

Kreissig's study, *Die Sozialen Zusammenhänge,* while correctly underlining the social and economic aspects, has been criticized for its all too one-sided treatment in reducing everything to a class struggle within Judaism. S. Applebaum, 'The Zealots: The Case for Revaluation', JRS 61(1971) 155-70, esp. 167f, also stresses the social aspects, but in a more balanced way, not neglecting other facets of the movement.

[9] Above, ch. 3, II.

[10] Hengel, 'Zeloten und Sikarier', 176f, n. 7, notes that with the exception of *Ant* 9:183, Josephus always uses it of those who are involved in opposition to Rome. His usage therefore corresponds to official Roman propaganda that does not admit any legitimate opposition, and thus discredits any movement of revolt, labeling its authors *latrones,* not *hostes.* Its application to Hezekiah would stem from Nicholas' pro-Herodian and anti-Jewish bias which would have been equally familiar with such Roman usage.

[11] It is not found in the parallel in *War,* and thus reflects the pro-Hasmonaean and anti-Herodian bias of *Ant.*

[12] Cf. ch. 2, n. 55, above, for the first Hasmonaean king. *War* 1:70 has the figure of 471 years, but it is also too large. However, there does appear to be a conscious desire to relate the events to the messianic expectations as outlined in the seventy weeks of *Dn* 9:24, as Thackeray notes, *Loeb Josephus,* II, 34f n.a. Cf. R. Meyer, *Der Prophet aus Galiläa,* Reprint Darmstadt, 1970, 60-70, on the messianic coloring of John Hyrcanus in such Sadducean sources as the *Testament of the Twelve Patriarchs, Test. Levi* 8:11-17; 17:11-18:14; *Jubilees* 31:11-12.

[13] W.R. Farmer, *Maccabees, Zealots and Josephus, An Enquiry into Jewish Nationalism in the Greco-Roman Period,* New York, Columbia Univ. Press 1956. His thesis of an ideological tradition between the Zealots and the Maccabees, has been cautiously received, mainly for lack of hard evidence. Cf. Hengel, *Die Zeloten,* 2f, and Applebaum, 160, n. 43. On the episode of the old man and the links with the story in 2 Macc 6:18-7:42 and the figure of Taxo in the *Assumption of Moses* 9:1-7, cf. F. Loftus, 'The Martyrdom of the Galilean Troglodytes (B.J. 1:312-3; A.J. XIV: 429-30). A Suggested *Traditionsgeschichte',* JQR 66(1976) 212-23, who argues for an original popular tale related to *Jer* 15:9 that has been adapted by different authors in the context of martyrologics.

[14] As such it serves his general theme of 'ἀνάγκη running through Jewish history and determining its outcome, though it should be noted that he does not include the story of Eleazar and his sons (*2 Macc* 7) in his account of the Maccabaean revolt.

[15] It is interesting to note that when Hyrcanus is addressed by Jews he is still called 'king': *Ant* 14:157, 172.

[16] Eissfeldt, *Introduction to the Old Testament,* 610-13.

[17] Schalit, *W.H.Hell.A.,* 344, n. 67.

[18] Cited from R.H. Charles, *The Apocrypha and Pseudepigrapha of the Old Testament,* 2 vols., Oxford 1913, 2, 648-52, with reference to A. Rahlfs, ed. *Septuaginta,* 2 vols., Stuttgart, 1935, 2, 486-8.

[19] There is an apparent inconsistency in this report, for at *Ant* 17:300 the Jews ask for αὐτονομία, yet at 314 they are willing to be good subjects of the Roman system. This was the only option open to them at the time that *Ant* was written, and thus we have another example of retrojection.

[20] Cf. below, ch. 8, I.

[21] Hengel, *Die Zeloten,* 333-6 and 'Zeloten und Sikarier', 179f, on Josephus' silence; W.R. Farmer, 'Judas, Simon and Athronges', NTS 4(1958) 147-55. On the contrary, Kreissig, *Die Sozialen Zusammenhänge,* 115f, sees this as a clear example of a class struggle.

[22] M. Hengel, *Gewalt und Gewaltlosigkeit. Zur Politischen Theologie in Neutestamentlicher Zeit.* Calwer Hefte 118, Stuttgart 1971, 34-7, points to the targum on *Gn* 49:10 which paints a warlike picture of the coming Messiah, as illustrative of popular beliefs rather than the heavenly saviour of *Dn.* On the contrary, M. de Jonge, art. χρίω *et cet. TDNT,* 9,514f doubts this. Cf. also his cautionary remarks on the alleged messianic features of Judas the Galilean and his clan, 'Josephus und die Zukunftserwartungen seines Volkes', in *Josephus-Studien* 205-19, esp. 216f.

[23] Stories of Herodian 'reluctance' to accept the office may be seen as addressed to the still current popular ideas concerning the sacral nature of kingship. *Ant* 14:386 relates that Herod did not expect kingship and had proposed his wife's son for it and at *Ant* 15:9f Antony has Antigonus put to death, recognizing that Herod would never have been accepted as long as the Hasmonaean lived. There is also the story in *M. Sot* 7:8 concerning Agrippa (probably the I), who was reluctant to continue the reading for the king from *Dt* 17:15 until the people assured him that he was their brother.

[24] Farmer, 'Judas, Simon and Athronges', points out that the Hasmonaean line must have still existed in its collaterals.

[25] Cf. above, ch. 3, II.

[26] Meyer, *Der Prophet aus Galiläa*, 70-81, esp. 73.

[27] Thus Hengel, *Die Zeloten*, 337, n. 3; Smith, 'Zealots and *Sicarii*', 15; J. Foakes Jackson, *Josephus and the Jews*, New York, 1930, 264. There is no completely satisfactory explanation of the fact that he is said to be a Gaulanite and to come from Gamala. Is Gamala in Upper Galilee confused with the better known one in Golan, as S. Klein, thinks *Neue Beiträge*, 8, followed by G. Dalman, *Orte und Wege Jesu*, Reprint Darmstadt 1969, 10 n. 2; Hengel, following J. Spencer Kennard, 'Judas of Galilee and his Clan', JQR 36(1945/6) 281-6, surmises that he may have escaped to Gamala in the Golan after his father's death, only to return to Galilee later.

[28] He is also mentioned at *War* 2:433; *Ant* 20:102.

[29] Thus Kennard, 'Judas of Galilee', followed by Hengel, *Die Zeloten*, 337f; Schürer, *Geschichte*, 1, 486f; Applebaum, 'The Zealots', 160f. The sons of Judas were executed about 47 C.E. during the procuratorship of Tiberius Alexander, *Ant* 20:102; Menahem who was murdered by the Zealots in 66 was said to have been his son also, though Hengel suggests grandson, *War* 2:433, and Eleazar the defender of Masada is also said to have been his son (*War* 7:253), though elsewhere his father's name is given as Jair (*War* 2:447). Rhoads, *Israel in Revolution*, 51, suggests that since Judas is said to have been a Γαυλανιτής from Gamala, Josephus is making a conscious effort to distinguish him from Judas the son of Hezekiah.

[30] *War* 2:118 says that it had nothing in common with the other sects, whereas *Ant* 18:23 identifies it with the Pharisees in all other respects except for its passion for liberty and refusal to call any man master except God. The former statement is readily explicable as part of the polemic of *War* in isolating the revolutionaries from the rest of Jewish life.

[31] *Die Zeloten*, 102.144.232.

[32] Rhoads, *Israel in Revolution*, 50.

[33] Applebaum, 'The Zealots', 161, makes the important point that Judas had opted for a charismatic, messianic interpretation of God's will, whereas other segments of Pharisaism based their understanding on the official interpretation of torah and halakhah, irrespective of the political regime.

[34] Meyer, *Tradition und Neuschöpfung*, has clearly outlined this aspect of Pharisaism. Cf. below, ch. 8.

[35] Hengel, *Die Zeloten*, 88f, describes the organization as being of necessity 'eine Art von Geheimbund'. Rhoads, *Israel in Revolution*, 59, n. 45, admits this possibility despite his thesis that there was no organized Zealot party before 67.

[36] *Israel in Revolution*, 52-9; cf. esp. notes 23 and 4.

[37] The question posed here is rather different from that of scholars who presume the revolutionary ethos of Galilee. A good example of how this can confuse the issue is G. Baumbach, 'Zeloten und Sikarier', ThLZ 90(1965) cols. 727-40, who presumes Galilean origin for the latter group because of their subsequent association with the family of Judas, despite the clear statement of *Ant* 20:185f that they originated in Judaea.

[38] J. Blintzler, 'Die Niedermetzelung von Galiläern durch Pilatus', Nov. Test. 2(1957) 24-49, esp. 32-7, where he discusses which of the known acts of Pilate, recorded by Josephus, might be linked with this episode. One possibility is the affair of the water conduit, *Ant* 18:62.

[39] Examples of this are the universal census under Quirinius (*Lk* 2:1) and the placing of the revolt of Theudas before that of Judas, (Ac 5:36f). Cf. H.J. Cadbury, *The Making of Luke-Acts*, London, S.P.C.K. 1961, 366f.

[40] Blintzler, 'Die Niedermetzelung', 43-7.

[41] Cohen, *Josephus in Galilee*, 274f, notes that the *Ant* account of this whole episode corresponds to an anti-Samaritan bias of this work as a whole, in that it is not one Galilean, but many (cf. *War* 2:232) that are killed, there is no mention of the Galilean preparation for war (*War* 2:233) and the fact that the Galileans killed many of their enemies is not referred to (*War* 2:235). However, this does not preclude the possibility of his treating the Galileans in a particular light also, especially in view of his presentation of Judas' philosophy earlier in the same work (*Ant* 18:23f). It also helps to underline the difficulties of the former general of the Galileans for a Roman readership of later times. On the notion of freedom as part of the ideology of the Fourth Philosophy cf. Hengel, *Die Zeloten*, 114-27 and G. Baumbach, 'Bemerkungen zum Freiheitsverständnis der zelotischen Bewegung', ThLZ 92(1967) 257f.

[42] *Jesus and the Zealots*, 356. His attempted corrective of what he considered a misrepresentation of his position, 'Jesus and the Zealots. A Correction', NTS 17(1971) 453, has been effectively answered by J.G. Davies, 'Zealot and Para-Zealot', NTS 19(1973) 483-5.

[43] *Die Sozialen Zusammenhänge*, 121.

[44] *Jesus the Jew*, 223-5.

[45] Cf. above n. 6. Cf. in addition, C.H. Dodd, *Historical Tradition in the Fourth Gospel*, Cambridge, Univ. Press, 1963, 217 and W.D. Davies, *The Gospel and the Land*, 337, n. 6, who apparently accepts the zealotism of Galilee, but refers to the unpublished 1973 dissertation of his student, F. Malinowski, *Galilee in Josephus*. However, this latter fails to carry through his initial insight that Jerusalem was the true center of the revolutionary ideology and is reduced to the circuitous argument that Galilee was revolutionary because Judas was called a Galilean, representing 'a way of thinking and acting of some Galileans' (237).

[46] For a survey, cf. N. Perrin, *The Kingdom of God in the Preaching of Jesus*, London, S.C.M. Press, 1963 and his subsequent studies, *Rediscovering the Teaching of Jesus*, London, S.C.M. Press, 1967, as well as *Jesus and the Language of the Kingdom. Symbol and Metaphor in New Testament Interpretation*, Philadelphia, Fortress Press, 1976. Cf. also, R. Schnackenburg, *Gottes Herrschaft und Reich*, Freiburg, 1959.

[47] Hoehner, *Herod Antipas*, 124-48, attempts to conflate the two reports, but minimizes the literary and theological differences between them. However, he rightly characterizes R. Eisler's attempt, *IHSOUS BASILEUS OU BASILEUSAS*, 2 vols. Heidlberg, 1929, 2, 66-96, to treat the Baptist movement as a zealot-style political one, as fantastic and unfounded.

[48] It is difficult to decide who precisely are covered by the term 'Herodians' in the gospels, as H. H. Rowley's survey of opinions makes clear, 'The Herodians in the Gospels', JTS 41(1940) 14-27. He opts for a general understanding of the term whereas others think of functionaries in the tetrarch's court. Of the Evangelists, Mark seems to have a particular interest in them as they occur in his gospel at 3:6; 8:15 and 12:13. E. Trocmé, *La Formation de L'Evangile selon Marc*, Paris, Presses Universitaires de France, 1963, 73-5, suggests that the combination of Herodians and Pharisees may reflect the time of Herod Agrippa I, who did enjoy the title king (cf. *Mk* 6:17), rather than the time of Antipas who was merely tetrarch. Hoehner, *Herod Antipas*, Appendix X, 331-42, approaches the question of the identification of the Herodians on the basis of some recent attempts to link them with the Essenes, and argues that they were indeed a religious group, to be identified however with the Boethusians.

[49] *Herod Antipas*, Appendix IX, 317-30. The term 'fox' applied to Antipas implies a cunning rather than a powerful person, *op. cit.* Appendix XI, 343-7.

[50] Dodd, *Historical Tradition*, 118, describes this as a tradition formed largely under the influence of a *testimonium* such as *Ps* 2, but 'by no means to be neglected'. Hoehner, *Herod Antipas*, 224-50, discusses the idea in great detail, arguing for its historicity, but without any new ideas on the question of jurisdiction which is the essential issue. If Sherwin-White is correct, against Mommsen, in seeing the *forum delicti* as the normal place of trial in the early principate as distinct from the *forum domicilii* of a later time *(Roman Society and Roman Law*, 28-31), then Antipas' involvement would have to be explained on the basis of the offense having been committed in Galilee as well as in Judaea in the narrower sense. However, *pace* Hoehner, Luke's account appears stylized and inconsequential, and so may have had apologetic rather than historical import in relation to the life of the church in the empire.

[51] Cf. the review of M. Hengel, JSS 14(1969) 231-40 as well as his *War Jesus Revolutionär?* Calwer Hefte 110, Stuttgart 1969; also E. Lohse's review, Nov.Test. 12(1970) 78; Davies, 'Zealot and Para-Zealot'; Davies, *The Gospel and the Land*, 340, n. 13. Brandon's response, 'Jesus and the Zealots', does not retract his basic thesis that ideologically Jesus and the Zealots were closely aligned. In particular to be noted are his repeated references to Jesus' boyhood in Galilee contributing to his revolutionary ideas (29.343f). On the question of Jesus' trial being a possible indicator of his zealotism cf. D.R. Catchpole, 'The Problem of the Historicity of the Sanhedrin Trial', in E. Bammel, ed. *The Trial of Jesus*, SBT 2nd series, 13, London, S.C.M. Press, 47-65, esp. 51-4, with a critical evaluation of Brandon's arguments.

[52] Contrast *Die Zeloten*, 344 with 'Zeloten und Sikarier', 186 and n. 37. In the latter article 187-9, Hengel has also defended his original opinion concerning the *qannaim* of rabbinic literature, maintaining that the term is a party designation in such texts as *ARNa* 6:8 and *M. Sanh* 9:6, against B. Salomonsen, 'Some remarks on the Zealots with special regard to the term *qannaim* in rabbinic literature', NTS 12(1966) 164-76, who had claimed that the term could refer to private people acting on behalf of the community as early as the Hasmonaean period. Cf. also, M. Borg, 'The Currency of the term Zealot', JTS 22(1971) 504-12, esp. 508.

[53] *Parables of Jesus*, 452. O. Cullmann, 'Le douzième apôtre', RHPR 42(1962) 133-40, has argued that Iscariot comes from the Latin *sicarius*, and that consequently the traitor Judas was also a member of the Zealots and to be identified with another Judas, designated *Kananaios* (sa for *Jn* 14:22) and *zēlōtēs* (*Vet. It.* for *Mt* 10:3). However, this explanation of Iscariot is extremely doubtful according to B. Gartner, *Iscariot*, English trans, Facet Books 29, Philadelphia 1971, 5-7, following the linguistic arguments of C.C. Torrey, 'The Name Iscariot', HTR 36(1943) 51-62. There is no basis for Cullman's statement that as many as six members of the Twelve were Zealots, *The State in the New Testament*, New York, Charles Scribner, 1957, 8f.

[54] Jeremias, *The Parables of Jesus*, 119; Sherwin-White, *Roman Society and Roman Law*, 131.

[55] G. Bornkamm, *Jesus of Nazareth*, English trans., London 1960, 66 and 201, n.4; Brandon, *Jesus and the Zealots*, 300f, n.5, cautiously; Catchpole, 'The Historicity of the Sanhedrin Trial', 54f, argues that the saying is either a critique of violence or an echo of the eschatological struggle of good and evil of the end-time, and so irrelevant to Brandon's thesis; this is the position of O. Betz, 'Jesu heiliger Krieg', Nov. Test. 2(1957) 125-9; D. Daube, *The New Testament and Rabbinic Judaism*, London 1957, 285-300, on the basis of rabbinic parallels, understands the saying about violence to refer to misinterpretation of the law of divorce.

[56] J. Yoder, *The Politics of Jesus*, Grand Rapids, Eerdumans, 1972,72; R.C. Tannehill, *The Sword of his Mouth*, Semeia Supplements 1, Philadelphia, Fortress Press, 1975, 67-77; O.J.F. Seitz, 'Love Your Enemies', NTS 16(1969) 39-54; J.D. Crossan, 'Jesus and Pacifism', in *No Famine in the Land: Studies in Honor of John L. McKenzie*, eds. J.W. Flanagan and A.W. Robinson, Missoula, Scholars' Press, 1975, 195-208; Hengel *Gewalt und Gewaltlosigkeit*, 40-4.

[57]M. Hengel, *Eigentum und Reichtum*, Stuttgart, 1973, esp. 31-8 and E. Bammel, art. πτωχὸς *TDNT*, VI, 888-915.

[58]Brandon attempts to turn the response of Jesus into a zealot-style slogan by detaching it totally from its present context, *Jesus and the Zealots*, 347. However, the effort is very unconvincing; cf. Bornkamm, *Jesus of Nazareth*, 121f.

[59]Hengel, 'Das Gleichnis von den Weingärtnern', esp. 85.

[60]*Jesus and the Zealots*, 42. 243f. 327.

[61]*Politics of Jesus*, 62, n.53

[62]P. Winter, *On the Trial of Jesus*, Berlin, 1961, esp. 137-48.

[63]*Politics of Jesus*, 58f; cf. 60, n. 53.

[64]*Historical Tradition*, 233-47.

[65]'Die Niedermetzelung', 44-8.

[66]*Historical Tradition*, 215; R.E. Brown, *The Gospel According to John*, 2 vols. *The Anchor Bible* 29 and 29A, New York, Doubleday, 1966 and 68, 1, 235 and 249; T.F. Glasson, *Moses in the Fourth Gospel*, SBT 40, London S.C.M., 29.

[67]I. de la Potterie, 'Jesus Roi et Juge d'après *Jn* 19:13', *Biblica* 41(1960) 217-47; W.A. Meeks, *The Prophet-King, Moses Traditions and the Johannine Christology*, Supplement to Nov. Test. XIV, Leiden, Brill, 1967, 87-91, who notes that Jesus' flight is not a rejection of kingship but only the worldly aspects of it (ἁρπάζειν), and besides his hour had not yet come.

[68]W.A. Meeks, 'Galilee and Judaea in the Fourth Gospel', JBL 85(1966) 159-69, esp. 166f.

[69]Dodd, *Historical Tradition*, 221.

[70]*Historical Tradition*, 112-15; 216f; 222.

[71]'Revolt in the Desert', NTS 8(1961/2) 135-41.

[72]*Jesus and the Language of the Kingdom*, 29f.

[73]Below chs. 8, III and 9, III.

[74]J. Gager, *Kingdom and Community. The Social World of Early Christianity*. Englewood Cliffs, N.J., Prentice-Hall, 1975, 29, citing P. Worsley, *The Trumpet Shall Sound. A Study of 'Cargo Cults' in Melanesia*, New York, Schoken Books, 1968, xii.

[75]Cf. my *The Twelve: Disciples and Apostles. An Introduction to the Theology of the First Three Gospels*, London, Sheed and Ward, 1968, 23-48, where I argue that the Twelve had a symbolic connotation for Jesus' audience in terms of the tribes of Israel (cf. *Mt* 19:28; *Lk* 22:28-30). It is significant that such ideas seem to have played a more vital role at Qumran and in apocalyptic circles generally: e.g. 1*QM* 2:1-3; *Test. Benj* 9:2; IV *Ezra* 13:39ff; *Apoc of Baruch* 62:5; 77:19;78:1. According to Jerome, in *Is* 9:1-2, the Hebrews who believed in Christ felt that the Galilean tribes of Zebulun and Naphtali, having been the first to have been taken into captivity, would be the first to be restored by seeing the light of Christ first. One might have expected that such ideas would have surfaced in pre-Christian Galilee also, or at least during the ministry of Jesus, but there is no trace in our sources of any such expectation. Instead we hear that Galilee will be laid desolate in the days of the coming of the Messiah, *M. Sot* 9:15.

[76]Cf. above, ch. 3, n. 42.

[77]C. Roth, 'The Debate on the Loyal Sacrifices', HTR 53(1960) 93-7, attempts, not very successfully, to isolate evidence in the rabbinic tradition that would support Josephus' account of the deliberations.

[78]Thus Hengel, *Die Zeloten*, 303; O. Michel, 'Studien zu Josephus. Simon bar Giora', NTS 14(1967/8) 402-8, links him with the strong-man *gibbôr* tradition in Judaism. G. Vermes, *Scripture and Tradition in Judaism*, Leiden. Brill, 1961, 56-60. claims that this tradition had messianic overtones. Cf. also Rhoads, *Israel in Revolution*, 140-8.

[79]This is the central thesis of *Die Zeloten*, reiterated against his critics in 'Zeloten und Sikarier', 179. Kreissig's study ignores this aspect completely in order to stress the social aspects of the struggle. Cf. above, n. 8.

[80]We can prescind from the question of whether or not the *sicarii* formed a separate group at this time and what their relationship to the Zealots was. Rhoads attempts to retain the name as a party designation for the war period only, and for those who eventually finished up at Masada, *Israel in Revolution*, 111-22; but has to admit that Josephus' usage would appear to indicate continuity between those of the same name in the reigns of Festus and Felix, *War* 2:254f; *Ant* 20:186; *Ac* 21:38. Smith is also prepared to admit their links with Josephus' Fourth Philosophy, but wishes to keep the term more general in the pre-war period, 'Zealots and *Sicarii*', 17f. Baumbach, 'Zeloten und Sikarier', is definitely in error in associating them with Galilee. Hengel, *Die Zeloten*, 47-52, sees the special name arising because of the tactics which the Zealots adopted from a certain stage. However, he too is prepared to allow that it may have been used in a more general sense by the Roman authorities for all freedom fighters in the pre-war period. In 'Zeloten und Sikarier', 190-3, he notes that Josephus' use of separate designations in the war period may be simply due to his desire to differentiate the different factions at that time.

[81]It is to this combination of priestly and lay groups in the winter of 67 C.E. that Smith, 'Zealots and *Sicarii*' 15, and Rhoads, *Israel in Revolution*, 97-111, esp. 103, attribute the founding of the Zealot party. However, the fact that many lesser priests lived in the Judaean countryside may be an indication that links between the two had been forged long before that, even if Josephus does not make that clear.

[82]This social tension is referred to in rabbinic literature also. Cf. below, ch.7, II, (ii).

[83]A. Büchler, *Die Priester und der Cultus im letzten Jahrzehnt des jerusalemischen Tempels*, 161ff and 168ff estimates that of the priests of the second temple, one fifth lived in Jerusalem, one tenth in Jericho and the rest were scattered throughout the Judaean countryside. By contrast the evidence for Galilean priests is slight, except for Sepphoris. Cf. below, ch.7, II, (ii).

[84]In particular, Farmer, *Maccabees, Zealots and Josephus*.

[85]E. Hobsbawn, 'Peasants and Politics', JPS 1(1974) 3-23, esp. 12f. He notes that such factors as seasonal farming lead to passivity as a traditional peasant strategy. 'But the times when Utopia can be conceived, let alone realized in terms of dismantling the superstructure of rule and exploitation, are few'.

[86]Cf. below, ch. 8, I, for the religious implications of this action.

[87]The repeated note of self-defense in *Life* concerning Josephus' lack of greed (63.80ff.298), suggests that there may be some real substance to the charge, which would not be very unusual for a Jerusalem priestly aristocrat, dealing with country-people.

[88]S.W. Mintz, 'Rural Proletariat and the Problem of Rural Proletarian Consciousness', JPS 1(1974) 291-325, esp. 305.

[89]Above ch. 3, n.40.

[90]The authenticity of this report seems assured by the fact that it appears also in the official *Commentary* of Vespasian, *Life* 342f, as Schalit notes, 'Josephus und Justus', 69f, n. 8, but who, however, surmises that the attack was instigated by Josephus and carried through by Justus. It seems better to regard it as part of the general series of attacks and counterattacks of Jews and Gentiles in 66, as Luther, *Josephus und Justus von Tiberias*, notes. Cf. *War* 2:459, where Hippos and Gadara are both mentioned in the list of places attacked by the Jews, but without any mention of Justus.

[91]Freyne, 'The Galileans', n.9.

[92]For an older view of Justus' zealotism cf. A. Baerwald, *Josephus in Galiläa. Sein Verhältnis zu den Parteien, inbesondere zu Justus von Tiberias*, Breslau, 1877, esp. 17-26. Schalit, 'Josephus und Justus', 68f, rightly attributes the animosity between the two to personal reasons, rather than to the zealotism of Justus. This personal reason is at least partly explicable in terms of tensions between Jerusalemites and independent-minded provincials.

[93]John is the enemy of Josephus in *Life* also, yet he is never called a λῃστής, brigand, in striking contrast with *War*, esp. 2:585-94. Cf. Rhoads, *Israel in Revolution*, 123f.

⁹⁴This is not at all unlikely since we hear of Niger the Peraean, the existing governor (τῷ δὲ ἄρχοντι τότε) of Idumaea, being suborned to act under Jesus son of Sapphas and Eleazar, son of Neus (or probably Ananias), on behalf of the revolutionary government (*War* 2:566).

⁹⁵Hengel, *Die Zeloten*, 381; H.P. Kingdon, 'Who were the Zealots and their Leaders in A.D. 66?', NTS 17(1970) 68-72. Rhoads, *Israel in Revolution*, 128f and Cohen, *Josephus in Galilee*, 390, suspect John's pacifism, as part of the apologetic of *Life*, used to illustrate the theme of ἀνάγκη.

⁹⁶Note the stress on Josephus' honesty and his inability to put a check to John, despite his own offical status, both apologetic themes of *Life*.

⁹⁷These connections have led Hengel to suggest that he may have been a member of the Pharisaic party himself, *Die Zeloten*, 381. C. Roth, 'The Pharisees and the Jewish Revolution of 66-73', JSS 7(1962) 63-80, esp. 69, has come to similar conclusions.

⁹⁸John's followers are called the σύνταγμα τῶν Γαλιλαίων by Josephus, *War* 4:558, and are said to have excelled all others in their audacity and ingenuity, having promoted John to power. F. Loftus, 'A Note on σύνταγμα τῶν Γαλιλαίων *B.J.* iv, 558', JQR 65(1975) 182-3, has argued that 'the Galileans' in this phrase does not refer to refugees from the province, but has rather the non-geographical connotation of 'rebel', which S. Zeitlin has also recently proposed for the designation 'Galilean' in *Life*, 'Who were the Galileans?', esp. 193.195.202. The cumulative result of Loftus' arguments is that even though not many Galileans were in the company of John in Jerusalem, the name became attached to his supporters because John himself was thought to be a Galilean. We can concur that the number of John's followers from Galilee was not very great, even though the 2,000 Tiberians of *Life* 354 may be included in the group, but the non-geographical use of the name Galilean is *a priori* unlikely and does not correspond to the data of *Life*. Cf. my critique of Zeitlin's position in 'The Galileans in the Light of Josephus' *Vita*.

⁹⁹Laqueur's study, *Der jüdische Historiker*, arguing that Josephus used a report he had sent to the Jerusalem authorities at the time of the delegation (*Rechenschaftsbericht*), as a source for *Life*, has given impetus to this view. Cf. Zeitlin, 'A Survey of Jewish Historiography' esp. 37-68, and Rhoads, *Israel in Revolution*, 129f.

¹⁰⁰This is one of the central points of Cohen's thesis, *Josephus in Galilee*, 195f. 350-5.

¹⁰¹*Life* 1-7. His Hasmonaean ancestry is not claimed in *War* 1:3, where only his priestly background is mentioned, but it occurs at *Ant* 16:187. Cohen, *Josephus in Galilee*, 208, n.33, considers it bogus in view of the pro-Hasmonaean and anti-Herodian traits of *Ant*.

¹⁰²*Josephus in Galilee*, 333.

¹⁰³Schalit, 'Josephus und Justus', 92; Drexler, 'Untersuchung zu Josephus' 296f; Zeitlin, 'Who were the Galileans?'; Freyne, 'The Galileans'.

¹⁰⁴Cohen's understanding of this episode, *Josephus in Galilee*, 373ff, seems rather contrived: Josephus persuaded the peasantry to provide him with funds to hire the bandits as mercenaries. He is never accused of this however, and the brigands can support Sepphoris against him, *Life* 104-10. Cohen argues that such passages as *Life* 244; *War* 2:581, where Josephus counsels moderation to his troops, show that they were previously accustomed to pillage. However, the language probably reflects a usual *topos* of generals addressing their armies, as the parallel with *Lk* 3:14, noted by Cohen, suggests, even if the line between brigands and mercenaries in the ancient world was rather thin. The incident in question took place in Upper Galilee, where Josephus never seems to have had any real authority, and thus John rather than Josephus was likely to have had greater influence with them, and in fact we hear of brigands in the area of Gischala later, *War* 4:84. Besides it is questionable if *War* 2:584 can be seen as a modification of *Life* 77f, since the former explicitly excludes the mercenaries (πλὴν τῶν μισθοφόρων) from the support of the village people.

¹⁰⁵Above, ch. 3, n.65.

¹⁰⁶*Jud. und Hell.* 558.

¹⁰⁷Hobsbawn, 'Peasants and Politics', 15.

Part Three
RELIGIOUS

CHAPTER SEVEN

THE GALILEANS AND THE TEMPLE.

Thus far we have attempted to separate the social and cultural aspects of life in Galilee from the distinctively religious ones, not however because we consider that these are areas of life divorced from each other. That is not true of any society, least of all a Jewish one, where religous conviction is the very foundation of national identity. Our purpose has been to isolate the various strands of life – political, cultural, social, religious – in order to see more clearly their interaction and mutual support. It is generally recognized by anthropologists and sociologists alike that religion, when viewed simply as a social phenomenon, can have a powerful integrating influence, insofar as it interprets the whole of life in a particular society as a reflection of, and in agreement with the ultimate vision of things which the religion in question espouses. Alternatively, it can function as an agent for social change when it offers another world-view conflicting with, or diametrically opposed to the accepted one in that society. This does not mean however that religion, even in ancient societies, is the more dominant influence to which social and cultural patterns are secondary and subservient. Rather, the interaction of world view (religion) and ethos (life-style, cultural patterns) must be seen as one of exchange and support, rather than dominance and subservience, as the anthropologist Clifford Geertz has insisted. Religion makes the ethos intellectually respectable and the ethos makes the religion emotionally satisfying. In other words religion is both the model *of* and the model *for* social order, at once reflecting the existing order and shaping it to the 'really real' world to which its own symbolic system refers.[1]

In the light of these considerations this final section of our study on the religion of Galilee can serve both as a conclusion drawn from our previous discussions and a test of their overall soundness. We have argued that the prevailing ethos was peasant and Jewish despite the fact that various aspects of hellenism had cast their shadow there from the very start. The conservative and relatively isolated character of peasant life seemed to warrant

259

that conclusion, but a consideration of the religious affiliation of the Galileans could affirm or challenge its correctness. Where were the basic religious loyalties of the Galilean peasant located? How did the symbol-system of those religious loyalties support and affirm the everyday life that had to be lived at the lowest level of the social ladder? As agents for social change emerged in the province – the cities, the Herodian aristocracy e.g. – are there increasing signs of dissatisfaction with the accepted symbol system, or was this so deeply rooted in the structures of the society that conformity to it prevailed? How effectively was the Jewish religion, through its symbol and belief systems, able to explain the anomalies of life in the province and continue to appeal to the emotions of the Galileans? These are the questions which we hope to address in this and subsequent chapters. By analyzing the available data in the light of these and similar questions it is to be hoped that the distinctive quality of Galilean religious loyalties may stand out more clearly. Certain questions pertaining to Judaism, Paganism and Christianity in the province may be addressed with more confidence than heretofore, given the many gaps in our knowledge of the situation there. Social and anthropological theory can never take the place of accurate information in making historical reconstructions, but they can illuminate the historical information available in a way that a mere enumeration of *realia* can never hope to accomplish.

In this chapter our focus is the temple, the primary religious symbol of Judaism as well as the related rituals of tithes, priesthood, sacrifices and pilgrimages. The fact that this symbol system was a storm-center within Judaism during the period in question, makes our study all the more significant as a starting point. Loyalties ranged from those who were in favor of replacing Yahweh worship there, the hellenizers of 175-163 B.C.E., to those who felt they could no longer identify with the restored cult after 163 B.C.E. because it was not sufficiently traditional, the Essenes. Several intermediate positions emerge within the total period, as we shall see, not the least interesting being that of Stephen, the first Christian martyr who challenges the idea that God lives in temples made with hands (*Ac* 7:48-50). A consideration of Galilean attitudes towards this primary symbol of Judaism, should prove particularly helpful for our overall conclusions, therefore.

I
PAGAN WORSHIP IN GALILEE — NEW SYMBOLS FOR OLD?

Any consideration of the religion of Galilee, even for Greco-Roman times, must seriously take into consideration, the possibility of the old Canaanite Baal worship persisting there side by side with the Yahweh worship throughout the centuries. The attempted reforms of Hezekiah and later Josiah, make it clear that a syncretistic fusion of the two deities was a constant danger in Judaea at the local Yahweh sanctuaries. This must have been even more true of the more remote northern kingdom, where Baal worship had at one stage been positively fostered by the ruling house (*1 Kgs* 18:18), and subsequent warnings of the prophets as well as the comments of the Deuteronomic redactor of the books of Kings make clear that the attraction of the *bamôth* or high places remained a constant threat there.[2] At the same time the fall of Samaria in 721 B.C.E. did not mean any conscious effort on the part of the Assyrians to eradicate Yahweh worship in the north, for as we have seen, only the aristocracy was replaced.[3] Besides, the tradition concerning the priest of Bethel (*2 Kgs* 17:27-29) who returned to instruct the new arrivals in the Yahweh religion is a definite indication that the Assyrians respected the religion of the people they had recently conquered, and saw its value in political terms within the newly-acquired province.

Against this background of the persistence of Canaanite 'nature' religion, even in Judaea, it would be unrealistic to expect a 'pure' Yahwism in Galilee, seeing that it was much more remote from the Yahweh cult center, and Yahwism had never been fostered there by the institutions of the state to the extent that it had been in the south. Peasant people have a capacity for combining in one acceptable religious synthesis ideas which the religious theorist regards as incompatible.[4] During the Babylonian captivity, when the Jerusalem temple was in ruins, religious affiliations in the north, no matter how Jerusalem and Yahweh-conscious they had become as a result of Josiah's reform attempts, had no alternative but to turn to local sanctuaries and cult centers in order to express their belief in the powers that determined life and death. What is particularly striking in the light of these circumstances is that when the sources again mention the north, attachment, even special devotion to the Jerusalem temple and its cult system, is presumed.[5] It may well be that the fall of Samaria in 721 B.C.E. had a more positive than negative effect on the Yahweh religion in the north, if only because it now called for a definite stance from its adherents, independently of the institutions of the state. Further links with Jerusalem may also have been forged if the theory of the northern provenance of Deuteronomy is maintained, and the possibility of emigration to the north from Judaea cannot be excluded for the time of the Babylonian crisis.[6] Whatever the causes, and they are no doubt complex, it would seem that there is every good reason to postulate the continuance of both Yahweh and Canaanite nature religions in the north throughout all the preceding centuries – a co-existence that within the framework of external influences of various kinds seems to have avoided the more crass forms of religious syncretism.

One positive reason for this assertion is the fact that in hellenistic times, both can be found, side by side, even though the Canaanite nature religion now reappears in hellenistic dress.[7] This can only mean that in the intervening centuries when our sources are silent a similar state of affairs also obtained, even if we can no longer document it in detail. Since our concern is with religious affiliation in Galilee for Greco-Roman times we must examine the evidence for this period closely, to see if any new factors have intervened. In particular, attitudes among the Jewish population must be scrutinized, since far-reaching changes were taking place at the center in Jerusalem even with regard to the cult. If the prevailing ethos of Galilean Judaism was hellenistic and syncretistic, surely it was from Galilee that one might expect the impetus for change in the Jewish religion, or at least active support and propagation, once this had been formulated by the aristocratic intelligentsia.

(i) *The Reform Attempt in Jerusalem.*

Recent studies in the background of the religious reform of Antiochus IV, Epiphanes, in 167 B.C.E. reported in such an abbreviated way in *1 Macc* 1:44-50, stress the fact that the impetus for the reform came not from the Seleucid king, but from the hellenized aristocratic party within Judaism, – 'the lawless men . . . who had made a covenant with the Gentiles' (*1 Macc* 1:11f.).[8] In particular Hengel's penetrating analysis of the immediate background stresses the fact that the reform party, centered on the Tobiad family, began their machinations by attempting to dismantle the Jewish theocratic state and establish Jerusalem as a *polis*, Antioch in Jerusalem, thereby curtailing what was in their view, the repressive control of Jewish affairs by the priestly aristocratic, Oniad family (*2 Macc* 4:7-17).[9] This control was clearly regarded as socially and economically counter-productive: 'since we separated ourselves from them (the Gentiles) many evils have come upon us' (*1 Macc* 1:11). At first they were content to supplant the conservative Onias IV with his brother Jason, but eventually he had to make way for Menelaus, who actually purchased the office from Antiochus IV with an offer of greater revenue than Jason was prepared to pay (*2 Macc* 4:23-27). With this move the hellenizing party was at once split and the supporters of Menelaus had effectively shown their disregard for Jewish religious tradition by accepting as high priest somebody other than an Oniad. In order to maintain control of the situation, they were now ready to reject the distinctively Jewish way of life represented by observance of the Jewish torah and the Jerusalem cult, and in this they had the active support of the king who actually issued a decree outlawing the practice of the Jewish religion, possibly in conformity with a general decree that 'the whole kingdom should be one people', and therefore, worship the one god.[10] What is significant in all this is the fact that social and economic possibilities, which were seen by this extreme party to be the advantages of hellenism, had actually led to a rejection of the Jewish religion and its replacement with another cult that seemed more in tune with the one world, one culture view of both Antiochus and the Menelaus faction.

The form of this new worship is particularly important for our purposes, since it offers a clue to what we might expect in Galilee also, should such developments have found an echo there. The temple at Jerusalem was to be turned into a shrine of Zeus Olympius, and its whole symbolic character changed by turning the sanctuary into a sacred grove and erecting a *massebah* or sacred stone over the altar of incense (*2 Macc* 6:2).

Thus the Yahweh worship regulated by Pentateuchal law was replaced by an older form similar to that which had actually been outlawed by Deuteronomy (*Dt* 16:21f), but was now reintroduced in a Greek guise as the worship of Zeus, who according to primitive Greek custom was also worshipped without a temple on a high mountain.[11] This explains why the new cult could be practiced in 'the cities of Judah' (*1 Macc* 1:44-51) also, and why the distinctive Jewish way of life which the torah represented had to be eradicated. The special relationship between Israel and Yahweh on which that way of life was based was to be abolished for a more universal and natural religion which could support the 'cosmic' aspirations of the hellenizers. In their desire to control the Jewish people, they had to control their symbol system and so they had been driven to abandon totally the accepted system, replacing it with an alien one, so deeply were culture and religion interwoven in the distinctive Jewish way of life. Control of the sources of power meant control of the symbol system on which the society was based, and for their vision of Jewish society to become a reality a religious ideology on which a new open society could be based had to be implemented.

One of the effects of the emergence of the Persian and Greek world empires was the move towards a syncretistic monotheism in which various local gods, Greek and Oriental alike, were seen as different expressions of the one supreme being who guided the universe.[12] In Palestine this trend had been particularly apparent in the Phoenician city states where the traditional Ba'al Shamēm, 'Lord of Heavens', had in the hellenistic period taken on universal traits and at the same time could be identified with Ζεὺς μεγιστός κεραυνίος, the god of thunder. He thus preserved some of his earlier characteristics as the god of rain and vegetation with the newly-acquired universal features expressed in the title 'Eternal Lord'.[13] This god had been worshipped at Tyre since the time of Hiram, Solomon's father-in-law, in the 9th century and possibly even earlier. And one of the most recently discovered inscriptions of a dedication of a temple door to the god is from Umm el-'Ammed, between Tyre and Acco, dated as late as 132 B.C.E.[14] The linking of this deity with Yahweh on the one hand and Zeus on the other was facilitated by the appellation ὕψιστος, 'Most High One'. This designation was at once an old one for Yahweh, El Elyon, that reappeared in the early hellenistic period with the increased reverence for the names of Yahweh, and it also described current beliefs in Ba'al Shamēm/Zeus as the supreme Lord of their respective pantheons.[15] Significantly the Jerusalem hellenizers had special links with Tyre, even to the point of sending an embassy to the Olympic games there, while Jason was still high priest, that is in the earlier years of the reform. It is interesting that on that occasion the Jewish high priest had no scruples about offering sacrifice to Heracles, who together with the consort Astarte was regarded as one of the family triad worshipped there.[16] Yet the Jews who brought the money for sacrifice eventually baulked and used it for other purposes (*2 Macc* 4:18-20). However, under Menelaus, no such scruple is apparent at Jerusalem, and no doubt with the support of the Syrian garrison that had been installed there, the extreme element felt free to openly persecute those who refused to obey the new reforms. Tyre's commercial success and prosperity would have made their god extremely popular with the Jewish hellenistic party and its aims, and some of the residents of Antioch in Jerusalem may have been from the Phoenician coast towns just as we find Phoenicians at Marisa and Shechem.[17]

The god Dionysus also seems to have been worshipped at Jerusalem, for we hear that the Jews were compelled to walk in processions wearing wreaths of ivy, the symbol of the god, on his feast day (*2 Macc* 6:7). Hengel is surely right in suggesting that this is not so much a sign of polytheism as the worship of the most high god under a different form.[18] As we shall see presently, Dionysus was particularly venerated at Scythopolis, but there is plenty of evidence of him on the coins of Tyre also. The Nabataeans also worshipped him as the graecized form of their supreme god, Dushara.[19] Besides, legend was current in antiquity that the Jewish god was really Dionysus, and Plutarch describes in detail how the feast of Tabernacles was really a feast in honor of the Greek god.[20] It is difficult to pin down the origin of this association, even though Scythopolis seems the most likely place for it to have emerged, and the fact that inscriptions to Zeus Ἀκραῖος and Zeus Bacchus have also been found there, would have made the triple identification, Zeus, Dionysus, Yahweh, quite feasible.[21] Thus the Dionysiac worship in Jerusalem could have been an attempt to replace a Yahweh festival with a suitable Greek one rather than the introduction of a second god side by side with Zeus Olympius.

(ii) *The Impact of the Reform in Galilee.*

We have already intimated that it was in Galilee that such development might have been expected to be most acceptable, if the ethos there had been as thoroughly hellenistic as some have suggested. Such a conclusion might appear all the more plausible given the alleged syncretistic nature of Yahwism there from the earlier period, and the continued encroachment on the interior by the territory of Tyre, already discussed in an earlier chapter.

More pertinent still is the development at Samaria, which can be gathered from a letter addressed to Antiochus by the Sidonians at Shechem in 166 B.C.E., the year after the reform had been instigated in Jerusalem (*Ant.* 12:257-61). These Sidonians are at pains to point out that they should not be identified with the Jews, and are happy to have the Zeus worship established at their sanctuary.[22] The fact that this move led to no counter-action in Samaria suggests a totally different religious and cultural atmosphere to Jerusalem and Judaea, where the resistance movement was able to match the hellenizers in their zeal for the law. This difference can only mean that at Samaria the hellenization of the ethos as a whole made the identification of the God of Gerizim with Zeus far less offensive to the worshippers there. Accordingly in this atmosphere of easy relationships no further attempt was made to change the 'semitic' style of life of the people and there was no persecution. It is interesting that in the wake of the destruction of their temple the Samaritans were able to continue worshipping 'on this mountain' (*Jn* 4:20),[23] that is, after the manner of the Zeus worship, as we have already seen. Whatever the origins of the Sidonians at Shechem – either a military settlement that had been planted there by the early Seleucids or a trading colony – it is presumably to their influence that the hellenization or syncretization of the Samaritan cultic traditions is due.[24] Evidence for such developments may be gleaned, not merely from the acceptance of the Zeus worship there, but also from the thoroughly hellenized picture of Abraham as an astrologer that emerges from two Hellenistic-Samaritan fragments found in Eusebius (*Praep. Evang.* IX, 17-22) and falsely attributed to Eupolemus by Alexander Polyhistor.[25]

Earlier when dealing with the transfer of power in Palestine from Ptolemies to Seleucids we saw how readily the north fell to the hands of the Seleucids once certain key centers had been taken over, and we suggested that this was due to the defection of the Ptolemaic officialdom. We also noted that the decree of Antiochus III allowing Jews to live κατὰ τοὺς πατρίους νόμους extended to the Jews of Galilee, so there was no conscious attempt to hellenize the Jewish religion prior to the reform of Antiochus IV.[26] Outside Jerusalem the process was rather one of assimilation if Samaria is any indication, especially through contact with the Phoenicians. The attitude of the Galilean Jews of the region bordering Ptolemais, Tyre and Sidon in appealing to their brothers in Judaea when harassed by their gentile neighbors is all the more significant therefore. Unfortunately the author of *1 Macc* treats of the episode in his usual manner from a narrow, Hasidic viewpoint, and so we are left in the dark about the immediate background to the trouble. However, it can be illuminated by seeing it as part of the attempt to extend the reform beyond the confines of Jerusalem. Even at Samaria, it was only after the Sidonians had made representation to the king to the effect that they had chosen 'to live according to the Greek manner', that the less discerning Seleucid officials, Nicanor and Apollonius desisted from harassing the natives. Similarly, according to *2 Macc* 6:8f, Ptolemy, presumably the governor to Coele-Syria and Phoenicia (cf. 4:45; 8:8) - that is the top ranking Seleucid official of the eparchy - had a decree issued to the neighboring Greek cities, that 'they should adopt the same policy towards the Jews and make them partake of the sacrifices, and should slay those who did not choose to change over to Greek customs'. This notice of a special decree came after the Dionysiac festival that was held in Jerusalem in honor of the new god that had been enshrined there, and presumably its effects continued to be felt outside Judaea even after the rededication of the temple in Jerusalem.

By directly linking the persecution of the Galilean Jews with the reform in Jerusalem, we can begin to answer some of the questions already posed about the demand for religious change in

the area, and better assess the true nature of Galilean religious
loyalties. Earlier we stressed that the action of Simon described in
1 Macc 5 was concentrated in that part of Galilee that bordered on
the Phoenician city terrorities as well as at Narbatta, which is best
located in the section of Samaria that bordered on the Carmel
range.[27] The real significance of this emerges when it is recalled
that Mt. Carmel, continued to be a center of pagan worship from
the period of the early monarchy to hellenistic and Roman times.
An inscription discovered there from the second century C.E.
links the god of Mt. Carmel with the god of Heliopolis (Baalbeck)
which at that stage was Zeus (Jupiter),[28] and already Ps.-Skylax
writing before 340 B.C.E., had made a similar connection between
Carmel and Zeus: ὄρος ἱερὸν Διός.[29] The Semitic equivalent is
generally recognized as Ba'al Shamēm, and the further identification with Hadad, a very ancient Syrian god also worshipped at
Baalbeck, has been suggested.[30] This supposition has been further
strengthened by the discovery of an early hellenistic inscription to
Hadad and his consort Atargatis in the region of Ptolemais.[31] For
a later period still we know from Tacitus that the sacred mountain
Carmel did not have an image or temple of its god, but only an
altar, 'ara tantum et reverentia.'[32] This means that the pattern of
worship at Carmel was very similar to, if not identical with that
which the hellenizers had sought to propagate in Jerusalem.
Indeed, one might go further and say that the new cult in Jerusalem was inspired by links with the Phoenician coast. In other
words, religious considerations reflect *and* create social, cultural
and economic links.[33] The persecution of the Jews of this area of
Galilee would mean therefore that they had refused to engage in
the religion of Carmel and its god despite the filip this had received
by the royal decree. This is all the more significant in that the
inscription from Kafr Yassif (9 Km NE of Ptolemais) mentioning
Hadad and Atargatis, is clearly a private family votive altar,
where the Semitic character of these gods is clearly retained. They
are further designated θεοι ἐπηκοοι, 'the gods who hear', a designation which suggests popular, private devotion of semitic worshippers.[34] Apparently, the private worship of the Carmel god (and
his consort) in their semitic dress was attractive to Greek-speaking,
and, from their names, presumably Greek-oriented country people
in the region of Ptolemais and was not confined to pilgrimages to

the mountain. The link between the Mt. Carmel god and Baalbeck is also significant, since Hadad the god of the latter center was originally a god of vegetation, and so might have been expected to appeal to the inhabitants of rural Galilee also. Therefore the Mt. Carmel cult center and its god should not have been unacceptable to Galilean country folk, yet this does not seem to have materialized, and their appeal for help to the Judaean resistance fighters is a clear indication that for them the god of the Phoenician city states or their world had no attraction. Elijah the great prophet of Yahweh who had once before conquered the Baal of the sacred place, Mt. Carmel, does not appear anywhere in Galilean traditions, now or later, as returning to reconquer the mountain. Rather, as we shall see, one of his concerns is said to be the Jerusalem temple and its cult.[35] In other words the political and cultural barriers we discovered in this area correspond with the deeper religious ones. There is apparently no great desire or attraction for Jews in this part of Galilee to adopt the religious symbols and worship of their neighbors, and this can only mean that the wider cultural and social gaps could not have been bridged by such a syncretism.

The conclusion is all the more interesting since it focuses on other possible centers to which Galilean Jews might have been attracted, had they been drawn to an alternative form of worship. One suggestion is Tabor (A(I) tabyrion) on the southern edge of Lower Galilee (*Life* 188), where the local Baal became Zeus Atabyrios and was worshipped in Rhodes, Sicily and Crimea even before Alexander, presumably because of commercial and trading links. The place was apparently a center of religious worship in the time of Hosea, though the prophet is critical of it (5:1), and it also was a prominent administrative center at the time of Antiochus III (Polybius, *Hist* V 70; *Ant* 13:396). Presumably then the cult center was thoroughly hellenized, but Eissfeldt argues that because the symbol of a bull is attached to the worship of Zeus Atabyrion in Rhodes, it can safely be identified with the mountain and weather gods such as Hadad.[36] The sanctuary would have been of the open-air variety, and the fact that Galilean Jews fled there first and subsequently to Jerusalem when Vespasian was rounding up the rebels in the province (*War* 4:54-61) might suggest that it had special religious significance for them at that time. Its importance seems to have been strategic rather than religious on the basis of Josephus' account, but that need not exclude some significant religious symbolism for this impressive mountain in the popular mind.[37] However, it does not seem to have been a center of thriving pagan worship, at least in hellenistic times, and the flight of some Jews from there to Jerusalem indicates that it did not function as a rival cult center for Galilean Jews.

Scythopolis presents a rather different picture. We have already discussed the legend linking it with Nysa, the place of banishment of Dionysus' nurse, so that at least from Seleucid times it was a center of worship for the god. As suggested already, the most plausible explanation for the Greek name of the city is that it comes from a colony of Scythian veterans planted there by the early Ptolemies,[38] who were also worshippers of the god Dionysus according to Herodotus (*Hist* IV, 79-80.108). So far only one inscription mentioning the god Dionysus has been found there on an altar originally belonging to the theatre of the city dating from second or third century B.C.E. A shrine situated on a high place dating from the same period has also been found, but no inscription has so far come to light identifying it definitively, and it is at least possible that it was a Zeus shrine, especially since, as mentioned, an inscription to Ζεὺς Ἀκραῖος has been unearthed in the city.[39] Even more important than these discoveries however, is the possibility that Yahweh the god of the Jews was first identified with Dionysus in this region. The most complete version of the identification is that given by Plutarch in which the Jewish feast of Tabernacles is described as a Dionysus festival, (*Quaest. Conviviales*, 6:1f). But it was also known to Tacitus, who dismisses the suggestion as unworthy of Dionysus (*Hist* V, 5).[40] If we are to seek any basis in reality for the identification it would seem that the Scythopolis area is the most likely location, given the fact of good Jewish/Gentile relations there throughout the centuries, with the one exception of the period immediately prior to the first Jewish revolt of 66 C.E.

While we might have expected religious hostilities in this area similar to those along the Phoenician coast just at the period of the reform, there were in fact no such disturbances. Judas Maccabaeus was able to destroy the temple of Atargatis at Carnaim

so, even though their main argument - the unliklihood of a temple being dedicated to a female goddess - is not all that telling, but so far no archaeological evidence from tel Dan supports the view that a temple did exist there in hellenistic times. At best then, one could see Dan as a cultic center with a serious attraction for Galilean Jews only insofar as it lived on in folk memory as a sacred place. In all probability even that link was broken after the Assyrians had deported the priestly leaders of the sanctuary, and the fact that the Pan grotto was not located on the actual site of the older sanctuary seems conclusive evidence that the earlier worship was not continued there.

Our search for an alternative cult center, whose symbol system might have replaced that of the Jerusalem temple for Galilean Jews, has not suggested any serious rivals. Literary evidence, allied to archaeological discoveries have indicated a number of pagan or syncretistic centers on the circumference of Galilee, at sites that had already been noted as such in Israelite times, and it is not surprising to find them still in existence, even thriving in hellenistic times. This is in line with the pattern of hellenistic religion that we know from elsewhere, but presumably, those same social, cultural and ethnic factors that had operated previously to make such centers unattractive, if not alien to the Israelite population, continued. Naturally the pattern is not uniform, as we have suggested, and can see from reading between the lines for the Beth Shean area. What is striking is that at no time in the whole period of our survey was there ever any attempt to build an alternative temple either pagan or syncretistic in Galilee itself. Tiberias had a royal palace and an amphitheatre that was hellenistic in style, but not a temple, and its founder, Herod Antipas apparently went to Jerusalem at Jewish festivals if only to maintain appearances (*Lk* 23:8-12). The aristocracy of Sepphoris were descended from the Jerusalem priesthood so that there was never any threat to Jerusalem from that quarter, and it may well have been this religious loyalty that prevented Sepphoris from adopting a more independent position when the opportunity was given it by Gabinius, as previously discussed.[48] Archaeological evidence from the Huleh basin, which lay outside Upper Galilee for the period of this enquiry, does suggest some worship of Athena and Zeus Heliopolis, but there is no evidence that this made any serious inroad even into Upper Galilee, but may rather be attributed to military garrisons at this cross-roads of the far north.[49] All this is in striking contrast to the picture in Trans-jordan, where what appears to have been a syncretistic temple was established by the Tobiad Hyrcanus at 'araq el Amir, and was apparently intended as a rival to the Jerusalem temple once the Seleucids had come to power in Palestine.[50] Besides there was the Atargatis temple at Carnaim, mentioned in 2 Macc 12:26. Galilee lacked any such influential native nobility, in the earlier period as we have seen, and without the impetus that such a thoroughly hellenized family in the area would provide, no such centripetal movement ever emerged there.[51]

Mention has already been made of the Samaritan temple on Mount Gerizim. By the first century C.E. the evidence of the New Testament and Josephus shows that Galilean Jewish attitudes towards this center were just as hostile as were those at Jerusalem. It is generally recognized that the thoroughgoing hellenization of the Shechem cult by the Sidonians there was the final wedge that irrevocably split the two communities, and this can only mean that the hellenized cult was unattractive to Galilean Jews also, thus confirming our earlier conclusions. One might have expected that this would not have been the case earlier, since the initial opposition between Samaria and Jerusalem after the Babylonian restoration was due to Judaea being recognized as an autonomous temple state by the Persians, and so was politically rather than religiously motivated.[52] Subsequently, more liberal-minded Jerusalem priests, reflecting a rift there even at an earlier stage, were prepared to intermarry with the Samaritans, to the great horror of their more conservative brothers (Ant 11:297ff. 307-11).[53] Apparently it was only after the placing of a Macedonian colony at Samaria itself by Alexander the Great that the Samaritan religionists moved to Shechem and with the aid of the dissident Jerusalem priests erected the temple on Mt. Gerizim, the ancient cultic site.[54] Despite the growing tensions between the two religious communities, a study of the Samaritan Pentateuch as well as their priestly lists has convinced scholars that the final rift did not come until Hasmonaean times, leading to the destruction by Hyrcanus in 128 B.C.E. Thus the existence of a separate cult center was no more decisive in making the final break than was the one at Leontopolis in Egypt.[55] Ben Sirach's conservative views about the sanctity of the Jerusalem cult contrasted with 'the degenerate people who dwell at Schechem'(*Sir* 50:25f) were not necessarily shared by all segments of Judaism of the time. At least in its early years there was no reason why Galilean Jews might not have supported the Shechem temple and still have regarded themselves as loyal to Israelite traditions.[56] Perhaps the anti-Samaritan polemic of Sirach carried on by *Judith* (5:16;9:2-4), *Jubilees* (30:5.7) and *Tar. Ps. Jonathan* to *Dt* 33:11 are signs that the Shechem temple did pose such a threat, but even then the message is addressed more to a Jerusalem than to a Galilean audience, and we have no other evidence which might be construed as Galilean support for Shechem. As we shall presently see, later evidence in fact suggests the opposite and supports the evidence of *1 Macc* 5 that even from an early period Galilean attachment to the Jerusalem temple was unwavering.

II
THE GALILEANS AND THE JERUSALEM TEMPLE

Our investigation so far has not indicated any great desire for radical change on the part of the Galilean Jews in regard to their central religious symbol system. Contrary expectations notwithstanding, we have not been able to find any positive traces of serious inroads of hellenistic religious syncretism there. Our task now is to probe more deeply into this Galilean attachment to the Jerusalem cult – its extent and motives – since many different attitudes can be detected among those who clung faithfully to traditional beliefs in the face of the hellenistic crisis.

. For one thing it seems important to distinguish between loyalty to the temple as such and loyalty to Jerusalem. Contrary to a widespread belief, the idea of the new Jerusalem is not identical with that of the new temple in the Jewish religious hopes for the post-exilic period, and the latter seems to have been secondary in many circles.[57] Of the two the new Jerusalem is much more prominent in apocalyptic, possibly because of attitudes such as those expressed in *Tobit* (14:5) and *Syr.Bar* (68:3) unfavorably contrasting the second temple with the earlier one.[58] Among those who did retain their loyalty to the temple one finds severe criticism of the existing cult and its ministers, as for example the

Qumran Essenes who considered their own community as the purified temple.[59] Even within less radical circles the emphasis seems to have changed from the temple itself to its rites as these could be conducted outside and independently of it, especially those of lustrations and common meals. This tendency can be seen at its mildest in Pharisaism which not merely extended the concept of the ritually clean into the everyday life, but also gained an increasing hold on the temple ritual (*Ant* 18:15), partly no doubt because of historical reasons, but also because the temple worship was integral to the Torah to which they were so totally committed.[60] But the same trend can be detected in other non-Essene baptist circles, even that of John the Baptizer, who claimed forgiveness of sins for his own ritual. Other groups are barely known, such as the Sabbaeans (Epiphanius, *Pan* XI), the Masbuthaeans (Hegesippus in Eusebius, *Eccles. Hist.* 4, 25.5) and the Dositheans, all of them linked with the Samaritan cult, as well as the Nazarenes from Gilead and Bashan.[61] These suggest that Judaism in its various forms was searching for complementary if not alternative ways to the temple, as an expression of its personal meaning for the individual.

It is against this background that we must attempt to evaluate the Galileans' attitudes. To what precisely were they attached – Jerusalem, the temple, or both? Do they share the dissatisfaction with certain developments in the Jewish cult reflected in the various groups just mentioned? Our answers to these questions will help to prepare the ground for the topic of our final chapter concerning Galilean Christianity, for according to Epiphanius there was a saying of Jesus preserved by the Ebionites directed against the temple cult: 'I came to abolish (κατάλυσαι) the sacrifices (θυσίας), and if you do not cease from sacrifice, the wrath (ὄργη) will not cease from you' (*Pan* XXX, 16.5). James, the brother of the Lord is also portrayed in the same light (*Pan* XXX, 16.5 and 7; XVIII, 1.4; Jerome, *In Is* 9:1), and Lohmeyer has built his thesis concerning Galilean Christianity of an earlier period on this evidence.[62] It would be imperative to see if any such attitudes are to be found in Jewish Galilee, and thus a possible criterion established for a discussion of Jewish Christian attitudes prior to 70 C.E. also.

(i) *The Galileans and Temple Offerings.*

We may take as our starting point for a discussion of Galilean attitudes towards temple offerings the tradition attributed to R. Judah in the Mishnah, *Ned* 2:4, where the topic under discussion is the correct interpretation of vows. A general principle has it that when the object of the vow is not clearly specified, the stricter interpretation of its meaning applies, whereas vows expressly defined may be interpreted more leniently. Various examples of how this operates are given, one of them based on the geographic differences between Galilee and Judea:

> Rabbi Judah says: if the vow was of undefined terumah, in Judea it is binding, but in Galilee it is not binding, since the men of Galilee know naught of the terumah of the temple chamber (שאין אנשי גליל מכירין את־תרומת הלשכן). And if the vow was of undefined votive things in Judea it is not binding, but in Galilee it is binding, since the people of Galilee know naught of things devoted to the priests (שאין אנשי גליל מכירין את־חרמי הכהנים).

Later we shall discuss the alleged lack of knowledge by the Galileans of 'the devoted things' (*herem*) for the priests, but for now we must concentrate on the *terumah* of the temple chamber.

Since the saying in question is attributed to Rabbi Judah, the head of the school at Usha in the second century C.E., our first question is to decide whether this piece of information is of any assistance in constructing the situation of an earlier period. The rabbinic material from the second century Usha school clearly reflects a polemical situation in which the *haber* or associate and the *'am ha-'aretz* are sharply differentiated by a number of issues, including that of vows, the subject of the present mishnah. According to *M. Dem* 2:3, R. Judah declared that the associate should not be profuse in vows, and in *M. Ned* 5:5 he again declares that the men of Galilee need not assign their share of the municipal property since their fathers have done so for them. In a *baraita* of the Babylonian Talmud the same rabbi gives as the reason for this the quarrelsome nature of the Galileans which led them to make vows rashly, so as not to benefit one another (*b.Ned* 48a). Perhaps then, *M.Ned* 2:4 should be read in the light of these traditions of

Rabbi Judah and reflect only the attitudes of the Galilean *'am ha-'aretz* of his own day. Its import would be that though generally unreliable in their vows, in this instance the Galileans pose no threat of defilement to the *haberîm* since their vow was not binding due to their ignorance of offerings for the temple. While not excluding this contemporary concern of Rabbi Judah, the example chosen to illustrate the principle being expounded, as well as the geographic distinction between the two regions, at least raises the question of differing attitudes to the temple and its offerings on the part of Galileans and Judaeans of an earlier period. Before dismissing the evidence entirely therefore, we will do well to examine it in the light of known general attitudes of an earlier period.[63]

The general meaning of *terumah* is 'an offering', but in the Mishnah it occurs almost 600 times in the technical sense of a heave-offering, that is a specific portion of the harvest (one fortieth to one eightieth) which had to be given to the priests, in accordance with the rules in the tractate of the same name.[64] However, in this instance it is specified as an offering of the temple chamber, that is the half shekel offering which is described as *terumah* throughout the tractate *Shekalîm* (cf. e.g. *M.Shek* 2:1f; 3:1). Underlying the legislation is the idea that once a thing is dedicated to the temple it is believed to participate in the holiness of the temple itself and so cannot be put to profane use. Thus any term in a vow that could conceivably apply to the temple had to be interpreted strictly unless otherwise specified, but in the case of the Galileans' use of *terumah* no such reference to the temple could be argued because of their ignorance of the *terumôth* for the temple chamber. What is the likelihood and circumstances of such Galilean ignorance in the pre-70 C.E. days?

Tannaitic tradition linked the half shekel offering that every adult male Jew was expected to pay to the temple annually for the provision of the daily sacrifices (*M.Shek* 4:1-4) with the arrangement of *Ex* 30:11-16 where Moses is commanded to take a half shekel offering from the Israelites on making a census of the people and use the money for the service of the tent of meeting, 'to make atonement for yourselves' (*p.Shek* 1,46a, *b.Meg* 29b; *M.Shek* 2:4). Nehemiah's arrangement for the restored community that each would give one third of a shekel for the service of the Lord's house (*Neh* 10:33f) is generally seen as the re-establishment of the Mosaic ordinance, the discrepancy in the amounts being variously explained. Yet there are problems about drawing such a direct line between the passages in *Ex* and *Neh* and the practice in New Testament times, especially when one examines the evidence for the later period.[65] For one thing, it is clear from the context that Nehemiah is not re-activating an old ordinance, but rather introducing a new one, which may have been due to the fact that the earlier decrees of Darius (*Es* 6:8ff) and Artaxerxes (*Es* 7:12ff) to the effect that the Persian administration would meet the temple costs, were either temporary or inadequate. Yet, apparently the Seleucids were prepared to accept similar responsibilities for the Jerusalem cult later (*Ant* 12:138ff; *2 Macc* 3:3 cf. *1 Macc* 10:40).[66] Against this background it is significant that there is no mention of the half shekel offering in documents that reflect the Persian and early hellenistic period, such as *Tob* 1:6-8; *2 Chron* 31 or *Jub* 13:26f. It is only in the sources from the Roman period that the obligation is presumed: Josephus, *Ant* 3:194-6; *War* 7:218; Philo, *De Leg. Spec.* 1:78; *Mt* 17:24. It is this evidence that has led J. Liver to conclude that the institution of the half shekel offering must be dated to Roman times, and he finds support for this conclusion in the *Megillath Ta'anit*, which declares that there is to be no fasting between the first and eighth of Nisan, during which time 'the daily offering was established'.[67] The old Hebrew *scholion* on this tells of a division between the Boethusians and the Sages on whether the sacrifices were to be provided by the whole community or by private individuals. The Sages were in favor of the sacrifices being provided for by the whole community from the temple chamber:

> 'and when they had gained mastery over them (the Boethusians) they fixed the regulation that all Israel would pay their shekels and deposit them in the temple chamber, and all the offerings would be provided by the community'.[68]

According to this evidence, the half shekel offering as a regulation for all Israel is to be dated to the Pharisaic control of the council, possibly during the reign of Solome Alexandra (cf. *Ant* 13:408-10).

Before deciding that the Galileans' ignorance of the temple *terumôth* was due to lack of Pharisaic influence on the populace there, it should be noted that a fragment from Qumran, *4 Q Ordinances*, dealing with cultic matters associated with such Old Testament texts as *Ez* 45:11; *Ex* 32:20; *Dt* 23.25f appears to also indicate a deviant atittude to the half shekel offering:

> 'that they gave every man a ransom for his soul, half
> (a shekel for an offering to the Lord). Only one (time)
> shall he give it all his days: the shekel is 20 gerah after
> the shekel of the sanctuary (11.6 and 7).[69]

It would appear that, according to this ordinance at least, the Qumranites were opposed to the annual offering for sacrifices which they considered illegitimate. Yet it is doubtful if we can forge links between the alleged Galilean ignorance of the temple *terumôth* and the critical stance of the Essenes, since the second part of *M.Ned* 2:4 presumes that they are prepared to offer *herem* – devoted offerings – to the temple, a direct contrast to the Essenes' reluctance, if not downright refusal to do so. As we shall presently see, the Galileans frequented the temple at the great pilgrimages and it was on these occasions that the shekels were brought to the temple chamber in formal procession 'with pomp' (*p. Shek*1,45d). Furthermore according to *M. Shek* 1:3 tables of money-changers were set out in the provinces to enable people to discharge their duty with Tyrian coinage, 'the money of the sanctuary'.[70]

It is difficult to conceive Galilean ignorance of the institution continuing for very long once the Pharisees had won their way with regard to all Israel being responsible. If Rabbi Judah's example has any relevance for the pre-70 period it can only mean that the Galileans did not observe the institution with any great enthusiasm, and there is evidence that they were not alone in their attitudes. Thus Rabban Johanan ben Zakkai bemoaning the fall of the temple chides his contemporaries for (among other failures) not being prepared to pay the half shekel offering, while at the same time paying fifty shekels to the government of the enemy (*Mek Ex* 19:1).[71] This critique takes on a special relevance for Galilee in the light of the Johanan's well known general charge of the province's neglect of torah, to be discussed in the next chapter. For the present it is sufficient to tentatively conclude that Galilean ignorance of the temple *terumôth*, if it is a genuine recollection of the period of the second temple, does not have to be understood as a critique of the temple as such, but merely an acceptance of the Sadducaean rather than the Pharisaic position on the matter of responsibility for the half shekel offering. Their attitude can be interpreted as conservative rather than neglectful, reflecting a refusal to adopt new ideas in religion anymore than in other walks of life, in line with peasant attitudes everywhere. Perhaps too the produce of the land rather than money, especially Tyrian money, was for these rural people a more fitting symbol of their worship of Yahweh.

(ii) *The Galileans and the Tithes.*

Josephus, at the beginning of *Life* stresses the fact that he is a descendent of one of the foremost priestly families, as recorded in the public registers which kept a stringent check on membership of such a privileged class within a hierocracy. The significance of this introduction emerges when later in the same work he tells us that he refused the tithes which the Galileans brought to him, even though *'they were his due as a priest'* (ἀλλ' οὐδὲ τὰς ὀφειλομένας μοι ὡς ἱερεῖ δεκάτας ἀπελάμβανον παρὰ τῶν κομιζόντων *Life* 80). In this magnanimous gesture he contrasts himself to his two companions, Joazar and Judas, who were also priests and before returning to Jerusalem amassed a large sum of money from the tithes which they accepted as their due (εὐπορήσαντες πολλῶν χρημάτων ἐκ τῶν δεδομένων αὐτοῖς δεκατῶν, *Life* 63). The fact that these two companions are not mentioned at all in the *War* account, as well as the whole apologetic tone of *Life* has caused some scepticism about these utterances. Certainly the immediate context of his remarks seems to be that of self-defense against specific charges made against him by Justus, and so he prefaces his response with an example of his magnanimity and selflessness.[72] For our present purposes, the significant aspect of the remark is the supposition of Josephus (and presumably Justus, if he is being directly addressed here) that the Galileans would have no hesitation in paying the tithes to Jerusalem priests. A similar attachment by the Galileans to priests from Jerusalem is further presupposed in the delegation subsequently sent to remove Josephus: they are told to ascertain whether or not Galilean loyalty to Josephus was due to the fact that he was a priest, and to assure them that two of their number were also priests (*Life* 198).

This attitude of the Galileans regarding priestly rights to the tithe offerings is all the more striking in view of the fact that a letter written to the men of Upper and Lower Galilee, by Rabbi Simeon ben Gamaliel and Rabban Johanan ben Zakkai, almost contemporaneously with the Josephus episode, gives a rather different impression: 'Let it be known to you that the fourth year has arrived, but still the sacred produce (קדשי־שמים) has not been removed. But now make haste and bring the olive heaps, for they hinder the confession (הודוי), and it is not we who have begun to write to you, but our fathers to your fathers.' The tone of this letter, more severe than that of an earlier one written by Rabban Gamaliel I, to the men of Lower Galilee reminding them that 'the time of removal had come to remove the tithes from the olive heaps', as well as the appeal to tradition 'for so our fathers wrote to your fathers', would seem to suggest that Galilean observance of the tithing laws was less than satisfactory, at least by the standards of the Jerusalem sages. We shall examine the details of this letter later,[73] but for now it is sufficient to note that there is question of the Galileans making haste to bring (תביאו) the sacred produce to Jerusalem. Clearly, we are dealing with a complex situation involving country – city tensions, and before drawing conclusions from these pieces of information regarding the Galilean religious attitudes we must attempt to situate them within the larger context of contemporary developments concerning the tithing laws.

The Deuteronomic centralization marked the beginning of far-reaching changes for the cultic institutions of Israel. Henceforth, all the offerings for cultic ministers were to be brought to Jerusalem (Dt 12:6; 14:22f; 18:1-6), thereby increasing the economic strength of the temple clergy and impoverishing the country priests, even though technically they too were entitled to participate in the temple services and could share in the offerings (Dt 18: 6-8). However, the repeated admonition to take care of the Levite in your midst 'who has no inheritance with you' and the linking of him with the stranger, the fatherless and the widow is ample testimony of the hardship many country priests experienced (Dt 12:12.18f; 14:27-29; 26:13). The third and sixth years were designated for the distribution of the tithes to the local poor, and this is a further indication of the social upheaval caused by the reform (Dt 14:22-29; 26:12-15).[74] The post-exilic situation reflects further changes. The Levites had experienced a loss of cultic rank on the return from Babylon, as evidenced in *Ez* 44:6-31,[75] and this was reflected in their social condition, for Nehemiah found that they had had to abandon the temple altogether because the tithes, their only source of income, were no longer given to them (*Neh* 13:5). Nehemiah regulated for this situation – first fruits were for the priests and the tithes were to go to the Levites (*Neh* 10:36-38a) who had to give a tithe of this tithe to the priests (*Neh* 18:26), but by the second century B.C.E. such writings as *Sir* (7:31f; 32:10f; 45:20f), *Judith* (11:13f), *Jubilees* (13:8.26f; 32:15), *I Macc* (3:46-54) and *Ps. Hecataeus* (cited in *Against Apion* 1:188), know only of tithes for the priests, with no mention of the Levites at all.[76] A further development in the tithing laws is the emergence of a second tithe, which the owner himself is to partake of in Jerusalem (*M.Ma'as Sch* 5:2-5) - apparently the combination of the one meal tithe of *Dt* 14:23 and the tithe for the Levite of *Nm* 18:21.[77] Yet a further addition is reflected in the Alexandrine and Vatican versions of *Tobit* 1:6-8 which has a third tithe, that of the poor man in the third and sixth years, thereby causing increased hardship for small landowners of the Roman period.[78] Even more remarkable is the fact that this third tithe for the poor man was to be discharged in Jerusalem, given the fact that in *Dt* it was originally connected with the local poor.

This survey of the situation in regard to tithing indicates that matters were by no means stable in the Greco-Roman period and one suspects that social and economic tensions of city-country and rich-poor were operative. Thus the purely religious significance of the tithes was likely to be disregarded or relegated to a secondary role, something that various halachic prescriptions also suggest. One can detect two different concerns involved. On the one hand, the withholding of the tithes meant a loss of revenue for the priests and penury for the lesser clergy and Levites. At the same time the non-observance of the tithe gave rise, in the view of the scribes, to *demai*-produce, that is not certainly tithed, and this endangered the purity of the *haberim* who had undertaken to live their lives in ritual purity. We shall defer until the next chapter a consideration of the Galileans' performance on that score in the eyes of the Jerusalem sages. Here we wish to consider their attitude to the tithes as an expression of their concern for the temple, conscious that the same obligation may be viewed in very different light by those who discharge it and by those who stand to benefit from its discharge.

We are best informed about the tithing situation for the immediate pre-70 period. Josephus tells us that during the high priesthood of Ishmael son of Phabi (59 C.E.) and later that of Ananias, the servants of the aristocratic priests went to the threshing floors to collect the tithes, using force against the local people where necessary and allowing the lesser priests to starve to death (*Ant* 20:181.206f;*b.Ket* 105b). This presupposes a situation in which the clergy themselves are divided on the basis of social status and access to the source of wealth, and the country people are reluctant to pay the tithes at all, or possibly wish to retain them for the local priest, as was their right according to the *halakhah (M. Betzah* 1:6; *T.Peah* 4:7). A *baraita* in both Talmuds fills out this picture further: Johanan the high priest who among other things did away with 'the avowal' in the mishnah under discussion (*M.Ma'as Sch* 5:15; *M.Sot* 9:15) is said to have sent inspectors through the country and found that while the separation of the *terumah* for the priest was separated, neither the tithe for the Levite nor the second tithe was observed. He accordingly decreed that the first and second tithes be separated, the former being given to a local priest and the latter discharged in Jerusalem (*b.Sot* 48a; *p.Sot* 9, 24a).[79] The fact that the abolition of the avowal has been dated by different scholars to the reign of John Hyrcanus I, that of Hyrcanus II, or the immediate pre-70 C.E. period – all with some reason – is indicative of the ongoing tensions that existed in the Hasmonaean state and thereafter between secular taxes and religious obligations as these impinged on the ordinary people.[80] In increasing numbers the landed aristocracy were themselves priests and undoubtedly this raised the question of why they should be paid a second time for the produce of the soil. For Galileans the bringing of tithes to Jerusalem must have created a particular hardship and that was why from its inception it was possible to redeem the second tithe and spend the money in Jerusalem (*Dt* 14:24f).

How are we to evaluate the Galilean attitudes in the light of this situation? Insofar as we can tell, Galilee did not have many lower class priests or Levites in the pre-70 period, and so was spared the social tensions of Judaea, a fact we noted earlier in contrasting the revolutionary ethos of both provinces.[81] Apparently, Josephus' and his colleagues' claims to the tithes were not questioned and we are justified in asking if this was because the Galilean country people had long been accustomed to paying the tithes to aristocratic priests within the province. Perhaps 'the willingness' of the Galileans was Josephus' way of covering up the extortionist practices of the aristocratic priestly families of which he was all too well aware. We have met priestly aristocratic landowners in Sepphoris already, Joseph ben Illem being a possible example in the time of Herod the Great (*T. Yoma* 1,4; *p. Yoma* 1,38d; *b Yoma* 12b; *Ant* 17:166f). In *Against Apion* 2:187 Josephus describes the function of the priests in Judaism in essentially secular and civil terms and that was his own role in Galilee also.[82] Presumably then, the reference to religious dues was simply for the edification of his readers, but for those who received them the tithes had ceased to have any real religious significance.

What were the real feelings of the Galileans? The letters from the Jerusalem sages seem to suggest some laxity on their part, and presumably the former were writing in their capacity as spokesmen for the council of the theocracy and not just as Pharisaic scribes concerned about *demai* produce for the *haberîm*, though of course this too was not excluded, once the Pharisees had taken effective control of the national *halakhah* – something that was to emerge more sharply in the post-70 situation.[83] The earlier letter of Gamaliel I speaks of the time of removal having come 'to bring out the tithes'. In view of the fact that a third similar letter from him to the men of the exile speaks of intercalating a month because the springtime had not yet arrived, it is doubtful if we can read from this expression alone laxity on the part of the Galileans and the men of the South (the addressees of the second letter), though undoubtedly the reminder was a timely one. Farmers have never been anxious to part with their produce! By contrast, the second letter from Simeon and Johanan speaks of the fourth year having come and that the delay of the Galileans is hindering the confession (הודוי cf. *Dt* 26:13). The problem apparently had been a perennial one since earlier remonstrations of a similar nature are referred to. The fact that the confession is hindered recalls the decree of Johanan the priest abolishing the confession, and one can only surmise that if this act is to be dated to an early time, it had been restored once Pharisaic control of the council had been effected. Mention of the arrival of the fourth year might suggest that the Galileans' laxity referred only to the poor man's tithe which was due in the third and sixth years. As discussed this too had tended to be centered on Jerusalem though originally intended for the local poor and one could easily sympathize with Galilean reluctance, given social and economic conditions in the homeland. However, the avowal or confession covered the discharge, not just of the poor man's tithe, but of all the tithing obligations apparently (*M Ma'as Sch* 5:10), so that the Galileans are being accused of a general laxity. Could it be that the restoration of the avowal or confession in Jerusalem – the Galileans are asked to hurry and '*bring*' (ותביאו) the olives – was not recognized in Galilee where Sadducean or priestly custom dominated the religious life? In that event we would be faced with a situation similar to that which obtained in regard to the half shekel offering, and we can understand why on the one hand tithes are discharged in the province to priestly aristocracy either native or sent from Jerusalem, like Josephus and his companions, and at the same time why the Pharisaic sages in control of the council are less than pleased with the situation. However, it should be noted that the Galileans are no different form other parts of the country since, as mentioned, a similar epistle was sent to the men of the South. Undoubtedly, we are dealing with practices which are seen rather differently from the center and the periphery of Jewish life, and it would be rash to conclude that the Galileans were less than attached to the temple and what it stood for just because social and economic considerations not of their making had determined their tithing habits.

The available evidence has necessitated focusing on the immediate pre-70 situation, but it seems legitimate to suggest that a similar situation must have obtained ever since Galilee's incorporation into the Jewish state and the emergence of a native landowning aristocracy. Tobit, a pious Galilean Jew, claimed to be alone of all his tribe (Naphtali) in going to Jerusalem for the feasts, bringing the proper offerings (*Tobit* 1:6-8), but given the didactic purpose of the work it is difficult to decide how representative he is of Galilean Jews of the early hellenistic period.

The wording of the decree of Caesar in favor in Hyrcanus II suggests that in his day at least, if not earlier, the tithes were controlled by the Hasmonaean aristocracy: 'they shall also pay tithes to Hyrcanus and his sons just as they paid to their fore-fathers' (*Ant* 14:203). The fall of Jerusalem was obviously a serious blow to all segments of the Jewish people who had put their hopes in the temple, including the Galileans, for whom it offered a focal point of their loyalties and a symbol of identity through centuries of living on the fringes of Jewish society and surrounded by a pagan life-style. However, once the temple no longer stood and with the increased economic burdens of the revolt and its aftermath, the tithes were not able to carry whatever religious weight they had previously retained for country people.[84] It may be that for a time at least some more devout souls continued with the pilgrimage to the temple mount, for we hear of a debate between Rabbis Meir and Judah concerning the personal use of goods for tithing on the journey to Jerusalem from Galilee (*M.Ma'as* 2:3). However, such devotion was only to be expected from the more fervent Jews and it is not surprising to find the laws of tithing observed by the followers of Bar Cochba also.[85] Like-wise we hear that the *haberim* in Galilee prepared their offerings in purity, hoping that Elijah would show how to bring them undefiled to Jerusalem (*b.Hag* 24b; *b.Nid* 6a). But this was in stark contrast to the majority, who we shall see, merited from the sages the uncomplimentary epithet *'am ha-'aretz* because of their failure to observe among other things, the tithing laws. Yet this 'negligence' in the post-70 period cannot be interpreted as dis-regard for the temple or its institutions in the earlier period in view of the economic and social aspects of the tithe which we have been considering.

(iii) *The Galileans and the Pilgrimage to Jerusalem.*

'Three times a year all the males shall appear before the Lord God' (*Ex* 23:17; *Dt* 16:16). Our task is to evaluate the importance Galilean Jews attached to this Deuteronomic commandment of the centralized cult. As we shall see there is plenty of evidence in our sources – Talmudic, Josephus and New Testament – to suggest that Galileans did take it seriously, but there is no great agreement on the way the pilgrimage affected the lives of the provincials or the spirit in which the obligation was carried out. Josephus (*War* 6:423f; cf. *T Pes* 4:3; *b.Pes* 64b) and Philo (*De Leg Spec* 1,69) mention huge crowds, but the former makes it clear that he was speaking of an exceptional year, and the latter's statements reflect the ideal rather than actual practice. Various regulations in rabbinic literature indicate that not all devout Jews made the pilgrimage on every occasion, a fact that is attested for Galilee also when we hear that in Judaea work continued until midday of the 14th of Nisan – the eve of Passover – whereas in Galilee they did not work at all that day, and the school of Shammai even prohibited work on the night before (*M.Pes* 4:6). It appears that the commandment was one of those immeasurable obligations mentioned at *M.Peah* 1:1, that is, each person fulfilled the obligation as best he could.

In rabbinic sources it is the spiritual aspect of the visit to Jerusalem that is particularly stressed and there can be no doubt that it was the occasion for the expression of great personal piety for many Jews, especially those from the Diaspora.[86] On the other hand Josephus seems to stress the social and political role of the pilgrimage – especially for Galilean Jews, so that naturally our attention is focused on his evidence rather than the more idealized and formal descriptions of the rabbis. In particular we must pay attention to the violence that could erupt on such occasions and attempt to evaluate its possible religious significance in the light of our earlier discussions.

The first such episode took place on the death of Herod the Great in 4 B.C.E. During the feast of Passover when many people were gathered in Jerusalem from the country and the Diaspora – Galileans are not explicitly mentioned – sympathizers of the Pharisaic scholars, Judas and Matthias whom Herod had executed (*Ant* 17:149-167), began to elicit support for the cause of the dead scholars from the countrypeople by mourning in the temple court. Archelaus intervened lest the whole crowd be infected with this fanaticism and this led to violence between the troops and the people. Eventually Archelaus suspended the festival altogether after slaughtering 3,000 of the pilgrims (*Ant* 17:213-18; *War* 2:8-13). However, the very next feast, that of Pentecost of the same year, saw increased crowds from the country present, 'not merely because of the religious observances but also because they resented the reckless insolence of Sabinius', the temporary Roman procurator left in Jerusalem to preserve the peace while Archelaus and Antipas were debating their respective cases in Rome. On this occasion Josephus does mention the places of origin of the pilgrims – Galilee, Idumaea, Jericho, Peraea and beyond the Jordan – with those from Judaea itself being the most militant. Apparently they organized themselves for battle and forming three divisions, encircled the Romans in the temple area. There was slaughter on all sides and the temple porticoes were set on fire. In the struggle that followed the Romans took possession of the temple chamber and carried off the dedicatory offerings (presumably the contributions from the half shekel offering), which incensed the Jews further.

In attempting to isolate the various aspects of this episode one is struck by the fact that it was Jerusalem Jews, and more precisely Pharisaic supporters of Judas and Matthias that were the prime instigators. The numerical presence of the country pilgrims was certainly an incentive, but the *War* as distinct from *Ant*, account suggests that they had already begun their protests even before the festival.[87] The fact that later the Jerusalemites attempt to blame the countrypeople for the trouble is a natural reaction, given their circumstances, but cannot disguise who the real leaders were (*Ant* 17:293). If we are correct in suggesting that the Galileans did not pay the half shekel offering as prescribed by the Pharisees, we can assume that they would have been less offended by the Roman seizure of these. Josephus mentions that greater crowds came for Pentecost than for Passover, and that many of them did not have particular religious motivation. If this is accurate it would suggest that some could go on the pilgrimage for all kinds of reasons other than purely religious ones – social, political, even economic – and that is only as we might expect. We have already argued that the subsequent disturbance in Galilee under Judas son of Hezekiah did not have a widespread popular support in the province, and we might suspect that Judas' desire for kingly rule would have been frowned on by the Pharisaic group who were at the center of the religious disturbances in Jerusalem.[88] In other words, while the Galilean pilgrims may well have been touched by the attitudes current in Jerusalem during these two feasts even to the point of becoming embroiled in the happenings, there does not seem to have been any great carryover when they returned to the province – either in resisting Judas' attempt, if indeed we are correct in surmising that the Pharisaic group would have been opposed to it on religious grounds, or alternatively, by throwing in their lot with him in a mass uprising against foreign rule. Given the provocation of having a sacred festival suspended, the offerings confiscated and probably some of their people murdered, one can only be struck by the passivity of Galilean religious affiliation, however much the occasion of the festival was used by more radical elements to foster national sentiments based on the common faith in Yahweh, giver of the land, which all the pilgrims shared.

No doubt it is in this perspective that we should see the episode of the Galileans whose blood Pilate mingled with their sacrifices, to which Luke alludes (*Lk* 13:1). It would be unwarranted to read into the episode a Galilean revolutionary ideology giving vent to its radical views on the occasion of the temple pilgrimage, given the undiscriminating handling of all disturbances by the Romans, but it would be equally one-sided to ignore that the pilgrimage did occasion displays of independence, and so must be seen as a powerfully evocative symbol for all Jews, even if the effects did not always survive the return journey to the provinces or the Diaspora. Both Josephus (*Ant* 20:105-12; *War* 2:224f,280f) and the New Testament (*Mt* 26:5; *Mk* 14:2; cf.*Lk* 23:25; *Jn* 18:3) indicate the possibility of tumult, and the extreme caution of Roman and Jewish officials on the occasion of the Jewish national festivals. Undoubtedly, agitators were able to exploit such opportunities to the full as can be seen from the period of the revolt (cf. *Ant* 20:208f; *War* 2:425f), yet the genuine feelings of community, as well as the memory of the mighty deeds of Yahweh in the past on behalf of his people which the cultic re-enactment evoked, must have stirred the emotions of the common people. For a brief period at least, all alike, rich and poor, city and country were supposedly united in a common religious experience and in such a frank atmosphere severe criticism of prevailing incongruities can be expected. Thus Jesus' cleansing of the temple (*Mk* 11:1-11) and his subsequent condemnation for having spoken against it (*Mk* 14:58) can be viewed in the light of the festival's expectations and tensions. Apparently, this prophetic action and word were seen by the Jerusalemites as a direct attack by a country outsider on the cherished source of their prosperity.[89] Perhaps also, being away from the restraining influences of home could have been a factor in countrypeople shedding their essentially conservative behavior while in Jerusalem, only to revert to a more cautious pattern subsequently . . . . There is no shortage of feasible explanations for what appears as an undoubted fact – the pilgrimage to Jerusalem did have very definite religious and national implications for Galilean, as well as other country Jews. In the case of the Galileans, however, this mood does not seem to have persisted at home, at least for the vast majority of the pilgrim population.

Another feature of the pilgrimage which the accounts of Josephus highlight is that it helped to sharpen the antagonism between the Galileans and the Samaritans. Luke tells us that the Samaritan villagers would not accept Jesus because his face was set to go to Jerusalem (*Lk* 9:53), and *Jn* 4:9.20f reflects a similar cultic opposition between Gerizim and Jerusalem. Despite the acceptance of the Zeus cult at the former center – or possibly because of it – the Samaritan religion continued unimpeded there and this led to the final break with Judaism. The destruction of their temple by John Hyrcanus in 128 B.C.E. must have caused a deep seated bitterness between the two communities that played itself out in the hostilities towards Jerusalem-bound pilgrims as reflected both in the New Testament and Josephus. The very fact of having to face physical danger as part of the pilgrimage experience must have heightened the Galilean awareness of their own religious identity and cemented their loyalty to the Jerusalem temple, even if the Jerusalemite aristocracy did not always appreciate such attachment. On the occasion of the disturbances of 52 C.E. for example, we hear that the magistrates of Jerusalem exhorted the populace not to bring destruction on themselves by avenging the blood of a single Galilean (*War* 2:237). At the same time the Galileans were not made to feel outsiders in the Jerusalem cult, as was the case with the Samaritans who were equiparated to Gentiles (*M. Shek* 1:5). Thus city/country social tensions, did not obliterate some sense of community within a common religious faith, at least during the festivals. Accordingly the counter-temple movement of the Samaritan prophet who led his country followers to Mt. Gerizim on the promise of finding for them the hidden temple vessels (*Ant* 18:85-9) won no support among Galilean peasants, nor did Pilate's brutal handling of the affair, on a par with his treatment of their own kinsmen in Jerusalem, forge bonds against the common oppressor. The Jerusalem temple remained the focus of the Galileans' loyalty to the end.

It is presumably in this light that we must understand the flight of various Galilean Jews to Jerusalem during the great revolt – John of Gischala and his followers, the 2,000 Tiberians referred to in *Life* 354 and the refugees from Tabor (*War* 4:61). However, our previous discussions about the revolutionary ethos of the province as well as the progress of the revolt there suggests caution in categorizing the whole Galilean populace as inspired with zeal for the temple. For one thing many did not even attempt to flee to Jerusalem, but turned to such local 'non-religious' centers as Tarichaeae, Jotapata, Gamala and Tiberias in their desire to escape the Romans' wrath. Not all can have been fired with religio-apocalyptic beliefs about salvation in Jerusalem, prophecies of which were rife among the people according to Josephus (*War* 6:285-7.310-15). As already mentioned, Josephus' blackening of John in the *War* account lies behind his description of the σύνταγμα τῶν Γαλιλαίων and their evil deeds in Jerusalem (*War* 4:558-60), especially their leader's disregard for the holiness of the temple and the purity laws (*War* 5:36f.100-2.563-5; 7:263f).[90] If John was no Zealot, neither was he a totally irreligious man as his earlier contacts with Simon ben Gamaliel suggest. It is doubtful, however, if his eventual flight to Jerusalem can be interpreted as the expression of an extreme hope in the temple and the expected salvation there. Thwarted of his ambitions in Galilee he may have hoped for more success in his desire for power in Jerusalem given his old associations in the city (*War* 4:126f), despite the fact that Josephus has him declare that 'he himself could never fear capture since the city was God's' (*War* 6:99. cf. *War* 5:564). It is difficult to differentiate fact and fiction in this picture, not only because of Josephus' bias, but also because of the apparent ambivalence of John's character. However, it is sufficient for our purposes to note, that even should we accept Josephus' numbers of those Galileans who came to Jerusalem, and were to allow that John

shared Zealot ideology about the temple, he is still unrepresenta-
tive of the Galilean attitudes as a whole. In other words, the
predominant loyalty to the Jerusalem temple among Galilean
Jews was realistic rather than apocalyptic and radical, no matter
how much occasional indications of more dramatic outbursts
during pilgrimages might suggest the contrary.

III
THE NATURE OF GALILEAN LOYALTY TO
THE TEMPLE

We have been attempting to penetrate Galilean religious
loyalties to the temple by examining the available evidence from
the perspective of how the temple and its institutions related to
the everyday life of Galilee. We have discovered what might
appear to be a surprising loyalty in the first century C.E. when
the sources are more informative, yet insofar as can be judged this
was not something new for Galilean Jews, but pre-dates our
period, presumably from Josiah's reform, and expresses itself also
in the failure to attract of alternative pagan or syncretistic cult
centers nearer home. The fact that the Galileans may not have
followed Pharisaic regulations concerning the half shekel
offering and do not appear to have been too scrupulous in regard
to tithing cannot be interpreted either as a total lack of interest in
the temple or as the critique of a sub-group, such as the Essenes,
whose extreme loyalty to the ideal of the temple made them critical of the existing institution. It would appear that the vast
majority of the inhabitants of the province did not share apocalyptic visionary ideas about either Jerusalem or the temple, such
as were current in certain circles, at least on the evidence of their
behaviour during the great revolt, yet there is no denying that the
pilgrimages did function as an emotional outlet for deeply-felt
loyalties that may have been all the more intense because of the
relative isolation and separation of rural Galilean life.

In attempting to evaluate the significance of this attachment,
which was very strong, yet realistic rather than fanatical, one
obvious factor is the relationship between temple and land. Such
early post-exilic prophets as Haggai (1:9ff; 2:14ff) and Zechariah
(14:17) used the motives of productivity of the soil and the freedom
from drought to encourage the rebuiding of the second temple,

and undoubtedly countrypeople, rather than the returned exiles were mainly responsible for the work. Such ideas were likely to have remained constant among countrypeople, and it was here that the significance of the existing temple lay for them. Their attachment was based on the belief that the God of the temple in Jerusalem was the one who provided them with the necessities of life from the land, and faithful worship of him was therefore of paramount importance. This explains why, during the affair of Caligula's statue, the peasants refused to sow their crops as long as any threat continued to the sovereignty of their God in Jerusalem (*War* 2:200). The fact that Petronius confronted the countrypeople on the issue near Ptolemais and again at Tiberias (cf. *Ant* 18:269ff) suggests that these ideas were held strongly by Galilean peasants, and significantly there is no threat of violence or armed resistance. Could it be then that this is the nerve center of Galilean attachment to the temple and does this explain their faithfulness to the pilgrimage as long as it stood?

This conclusion might not appear very likely in view of the apparent apathy in regard to the tithes and temple *terumôth* we have encountered. However, it should be remembered that tithes were only one of the several offerings from the land that tied countrypeople to the temple, and as we have seen, it was the one that became most easily confused with a civil tax for the aristocratic landowners in the prevailing economic conditions. Those whose livelihood depended on retaining a tenuous link with the land were in no position to challenge the aristocracy by following Pharisaic *halakhah*, as long as the institutions of the state supported the Sadducean aristocracy, no matter what position those Pharisees had succeeded in attaining within the council. Thus the Galileans paid their taxes in the province, but without attaching too much significance to them. We have no reason to doubt that the picture of *M. Bikk* 3:2; *M. Ta'an* 4:2, portraying devout countrypeople gathering to bring their offerings, also applied to Galilean Jews once the *ma'amadoth* system had been set up there (cf. *p. Ta'an* IV, 69a). Such occasions would have kept alive the sense of Yahweh, giver of the land, no matter how corrupt the priestly aristocracy had become or how alienated the peasants may have felt from them, as can be sensed in the Galileans' hatred for Sepphoris in the immediate pre-revolt period.

At the same time the Galileans did not share any of the ideologies of the land current in the first century. Unlike the Essenes who considered their exile as 'atonement for the land' (*1Q* S8:4-7;9:3ff; *CD* 1:16; 8:1),[91] there is no evidence that the Galileans considered themselves in religious exile from the land of Israel, despite the fact that Samaria separated them from their true cultic center, and they were surrounded by Gentiles. While zeal for Temple and Torah was the center of the Zealots' philosophy, the notion of the purity of the land seems also to have played a part in their thinking.[92] Once again there is no indication that such radical ideas found particularly powerful expression in Galilee, even though this might have been anticipated. After the fall of the temple the sacredness of the land was particularly stressed by the rabbis, and the Galileans' refusal to identify with many of the stringent rules that at an earlier period had bound temple and land together so intimately, shows that they no longer shared such a sacral view of the land.[93] For them the land represented their livelihood and was not primarily a symbol of the *Heilsgeschichte*, as was the case with the more extreme elements, and while the temple survived they showed their gratitude for fruitfulness of the earth by going on pilgrimage to Yahweh's shrine at Jerusalem. The fabric of life in Galilee had for too long been shaped by non-Israelite influences for any Jewish ideology that attempted to stress the uniqueness of Israel to survive there without a violent confrontation with other elements in the ethos, and the relative peace in the province would seem to indicate that in fact no such ideology took root there. We may conclude that for the Galilean peasants the Jerusalem temple was not the center of messianic hope but the source of their confidence in the ongoing struggle for the necessities of life, and this 'attenuated' understanding of the temple and its symbolism may have been the ultimate reason for their continued faithfulness to the Yahweh shrine through the centuries, despite the vicissitudes of history.

We must not, however, confine Galilean Judaism to the peasant class, no matter how much the small landowner or tenant farmer constituted the bulk of the population there. We have already seen that following the Hasmonaean conquests, a Jewish aristocracy emerged to replace their hellenistic counterparts, comprised of the landlord class. At first common faith in Yahweh was able to completely bridge the social gap between them and the peasants and relieve the inevitable tensions that exist between these two classes in any agrarian society. A rapid review of events we have covered more than once suggests a pattern of loyalty to the temple being used by the new aristocracy as a way of overcoming the social barrier and of even exploiting the lower class. We find Galilean mothers protesting in the temple (*Ant* 14:168) on the occasion of Herod's murder of Hezekiah, a Galilean chief, thereby appealing to religious loyalty to vindicate what was essentially a political and social injustice in the eyes of the old aristocracy at the hands of the Idumaean parvenus. Antigonus may have begun his struggle against Herod in Galilee, partly at least in the hope of evoking a response from the religious loyalties of the peasants, but without much success, as we have seen. Even when the Hasmonaean aristocracy was replaced by a Herodian one, matters do not seem to have changed appreciably, for Herod showed his astute political sense in terms of Jewish religious susceptibilities as long as no threat to his own domination was present, as is exemplified by his marriage to a Hasmonaean princess and his rebuilding program for the temple. Were Joseph ben Illem and his cousin, the high priest, typical of the new nobility of Galilee, Jewish in externals only? The subsequent Herods retained an interest in the high priesthood, we have seen, and the high praise for Agrippa I in Jewish tradition is a good indication that observance of and regard for the religious practices of the people could pay off handsomely in terms of popular esteem. Presumably this explains Antipas' presence in Jerusalem at feast times (*Lk* 23:7). Once he is said to have offered sacrifice there together with Vitellius, the Roman general, to the great delight of the crowds (*Ant* 18:122f). Agrippa II's appeal to the revolutionaries on the eve of the first revolt, even if it is a Josephan construction, is surely typical of overall strategy.

Undoubtedly similar attitudes prevailed among the other nobles of the province, no less aware of the social implications of the external observance of their faith in their relations with the peasant stock of the province. Many may have lived in Jerusalem, their agents conducting the affairs in Galilee as certain rabbinic indications suggest, with the social attraction of the metropolis being readily clothed in a religious garb for the benefit of the countryfolk. The religious posturing of Josephus as portrayed in *Life* has more than a little probability when seen in this perspective, as well as his repeated appeal to ὁμοφυλία to quieten passions that had been aroused by cultural and social inequalities. Thus, for aristocrat and peasant alike the pilgrimage as an expression of a common faith could function in very different ways and have very different motivations when viewed in the light of their respective positions within the social fabric of life in the province.

NOTES FOR CHAPTER 7

[1]'Religion as a Cultural System', in *Anthropological Approaches to the Study of Religion*, ed. M. Banton, A.S.A. Monograph series, 3, London, 1966, 1-46, esp. 3f.

[2]R. de Vaux, *Ancient Israel*, 284-8; cf. *Am* 7:9; *Jer* 7:31; *2 Kgs* 21:3ff; 23:4ff; *Zeph* 1:4, with reference to the Assyrian cult even in Jerusalem.

[3]Cf. above, ch. 2, n. 10.

[4]Above, n. 2 and Alt, 'Die Umgestaltung Galiläas', *G.P.* 5, 415-17.

[5]*1 Macc* 5, *Tob* and *Jdt* are our earliest literary witnesses.

[6]G. von Rad, *Studies in Deuteronomy*, English trans. London, S.C.M. 1953; Noth, *The History of Israel*, 275f; de Vaux, *Ancient Israel*, 338.

[7]D. Flusser, 'Paganism in Palestine', *Compendia*, 2, 1065-1100. Cf. especially, 1070f, on Mekal and Resheph, two Syro-Canaanite gods who reappear in hellenistic Palestine.

[8]Thus, e.g. Tcherikover, *Hellenistic Civilization*; Bickerman, *Der Gott der Makkabäer*, and *From Esdras to the Last of the Maccabees*.

[9]*Jud. und Hell.*, esp. 486-503.

[10]Thus *1 Macc* 1:41f, apparently supported by *Dn* 11:37-9a. However, after a detailed discussion, Hengel, *Jud. und Hell.*, 516-24, feels that originally there can only have been question of a harmless decree of loyalty, linking the worship of Zeus Olympius with the ruler cult.

[11]Hengel, *Jud. und Hell.*, 538ff, who argues that the desolating sacrilege does not mean the introduction of a Greek cult form, but rather the placing over the altar of sacrifice of a *massebah* or sacred stone, a widely circulated cult object in the Syro-Phoenician realm and corresponding with the form of Zeus worship even on Mt. Olympus.

[12]J. Teixidor, *The Pagan God. Popular Religion in the Greco-Roman Near East*, Princeton Univ. Press, N. Jersey, 1977, 13-17 and *passim*, basing himself on the inscriptions. *The Letter of Aristeas*, 15f, suggests that such trends were acceptable in Diaspora Judaism also.

[13]*Ba'al Shamēm* is certainly known from Aramaic and Phoenician inscriptions of the 10th century and thereafter, and possibly even as early as the 14th century B.C.E. yet is also attested in the Palmyra inscriptions of the 2nd-4th centuries C.E., where the epithet *mr' 'lm'* occurs. Teixidor *The Pagan God*, 28-30, thinks that originally this may have been a general name applicable to the head of any pantheon considered mainly as a god of rain and vegetation, but developing universal traits in the hellenistic period as the Palmyra identification suggests. However, a recent survey of the evidence by R.A. Oden jn., *'Ba'al Shamēm* and 'El', CBQ 34(1977) 457-73, taking account of earlier secondary literature argues that even in the earlier inscriptions *Ba'al Shamēm* had a very definite character as head of the pantheon and protector of kings, traits which he considers identify him with the Canaanite 'Ēl rather than the Syrian Hadad or the Philistine Dagon.

[14]Josephus, *Ant* 8:144-8; *Against Apion* 1:116ff, citing from a certain Menander who is said to have translated the Tyrian records from Phoenician into Greek, claims that Hiram, the contemporary of Solomon, built a temple to Zeus Olympios. As Oden observes, 'Ba'al', 460, notes 13 and 14, since *olympios* is often the equivalent for *ouranos* in hellenistic times, most commentators agree that this notice of Joesphus refers to *Ba'al Shamēm*. The Umm el-'Ammed inscription is to be dated to the year 132 B.C.E., according to Teixidor, *The Pagan God*, 40ff.

[15]On ὕψιστος as an epithet for Zeus and the LXX translation for Yahweh cf. W. Bertram, *TDNT*, 8, 614-20; Hengel; *Jud. und Hell.*, 545, notes 243 and 44 with relevant literature and sources.

[16]Heracles is the Greek equivalent for Melqart, and is mentioned with Astarte in the Josephan citation, *Ant* 8:146. Melqart and Astarte appear after *Ba'al Shamēm* in an early seventh century B.C.E. treaty between Esharhaddon, the king of Assyria and the *Ba'alim* of Tyre. Cf. Oden, 'Ba'al', 463 and Teixidor, *The Pagan God*, 34f.

17For Marisa cf. *OGIS* 593: Ἀπολλόφανης ἄρξας τῶν ἐν Μαρίσηι Σιδωνίων and Shechem, *Ant* 11:344; 12:257ff.

18Thus Hengel, *Jud. und Hell.*, 546f, agreeing with Tcherikover, *Hellenistic Civilization*, 182, but against Bickerman, *Der Gott der Makkabäer*, 111-16.

19Teixidor, *The Pagan God*, 70.

20Cf. below, n.40.

21B. Lifshitz, 'Der Kult des Zeus Akraios', ZDPV 77(1961) 186-90. However, the reading is disputed as Hengel, *Jud. und Hell.*, 521, n. 174 and 547, n. 248, observes, following the critical comments of H. Seyrig, 'Note sur les Cultes des Scythopolis à l'époque romaine', Syria 39(1962) 207-11.

22E. Bickerman, 'Un document relatif à la persécution d'Antiochus IV Épiphane', RHR 115(1937) 188-221, has conclusively shown the authenticity of this letter. Their temple was without a name and therefore deprived in Greek eyes and the object of derision, e.g. Juvenal, *Satires*, 14:97. Clearly they wished to have their own form of Zeus worship, different from the Zeus Olympios of Jerusalem, whether we opt for Josephus' Zeus *hellenios* (*Ant* 12:261.3) or *zenios* (*2 Macc* 6:2). Hengel, *Jud. und Hell.*, 536, n. 216, prefers the latter and makes several suggestions as to its origins, as e.g. that according to the anonymous Samaritan (Eusebius, *Praep. Evang.* IX,17.5) Abraham ξενισθῆναι at Gerizim.

23R.J. Bull, 'An Archaeological Footnote to "Our Fathers Worshipped on this Mountain"', *Jn* iv.20', NTS 23(1977) 460-2, notes that the ruins of the hellenistic temple destroyed by John Hyrcanus would have been visible from Jacob's well in the first century C.E.

24Cf. above, n.17. Bickerman, 'Un document', 204ff, regards the term 'Sidonian' as equivalent to 'Phoenician' which in turn stands for 'Canaanite', arguing from *Gn* 10:12 (Canaan is the father of Sidon) and the LXX translation of 'Canaanite' by 'Phoenician' (*Ex* 6:15; *Jos* 5:1.12; *Jb* 40:30; *Is* 23:2) as well as 'Sidon' and 'Sidonian' by 'Phoenicia' and 'Phoenician' (*Dt* 3:9). Strabo, *Geographica*, 16,2.34, says that the population of Samaria, Galilee, Jericho and Philadelphia was made up of Egyptian, Phoenician and Arabian tribes, while the Jews were descended from the Egyptians. Rostovtzeff, *SEHHW* 3, 1536, n. 134, seeks to explain them in relation to the Sidonian traders at Marisa, Hengel, *Jud. und Hell.*, 535f, n. 215 sees no contradictions in both suggestions: originally they were a trading colony and at the time of crisis the Samaritans joined forces with them because of the ancient relationship, real or imagined, which was a typical feature of the mixing of peoples in hellenistic times. On the other hand H. Kippenberg, *Gerizim und Synagoge. Traditionsgeschichtliche Untersuchungen zur Samaritanischen Religion der aramäischen Periode*, Religionsgeschichtliche Versuche und Vorarbeiten, 30, Berlin 1970, 74-80, follows M. Delcor, 'Vom Sichem der hellenistischen Epoche zum Sychar des Neuen Testamentes', ZDPV 7(1962) 34-48, esp. 37, in regarding the Sidonians at Shechem as being originally a military colony. At all events Hengel's conclusion stands, namely that they had influenced the whole Samaritan people rather than constituting a small but powerful enclave there.

25Hengel, *Jud. und Hell.*, 162-9, sees the work as an attempt to build a bridge between Babylonian and Greek cultures on the basis of biblical traditions. Cf. also, Stern, *Greek and Latin Writers*, 157-64 and B. Wacholder, 'Pseudo-Eupolemus. Two Greek Fragments on the Life of Abraham', HUCA 34(1963) 83-113.

26Above, ch. 2, III.

27Above, ch. 2, n. 37.

28M. Avi-Yonah, 'Mount Carmel and the God of Baalbeck', IEJ 2(1951) 118-24. It reads: ΔΙΙ ΗΛΙΟΠΟΛΕΙΤΗ ΚΑΡΜΗΛΩ .

29Cited by Hengel, *Jud. und Hell.*, 474, n. 24, from C. Müller, *Geographica Graeca Minora*, Paris, 1855-61, 1, 79. On the Heliopolitan Zeus, one of the best known gods of antiquity, cf. A.B. Cook, *Zeus. A Study in Ancient Religion*, 3 vols., Cambridge 1914-40, 1, 549ff.

30Thus Avi-Yonah, 'Mount Carmel', 122; Teixidor, *The Pagan God*, 53f; Flusser, 'Paganism', *Compendia*, 2, 1072f. However, Oden, '*Ba'al*', 470, considers it an unlikely equation, since Hadad as described in the Ugaritic texts does not correspond with the usual features of *Ba'al Shamēm*. However, the fact that at Baalbeck at least he became identified with the Sun God who gave his name to the city would seem to suggest that he could have been identified with *Ba'al Shamēm*, especially if this latter title had a certain fluidity about it that allowed it to be used of different gods. According to Macrobius, *Saturnalia* 1,23.10, Hadad was the supreme god of Baalbeck.

³¹Cf. M. Avi-Yonah, 'Syrian Gods at Ptolemais-Accho', IEJ 9(1959) 1-12. The fact that the gods are called by their semitic names, as well as the form of the script, suggests an early date to the editor.

³²*Hist.* 2,78. According to Suetonius, Vespasian consulted 'apud Iudaeam Carmeli dei oraculum' (*Lives, Vespasian* 5). The priests of the Ba'al of Carmel in Elijah's day also come to mind. According to Macrobius the god of Baalbeck had similar oracular powers; cf. Teixidor, *The Pagan God*, 58f.

³³Cf. Hengel, *Jud. und Hell.*, 548-53 on the universalist ideology of the hellenizers, whose abandonment of the particularism of Judaism should not be seen as a sign of religious degeneracy, but rather the outcome of philosophical speculations about the world that had infiltrated certain levels of Palestinian thinking for some time.

³⁴Thus Teixidor, *The Pagan God*, 7ff and Avi-Yonah, 'Syrian Gods', 5ff, who contrasts it with the classical Greek conception. The Latin equivalent is *propitius*.

³⁵Below, ch. 8, III.

³⁶DeVaux, *Ancient Israel*, 280; Hengel, *Jud. und Hell.*, 474, n. 24; Alt, 'Galiläas Verhältnis', *G.P.* 4, 404f, n. 4, sees the possibility of a shrine there in hellenistic times on the basis of *Dt* 33:19; *Hos* 5:1. However no such shrine is mentioned anywhere, but according to *T.Ros ha-Sh* 2:2 it was one of the mountains from which flares were sent up to signal the new year.

³⁷For the tradition linking this mountain with the transfiguration of Jesus cf. C. Kopp, *The Holy Places of the Gospels*, English trans. London, 1964, 242-7.

³⁸Above, ch. 4, n. 22.

³⁹Flusser, 'Paganism', *Compendia*, 2, 1083f, basing himself on the article of A. Ovadya, 'Greek Religions in Beth Shean/Scythopolis in the Greco-Roman Period', *Eretz Israel* 12(1975) 116-24 (Hebrew) and paying special attention to the inscriptions. Cf. above, n. 21.

⁴⁰Stern, *Greek and Latin Authors*, 560, suggests that the link between the god of the Jews and Dionysus was due to the latter's identification with Sabazius, a Phrygian deity. According to the Roman author of the first century, Valerius Maximius, Jews were expelled from Rome for attempting 'to infect the Roman customs with the cult of Jupiter Sabazius by the consul for the year 139 B.C.E., Cornelius Hispalus. Stern suggests that the epithet Sabbaôth for Yahweh probably facilitated the link, *op cit*, 358f. Even then Scythopolis is the natural place for the linking of Yahweh and Dionysus, considering the existing relations between Jews and Gentiles and the prominence of the latter god there.

⁴¹Above, ch. 4, I,(ii). There we speculated that since the city never presented the same hostile front to Galilean Jews as did Ptolemais, it might have been a possible center of attraction for country people from a wider area.

⁴²O. Michel, O. Bauernfeind, O. Betz, 'Der Temple der goldenen Kuh. Bemerkungen zur Polemik im Spätjudentum', ZNW 48(1957) 197-212, esp. 197, n. 3; Aharoni, *The Land of the Bible*, 29f.

⁴³Hengel, *Jud. und Hell.*, 264, n. 6 and 481.

⁴⁴De Vaux, *Ancient Israel*, 307f.

⁴⁵De Vaux, *Ancient Israel*, 335; Michel, Bauernfeind, Betz, 'Der Temple der goldenen Kuh'. 199-202.

⁴⁶W. Albright, *Archaeology and the Religion of Israel*, Baltimore, 1946, 172f.

⁴⁷Cf. *Ant* 8:226 for his addition to *1 Kgs* 12:28, a speech of Jeroboam saying that God is everywhere, and so cannot be tied to any one place.

⁴⁸Above, ch. 3, I.

⁴⁹F. Abel, 'Inscriptions de Transjordan et de Haute Galilée' RB 5(1908) 568-77.

[50]Hengel, *Jud. und Hell.*, 496-503, esp. 499 where he describes it as a 'Konkurrenztempel zu Jerusalem'. P.W. Lapp, 'The Second and Third Campaigns at 'Araq el 'Emir', BASOR 171(1963) 8-38, whose report of the archaeological finds has convinced Hengel that there is question of a temple there and not a palace.

[51]Tcherikover, *Mizraim*, 53 and *W.H.Hell.A.*, 98, notes the conclusion of *PCZ* 59076, a letter of Toubias to Apollonios: πόλλη χάρις τοῖς θεοῖς and observes that such a greeting on the mouth of a Jew is most significant.

[52]Cf. above, ch. 2, n. 5.

[53]For a discussion of the dating of the episode related by Josephus, cf. Markus, *Loeb Josephus*, 6, Appendix B, 'Josephus and the Samaritan Schism', 498-511, esp. 509, who opts for a date 430 B.C.E. in terms of the schism, but does not preclude the possibility of the temple being built closer to the Greek period, the date of Josephus. F. Moore Cross, 'Aspects of Samaritan and Jewish History in late Persian and Hellenistic Times', HTR 59(1966) 201-211, esp. 203-5, arguing from the Samaritian papyri from W. Daliah, concludes for a later date, thus agreeing with Josephus. Archaeological evidence supports this, apparently, G. Wright, 'The Samaritans at Shechem', HTR 55(1962) 357-66, and R.J. Bull and G.E. Wright, 'Newly Discovered Temples on Mt. Gerizim in Jordan', HTR 58(1965) 234-7.

[54]Cross, 'Aspects', 207-10; Kippenberg, *Gerizim und Synagoge*, 60-73; Alt, 'Zur Geschichte der Grenze', *Kl. Schr.* 2, 357-62.

[55]De Vaux, *Ancient Israel*, 340-2, deals with the temple of the Jewish colony at Elephantine in Egypt, dating from the sixth century B.C.E. The fact that they wrote to the governor of Judaea, Bagoas and to the high priest in Jerusalem, Johanan, seeking support for the rebuilding of their temple which had been destroyed in 410 B.C.E. shows that in their view a separate temple did not cut them off from their brothers in the homeland. They received no reply to either letter and wrote again to Bagoas three years later, indicating that the Jerusalem priests did not agree with their position on the basis of *Dt*. At a later date Onias IV, after the murder of his father built a temple at Leontopolis with the permission of the Egyptian monarch (*Ant* 13:62-73; *War* 7:426ff). This temple was not condemned outright by the rabbis, but Josephus accuses Onias of bad faith (*M. Men* 13:10; *War* 7:426-32). Perhaps the reason for such tolerance, if not acceptance, is the fact that Onias reputedly justified his action by the prophecy of *Is* that an altar would be built for Yahweh in Egypt (*Is* 19:19), or because the law of *Dt* did not apply with the same rigor outside the territory of the tribes *Jos* 22:26-8.

[56]Kippenberg, *Gerizim und Synagoge*, 87-92. Apparently *Gn* 34, the story of the destruction of the heathen people of the Shechem by Simeon and Levi, served as the basis for a midrashic interpretation of the Hasmonaean destruction later, since according to *Ant* 1:337-40, it was during a feast, when the Sichemites were given over to indulgence and revelry that Simeon and Levi surprised them and destroyed their whole male population. Theodotus, a Samaritan author, composed a poem about the incident, Eusebius, *Praep. Evang.* IX,22.

[57]*Rev* 21:2.22 is a Christian reflection of this thinking, which, contrary to H. Strack-P. Billerbeck, *Kommentar zum Neuen Testament aus Talmud und Midrasch*, 5 vols., 1922-56, 4, 884, is as old as *2 Is*.

[58]P. Volz, *Die Eschatologie der jüdischen Gemeinde im neutestamentlichen Zeitalter*, 2 ed. Tübingen, 1934, 371ff. E. Lohse, art Σιων *TDNT* 7, 325-7; L. Gaston, *No Stone on Another. Studies in the Significance of the Fall of Jerusalem in the Synoptic Gospels*, Suppl. to Nov. Test. XXIII, Leiden, Brill, 1970, 105-12; G. von Rad, *Theology of the Old Testament*, 2 vols., English trans., London, Oliver and Boyd, 1965, 1, 46f and 2, 155-69, 239f, 280f, 293f, deals extensively with the origin and development of the Zion tradition in the Old Testament. One should note however the cautionary remarks of Davies, *The Gospel and the Land*, 144 and 150-4, claiming that the two realities of temple and land can easily become interchangeable in late Jewish thought.

[59] *1Q pHab* 9:3-7; 12:7-9; *4Q Test* 28-30, all reflect the community's dissatisfaction with the existing Jerusalem cult. The condemnation of the wicked priest, whoever is intended, is a further indication of the community's attitudes: *1Q pHab* 11:4-8; 8:8-13; 9:9-12. Cf. J. Murphy-O'Connor, 'The Essenes and their History', RB 81(1974) 215-44, esp. 216, for a summary of the various opinions, and 229-33 for his own identification of the wicked priest with the Maccabaean Jonathan. The question of Essene sacrifices is also disputed, depending on how such passages as *CD* 6:11-14. 20 are interpreted and the way in which they can be reconciled with Josephus' claim that 'they send offerings to the temple, but offer no sacrifices, since the purifications to which they are accustomed are different' (*Ant* 18:19). The possibility of their offering sacrifices in the desert cannot be ruled out according to Gaston and others, *No Stone on Another*, 124f. However, it seems more likely that they spiritualized the concept of the cult as G. Klinzing, *Die Umdeutung des Kultus ın der Qumrangemeinde und ım Neuen Testament*, Göttingen 1971, esp. 155-67, argues. The concept of the community itself as the new temple points in a similar direction: *4QFlor* 1:1-13; 1QS 8:1-10; 5:5-7; 9:3-6. Cf. B. Gärtner, *The Temple in the Community in Qumran and the New Testament*, SNTS Monographs 1, Cambridge, Univ. Press, 1965, 16-44; Gaston, *No Stone on Another*, 163-76.

[60] R. Meyer, *Tradition und Neuschöpfung*, esp.; 15-23. On the Pharisaic control of the cult, Safrai, 'Jewish Self-Government', *Compendia* 1, 396f with reference to M. *Midd* 5:3; M. *Yom* 1:5; M. *Sukk* 4:9.

[61] Gaston, *No Stone on Another*, 132-40; M. Black, *The Dead Sea Scrolls and Christian Origins*, New York, Scribner, 48-74. Cf. also J. Bowman, 'Contact between Samaritan Sects and Qumran?' VT 7(1957) 184-9.

[62] Cf. below, ch. 9, I, (iii).

[63] According to *War* 7:218 the half shekel offering went to the Romans after 70, and so was not likely to have created inner Jewish strife in the same way as other religious dues did in the second century C.E.

[64] Cf. H. Danby, *The Mishnah*, Oxford 1933, appendix 1, 48 and also M. Jastrow, *A Dictionary of the Targumim, the Talmud babli and yerushalmi and the Midrashic Literature*, 2 vols. New York, 1950, *sub voce*.

[65] J. Liver, 'The Half Shekel Offering in Biblical and post-Biblical Literature', HTR 56(1963) 173-98.

[66] This was a common practice of hellenistic monarchies as is pointed out by Tcherikover, *Hellenistic Civilisation*, 82ff and by Bickerman, 'La charte séleucide', 13, n. 3. On the authenticity of the earlier decrees cf. R. de Vaux, 'Les Décrets de Cyrus et de Darius sur la reconstruction de temple', RB 46(1937) 29-57.

[67] Liver, 'The Half Shekel Offering', 188-90; cf. also S. Safrai, *Pilgrimage at the Time of the Second Temple*, (Hebrew), Tel Aviv, 1965, 55.

[68] Lichtenstein, 'Die Fastenrolle', esp. 290-2, for a discussion of the historical reliability of the scholion. J. le Moyne, *Les Sadducées*, Paris, 1972, 200, prefers the shorter version of the same tradition as found in b. *Men* 65a, where the Sadducees, not the Boethusians are the opponents of the scribes. The latter are normally dated to the reign of Herod the Great, *Ant* 15:320ff.

[69] Originally published by J.M. Allegro, 'An Unpublished Fragment of Essene Halachah', JSS 6(1961) 71-3; Cf. *D.J.D.* V. For an interpretation and discussion cf. Liver, 'The Half Shekel Offering', 190-9.

[70] M. *Bek* 8:7: b. *Bek* 50a: 'the shekels of the sanctuary in Tyrian coinage'; T. *Ketub* 13:3: 'Wherever in the torah money is mentioned it is Tyrian currency', according to R. Simeon ben Gamaliel, II, (c.a. 130 C.E.). Josephus calls the shekel a νόμισμα 'Εβραίων, *Ant* 3:195, presumably because of its wide currency in Palestine. Cf. also, Ben David, *Jerusalem und Tyros*, esp. table II, page 8 and 19-24.

[71] *Mekilta de Rabbi Jischmael*, ed. J.Z. Lauterbach, 3 vols., Philadelphia, 1949, 2, 193f.

[72] Schalit, 'Josephus und Justus', esp. 69f, n. 8. Cf. also the personal testimonies to his character, *Life* 259.285.

[73] Because of apparent similarity of style it has been argued that there was in fact only one series, but on closer examination one notices that the addresses and

tone are different as well as the place of composition, Gamaliel dictating his from the temple steps and Simeon and Johanan theirs from the upper market beside the refuse gate of the city. The former series appears in several rabbinic passages in identical form: *T. Sanh* 2:2; *p. Sanh* 1,18d; *p. Ma'as Sch* 5:56b and *b. Sanh* 11b. The Gamaliel in question is not further specified, but it is probable that Gamaliel I, the teacher of Paul, not his grandson Rabban Gamaliel II, the successor of Johanan in Jamnia is the author: cf. W. Bacher, *Die Agada der Tannaiten*, Stuttgart, 1903, 1, 73-95, esp. 79; A. Büchler, *Das Sanhedrion in Jerusalem und das Grosse Beth Din in der Quaderkammer des Jerusalemischen Tempels*, Vienna, 1902, 115-8. The second series is found in *Midrash Tannaim*, ed. D. Hoffmann, 1909, 175f, (*Dt* 26:13); cf. H. Mantel, *Studies in the History of the Sanhedrin*, Cambridge, Mass., 1961, 28-31,

[74] O. Eissfeldt, *Erstlinge undZehnten im Alten Testament*, BWANT, 22, Leipzig, 1917 is the classic study.

[75] M. Stern, 'Aspects of Jewish Society: The Priesthood and other Classes', *Compendia*, 2, 561-630, esp. 596-9; Eissfeldt, *Erstlinge und Zehnten*, 152-61, esp. 159f.

[76] B. Schaller, 'Hekataios von Abdara über die Juden', ZNW 54(1963) 15-31, esp. 23-5, summarizing the evidence. He argues that the citation in *Against Apion* 1:188 cannot be earlier than 100 B.C.E. and his conclusions have been adopted by J. Jeremias, *Jerusalem at the Time of Jesus*, English trans. London, S.C.M. Press, 200, n. 173, from whom we have taken the nomenclature Pseudo-Hecataeus. Both Philo and Josephus appear to have conflicting information about the tithing laws. The former follows the Pentateuchal law in *De Spec. Leg.* 1:156f whereas in *De Virt.* 95 he mentions that the tithes are for the priests with no recognition of the Levites. S. Belkin, *Philo and the Oral Law*, Cambridge, Mass., 1940, 67-71 and Jeremias, *Jerusalem*, 107f, discuss the matter, the former accepting, the latter sceptical of Philo's knowledge of actual institutions. Josephus speaks of paying a tithe of the produce of the ground annually to the Levites 'along with the priests', *Ant* 4:68, appearing to include the two together, yet in the very next verse he speaks of Moses instructing the Levites to deduct a tithe of that which they annually receive and give it to the priests. Similarly at *Ant* 4:205 priests and Levites are mentioned together in an oblique reference to the first tithe, yet at 4:240 the first tithe is for the Levite alone. Apparently, Josephus is following Pentateuchal law for the most part, and when priests are also mentioned as recipients, he is reflecting the experience of his own day.

[77] Eissfeldt, *Erstlinge und Zehnten*, 110.118f. The earliest indication of this second tithe is the LXX to *Dt* 26:12 where there is mention of τὸ δεύτερον ἐπιδέκατον .

[78] For a full discussion of the differing recensions of this passage cf. Jeremias, *Jerusalem*, 135f, n. 27.

[79] R. Meyer, 'Die Angebliche Demaj-Gesetz Hyrkans I', ZNW 38(1939) 124-31, discusses the tradition history of these passages in a convincing way. He argues that the mention of Demai produce in the Babylonian version is a later accretion and that originally there was question of the high priest issuing a decree to the whole people to ensure that the priests received their income. Such a decree, he believes, should be dated to the first century C.E. and not ot the reign of John Hyrcanus, as is sometimes supposed, which had become for the rabbis the ideal time of the past, 'for in his day nobody had to inquire about doubtful produce' (*M. Sot* 9:10). Cf. however, the following note about the dating of these decrees.

[80] A. Oppenheimer,*The 'Am Ha-Aretz. A Study in the Social History of the Jewish People in the Hellenistic-Roman Period*, English trans. Leiden, Brill, 1977, 34, sees the abolition as a sign of the transfer of these religious dues into state taxes by the Hasmonaean state, already in the days of John Hyrcanus. Safrai, 'Religion in Everyday Life', *Compendia*, 2, 822, sees the possibility of a reference to Hyrcanus II, who along with his sons was authorized to receive the tithes (*Ant* 14:202). Meyer, 'Die Angebliche Demaj-Gesetz', and Büchler, *Der Galiläische 'Am-Ha 'Ares*, 17f, n. 1, and *Das Sanhedrion*, 91ff, think of the period immediately prior to the first revolt, and the latter identifies Johanan with Ananus, the high priest of the time, *Ant* 20:199.

[81] Above, ch. 6, n. 83, It is doubtful if *p.Ta'an* IV, 69a referring to wagons laden with gifts for the temple in the Galilean towns of Migdal, Sikhnin and Chabul can be used to prove the existence of Galilean priests prior to 70, even though there is mention of priestly garments on the wagons coming from Migdal (cf. *1 Macc* 3:49), as Büchler, 'Die Schauplätze des Bar-Kochbakrieges', 199f and Klein, *Neue Beiträge*, 36, think. The latter recognizes that the passage has been subject to later rabbinic moralizing and in all probability the reference to priests also reflects the post-135 period. According to the 9th century poems of Calir, examined by Klein, *Beiträge*, esp. 12-21 and 94f, most of the courses came to reside in Galilee then. Cf. also M. Avi-Yonah, 'The Caesarean Inscription of the 24 priestly Courses' IEJ 12(1962) 137-9.

[82] τὰ κοινὰ διοικοῦντες citing from (Ps) Hecataeus of Abdera *Against Apion* 1:188; cf. also *Ib* 2,187. Belkin, *Philo and the Oral Law*, 72, n.23, sees this secular description of the role of the priest by Josephus as part of the apologetic of this work, but surely this also corresponded to the realities of the situation.

[83] We agree with Safrai, 'Jewish Self-Government', *Compendia*, 1, esp. 383-9 and 396, that it is better to interpret the available evidence to signify one Jewish body, despite the differing names by which it was called in rabbinic sources. The growing Pharisaic influence can be easily documented from Josephus (*Ant* 18:17; *Life* 190ff.216) and the New Testament (*Ac* 5:34ff).

[84] Oppenheimer, *The 'Am ha-Aretz, 43, pointing to a halakhah* in *p. Shek 8*, 51b: 'It was taught: One may nowadays neither consecrate anything nor make a valuation vow, nor declare anything devoted nor separate terumôth and tithes'.

[85] Cf. e.g. *D.J.D.*, II, 224f.

[86] I. Elborgen, 'Die Feier der drei Wahlfahrtsfeste im Zweitem Tempel', in *Bericht der Hochschule für die Wissenschaft des Judentums in Berlin*, 1929, 27-46; S. Safrai, 'Pilgrimage to Jerusalem at the End of the Second Temple Period', in *Studies on the Jewish Background of the New Testament*, O. Michel et al., Assen. Van Gorcum, 1969, 12-21.

[87] According to the former version there had been rioting in the temple before the Passover crowds assembled and Archelaus had actually sent his general to appease the crowds, but to no avail.

[88] Cf. above, ch. 6, I.

[89] Cf. the illuminating study from a socio-economic as well as religious perspective by G. Theissen, 'Die Tempelweissagung Jesu. Prophetie im Spannungsfeld von Stadt und Land', TZ 32(1976) 144-58. He argues that Jesus' prophecy about the new temple, closely related to his cleansing action, should be seen in the light of the social tension between city and country in first century Judaism, which often manifested itself at the feasts, and insofar as it was directed against the temple could be interpreted as questioning the whole basis of social and economic life in the city. Stephen's fate in being stoned by the Jerusalem mob is another example of such tensions.

[90] Above ch. 6, n. 8.

[91] Davies, *The Gospel and the Land*, 52-4.

[92] Hengel, *Die Zeloten* 201ff, considers purity of the land in terms of insisting that foreigners be circumcised, was part of the Zealot ideology. Cf. below ch. 8, n. 28. Nevertheless there are not the same explicit references to the land as one finds for Maccabaean times: *1 Macc* 3:1-9; *Ant* 12:285f. Cf. also above ch. 3, n. 51.

[93] Davies, *The Gospel and the Land*, 54-74.

[94] Cf. above ch. 6, n. 23. It should be noted however, that despite the praise for Agrippa I, both in rabbinic literature and Josephus (*Ant* 19:292f.328-31), he celebrated games at Caesarea and endowed the city of Berytus in the best hellenistic tradition (*Ant* 19:335-7 and 343-6). Besides, the later Herodian interest in the highpriesthood had a definite political motivation, something that was not appreciated by the priestly aristocracy, as is clear from *Ant* 19:313-6 (Agrippa I) and *Ant* 20:189-96.216 (Agrippa II)). This may have had the subtle effect of ingratiating the Herodians with the country people.

[95] Cf. H. Lindner, *Die Geschichtsauffassung des Flavius Josephus im Bellum Judaicum*, AGJU 12, Leiden, Brill, 1972.

CHAPTER EIGHT

GALILEE AND THE HALAKHAH.

Our investigations in the last chapter have suggested that the pilgrimage to the Yahweh shrine in Jerusalem was the focal point of Galilean piety. Yet it could be argued that by itself this was scarcely adequate to maintain religious identity, given the many other social and cultural cross-currents in the province. One can easily understand a mood of optimism, even euphoria, being engendered by the pilgrimage experience, especially when contrasted with everyday life as this had to be lived out by the small farmer or tenant in the relative isolation of village life, often in dire economic need. What was to provide the motivation to continue to live a distinctively Jewish way of life on the return to such circumstances, especially if the common-sense world of the everyday seemed at odds with the really real world celebrated in the temple ritual? Did one abandon the religious beliefs altogether when faced with the glaring differences between the promises of the cult and the stark reality of the everyday? On the evidence available there is no indication of any such wholesale disaffection with the Jewish beliefs in Galilee, but on the contrary we have found a remarkable fidelity in the face of trying social and cultural conditions. The alternative was to attempt to bridge the gap in some other way at the religious and emotional levels, and in this regard one immediately thinks of Pharisaism which had developed precisely with this purpose of recreating the religious conditions of the cult in the everyday life of the people.

However, before we can discuss the successes and failures of this movement in relationship to Galilee it is necessary to clarify a number of concepts that seem to be particularly relevant to our topic. At the outset a very clear distinction must be drawn between the pre- and post-70 situations, for what was one of several different sectarian responses within Judaism prior to the first revolt was afterwards to become identified with normative Judaism. Naturally, the later rabbinic sources tend to blur that distinction and transpose backwards onto the earlier period concepts and attitudes of its own situation, thereby appropriating

305

Pharisaism for itself. This process is facilitated by the fact that central concepts such as *haber* and *'am ha-'aretz* are relevant to both periods, but as we shall see with rather different connotations because of the changed situation. Accordingly, non-rabbinic sources such as Josephus and the Gospels become extremely important in our efforts to differentiate the two periods.[1]

The Pharisees, as a sect, were concerned with extending the holiness of the temple to the everyday life in the world. To achieve this they were particularly careful about eating ordinary food (חולין) in a state of ritual cleanliness and observing the tithing laws strictly.[2] Some at least of the Pharisees were organized in fellowships (*haburôth*) with stringent rules of admission and expulsion, representing a more radical commitment to the Pharisaic ideal, as is clear from a number of recurrent expressions such as 'taking on oneself', or 'being accepted as a *haber*'.[3] It would appear then that even within Pharisaism there were degrees of strictness, and this finds expression in such passages as *T. Demai* 6:6 where the houses of Shammai and Hillel are divided on the question to whom may one sell olives: according to the Shammaites it could only be to a fellow-*haber*, whereas the Hillelites permitted it to 'one who separates tithes' (למעשר). Or again, we hear that according to the house of Shammai a Pharisee who has a discharge shall not eat with an *'am ha-'aretz* who has a discharge (one of the fathers of uncleanness according to *M.Kelim* 1:1) but the house of Hillel permits it (*T. Shabb* 1:15).[4] These differences of opinion between *haber* and ordinary Pharisee on how strictly the essentials of tithing and purity laws were to be observed should not obscure the fact that all alike stand over against the *'am ha-'aretz*, who in many Talmudic texts are defined as being non-observant in these matters. Consequently they are to be avoided by the Pharisees as a possible source of uncleaness (*M.Hag* 2:7).[5] Nevertheless, the Pharisees did not cut themselves off completely from the *'am ha-'aretz*, as the previous discussions indicate, and apparently during the great religious festivals, in particular, the dividing lines were less rigid, when it was presumed that all the people had observed the necessary purity laws and the emphasis was on the unity of the people. Thus we hear that 'our rabbis taught that the impurity of the *'am ha-'aretz* was purified on a festival' (*b.Betz* 11b; *b.Hag* 26a).[6] Even during the year the wife of a *haber* was allowed to lend certain utensils to the wife of an *'am ha-'aretz* in the interests of peace, provided there was no assistance to the breaking of the purity laws (*M.Gitt* 5:9).

Despite the demise of the Pharisaic sect or at least despite its absorption into rabbinic Judaism, this understanding of the *'am ha-'aretz* as unreliable in regard to the purity laws and negligent in tithing was continued and further developed in the post-70 situation, reaching its climax in the Ushan period apparently, under Rabbis Meir and Judah.[7] Yet, side by side with this another conception of the *'am ha-'aretz* developed in the Jamnia period which emphasizes, not their failure to observe the purity laws, but their lack of study of the torah.[8] This understanding is normally associated with Hillel's dictum: 'an uncultured person is not sinfearing, neither is an *'am ha-'aretz* pious' (*M.Ab* 2:6). *Jn* 7:49, 'this people who do not know the law is accursed', seems to attest to a similar contrast and this evidence presupposes that it was a relatively early distinction.[9] Certainly in the Jamnia period study of the torah was to move to the center of Jewish life, replacing the temple as the primary religious symbol of Judaism, and all previous distinctions within the people were now replaced by this single one - those who were students of the torah, following the instruction of the wise (*talmîdı hakhamîm*), and those who were not. Neusner, in particular, has stressed that this change of emphasis is to be associated with the presence in Jamnia, not only of pre-70 Pharisees such as Eliezer ben Hyrcanus, but more significantly of pre-70 scribes like Johanan ben Zakkai and others, who are able to suggest a replacement for the cult, as distinct from the Pharisees whose concern was to replicate it, and hope for its restoration.[10] The disciples of the sages inherited the title and the framework of the earlier Pharisaic associations, except that now the opposition to the *'am ha-'aretz* had become hardened into downright hostility and even social deprivation within the community until political and social conditions of the third century brought about a change of attitude (cf. *b Pesh* 49a).[11]

This brief discussion of Pharisees, *haberîm* and *'am ha-'aretz* has particular importance for our study of Galilean attitudes in view of the fact that several times in rabbinic literature their inferior knowledge of the torah is alluded to (*b.Erub* 53a/b; *ARN* a 28a, ed. Schechter), and in the discussions of the Ushan school about the '*am ha-'aretz* it is presumably Galileans that are primarily involved. However, in view of what we have been saying about the changed situation in the pre and post-70 periods the Galileans' attitude towards *halakhah* needs to be thoroughly re-examined, especially since the only full length study of the topic until recently, that of A. Büchler, *Der Galiläische 'Am Ha-' Aretz des Zweiten Jahrhunderts* (1906), has for long been regarded as onesided and erroneous.[12] In brief, Büchler's thesis – partly a reaction to Christian scholars who had attempted to make Jesus the champion of the '*am ha-'aretz* – was, that as a term denigrating those who did not observe tithing and ritual purity laws, it emerged only in the Ushan period, that is after 135 C.E. It was then that the sages had moved to Galilee and attempted to goad the natives into stricter observance of these laws. They were addressed in particular to the Aaronides, or priests who had migrated to the province in great numbers after the two revolts and were failing to observe the ritual laws in regard to *terumôth* or priestly offerings. By thus relegating the rabbinic discussions concerning the purity laws, sabbatical year regulations and the tithe to Galilee of the post-135 era, Büchler was able to challenge the position of those scholars who saw Jesus as the enemy of legalistic Judaism; in effect, he claimed, the Judaism of Christian apologists only existed in the second century C.E.

The most thorough rebuttal of Büchler's arguments was left to a Jewish scholar, Aharon Oppenheimer, whose historico-critical approach to the talmudic sources as well as his use of extra-Talmudic *halakhah* (Josephus, Apocrypha, Philo, Qumran), enabled him to trace the development of the '*am ha-' aretz* from early hellenistic times through the third century C.E. We cannot here examine in detail his reconstruction, which in its main lines is convincing and lucid, but rather we wish to raise a question arising from his study that bears directly on Galilee and the *halakhah*. Oppenheimer is surely correct in insisting that, as used in rabbinic sources, the term '*am ha-' aretz* should not be confined to any one strand of the Jewish people, but can be used indiscriminately of peasant and aristocrat alike insofar as they do not observe the prescriptions of the *haburôth*, or follow the instruction of the sages (cf. *M.Hor* 3:8).[13] However, in attempting to free the concept from 'the Procurstean bed of

time and locality', he has in our opinion overlooked certain
aspects of Galilean life and history which have given a distinctive character to its relations with *halakhah*, both before and
after 70 C.E.[14]

The following survey of halakhic attitudes in Galilee is undertaken with the intention of underlining those circumstances more
thoroughly and suggesting their likely impact on Jewish life
there. It is not that Galilee was totally lacking *halakhah*, a
position Oppenheimer seems to be arguing against. Its continued
loyalty to Judaism insured that. Our question rather is which
halakhah was likely to have most appeal for its inhabitants
given the social and historical conditions that obtained there.

I
GALILEE AND THE HALAKHAH PRIOR TO 70 C.E.

In the previous chapter we have already encountered apparent
Galilean ignoring, if not ignorance of Pharisaic *halakhah* with
regard to temple obligations. Yet this in no way impaired their
attachment to the temple, it would seem, nor did it exclude them
from the ambit of the Jewish religious community. As long as the
temple stood it represented a polivalent symbol system that was
not the preserve of any one group even if one sect (the Pharisees)
dominated official policy in regard to it in the closing years,
as Josephus maintains (*Ant* 18:17). We must now consider whether
what we have already discovered about Galilee in relation to
Pharisaic *halakhah* is equally true when viewed from a broader
perspective. Does a consideration of all the pre-70 evidence point
in the same direction and confirm the impressions already
gleaned; and in that event are there any possible reasons that
suggest themselves for the non-acceptance that might be the result
of conditions specific to Galilee? Since Pharisaism cannot be
treated as a monolithic phenomenon, as we have seen, is there a
rejection of their whole system or merely certain, more extreme
expressions of it?

Josephus' *Life* seems a good starting-point for our deliberations, since, as we have seen, it gives us some good insights into
the inner working of the life in the province in the immediate pre-
70 period. Repeatedly in this work the author stresses his regard
for Jewish piety in his handling of affairs in Galilee, and like
many other facets of the *personalia* in the work this evidence is

suspected of reflecting his own concerns at the time *Life* was written, rather than the historical actualities of the past.[15] However, his Pharisaism is only explicitly mentioned at the outset where he relates that since the age of nineteen he had begun to govern his life by the rules of the Pharisees. Now, some years later he had supported the cause of two young men who had been sent to Rome as prisoners, once he had heard of their fidelity to Jewish dietary laws (*Life* 12.14). Elsewhere Josephus shows concern for returning stolen booty 'since we are forbidden by our laws to rob even an enemy' (*Life* 128; cf. *War* 2:597); he dismissed his army on the eve of the sabbath in order not to annoy the inhabitants of Tarichaeae (*Life* 158; *War* 2:634), and he refused to recall them, 'since bearing of arms on the Sabbath was forbidden by our laws' (*Life* 161);[16] his only reason for marrying a wife from those taken captive – a violation of Jewish law for a priest (*Against Apion* 1:135; *Ant* 3:276; 13:292) – was orders from the emperor (*Life* 414) and his greatest consolation at the fall of the temple is to be able to rescue some Jews and scrolls (*Life* 418). Of this evidence only that referring to the sabbath at Tarichaeae is relevant to Galilee itself, and is of interest in that Tarichaeae figures in other evidence to be examined shortly, also.

Whether or not Josephus' Pharisaism is contrived, that of his opponents in the Jewish delegation can scarcely have been an invention. The delegation sent to Galilee at the instigation of Simeon ben Gamaliel, himself a distinguished Pharisaic sage and friend of John of Gischala (*Life* 190-2; 197f), consisted of three Pharisees. In their efforts to oust Josephus they were told to emphasize to the people that they too were not ignorant of the customs of the fathers should this prove to be the basis for his popularity with the Galileans. Does this mean that the council in Jerusalem considered that the inhabitants of the province would be particularly influenced by such qualities in its delegates – Josephus or those sent to replace him? It is difficult to generalize from such scanty information. Simeon must have been aware of Galilean attitudes to the tithing laws in view of his letter already discussed. Furthermore, if Josephus' Pharisaism was contrived and that of the delegation genuine, then the latter's failure to convince the Galilean populace at large is itself indicative. At the same time Simeon's friendship with John of Gischala should be noted, and even if Hengel's suggestion that John himself was a Pharisee cannot be verified, their contacts show that leading Pharisees were not anathema at least to certain circles in Galilee.[17]

Apart from these rather inconclusive generalizations a number of specific episodes in *Life* point to rather extreme Jewish sectarian views whose significance must be explored. These are the destruction of Herod's palace at Tiberias, the incident of the refugee gentile noblemen and the question of kosher oil for the Jews of Caesarea Philippi. All three are significant in themselves, but taken together they seem to reflect certain prescriptions of the 18 *halakhôth* stemming from the school of Shammai, referred to in rabbinic literature, which several scholars date to the take-over of the Jerusalem council by more extreme (Shammaitic) elements in the days immediately prior to the first revolt.[18] If this estimation is correct does it help us in determining the general *halakhic* situation in Galilee? Let us examine each case individually.

We have already discussed the destruction of Herod's palace as a possible pointer to the revolutionary ethos of Galilee, but now we wish to highlight its religious aspects. Josephus expressly states that the palace had animal representations, 'prohibited by Jewish law' (*Life* 65). This was the reason for the decree from Jerusalem to destroy it which both he and leading opinion in the city were reluctant to implement. Elsewhere we hear that Jesus, son of Sapphias, the ringleader of the mob who destroyed the palace, appeared in the hippodrome at Tarichaeae brandishing the laws of Moses and accusing Josephus of being about to betray them (*Life* 134f). The fact that in all probability the palace had been in existence for close on fifty years without any such opposition being raised against it suggests that the issue was just then a particularly sensitive one, presumably inspired by Zealot ideals.[19] Their ideology forbade images of any kind, as can be seen from the coins of the Jewish revolt,[20] even though general practice had apparently varied considerably, and there was no effective general ban on animal or even human representations in private homes, granted that all the examples come from aristocratic, and therefore hellenized Jewish families.[21]

The decision in regard to Herod's palace then is at least a reflection of a new and more radical mood within Judaism that apparently had originated with Eleazar, the temple captain and son of

Ananias, the high priest, who, according to Josephus, had laid the foundations for war by persuading those in charge of the temple not to accept sacrifices from a foreigner (*War* 2:409; *b Gitt* 56a). It is difficult to say whether the decision about Herod's palace was an individual one or reflected a general decree of the period, since we hear of no similar incident elsewhere, yet the policy it reflects seems to correspond with that of the Zealots concerning the coins.[22] It might appear surprising that there were those at Tiberias who were eager to comply with the decree in view of the fact that it was an Herodian foundation and inhabited by less than meticulous Jews, if Josephus' account of its being founded on a cemetery has any substance (*Ant* 18:37f).[23] However, we have attempted to explain the social reasons for such a pocket of Jewish resistance at this center earlier, and presumably strict Pharisaism of an earlier period had to find its way around certain unpleasant situations not of its own making, just as the rabbis of the second century also had to do.[24]

The second specific incident from *Life* bearing on our discussion of the *halakhah* in Galilee is that concerning the refugee gentile noblemen. Josephus had billeted at Tarichaeae the deserters from king Agrippa II who had come, apparently, to throw in their lot with the Jewish resistance, bringing their arms, men and money (*Life* 112-14). His action was, no doubt, inspired by the need for support for his command in Galilee, though it also complied with Jewish laws of hospitality for the foreigner (*gēr*).[25] However, Josephus' opponents exploited the issue by convincing the masses that the presence of these foreign 'sorcerers' made it impossible for them to defeat the Romans, and eventually they had to be given safe conduct to the other side of the lake (*Life* 149-154).[26] Assuming that the instigators of the trouble were the same zealot fanatics who had destroyed Herod's palace, it is significant that their appeal to the people was made in terms of popular religious beliefs (sorcery), rather than ritual laws of purity which might have reflected rigorist sectarian attitudes shared by the people at large. At the same time one cannot ignore the fact that it seems to have been the people (significantly called Ἰουδαίοι, not Γαλιλαίοι) who raised the issue initially, and this can only be interpreted as a hypersensitive reaction, given the fact that gentiles must have been part of everyday life in Galilee, and later rabbinic attitudes to gentiles varied considerably.[27] Before deciding that the people's reaction had a similar motivation to that of the Jerusalem council who at this time had banned gentile marriages as part of the provisions of the 18 *halakhôth*,[28] it should be remembered that Tarichaeae must have felt itself particularly vulnerable, since it belonged to Agrippa II's kingdom until the Jerusalem council had taken it over. Naturally, the presence of noblemen from that realm, presumably ready for action, would have been treated with a good deal of suspicion, and it could have been exploited for their own aims by a few fanatics. We hear of a Galilean missionary Eleazar, 'who had a reputation for being extremely strict concerning ancestral laws' exhorting Izates, the king of Adiabne to have himself circumcised earlier in the first century C.E. (*Ant* 20:43), and the Ituraeans on the borders of Upper Galilee had been circumcised by Aristobulus I (*Ant* 13:319). However, these examples are too remote in time and place to argue for particularly keenly felt Galilean atittudes towards circumcision. One can see reasons why people who had held on to their Jewish religion in the cross-cultural situation in which they lived might have been sensitive on the issue as a basic hallmark of Jewish faith rather than for sectarian halakhic motives. Yet in all probability the incident does reflect the sensitive concerns of the times, without implying that all Galileans felt equally about the issue.

One final piece of evidence from *Life* concerns the use of native oil by the Jewish inhabitants of Caesarea Philippi, which John of Gischala exploited so unashamedly (*Life* 74; *War* 2:591). Irrespective of whether the Seleucid who made a grant to the Jews of Antioch to pay for their own oil, was Seleucus I, Nicator (312-280 B.C.E.), as Josephus says (*Ant* 12:119f), or Antiochus III (223-187 B.C.E.), as most scholars think,[29] the concession shows that the question of the Jewish use of pagan oil had been an issue since early hellenistic times. The mention of the gymnasiarchs as administrators of the relief suggests the use of oil in the gymnasia for the anointing of the body, the full religious implications of which were to be revealed in Palestine later during the hellenistic reform (cf. *2 Macc* 4:7-17). It is possible that the newly-arrived Greeks imported their own oil and no doubt were followed in this by the native hellenized aristocracy, so that Jewish halakhic

attitudes would have begun to be formed at an early stage as part
of the resistance on religious grounds to a whole different way of
life (cf. *Judith* 10:5; *Dn* 1:8).[30] It has been suggested by Hoenig in
particular that the avoidance of gentile oil at the early period was
due to fear of involvement in idolatrous sacrifices, oil being
especially associated with cult in the ancient world, and had
nothing to do with ritual laws of purity.[31] This seems an over-
statement however, in view of the fact that the purity laws had
originated in the cult.[32] Certainly, care in regard to the oil and
wine for sacrifice was an integral part of priestly *halakhah* from
an early stage (*M.Midd* 2:5; *War* 5:562-5), and inevitably a similar
attitude would have extended to the daily use of oil by those who
embraced the Pharisaic way of life. It was in line with this extension that oil appears in an early list of forbidden gentile food
which probably formed the basis for the later 18 *halakhôth* (*M.Ab.
Zar* 2:6).[33] Another mishnah draws a distinction on geographic
lines in regard to the purity of wine and oil: they are presumed to
be kept in ritual purity all the year round in Judaea when they are
designated for the temple, whereas heave offerings can only be
presumed to be ritually pure during the harvest time (*M. Hag* 3:5).[34]
The Talmuds explain that Galilee cannot share the same presumption since it is separated from Judaea by a strip of Cuthaean
territory (*b.Hag* 24b *p. Hag* 3:79a). Apparently, the nearer to the
temple the greater the likelihood that the purity laws would be
observed, but this need not be seen as reflecting Galilean laxity
in the earlier period.[35] Certainly, according to *Life* (and *War*)
Galilean olives are acceptable to the Jews of Caesarea Philippi,
presumably for extra-cultic use. In the light of the discussion this
suggests that the Galileans were not irresponsible in their preparation of oil, or at least it was more acceptable than pagan produce
to the beleaguered Jews of Caesarea.

It is indeed striking that these three examples from Galilean
life immediately prior to the great revolt suggest links with the
more radical expression of Jewish separation which was the
underlying support for the revolt. Of the three, the incident concerning Herod's palace is the most obvious example of such
prompting, and the questions of circumcision and Jewish oil in
all probability were similarly inspired. What does this tell us
about Galilee and the *halakôth*? For one thing if a direct link is

claimed with the 18 *halakôth* passed in Jerusalem it could be suggested that Galilee was very much the concern of those who fashioned those enactments. Could this mean that the lines of Jewish separatism in the province were blurred or in danger of becoming so in the eyes of the Jerusalem-based radicals? In that event one must note that on the basis of the, admittedly scanty evidence, the measures did not have any gret success. A sporadic outburst in Tiberias, with the same faction continuing the trouble at Tarichaeae, and swaying the general populace to their side for a moment, were the only real victories, it would seem. However, it is not always possible to guage the true feelings of a region at a moment of extreme crisis, so we must look to our other sources – rabbinic literature and the gospels – for Galilean halakhic attitudes in the pre-70 period.

In view of his later importance for Judaism in the Jamnia period, the tradition that links Johanan ben Zakkai with the Galilean town of Arav (9 K. N.N.E of Sepphoris) is the single most important piece of rabbinic evidence for the pre-70 period (*b.Shabb* 146a; *M. Shabb* 16:7; 22:3). If the tradition that links Johanan with Hillel is reliable then in all probability it was after the latter's death that Johanan moved to the north, and it is for these reasons that Neusner dates the sojourn between the years 20 and 40 C.F.[36] Johanan's famous woe: 'Galilee, Galilee! You hate the torah! Your end will be to be besieged' (*p Shabb* 16,15d), attributed to him by a third century Amora, Ulla, has been judged by Neusner to be pseudepigraphic,[37] but on the basis of the traditions ascribed to Johanan for the pre-70 period in general, and more importantly for his Galilean sojourn, it can only be an accurate impression of his feelings.[38] Presumably, Johanan went to Galilee as the representative of Jerusalem scribism rather than as an advocate fo the Pharisaic sect, and we must be careful to keep the two separate no matter how much our sources tend to identify them, or how closely their views corresponded in practice.[39] The gospels also mention Scribes from Jerusalem, and as we shall see, it is they rather than the local Pharisees who seem to be at odds with native piety.

Two stories relating to Johanan in Galilee may help to illustrate the tensions inherent in the situation. The first concerns Johanan's associate Hanina ben Dosa, who clearly was not a teacher despite the ascription of the title rabbi to him in later tradition.[40] Hanina's cure of Johanan's son is related in *b. Ber* 34b and despite being the beneficiary of the healer's prayer, Johanan contrasts himself with him as a prince to a servant in the house of a king. Clearly, institutional religion was not too enamoured of the charismatics' popular appeal. The second incident concerns one of Johanan's pupils (R. Josua according to the *ARN* version)[42] who was sent to investigate a *hasid* living at Beth Rama (or Ramat beth- Anath) and, though a priest and follower of the instruction of the *hasidim* (משנת חסידים), is said to have known nothing about the biblical verse relating to the possibility of stoves and ovens becoming unclean (*Lv* 11:35).[43] The episode is told as an illustration of the saying in *M. Ab* 1:13, 'he who does not serve the scholars deserves to die', and is clearly intended as a criticism of those *hasidim* who were not overly concerned with the purity laws, despite their renown as holy men. While it is not possible to date either episode to the historical Johanan's stay in Galilee with any degree of certainty, both surely reflect the kind of inevitable tensions that must have arisen between the recognized practitioners of the pious way of life within the province, and those who came from outside, especially Jerusalem.

This appears to be the correct place to discuss the distinctive Galilean practices and customs that are frequently referred to in rabbinic literature. Do these differences amount to a distinctive Galilean *halakhah*, and if so in what circumstances was it developed? Finkelstein has addressed himself to this question and attempts to explain the differences on the basis of patrician and plebeian conditions in Jerusalem, represented by the Shammaites and Hillelites, which were subsequently transferred to Galilee, dominated as it was by the Shammaitic patrician class of land-owners.[44] Thus stated, there are a number of unproven and un-provable assertions in this thesis, like the patrician background of the Shammaites or their domination of life in Galilee. Yet the suggestion bears further consideration in the light of our earlier discussion of the history and social conditions in Galilee. The distinction between Judaea and Galilee was in part geographic and climatic, as *M. Shab* 9:2 recognizes. Historically, the division between the two provinces goes back at least to the division of the whole Jewish territory by Pompey, when for a time, Galilee had its own (aristocratic) council. We are not in a position to say if this continued in a limited, specifically religious capacity later, yet the fact that Josephus could set up a local council for dealing with civil and criminal cases, suggests that the notion would not be altogether foreign to Jewish organization. According to *M. Ned* 5:5 the Galileans' fathers had handed over their share in public things to the *nasi*, and depending on what is meant by 'public things' this could be a pre-70 reference.[45] Likewise the letters of the sages regarding tithes speak of similar communications to the Galilean fathers. Thus these two pieces of evidence seem to suggest one central control of Jewish religious practice which would make the emergence of an independent *halakhah* within the province unlikely in the earlier period. In the previous chapter we argued that the Sadducean, rather than the Pharisaic approach to the half shekel offering was followed there, and this would indicate a certain degree of flexibility in such matters. Furthermore, if the dominant social class was Sadducean, in all probability they controlled religious matters also, and it may have been to counteract such influence that Pharisaic scribes like Johanan went to the area.

Specifically, the differences cover a number of areas: weights and measures, the Galilean ones being only half the volume of the Judaean, (*M. Keth* 5:9; *M. Hull* 11:2; *M. Ter* 10:8; *p. Kel* 5:11a); customs relating to the eve of the feasts of Passover and the Day of Atonement (*M. Pesh* 4:5; *M. Hull* 5:3); funeral rites and customs (*p. Mo Kat.* 3,5; *Sem.* 3:6, 10:15; *b. Shabb* 153a); marriage law and divorce (*M. Keth* 1:5; 4:12; *b. Keth* 12a).

Can this evidence support the hypothesis that Finkelstein wishes to construct? Metrology was not so highly developed in Palestine as to exclude local customs, and the hellenistic monarchies did not achieve a totally centralized system either, so that differences in weights and measures are not significant once their relative volume had been worked out for tithing and other sacred obligations.[46] The customs relating to the eves of the two feasts are best interpreted as a more literal following of the relevant biblical verses (*Nm* 28:18.28, Passover; *Lv* 22:28, Day of Atonement), but this would point to the Sadducean *halakhah*, rather than to that of the school of Shammai. Custom differed from place to place according to *b. Shabb* 153a, and thus Finkelstein's suggestions about the reserve of the Galileans at funerals or their modesty at marriages seem rather far-fetched.[47] More significant is the agreement of the Galileans with the men of Jerusalem over against the Judaeans regarding the rights of the widow. According to the former she had a contractual right to be supported from her ex-husband's property as long as she remained a widow, whereas the latter were free to pay her a fixed dowry and dismiss her (*M.Keth* 4:12). The remark of *p.Keth* 4:29b to the effect that the Galileans were more concerned with honor than with money is scarcely an adequate explanation of the difference. Once again one might point to a more rigid adherence to the biblical laws protecting the widow (e.g. *Ex* 22:21; *Dt* 10:18; 24:17-21; 26:12f; 27:19) as the source of the Galilean (and Jerusalem) attitude. However, the mishnah itself points to a more immediate source for the custom, namely an ordinance of the *Beth dîn*. Galilean life in religious, as well as other matters, had gladly come under the control of the Jerusalem council and in the early days was happy to accept the decrees of that central religious authority in Judaism without cavil. Once a certain custom had been established, loyalty demanded adherence to that way. Thus the Galileans did not recognize or indeed require the Pharisaic changes to the *halakhah,* often designed to meet new social conditions that did not obtain among them. It is this circumstance, rooted in the history and social stratification of the province, rather than Finkelstein's 'patrician Shammaites' that explains the apparent conservatism of Jewish customs there.[48]

One possible source of Galilean contact with *halakhah* other than that of the Jerusalem sages is the *Beney Bathyra* who recur from time to time in rabbinic literature. We first hear of them in Babylonia opposed to Hillel on the question of working on the eve of Passover when that day fell on a sabbath, being inclined to the more stringent view until Hillel was able to cite Palestinian authority in favor of his opinion (*p. Pesh* 6,34b). Hillel reproached them for not studying under Shammaiah and Abtalion in their own country thereby not being dependent on the opinion of a Babylonian sage.[49] Subsequently we meet them at Jamnia opposing Johanan ben Zakkai's transference of temple ritual to the synagogue (*b. Ros ha-Sh.*29b).[50] Several scholars assume that their name is derived from βαθυρα in Batanaea, in the district where Babylonian

Jews had been planted by Herod the Great and had proved to be a real support against the marauders of Transjordan for fellow Babylonians on pilgrimage to Jerusalem.[51] In fact Josephus says that many Jews from all parts 'devoted to ancestral customs' flocked to the territory, apparently not merely because of the tax concessions that lasted as long as Herod lived (*Ant* 17:26-31). Unfortunately we have no more precise information on Zamaris' religious views, nor of those who migrated to his territory. However, we do find his ancestors maintaining both their loyalty to the Herods and their Jewish faith at the time of the first revolt. One of his descendants Philip ben Jacimus played a significant, though ambivalent part in the events of 66 C.E. being apparently on the side of moderation both in Jerusalem and at Gamala.[52] Kinsmen of his in Jerusalem were also on the side of the moderates (*Life* 46f) and good relations seem to have existed between the 'Babylonian' Jews and those in Caesarea Philippi (*Life* 55). Presumably further contacts between these Jews and those of Galilee can be presupposed, a fact that may explain the confusion in regard to Judas the Galilean or the Gaulanite (*Ant* 18:4; *War* 2:118) and Josephus' appointment to the two Galilees and Gamala (*War* 2:568). In fact we hear of refugees from Trachonitis and Gaulanitis at Tarichaeae during the revolt (*War* 3:542), and in turn the Galileans helped out their fellow Jews during the siege of Gamala. Recent archaeological reports suggest more lasting relations between Upper Galilee and the western Gaulan both in terms of linguistic regionalism and the overall material culture and thus the scattered contacts suggested by literary sources take on a wider significance.[53] It might seem strange to suggest that new arrivals could have been the source for certain Galilean practices and attitudes, and perhaps the influences were mutual, rather than one-sided. Naturally any conclusions must be extremely tentative, yet it is suggestive to find some correspondence both in general and detail between Galilean *halakhic* attitudes and those of the *Beney Bathyra*, as opposed to those of Jerusalem sages.

Finally, we can turn to the gospel evidence and examine it against the sporadic, and apparently unsuccessful Pharisaic presence in Galilee, prior to 70 C.E. that can be discerned from Josephus and the rabbinic sources. It is generally recognized that the picture of the Pharisees which emerges from the pages of the

New Testament is colored by the early Christian community's experiences with Judaism during the formative period of the synoptic tradition. In particular the sharp polemic of *Mt.* is considered to reflect the tensions of the Jamnia period, but to some degree these same tendencies can be detected in the other three gospels also.[54] Thus the Pharisees of the New Testament, in the words of Jacob Neusner, 'serve as a narrative convention. Whenever the narrator needs someone to ask a question that allows a stunning response on the part of Jesus, he calls forth the Pharisees. When a villain is needed to exemplify obviously unsavoury spiritual traits he calls forth the Pharisees.'[55] The more obvious examples of this characterization are: the lack of interest in any intra-Pharisaic differences; the suggestion that the Pharisees are the only or the dominant spiritual force in Judaism;[56] the linking of the Pharisees with other groups, especially the scribes, to the point that 'Scribes and Pharisees' become an almost technical term for the opponents of Jesus, without scarcely any attempt to differentiate between them.[57] The fact that the Pharisees and Christians agree on the idea of resurrection from the dead (*Mk* 12:18-27 and par.) does not alleviate the overall impression made by the sheer volume of material that has Jesus (or his disciples) in radical opposition to the Pharisees, their teachings and practices.[58]

When all this development in the tradition has been granted, it still does not seem possible to eliminate completely a genuine confrontation between Jesus and Pharisaism. For one thing, even Bultmann recognizes that the saying of Jesus embedded in a controversy story may be authentic even when the setting is the product of the early Christian community.[59] And a number of the gospel controversy stories deal explicitly with topics that were central to Pharisaic teaching: the sabbath observance (*Mk* 2:23-8 and par.) fasting (*Mk* 2:18-22 and par.); the observance of purity laws (*Mk* 7:1-23 and par.) and divorce (*Mk* 10:2-12). When all these passages have been subjected to a thorough form and redaction-critical analysis they still leave no reasonable doubt that Jesus was at odds with the Pharisees on a number of crucial points in their piety.[60] And an examination of his own teaching, as this can be gleaned e.g. from the parables, suggests a totally different conception of God, so graphically portrayed in the parable of the Pharisee and the Publican (*Lk* 18:10-14).[61]

Where did such a confrontation between Jesus and Pharisaism take place? Here we run into the difficult question of gospel geography and the possibility of the patent Galilee/Jerusalem tensions being the result of early intra-Christian polemics – a problem we hope to address in the final chapter of this study.[62] Besides, all would agree that the present framework of the gospels is secondary, so that the location of a particular controversy within the Galilean section of the gospel does not necessarily prove that a confrontation took place there, unless the episode as a whole is tightly anchored to the particular geographic situation to which it is attributed, as e.g. the story of the Gadarene demoniac (*Mk* 5:1-19 and par.).[63] Nevertheless, a few indications within the gospels may help towards a solution of the question posed in terms of the concerns of this chapter – Pharisaism in Galilee. The parable of the Pharisee and the Publican at least suggests that Jerusalem rather than Galilee was the place where a Galilean locates the Pharisees, though undoubtedly the verb ἀναβαίνειν could indicate the idea of the pilgrimage to Jerusalem (cf. *Jn* 7:8). More significant is the evidence of Luke's gospel, especially since the third evangelist seems to be better informed on a number of points about Pharisaism.[64] On three occasions we hear of Jesus being at table with Pharisees (*Lk* 7:36; 11:37; 14:1) in a Galilean setting, at least in the first two instances. These passages seem to be free of the more polemical overtones of the tradition, but taken in isolation they would be open to the objection just raised – we have no warrant for concluding from their gospel location to their original setting. However, *Lk* 13:31ff., which concerns a friendly attitude between Pharisees and Jesus, strongly suggests the presence of some Pharisees in Galilee. Bultmann describes the episode as 'in the strict sense a piece of biographical material',[65] and the fact that Jesus is being warned about Herod Antipas means that it took place within his jurisdiction, probably in Galilee, since we have no evidence of a ministry of Jesus in Peraea.[66] The fact that there is no mention of scribes in this episode is significant since Luke is aware of the distinction between scribism as a profession (*Lk* 11:46-52; 20:46) and Pharisaism as a way of life (*Lk* 11:39-42.44),[67] and the conclusion seems justified that there were Pharisees living in Herod's territory during Jesus' ministry. At the same time there is an important notice at *Mk* 3:22, repeated at 7:1 which should not be overlooked: scribes

(γραμματεῖς) from Jerusalem came and accused Jesus of being
possessed by Beelzebul (3:22), and at 7:1 we hear of the 'Pharisees
gathering together with some of the scribes who had come from
Jerusalem' (R.S.V.). Both verses show signs of Markan editorial
writing,[68] yet this does not invalidate the information for our
purposes of discussing the pre-70 situation in Galilee. The
correspondence with Luke is striking, in that Mark too seems to
attribute a Pharisaic presence to Galilee and a scribal mission
from Jerusalem to support it.

Surveying this evidence from our sources for pre-70 Judaism in
Galilee a number of points seem to be established. Pharisaism had
made certain inroads into the province prior to 70 C.E. and both
Josephus and the gospels suggest that its greatest successes were
in the settlements along the lake front – Tiberias, Tarichaeae,
Caesarea Philippi, and probably Caphernaum, Corozain and
Bethsaida also. It is not possible to say how extensively it dominated life elsewhere, but the likelihood is that the Γαλιλαῖοι
ἀπὸ τῆς χώρας of Josephus, namely the rural people, would be
termed 'am ha-' aretz by the Pharisees on religious grounds. Yet
if the gospels are at all reliable the Pharisees of Galilee do not
appear to be overly rigid in terms of their contacts with those who
were not of that persuasion, as their discussions with Jesus
indicate. One finds no traces of Pharisaic haburôth of the more
strict observance in the available evidence. The attempt by zealot
extremists to radicalize this Galilean Pharisaism in the immediate
pre-70 period seems to have met with only a limited success, and
the very prescriptions which would appear to have Galilee particularly in mind, or at least had a very real echo there, suggest that
in the pre-70 period the lines between Pharisee and 'am ha-' aretz
were not rigidly drawn. Neither did Jerusalem scribism have any
great success in Galilee in ousting the Sadducean domination of
the ethos there. This was not due to any great bonds between
peasant and aristocratic landowner, but rather because initially
Galilean Judaism had entered the mainstream of Jewish life in
Palestine under the old hierocracy, and loyalty to a way of life
that was built on the written torah suited the agrarian circumstances of these people. Religious conservatism and relative
social stability combined to make the scribal way of life both
unnecessary and unattractive to the peasants. In the eyes of the

scribe both wealthy landowner and peasant were alike *'am ha-'aretz* insofar as they refused to accept his way, but as long as the temple stood such divisions were not so obvious even for those directly involved. We must now turn to the evidence from the Jamnia period to see how the changes within Judaism which we have outlined at the outset worked themselves out in the province in the wake of the religious and social upheaval of the revolt against Rome.

II
GALILEE'S RESPONSE TO THE RE-ORGANIZATION OF JAMNIA

At the beginning of this chapter we have underlined the change that took place within Judaism with the destruction of the temple. The study of the torah now became the central reality of Jewish life and all previous divisions tended to be obliterated in the one overarching concern to establish 'another way' for the pious Jew. However, the reorganization did not take place immediately and many of the older tensions continued to be identifiable for some time, especially as long as influential figures from the pre-70 period lived. All this re-organization was possible, of course, because Rome made no attempt to wipe out the Jewish religion, despite allowing (or causing) the temple to be burned in 70.[69] Within the confines of tight political control that response was most likely to succeed which divorced Judaism from political and national concerns and concentrated on its purely religious aspects. It was this that Johanan ben Zakkai perceived and on this insight he was able to refashion Judaism by explaining the calamity in terms of Israel's sin and pointing the way of atonement through acts of loving kindness, based on a more faithful observance of the will of God.[70] In these circumstances study of the law was to become the alternative way, and Johanan's background as a Jerusalem scribe made it possible for him to become the active propagator of the 'new' religion.

His earliest enactments deal with liturgical matters that called for urgent attention now that the temple no longer existed. Johanan's principle in these enactments dealing with the new year festival, the *lulav*, the wave offering, the new moon, offerings from proselytes and those dedicated to the temple, was to transfer the sacredness of the temple to the *Beth dîn*, thereby investing the latter with a greater authority. No civil or criminal cases are mentioned in the earliest enactments, but Johanan's action in taking responsibility for liturgical matters was tantamount to replacing the priest with the scribe at the center of Jewish life.[71] The victory of scribism was not absolutely secured however, as divisions between the schools stemming from the pre-70 days tended to disrupt the unity of the nation. A number of stories in rabbinic sources such as the excommunication of R. Eliezer, the deposition of Johanan's successor R. Gamaliel II, and the *bath qôl* or heavenly voice favoring the Hillelites, have left the barest ripple of what must have been a stormy passage.[72] We know nothing of other currents which had been driven underground, but the Bar Cochba revolt is a sure indication that they were able to re-emerge and have some influence on the inner life of Judaism, while the bitter opposition to the *minim* or Jewish Christians, attested both in Rabbinic and Christian sources, is a clear pointer to the struggle that was going on for the soul of Judaism. With all this in mind it is time to turn to Galilee and consider its response to the changing situation.

The first indication of the increased contacts between Galilee and Judaea is the number of journeys made by leading rabbis from the south. This suggests an intensification of the program already initiated by Johanan ben Zakkai prior to 70, which reaped little success apparently. There is no suggestion that Johanan ever returned to Galilee, but we do find such leaders from Jamnia as Rabban Gamaliel II and R. Eliezer active in the province at various centers. It is difficult to decide how official these visits were, but one can see the authority of the visiting rabbi recognized in various ways – a formal decision given or a request for clarification presented by the locals, and this suggests a more active involvement with torah on the part of some Galileans at least. Thus we hear of Rabban Gamaliel 'going from place to place', at Ecdippa answering a query of the local ruler of the synagogue (*T. Ter* 2:13), and we also meet him at Tiberias (*b. Shabb* 115a; *M. Erub* 10:10), Sepphoris (*T. Shabb* 15:8) and Kephar 'Uthnai (*M. Gitt* 1:5). In Tiberias at least he was accompanied by elders, suggesting an official visit. Rabbi Eliezer was at Sepphoris certainly, for it is there that he encountered the heretic (*T. Hull* 2:24), but we also find him in Upper Galilee and Caesarea Philippi answering questions concerning the feast of Tabernacles (*b. Sukk* 28a; *T. Sukk* 1:9). We know from *M. Hall* 4:7 that these two influential rabbis differed on the question of whether Jews who had leased land in Syria should be subject to sabbatical year and tithing laws, the former declaring them exempt, the latter holding them bound, but it is difficult to decide whether these journeys represented the attempts of rivals to control the northern province, or are a common effort to win Galilee for the torah.[73]

For some scholars R. Eliezer represented the Shammaitic tradition at his school in Lydda and this has been linked by Büchler to the alleged Shammaism of Galilee.[74] However, Neusner's detailed study of Eliezer's legal traditions has shown that in some instances he agreed with the Hillelites and in others with the Shammaites and in some cases he concurred with neither.[75] Eliezer then represented pre-70 Pharisaism rather than scribism, and it is precisely in this guise that we find him functioning in Galilee also – he has no independent ruling on the number of cases presented to him, but is merely the mouthpiece of earlier tradition (*b. Sukk.* 28a).[76] Rabban Gamaliel's rulings in Galilee cover a number of different issues in a more independent way. At Ecdippa he dealt with the question of heave offerings from fourth year trees that had been bought from a non-Jew in Syria; at Tiberias he responded to questions concerning the Sabbath; at Sepphoris he ruled on circumcision and the sabbath and at Kephar 'Uthnai on a Samaritan witnessing to a marriage contract. This list, if it is at all indicative, suggests that Gamaliel at least was more concerned with basics of Jewish life as these were touched by the new situation, and not with the details of the *haburôth*, such as we find later with R. Meir and R. Judah. Thus there is no evidence that either of these two Jamnia rabbis was involved in a personal struggle for power in Galilee, though we can recognize in the approach of each the different concerns which they represent.

It is also noteworthy that native Galilean scribes emerge in our sources for this period. Büchler has given a long list of Galilean teachers of the Jamnia period, but even he admits that some of those listed are at best probable.[77] Klein also has a tendency to generalize from a few that can be listed by name to a total situation, both for the period before and after 70.[78] At best such generalizations are merely guesswork, and it is better to attempt to evaluate the trends that are exemplified by those Galilean teachers we know of for certain. In this connection the notice of *M. Ta'an* 2:5 is instructive: in the days of R. Halafta and R. Hananiah ben Teradion (the former at Sepphoris, the latter at Sikhnin according to *b. Ta'an* 16a; *b. Ros ha-Sh.* 27a) on days of fasting the custom was introduced to the synagogue of reading the whole seventh benediction without the people interrupting with 'Amen'. The sages were informed about this and declared that this practice only took place on the temple mount and at the eastern gate, presumably because the blessing in question refers to Abraham's blessing on Mt. Moriah, an old name for Jerusalem.[79] One can detect here a trend similar to that of Johanan's liturgical ordinances at Jamnia, with the synagogue replacing the temple as the sacral center of Jewish life.[80] Significantly, in another *baraita* we hear that R. Halafta had gone to meet Rabban Gamaliel at Tiberias and, on finding him reading the book of Job in Greek, he reminded him that his grandfather Gamaliel I had once rejected a similar translation on the temple mount in Jerusalem (*b. Shabb* 115a; *T. Shabb* 13:2). Clearly, Halafta had been in Jerusalem prior to 70, apparently belonging to the scribal class there, and this explains his transferring of the temple ritual to the synagogue, as well as the possible reprimand to R. Gamaliel. The same suggestion would apply to his contemporary, R. Hananiah ben Teradion who is said to have had a *Beth din* at Sikhnin (*b. Sanh* 32b). However, it is idle to speculate further whether or not both men were native Galileans or had migrated to Galilee later.[81] Prior to 70 Jerusalem was the center of scribism, even if some did move to the provinces in a more or less temporary capacity. Native or not, we have seen that the available evidence suggests that such scribal missions were less than successful, so that it would be unwise to use the example of these two rabbis as illustrative of far-reaching trends in Galilee in that earlier period.

After 70 we meet Galilean students of *halakhah* in the south with greater frequency and this can only mean that the changed situation had begun to have its effects there also. Foremost of these is R. Jose, the Galilean, whose epithet suggests not merely that he came from Galilee but that his main activity was outside the province.[82] It comes as little surprise to find him the tradent of the custom of his native province already discussed regarding the eve of the Day of Atonement (*M. Hull* 5:3). According to *b. Erub* 53b he was reprimanded by the wife of R. Meir as a foolish Galilean for inquiring from a woman about the correct road to Lydda, but since this section of the Talmud deals with Galilean ignorance of torah, the episode can be dismissed at least as far as R. Jose is personally concerned. Similarly we hear of R. Simeon ben Yohai relating the views of his teacher R. Aqiba to his colleagues in Galilee concerning the defilement of an offering before the tossing of the blood (*M. Meil* 1:2), and they disagreed with the opinion (*T. Meil* 1:5; *b. Meil* 7a). Another Galilean student from this period is R. Johanan ben Nuri, who discussed a series of rulings of R. Aqiba with R. Halafta in Sepphoris, and the latter disagreed with the decisions (*T. Maʻas Sch* 1:13; *T. Bab.Bath* 2:10; *T. ʼAhil* 5:8). These exchanges suggest that the contacts between the two provinces on the matter of *halakhah* were much more frequent than in the earlier period, yet a certain amount of independence still prevailed, even if the Judaean schools had a special attraction for some Galileans.

We must not be lured into the position of those who wish to generalize from various examples to a total picture, however. Certainly the invitation of the Judaean teachers who migrated to Usha after 135 is helpful: the assembled rabbis invited the זקני־הגליל to join them: 'everyone who has learned come and teach, and everyone who has not learned come and learn' (*Cant R* 2:5). This suggests that there were in Galilee at that period those who had not studied the torah, the *ʻam ha-ʼaretz le torah* according to Oppenheimer's designation. At approximately the same time the references to what constitutes an *ʻam ha-ʼaretz le mitzwôth* seem to have increased, as the discussions of R. Meir and R. Judah with the sages on what constituted a *habēr* and an *ʻam ha-ʼ aretz* suggest (*M. Demai* 2:3; *T. Demai* 2:2; *b. Berak* 47b; *T. Ab Zar* 3:10). Oppenheimer is surely correct in emphasizing that these debates may have been intensified in the Ushan period as a result of the second defeat by Rome, but that they were not initiated then for the first time.[83] At the same time it does not seem possible to distinguish absolutely between two different types of *ʻammei ha-ʼaretz*, the one contrasted with the *talmîdî hakhamîm* and the other with the *haberîm*. Rather, with the increased centrality of torah study as the essential task of the pious Jew, the concerns of the *talmîdey hakhamîm* must have also extended to observance of these *mitzwôth* demanded from a *haber* in the post-70 period, since those very *mitzwôth* (tithing and ritual purity) had their roots in the written torah and had been further elaborated in the oral torah of the sages.[84] Thus, there were *'am ha-'aretz le mitzwôth* in Galilee in the Ushan period, at least by R. Meir's and R. Judah's standards, and this can only mean that the whole population of the province had not yet accepted the centrality of the sages and their teaching for the Jewish way of life. And this conclusion is further corroborated by the fact that in the interests of peace and harmony the sages of the third century mollified considerably their attitudes towards the *'am ha-'aretz*.[85] Furthermore, the various references in talmudic literature, already referred to, dealing with the inferiority of the Galileans' knowledge of torah cannot be simply dismissed, and presumably reflect the ongoing struggle of the sages with Galilean recalcitrance in this matter.[86] Likewise there is the woe on Galilee attributed to Johanan ben Zakkai by Ulla, the third century Amora, which presumably reflects the provinces neglect of torah even in his day. Reference can also be made to the apocalyptic passage in *M. Sotah* 9:15 which enumerates among other signs of the Messiah's coming the desolation of Galilee and the increase of sin and lawlessness.[87] One can detect here the frustration of rabbinic thought concerning its own failures in the province, and yet the consolation that, perhaps, that very obstinacy might be a sign of hope.

All these indications from later rabbinic sources suggest caution in contrasting pre- and post-70 C.E. attitudes towards *halakhah* in Galilee. Just as in the first century when Pharisaism, but not the Jerusalem sages, had a limited success there, so in the second the sages do not appear to have been totally successful in winning the province for their way, based on the study of the torah and the stricter observance of the ideals of the *haburôth*. This was no longer the mark of the dutiful sectarian but the essential lifestyle of the pious Israelite who had put the torah in its twofold expression at the center of his life. Galilee's increase in concern for *halakhah* can be readily attributed to the loss of the temple and the consciousness that the social upheaval of the revolt was just punishment for its earlier failures.[88] It is not possible to confine the concept '*am ha-'aretz* to the Aaronides as Büchler attempts to do, since many of the references have a much wider scope than priestly failure with tithes and ritual purity. At the same time we cannot any longer maintain the identity of '*am ha-'aretz* with the Galilean peasants since it has now become a term for all who do not go the way of the torah, no matter what their social situation. We already discussed the differing social situation of Galilee and Judaea after the first revolt when the latter fell foul of the '*annasîm* and *mesiqîn* and was also subject to the usurping occupant – all Jewish collaborationists who were more concerned with the material benefits their loyalty to Rome might bring than with the spiritual renewal of the nation.[89] Presumably, these Jews too would have earned the epithet '*am ha-'aretz* from the Jamnia teachers who were still attempting to ignore the changed social situation in the Judaean courts (*M. Gitt* 5:6).[90] It is altogether possible then that the main object of the sages' attacks in the Jamnia and early Ushan periods was not the older Galilean peasants but the newly arrived landowners and their offspring who had never had any desire to become involved with Rome and were now rewarded for their loyalty. Besides many of the peasants of older stock had either perished, fled or been sold into slavery, and this change of population needs to be remembered when one attempts to assess the halakhic tendencies in the province after 70, as contrasted with those of earlier times.

III
POSSIBLE ALTERNATIVES TO PHARISAISM IN GALILEE

Our discussion of halakhic attitudes in Galilee has been set in the context of Geertz's comment that all religion needs a motivating force to bridge the gap between the mood that is evoked by the cult and the return to the routine world of everyday life. Pharisaism seemed to be the most likely possibility since within the spectrum of various alternative expressions of the Jewish faith in the pre-70 period it had the widest popular appeal, and in the wake of the threat to the Jewish religion which the hellenistic reform had posed it had developed specifically to meet the need that Geertz speaks about. Before attempting to suggest possible reasons for the relative failure of Pharisaism in Galilee and as a way of isolating the problem further, it seems advisable to search for traces of other forms of religious practice in the province, always remembering that we are dealing with an essentially Jewish situation where popular forms of religion like the mystery cults were not likely to make any great inroads, at least in an explicit way.

The most obvious alternative within Judaism is not to be sought in one of the other Jewish sects – the Zealots or the Essenes – who were concerned with mapping out a detailed way of life apart from the temple. We have already queried the assumption of many contemporary scholars that Galilee was the home of Zealotism, on the basis of lack of sufficient evidence for a revolutionary ethos there. If the eighteen *halakhôth* of the immediate pre-70 period were in fact directed at Galilee, this conclusion is only confirmed in that they represent an effort of Shammaitic Pharisaism to extend its views to Galilee similar to what Hillelite Pharisaism had attempted earlier through Johanan ben Zakkai. And there is no evidence that the former were any more successful than the latter. Nor is there any warrant for locating the Essenes in the province, even though Josephus does not appear to restrict them to the Judaean desert (*War* 2:124 ἐν ἑκάστῃ (πόλει) μετοικοῦσιν πολλοί; cf. *1 Macc* 2:29). The most significant alternative from our sources is undoubtedly the holy man or *hasîd*, whom we meet in Galilee in the person of Hanina ben Dosa. Certain aspects of the popularity of Jesus of Nazareth with the Galilean country-people could also be explained in this light, even if it does not seem possible to reduce him to being simply a *hasîd*, as Vermes attempts to do.[91]

We find Hanina active at Arav, located about six miles northeast of Sepphoris, and the pupil of Johanan, apparently in the pre-70 C.E. period.[92] This does not mean that he was a Galilean scribe, however, for he is designated 'a man of deed' in one of the earliest references to him (*M. Sot* 9:15) and there is not one piece of halakhic tradition ascribed to him in all the rabbinic sources. The expression 'man of deed' has been taken to mean 'a miracle worker' (Vermes) or a man of piety (Büchler) or a promoter of public welfare (Safrai),[93] and on the basis of the traditions about him the former would appear to be the most likely designation since it is primarily as a healer that we meet him. However, as we shall see, this need not exclude the other aspects also, once attention is paid to the social aspects of his deeds. Furthermore, we do find a series of sayings attributed to him that are general in character but suggest a broad and open view of the religious life with the emphasis on action: 'Any man whose fear of sin precedes his wisdom endures; but if his wisdom precedes his fear of sin, his wisdom will not endure. Any man whose deeds exceed his wisdom, his wisdom will not endure. Any man whose deeds exceed his wisdom, his wisdom will endure; but if his wisdom exceeds his deeds, his wisdom will not endure. Any man with whom men are pleased, God is pleased with him; but any man with whom men are displeased, God too, is displeased with him' (*M. Ab.* 3:10f). Vermes has detected two different tendencies in the tradition about Hanina. On the one hand there is a desire to 'rabbinize' him and to downplay, if not discredit, his miracles, but there is also clear evidence of an Hanina legend in the late first and second century C.E. in Galilee in which his healing and rain-giving deeds are attributed cosmic significance (*b. Ta'an* 24b).[94] He and his companions are 'the men of truth' whom Moses was to appoint as his helpers and judges (*Ex* 18:21, *Mekhilta*), or again we hear that the world to come was created for him (*b. Ber* 61b).

In attempting to assess the significance of the Hanina of history and legend for Galilean Jewish loyalties of the first and second centuries C.E., the conscious assimilation of the tradition to the figure of Elijah seems significant. This can be seen not merely from the type of miracles attributed to Hanina – cures of the sick, a rain miracle during a drought, the miraculous multiplication of oil – but also in his very posture at prayer – head between the knees (cf. *2 Kgs* 18:42). It is also noteworthy that of the many aspects of Elijah's return reflected both in late Jewish sources and in the New Testament itself – that of end-time helper in general, end-time high-priest, messianic precursor or precursor of God himself[95] – the aspect that comes to the fore in these stories of Hanina is 'the historical' Elijah's mighty deeds for those in need. This observation is all the more significant since Elijah was a northern prophet and the New Testament shows that popular opinion in Galilee could easily identify a prophetic-style figure with Elijah even before the Hanina legend began to be developed (cf.*Mk* 8:23; *Jn* 1:21).[96] Could it be that in the prophet's homeland the popular mind had retained a memory of him that was neither eschatological nor apocalyptic in nature, and that therefore differed from the hopes associated with him in more developed sectarian circles of Judaism?[97] We shall explore this possibility presently, but it should be noted now that there is no evidence for suggesting that the traditions linking both Jesus and Hanina with Elijah were developed in conscious relationship with each other. Rather *both* reflect from different historical and religious situations a Galilean interest in the particular aspect of Elijah which was likely to appeal to the popular religious mind.[98]

It must be immediately admitted that even with the discovery of such an interest in popular aspects of the Elijah legend in first century Galilee we are far from having settled the question to which we are seeking an answer – what alternative motivation did the figure of the *hasid* offer for the continued adherence to the Jewish religion? It may well be that there were companies of such *hasidim* with their own life-style and piety living on the fringes of life, but unless some links could be forged between them and the ordinary people their impact was likely to have been marginal.[99] It is here that the social significance of such holy men in relation to the society around them must be seriously evaluated. It seems legitimate to borrow Peter Brown's distinction between monastic life in Egypt and Syria for later times and apply it, *mutatis mutandis,* to Galilean and Judaean Jewish ascetics of an earlier period. In Egypt a man had to transplant the ways of the world to the desert if he was to survive at all, and this 'exercised a discreet and irresistible pressure in the direction of an inward-looking and earnest attention to the hard business of survival', whereas in Syria the physical contrast between desert and habitable land was never so stark and so the holy man was able to live on the fringes of society and highlight more clearly by his different life-style the gulf that separated him from the rest of men.[100] The Judaean landscape lent iself more to the Egyptian-type monasticism, whereas in Galilee no such physical contrast existed and so the holy man could impinge more palpably on the rest of life there. Itinerant radicalism may well have accentuated this influence, as the holy man moved from place to place and he may even have acted as spokesman for local needs with the authorities or settled cases of legal dispute among village people (cf. *Lk* 12:13f).[101] In an ethos where physical evil was attributed to demonic and hostile forces, the ability to overcome such obvious manifestations of evil as sickness or natural catastrophe seen as punishment for moral wrongdoing gave the holy man a very important social as well as religious role in the community.[102] In any age it is difficult to draw a clear line between what might be regarded as orthodox religious belief in the power of God and superstitious trust in magic spells and sorcery, especially at the practical as distinct from the theoretical level. There is enough evidence to suggest that Palestinian Judaism was not immune from this latter form of belief and its practice,[103] and the popularity of the holy man there suggests that Galilee may have been particularly susceptible in this regard. In such an atmosphere the holy man takes on an even added significance, and is in a certain tension with the temple as the official place of divine power and presence.[104] In the previous chapter we could not find any traces of Galilean opposition to or critique of the temple, much less its spiritualization, as among the Essenes and early Christians. Yet it appeared that its function as a religious symbol was somewhat attenuated, closely related, we suggested, to the peasants' struggle with nature and therefore less likely to inspire revolutionary action as long as some links with the land could be maintained. The holy man would seem to be the natural supplement to this 'pilgrimage' type of religion, not necessarily opposed to that of the temple, even if such characters as Hanina and Jesus display independence if not superiority on occasion.[105]

It would be foolhardy to attempt any estimate of the success of the Pharisaic *halakhah* in Galilee over against the older and more popular forms of belief and practice. As stressed more than once, the dominant ethos there was rural and peasant, and in those circumstances one can readily appreciate why Pharisaism, which had particular appeal with the townspeople according to *Ant* 18:15, that is, among the emerging middle class, would have had little attraction for people from the country. The Pharisaic 'revolution', as Rivkin calls it, was an attempt to forge a new understanding of God and *halakhah* to meet the needs of the Jew in the urban context of the hellenistic age, a situation that Pentateuchal religion could not deal with.[106] While the crisis of

70 did bring about a definite increase of interest in the other way of *halakhah* it could not be expected to take over completely, since some peasants did survive the catastrophe. With the apparent continued interest in the figure of the *hasid*, it seems pertinent to ask whether Christianity might not be expected to fare better in Galilee. It is to this question that we must now turn in our closing chapter.

NOTES FOR CHAPTER 8

¹This is not to suggest that these sources are free of all *tendenzen* in regard to Pharisaism. Josephus' concern seems to have been to convince the Romans that they should support the successors of the Pharisees as rulers of the Jewish people, especially in his treatment of the party in *Ant*, as M. Smith has argued, 'Palestinian Judaism in the First Century', in *Israel: Its Role in Civilization*, ed. M. Davis, New York, Harper and Row, 1956, esp. 75f. Cf. also, J. Neusner, *From Politics to Piety. The Emergence of Pharisaic Judaism*, Englewood Cliffs, N.J., Prentice Hall, 1973, 45-64. On the Gospels' portrayal of the Pharisees, cf. Neusner, *op. ci'.*, 67-80 and H. Weiss, 'Der Pharisäismus im Lichte der Überlieferung des Neuen Testaments', Beitrag to Meyer, *Tradition und Neuschöpfung*, 91-132, and *TDNT* 9, art. Φαρισαῖος.

²This depiction is based on a number of recent studies, among which those of Meyer, *Tradition und Neuschöpfung*, and art. Φαρισαῖος in *TDNT* 9, 11-35, and Neusner, *The Rabbinic Traditions about the Pharisees before 70*, 3 vols. Leiden, Brill, 1971, *From Politics to Piety*, '"Pharisaic-Rabbinic" Judaism: A Clarification' *HR* 12(1973) 250-70, have been found most helpful. Cf. however, the very different treatment by E. Rivkin, 'Defining the Pharisees: The Tannaitic Sources', *HUCA* 40/41 (1969/70) 205-49, art. 'Pharisees' *IDB* Suppl. vol., 657-63, who denies any necessary connection between the Pharisees and the *haberim* and defines the former as 'that scholar class that created the concept of the twofold law, carried it to triumphant victory over the Sadducees and made it operative in society' ('Defining the Pharisees', 248); cf. in addition his 'The Internal City: Judaism and Urbanization', *JSSR* 5(1966) 225-40. Rivkin contends that the usual understanding of the Pharisees as a sect of ritual purists is based on the false assumption that they can be identified with the *perushim* of *M.Hag* 2:7, who can be rendered unclean by the garments of the *'am-ha-'aretz*. He attempts to set up criteria other than the merely linguistic ones for detemining when tannaitic texts are actually dealing with the Pharisees. For a discussion of Rivkin's methodology, cf. D. Ellenson, 'Ellis Rivkin and the Problem of Pharisaic History', *JAAR* 43(1975) 787-802. The call for a clear methodology is laudable, but it seems that in confining Pharisees to a teaching class only he has gone beyond the evidence of the New Testament (cf. *Lk* 11:37.45; which distinguishes Pharisaic from Scribal concerns) and Josephus (cf. *Ant* 18:15, which speaks about their way of life as well as their teaching) both of which should also be taken into account in his methodology. The views of Meyer, *Tradition und Neuschöpfung*, esp. 33-43, can perhaps suggest a rapprochement between the two positions: he concludes his section 'Pharisäische Weisheit und Schriftgelehrsamkeit' as follows: 'Das bedeutete aber, dass der Schriftgelehrte, gerade in seiner Eigenschaft als Sofer, das heisst als Tradent und Interpret der Tora, fur die innere und aussere Existenz der *Perusim* beziehungsweise *Haberim* lebensnotwendig war'.

³Meyer seems to suggest that all Pharisees were organized in *haburôth*, even though he does admit of certain grades of *haberim* on the basis of the rabbinic evidence, *Tradition und Neuschöpfung*, 23ff, and *TDNT*, 9, 16-20. This is also the view of Jeremias, *Jerusalem in the Time of Jesus* 247 and 251, n.3. Others are less certain: G.F. Moore, *Judaism in the First Centuries of the Christian Era. The Age of the Tannaim*, 3 vols. Cambridge, Harvard Univ. Press, 1927, 3, 26; J. Neusner, 'The Fellowship in the Second Jewish Commonwealth', *HTR* 53(1960) 125-42, esp. 125, n.1; E.P. Sanders, *Paul and Palestinian Judaism*, Philadelphia, Fortress Press, 1977, 154; Oppenheimer, *The 'Am ha-Aretz*, 118-60. On 119, n.4, he gives the various references in rabbinic literature to the expressions cited in the text. Cf. also C-H Hunzinger, 'Spüren Pharisäischer Institutionen in der frühen rabbinischen Überlieferung', in *Tradition und Glaube, Festgabe für Karl Georg Kuhn*, Göttingen, Vandenhoeck und Ruprecht, 1971, 147-56, with reference to the practice of excommunication in rabbinic literature.

⁴*M. Ed* 1:14 gives another such dispute where the Shammaites and Hillelites differ concerning the degree of impurity of an earthenware vessel of an *'Am ha-Aretz*.

In this instance the Hillelites yielded to the opinion of their opponents. The mishnah in question comes from the Jamnia period when a serious attempt was made to reconcile the diverging views of the earlier period. Cf. Oppenheimer, *The 'Am ha-Aretz*, 88, and Neusner, *From Politics to Piety*, 100-3.

⁵Oppenheimer, *The 'Am ha-Aretz*, 60, n. 119, shows that this is an early (i.e. pre-70) mishnah on the basis of a comparison with *T. Hag* 3:2f, the parallel text, where additional names of Jamnia rabbis are introduced. Accordingly, Rivkin's relegation of the passage to his category of doubtful references to the Pharisees, 'Defining the Pharisees', 239, appears unwarranted. His argumentation is only valid if one accepts his definition that the certain Pharisaic texts *'without exception'* have the *perushim* stating a legal position, and never themselves the subject of the law. Cf. above. n. 2.

⁶Oppenheimer, *The 'Am ha-Aretz*, 156-60, discussing the example of *b.Sukk.* 43b., where Pharisees and *'Am ha-'Aretz* agree against the Boethusians in regard to a particular rite. Despite the polemics of the chapter, *Jn* 7 suggests a similar situation on the occasion of a feast. Cf. also Oppenheimer's discussion of cases where there is a desire not to widen social divisions created by the purity laws, *op. cit.* 92-6.

⁷There were good social reasons for this as Oppenheimer, *The 'Am ha-Aretz*, 115, points out, namely the historical interest of the Ushan sages in the period of the second temple because of the continuing hope that the temple would be rebuilt; the collecting and sifting of *halakhôth* from earlier times preparatory to the redaction of the Mishnah; insistence on the religious-national practices, especially the tithing and purity laws, which were probably suspended in the wake of the persecution of Hadrian. Büchler, *Der Galiläische 'Am ha-Ares*, uses such Ushan traditions as *T.Dem* 2:2; *T. Ab. Zar.* 3:10; *M. Dem* 2:3; *b. Ber* 47b, all dealing with the views of Rabbis Meir and Judah on what constitutes an *'am ha-'aretz* and a *haber*, as a proof that these concepts emerged only in the Ushan period. However, he mistakes the attribution of a particular *halakhah* to a Rabbi with its origin, as Oppenheimer points out, and the latter has convincingly shown that the issues are much earlier, and rooted in the economic and social fabric of life in Palestine since Hasmonaean times, at least, *op. cit.* 6, 69-79 (tithes) and 83-96 (purity laws). Cf. above ch. 7. notes 79 and 80.

⁸Büchler, *Der Galiläische 'Am ha-Ares*, 18-26, insists that this understanding of the *'am ha-'aretz* was to be found in Judaea in the Jamnia period, but not in Galilee. Cf. also Oppenheimer, The *'Am ha-Aretz*, 97-106. Cf. *M. Sotah* 9:15; *b.Ber* 47b, for two detailed descriptions of what constitutes an *'am ha-'aretz*, the former stressing a lack of concern for spiritual things in general and the latter a neglect of such distinctive Jewish practices as the recitation of the *Shema'*, the wearing of *tefillin* and the placing of *mezuzah* at the door. It climaxes with the following: 'Others again said: Anyone who has learned Scripture and Mishnah, but has not ministered to the *talmidey hakhamim* is an *'am ha-'aretz.'*

⁹Oppenheimer, *The 'Am ha-Aretz*, 103-5, argues to the lateness of this dictum which he attributes to R. Hillel, a third century C.E. teacher, but his arguments, based on variant MS reading, are not very convincing, especially in view of the Johannine verse.

¹⁰'"Pharisaic-Rabbinic" Judaism', 140f; *Eliezer ben Hyrcanus. The Traditions and the Man*, 2 vols. Studies in Judaism in Late Antiquity, III and IV, Leiden, Brill, 1973, 2, 140f. Oppenheimer, *The 'Am ha-Aretz*, 183f, lists the rejection of the sects, the rise of the sages to the role of political and national builders and the replacement of the temple by the torah at the center of Jewish life as reasons for this development.

¹¹This aspect of the struggle has been underlined particularly by R. Meyer, 'Der 'Am ha-Ares. Ein Beitrag zur Religionssoziologie Palästinas im ersten und zweiten Jahrhundert', *Judaica* 3(1947) 169-99, esp. 192-5.

¹²Cf. already the critical remarks of E. Schürer, *Theologische Literaturzeitung*, nr. 23(1906) 619f, who points out the forced interpretation of many rabbinic passages such as *M. Hag* 2:5; *b.Ber* 47b in order to restrict their meaning to priest alone.

¹³*The 'Am ha-Aretz*, 18-22, Meyer, 'Der 'Am ha-Ares.' 197, sees this as the reason why the social ostracization did not lead to violent conflict.

[14]While disclaiming any significance to the distinction between town and country in discussing the nature of the concept, *The 'Am ha-Aretz*, 19f, Oppenheimer later seems to recognize that such distinctions did play a real part in determining attitudes to the tithes (*op. cit.* 71).

[15]This is stressed by Cohen, *Josephus in Galilee*, 267-78, 393 and by Rajak, 'Justus of Tiberias', 357. A comparison with *War* at the relevant passages shows no such concern.

[16]According to *Ant* 12:276 Mattathias allowed fighting on the Sabbath, and according to *War* 2:517 the Jews also attacked the army of Cestius on that day. On the other hand they observed the rule stated in *Jubilees* 50:12 during Pompey's siege, *Ant* 14:63. Observance of the Sabbath was a cornerstone of Jewish piety (Cf. already *Ant* 13:337 for Galilee) and differences of opinion between the sects dealt only with what constituted a violation. Cf. in general E. Lohse, art. σάββατον *TDNT* 7, 1-35, esp. 8f on the question of fighting on the sabbath.

[17]Above ch. 6, n. 95. The precise meaning of παλαιός is uncertain, for it could signify 'of long standing' or 'at one time'. The encomium on Simon *Life* 190-2, does not detract from the information, since Josephus says that Simon was at that time at variance with him (τότε).

[18]For a dicsussion cf. Hengel, *Die Zeloten*, 204-11. The rabbinic references are *p. Shabb* 1,3c; *b. Shabb* 17b; *b.Ab.Zar* 36a and *b. M. Shabb* 1:4 briefly mentions a blood-bath. Twelve different types of food are excluded as well as the Greek language, their witness, their gifts, their sons and daughters and their first fruits, 'their' referring to gentiles. H. Graetz, whose views have been followed by most scholars, including Hengel, dates them to the period just before the first revolt, *Geschichte der Juden*, III, 809. There is no mention of images in this list, but C. Roth, 'An ordinance against Images in Jerusalem', HTR 49(1956) 151-64, on 176, n.13, tentatively suggests צִיּוּר (picture) for צִיר (brine).

[19]Roth, 'An Ordinance against Images', 173-5, links the κοινόν of Jerusalem mentioned at *Life* 65.310 with the body that passed the 18 *halakhôth* of the same period.

[20]Cf. Roth, 'The Historical Implications of the Jewish Coinage'; ch. 3 above, n. 51.

[21]Josephus is a good example of this double standard, since in several places he mentions the law that forbids any representations: *Ant* 3:91; 8:195; *Against Apion* 2:74f, yet reports without comment the fact that some Jewish aristocratic homes had such representations: *Ant* 12:230 (John Hyrcanus); 14:34 (Aristobulus II); 15:26 (Alexandra II); 19:357 (Agrippa). J. Gutmann, 'The Second Commandment and the Image in Judaism', HUCA 32(1961) 161-74, esp. 172, n. 10, speculates that in the light of the above evidence Josephus would have been anxious to show the Zealots of Tiberias where his true loyalties lay. However, apart from the doubtful case of the 18 *halakhôth* (cf. above n. 18) there does not seem to have been any general ban on images, as the saying of Eleazar ben Saddoc (c. 100 C.E.) indicates: 'There were all kinds of representations in Jerusalem except for human figures' (*T. Ab.Zar.* 5:2). In general cf. Meyer, 'Die Figurendarstellung in der Kunst des späthellenistischen Judentums', 12f, who notes that all the examples cited come from those who had not accepted the Pharisaic-rabbinic dogma of the sanctification of the everyday through the law and with it the prohibition against images in the non-cultic sphere.

[22]Hengel, *Die Zeloten*, 198, regards Roth's emendation to include a ban on images in the 18 *halakhôth* (above n. 18) doubtful.

[23]Above ch.4, notes 65 and 6. Büchler, *Der Galilaische 'Am ha-Ares*, 94-6 points to the rabbinic tradition in *b. Shabb* 33b and *p. Shabb* 9. 38d where only a few graves were protruding, and therefore concludes that the whole city was not regarded as unclean. His conclusion that, because Rabbis such as Johanan ben Zakkai visited the city before the cleansing, the problem of Jews inhabiting the place referred to by Josephus as well as the legend of the cleansing could only have concerned priests, appears to be another example of his special pleading in support of his overall thesis. Cf. above, n. 12.

[24]*M. Ab. Zar.* 3:4 relates the reply of Rabban Gamaliel when questioned by a certain Proklos why he visited the bath of Aphrodite in Acre, the burden of which

is, that because men disregard the statue as they enter and exit, she is not really a goddess, and so there is no violation of the command not to worship their gods (*Dt* 12:3).

²⁵ Moore, *Judaism*, 1, 328f; de Vaux, *Ancient Israel*, 74f. The fact that these men seem to have transferred their allegiance on a permanent basis put them in the category of *gēr* rather than *nokri'*, though not called proselytes by Josephus for whom there were special regulations. Cf. also the articles on ξένος and προσήλυτος., in *TDNT* 5, 1-36 and 6, 727-44.

²⁶ Is Josephus here underlining his maganimity for Roman readers or answering a charge of Justus? There is certainly a danger of reading everything in *Life* from this latter perspective. It is noteworthy that the episode is linked with charges that Josephus was a collaborationist, *Life* 129.132.

²⁷ Sanders, *Paul and Palestinian Judaism*, 209f, has a good discussion of the differing attitudes on this question.

²⁸ Above, n. 18. Hengel, *Die Zeloten*, 203f, notes that circumcision was an issue at *War* 2:454, where the rebels are said to have compelled the captain of Herod's palace to be circumcised in order to save his life. He sees the compulsory circumcision as having its roots in Maccabaean times: *1 Macc* 1:61; 3:8; *2 Macc* 8:3, and links the Galilean episode with the Zealot ideal of purity of the land. Cf. above ch. 7, n. 92. It should be noted however that during the conquests of Hyrcanus circumcision was imposed on the conquered peoples without any particular appeal to sectarian concerns (*Ant* 13:257.318f).

²⁹ Marcus, *Loeb Josephus*, 7, 737-42, Appendix C, 'The Early Seleucid Rulers and the Jews'.

³⁰ Hengel, *Jud. und Hell.*, 85f, n. 332. The early enactment of Jose ben Joezer and Jose ben Johanan, who were the second pair of Pharisaic teachers, decreed that glassware also was subject to impurity and may have been directed against the same practice according to Oppenheimer, *The 'Am ha-Aretz*, 57, n. 113. Cf. above ch. 5, n. 84 and 85.

³¹ S. Hoenig, 'Oil and Pagan Defilement', JQR 61(1970/1) 63-75, esp. 66-9.

³² J. Baumgarten, 'The Essene Avoidance of Oil and the Laws of Purity', RQ 6(1967/8) 184-92, interprets *CD* 12:15-7, as concern for the purity laws rather than rejection of sacrifice or avoidance of luxurious living. Cf. *War* 2:123: 'Oil they (the Essenes) consider defiling'.

³³ Graetz, *Geschichte*, 3, 807f.

³⁴ Eupolemus, writing about 150 B.C.E., in a fragment preserved in Eusebius (*Praep. Evang.* IX, 33.1) mentions supplies of food for Jerusalem coming from different regions: oil from Judaea, fatstock from Arabia and wheat from Galilee, Samaria and Moab and Ammon and Gilead. This was before Galilee had been officially integrated into the Jewish land, and significantly its oil is not for use.

³⁵ Thus Oppenheimer, *The 'Am ha-Aretz*, 204, following Safrai, *Pilgrimage* (Hebrew) 44-6, who regards the explanation of the Talmuds as not reflecting the historical situation of the actual *halakhah* in question, and notes the other geographical data of the same Mishnah.

³⁶ *A Life of Rabban Johanan ben Zakkai*, Studia Post-Biblica 7, Leiden, Brill, 1962, 23-6, discusses this tradition and notes the apologetic concerns of a later time, but nevertheless dates his career in relation to Hillel (p. 27).

³⁷ Above ch. 5, n. 58 for Neusner's views on the authenticity of the saying and *ib.* n. 55 for the meaning of *siqarikon*.

³⁸ The two cases brought to him *M. Shabb* 16:7;22:3 deal with the *trivia* of Sabbath violation.

³⁹ Cf above, notes 2 and 10.

⁴⁰ G. Vermes, 'Hanina ben Dosa. A Controversial Galilean Saint from the First Century of the Christian Era', JJS 23(1972) 28-50 and 24(1973) 51-64, 61, (hereafter 'Hanina ben Dosa', I and II) against A. Büchler, *Types of Jewish Palestinian Piety From 70 B.C.E. to 70 C.E. The Ancient Pious Man*, Reprint, New York, Ktav, 1968, 89. Cf. below, n. 92.

[41] Thus Neusner, *A Life of Rabban Johanan ben Zakkai,* 30f; Vermes, 'Hanina ben Dosa', I, 32, describes the contrast as follows: a favorite slave is in a position to procure some favor from his master more speedily than is a prince who must follow the rules of protocol.

[42] *ARNB*, ch. 27 reads Ramath bene-Anat whereas *ARNA* has Beth Ramah. The former is unknown, and Neubauer (reading Bet Ramtah) locates the latter across the Jordan from Jericho, *Géographie*, 198. According to A. Salderini, *The Fathers According to Rabbi Nathan*, Studies in Judaism in Late Antiquity, Leiden, Brill, 1975, 163, n. 32. Ms. N reads Ramat Beth-Anat, which is very similar to Rum Bet Anat of *T. Mik* 6:3 and is usually located in Galilee. Cf. above, ch. 4, n. 15 and ch. 5, n. 7.

[43] S. Safrai, 'Teaching of Pietists in Mishnaic Literature', JJS 16(1965) 15-33, esp. 25ff, examines the various traditions of this anecdote; cf. also Büchler, *Der Galiläische 'Am ha-Arets*, 90ff. Safrai believes that the expression refers to a definite current in the *halakhah*, having certain affinity with the Rabbis but with its own individual lines.

[44] L. Finkelstein, *The Pharisees. The Sociological Background to their Faith*, 2 vols. 3 ed., Philadelphia, The Jewish Publication Society of America, 1962, 43-60.

[45] *b. Sanh* 11b presumes that a local *Beth Dîn* could decide about intercalation. However, this may be purely theoretic in view of Gamaliel I's letter on this matter mentioned above. 'Public things' could refer to such as the temple mount, its courts and wells for the pilgrims which were considered to belong to all Israel. Mantel, *Studies in the Sanhedrin*, 29, considers the title *nasi'* to be early, but is criticized by Hengel, 'Die Synagogeninschrift von Stobi', 153, n. 24; cf. above, ch. 3, n. 60, however, where it is suggested that at least the office of *nasi* would seem to have existed from Maccabaean times.

[46] De Vaux, *Ancient Israel*, 194-209 and Rostovtzeff, *SEHHW* 1, 451-5 and 2,1296-1300.

[47] *The Pharisees*, 1, 48-50 and 43-7. He does accept that the Judaean custom of inspection of the marriage bed may be the survival of a very ancient rite, 2, 829, n. 10. Oppenheimer, *The 'Am ha-Aretz*, 215f, makes no attempt to probe behind these customs for possible social reasons, simply commenting, 'a more beautiful custom'. Cf. above, n. 14.

[48] Oppenheimer, *The 'Am ha-Aretz*, 200-17, is at pains to show that at least some Galileans were concerned both with the study of the torah in general and the detailed *halakhôth*, in his desire to refute Büchler's thesis. While his criticism of the latter is in its general lines correct, it has led him at times to ignore the real differences in regard to *halakhah* in general between the pre- and post- 70 periods, and the historical and social factors that made for special attitudes in Galilee. In this instance all the examples he cites come from the Jamnia period, but what does this say about the earlier situation? Cf. n. 10 above.

[49] Moore, *Judaism*, 1, 78f, calls this an old *baraita*, but it seems likely that its form is determined by debates about the authority of Hillel at a later time.

[50] J. Neusner, *First Century Judaism in Crisis. Yohanan ben Zakkai and the Renaissance of Torah*, Nashville, Abingdon Press, 1975, 184ff; 'Studies in the *Taqqanôt* of Yavneh', HTR 63(1970) 183-98, esp. 193f, where he argues that insofar as the tradition supports a central authority and suppresses opposition from opposing groups it must have come from Yavneh.

[51] Thus, Moore, *Judaism*, 1, 78, n. 2; Neusner, *From Politics to Piety*, 27.

[52] Above, chs. 3, n. 55 and 4, notes 82 and 3.

[53] Meyers, 'Regionalism', 97 and 99; cf. above, ch. 4, n. 102. On the basis of our discussions in ch. 1 this is an example of human factors, religious and social, overcoming natural barriers to exchange and communication.

[54] Above, n. 1. Cf. Davies, *The Setting of the Sermon on the Mount*, 256-315; W. Trilling, *Das Wahre Israel, Studien zur Theologie des Matthäusevangeliums*, 3 ed., SANT, Munich, Kösel, 1964, 90-7; R. Hummel, *Die Auseinandersetzung*

zwischen Kirche und Judentum im Matthäusevaneliums, Beiträge zur Evangelischen Theologie, 33, Munich, Kaiser, 1963, 26-35; G. Barth, 'Matthew's Understanding of the Law', in *Tradition and Interpretation in Matthew*, G. Bornkamm, G. Barth, H.J. Held, English trans., London, S.C.M. 1963, esp. 85-95.

[55] From *Politics to Piety*, 72.

[56] In this connection the absence of the Pharisees from the trial of Jesus is significant, but it does not warrant P. Winter's conclusion, *On the Trial of Jesus*, Berlin 1961, 124f, that all polemical aspects of Jesus' relation with the Pharisees in the gospels are secondary.

[57] Weiss, art Φαρισαῖος , *TDNT* 9, 38f. The characterization of Jesus' opponents in *Jn* as 'Ιουδαῖοι is a further stage of this development.

[58] We should not overlook the pro-Pharisaic views in *Mt* 23:3.23; 13:52; or the fact that Nicodemus, 'a teacher in Israel', is favorable to Jesus in *Jn*. These indications suggest that all contact between the two groups is not precluded. Cf. H. Merkel, 'Jesus und die Pharisäer', NTS 14(1968) 194-208, esp. 198-200 who says that *Mt's* criticism of the Pharisees is 'scharf' but never 'prinzipiell', and Weiss, *TDNT* 9, 44f, who notes *Jn's* rejection of Pharisaic teaching (*Jn* 8:30; 9:16) but without condemning the Pharisees themselves.

[59] R. Bultmann, *The History of the Synoptic Tradition*, English trans. 2 ed. Oxford, Blackwell, 1968, 50.

[60] Cf. in particular, Merkel, 'Jesus und die Pharisäer', esp. 202-7, and Weiss, *TDNT* 9, 41, notes 167 and 9 with other studies cited there.

[61] Jeremias, *The Parables*, 139ff; E. Linnemann, *Parables of Jesus. Introduction and Exposition*, English trans., London, S.P.C.K., 1966, 58-64.

[62] Below, ch. 9, II.

[63] The Q saying. *Lk* 10:13-15; *Mt* 11:20-4 mentions three Galilean locations, Corozain, Caphernaum and Bethsaida, all along the lake-front, where Jesus' preaching was unsuccessful, yet it is not clear that the opposition came from the Pharisees. On the Galilean controversy cycle and their artificial (that is, literary rather than biographical) features cf. Joanna Dewey, 'The Literary Structure of the Controversy Stories in *Mk* 2:1-3:6', JBL 99(1973) 394-401.

[64] On Luke's more 'historical' and less polemical attitudes cf. Weiss, *TDNT* 9, 36 and 45, and Jeremias, *Jerusalem at the Time of Jesus*,253f.

[65] *The History of the Synoptic Tradition*, 35.

[66] Hoehner, *Herod Antipas*, 146-9 argues that there is nothing in the gospels to contradict the information of Josephus, *Ant* 18:112, that John was put to death in Machaerus in Peraea. However, Tiberias seems to have been Antipas' usual place of residence and it is in Galilee that the incident of *Lk* 13:31 should be located.

[67] Above, notes 10 and 64.

[68] Cf. V. Taylor's analysis of these verses from the point of view of style and vocabulary, *The Gospel according to Saint Mark*, London, Macmillan, 1963, 263f. 334. Oppenheimer, *The 'Am ha-Aretz*, 205 and 10, thinks that these references do not exclude Galilean scribes also, but there is little evidence for any active in the province, apart from Johanan ben Zakkai, before 70 C.E. Cf. below, n. 78.

[69] Neusner, *First Century Judaism in Crisis*, 148-53.

[70] *Mek R. Ishmael*, trans. Lauterbach, 2, 193f; *ARNA*, Goldin ed. 94. Neusner, *A Life of Rabban Yohanan ben Zakkai*, 147-68; *First Century Judaism in Crisis*, 166-9.

[71] Neusner, 'Studies in the *Taqqanôt* of Yavneh'.

[72] *b. Bab Mez* 59a and b; *p. Mo Kat* 3,1. Neusner, *Eliezer ben Hyracanus*, 422-7 and 2, 345. On the deposition of Gamaliel, cf. Graetz, *History of the Jews*, 3 vols. Philadelphia, 1902, 2, 340-2. *p. Sukk* 2,8 tells of the *Bath Qôl* that favored the Hillelites; cf. Neusner, *From Politics to Piety* 100-3 and Davies, *The Setting of the Sermon on the Mount*, 262-6.

[73] Oppenheimer, *The 'Am ha-Aretz*, 212f.

[74] Büchler, *Der Galiläische 'Am ha-Ares*, 278ff. It is also implied by Finkelstein, *The Pharisees*, 1, 43-61 who speaks of the Shammaites and the wealthy patricians dominating Galilean halakhic attitudes. A. Finkel, *The Pharisees and the Teacher of Nazareth*, AGSU 4, 2 ed., Leiden, Brill, 1974, 129, goes so far as to say that Shammai was a Galilean, but without any greater evidence than a reference to I. Abrahams' *(Studies in Pharisaism and the Gospels*, Reprint, New York, Ktav, 1967, 15) surmise that perhaps this was so. Cf. the critical comments of Vermes, *Jesus the Jew*, 56 and 238, n. 79.

[75] *Eliezer ben Hyrcanus*, 2, 309.351.399.416.

[76] *Eliezer ben Hyrcanus* 1, 141f. At *b. Hull* 62a he comments on the practices of the men of Upper Galilee.

[77] *Der Galiläische 'Am ha-Ares*, 274-336. On p. 336 he writes: 'teils erwiesenen teils vermuteten'. (Italics mine).

[78] *Galiläa vor der Makkabäerzeit*, 39-43. He lists R. Hanina, R. Yohanan, Eleazar, the Galilean who insisted on circumcision for Izates the king of Adiabne (*Ant* 20:43); Nittaj of Arbela (*M. Hag* 2:2; *M. Ab* 1:6f); Abba Jose Halifkuri from near Tibi'in (*M. Maksh* 1:3) and the unnamed teacher of the young Alexander Jannaeus who is said to have been educated in Galilee (Ant 13:322). Over a period of 150 years this is clearly a very small number even if it could be shown that they were all Pharisaic scribes and were more successful than Johanan ben Zakkai.

[79] Büchler, *Der Galiläische 'Am ha-Ares*, 277, n. 2; Klein, *Neue Beiträge*, 20f.

[80] S. Krauss, *Synagogale Altertümer*, Reprint Darmstadt 1966, 93-102. Cf. M. Hengel, 'Proseuche und Synagoge' in *Tradition und Glaube*, 157-84, with a detailed study of synagogue inscriptions from the Diaspora and Palestine. He shows that proseuche (house of prayer) was more typical of the Diaspora, in the absence of an alternative sacred place, whereas the more secular 'synagogue' was the usual Palestinian translation of Beth Kenesseth, even when the place had a sacral as well as secular character, something that the gospels amply testify. At Tiberias both aspects of the synagogue are apparent (cf. *Life* 277.280.293ff) but the diaspora designation 'proseuche' is used, which Hengel describes as 'fremd und vornehm klingenden der Diaspora'. He maintains that the gradual infiltration by the Palestinian designation 'synagogue' in the Diaspora is a sign of the increasing influence of the homeland, especially after 70, when the synagogue had filled the religious vacuum created by the destruction of the temple there also.

[81] Büchler, *Die Priester*, 39-41, believes that the group frequently described in the Babylonian Talmud as 'the holy congregation of Jerusalem' were Jerusalmites who fled to Galilee and especially Sepphoris after 70, and were extremely strict in their dealings with the *'am ha-'aretz*. S. Safrai, 'The Holy Congregation of Jerusalem', St Hier 23(1972) 62-78 concurs, pointing to *T.Dem* 2:2 contrasted with *M. Dem* 2:2 and *T.Dem* 2:9 compared with *b.Bek* 31a, for the stricter attitudes. He concludes that they were the disciples of R. Meir, who, conscious of the holiness of Jerusalem, resettled there in the second century. Jeremias, *Jerusalem at the Time of Jesus*, 247-9, dates them to the first century, and believes the expression designates a Pharisaic group existing in Jerusalem before 70. The former view is the more likely and one can recognize from it the sense of 'exile' that some at least experienced in Galilee in the second century.

[82] Büchler, *Der Galiläische 'Am ha-Arets*, 300-7, attempts rather unsuccessfully to make him a Shammaite. Cf. above, n. 74.

[83] Above, n. 7.

[84] Oppenheimer, *The 'Am ha-Aretz*, 170f, clearly recognizes this, pointing to the fact that *haber* is frequently equiparated with *talmid* - *b.Bab Bath* 75a; *p. Mo Kat* 3, 81d. However, he does not seem to address the question of this relationship in his long treatment of the *haberim* (119-56) and thus fails to work out what, if any were the practical differences between the two in the post-70 period.

[85]Meyer, 'Der 'Am ha-Ares', 198f, with reference to *b.Bab Mez* 33b; *b.Sanh 96a*. Oppenheimer, *The 'Am ha-Aretz*, 188-95, points to the political and social reasons underlying this change in the third century.

[86]*b. Erub* 53a and b. Oppenheimer, *The 'Am ha-Aretz*, 206f and 210, dismisses this as insignificant, but there must be some basis for it in tensions between the two provinces, however formalized it had become.

[87]Cf. G. Scholem, 'Towards Understanding of the Messianic Idea in Judaism', in *The Messianic Idea in Judaism and Other Essays on Jewish Spirituality*, New York, Schocken, 1971, 1-37, esp. 12f.

[88]Above, notes 10 and 11.

[89]Above, ch. 5, notes 55 and 6. We have also discussed the question of Galilean involvement in the Bar Cochba struggle, ch. 3, n. 65. Oppenheimer's evidence from rabbinic sources, *The 'Am ha-Aretz*, 207, n. 27. does not substantially alter the picture: *T. Bab Kam* 8:14 (destruction because of rearing of small cattle and trying of civil cases with only one judge); *p. Ta'an* 4, 69a (destruction of Galilean towns); *T.Peah* 7:1 (scarcity of olives because of Hadrian the wicked) etc. None of these passages speaks of Galilean participation in the war, but of course this does not preclude greater Roman presence in the province with the consequent social upheaval afterwards.

[90]The expression found in *M.Ab* 3:10: *battē kenesi' ōth sel-'ammēi ha-'ares*, is explained by Meyer, 'Der 'Am ha-Ares'. 175f, n.26, as referring to the first century C.E. situation in which the Pharisees had not yet taken over all the synagogues of Palestine, and which could still be used as places of secular activity (cf. above, n. 80). He surmises that these were to be found especially in Galilee. Cf. W. Schrage, art. συναγωγή *TDNT* 7 778-852, esp. 821-5 for the various purposes of the synagogue in Jewish life.

[91]*Jesus the Jew*, Cf. my review, *The Furrow*, (1974) 517-20.

[92]*b.Ber* 34b; *p.Ber* I, 9d. The former makes him a pupil of Johanan, but Vermes, 'Hanina ben Dosa', II, 61 thinks this unlikely. The more precise dating of his career depends on some association with Johanan during the latter's Galilean sojourn, which Neusner, *A Life of Rabban Yohanan*, 47, dates to between 20-40 C.E. Vermes, 'Hanina ben Dosa', II, 59-61, gives circumstantial evidence: the healing of Nehuniah's daughter (*b.Bab Kam* 50a) who was probably the ditch-digger mentioned in *M. Shek* 5:1, and so in the active service of the temple; according to *Qoh R* 1:1, he wished to send a stone to Jerusalem for the temple with his fellow townsmen. In other words the tradition places him in the pre-70 period.

[93]Vermes, 'Hanina ben Dosa', I, 38f; Büchler, *Types of Jewish Palestinian Piety*, 83-7; Safrai, 'The Pietists', 16.

[94]'Hanina ben Dosa', II, 61ff.

[95]J. Jeremias, art. 'Ηλ(ε)ίας , *TDNT* 2, 928-41, esp. 933f; Strack-Billerbeck, *Kommentar*, 4, 781ff.

[96]Cf. R. Meyer, *Der Prophet aus Galiläa*, Reprint Darmstadt 1970, 32-7, for a good summary of the Elijah traits in the Jesus traditions of the gospels: He instances the call of the disciples (*Mk* 1:16-20 = *1 Kgs* 19:19-21) the Gethsemane scene (*Mk* 14:32-42 = *1 Kgs* 19:3b-9b), and the unwelcoming Samaritans (*Lk* 9:52b-6 = *2 Kgs* 1:9-15); the raising of the widow's son at Naim (*Lk* 7:11-15 = *1 Kgs* 17:17ff).. Cf. also J.L. Martyn, 'We have found Elijah', in *Jews, Greeks and Christians. Religious Culture in Late Antiquity. Essays in Honour of W.D. Davies*, ed. R. Hammerton-Kelly and R. Scroggs, Leiden, Brill, 1976, 181-219.

[97]Hengel, *Die Zeloten*, 167-75, deals with the Jewish traditions linking Elijah with Phineas and the highpriesthood, pointing to the fact that such a tradition was current in first century Judaism but that the sages were critical of it.

[98]Vermes, *Jesus the Jew*, seeks to identify Jesus and Hanina as two Galilean *hasidim*. However, the stories about them cast in the Elijah mould would have had to have been developed in different circles, probably those of disciples, no matter how much each drew on popular religious beliefs. The Hanina cycle was criticized by more orthodox circles, and so could scarcely have been developed as a conscious attempt to counteract the Jesus cycle in use among Christian missionaries.

[99]Safrai, 'The Pietists', 25f on the משנת חסידים .

[100]'The Rise and Function of the Holy Man in Late Antiquity', JRS 61(1971) 80-100, esp. 82f.

[101]G. Theissen, 'Wanderradikalismus: Literatursoziologische Aspekte der Uberlieferung von Worten Jesu im Urchristentum', ZTK 70(1973) 245-71, has underlined how strongly this factor comes into play in understanding Jesus' sayings on discipleship and their meaning for early Christian missionizing. The rural color of the sayings makes it likely that the Galilean ministry of Jesus and the first Christian missionaries there is their immediate background.

[102]P. Brown, 'Sorcery, Demons and the Rise of Christianity' in *Witchcraft: Confessions and Accusations*, ed. M. Douglas, ASA monographs 9, London, Tavistock, 17-45, though dealing with late antiquity has some things to say that are pertinent to the earlier period also, when he writes thus, "'My thesis is that a precise malaise in the structures of the governing classes of the Roman Empire (especially in its eastern, Greek-speaking half) forced the ubiquitous sorcery beliefs of ancient man to a flash-point of accusations in the mid-fourth century . . . . . These (accusations) reach a peak at a time of maximum conflict in the 'new' society of the mid-fourth century'. Again we can back-date Brown's comments to our own period, since a similar wave of uncertainty struck the Jewish governing class, much earlier, even if the fear of the sorcerer's powers did not reach the same proportions as in the late empire. Cf. the following note.

[103]Hengel, *Jud und Hell.*, 239f, notes the widely diffused picture of Solomon as a magician in the Greco-Roman period: *Ant* 8:44f; *Syr Bar* 77:25; *Ps Philo* 60:2. He notes that this was an area where Jewish and hellenistic syncretism readily collaborated. Cf. *op. cit.*, 438ff on Essene magic. Note also S. Baron, *A Social and Religious History of the Jews.* 10 vols. 2ed., Philadelphia, Jewish Publication Society of America, 1952, 2, 21 and 336, n. 25. It is worth noting the interest of the 'sophisticated' Herodians in sorcery, *War* 2:112; *Ant* 20:142, as well as the common people, *Life* 149. This may well explain Antipas' desire to see Jesus based on reports about him, *Lk* 23:8, as well as the charge by the Scribes and Pharisees from Jerusalem that Jesus cast out demons by Beelzebul, *Mk* 3:22. Beelzebul may refer to a Syrian god, 'Lord of the Heights'; cf. Taylor, *St. Mark*, 238f. M. Limbeck, 'Jesus und die Wirklichkeit des Bösen', in *Teufelsglaube*, H. Haag, Tübingen, Katzmann, 1974, 273-318. esp. 294-303, has put forward a different understanding of this charge. He maintains that in the light of contemporary Jewish practice a charge that Jesus was in league with Satan would have made very little sense. Instead Beelzebul 'lord of the dwelling' was a name for Jesus himself which his opponents had concocted (cf. *Mt* 10:25), since Jewish exorcists were practicing in the name of Jesus and the matter was of some concern in orthodox circles (cf. *Mk* 9:38f; *Ac* 19:13f). This would also explain the point of Jesus' counter-question: 'by whom do your children cast them out?' (*Lk* 11:19). It was only when the controversy was translated into Greek that the significance of the name was mistaken and Beelzebul identified with the 'prince of demons'.

[104]J.Z. Smith, 'The Temple and the Magician', in *God's Christ and his People. Studies in Honour of Nils Alstrup Dahl*, ed. J. Jervell and W. Meeks, Oslo, Bergen, Tromso, Universitetsforlaget, 1977, 233-47, esp. 238f, with an approving citation from P. Brown, *The World of Late Antiquity*, London, Thames, 1971, 102f. Brown had written that the emergence of the holy man at the expense of the temple marked the end of the classical world, and Smith claims that the holy man was already filling the same sociological niche since the second century B.C.E.

[105]For Hanina there is the tradition of *Qoh R* 1:1, concerning his desire ot send a stone (presumably for the rebuilding program), yet his reluctance to go there himself. His sphere of action was outside and largely independent of the temple. For Jesus' relationship to the temple cf. above, ch. 7, n. 89 and the article by Theissen cited there.

[106]E. Rivkin, 'The Internal City: Judaism and Urbanisation', despite our earlier reservations about his understanding of the Pharisees (above n. 2), has a brilliant analysis of the Pharisaic phenomenon within Judaism in relation to the dominant urban trend of the hellenistic world.

CHAPTER NINE
CHRISTIANITY IN GALILEE

In the last chapter we saw that Pharisaic, and later rabbinic *halakhah* received only a limited response in Galilee despite the best efforts of Jerusalem-based Pharisaic scribes and the teachers of Jamnia.[1] The presumption must be that these latter did have a greater degree of success given the changed religious climate of Judaism after 70. Yet it is natural to think of Christianity as the major alternative to the *halakhah* that we felt impelled to look for, given the fact that its founder Jesus was a Galilean and initially at least enjoyed great popularity there. Besides, all the gospels written about the year 70 or afterwards have a very positive attitude towards Galilee, especially in contrast to Judaea, and in particular Jerusalem. Indeed there is evidence that 'Galilean' had quite early become a name for Christians in certain quarters, and continued to be so used as late as the fourth century Emperor Julian.[2] In this chapter we intend to examine the place of Christianity within the religious spectrum of Galilee against the background and circumstances already discussed, hopefully making some contribution to this much discussed question of primitive Christian history.

I
CHRISTIANITY IN GALILEE

One might be forgiven for assuming that we have plenty of information on Christianity in Galilee, seeing that the term 'Galilean Christianity' is so frequently employed in contemporary New Testament studies.[3] Yet the truth is that *direct* information on the existence or nature of Christianity in the province is extremely limited, if for the moment we leave aside the gospels, for reasons that will emerge later.

(i) *Acts and Galilean Christianity.*

Within the New Testament *Ac* 9:31 is the single piece of direct information that we have, and given the fact that this is a Lukan summary, one of the many that punctuates this writing as a

344

literary device of the author, it cannot be said to give too much away.[4] The church throughout all Judaea and Samaria and Galilee had peace, 'and it was built up and advanced in the fear of the Lord and in the consolation of the Holy Spirit'. Considering the author's silence about Galilee at points in his narrative where we might have expected the province to be mentioned, e.g. 1:8; 8:1.4, one can only judge this particular reference as unexpected. Apparently Luke assumes that Christianity was well established in Galilee at the time of Paul's conversion, but it is unfortunate that he has given us no clue as to how it got there or the extent of its popularity. We have no story of any evangelism there, legendary or otherwise, comparable to those of Philip in Samaria and Gaza (*Ac* 8) or Peter at Lydda, Joppa and Caesarea (*Ac* 9:32-10:48). In this respect the absence of any mention of Galilee in the notice of 8:1 is most surprising. The Hellenists who were dispersed from Jerusalem in the persecution that followed Stephen's martyrdom are said to have gone to Judaea and Samaria (does κατὰ τὰς χώρας mean the country districts of these provinces?) preaching the word. One might have expected that they would have also gone to Galilee, but this is not mentioned, and we are left to conjecture the reasons for this omission on their part, or Luke's, or both.

This lack of information about post-Easter evangelism in Galilee has led to a variety of opinions on the matter, all of them starting from the most tenuous of arguments, the one from silence. In general, two differing views are put forward, depending on whether or not Luke's picture of the early church emerging in Jerusalem is considered reliable or not. For those who accept the trustworthiness of the account in *Acts*, at least in its broad lines, a variety of reasons are given for Luke's failure to treat of the beginning of the church in Galilee. The most simple explanation is that he did not have any information on the matter or that it did not suit his concerns, since he does not tell us about emerging Christianity at other centers also, notably Damascus and Rome, even though his narrative presupposes Christian communities in these cities.[5] It has also been suggested that Galilee is included in his references to Judaea at 1:8 and 8:1.4 since his geographical understanding of Judaea seems to be more in line with Roman usage covering the whole Jewish territory, *pace* Conzelmann.[6] Another suggestion is that the evangelization of Galilee was in

Luke's view the work of Jesus (cf.*Ac* 10:37) and so the gospel narratives about the missions of the Twelve and the Seventy(two) (*Lk* 9:1-6; 10:1-11) would already have given his views on the matter.[7] Or again, it is pointed out that 'the brothers of the Lord' are, as early as *1 Cor*, presumed to have been engaged in evangelism (9:5f) and Galilee, their homeland, is the most natural place to locate their activity, even if Luke passes it over in silence, not to destroy his picture of the church emerging around the Twelve in Jerusalem.[8] There is nothing inherently improbable about any or all of these positions, and should we accept Luke's view of the matter Galilean Christianity must have played a rather insignificant role in the subsequent development, unless of course, he has suppressed evidence, something he has in fact been accused of.

At the same time a number of scholars are not particularly convinced by Luke's presentation of Christian origins based on the Twelve in Jerusalem. Arguing from the prominence of Galilee in the post-resurrection narratives of all four gospels these writers contend that Galilee, not Jerusalem was the first home of Christianity, and that it was from there that the evangelism of Palestine as a whole, including Jerusalem, took place.[9] Certainly, weighty arguments can be given for making the Galilean rather than the Jerusalem appearances the earlier ones, since it seems unlikely that they would have been fabricated later once the Jerusalem tradition had been established.[10] Besides it is possible to argue that within the present gospels, with the exception of Luke, there is a subordination of the Jerusalem appearances to the Galilean ones. Mark gives no Jerusalem appearance but promises that the Risen Lord will be seen in Galilee (*Mk* 16:7), and Matthew has the Jerusalem appearance to the women serve as an introduction to the Galilean one to the Twelve which establishes the universal mission (28:16). Assuming that *Jn* 21 refers to the Sea of Tiberias, this appendix, stemming from the Johannine circle, gives the final word to Galilee also. Indeed it could be argued with good reason that Luke too is familiar with this tradition, but that for his own reasons he has projected it back into the ministry of Jesus (*Lk* 5:1-11).

Even if it were established that the Galilean appearance was the earlier and more authoritative one, this does not of itself prove that the true home of post-Easter Christianity was in Galilee, however. Given the apocalyptic atmosphere of early Christianity that all seem agreed on, nothing would be more natural than that the Twelve should have returned to Jerusalem, there to await the second coming of Jesus - an attitude exemplified later in the action of many Jews at the time of the Jewish revolt (*War* 6:285f). However, other features of early Christianity are seen to reflect Galilean conditions, real or imagined, also. Thus, while Schmithals is prepared to consider Bauer's idea that the Hellenists came from Galilee he himself prefers Antioch and locates the Hebrews in Galilee. Kasting also locates the earlier expansion center of Christianity in Galilee and argues that this movement went in two different directions, one to Jerusalem centered on the Twelve and the other to Syria where one can detect the first hellenizing tendencies of early Christianity. It was from Galilee also that Damascus must have been evangelized according to Kasting and the many local Galilean traditions of Mark's gospel are for him a pointer that Christian communities were established at these centers.[12] Thus in the earliest evangelist's view Galilee would be the starting place for the Gentile mission rather than the place of the Parousia.[13]

(ii) *Rabbinic Evidence.*

Before pursuing this line of inquiry further, namely the significance of Galilee in the gospels, we shall do well to search for other signs of Christianity there, even from later times. One thinks immediately of the *minîm* of rabbinic literature as evidence for *some* Christians in Galilee in the second and third centuries. The problem with these references is that it is not at all certain that *minîm* always refers to Jewish *Christian* heretics, and the nature of the polemical remarks does not help very much in deciding the issue.[14] Two examples from the early Tannaitic period are, however, illustrative of Christian confrontation with Rabbinic Judaism, and they may well serve as pointers to the situation in Galilee, at least for our period. Both deal with a *mîn*, Jacob, whose place of origin is variously described as Kefar Sekhaniah (Sikhnin) or Samma - the former, the more likely, being identified with Sogane in Galilee, the latter a southern Judaean town.[15] In all probability he was a Galilean Christian, for it is with him that R. Eliezer had the discussion in Sepphoris that eventually led to the latter's arrest by the Romans. The first tradition about Jacob has him as a miracle worker, possibly following the model of the Galilean Jewish *hasîdîm* already discussed.[16] His healing powers are to be repudiated even if it means losing one's life,something that a certain ben Damah learned to his cost too late (*T.Hull* 2:22f; *p.Shabb* 1,14b; *b Ab.Zar* 27b). In the second tradition he and R. Eliezer agree on a matter of *minnût* (according to one version, *T. Hull* 2:24) or torah (according to another, *b Ab. Zar* 16b-17a). This incident made R. Eliezer suspect in the eyes of the authorities and he was arraigned before the *hegemōn* or governor, probably in Caesarea. Lieberman has argued that the incident should be dated to the persecution of Christians by Trajan and is therefore an indication that they were to be found in Galilee after the year 100 C.E.[17] Perhaps more interesting still is the fact that Jacob was anxious to dialogue with the influential rabbi on matters of torah and Eliezer could be anonymously denounced, presumably because there was still no clear distinction between Jew and Jewish Christian in Palestine despite the condemnation of the *nozrîm* and *minîm* that had been introduced into the eighteen benedictions some time before this.[18] This can also be corroborated for the slightly earlier period of Domitian, when, according to Eusebius' report taken from Hegesippus, the grandsons of Judas, the brother of the Lord, were also delated to the officer (*evocatus*) and brought before the emperor because they were of the family of David (*Eccles. Hist.* 3,19). One gets the impression from these texts - and it can be no more than that - that by the end of the first and early in the second century C.E. there was a minority of Christians in Galilee who were Jewish Christian in origin and background and who were gradually being isolated within the total Jewish community because of the growing rift between church and synagogue.

(iii) *Later Christian Sources.*

Following this lead further, it is important to discuss the place of Galilean Christianty in the context of Palestinian Jewish Christianity as a whole, especially in view of the fact that the post-70 heretical forms of this latter, namely the Ebionites and the Nazoraeans, have been used to document the attitudes of the former by Lohmeyer and other scholars. The links that can be forged between the two are dependent on a number of facts about which it unfortunately does not seem possible to have complete certainty. The main problem concerns the flight of the Jerusalem Christians to Pella prior to the first Jewish revolt as reported by Eusebius (*Eccles. Hist.* 3, 5), something that has been rejected by a number of scholars as a later legend, but which has been ably defended most recently by M. Simon.[19] However, even allowing for the reality of the flight, it still seems a rather long way from this, presumably, small group of fugitives, some of whom may have later returned to Jerusalem,[20] and the groups described by Epiphanius. Our question then becomes twofold: what are the links between pre-70 Jerusalem Christianity and the later Christian sectarians of the Transjordan region and secondly, how are Galilean Christians connected with one or both movements?

Looking at the problem from the perspective of the later situation, two different groups appear in the Transjordan region, the Ebionites and the Nazoraeans. Even this fact alone suggests that they cannot all be seen as the direct descendants of the Jerusalem Christians, unless we suppose that there were different segments in that church even after the hellenists had been pushed out. But there is considerable confusion concerning these two sects and their interrelationship. Jerome (*Letters* 112,13) says that the Jewish title for all Jewish Christians was Nazarenes (Nazorenes), a designation that is found commonly for all Christians in Persian and Mohammedan sources.[21] Epiphanius concurs with this (*Pan.* XX, 4) while also describing a Jewish Christian and a Jewish sect of a similar, if not the same name. Even though he attempts to distinguish between these two sects, treating of the Ναϭαραῖοι in chapter XIX (cf.XXIX,6) and the Christian Ναʒωραῖοι in chapter XXIX, one cannot avoid the impression that his description of the Jewish Christian sect is colored both by his account of the earlier Jewish one and that of the Ebionites to follow in chapter XXX.[22] This naturally raises questions about the indentity of the Christian Nazoraeans, who unlike the Ebionites, do not appear in any of the other early lists of Christian heretics. This is especially true seeing that Epiphanius does not seem to have even read their gospel, much less have had any personal contact with them. In one part of his treatment of the

Christian Nazoraioi he suggests that they were a very early Jewish group devoted to circumcision and the law who came to believe in Jesus and named themselves after his native place (XXIX, 5), whereas later he says that they originated from the Jewish Christians who fled to Pella and that they flourished in Boröa (Aleppo) in Coele-Syria as well as in the Dekapolis around Pella and in a town of Batanaea called Cochaba (XXIX, 8).[23] This geographic location is all the more significant since it is in the same region that the Jewish Nasaraeans are located (XIX, 1), and subsequently the Ebionites are also explicitly associated with the town of Cochaba (XXX, 2). The Christian Nazoraioi, according to Epiphanius, followed the Jewish law in regard to circumcision, the sabbath and other ceremonies, yet he is not able to impute to them any heretical views on the nature of Christ and apparently they followed a full version of Matthew's gospel in Aramaic, as well as the Jewish scriptures (XXIX, 7,9). Indeed Epiphanius uses very little of his usual rhetorical invective against them and one is justified in asking if in fact these Nazoraioi are not orthodox Jewish Christians, isolated perhaps in the Coele-Syria region from the mainstream of Christian development, especially in the Pauline churches, and so retaining close links with their Jewish past.

Despite the similarity of names they do not seem to have had anything in common with the Jewish sect described by Epiphanius, whose rejection of the Jewish cult and acceptance of a secret revelation to Moses rather than the (falsified) public one of the Pentateuch suggest a fringe Jewish gnostic group. Thus, it could be argued, that the Christian Nazoraioi, are in fact the legitimate heirs to the Jerusalem Jewish Christians who retained or applied to themselves an early name for the Jewish followers of Jesus of Nazareth current among their Jewish brothers (cf. *Ac* 24:5) and were attached to a Hebrew (Aramaic?) version of Matthew's gospel. Indeed this conclusion seems supported by an examination both of extant fragments of this gospel and the Nazoraean interpretations of Isaiah to be found in Jerome's commentary on that prophet. Though their gospel is apparently later than canonical Matthew, its divergencies from it could possibly be explained by the fact that they shared common sources that had been reworked in different circles, while the citations of Isaiah also suggest a different circle to that of canonical Matthew.[24]

Our information on the Ebionites is considerably more substantial, but no less problematical, partly due to the other early testimonies to their existence such as Justin Martyr, Irenaeus, Origin, Eusebius and Jerome, as well as Epiphanius, and partly due to the complex *Ps. Clementine* collection, one of whose sources, the *Kerygmata Petrou* has been identified with the Ebionite *Periodou Petrou dia Klementos* mentioned by Epiphanius (XXX,15).[25] Apparently their name is not to be derived from a founder Ebion but is a latinized form from the Greek of an original Aramaic word *'ebyônāyê'*, meaning 'poor'.[26] They too are located by him in the same general area as the Nazoraioi, including the town of Cochaba, and are also associated with the flight to Pella of the early Christians (XXX,2). They followed a truncated version of the gospel of Matthew that omitted the story of the virgin birth in line with their doctrine of Jesus being only a man. It has been suggested that Epiphanius has confused their beliefs and practices with those of the Elchesaites, an early Christian gnostic-baptist group, but it may well be that the various lustrations which he attributed to them (XXX,17) are due to real contacts with that baptist group and indeed with the Essenes also.[27] Despite their heretical beliefs concerning the person of Christ and their dualistic ideas it is natural to see them closely related to the Nazoraioi, and one of the two different groups of Ebionites mentioned by Eusebius (*Eccles. Hist.* 3, 27) and Origen (*Contra Celsum* 5, 61.65) - one being more orthodox the other heterodox - have been identified by some scholars with the Nazoraioi, even though they are not explicitly so called by these writers.[28] One doctrine of the Ebionites which Epiphanius mentions identifies them more closely with the pre-Christian Nasaraioi rather than with the Christian Nazoraioi, however, namely the rejection of the Jewish cult by both groups. Thus the Ebionite Gospel has the following saying attributed to Jesus: 'Because I have come to destroy ($\kappa\alpha\tau\alpha\lambda\hat{\upsilon}\sigma\alpha\iota$) the sacrifices; and if you do not cease from sacrifice, the wrath shall not cease from you' (XXX,16). Clearly, however the relationship between the Ebionites and the Nazoraioi is to be worked out, it is important to

recognize that a number of external influences have been operative on their different development in the Transjordan region
during the second century. One cannot therefore take their beliefs
and practices *in toto* and use them for determining trends and
attitudes in early Christianity, and more specifically in Galilean
Christianity, as Lohmeyer seeks to do.

Before dismissing the attempt as totally futile however, we must
return to our question already posed - are there any links that can
be forged between this later, part heterodox, part orthodox but
conservative Christianity and Galilee? To answer this a number
of factors have to be considered. Firstly, on the assumption that
some historical credence may be given to the story of the flight to
Pella, it is legitimate to look for earlier traditions in this Trans-
jordanian Christianity belonging to pre-70 Jerusalem Christians,
but it is not clear how these could be termed Galilean even if they
could be isolated with confidence. Here the influence of James,
the brother of the Lord, looms very large in any weighing of the
evidence. On the one hand it is usual to identify him with Galilee
initially, seeing that he was not a member of the group of the
Twelve, yet on the basis of *Gal* and *Ac*, as well as later sources, it is
at Jerusalem that he had his greatest sphere of influence, and the
testimony of *Gal* 2 suggests that this was relatively early. Mention
has already been made of *1 Cor* 9:5 as witnessing to an actual
mission of the brothers of the Lord, yet this is an inference from
the text and there is no explicit mention of a mission there.[29] In
the time of Domitian, we have noted, others of the Lord's family
were living in Galilee (presumably, but not explicitly stated,
Eusebius *Eccles. Hist.* 3, 19), and they are delated, not for active
missionary propaganda but because they belonged to the house
of David, as it was claimed. More promising is the evidence of
Julius Africanus (c. 170 C.E.) in his letter to Aristides, namely
that the *desposynoi*, that is the cousins of the Lord 'from the
Jewish villages of Nazara and Cochaba traversed the rest of the
land expounding their genealogy from the book of Chronicles
as far as they went' *(Eccles. Hist.* 1,7.15). The context is a discussion of the differing genealogies of *Mt* and *Lk* and it is possible
that in the second century different people laid claim to being
cousins of the Lord within the Jewish Christian community,
relying on the differing genealogies.[30] What is significant for

our purposes is that Nazareth and Cochaba are explicitly mentioned, the latter we have seen, being one of the centers of Naz-
oraioi/Ebionite Christianity in Transjordan. Does this mean that
there were direct links in the second century between the Galilean
and Nazoraean Christians of Transjordan? Admittedly, it is
precarious evidence upon which to build an hypothesis about
the situation a century earlier. Perhaps contacts were established
with Nazareth by the Nazoraioi of Cochaba in an attempt to
establish their legitimacy by tracing their origins not just to the
town to which they owed their name, but also with the brothers
of the Lord within the Christian community there. However,
this can only remain conjecture in the absence of other information and clearly there is not sufficient evidence in this notice
alone on which to base common theological ideas and practices.

Mention has already been made of the gospel of the Nazoraioi
and their interpretations of Isaiah preserved by Jerome, which
may provide a further lead towards understanding this group
and their background.[31] Their interpretation of *Is* 8:23f is particularly significant since the M.T. and the LXX, followed by
Matthew (4:15f), all have a clear reference to Galilee, but the
Nazoraioi apparently understood the passage differently.
According to Jerome they interpreted the passage as follows:

> With the coming of Christ and the success of his preach-
> ing first the land of Zebulun and Naphtali was freed
> from the errors of the Scribes and Pharisees, and he re-
> moved the heavy yoke of Jewish tradition from their
> necks. Afterwards through the gospel of the apostle
> Paul, who was the last of all the apostles, preaching
> was made heavier, that is it was multiplied, and the
> gospel of Christ shone among the borders of the gen-
> tiles *(termini gentium)* and the way of the universal
> sea *(viam universi maris)*.

The Nazoraioi distinguished two stages of the Christian
mission, that of Christ to the Jews in the land of Zebulun and
Naphtali and that of Paul to the gentiles. Galilee is no longer
mentioned explicitly, but instead becomes *'termini gentium'*
'the borders of the gentiles', presumably based on Symmachus
who renders *galîl haggoyîm* (M.T.) by ὅριον τῶν ἐθνῶν.[32] It might
appear then that the Nazoraioi, following Symmachus, regarded

Galilee as gentile territory, but in reality they have purposely omitted mentioning it, calling the territory instead by its biblical name 'Land of Zebulun and Land of Naphtali'. They thereby rejected its gentile connotations and associated themselves with the more ancient Iraelite traditions concerning it.

In their opinion Galilee was evangelized by Jesus, who, had opposed the Scribes and Pharisees and their traditions, a theme found in their interpretations of *Is* 8:14 and 8:19-22 also.[33] This would corroborate the notice of Julius Africanus just discussed, whereby it may be surmised that they sought to establish their own relationship to the Lord and his family directly. In that event it was this concern to establish their legitimacy rather than the need to forge links with existing churches in Galilee at a later date that determined their interpretation of the Isaian text. We can only presume that either there were no churches there at that later stage or that they were sufficiently insignificant in terms of the great church not to warrant such links being established.

The attempt of Lohmeyer to reconstruct other aspects of Galilean Christianity on the basis of alleged Ebionite practices and beliefs has been largely rejected. One reason has already been suggested, namely, the later development of the Ebionites in the Transjordan region does not make them the most trustworthy repository of pre-70 Jerusalem Christians, even if it were allowed that a strong Galilean influence had entered that church with the emergence of James as its leader. The ideal of poverty for example, both as practiced by the Ebionites (*Pan.* XXX,17) and the early Christians of Acts (*Ac* 2:44f; 4:32-35) has now to be seen against the background of the Qumran documents, where poverty, or at least a community of goods, was an integral part of Jewish ascetical practice, even before Jesus.[34] It seems arbitrary then to suggest that this was a distinctive feature of Galilean Christianity, even if the form it took for the wandering preachers of the Galilean mission (cf. *Mt* 10:9f) and the settled community of Jerusalem differed according to life-style and circumstance.[25] Even more problematic is the Son of Man expectation and the anti-temple attitudes attributed to the Galileans on the basis of Hegesippus' account of the death of James

(*Eccles. Hist.* 3, 23), according to which James the Just, proclaiming Jesus as the returning Son of Man, refused to divert the people from coming to him 'the door of salvation' and was cast down from the temple and clubbed to death. Schoeps has argued that underlying this account and that of the *Anabathmoi Iakobou* to be found in the *Ps. Clementine Recensions I*, 66-71 are the remains of the Ebionite Acts, referred to by Epiphanius (*Pan.* XXX,16), according to which James also spoke against the temple, the sacrifices and the altar of incense. These, it is maintained, contain good, old tradition, according to which it was James not Stephen, who led the first attack on the Jerusalem cult. The Ebionites, for whom James was the most important figure from the apostolic age, would have preserved this tradition, admittedly using it in a confused mixture of fact and legend as they came to write their own Acts of the Apostles in the second century, counteracting the Lukan version which had been composed for the great church.[36] We have already seen that the anti-cult stance of the Ebionite Jesus has more in common with the pre-Christian Jewish Nasaraioi, or for that matter with the Qumran Essenes, than it has with the Nazoraioi, who in this regard are more representative of the Jerusalem Christians' attitudes, including James, as these are described in Acts (*Ac* 2:46; 3:1; 21:20-26). In an earlier chapter we have seen the attachment to the temple of the Galilean Jews and it would come as some surprise to find such a strong anti-temple thrust among Galilean Christians of this stock, given Jesus' own attitude to the temple.[37]

This attempt to find good pre-70 traditions in second century material is not convincing, but even should it prove possible to achieve a satisfactory source analysis of the *Ps. Clementines* it will call for much greater sifting of evidence before specifically Galilean traditions can be confidently identified based on these sources alone. Indeed Epiphanius himself would seem to preclude any identification of Ebionite Christianity with Galilee, for in chapter XXX of *Pan.* he has a lengthy excursus on one Joseph of Tiberias who, though belonging to the intimate circle of the Patriarch, became a Christian and was granted permission by the Emperor Constantine to build churches at Tiberias, Diocaesarea (Sepphoris), Nazareth, Caphernaum and other places (XXX,4.11), where no churches had ever been previously built. Christianity in Galilee is certainly an underground minority in this account, which Epiphanius says he heard from Joseph himself when the latter lived in Scythopolis.[38] Besides, the Hebrew Matthew, a translation of John's gospel and Acts of the Apostles were also secretly kept by the Jewish Christians of Tiberias in their *genizah*. Certainly for Epiphanius Galilee is not the home of Ebionism nor does he presume any contacts between them and the Christians of the province.

Our search for evidence of Galilean Christianity has taken us from Acts of the Apostles to Rabbinic sources and the Patristic writings with largely negative results. We have found a Christian minority there, Jewish Christian in background and origin, possibly having contact with the Nazoraioi of the Transjordan region, where Christianity seems to have flourished both in its heterodox and orthodox but conservative forms. We must now turn to the gospels as a final possible source for Galilean Christianity, since, it is alleged, they contain Galilean traditions of the post-Easter Galilean church.

II

THE TOPOGRAPHY OF THE GOSPELS
AND GALILEAN CHRISTIANITY

Lohmeyer's attempt to reconstruct Galilean Christianity based on what he conceived to be its authentic voices of a later period, namely the Ebionite and Nazoraean sources, has not won wide acceptance. In the light of our discussion of these sources one can easily recognise the weakness of his method in attempting to reconstruct earlier beliefs from later sources that have been in contact with alien and outside influences. Yet the question he posed, namely, how far it is possible to decipher the concerns of local Christian churches from the traditions of the gospels, remains very much with us and has received considerable attention through the use of form and redaction critical methods. In particular the geography of the gospels has been examined for its symbolic value, and the wide popularity of H. Conzelmann's study of Luke, stressing the theological relevance of its geography, may be taken as an indication of the importance of topography in contemporary gospel studies.[39] However, it does not mean that as yet a convincing methodology has been worked out for evaluating the geographical references of the gospels. For example, the geography of Mark's gospel has been interpreted in very different ways: as biographical reminiscences from the life of Jesus (Hengel); as having purely symbolic intent (Lohmeyer, Marxsen); or with reference to cultic and mission concerns of the early Church (*Ortsgemeinde Legitimierung*, Schille).[40] Clearly there is need to integrate the geography of the various gospels with the larger concerns of the Evangelists, keeping these various possibilities in mind, and we shall attempt therefore to interpret the references to Galilee and Galilean centres in this way. Hopefully such an examination will give some further hints about what, if any form of Christianity we may hope to find in Galilee and point the way for some concluding reflections of a broader nature based on the study of Galilean life which we have presented.

(i) The Gospel of Mark

The gospel of Mark is the obvious starting point since both Lohmeyer and after him Marxsen, consider the references to Galilee in this work to have a special significance in relation to early Christianity there. For the former the Markan Galilee is a larger territory than that normally associated with the name, including the Transjordan area as well as the districts of Tyre and Sidon and Caesarea Philippi—'a Christian Galilee, if one may so express it'.[41] From this starting point of the geography he goes on to develop the characteristics of Christian Galilee —a community awaiting the return of the Son of Man, and practising a similar ascetic to that of the later Ebionites. Marxsen also focuses on Galilee, seen as the place of the Parousia on the basis of 14:28 and 16:7, yet he does not feel free to postulate a native Christian community in Galilee, identifying Galilean Christians with those from Jerusalem who may have sojourned there on their way to Pella.[42] The gospel is written by somebody with a special interest in Galilee who summons Christians to meet the coming Christ there just as his earthly life was also a (secret) epiphany in Galilee. Marxsen claims that all the references to Galilee in the gospel are redactional, something that others too have underlined.[43] However, since four of these occur in chapter one, (vv.9.14.28.39) it would seem that for the Evangelist Galilee is closely associated with the preaching of Jesus (cf. κηρύσσειν of vv.14.39.45) rather than with his second coming.[44] It is the place of the good news as first proclaimed by Jesus and this has to be taken into account in any interpretation of the command to return there at the end of the gospel, especially if it is agreed that the work originally ended at 16:8 without any appearance of the Risen One.[45] The disciples and Peter, and with them presumably the Christian readers, are directed to Galilee to encounter the Risen Christ as Messiah and Son of God, who is the content as well as bringer of the good news according to 1:1 (cf. 8:29 and 15:39). Thus, interest in Galilee cannot be divorced from the concern for the proclamation of the church and its Christology in the present, however much that may be shaped by the hope of the coming Son of Man (cf. 14:62).[46]

This suggestion calling for the geography of the gospel—especially the references to Galilee—to be interpreted in the light of the larger concerns of the Evangelist sheds light also on the other important passage, 3:7ff, which, all are agreed, is a Markan summary in its present form, even if there is an underlying *Vorlage*. Its strategic location within the Markan framework is also widely conceded, representing a transition from the rejection of Jesus by the Jewish religious and political leaders (3:5f) to the formation of the inner circle of the Twelve who are to be at the centre of the stage subsequently (3:13-19).[47] In this list of places Galilee seems to be distinguished from the other geographic areas in that it is said that a crowd from Galilee 'followed', whereas those from the other regions came to him. But this is a natural way to describe the situation seeing that Jesus was actually then working in Galilee, and later he is said to have done a tour from Tyre through Sidon to the Sea of Galilee and into the Decapolis (7:31), to the unknown Dalmanutha (8:10), to Bethsaida (8:22) and to the territory of Caesarea Philippi (8:27). Clearly Mark does not intend to confine the movement of Jesus to Galilee, or suggest that he can be encountered as saviour only there (cf. 5:19f). Yet 3:7 does show clearly, contrary to Lohmeyer's view, that Mark does not identify

Galilee with the whole of northern Palestine, for he differentiates it from πέραν τοῦ 'Ιορδάνου and πέρι Τύρον καὶ Σιδῶνα . It seems natural, therefore, to relate the enumeration of places in these verses to the scene of the election of the Twelve which follows immediately and stresses the apostolic and missionary nature of their vocation (ἀποστέλλειν and κηρύσσειν v.14). It must remain a moot point whether Mark wishes to include the Christian communities known to him in his own day or simply wanted to paint a universal picture of Jew and Gentile as the appropriate mission field of the church. Even if the former were the case, it would not necessarily follow that he was pointing to a Galilean church, side by side with others, some of which we know of independently from *Acts* (2:3-7; Tyre; *passim*, Jerusalem). Galilee has already been identified by him as the place of the first proclamation of the gospel by Jesus, and at 3:7 it probably formed part of the *Vorlage* to which the final redactor has added the other place-names.[48] It could then be argued that it is in these places, not Galilee, that Christian communities are to be found for the Evangelist.

A consideration of the geographical data of Mark's gospel does not suggest that Galilee was important to him because it was the place of the expected Parousia or because it was an influential Christian centre in his day. Rather it was significant as the place of the first ministry of Jesus, which was an integral part of the gospel story, and had to be included in any authentic proclamation by the later church. Yet the Galilean happenings had to be properly understood and that explains why it is necessary to return there to discover their true meaning as Mark has presented it, illumined by the Easter experience. Unlike many contemporary writers Mark does not separate the Jesus of history and the Christ of faith and consequently he can present the ministry of Jesus' 'doing good' in Galilee in the light of the Easter faith in Jesus just as the present life of the church can be reflected in the problems and difficulties of the original group of followers.[49] Inevitably then, Galilee had to figure prominently in the Markan account but without thereby suggesting that it was the primary focus of the Evangelist's concern *when he wrote*. Though we cannot agree with Schille's highly imaginative reconstruction of Christian origins based on north

Galilean (missionary) lower Jordan (baptist) and Jericho (cultic) traditions, he is surely correct in emphasising against Bultmann that place and personal names in individual stories should not be considered late and legendary.[50] The one story in Mark that seems to be rooted to a definite geographical area in this way is that of the Gerasene demoniac (5:1-19) and the Evangelist links this and another cure to the Dekapolis region, 5:20; 7:31. This could suggest that that was the general area in which the gospel originated. Recently, H. Clark Kee has also suggested that region as the home of the Markan community on the basis of the socio-cultural patterns reflected by the work as a whole.[51] It is virtually impossible to reach anything like certainty on this question since other regions could equally well reflect similar patterns. For our purposes, however, the important inference seems to be that there is nothing in the topographical references of the gospel which demands that it be attributed to a Galilean Christian community, and much indicating that it should not.

(ii) The Gospel of Matthew

Turning next to Matthew's gospel we find that the command to meet the Risen Lord in Galilee is now explicitly linked to the mission, for the Twelve 'proceeded to Galilee to the mountain that Jesus had commanded them' (Mt 28:16; cf. v.7) there to receive their universal mission. The very mention of the mountain here tends to divert attention from Galilee as a geographical place of importance for Matthew and points instead to the Christophany and commission to follow. One thinks of Mt. Sion as the eschatological meeting place of 'all the nations' according to Jewish tradition.[52] Matthew seems concerned to show that though the mission of the church to all the nations originated on a mountain in Galilee rather than in Jerusalem his claims that this community is the messianic assembly are still valid. He was equally concerned to show in the infancy narratives how Jesus' association with the place came about (2:22f) and did not take from his Messiahship.[53] Does this apologetic approach suggest that Galilee was still important, or is Matthew concerned to vindicate the history of Jesus and the early mission?

Elsewhere, one's attention is drawn to the introduction to the public ministry of Jesus at 4:12-17 and its relationship to the subsequent presentation of that ministry in chapters 5-7 (word) and chapters 8-9 (deed). The notice that Jesus began his public ministry in Galilee after the arrest of John is common to Mark also, though Matthew's use of the verb ἀναχώρειν, 'to withdraw', may wish to suggest that it was not possible for him to conduct his ministry elsewhere.[54] Moreover, there are two significant additions to Mark. Firstly, he is said to have left Nazareth, where his previous permanent abode may be presumed to have been located (cf. 2:22f), and to have taken up residence (κατῴκησεν) at Caphernaum. This focus on Caphernaum is a particular concern of the Evangelist, for at 9:1 he describes it as Jesus' own city. Yet before concluding that Matthew knows of a Christian community there in his day one must take account of the woes uttered against it as well as Corozain and Bethsaida (11:20-24), in which Matthew over against Luke (=Q) stresses the judgment on Caphernaum in terms of the fate of Sodom. There were *some* Christians there it would seem, for, according to an admittedly late Jewish source (*Qoh R.* 1:8), Hananiah the nephew of R. Josua (c. 130 C.E.) was put under a spell by the *minim* of Kephar Nahum and so had to abandon the land of Israel for Babylon.[55] The story at least reflects a criticism of Jewish teachers who had dealings with Christians (assuming that they are the *minim* in question), but one need only surmise a small Christian group there that had now become clearly isolated from the synagogue, for such a situation to arise. Nor has archaeology been able to convincingly uncover any sizable traces of early Christianity at Caphernaum, beyond the suggestion of an early Jewish-Christian house church.[56]

More significant then is Matthew's second addition to the Markan source, the text from *Is* 8:23f, introduced by the standard Matthean formula for introducing his fulfilment texts. We have already noted the Nazoraioi's independent use of this text, related presumably to their own situation, and Matthew has also made certain adjustments to the LXX and M.T. texts. Thus there is a shift in tense from future to past to indicate that the event of salvation had already taken place. Furthermore the phrase ὁ λαός ὁ πορεύομενος has become ὁ λαός ὁ καθήμενος, pointing out that Jesus was the light for those actually inhabiting those parts, not those exiled from it as in the M.T. text.[57] Clearly for Matthew Galilee was the initial place of the gospel, because it was the place where the proclamation of Jesus first took place. Yet his citation and adaptation of the text of Isaiah suggests a vindication of his claims against Jewish objections, rather than a desire to extol Galilee as a sacred place.[58]

Does this mean that Galilean Christianity had little significance for him in his own day? Before definitely drawing this conclusion it is necessary to consider Matthew's handling of the other geographical data. At 4:23-25 he has composed a summary that is clearly intended as an introduction to the sermon and miracle activities of Jesus to be recapitulated by way of inclusion at 9:35-7. A detailed examination of the first of these summaries shows that we are dealing with a compilation based on traditional material drawn from several places in Mark combined with Matthean editorial writing.[59] While Galilee is still retained as the focal point of Jesus' ministry and following (vv. 23-25 based on *Mk* 1:15.28.39), a new element occurs at 4:24—his fame spread throughout all Syria (*Mk* 1:28 has 'throughout all the surrounding region of Galilee'). In the concluding list of places (v.25), based on *Mk* 3:7f, Idumaea and Tyre and Sidon are missing, but all are now said to follow him—from Galilee, the Dekapolis, Jerusalem and Judaea and from beyond the Jordan. At first sight it seems strange that Matthew drops all geographic references in the second summary at 9:35-7 especially in view of the fact that it seems to have been consciously constructed on the model of 4:23-5. We shall return to this point presently, but it is necessary first of all to evaluate the geographical data of the earlier summary. The mention of Syria seems to be particularly significant, however difficult it is to decide which precise territory is meant by this term. Its significance is even further enhanced if, as is widely assumed Matthew's gospel took its final form in the post-Jamnia period, for rabbinic evidence from this period shows a genuine concern to equiparate Syria and the land of Israel, and, as is well known, Matthew reflects a situation where church and synagogue are in the process of separating and engaged in bitter antagonism with each other.[60] The failure to mention Tyre and Sidon at v.25

may be due to the fact that they are included in 'all Syria' for at least they are retained elsewhere (15:21), whereas this is the only mention of the Dekapolis, based presumably on the Markan source, but omitted elsewhere at the parallels to *Mk* 5:20; 7:31, that is, *Mt* 8:34; 15:29. Presumably the reason for passing over this area in these later stories is his lack of concern with the development of the mission in that region, and his desire to confine the actual portrayal of Jesus to the land of Israel insofar as this was feasible, given the material he had to work with.[61]

We may now address the question previously posed, namely the absence of any geographic references in the summary of 9:35-7 which corresponds to 4:23-5. In particular 9:35 follows 4:23 verbatim except that ἐν ὅλῃ τῇ Γαλιλαίᾳ of the latter verse is replaced by τάς πόλεις πάσας καὶ τάς κώμας in the former; otherwise they are identical. Surprising as this omission seems, it is possible to explain it in the light of the succeeding chapter 10, the missionary discourse, which all recognise to be a Matthean conflation, at once stressing the particularity of the mission to Israel for apologetic purposes (10:5b-6.23) and yet reflecting its actual extension to non-Jewish areas also (cf. governors and kings, v.18). Galilee as the place of Jesus' ministry, which had to be vindicated by an appeal to Scripture, has receded somewhat from the Evangelist's perspective and instead the 'lost sheep of the house of Israel' or 'all the cities of Israel' are theological expressions for all the Jewish territory where the mission of Jesus and subsequently that of the church was conducted.[63] The rejection of this mission by Israel is consciously linked to the judgment of God on Jerusalem whose destruction is seen as the punishment of an unfaithful people and its city (23:29-39).[64]

Summing up Matthew's geographical data in relation to Galilee we can say that he recognises that it was the place of Jesus' ministry, at least initially, and this has to be justified in terms of Scripture. However, we have not found any further evidence of a particular interest in Galilee in this gospel. Indeed it could be argued that for Matthew Palestinian concerns are a matter of the past which for the most part proved unsuccessful and thus the gospel is addressed to 'all the nations', an expression which does not positively exclude the Jews, but has its sights

consciously set towards a universal mission.[65] The warnings
and advice for intending missionaries in chapter 10, especially
vv.10-23 has been understood to reflect the contemporary
situation at the time of the writer, but even these fit as easily
into a hellenistic background as a Palestinian one, despite
the apparent restriction of the mission to Israel. It is not surprising then that many scholars have suggested Syria rather
than Palestine as the place of composition of this gospel, despite
its Jewishness. This would explain the mention of Syria at 4:24,
the single piece of geographic information not found in
Matthew's sources. It would also help to explain the polemical
tone of the gospel in relation to the synagogue when we remem-
ber that the post-70 rabbis wished to equiparate Syria with the
Eretz Israel. Of course Syria is still a very broad area and it seems
difficult to pin it down more accurately.[66] Perhaps the popularity
of the gospel of Matthew with the Nazoraioi and the Ebionites
can be taken as a pointer that it was in southern Syria that the
gospel was written and continued to circulate. At all events it
seems we can exclude Galilee either as its place of composition
or as the area of most current concern to the Evangelist when
he wrote.

(iii) The Gospel of Luke

Mention has already been made of Conzelmann's thesis
which highlights the geography of Luke in relation to his
theology of Jesus' ministry. In particular Galilee is supposed to
correspond to the Satan-free period of the ministry when the
official witnesses were gathered for the journey to Jerusalem. As
a distinct region in Palestine Galilee has no importance for
Luke and this explains why the geography is rather hazy, representing, in Conzelmann's view, a picture of the country 'from
abroad' where Galilee and Judaea are adjacent and Samaria
is thought to border both of them.[67] A number of objections
have been made to this understanding of Luke. For one thing
the Satan-free period has been challenged by a number of critics
as putting too much emphasis on the ἄχρι χαιροῦ of Lk 4:13
in the light of other data concerning Satan during the ministry.[68]
More significant for our present purposes is the conception of

Luke's geography as being highly symbolic, though hazy from a topographical point of view. Davies' point is well taken, that if Luke had such a vague conception of Galilee and Judaea as distinct regions topographically, it is highly unlikely that he would have given to each such a charged symbolic significance.[69] Furthermore, Conzelmann's handling of such passages as 9:51-6 (rejection by Samaritan villages) and 13:31-3 (response of Jesus to the threat of Herod in Galilee), which are essential to his overall thesis of a journey is not wholly convincing and so we must attempt to reassess Luke's geographical data with special reference to Galilee.[70]

By contrast with Matthew, Luke can take for granted the fact that Galilee is Jesus' homeland (*Lk* 1:26; 2:4.39) and he does not have to give any scriptural or other rationale for it.[71] Likewise the initial phase of the public ministry is located in Galilee following Mark (*Lk* 4:14), and even though rejected at Nazareth he can still continue to minister in that region transferring instead to Caphernaum, 'a city of Galilee'—a specification that is an addition to the source (*Lk* 4:31 = *Mk* 1:21). Again at 5:17 we hear that Pharisees and teachers of the law had come from Galilee and Judaea and Jerusalem to hear Jesus. Conzelmann sees this geographic combination as a fixed pattern in Luke for Jesus' ministry, while at the same time arguing that 'Judaea' is the correct reading for the place of Jesus' activity at 4:44, basing himself on 7:17 and 23:5, where 'Judaea' seems to stand for the whole area of Jesus' activity and sphere of influence.[72] It is on the basis of these references that he claims that while Galilee and Judaea are clearly distinguished as regions, only the latter has any significance of its own for Luke—because of Jerusalem. However, it seems that a less forced understanding of Luke's geography is possible on the assumption that Judaea stands for the whole of Jewish territory. Even if Galilee had its own tetrarch at the time of Jesus' ministry (cf. 3:1), by the time of Luke's writing the whole Jewish territory consisted of the province of Judaea, and this is the meaning that would be intelligible to Luke's non-Jewish readers. Galilee is still remembered as having been a separate region at the time of Jesus, but is now part of a larger whole. Thus Luke can easily slip from Judaea simply to Galilee and Judaea, (4:44 contrasted with

5:17) but this should not be interpreted as a lack of interest in the former area as a region of its own at least in relation to the time of Jesus. Conzelmann himself is prepared to accept that explicit mention of Galilee as part of Judaea at 23:5 is to prepare for the trial before Herod to follow, but wrongly, in my view, describes this as a pre-Lukan formula.[73] Again we hear of the women who had come up with him from Galilee (23:49.55), and the Twelve are twice described as Γαλιλαῖοι at Ac 1:11; 2:7 just as Jesus too is a Γαλιλαῖος (22:59; 23:6).

It seems unwarranted then to suggest that Luke has no interest in Galilee, 'apart from the Galileans'. Admittedly there are no appearances in Galilee and Mark's command to the disciples to return there is changed into a recollection of what Jesus had told them while he was still in Galilee (24:6).[74] However, the reason for this concentration on Jerusalem has been recognised by all commentators as being related to the Lukan scheme of history and the concern to portray the mission inaugurated from there. Consequently this cannot be interpreted as a rejection of Galilee or its place in the Christian story of beginnings as told by Luke. At the time of writing the second volume his concern is to show that the gospel was not tied to Palestine but was truly universal in its scope, and so it can be fairly surmised that Galilee is passed over as relatively unimportant to his present concerns. For that very reason the almost casual mention of the region at Ac 9:31 might be considered all the more significant in terms of possible Christian communities there, however little it suits Luke's overall purpose to describe their origin and nature. However, when one weighs all the evidence for Luke's treatment of Galilee it is difficult to avoid the conclusion that it is important to him as the historical starting point of Jesus' ministry. As is well known, Luke is anxious to tie the witness of the church to that of Jesus, and one of the ways he achieves this is by stressing the importance of the Twelve as witnesses of Jesus' life 'from the beginning', to the virtual exclusion of Paul from the role of an apostle.[75] It is highly significant then that their Galilean origins are twice alluded to (Ac 1:11; 2:7), as is that of the women who in his account are the first to spread the word of the resurrection. Far from showing no interest in Galilee as a region this seems to be a very conscious highlighting of it, no matter how much its significance lies in its association with the beginnings of Luke's story, and so is connected with the past rather than the present. In stressing the historical rather than the symbolic significance of Galilee we are not of course necessarily suggesting that everything reported by Luke in Galilee actually happened there. It is the *fact* of Galilee rather than the *details* that is important for him, and so as in the case of the other Synoptists, we must leave as an open question the reality of a specific Galilean Christianity in Luke's day. All we can say is that if such actually existed it was of less concern to Luke than was the fact that Galilee was enshrined in Christian tradition as the starting place of Jesus' ministry.

(iv) The Fourth Gospel

A recent trend in the study of the Fourth Gospel has been concerned with uncovering the various stages in the life of the community from which this work emerged.[76] This gospel is particularly inviting for such an approach since it has long been recognised that it reflects a quite distinctive and original development within primitive Christianity to be attributed not just to one individual author, but to a circle or group, sometimes more precisely described as a school.[77] Moreover, because of the highly distinctive theological re-interpretation of Jesus' ministry it is considered possible to detect community interests and concerns within the work, in a way that *Redaktionsgeschichte* has been successfully applied to the study of the other gospels. The debate about the cultural and religious matrix of this church has also been much discussed, fluctuating from hellenistic to Jewish, with several intermediary positions. More recently the view seems to be prevailing that Johannine Christianity had its origins close to Palestinian Judaism, and naturally this has thrown the geography of the gospel into much greater prominence.[78]

Since our concern is to uncover evidence that points to a Galilean Christian community we shall once again confine ourselves to the way in which geographical data are handled, conscious that each reference has to be examined in the light of various layers within the work. In this regard Samaria is a particularly outstanding example because of the positive response to Jesus on the part of the Samaritans in chapter 4, a section that seems to have been inserted into a previously existing framework of a journey from Judaea to Galilee (4:1-3.43). A number of scholars have argued for definite traces of Samaritan influences in John's gospel as a whole, ranging from language to theology. In particular the study of W. Meeks has shown that the notion of the prophet-king—central to Johannine Christology —may have been worked out in interaction with Samaritan Jewish circles that thought of Moses in these categories.[79] More recently another influential student of John, R.E. Brown, has also advocated similar influences in the early stages of the Johannine community in terms of a large influx of Samaritan Christians into the original group that had originated in Baptist circles. These new arrivals acted as a catalyst in alien-ating the original group from orthodox Judaism and in develop-ing a 'high' Christology that stressed the strangeness of Jesus as the one 'from above' and his community that 'is not of this world'. Brown also postulates a Gentile element in this circle, pointing to such passages in the gospel as 7:35 and 12:20-23.[80] Since Christianity in Samaria originated with the hellenists who had been expelled from Jerusalem following the death of Stephen (*Ac* 8:4-25) it is natural to connect these with the gentile influences in the Johannine church, something that seems to be reinforced by the anti-temple polemic of Stephen and the new understanding of worship that the Samaritan Christians have acquired (*Jn* 4:21).[81] A sure indication that these Samaritan Christians are fully integrated into the Johannine circle comes at *Jn* 8:48, where the ironic taunt (usually indicating the truth of the assertion at another level for John) is thrown at Jesus: 'Are we not right after all in saying that you are a Samaritan, and possessed besides?' Significantly, the latter accusation is denied by Jesus, but not the former, since the epithet Samaritan can be 'positively appropriated' not merely by the community but by its Christ-figure.[82]

Is it possible to view Galilee and the Galileans in a similar light? The opening reference to our territory occurs at 1:43 where it is said that Jesus transferred to Galilee, there to find other disciples after the original two had joined him from

John's circle while in the south. The commentators have recognised the syntactical awkwardness of this verse, and the most logical explanation is that a later redactor has introduced it into an earlier *Vorlage*, to stress the active role of Jesus in calling the first disciples, but also in our view, to make a positive association with Galilee from the very start.[83] This makes the first disciples Galileans, and one of them Nathanael (significantly from Cana, cf. 21:3) is described as 'an Israelite in whom there is no guile' when he professes Jesus as 'the Son of God, the King of Israel', and is promised still greater things, which will link heaven with earth in a new way. The fulfilment of this promise takes place at Cana which is chosen as the place of Jesus' first manifestation of his glory, leading to the faith of his disciples. It is described as Κάνα τῆς Γαλιλαίας in all, four times: 2:1.11; 4:46; 21:2—a concentration that can scarcely have been for purely geographic reasons. In particular the two Cana miracles are drawn closely together by the conscious recalling of the first in the introduction to the second at 4:46, which is subsequently described as a second sign (δεύτερον σημεῖον) which Jesus had performed on coming from Judaea to Galilee. Clearly in the mind of the author both episodes are to be equiparated as highly significant faith-events,[84] even if, as we shall see, there is need for a warning in the second instance. The royal official is capable of sharing in the faith experience of the disciples, for like the Samaritans of the previous episode but unlike the Jerusalem Jews of the succeeding one, he believes in Jesus' word (cf. 4:41.50; 5:47).

The second Cana sign calls for our special attention in view of its immediate context, for the assertion is repeated five times within the pericope that Jesus came from Judaea into Galilee: *Jn* 4:43.45.46.47.54. There seems to be a particular emphasis here, all the more significant seeing that the first two enclose the proverb, known also from the Synoptics: 'No prophet is accepted in his own (ἐν τῇ ἰδίᾳ) country', and the second notes explicitly that the Galileans received Jesus. The most obvious meaning of the proverb seems to be that, in contrast to the Synoptics, the Fourth Gospel regards Judaea, not Galilee (more specifically Nazareth) as Jesus' πατρίς, especially since the qualifier ἰδίος has clear echoes of the rejection already stated in the prologue (*Jn* 1:11).[85] Not all commentators accept that interpretation and various attempts have been made to bring it into line with the Synoptic use but none of them are overly convincing. Of special importance is the view that sees the succeeding miracle as an example of 'the unsatisfactory faith of the Galileans, a faith based on a crude dependence on signs and wonders', as Brown puts it.[86] This view of the episode is largely based on the negative tone of v.48: 'Unless you see signs and wonders (σημεῖα καὶ τέρατα) you do not believe'—a statement that has to be attributed to the final editor, as well as the more positive designation of the event as a σημεῖον in the full Johannine sense already alluded to.

There is an undoubted tension here but this can to a great extent be resolved by recognising that σημεῖα καὶ τέρατα refers to a faith based on an external display of miraculous power and has to be carefully distinguished from the full Johannine faith coming from the unique conception of sign that is proper to the Fourth Gospel.[87] Indeed the Galileans reception of Jesus can very easily be of the former kind as is explicitly stated at 4:45—they received him having seen all that he did in Jerusalem at the feast. This explains the emphatic tone of the warning (οὐ μὴ) of v.48 and the address which is in the second person plural (πιστεύσητε), appearing to ignore the 'blind' faith of the centurion in coming to Jesus initially. Not surprisingly a similar warning is addressed to the Galilean crowds at 6:26 after the first feeding miracle, and in view of the interest shown in 'the men of deeds' discussed in the previous chapter this type of enthusiasm in Galilee need not surprise us. What is important is the fact that individual Galileans can make the transition from the one type of faith to the other and be fully integrated into the discipleship community.

If this understanding of the story is correct it would seem to suggest two distinctive types of Galilean Christians within the perspective of the Fourth Gospel—those whose faith was regarded as essentially superficial and those who had come to full discipleship faith by recognising the true source of Jesus' glory through his signs, like his disciples at Cana. We can put this theory to the test by a consideration of *Jn* 7:40-52 where Galilee and Galilean attitudes come to the fore as part of a discussion about Jesus' nature. The overall context is the Feast of Tabernacles in Jerusalem, whither Jesus had gone (in secret) after rejecting his brother's suggestion that he leave Galilee, go to Judaea and show the world the mighty deeds he was doing—an attitude that suggests to the Evangelist that they did not believe in him (7:5). The passage of particular interest has a very definite structure—chiasmic according to Meeks.[88] Two titles of some significance to the Johannine community—the prophet and the Christ—are denied to Jesus by his opponents arguing from Scripture for precisely the same reason: because he is from Galilee. There is general agreement that Johannine irony is at play here—either Jesus does fulfill the requirements of Scripture but his opponents are unaware of it, or the question of his human origins is of no consequence since he is really from above, (cf. 7:27-9.33), a question that is ignored by his opponents though it is central to the argument. Insofar as Nicodemus is prepared to learn from 'the things which he has done' he is pilloried as being from Galilee for such open-mindedness, and the temple guard are equally repri-manded for their statement: 'no man has ever spoken like this man'. Only this people who is accursed and does not know the law could think such things. From a Jerusalem Jewish per-spective then one was as equally reprehensible as the other—being from Galilee or belonging to the *'am ha-'aretz.*

Before deciding that the passage is just another piece of anti-Jewish polemic however, it should be noted that the two titles under discussion here and thought of as representative of Galilean attitudes also occur in chapter 6 (v.14f), where an over-enthusiastic Galilean crowd, proclaiming Jesus to be the *prophet* wanted to take him by force and make him *king*. Jesus rejects these overtures and in the subsequent discourse shows that he is greater than Moses (the prophet according to *Dt* 18:18) in that he is uniquely 'from above' (v.38.41.46.57) and his human origins are of no consequence (v.42f). The scene is set in Galilee, 'in the synagogue at Caphernaum', but those who reject Jesus' claim are called 'the Jews' (vv.41.52), and many of his own disciples 'drew back and did not walk with him'. The parallels with chapter 7 are sufficient to suggest that Galilean Jews were prepared to attribute both titles to Jesus but in such a way that they were unacceptable to the Johannine author.[89] It is suggestive that it was in the Caphernaum synagogue that the seeds for the division were sown. It was there that Jesus had gone with his disciples 'and his brothers' after the first Cana miracle (2:12), but in contrast to the Synoptics Cana seems to be more important in the Johannine perspective.[90]

One gets the distinct impression that the debates between different Jewish parties and Jesus are representative rather than real so that in all probability we are dealing with issues that were of concern to the author towards the end of the first century, when church and synagogue had clearly separated. Our discussion of the place and significance of Galilee in John suggests that it differs somewhat from the Synoptic presentation in that genuine Galilean attitudes, both Jewish and Christian, are under discussion. It remains to test these observations in the light of the larger picture we have painted.

III
CHRISTIANITY IN GALILEE: SOME REFLECTIONS

Our search for positive signs of Christianity in Galilee, either from the gospels or from other early sources, Jewish and Christian, has not been very successful. *Possible* links with Jewish Christianity as this emerged in the Transjordan region in the later sources, are suggested through the figures of 'the brothers of the Lord', but these are extremely tenuous and certainly do not warrant Lohmeyer's attempted reconstruction. Presumably such Jewish Christians would be represented by the occasional *mîn* that we meet in rabbinic sources at various Galilean centres still closely allied to Judaism. The Johannine community offered slightly better prospects inasmuch as the positive evaluation of Galilee and Galileans in the Fourth Gospel alongside that of the Samaritans, points to another type of Galilean Christian whose cultural and theological orientation is different. It has been suggested that it is due to the influx of these latter that we are to explain the high Christology of this work which gave the Johannine circle a very distinctive outlook, radically differentiating it from synagogue Judaism and other Christian groups alike. If these, admittedly, slender indications have any merit two rather different versions of Christianity—not easily reconciled, if the Johannine community is any indication—may have been present in Galilee, at least as marginal minorities within the larger religious and cultural spectrum of the province. Some obvious questions immediately arise: where exactly are we to locate these Christian minorities within Galilean life?; and in the light of our study what roles were they expected to play in that society and what factors were likely to shape their beliefs and life-style? With such questions as these in mind it may at least be possible to check the truth or otherwise of our tentative findings in the earlier part of this chapter.

We have already touched on the role of Jesus of Nazareth in Galilean life more than once and it is with him that we must begin our treatment of early Galilean Jewish Christianity.[91] *A priori*, it is altogether probable that his attitudes and life-style would be closely reflected by other Galilean Jews who might have been prompted to attach themselves to this movement both during his life-time and immediately after his death. We have contended that Jesus refused to be cast in the role of a political agitator there, even when such intentions could have been imputed to his words and deeds. The figure of the *hasid* or holy man, operating in an unstructured way is certainly a more suitable model for understanding *some* aspects of Jesus' ministry in Galilee and we have seen that such figures had a very definite function within Galilean Jewish peasant life. At the same time it is only hypercritical scholarship that ignores or rejects Jesus' teaching as unimportant in locating him within the spectrum of Galilean life of his own day.[92] The sayings tradition is at least as 'primitive' as that of his mighty deeds, and hence a balanced assessment of the role of Jesus within Galilean religious life has to see him as *both* teacher and doer of mighty deeds. Given the way in which eschatological prophet, wisdom teacher and charismatic wonder-worker were inextricably interwoven in the popular religious imagination of first century Palestine[93] it was virtually impossible for Jesus to have engaged in his proclamation of the coming Kingdom without combining both aspects in his ministry, while at the same time not conforming to the recognised scribal teaching pattern that we know from the later Rabbinate. This does not prevent certain aspects of his ministry being more popular with different segments of the population, and no doubt his role as wonder-working charismatic caught the attention of the un-lettered country folk, corresponding to the image of the holy man discovered in the preceding chapter. It is quite possible then that there were those in Galilee whose attachment to Jesus was and remained of this superficial kind without being radically touched by his message or its claims and that after his death some of his followers were 'received' for the same reasons.[94]

What of Jesus' more permanent followers of Galilean origin? The fact that a whole body of sayings has been transmitted in his name advocating attitudes of homelessness, separation from the family and poverty as the sure way to enter the kingdom he proclaimed and share in the glory of the coming Son of Man, is a clear indication that such a life-style was actually adopted by some at least of his followers and taken extremely seriously by them.[95] Having its origins in Jesus' own attitudes this move-ment must have further developed after his death, as one can detect from the combination of his sayings with those of early Christian prophets within the same tradition. The difficulty that form criticism has experienced in deciphering authentic Jesus sayings from those of early Christian prophets who adopted his life-style is an indication of how closely these latter consciously imitated the former in every aspect of their ministry.[96] Like him their life-style was that of the wandering charismatic, combining in the name of the coming Son of Man prophetic-style utterance, wisdom instruction and mighty deeds in exchange for lodging and sustenance. The fact that these charis-matics adopted an itinerant life-style suggests at most a very loosely organised structure holding them together, yet their attachment to Jesus and his way ensured that the movement did not become an amorphous set of splinter groups. Adding further stability must have been members of local communities who were attracted by the message and style yet for economic or other reasons did not feel totally free to embark on it them-selves.[97] It does not seem possible or necessary to distinguish such communities clearly from Judaism at this early stage, given the variety of conflicting and messianic-style movements, both political and religious, within pre-70 Palestinian Judaism. That they were for the most part based in the rural areas seems to be reflected both by the tenor of the sayings themselves as well as the fact that major centres are ignored (e.g. Sepphoris and Tiberias) and others are presumed not to have been visited, Samaria, Tyre and Sidon or Caesarea (cf. *Mk* 7:31; 8:27; *Mt* 10:5b.6; 11:50ff).[98] However, the movement must have eventually attempted to set foot in the larger centres of population, possibly following a trend of flight from the land, where opposition from the more established form of Judaism just then attempting to establish itself could be expected. This explains the stress on the possibility of persecution that is such a strong feature of the sayings. Such persecution is the inevitable outcome of the prophetic call (*Mt* 23:34-6) yet it can be undertaken with equanimity since they will not have completed all the cities of Israel before the Son of Man comes (*Mt* 10:23).[99]

It is not possible to confine this movement of Palestinian Jewish Christianity to Galilee, or even to Palestine itself, since the Pauline letters as well as the *Didachē* suggests that it was a widespread phenomenon in early Christianity side by side with the more settled Pauline churches. Yet it would be equally naive to ignore the fact that Galilee was its natural home as the missions of the Twelve and the Seventy (two) in the lifetime of Jesus already strongly suggest.[100] If this is in fact true it is surprising that we have not met more definite traces of this movement in our other sources, where Galilee is for the most part a memory from the past, and we meet the occasional isolated *mîn* still functioning on the fringes of Judaism, but with no apparent Christian community there. This, coupled with the strong condemnation of some Galilean centres (*Mt* 11:20-4; *Lk* 10:13-5), would seem to suggest that the movement was largely a failure in Galilee and it is interesting to speculate why and when this might have occurred. The fact that James the brother of the Lord seems to have transferred (from Galilee) to Jerusalem may already suggest that the movement was no longer welcome in Jesus' homeland. However, the transfer could have been equally motivated by the religious attraction of the holy city, a constant factor for Galilean religious loyalties, we have seen. It is not certain whether James was himself an active member of the movement, for even though we hear of the brothers of the Lord possibly engaged in missionary activity (1 *Cor* 9:5; Euseb. *Eccles. Hist.* 1,7) later tradition suggests that his own piety was that of a *nazir* (Euseb. *Eccles Hist.* 2, 23.4-6). If James' departure from the homeland had been caused by the threat of persecution there, Jerusalem was scarcely the place to have attracted him, given the fate of Jesus and Stephen, the former at the hands of the Jewish religious aristocracy which was eventually to be instrumental in having James removed also (*Ant* 20:200). The likelihood then is that James came to Jerusalem because of the religious symbolism of the holy city, and he is scarcely representative of the common trend of the Jesus movement as a whole, among whom flight from Jerusalem was the advice that was most commonly shared (cf. *Mk* 13:16ff). The movement away from Jerusalem had already begun for another segment of early Christianity, the Hellenists, after the death of Stephen, and the probability is that it was these rather than the predominantly Aramaic-speaking prophets of Galilee that first carried on a mission outside Palestine. Presumably, however, contacts were established through a common life-style and because of persecution. The sayings of Jesus supported both groups and these were translated and adapted to new situations and circumstances.[101] Besides, the effects of the revolt in Galilee would have had serious consequences for the wandering charismatics there. The flight from the land as well as the wholesale slaughter must have robbed them of their natural constituency and support among the country people. By the end of the Galilean campaign the circumstances were ripe even for settled communities to emigrate in order to escape the consequences of the Roman settlement, and in view of the cultural and commercial links between Lower Galilee and the Transjordan, one naturally thinks of this region as one place of refuge.[102] Previously we have queried the common assumption that as a revolutionary centre Galilee was fertile ground for apocalyptic hope. Yet this general conclusion need not exclude an apocalyptic mood there among the followers of Jesus, especially given the fringe nature of these early Christian prophets as wandering radicals and their support communities. After 70 however, they would have had to compete with an intensified campaign by the reorganised

Judaism emanating from Jamnia as we have seen. We have already noted the mention of Syria in Matthew's gospel as a possible pointer to the home of that community, but we are reminded that the post-70 rabbis also showed interest in including Syria within the boundaries of Eretz Israel.[103] This concern could have been at least partially due to a desire to counteract greater activity by the Christian prophets there among the emegrées from northern Palestine, as the so-called 'Q community' moved to other centres, perhaps even Antioch itself. Such a depiction of events would explain how eventually a sayings tradition that reflects a loosely organised, prophetic-charismatic movement, apocalyptic in tone, yet particularist in scope, was eventually fused with traditions of an organised congregation with a universal mission outlook. At that point however, its Galilean roots were merely a memory from the past and the barest remnants of the type of Jewish Christianity it once represented survived as fossils that would prove no threat to the new aggressive Judaism that would soon invade the province.

The Johannine community reflected a rather different kind of Galilean Christian, and it remains to pursue that indication further. Our argument has been that the Fourth Gospel believes that Galilean Christians were capable of making the transition from a faith in Jesus as the wonder-working charismatic to a deeper one that recognises him as the Man from heaven who reveals the Father to them. In its present (finished) state the Fourth Gospel envisages a number of different attitudes towards Jesus—six in all according to Brown[104]—which can be taken to reflect the current situation of the writer's day. The average Galilean attitude is unsatisfactory as far as the Evangelist is concerned, as we have seen, since their enthusiasm for Jesus is based on his wonder-working achievement (4:48; 6:25). Their attitude is typified by that of 'the brothers of the Lord' who recommended Jesus to show himself to the world, since nobody did the works he did in secret. For the Evangelist, however, such sentiments are an indication of their unbelief (7:1-6). Yet there seems little to differentiate their views from those of the wandering charismatics that lie behind the sayings tradition, and clearly the Johannine circle has adopted a very critical stance towards other Christian groups that do not share their own point of view.[105] Yet the Galileans *as such* are never criticised, for in chapter 6 insofar as their murmuring in the synagogue at Caphernaum suggests non-acceptance of Jesus as the bread of life they are designated 'Jews'. Is the author thereby throwing out a line to Galilean Jews in the hope that others might join the Johannine circle, following the example of the first disciples and the royal official ($\beta\alpha\sigma\iota\lambda\iota\sigma\kappa\grave{o}s$) from Caphernaum? It is at least noteworthy that whereas many Samaritans come to believe in Jesus, a situation that is clearly the result of the community's missionary activity (4:35-8), no such influx of Galileans is reported even though the possibility is clearly envisaged.

If then Galileans are being encouraged to join a community one of whose constitutive elements had a Samaritan background —something that seems highly probable—the obvious question to be asked is, which stratum of Galilean society was most likely to be open to the idea? As both the gospels and Josephus make clear the animosity between Samaritans (that is the country residents of the territory) and the Galilean Jewish peasants was intense.[106] Religion was certainly a very important factor both in creating and fostering this hostility as our study has made clear and Christianity was no more likely to be successful in bridging this gap than Judaism had been before it, especially since Jesus and his followers were known as Galileans. We must then turn elsewhere in Galilee, and the Johannine author, describing the Caphernaum official as a $\beta\alpha\sigma\iota\lambda\iota\sigma\kappa\grave{o}s$ may have suggested the proper direction in which to look. In all probability this term is more original than the Q $\dot{\epsilon}\kappa\alpha\tau\text{o}\nu\tau\acute{\alpha}\rho\kappa\text{o}s$, and thus whether we translate it as royal official (Brown) or nobleman (Fortna) the likelihood is that there is question of a hellenised Jew of Herodian background or association.[107] As such he belonged to a culturally more mobile stratum of society than the peasants and if other sufficiently significant factors were operative a Samarian component would not have prevented his joining the Johannine community. It should be remembered that Christianity had come to Samaria *via* the Hellenists from Jerusalem, and so presumably bore the hallmarks of its origin. Accordingly, a common cultural ethos rather than a shared religious point of view may have been the motivating force that could have been expected to draw some Galileans at least to join the Johannine circle.[108] The religious situation of such hellenised Jews in Galilee in the Jamnia period may not have been all that congenial and the possibility must have been very real that some might find their spiritual home in a religious climate that considered the cultic aspirations of Judaism to have been fulfilled in Christ, rather than in one where a sharpening of *halakhic* demands replaced those aspirations. Johanan ben Zakkai had not had much success in Galilee earlier, and the Pharisaic delegation from Jerusalem made little progress in unseating Josephus. If the priestly and Herodian aristocracy of Galilee were prompted to seek an alternative religious symbol system in the post-70 period it could well be that a temple oriented theology had ultimately more appeal for them than 'the other way' of Johanan. As already documented, the Galilean *'am ha-'aretz* continued to be the bane of the rabbinic *haberim* in the second century, and the term was now applied to all—irrespective of social status—who did not adopt the way of the *halakhah* in all its rigor. Perhaps then, John's ironic dismissal of 'this people who does not know the law that is accursed' by the Pharisees (*Jn* 7:49) has a polemical *and* missionising edge to it, as the gospel circulated towards the end of the first century. The fact that we meet Ἰυδαῖοι in Galilee in ch. 6 even in the synagogue of Caphernaum, suggests that it is no longer an open field, like Samaria. Yet the fact that the first Galilean disciples had come to see greater things in Jesus than a purely Jewish understanding held out hope. In this regard we cannot forget the tantalising piece of evidence that Epiphanius records for us to the effect that τίνες τῶν ἀπὸ Ἰουδαίων πεπιστευκότων knew of a copy of the Fourth Gospel translated from Greek into Hebrew in, of all places, Tiberias. In the light of the above suggestions it may not be so strange after all.

We have deliberately entitled this final section of our study 'Reflections', since what has been said has had to be so conjectural and tentative as not to warrant the status of hypothesis. Nevertheless, enough correspondences have emerged between Galilean life in general and the scanty evidence we have about primitive Christianity's varied development to suggest that the latter can be plausibly fitted into the larger picture, lighting up several obscure areas of the development in the process. In terms of the overall purpose of this study, namely the understanding of a religious tradition within the larger social world to which it contributes and by which it is shaped, it is gratifying to be able to point to these correspondences as a small but significant confirmation of the overall thesis. At the same time, reflecting on early Christianity in the context of Galilean Judaism is a painful reminder that even in the very home of the Mishnah and Gospel the tensions between these two western religions that have cast such a dark shadow over our twentieth century were already in evidence in the first.

NOTES FOR CHAPTER 9

[1] Above chs. 7, II and 8, III.

[2] Christian writers used the name 'Galilean' for a Jewish sect, presumed to be the Zealots; cf. above, ch. 6, n. 6. Nevertheless it was also in vogue in New Testament times for the followers of Jesus: *Ac* 1:12; 2:7; 3:6; 4:10; 24:5; *Jn* 1:46; 4:45; 7:41f.52. The later in *Acta Theodoti Ancyrani*, c.xxxi dub Theodotus προστάτης τῶν Γαλιλαίων as a term of opprobrium. Julian had also used it in this way according to Gregory Nazianzus, *Orat.* IV. Cf. A. Harnack, *The Mission and Expansion of Christianity in the First Three Centuries*, English trans., New York, Harper Torchback, 1961, 401f, n. 1.

[3] Stemberger, 'Galilee-Land of Salvation?' in Davies, *The Land*, 409-38, has an excellent discussion of the topic, primarily directed at Lohmeyer's study *Galilee und Jerusalem*, FRLANT, 34, Göttingen 1936.

[4] J.A. Fitzmyer, in *Jerome Biblical Commentary*, eds. R.E. Brown, J.A. Fitzmyer and R. Murphy, London, Chapman, 1968, 166; H.J. Cadbury, 'The Summaries of Acts' in Jackson-Lake. *The Beginnings of Christianity*, 5, 392-402; J. Dupont, *Études sur les Actes des Apôtres*, Paris, Cerf, 1964, 425f, n.9, point to vocabulary and style.

[5] Dupont, *Études*, 413, n. 68, writes: 'un certain schématisme'; E. Haenchen, *Die Apostelgeschichte*, 13 ed Meyer's Kritische Exegetischer Kommentar über das Neue Testament, Göttingen, Vandenhoeck and Ruprecht, 1961, 280: 'über. dessen Christianisierung Lukas, anscheinend kein Material besass'.

[6] H. Conzelmann, *The Theology of St. Luke*, English trans. London, Faber, 1960, 40, n. 4. Cf. *Lk* 6:18 with *Mk* 3:8. At *Lk* 4:44; 5:17 Jesus is said to preach in the synagogues of Judaea. Cf. also *Lk* 23:5; *Ac* 10:37. Elsewhere, Conzelmann cites Pliny, *Nat. Hist.*, V, 70: 'Supra Idumaeam et Samariam Judaea longe lateque funditur. Pars ejus, Syriae juncta Galilaea vocatur'. (*Die Apostelgeschichte*, Handbuch zum Neues Testament, Tübingen, Mohr, 60). Josephus also uses Judaea to cover the whole of Jewish Palestine, cf. above ch. 2, notes 40 and 43.

[7] Conzelmann, *Die Apostelgeschichte*, 60.

[8] Eusebius, *Eccles. Hist.* 1,7, says that the family of the Lord, the *desposynoi*, from the Jewish villages of Nazara and Cochaba traversed the countryside and expounded the genealogy of their descent. Cf. Lohmeyer, *Galiläa und Jerusalem*, 52-4; W. Schmithals, *Paul and James*, SBT 47, English trans. London, S.C.M., 1965, 35; H. Kasting, *Die Anfänge Christlichen Mission*, Munich, Kaiser, 1969, 67.

[9] This is the starting point for Lohmeyer's thesis.

[10] Kasting, *Die Anfänge*, 82-6; Jackson-Lake, *The Beginnings*, 1, 302-4, opts for Galilee as the place of the earliest appearance, after which the apostles moved to Jerusalem for eschatological reasons. Lake, however, in a later note, (5, 7-16) wavers somewhat. For a modern discussion and a tentative hypothesis placing the earliest experience in Galilee, cf. R. Brown, *The Virginal Conception and the Bodily Resurrection of Jesus*, London, Chapman, 1973, esp. 99-110.

[11] Schmithals, *Paul and James*, 28f., n. 55, citing W. Bauer, 'Jesus der Galiläer', in *Festgabe für Adolf Jülicher*, Tübingen 1927, 16-34, here, 32f. Schmithals himself believes that the church of the Hellenists was located in Antioch first, and sees Nicolas of Antioch, a proselyte and one of the seven, as an important bridge person with the Jerusalem church. M. Hengel, 'Die Ursprünge der Christlichen Mission', NTS 18 (1971) 15-38, esp. 27, n. 42, and 'Zwischen Jesus und Paulus. Die 'Hellenisten', die 'Sieben' und Stephanus', ZTK 72(1975) 151-206, has shown in great detail the presence of hellenistic influences in Jerusalem prior to Christianity, and therefore exposed the weakness of Schmithals' position.

[12] *Die Anfänge*, 89-95, following Schmithals, but based on very general views about the nature and extent of hellenism in Galilee.

[13] G. Boobyer, 'Galilee and Galileans in St. Mark's Gospel', BJRL 35(1953) 334-48, had already attacked Lohmeyer's position, pointing to such passages as *Ez* 47:10

(LXX) where Galilee is the land of gentile salvation rather than the place of messianic appearances. Cf. now Stemberger's critique of both Lohmeyer and Marxsen, 'Galilee – Land of Salvation?', esp. 415 ff.

[14] The chief texts have been collected by R.T. Herford, *Christianity in Talmud and Midrash*, Reprint, Clifton, New Jersey, 1966, but the evidence is treated rather uncritically. Cf. also, A. Büchler, 'Uber die *minim* von Sepphoris und Tiberias in 2 und 3 Jh', *Cohenfestschrift*, Judaica, 1912, 91-102, K. G. Kuhn, 'Gilgonim und Sifre minim', in *Judentum, Urchristentum, Kriche, Festschrift J. Jeremias*, Beih. ZNW 26, Berlin, Töpelmann, 1964, 24-61, is critical of both positions. On p. 55. he points out that the story of Imma Shalom, the sister of Rabban Gamaliel II coming before a Christian judge who uses the gospel, *b. Shabb*, 116a and b, is impossible in first century Palestine. Against Büchler, he claims that the parallelism between the rabbinic anecdotes e.g. in *b. Sanh* 38a and b and Justin's dialogue with Trypho, shows that the former are controversies with hellenistic Christians and not Jewish Christians as Büchler had maintained (*art. cit.* 39, n. 32).

[15] Klein, *Neue Beiträge*, 21, and Schlatter, *Geschichte Israels* 366.

[16] Above, ch. 8, III.

[17] The relevant text and a discussion about its tradition is found in Neusner, *Eliezer ben Hyrcanus*, 1, 400-3. S. Lieberman, 'Roman Legal Institutions in early Rabbinics and the *Acta Martyrum*', JQR 35(1944) 1-57, esp. 19-24, dates the episode before Trajan's letter to Pliny. It is unlikely to have happened after his excommunication, against Herford, *Christianity*, 142, since his disciples gathered around him.

[18] On the dating and the original text of the *birkath ha-minim*, which apparently included Jewish Christians, cf. K.G. Kuhn, *Achtzehngebet, und Vaterunser und der Reim*, Tübingen, 1950, 18ff; cf. also W. Davies, *Setting of the Sermon on the Mount*, 274-6.

[19] M. Simon 'La migration à Pella. Légende ou Réalité?' RSR 60(1972) = *Judéo-Christianisme. Recherches historiques et théologiques offertes en homage au Cardinal Jean Daniélou*, 37-74, taking special account of the arguments against its historicity advanced by J. Munck, 'Jewish Christianity in post-Apostolic Times' NTS 6(1959/60) 103-116, esp. 103f; G. Strecker, *Das Judenchristentum in den Pseudoclementinen*, Berlin 1958, esp. 229-31; and Brandon, *Jesus and the Zealots*, 210f; Simon proposes changing the date to 62 C.E. immediately after the death of James, and this would not do any violence to Eusebius, since he (or Hegesippus?) has linked the episode to the outbreak of the Jewish war in a tendentious manner, pointing to the judgment of God on Judaism.

[20] Simon, 'La migration', 52f, argues that the accounts of the election of Symeon, the son of Clophas as James' successor, (Eusebius, *Eccles. Hist.* 3, 11; 4, 22) at least indicate the return of some Jerusalem Christians, even though the church was subsequently subordinate to that of Caesarea. Eusebius' account could then be seen as an attempt to establish its orthodoxy over against the Ebionites. H. von Campenhausen, 'The Authority of Jesus' relatives in the Early Church' in *Jerusalem and Rome*, H. von Campenhausen and H. Chadwick, Facet Books, History Series 4, Philadelphia, Fortress, 1966, 1-19, regards the whole account as based on the concerns of Eusebius' own day, and is at pains to show that the idea of episcopal succession that is suggested is a later fabrication. Even granting this however, the reports at least indicates a Jerusalem church after 70, and Simon's point would still be valid.,

[21] The adjectives Ναζωραῖος and Ναζαρηνός appear in the gospels and *Ac*, the former being preferred by *Lk*, *Mt* and *Jn* and the latter by *Mk*. As applied to Jesus it is equivalent to ὁ ἀπὸ Ναζαρέθ (cf. *Ac* 2:22 with 10:37; *Mt* 26:71 with 21:11; 2:3). It is natural therefore to derive the name Nazoraioi as applied to the early Christians from the native place of their founder, despite various attempts to discredit such a derivation. G.F. Moore, 'Nazarene and Nazareth', Appendix B, *The Beginnings of Christianity*, 1, 426-32, has responded to such attempts. He notes that the name for Jesus in Jewish sources is ישו הנוצרי and even though a problem arises as to how

ע can be rendered by ṣ in Greek, Moore believes that no more recondite argument is required than the false linking of Ναζωραῖος with Ναζιραῖος (nazir), something that would have been facilitated if Epiphanius is correct about the pre-Christian Jewish sect of the Ναζαραῖοι. Cf. also Harnack, *Mission and Expansion*, 401-3, n. 1.

[22]H.J. Schoeps, *Theologie und Geschichte des Judenchristentums*, Tübingen, Mohr, 1949, 19f, following A. Schmidke, *Neue Fragmente zu den Judenchristlichen Evangelien*, Leipzig 1911, (T.U. 37,1), rejects this report as nothing but a collection of different traditions, fused together here by Epiphanius, but with little historical value beyond the fact that there was a 'great church' group of Nazoraioi in Beröa. He thus identifies the Nazoraioi and the Ebionites of Transjordan. However, this seems an unnecessary rejection of all the evidence concerning the Nazoraioi, for, as A. Hilgenfeldt had pointed out, they are decidedly different from the Nasaraeans of ch. XIX, *Judentum und Judenchristentum*, Reprint Darmstadt, 1966, 83-9, esp. 87. Besides the heretical, 'zum teil', Ebionite views of the Nazoraioi are not as evident as Schoeps maintains. Simon, 'La migration' 47-9, argues that the Christian Nazoraioi are the continuation of the Jerusalem church, whereas the Ebionites are one element of that church, mingled with the pre-Christian Nasaraeans, who also wanted to claim their parentage in the Jerusalem church and had their own version of this in the Ps.-Clementine literature. A.F.J. Klijn, 'The Study of Jewish Christianity', NTS 20(1974/5) 419-31, esp. 429f, avoids the term heretical and speaks of vulgar Christianity, sharing a variety of ideas partly influenced by religious developments in the Greco-Roman world.

[23]Jerome, *De Vir. Illus.* 3, also located them in Boröa, but J.N.D. Kelly, *Jerome* New York, Harper and Row, 1975, 65, believes that he did not have access to their gospel, despite his claims, for he could not have failed to notice the discrepancies with Matthew's.

[24]P. Vielhauer, 'Jewish Christian Gospels', in *New Testament Apocrypha*, ed. R. Hennecke and W. Schneemelcher, English trans., London, Lutterworth 1963 and 65, 1, 117-65, following M. Dibelius, *From Tradition to Gospel*, English trans., New York, Scribner, 21, thinks that the gospel of the Nazoraioi is an expansion in Aramaic of Greek *Mt*, since from the point of view of *traditionsgeschichte* its expansions are secondary and not reflections of an Ur-Matthäus. However, A.F.J. Klijn, 'Jerome's Quotations from a Nazoraean Interpretation of Isaiah', *Judéo-Christianisme*, 241-55, has correctly pointed out that a common background of sources, reworked in different circles, would best explain the similarities and differences in the use of *Is* by *Mt* and the *Gospel of the Nazoraeans*. Cf. in particular his conclusions and suggestions, 254f. Vielhauer's view is based on a too rigid notion of what constitutes a tendency or development of a tradition.

[25]Schoeps, *Theologie und Geschichte*, 14-21, arguing for the use of the *Ps-Clementines* as a source for Ebionite history; cf. below n.36. Cf. also Hilgenfeldt. *Judentum und Judenchristentum* and A.F.J. Klijn and G.J. Reinink, *Patristic Evidence for Jewish-Christian Sects*, Leiden, 1973.

[26]J. Fitzmyer, 'The Qumran Scrolls, The Ebionites, and their Literature', originally published in TS 16(1955) 335-72, reprinted in *Essays*, 435-80, from which page references are given; here 438.

[27]Thus Fitzmyer, 'The Qumran Scrolls', 444ff, n. 17, following J. Thomas, *Le Mouvment Baptiste en Palestine et Syrie, (150 a. J.-C. -300 apr. J.-C.)*, Gembloux, Ducolet, 171-83, against Schoeps, who seeks to exclude all gnostic influences from the Ebionites, attributing them to the Elchesaites instead. As Fitzmyer notes, Epiphanius is aware of a difference between Ebion and the later Ebionites, which may be due to these latter's contact with the Elchesaites.

[28]Fitzmyer, 'The Qumran Scrolls', 442-4, even though he admits that there is some difficulty with the identification.

[29]This is correctly observed by L.E. Elliot-Binns, *Galilean Christianity*, S.B.T. 16. London, S.C.M. 1956, 65, against those who assume such a mission, e.g. Schmithals, *Paul and James*, 35, Kasting, *Die Anfänge*, 67, Lohmeyer, *Galilaa und Jerusalem*, 68.

[30]Cf. above, n. 20 on the continuing influence in the family.

[31]Klijn, 'Jerome's Quotations from a Nazoraean Interpretation of Isaiah'.

[32]Klijn, 'Jerome's Quotations', 244; cf. Jerome, *In Isaiam*, 121. Symmachus seems to regard Galilee as border country, translating *Joel* 3:4 ὅρια, and *Ez* 47:8 τὸ μεθόριον τὸ ἀνατολικόν. This suggests to Schoeps, *Theologie und Geschichte*, 275, n. 2, that he himself lived in the north or east of Palestine.

[33]Klijn, 'Jerome's Quotations', 250, n. 46, suggests that this indicates a time when they had broken with official Judaism.

[34]Fitzmyer, 'The Qumran Scrolls', 476f, and his more recent, 'Jewish Christianity in Acts' in the Light of the Qumran Scrolls', *Essays*, 271-303, esp. 284-8.

[35]Cf. Theissen's underlining of the socio-economic situation presumed by the Jesus' sayings, 'Wanderradikalismus'.

[36]This is the burden of a lengthy excursus in Schoeps, 'Die Frage Ebionetischer Acta Apostolorum', *Theologie und Geschichte*, 381-456. For a survey of the source criticism study of the Ps-Clementines in general, and his own cautious remarks about the feasibility of the enterprise, cf. Fitzmyer, 'The Qumran Scrolls', 447-53. More recenty J.L. Martyn, 'Clementine Recognitions, 1, 33-71, Jewish Christianity and the Fourth Gospel', in *God's Christ and His People*, 265-93, has reopened the question with special attention to a possible relation between the Recognitions and the tradition of the Fourth Gospel. He concludes that the author of Recognitions knew canonical Acts and a piece of tradition, also known in the community of the Fourth Gospel, which had been fashioned in the situation of Jewish Christians being tried before the *Beth Din*. The author, a skillful literateur, reworked these into a vivid account, but this should not mislead us to think that he was preserving accurate information from the first century. (p. 391).

[37]Above, ch. 7, n. 89.

[38]Martyn, 'Clementine Recognitions', 295, n. 58, notes this evidence also, but is doubtful if it can be made to mean that the Fourth Gospoel was read and interpreted by *non-gnosticizing* Jewish Christians.

[39] *The Theology of Saint Luke.* This study is partly based on his earlier, unpublished Tübingen dissertation (1951), *Die Geographischen Vorstellungen im Lukasevangelium.* Several studies of R. H. Lightfoot had already raised the question in the English speaking world: *Locality and Doctrine in the Gospels*, London, 1938; *The Gospel Message of Mark*, Oxford Paperback, 1962.

[40]Hengel, 'Zwischen Jesus und Paulus', 164, n. 48, writes: 'Die Evangelien geben für unsere Kenntnis galiläischer Gemeinden kaum etwas her, sondern nur für das Wirken Jesu in Galiläa'; cf. Lohmeyer, *Galiläa und Jerusalem*, 13f, and W. Marxsen, *Der Evangelist Markus.* Studien zur Redaktionsgeschichte des Evangeliums, FRLANT 67, Göttingen 1956, 12-4; G. Schille, 'Die Topographie des Markusevangeliums, ihre Hintergründe und ihre Einordnung', ZDPV 73(1957) 133-66, esp 138f.

[41] *Galiläa und Jerusalem*, 27. Stemberger, 'Galilee—Land of Salvation?' 415-21, shows that there is no warrant for such an extended understanding of Galilee, either in *Mark* or the contemporary sources.

[42] *Der Evangelist Markus*, 54f, 76; *Introduction to the New Testament*, English trans. Oxford, Blackwell, 1968, 138f; Davies, *The Gospel and the Land*, 222-35, effectively critiques the view of N. Wieder, *The Judaean Scrolls and Karaism*, London, 1962, that Galilee was the place of the Messiah according to Karaite sources; Klijn, 'Jerome's Quotations' 251, n. 46, cites the *Gospel of the Hebrews* to the effect that because the Galilean tribes were first into exile, they would be the first to receive the light of salvation, but he doubts if there was any explicit mention of Galilee in the text in question.

[43] *Der Evangelist Markus*, 35-59; Lohmeyer, *Galiläa und Jerusalem*, 26; J. M. van Cangh, 'La Galilée dans l'Évangile de Marc: un Lieu Théologique?', RB 79(1972) 59-76, esp. 68-72. Stemberger's attempt to challenge this position is not altogether successful, since even when some references can plausibly be attributed to the tradition, they too must be interpreted in the light of the overall emphasis of the finished work. ('Galilee—Land of Salvation', 431-5).

[44] *Mk* 9:30, the second prediction of the passion taking place 'in secret' in Galilee does not contradict this position, but rather confirms it since it points to the future when the Galilean gospel will be understood in the light of the Jerusalem experience. The verse is certainly redactional as N. Perrin, *What is Redaction Criticism?* Philadelphia, Fortress 1969, 44, shows.

[45] Cf. B. Metzger and others, *A Textual Commentary on the Greek New Testament*, United Bible Societies, London and New York, 1970, 122-6; W. Farmer, *The Last Twelve Verses of Mark*, S.N.T.S. Monographs 25, Cambridge. Univ. Press, after examining internal and external evidence favours the view that the long ending comes from the redactor, Mark.

[46] A number of recent studies stress the importance of εὐαγγέλιον as determinative of the content of *Mark*, pointing out that at 8:35 and 10:39, losing one's life or doing something for the sake of (ἕνεκεν) Jesus and the gospel are equiparated. Cf. Marxsen, *Der Evangelist Markus*, 83-92; P. Lamarche, 'Commencement de l'Évangile de Jésus Christ,'*NRT* 102(1970) 1024-36; R. Schnackenburg, 'Das Evangelium im Verständnis des ältesten Evangelisten' in *Orientierung an Jesus. Zur Theologie der Synoptiker*, ed. P. Hoffmann, Freiburg, 1973, 309-24, esp. 317f; L. Keck, 'The Introduction to Mark's Gospel', NTS 12(1966) 352-70.

[47] In my study, *The Twelve: Disciples and Apostles. An Introduction to the Theology of the First Three Gospels*, London, Sheed and Ward, 1968, 63-72 and 81-90, I have discussed the redactional activity of Mark in terms of the location and formulation of this passage.

[48] For a discussion of the tradition and redaction of these verses, both stressing the pre-Markan *Vorlage*, cf. L. Keck, 'Mk 3:7-12 and Markan Christology', JBL 84(1965) 341-58; K. Stock, *Boten aus dem Mit-Ihm Sein*, Analecta Biblica 70, Rome, P.I.B. Press, 1975, 55-65. The number of textual variants are already indicative of the awkwardness of the redactional activity, which has not been recognised by Taylor, *The Gospel according to St. Mark*, 55, n. 37, who tries to remove the difficulty by ignoring the difference between Galilee and the other places mentioned.

[49] This point was already forcefully made by J.M. Robinson, *The Problem of History in Mark*, SBT 21, London, S.C.M., 1957. More recently the disciples in Mark have been the focus of much attention as indicative of the Markan ecclesiology: T. Weeden, 'The Heresy that necessitated Mark's Gospel', ZNW 59(1968) 145-58; P. S. Minear, 'Audience Criticism and Markan Ecclesiology' in *Neues Testament und Geschichte, Festschrift Oscar Cullman*, Tübingen, Mohr, 1972, 79-90; E. Best, 'The Role of the Disciples in Mark' NTS 23(1977) 377-401.

[50] 'Topographie des Markusevangeliums', 137f, and elsewhere in his writings; for a presentation and critique of Schille's method of gospel study, cf. W. Feneberg, *Der Markusprolog. Studien zur Formbestimmung des Evangeliums*, SANT 36, Munich, Kösel, 1974, 79-119.

[51] H. Clark Kee, *Community of the New Age. Studies in Mark's Gospel*, Philadelphia, Westminster, 1977, 100-105.

[52] Cf. *Mt* 5:1; 15:29; 17:1. Davies, *Setting of the Sermon on the Mount*, 60, after a careful examination of the arguments for an exodus typology in *Mt*, doubts that there is any conscious reference to Sinai.

[53] K. Stendahl, 'Quis et Unde? An Analysis of Mt 1-2', in *Judentum, Urchristentum, Kirche*, 94-105, esp. 97-9; R. Brown, *The Birth of the Messiah*, New York, Doubleday, 1977, esp. 179f develops Stendahl's insight further, that Matthew's concern in ch. 2 is to answer the type of objection encountered in *Jn* 1:45f; 7:52, namely ubi? (where?) and unde? (whence?) does the Messiah come from. Earlier 106f, he had pointed to the literary links between Mt 2:22f and 4:12-16, suggesting the same concerns for the start of the ministry—the transfer to Caphernaum is substantiated by the expression ὁδὸν θαλάσσης in the Scripture text.

[54] This would appear to be a favourite verb of Matthew, probably reflecting the theological move from Israel to the nations as a theme of his work: Mt 2:12.13.14.22; 4:12; 9:24; 12:15; 14:13; 27:5; that is 9 times, compared with one usage each by Mark and John and two by Luke in *Ac*.

[55] Cf. Herford, *Christianity in Talmud and Midrash*, 215.

[56] G. Foerster, 'Notes on Recent Excavations at Caphernaum', IEJ 21(1971) 207-11, is critical of V. Corbo's too ready assumption that he has uncovered a first century house church beneath the octagonal building of a later date, *The House of St. Peter at Caphernaum*, Publications of the *Studium Biblicum Franciscanum* 5, Jerusalem 1969. According to Foerster the hall which Corbo claims to have been the church shows no signs that it was a place of worship in the first century.

[57] K. Stendahl, *The School of St. Matthew*, Philadelphia, Fortress, 2 ed. 104-6. He suggests that an alternative explanation for the change might be the monotony of the double καθήμενος.

[58] This has been pointed out in particular by G. Strecker, 'The Concept of History in Matthew', JAAR 25(1967) 220-30, esp. 221f, who sees the use of O.T. quotations in relation to the various geographical locations of the gospel—Bethlehem, Egypt, Nazareth, Caphernaum—as a sign of the author's 'historicizing' tendency to show that the promises of God have been fulfilled in the past life of Jesus.

[59] For an analysis cf. *The Twelve*, 72-7.

[60] D.R.A. Hare, *The Theme of Jewish Persecution of Christians in the Gospel according to St. Matthew*, S.N.T.S. monographs 6, Cambridge, Univ. Press, 1967, esp. ch. 3, shows that it is Christian missionaries that are being persecuted, but assigns the persecution to the past (167-71). R. Hummel, *Die Auseinandersetzung zwischen Kirche und Judentum im Matthäusevangelium*, 26-33, claims that the gospel must have been written before the introduction of the *birkath ha-minim*, against G. Kilpatrick, *The Origins of the Gospel according to St. Matthew*, Oxford, Clarendon, 1946, 110f, who had pointed to the constant reference to 'their synagogues' 4:23; 9:35; 10:17; 12:9; 13:54; 23:34. Hummel argues that there is no hint of excommunication in *Mt* where we might expect it, e.g., 5:11 (cf.ἀφορίζειν *Lk* 6:22), and 23:2f where Matthew presupposes Pharisaic control of the synagogue but is antagonistic towards their attitude, not their position. Davies, *The Setting of the Sermon on the Mount*, 256-315, discusses the relation of *Mt* to Jamnia Judaism, esp. 295f for the rabbinic decrees about Syria.

[61] W. Trilling, *Das Wahre Israel. Studien zur Theologie des Matthäus-Evangeliums* SANT 10, Munich, Kösel, 1964, 130-7, deals with Matthew's redaction of the Markan geographic data. *Mt* 15:29-31 = *Mk* 7:31-7, the introduction to the second feeding miracle, is particularly significant, for even though the setting is in the region of Tyre and Sidon (15:21), the only occasion in *Mt* where Jesus works outside Israel, we hear him utter his most particularistic saying of all, 15:24, and the crowds that are healed glorify the God of Israel, 15:31.

[62] Trilling, *Das Wahre Israel*, 102f, ascribes the particularism to the apologetic concerns of the author. Hare, *The Theme of Jewish Persecution*, 102 and 127, thinks that συνέδρια is a Diaspora rather than a Palestinian institution, on the basis of *War* 2:273.

[63] *Eretz Israel* is the constant rabbinic expression for Palestine, and it may well be this fact that influences Matthew's usage in this chapter; cf. Strack-Billerbeck, *Kommentar zum Neuen Testament*, 1, 90. Matthew also uses the expression γῆ Ἰσραήλ at 2:20.21. According to Stendahl, *The School of St. Matthew*, 104, this may explain a minor change in *Is* 8:23f, when he writes γῆ for χώρα (LXX) at 4:15.

[64] The verbal and thematic links between *Mt* 10 and 23 are striking as I have noted in *The Twelve*, 180; cf. also Hare, *The Theme of Jewish Persecution*, 80-96. For him *Mt* 10:23 is a 'fulfilled prophecy' because of the recurrence of the motif at 23:34.

[65] Cf. recent discussion of the question in J. Meier, 'Nations or Gentiles in Mt 28:19', CBQ 39(1977) 94-102.

[66] Trilling, *Das Wahre Israel*, 135, opts for the larger territory, while Hare, *The Theme of Jewish Persecution*, 168, mentions Antioch and other Syrian cities. For a full discussion cf. W. Kummel, *Introduction to the New Testament*, English trans. London, S.C.M., 1966, 84.

[67] Conzelmann, *The Theology of St. Luke*, 18-94, esp. 40f and 69f.

⁶⁸ Davies, *The Gospel and the Land*, 249f; S. Brown,*Apostacy and Perseverance in the Theology of Luke*, Analecta Biblica 36, Rome, P.I.B. press, 1969, 6-12, both pointing to such passages as *Lk* 10:18; 11:14-22; 13:11-17.

⁶⁹ *The Gospel and the Land*, 247f.

⁷⁰ *The Theology of St. Luke*, 65 and 68. In regard to the former passage he suggests that Luke does not locate the journey in Samaria, since elsewhere, e.g., after the rejection at Nazareth and Gadara, Jesus does not return. However it seems difficult to interpret εἰς ἑτέραν κώμην of 9:56 in any other way except another *Samaritan* village. He also seems to minimise the reference to Herod, i.e. Galilee, in the second passage, by ascribing it to the tradition, and claiming that the notice serves only to highlight the theological necessity of the journey for Luke. Admittedly, *Lk* 17:11, διὰ μέσον Σαμαρείας καὶ Γαλιλαίας , does seem to support his view that for Luke Galilee and Judaea were adjacent, with Samaria a border country of each. Yet even in this instance the mention of Samaria first is strange unless Luke believes that the journey is now in Samaria, and Galilee is referred to for the reason proposed below, n. 72.

⁷¹ It is the birth at Bethlehem that causes him more concern, resulting in the confused account of the census. Cf. Brown, *The Birth of the Messiah*, 413f and 547-55.

⁷² Judaea alone is judged to be the *lectio difficilior* by the editors of *The Greek New Testament*, giving it the rating (B); cf. *A Textual Commentary*, 137. Conzelmann appears to be somewhat inconsistent here: on the one hand he argues that Judaea alone is the correct reading for Jesus' sphere of activity at *Lk* 4:44 (p. 40f), yet claims that Galilee, Judaea, Jerusalem is a fixed pattern for Luke on the basis of 6:19 (sic, 5:17?), *Ac* 1:18 (sic, *Ac* 1:22?), *Ac* 10:37-9 (p. 43, n. 3). The fact that Tacitus, *Annal.* XII, 54; Josephus, *Ant* 12:421; 13:174; *War* 1:309; and Pliny, *Nat. Hist.* V, 68, all use Judaea in this official Roman sense lends weight to our suggestion. Cf. above, n. 6.

⁷³ *The Theology of St. Luke*, 86, n. 1, without any reference to language or style.

⁷⁴ It would be wrong to see the apparent concentration on Galilee to the exclusion of other areas in the first half of the gospel as a sign of Luke's symbolic understanding of the region. Bethsaida is mentioned at 9:10, even though it lay outside Galilee, and Jesus visited the country of the Gerasenes (8:26) which is described as being opposite Galilee. The mention of Tyre and Sidon in the source Mark (7:24-31) that does not appear in Luke is part of the 'great omission'. This leaves the absence of Caesarea Philippi (*Mk* 8:27 missing at *Lk* 9:18) alone unexplained.

⁷⁵ Cf. my *The Twelve*, 218-55, and G. Klein, *Die Zwölf Apostel. Ursprung und Gehalt einer Idee*, FRLANT 77, Göttingen 1961, esp. 202-17, though with very different explanations of the Lukan emphasis on the Twelve as the only apostles, to the virtual exclusion of Paul.

⁷⁶ R. E. Brown, 'Johannine Ecclesiology—The Community's Origins', Interpretation 31(1977) 379-93 in discussion with J. L. Martyn, 'Glimpses into the History of the Johannine Community' in *L'Évangile de Jean: Sources, Rédaction, Théologie*, M. de Jonge ed. BETL 44, Gembloux, Ducolot, 1977, 149-75, and G. Richter, 'Präsentische und futurische Eschatologie im 4 Evangelium', in *Gegenwart und Kommendes Reich: Schülergabe Anton Vögtle zum 65 Geburtstag*, ed. P. Fiedler and D. Zeller, Stuttgart, Katholisches Biblewerk, 1975, 117-52.

⁷⁷ R. A. Culpepper, *The Johannine School*, S.B.L. Dissertation Ser. 26, Missoula, Scholars' Press, 1975; E. S. Fiorenza, 'The Quest for the Johannine School: the Apocalypse and the Fourth Gospel', NTS 23(1977) 402-28.

⁷⁸ J. A. T. Robinson had argued for this position in 'A New Look at the Fourth Gospel', in *Twelve New Testament Essays*, SBT 34, London, S.C.M., 1962, 94-106, against C. H. Dodd, *The Interpretation of the Fourth Gospel*, Cambridge, Univ. Press, 1953, who locates it in a hellenistic milieu. More recently C. K. Barrett has discussed the question in *The Gospel of John and Judaism*, Philadelphia, Fortress, 1975, claiming that it is part Jewish, part Gentile in its concerns, 19. Cf. also, J. L. Martyn, *History and Theology in the Fourth Gospel*, New York, Harper and

Row, 1963, and more recently, 'Glimpses', arguing for a strong interaction between the Johannine community and post-70 Judaism. On the question of the topography of the gospel in relation to its theological concerns cf. K. Kundsin, *Topologische Überlieferungsstoffe im Johannes-Evangelium: Eine Untersuchung*, FRLANT 22, Göttingen, 1925; R. T. Fortna, 'Theological Use of Locale in the Fourth Gospel' in *Gospel Studies in Honor of S. E. Johnson*, Ang. theol. Rev. Suppl. ser. 3, ed. M. Shepphard and E. C. Hobbs, March 1974, 58-95.

[79] Thus W.A. Meeks, *The Prophet-King. Moses Tradition and the Fourth Gospel*, Suppl. Nov. Test. XIV, Leiden, Brill, 1967, esp. 216-57 on Moses as prophet-king in the Samaritan sources; E.D. Freed, 'Did John write his Gospel partly to win Samaritan Converts?', Nov. Test. 12(1970) 241-56; C.H. Scobie, 'The Origins and Development of Samaritan Christianity', NTS 19(1973) 390-414, esp. 401-8. Cf. also n. 81 for the views of O. Cullmann.

[80] Brown, 'Johannine Ecclesiology', 390f. W.A. Meeks, 'The Man from Heaven in Johannine Sectarianism', JBL 91(1972) 44-72, has argued most convincingly for a sense of alienation within the Johannine community as instrumental in shaping the unique Christological myth of the descending/ascending redeemer. However, insofar as Meeks' stress on the isolation of the group would seem to exclude any sense of mission in the Fourth Gospel, we cannot fully accept his thesis.

[81] This connection has been argued strongly by O. Cullmann, in a number of his publications: 'L'Opposition contre le temple de Jerusalem: motif commun de la théologie johannique et du monde ambiant', NTS 5(1958) 157-173; 'La Samarie et les origines de la mission Chrétienne. Qui sont l'alloi de Jean IV, 38' in *Annuaire del 'École Pratique des Hautes Études*, Paris, 1953/4, and most recently in *The Johannine Circle*, Philadelphia, Westminster, 1976, 43 and 87.

[82] Meeks, *The Prophet King*, 313f; also, 'Galilee and Jerusalem in the Fourth Gospel', JBL 85(1966) 159-69, esp. 168.

[83] Martyn, 'Glimpses', 152f.

[84] A. Feuillet, 'The Second Cana Miracle', in *Johannine Studies*, English trans. New York, Alba House, 1964, 39-52.

[85] Thus Meeks, *The Prophet King*, 40; 'Galilee and Jerusalem', 163.

[86] *John*, I, 187f.

[87] R.T. Fortna. *The Gospel of Signs: A Reconstruction of the Narrative Source Underlying the Fourth Gospel*, S.N.T.S. Monographs 11, Cambridge, Univ. Press, 1970, 40, and 'Source and Redaction in the Fourth Gospel's Portrayal of Jesus' Signs', JBL 89(1970) 151-66, esp. 153, regards the traditional phrase σημεῖα καὶ τέρατα as a description of an inadequate approach in terms of the Fourth Gospel's understanding of Jesus' signs.

[88] 'Galilee and Jerusalem', 160f, with a discussion of the possible irony of these verses.

[89] Above, ch. 6, n. 67. Cf. however, the corrective of Meeks' position regarding the importance of these two titles for John suggested by M. de Jonge, 'Jesus as Prophet and King in the Fourth Gospel', ETL 49(1973) 160-77, who claims that 'Jesus' kingship and his prophetic mission are both redefined in terms of the unique relationship between Father and Son', (p. 162).

[90] The fact that Caphernaum is regarded by the Evangelist as a Jewish rather than a Christian center (*Jn* 6:59) would explain the emergence of Cana as the place of the revelation of Jesus' glory (2:11; 4:46). Cf. Kundsin, *Topologische Überlieferungsstoffe*, 69-71, endorsed by Fortna, 'Theological Use of Locale', 76, n. 61.

[91] Above ch. 6, section II and ch. 8, section III.

[92] This is one of the main criticisms that can be levelled at Vermes' study, *Jesus the Jew*. A subsequent volume is promised that will study the teaching of Jesus against the Galilean background, but already by focusing on the deeds alone and the suggested parallels with the *hasid* tradition the lines would appear to have been irrevocably drawn. More recently M. Smith, *Jesus the Magician*, New York, Harper and Row, 1978, has interpreted the gospel material against the background

of magic in the ancient world and the opinions that circulated about Jesus among 'outsiders', as distinct from the official 'revised' version of the gospels. He argues that Jesus fits perfectly the role of the magician and was so understood by his contemporaries. Irrespective of one's opinion of the relevance of some, at least of the evidence that Smith has marshaled to prove his case and the validity of some of his historical reconstruction and argumentation, the fact that his treatment of the tradition about Jesus' teaching is brief and dismissive (pp. 22f.129-37) causes concern about the objectivity of his approach. On the other hand the 'Scandanavian approach' of H. Reisenfeld, *The Gospel Tradition and its Beginnings. A Study in the Limits of Formgeschichte*, London 1957 and B. Gerhardson, *Memory and Manuscript. Oral Tradition and Written Transmission in Rabbinic Judaism and Early Christianity*, Lund, Gleerup, 1961, while restoring a balance in gospel studies, has been rightly criticized for imposing too rigid a pattern on early Christian tradition. Cf. the criticism of Davies, *Setting of the Sermon on the Mount*, 464-80, and Gerhardson's recent reply to his critics, *Die Anfänge der Evangeliontradition*, Wuppertal, Brockhaus, 1977.

[93] *Lk* 24:19 expresses this popular idea well: ἀνὴρ προφήτης δυνατὸς ἐν ἔργῳ καὶ λόγῳ. According to *Ac* 7:22 the contemporary view of Moses was that he too shared gifts of wisdom and mighty deeds. Cf. in detail K. Berger, 'Die königlichen Messiastraditionen des Neuen Testaments', NTS 20(1973) 1-45, where the charismatic *and* wisdom aspects of various New Testament christological titles are illustrated. Cf. also, M. Hengel, *Nachfolge und Charisma. Eine Exegetisch-religionsgeschichtliche Studie zu Mt 8,21f, und Jesu Ruf in der Nachfolge*, Beih. ZNW, Berlin, Töplemann, 1968.

[94] Cf. above, ch. 8, n. 103 and ch. 9, section I, ii, for evidence of Jewish miracle workers using the name of Jesus. Hengel, *Nachfolge und Charisma*, 73f, points to the gospel evidence for the popularity of the disciples healing activity in Galilee: *Mk* 6:31; *Lk* 10:17.19f. Cf. also, Smith, *Jesus the Magician*, 48 and 179, note on *T. Hull* 2:22f.

[95] This evidence from the gospels has been brilliantly analysed by Theissen in a number of his publications dealing with the social setting of the gospel tradition: 'Wanderradikalismus',' "Wir haben alles verlassen" (Mk 10:28). Nachfolge und soziale Entwurzelung in der jüdisch-palästinischen Gesellschaft des 1 Jahrhunderts n. Ch.', Nov. Test. 19(1977) 161-96; *Sociology of Early Palestinian Christianity*, English trans. Philadelphia, Fortress, 1977. By contrast an earlier study of S.E. Johnson,' Jesus and First Century Galilee', in *In Memoriam E. Lohmeyer*, 73-88, though providing many useful insights, is ultimately inadequate because of insufficient attention to the socio-cultural situation in the province.

[96] Bultmann, *The History of the Synoptic Tradition*, 127f. For a recent informative discussion stressing the control of prophetic words in the early community cf. J. Dunn, 'Prophetic 'I'-Sayings and the Jesus Tradition: The Importance of Testing Utterances in Early Christianity', NTS 24(1978) 175-98; though cf. the critical approach of D. Hill, "On the Evidence for the Creative Role of Christian Prophets', NTS 20(1974) 262-74. Hengel, *Nachfolge und Charisma*, 91f, cautiously endorses the suggestion of H. Schürmann, 'Die vorösterlichen Anfänge der Logientradition' in H. Ristow and K. Matthiae ed. *Der historische Jesus und der kerygmatische Christus*, Berlin 1916, 342-70, that some of the sayings have a *Sitz im Leben Jesu* in terms of the mission of the Twelve, without however going so far as to claim that Jesus had deliberately shaped his words so that they could be remembered. Cf. above n. 92.

[97] The question of the *Q* community and its *Sitz im Leben* has been much discussed in recent writing without any definitive conclusions emerging. For good summaries of the current position cf. M. Devisch, 'Le Document Q, source de Matthieu. Problematique Actuelle', in *L'Évangile selon Matthieu. Rédaction et Théologie*, ed. M. Didier BETL 24, Gembloux, Ducolot, 71-97, and more recently, R.A. Edwards, *A Theology of Q. Eschatology, Prophecy, Wisdom*, Philadelphia,

Fortress, 1976, stressing the interconnection of the three motifs of the title in the Q material. The problem is compounded because of the difficulty in deciding the extent of Matthaean and Lukan redaction of possible Q material. From the present point of view the most interesting suggestions are those of P. Hoffmann, *Studien zur Theologie der Logienquelle*, Münster, Aschendorff, 1972, suggesting that the community found itself in direct opposition to the Zealot ideology, and S. Schulz, *Q. Die Spruchquelle der Evangelisten* Zürich, Theologischer Verlag, 1972, arguing for two layers to Q, one Palestinian, the other hellenistic. Needless to say neither view has won widespread acceptance. The study of Theissen promises to break new ground. He speaks of sympathisers of the charismatics within the local communities on the analogy of the Essenes (*War* 2:124ff), *Sociology*, 17-23.

[98] The rural context of many of the instructions in the *Epistle of James* lead L.E. Elliot-Binns to attribute this work to Galilean Christians of an early period, even though he does not accept the ascription of the work to James, the brother of the Lord, *Galilean Christianity*, 45-53. There is no way of verifying such an hypothesis however, especially in view of the many unresolved questions about the work. Cf. M. Dibelius, *James*, English trans. of rev, German ed. Philadelphia, Fortress, 1976, 25, n. 73 warns against over-precision in attempting to locate the work in view of its lack of a distinctive theological point of view, something Lohmeyer, *Galiläa und Jerusalem*, 66f, has also attempted. The fact that there are a number of echoes of the sayings of Jesus in the letter might seem to support the position being developed here, namely that many of the sayings of Jesus were current in Galilean circles initially, yet as Davies, *The Setting of the Sermon on the Mount*, 401ff, points out, it is curious that so few of these parallels are with Q sayings.

[99] For a discussion of these two saying from the point of view of Christian prophecy cf. the studies of M. Eugene Boring: 'Christian Prophecy and *Mt* 10:23, A Test Exegesis', *SBL Seminar Papers*, ed. G. McRae, Missoula, Scholars' Press, 1976, 127-34, and 'Christian Prophecy and Matthew 23:34-6'; A Test Exegesis', *SBL Seminar Papers*, ed P.J. Achtemeier, Missoula, Scholars Press, 1977, 117-26.

[100] Cf. Hengel's defense of the basic historicity of these mission accounts, *Nachfolge und Charisma*, 82-9.

[101] Hengel, 'Zwischen Jesus und Paulus', 200f, stresses the role of the Hellenists in regard to the translation, adaptation and transmission of the sayings of Jesus. However, he would not exclude an earlier Aramaic version also (cf. above n. 96). Schulz, *Die Spruchquelle*, has also advocated two different versions of Q, but with a too rigid notion of what constitutes hellenistic and Palestinian.

[102] This emigration might also explain the emphasis on the Dekapolis in *Mk*, already discussed above, n. 51. The pre-Markan catena of miracle stories could have originated among these prophets also, later to become associated with the areas to which they had migrated. This need not mean that Mark knew Q, though this is not a closed issue, but only that the different types of material, sayings and narratives stem from the same group within early Christianity initially. *Mt* 8:5-13; *Lk* 7:1-10, the cure of the centurion's son indicates the presence of some miracle material in Q, despite the effort of Edwards, *A Theology of Q*, 93f, to confine the Q element to the dialogue because of the narrative discrepancies.

[103] Above, ch. 8, section II and ch. 9, n.60.

[104] 'Other Sheep not of This Fold', 9f.

[105] Fortna's attempt to reconstruct a detailed signs source behind the Fourth Gospel has been judged as less than totally successful by many scholars. Yet, as Brown, 'Johannine Ecclesiology', 385, notes, there were some stories of Jesus' miracle working activity available to the Evangelist and probably coming from the oldest layer of the gospel. These cannot have differed very much, either in tone or purpose from those which Mark had available to him. (Cf. above n. 102). Perhaps the theological and structural similarities between *Mk* and *Jn* that some scholars

have pointed to may be due to the fact that both were dealing in different ways with the same problem of an inadequate acceptance of Jesus, based on the activity of the wandering charismatics and their portrait of Jesus.

[106] *Lk* 9:52f; *Jn* 4:9; *Ant* 20:118-36; *War* 2:232-46.

[107] Bultmann, *The History of the Synoptic Tradition*, 38f, believes that the adaptation was made because of the Synoptists' desire to introduce a Jew/Gentile element into the story. Cf. Fortna, *The Gospel of Signs*, 45, who attributes the adaptation to *Q*, and Brown, *John*, I, 190, who notes that the term βασιλισκὸς does not preclude the official from being a soldier, since it is used for Herodian troops by Josephus, *Life*, 400.

[108] The missionary attitude of the Fourth Gospel has been noted by many scholars: Dodd, *The Interpretation of the Fourth Gospel*, Barrett, *The Gospel of John and Judaism*, 19f; G. McRae, 'The Fourth Gospel and *Religionsgeschichte*', CBQ 32(1970) 13-24. There is evidence of increased rabbinic concern with Samaria also, Neusner, *Eliezer ben Hyrcanus* 1, 41-3; 2, 348-50. Fortna comes nearest to our own position in regard to these concerns, 'Theological Use of Locale', 84-9, but without sufficient attention to the religious competition in Palestine in general, and Galilee in particular, in the post-70 period.

RETROSPECT

Looking back over this study of Galilean Judaism, a number of significant answers to the questions posed in the introduction have emerged. To catalogue these briefly may serve as a fitting conclusion to our enquiry.

(1) Despite the fact that our sources are silent for a number of centuries it does not seem probable that belief in Yahweh and loyalty to the Israelite religion were ever totally destroyed in the northern region of Palestine, especially among the country people. The fact that the Samaritan temple was not considered an attractive alternative is itself indicative of the quality of their adherence. As a result, there is little or no evidence for the 'judaising' of the north by the conquering Hasmonaeans once the barriers of the Greek cities had been destroyed. Rather, Galilean Judaism was now politically reunited with what had always been its cultural and religious center.

(2) While hellenism, especially in terms of land-ownership and control over the produce of the land, made its full impact in Galilee as well as elsewhere in the Ptolemaic and Seleucid period a considerable number of Galilean peasants would appear to have maintained some tenuous links with the land. This was to prove a very significant factor in their subsequent political and religious responses, but it also contributed to a definite feeling of alienation towards the cities, even, or perhaps more especially, when these were Jewish foundations but with aristocratic bias, either Sadducean (Sepphoris) or Herodian (Tiberias).

(3) Galilean political attitudes were not at all so radical or sharply defined as has often been suggested. Galilean Judaism had for long learned to live with the non-Jew, and when given the opportunity by Gabinius showed no great desire to establish itself in independence from its natural cultural and cultic center, Jerusalem. The growing dissatisfaction with Roman rule at the center was cushioned somewhat for the Galileans, especially by the long reign of Antipas, and so Zealotism got a cautious response within the province. It was inevitably embroiled in the revolt against Rome, once a Jewish governor arrived there

392

and had to bear its full share of the Roman conquest. The resistance within the province was easily contained by the Romans however and though their handling of the situation was at first efficiently brutal, in the subsequent settlement Galilee may have fared better than Judaea.

(4) As country people for the most part the Galileans were more likely to have been influenced by popular hellenistic syncretism rather than by Greek philosophical ideas. Yet the available evidence strongly suggests that the Jerusalem temple continued to exercise a powerful attraction for them, and this was able to express itself in pilgrimages and a general observance of the tithes. It may be that for them the temple's attraction was related to their struggle for the land and its produce, and hence we find Galileans as militant as the inhabitants of any other area of the country on the occasion of the feasts, only to revert to much more cautious and less conspicious attitudes once they had returned to the remoteness of village life.

(5) As long as the temple survived, the 'other way' of the *halakhah* had little attraction for the country people, and there were few Pharisaic scribes active in the province though occasional attempts to extend their influence to the region can be seen from the ministry of Jesus and the mission of Johanan ben Zakkai. This is understandable since Pharisaism as a way of life was more suited to the middle class townspeople. Instead, considered as mediator of the power of the divine presence, the holy man appears to have been a far greater attraction among the village population as the bridge between the temple holiness and everyday life. After 70 C.E. however, there was a much more concerted effort to win Galilee for the *halakhah*, and partial success at least can be seen in the occurrence of native Galilean rabbis, active both in the province and at Jamnia, as well as in the journeys of the leading Jewish figures to the province. Yet the fact that the *'am ha-'aretz* were still present there after 135 C.E. when rabbinic Judaism was forced to make its home in Galilee, shows that the efforts of the Jamnian period were not altogether successful.

(6) The search for any clear indications of Christianity in Galilee in the first century proved for the most part fruitless. This may have been due to the nature and scarcity of our

sources. However, in considering an appropriate *Sitz im Leben* for *Q* and the Fourth Gospel some avenues of exploration suggested themselves, and it seemed permissible to differentiate two forms of Christianity in the province. The older one was Jewish Christian, closely modeled on Jesus' life and his words on discipleship. The disruption of life in the province during the revolt and its immediate aftermath must have drastically curtailed this movement of wandering teachers, possibly even put an end to it altogether. Yet the situation in Palestine after 70 did have possibilities for the various religious groups who survived the destruction, and it seemed that the Johannine community seized the opportunity to make converts to its distinctive point of view among certain strands of Galilean Jews, but little can be said about the outcome of such overtures. It may well be that Galilee still holds the key to its own Christian past in terms of the archaeology of later Christian centers, but for now at least, the judgment must be that it was never very extensive.

ABBREVIATIONS

Standard abbreviations are used for the biblical books, apocrypha, pseudepigrapha, Dead Sea Scrolls, tractates of the Mishnah, Tosephta and Talmuds, as well as Classical and Christian authors. Slight variations of a personal nature are easily identifiable.

AASOR	Annual of the American Schools of Oriental Research.
AGSU	Arbeiten zur Geschichte des Spätjudentums und Urchristentums.
AJPh	American Journal of Philology.
Ant	Jewish Antiquities of Flavius Josephus.
ARW	Archiv für Religionswissenschaft.
b	Babylonian Talmud.
BA	The Biblical Archaeologist.
BASOR	Bulletin of the American Schools of Oriental Research.
BJRL	Bulletin of the John Rylands Library.
CBQ	Catholic Biblical Quarterly.
CIJ	Corpus Inscriptionum Judaicarum.
CPJ	Corpus Papyrorum Judaicarum.
Compendia	Compendia Rerum Judaicarum ad Novum Testamentum.
CQ	Classical Quarterly.
DJD	Discoveries in the Judaean Desert.
ET	Evangelische Theologie.
ETL	Ephemerides Theologicae Lovanienses.
FRLANT	Forschungen zur Religion und Literatur des Alten und Neuen Testaments.
G.P.	A. Alt, Galiläische Problemen.
HR	History of Religions.
HTR	Harvard Theological Review.
HUCA	Hebrew Union College Annual.
IDB	Interpreters Dictionary of the Bible.
IEJ	Israel Exploration Journal.
JAAR	Journal of the American Academy of Religion.
JBL	Journal of Biblical Literature.

JJS	Journal of Jewish Studies.
JPS	Journal of Peasant Studies.
JQR	Jewish Quarterly Review.
JRS	Journal of Roman Studies.
JSJ	Journal for the Study of Judaism.
JSS	Journal of Semitic Studies.
JTS	Journal of Theological Studies.
LCL	Loeb Classical Library.
M	Mishnah.
Mizraim	V. Tcherikover, Palestine Under the Ptolemies.
MGWJ	Monatschrift für Geschichte und Wissenschaft des Judentums.
Nov. Test.	Novum Testamentum.
NTS	New Testament Studies.
OGIS	W. Dittenberger, Orientis Graeci Inscriptiones Selectae.
p	Palestinian (Yerushalmi) Targum.
PCZ	Zenon Papyri, edited C.C. Edgar.
PColZ	Zenon Papyri at Colombia, ed. W. Westermann et al.
PEQ	Palestinian Exploration Quarterly.
PG	Patrologia Graeca, J.-B. Migne.
PJB	Palästinajahrbuch.
PL	Patrologia Latina, J.-B. Migne.
PSI	Publicazioni della Societa Italiana, ed. G. Vitelli et al.
PW	Paulys Realencyclopädie der Classischen Altertumswissensschaft.
RB	Revue Biblique.
REJ	Revue des Études Juives.
RHPR	Revue d'Histoire et de Philosophie Religieuses.
RHR	Revue de l'Histoire des Religions.
RIDA	Revue Internationale des Droits de l'Antiquite.
RQ	Revue de Qumran.
RSR	Recherches Sciences Religieuses.
SANT	Studien zum Alten und Neuen Testaments.
SBT	Studies in Biblical Theology.
SEHHW	Social and Economic History of the Hellenistic World, M. Rostovtzeff.

SEHRE	Social and Economic History of the Roman Empire, M. Rostovtzeff.
T	Tosephta.
TAPA	Transactions of the American Philological Association.
TDNT	Thcological Dictionary of the New Testament.
ThLB	Theologische Literatur Blatter.
ThLZ	Theologische Literaturzeitung.
TZ	Theologische Zeitschrift.
VT	Vetus Testamentum.
W.H.Hell.A.	A. Schalit, ed. World History of the Jewish People, Hellenistic Age.
W.H.Her.P.	M.Avi-Yonah, ed. World History of the Jewish People, Herodian Period.
ZAW	Zeitschrift für die Alttestamentliche Wissenschaft.
ZDPV	Zeitschrift des Deutschen Palästina-Vereins.
ZNW	Zeitschrift für die Neutestamentliche Wissenschaft.
ZTK	Zeitschrift für Theologie und Kirche.

BIBLIOGRAPHY

I. PRIMARY SOURCES.

(i) Bible and Related Books.

- *Biblia Hebraica*, ed. R. Kittel, 12th ed. Stuttgart, 1961.
- *Septuaginta*, 2 vols., ed. A. Rahlfs, 7th ed. Stuttgart, 1962.
- *The Apocrypha and Pseudepigrapha of the Old Testament*, 2 vols., ed. R.H. Charles, Oxford, 1913.
- *Die Apokryphen und Pseudepigraphen* des Alten Testaments, 2 vols. ed. E. Kautzsch, Tübingen, 1900.
- *Novum Testamentum Graece*, ed. E. Nestle and K. Aland, 25th ed., Stuttgart, 1963.
- *The Greek New Testament*, ed. K. Aland et al., Stuttgart, United Bible Societies, 3rd ed., 1974.
- *The New Testament Apocrypha*, 2 vols., ed. E. Hennecke and W. Schneemelcher, English, trans., London, 1963-5.

(ii). Rabbinic Sources.

- *Aboth de Rabbi Nathan*, ed. S. Schechter, reprint, New York, 1967.
- *Babylonische Talmud, (Der)*, ed. L. Goldschmidt, 12 vols., Berlin, 1929-36.
- *Babylonian Talmud, (The)*, English trans., ed. I. Epstein, 18 vols., Reprint, London, Soncino Press, 1961.
- *Fathers according to Rabbi Nathan, (The)* English trans., J. Goldin, New Haven, 1955.
- *Midrash Rabbah*, English trans., H. Freedman and M. Simon, 10 vols., London, Soncino Press, 1951.
- 'Megillath Ta'anith,' H. Lichtenstein, HUCA 8/9(1932) 257-351.
- *Mekilta de Rabbi Ischmael*, 3 vols., J. Lauterbach, Philadelphia, 1949.
- *Mishnah, (The)*, English trans. H. Danby, Reprint, Oxford, Clarendon, 1972.
- *Mishnah (Shishnah Sidre)*, 6 vols. Jerusalem/Tel Aviv, 1958-.

- *Palestinian Talmud, (The)*, Krotoshin ed., Reprint, New York, 1949.
- *Talmud de Jérusalem, (Le)*, French trans. M. Schwab, Paris 1871-90.
- *Tosephta*, ed. M.S. Zuckermandel, Reprint, Jerusalem, 1963.
- *Tosefta Ki-Fshutah*, S. Liebermann, 4 vols., New York, 1955-73.

(iii). Qumran Literature.

- *Discoveries in the Judaean Desert*, 5 vols., eds. D. Barthèlmy, J.T. Milik, P. Benoit, R. deVaux, J. Sanders, J. Allegro, Oxford, Clarendon, 1955-68.
- *Essene Writings from Qumran (The)*, A. Dupont-Sommer, English trans. Oxford, 1962.
- *Texte aus Qumran, (Die)*, Hebräisch und Deutsch, 2nd ed. Darmstadt, 1971.

(iv). Jewish Christian and Pagan Writers.

- Epiphanius, *Panarion Haeresum*, ed. K. Holl. Leipzig, 1915-33.
- Eusebius, *The Ecclesiastical History*, LCL, 2 vols., trans. K. Lake and J.E.L. Oulton, London. Heinemann, 1926-32.
- *Das Onomasticon der Biblishcen Ortsnamen*, ed. F. Klostermann Reprint, Darmstadt, 1966.
- Josephus Flavius, *Jewish Antiquities, Jewish War, The Life and Contra Apionem*, LCL 9 vols., trans. H. St.J. Thakeray, R. Marcus and L.H. Feldman, London, Heinemann, 1925-65.
- *De Bello Judaico*, ed. and trans. O. Michel and O. Bauernfeind, 3 vols., Darmstadt, 1959-67.
- *Josephi Flavii Opera*, ed. B. Niese, 7 vols., Berlin 1887-95.
- Jakoby, F., *Die Fragmente der griechischen Historiker*, 14 vols. Berlin, 1925-58.
- Migne, J.-P., *Patrologia Graeca*, Paris, 1857-.
  Patrologia Latina, Paris, 1844-.
- Müller, C. and Th., *Fragmenta Historicorum Graecum*, Paris, 1841-72.

- Philo, 10 vols. and 2 supplementary vols., trans. F.H. Colson et al., London, Heinemann, 1929-61.
- Pliny, *Natural History*, LCL 10 vols. trans. H. Rackham, London, Heinemann, 1938-63.
- Polybius, *The Histories*, LCL, 6 vols. trans. W.R. Paton, London, Heinemann, 1922-7.
- Stern, M., *Greek and Latin Authors on Jews and Judaism*, vol. 1, Jerusalem, Masada Publishing House, 1976.
- Strabo, *The Geography of Strabo*, LCL, 8 vols. trans. H.L. Jones, London, Heinemann, 1917-32.
- Tacitus, *The Histories*, LCL 2 vols. trans. C.H. Moore, London, Heinemann, 1925-31.
- *The Annals*, LCL 3 vols. trans. J. Jackson, London, Heinemann, 1931-7.

(v). Inscriptions, Papyri.

Corpus Inscriptionum Judaicarum, 2 vols., ed. J.-B. Frey, Rome 1936-52.

Corpus Papyrorum Judaicarum, 3 vols. ed. V. Tcherikover and A. Fuchs, Cambridge, Mass., 1957-64.

Landau, Y.H., 'A Greek Inscription found near Hefzibah', IEJ 16(1966) 54-70.

Orientis Graeci Inscriptiones Selectae, ed. W. Dittenberger, Leipzig, 1903-5.

Publicazioni della Societa Italiana. Papiri Graeci e Latini, ed. G. Vitelli vols. IV-VI, Florence 1917-20 (=PSI).

Roberts, L. and J., *Bulletin Épigraphique*, REG 75(1962).

Schwabe, M., 'Greek Inscriptions found at Beth Shearim in the Fifth Excavation Season', IEJ 4(1954) 249-61.

Welles, C.B., *Royal Correspondence in the Hellenistic Period*. New Haven 1934.

Zenon Papyri, ed. C.C. Edgar, vols. I-IV, *Catalogue General des Antiquités Égyptiennes du Musée du Caire*, Cairo, 1925-40, (=PCZ).

Zenon Papyri, Business Papers of the Third Century dealing with Egypt and Palestine, ed. W. Westermann and E.S. Hasenoehrl, 2 vols. New York, 1934-40, (=PColZ).

(vi). Dictionaries, Encyclopedias, etc.

Bauer, W., *A Greek English Lexicon of the New Testament and Other Early Christian Literature*, Rev. and trans. W. Arndt and F.W. Gingrisch Chicago, Univ. Press, 1957.

Cambridge Ancient History, 12 vols. 2nd ed. Cambridge, Univ. Press, 1924-39.

Compendia Rerum Judaicarum ad Novum Testamentum. The Jewish People in the First Century. Historical Geography, Political History, Social, Cultural and Religious Life and Institutions, Vol. 1, 1974, Assen, Van Gorcum, Vol. 2, Philadelphia, Fortress, 1976. Eds. S. Safrai and M. Stern.

A Dictionary of the Targumim, The Talmud Babyli and Yerushalmi and the Midrashic Literature, M. Jastrow, New York 1950.

Encyclopaedia Judaica, 10 vols., Jerusalem, Keter Publishing Co., 1971.

Interpreters Dictionary of the Bible, ed. G. Buttrick, 5 vols. Nashville, Abingdon, 1962-76.

Jewish Encyclopedia, (The), 12 vols., ed. I. Singer, New York-London, 1901-7.

Jerome Biblical Commentary, (The), ed. R.E. Brown, J. Fitzmyer, R. Murphy, London, Chapman, 1968.

Namenswörterbuch zu Flavius Josephus, ed. A. Schalit, Leiden, Brill, 1968.

Paulys Realencyclopädie der Classischen Altertumswissenschaft, rev. ed. G. Wissowa, W. Kroll, Stuttgart, 1950ff.

Reallexicon für Antike und Christentum, ed. Th Klauser, Stuttgart, 1950-.

Theological Dictionary of the New Testament, 10 vols. ed. G. Kittel and G. Friedrich, English trans., Grand Rapids, Eerdmans, 1968-.

The World History of the Jewish People. First Series: The Ancient World: vol. 6, *The Hellenistic Age*, ed. A. Schalit; vol. 7, *The Herodian Period*, ed. M. Avi-Yonah, Jerusalem, Masada Publishing House, 1972 and 1975.

II. MODERN BOOKS AND ARTICLES

ABEL, F.M.
- 'Inscriptions de Transjordan et de Haute Galilée' RB 5 (1908), 568-77.
- 'La liste géographique du Papyrus 71 de Zénon', RB 32 (1932), 409-15.
- *Géographie de la Palestine*, 2 vols., Etudes Bibliques, Paris 1938.
- *Histoire de la Palestine*, 2 vols., Paris 1952.

ABRAHAMS, I.
- *Studies in Pharisaism and the Gospels*, Reprint, New York Ktav, 1967.

AHARONI, Y.
- *The Land of the Bible*, English trans., London, Burns Oates, 1967.

AHARONI, Y. and AVI-YONAH
- *The Macmillan Bible Atlas*, New York/London, 1968.

ALBRIGHT, W.F.
- *Archaeology and the Religion of Israel*, Baltimore, 1946.

ALLEGRO, J.M.
- 'An Unpublished Fragment of Essene Halachah', JSS 6 (1961), 71-3.

ALLON, G.
- 'The Attitude of the Pharisees to the Roman Government and the House of Herod' Scripta Hierosolymitana 7, Jerusalem 1961, 53-78.

ALT, A.
- 'Eine Galiläische Ortsliste in *Jos* 19' ZAW 4 (1927), 59-81.
- 'Die Reiterstadt Gaba', ZDPV 62 (1939), 3-21.
- *Kleine Schriften zur Geschichte des Volkes Israel*, 3 vols., Munich, 1953-64.
- 'The Settlement of the Israelites in Palestine', in *Essays on Old Testament Religion*, English trans. Oxford, B.A. Blackwell, 1966.

AMIRAM, D.H.K.
- 'The Pattern of Settlement in Palestine', IEJ 3 (1953), 65-78, 192-209, 250-59.
- 'Sites and Settlements in the Mountains of Lower Galilee', IEJ 6 (1956), 69-77.

APPLEBAUM, S.
- 'The Zealots: The Case for Revaluation', JRS 61 (1971), 155-70.
- 'Economic Life in Palestine', in *Compendia Rerum Judaicarum ad Novum Testamentum*. ed. M. Stern and S. Safrai, 2, 631-700.

AVI-YONAH, M.
- 'Mosaic Pavements in Palestine', QDAP 2 (1933), 136ff and 3 (1934), 26ff.
- 'The Foundation of Tiberias' IEJ 1 (1950), 160-69.
- 'Mount Carmel and the God of Baalbeck', IEJ 2 (1951), 118-24.
- 'The Missing Fortress of Flavius Josephus', IEJ 3 (1953), 94-8.
- 'Syrian Gods at Ptolemais-Accho', IEJ 9 (1959), 1-12.
- *Israel: Ancient Mosaics, U.N.E.S.C.O. World Art Series*, 14, Paris, 1960.
- 'Scythopolis', IEJ 12 (1962), 123-34.
- 'The Caesarean Inscription of the 24 priestly Courses', IEJ 12 (1962) 137-9.
- *The Holy Land from the Persian to the Arab Conquests. An Historical Geography*, Grand Rapids, Baker Books, 1966.

AVI-YONAH, M. and BARAS, Z.
- *The World History of the Jewish People. First Series, Vol. 7, The Herodian Period*, Jerusalem, Masada Publishing Co. 1975.

BACHER, W.
- *Die Aggada der Tannaiten, Vol. I, Von Hillel bis Akiba*, 2nd ed. Strassbourg, 1902.

BADIAN, E.
- 'Patron-State and Client-State', reprint from *Roman Imperialism in the Late Republic*, Oxford, B. Blackwell, 1948.

BAERWALD, A.
- *Josephus in Galiläa. Sein Verhaltnis zu den Parteien, inbesondere zu Justus von Tiberias*, Breslau, 1877.

BALY, D.
- *The Geography of the Bible*, New York, Harper and Row, 1957.

BAMMEL, E.
- 'Die Neuordnung des Pompeius und das römisch-judisch Bundnis', ZDPV 75 (1959) 76-88.
- 'The Organisation of Palestine by Gabinius', JJS 4 (1959) 159-62.
- ed. *The Trial of Jesus*, SBT 2nd series, 13, London, S.C.M. 1970.
BANTON, M.
- ed. *Anthropological Approaches to the Study of Religion*, A.S.A. Monographs 3, London, 1966.
BARON, S.
- *A Social and Religious History of the Jews*, 10 vols, 2ed. Philadelphia, Jewish Publication Society of America, 1952.
BARR, J.
-'Which Language Did Jesus Speak? Some Remarks of a Semitist' BJRL 53 (1970) 9-29.
BARRETT, C.K.
- *The Gospel of John and Judaism*, Philadelphia, Fortress, 1974.
BARTH, G.
- 'Matthew's Understanding of the Law', in *Tradition and Interpretation in Matthew*, G. Bornkamm, G. Barth, H.J. Held, English trans., London, S.C.M. 1963.
BAUER, W.
- 'Jesus der Galiläer', in *Festschrift für Adolf Jülicher*, Tübingen, 1927.
- *Aufsätze und Kleine Schriften*, ed. G. Strecker, Tübingen, Mohr, 1967.
BAUMBACH, G.
- 'Zeloten und Sikarier', ThLZ 90(1965) cols. 727-40.
- 'Bemerkungen zum Freiheitsverständnis der zelotischen Bewegung', ThLZ 92(1967) cols. 257f.
BAUMGARTEN, J.
- 'The Essene Avoidance of Oil and the Laws of Purity', RQ 6(1967/8) 184-92.
BELKIN, S.
- *Philo and the Oral Law*, Cambridge, Mass. 1940.

BEN-DAVID, A.
- *Jerusalem und Tyros. Ein Beitrag zur Palästinensischen Münz- und Wirtschaftsgeschichte (126 a.C.-57 p.C.)*, Tübingen, 1969.

BEN-ZEVI, I.
- 'The Beth Shean Valley', IEJ 11(1961) 198-202.

BERGER, K.
- 'Die königlichen Messiastraditionen des Neuen Testaments', NTS 30(1973) 1-45.

BERTRAM, W.
- 'Der Hellenismus in der Urheimat des Evangeliums', ARW 32(1935) 265-81.

BEST, E.
- 'The Role of the Disciples in Mark', NTS 23(1977) 377-401.

BETZ, O.
- 'Jesu heiliger Krieg', Nov Test 2(1957) 125-9.

BEVAN, E.R.
- *Jerusalem Under the High Priests*, London 1924 (Reprt. 1952).

BICKERMAN, E.
- 'La Charte Séleucide de Jérusalem', REJ 100(1935) 4-35.
- *Der Gott der Makkabäer*, Berlin 1937.
- 'Un document relatif à la persécution d'Antiochus IV, Épiphane', RHR 115(1937) 188-221.
- *Institutions des Séleucids*, Paris 1938.
- 'Sur une Inscription grecque de Sidon', in *Mélanges Syriens offerts a M.R. Dussaud*, Paris, 1939, 91-9.
- 'Les Privilèges Juifs' in *Mélanges Isidore Levy*, Brussels, 1955, 11-34.
- 'La Coele-Syrie. Notes de géographie historique', RB 54(1947) 256-68.
- *From Ezra to the last of the Maccabees. The Foundations of Post-Biblical Judaism*, New York, Shocken, 1962.

BIETENHARDT, H.
- 'Die Dekapolis von Pompeius bis Traian. Ein Kapitel aus der neutestamentlichen Zeitgeschichte', ZDPV 79(1963) 24-58.

BIRNBAUM, S.A.
- 'Bar Kokhba and Akiba', PEQ 86(1954) 23-33.
BLACK, M.
- *The Dead Sea Scrolls and Christian Origins*, New York, Scribner.
- *An Aramaic Approach to the Gospels and Acts*, 3ed. Oxford, Clarendon, 1963.
BLINTZLER, J.
- 'Die Niedermetzelung von Galiläern durch Pilatus', Nov Test 2(1957) 24-49.
BOOBYER, G.
- 'Galilee and Galileans in St. Mark's Gospel', BJRL 35(1953) 334-48.
BORING, M.E.
- 'Christian Prophecy and Mt 10:23; A Test Exegesis', in SBL Seminar Papers, 1966, Missoula, Scholars' Press, 127-34.
- 'Christian Prophecy and Mt 23:34-6; A Test Exegesis', SBL Seminar Papers 1977, Missoula, Scholars' Press, 117-26.
BORG, M.
- 'The Currency of the Term Zealot', JTS 22(1971) 504-12.
BORNKAMM, G.
- *Jesus of Nazareth*, English trans. London, S.C.M. 1960.
BOWMAN, J.
- 'Contact between Samaritan Sects and Qumran', VT 7(1957) 184-9.
BRANDON, S.F.G.
- *Jesus and the Zealots*, Manchester, Univ. Press, 1967.
- 'Jesus and the Zealots: A Correction', NTS 17(1971) 453.
BRAUNERT, H.
- 'Der Römische Provinzialcensus und der Schätzungsbericht des Lukas-Evangeliums', Historia 6(1957) 192-214.
BRIANT, P.
- '*Laoi* et Esclaves Ruraux', in *Actes du Colloque 1972 sur l'esclavage*, Paris, 1974, 93-133.
BROSHI, M.
- 'La population de l'ancienne Jérusalem', RB 82(1975) 5-17.
BROWN, R.E.
- *The Gospel according to John*, 2 vols. Anchor Bible 29 and 29A, New York, Doubleday, 1966 and 68.

- *The Virginal Conception and the Bodily Resurrection of Jesus*, London, Chapman, 1973.
- *The Birth of the Messiah*, New York, Doubleday, 1977.
- 'Johannine Ecclesiology - The Community's Origins', Interpretation 31(1977) 379-93.
- "Other Sheep not of This Fold", The Johannine Perspective on Christian Diversity in the Late First Century', JBL 97(1978) 5-22.

BROWN, P.
- *The World of Late Antiquity*, London, Thames, 1971.
- 'The Rise and Function of the Holy Man in Late Antiquity', JRS 61(1971) 80-100.
- 'Sorcery, Demons and the Rise of Christianity', in *Witchcraft: Confessions and Accusations*, ed. M. Douglas, ASA Monographs 9, London, Tavistock, 1970, 17-45.

BROWN, S.
- *Apostacy and Perseverance in the Theology of Luke*, Analecta Biblica 36, Rome, P.I.B. Press, 1969.

BÜCHLER, A.
- *Die Priester und der Cultus im letzten Jahrzent des Jerusalemischen Tempels*, Vienna 1895.
- *Das Sanhedrion in Jerusalem und das Grosse Beth Din in der Quaderkammer des Jerusalemischen Tempels*, Vienna 1902.
- 'Die Schauplatz des Bar Kochba-Krieges', JQR 16(1904) 192-205.
- *The Economic Conditions of Judaea after the Destruction of the Second Temple*, Jewish College Publications, 4, London, 1912.
- *The Political and Social Leaders of the Jewish Community od Sepphoris in the Second and Third Centuries*, Jewish College Publications, 6, London, 1914.
- 'The Priestly Dues and the Roman Taxes in the Edicts of Caesar', in *Studies in Jewish History*, Univ. Press, 1956.
- *Types of Jewish Palestinian Piety from 70 B.C.E.-70 C.E. The Ancient Pious Man*, Reprint, New York, Ktav, 1968.
- *Der Galiläische 'Am ha'Aretz des zweiten Jahrhunderts*, Reprint Hildesheim, Olms, 1968.

- 'Uber die Minîm von Sepphoris und Tiberias in 2 und 3 Jahrhunderten', *Cohenfestschrift*, Judaica, 1912.

BULL, R.J.
- 'An Archaeological Footnote to "Our Fathers worshipped on this Mountain", Jn iv, 20, NTS 23(1977) 460-2.

BULL, R.J., and WRIGHT, G.E.
- 'Newly Discovered Temples on Mt. Gerizim in Jordan', HTR 58(1965) 234-7.

BYATT, A.
- 'Josephus and Population Numbers in First Century Palestine', PEQ 105(1973) 51-60.

BULTMANN, R.
- *The History of the Synoptic Tradition*, English trans. Oxford, Blackwell, 1968.

CADBURY, H.J.
- 'The Summaries of Acts' in *The Beginnings of Christianity*, 5, 392-402, ed. Jackson-Lake.
- *The Making of Luke-Acts*, London, S.P.C.K., 1961.

CATCHPOLE, D.R.
- 'The Problem of the Historicity of the Sanhedrein Trial', in E. Bammel, ed. *The Trial of Jesus*, SBT 2nd series, 13 London, 1970, S.C.M. Press, 47-65.

CERFAUX, L.
- 'L'inscription Funéraire de Nazareth à la Lumière de l'histoire Religieuse', RIDA 5(1958) 347-63.

CHADWICK, H.
- 'Justin's Defense of Christianity', BJRL 47(1965) 275-297.

CLAIBURN, W.E.
- 'The Fiscal Basis for Josiah's Reform', JBL 92(1973) 11-22.

CLARK, KENNETH W.
- 'Worship in the Jerusalem Temple after A.D. 70', NTS 6(1970) 269-80.

COHEN, G.M.
- 'The Hellenistic Military Colony: A Herodian Example', TAPA 103(1972) 83-95.

COHEN, S.
- *Josephus in Galilee and Rome: His Vita and Development as a Historian*, Columbia University, Ph.D. 1975, Ann Arbor, University Microfilms.

COLIN, J.
- 'La Galilée de l'Évangile et les villes paiennes de la Palestine' Ant. Class. 34(1965) 182-192.

CONZELMANN, H.
- *The Theology of Luke*, English trans. London, Faber, 1960.

COOK, A.B.
- *Zeus. A Study in Ancient Religion*, 3 vols., Cambridge, 1914-40.

CORBO, B.
- *The House of St. Peter at Caphernaum*, Publications of the Studium Biblicum Franciscanum 5, Jerusalem, 1969.

CROSS, F. MOORE
- 'Aspects of Samaritan and Jewish History in Late Persian and Hellenistic Times', HTR 59(1966) 201-11.

CROSSAN, J.D.
- 'Jesus and Pacifism, in *No Famine in the Land: Studies in Honour of John L. McKenzie*, Missoula, Scholars' Press, 1975, 195-208.

CULLMANN, O.
- 'La Samarie et les origines de la mission Chrétienne. Qui sont l'*alloi* de Jean IV, 38' in *Annuaire del'École Pratique des Hautes Études*, Paris, 1953/4.
- 'L'opposition contre la temple de Jérusalem: motif commun de la théologie johannique et du monde ambiant', NTS 5(1958) 157-173.
- 'Le douzième apotre', RHPR 42(1962) 133-40.
- *The Johannine Circle*, Philadelphia, Westminster, 1976.
- *The State of the New Testament*, London, S.C.M. 1956.

CULPEPPER, R.A.
- *The Johannine School*, S.B.L. Dissertation Ser. 26, Missoula, Scholars' Press, 1975.

DALMAN, G.
- *Arbeit und Sitte in Palästina*. 7 vols., Reprint, Hildesheim, Olms. 1964.
- *Orte und Wege Jesu*, Reprint, Darmstadt, 1968.
- *The Words of Jesus Considered in the Light of Post-Biblical Jewish Writings and the Aramaic Language*. English Translation, Edinburgh, 1902.

- *Jesus-Jeshua. Studies in the Gospels*. English Translation, Reprint, Ktav. London, 1929.

DAVIES, J.G.
- 'Zealot and Para-Zealot', NTS 19(1973) 483-5.

DAVIES, W.D.
- *The Setting of the Sermon on the Mount*, Cambridge, Univ. Press, 1964.
- *The Gospel and The Land*, Berkley, Univ. of California Press, 1974.

DAUBE, D.
- *The New Testament and Rabbinic Judaism*, London 1957.

de JONGE, M.
- 'Josephus und die Zukunftserwartungen seines Volkes' in *Josephus-Studien. Festschrift für Otto Michel*, Göttingen, Vandenhoeck und Ruprecht, 1974, 205-19.
- 'Jesus as Prophet and King in the Fourth Gospel', ETL 49(1973) 160-77.

DELCOR, M.
- 'Vom Sichem der hellenistischen Epoche zur Sychar des Neuen Testamentes', ZDPV 7(1962) 34-48.

DERENBOURG, J.
- *Essai sur l'Histoire et la Geographie de la Palestine d'après les Talmuds et les Autres Sources Rabbiniques. Prémier Parti: Histoire de las Palestine depuis Cyrus jusqu'à Adrien*. Reprint, Farnborough, Gregg, 1971.

DERRETT, J.M.
- 'Law in the New Testament: Si scandalizaverit te manus tua abscide illum', RIDA 20(1973) 11-41.

DeVAUX, R.
- *Ancient Israel. Its Life and Institutions*, 2nd ed. London, Darton Longman and Todd, 1965.

DEVISCH, M.
'Le Document Q, source de Matthieu. Problematique Actuelle', in *L'Évangile selon Matthieu. Rédaction et Théologie*, Gembloux Ducolet, 1971.

DEWEY, J.
- 'The Literary Structure of the Controversy Stories in *Mk* 2:1-3:6', JBL 99(1973) 394-401.

DIBELIUS, M.
- *From Tradition to Gospel,* English trans. New York, Scribners.

DODD, C.H.
- *The Interpretation of the Fourth Gospel,* Cambridge, Univ. Press 1953.
- *Historical Tradition in the Fourth Gospel,* Cambridge, Univ. Press, 1963.

DONAHUE, J.R.
- 'Tax Collectors and Sinners. An Attempt at an Identification' CBQ 33(1971) 39-61.

DREXLER, H.
- 'Untersuchungen zu Josephus und zur Geschichte des jüdischen Aufstandes 66-70', Klio 19(1925) 277-312.

DUNN, J.
- 'Prophetic 'I'-Sayings and the Jesus Tradition: the Importance of Testing Utterances in Early Christianity', NTS 24(1978) 175-98.

DUPONT, J.
- *Études sur les Actes des Apotres,* Paris, Cerf, 1967.

EDWARDS, R.A.
- *A Theology of Q. Eschatology, Prophecy, Wisdom,* Philadelphia, Fortress, 1976.

EISLER, R.
- *IHSOUS BASILEUS OU BASILEUSAS,* 2 vols. Heidleberg, 1929.

EISSFELDT, O.
- *Erstlinge und Zehnten im Alten Testament,* BWAT 22, Leipzig, 1917.
- *The Old Testament. An Introduction.* English trans. Oxford, Blackwell, 1965.

ELBORGEN, I.
- 'Die Feier der drei Wahlfahrtsfeste im zweiten Tempel', in *Bericht der Hochschule für die Wissenschaft des Judentums in Berlin,* 1929, 27-46.

ELLENSON, D.
- 'Ellis Rivkin and the Problem of Pharisaic History', JAAR 43(1975) 787-802.

ELLIOTT-BINNS, L.E.
- *Galilean Christianity*, SBT 16, London, S.C.M., 195.
EFRAT, E. and ORNI, E.
- *Geography of Israel*, 3rd rev. ed. New York, American Heritage Co. 1971.

FARMER, W.R.
- *Maccabees, Zealots and Josephus. An Enquiry into Jewish Nationalism in the Greco-Roman Period*, New York, Columbia Univ. Press, 1956.
- 'Judas, Simon and Athronges', NTS 4(1958) 147-55.
- *The Last Twelve Verses of Mark*, S.N.T.S. Monographs 25, Cambridge, Univ. Press, 1974.
FENEBERG, W.
- *Der Markusprolog. Studien zür Formbestimmung des Evangeliums*, SANT 36, Munich, Kösel, 1974.
FUEILLET, A.
- 'The Second Cana Miracle' in *Johannine Studies*, English trans. New York, Alba, 1964.
FINKEL, A.
- *The Pharisees and the Teacher of Nazareth*, AGSU 4, 2nd ed. Leiden, Brill, 1974.
FINKELSTEIN, L.
- *The Pharisees. The Sociological Background to Their Faith*, 2 vols. 3rd ed. rev. Philadelphia, The Jewish Publication Society of America, 1962.
FIORENZA, E., SCHÜSSLER
- 'The Quest for the Johannine School: The Apocalypse and the Fourth Gospel, NTS 23(1977) 402-28.
FITZMYER, J.A.
- *Essays on the Semitic Background to the New Testament*, London, 1971.
- 'The Languages of Palestine in the First Century', CBQ 30(1972) 501-31.
FLANAGAN, J.W., and ROBINSON, A.W. eds.
- *No Famine in the Land: Studies in Hounour of J.L. McKenzie*, Missoula, Scholars' Press, 1975.
FLUSSER, D.
- 'Paganism in Palestine', in *Compendia Rerum Judaicarum ad Novum Testamentum*, 2, 1065-1100.

FOERSTER, G.
- 'Notes on Recent Excavations at Caphernaum', IEJ 21(1971) 207-11.

FOHRER, E.
- *Die Provinzeinteilung des Assyrischen Reiches*, Leipzig, 1920.

FORTINA, R.T.
- *The Gospel of Signs: A Reconstruction of the Narrative Source Underlying the Fourth Gospel*, S.N.T.S. Monographs 11, Cambridge, Univ. Press, 1970.
- 'Source and Redaction in the Fourth Gospel's Portrayal of Jesus' Signs', JBL 89(1970) 151-66.
- 'Theological Use of Locale in the Fourth Gospel', in Anglican Theological Review, Suppl. ser, 3, eds. M. Sheppard and E.C. Hobbs, 1974.

FRANK, T.
- ed. *An Economic Survey of Ancient Rome*, 4 vols, Baltimore, 1938-40.

FREED, E.D.
- 'Did John write his Gospel partly to win Samaritan Converts?' Nov. Test. 12(1970) 241-56.

FREYNE, S.
- *The Twelve: Disciples and Apostles. An Introduction to the Theology of the First Three Gospels*, London, Sheed and Ward, 1968.
- Review of G. Vermes, *Jesus the Jew*, The Furrow, (1974) 517-20.
- 'The Galileans in the Light of Josephus' Vita', forthcoming, NTS.

GAGER, J.
- *Kingdom and Community. The Social World of Early Christianity*, Englewood Cliffs, N. Jersey, Prentice Hall, 1975.

GALLING, K.
- 'Judäa, Galiläa und der Osten im Jahre 163/4 v. Chr.', PJB 36(1940) 43-77.

GIL, M.
- 'Land Ownership in Palestine under Roman Rule', RIDA 17(1970) 11-53.

GARNSEY, P.
- 'Peasants in Ancient Roman Society', JPS 2(1975) 222-35.
GÄRTNER, B.
- *Iscariot*, Facet Books 29, English trans., Philadelphia, Fortress, 1971.
GASTON, L.
- *No Stone on Another. Studies on the Significance of the Fall of Jerusalem in the Synoptic Gospels*, Suppl. to Nov Test XXIII, Leiden, Brill, 1970.
GERHARDSON, G.
- *Memory and Manuscript. Oral Tradition and Written Transmission in Rabbinic Judaism and Early Christianity*, Lund, Gleerup, 1961.
- *Die Anfänge der Evangelientradition*, Wuppertal, Brockhaus, 1977.
GLASSON, T.F.
- *Moses in the Fourth Gospel*, SBT 40, London, S.C.M. 1963.
GOLAMB, B. and KEDAR, J.
- 'Ancient Agriculture in the Galilean Mountains', IEJ 3(1953) 94-8.
GOODENOUGH, E.R.
- *Jewish Symbols in the Greco-Roman World*, 13 vols. New York, 1953.
GRAETZ, H.
- *Geschichte der Juden*, 3 vols. Leipzig, 1905.
GRANT, F.C.
- *The Economic Background to the Gospels*, Oxford, Clarendon 1923.
GRUNDMANN, W.
- *Jesus der Galiläer und das Judentum*, Leipzig 1941.
GUTMANN, J.
- 'The Second Commandment and the Image in Judaism', HUCA 32(1961) 161-74.

HAENCHEN, E.
- *Die Apostelgeschichte*, 13th ed. Meyer's Kritische Exegetische Kommentar über das Neue Testament*, Göttingen, Vandenhoek and Ruprecht, 1961.

HARE, D.R.A.
- *The Theme of Jewish Persecution of Christians in the Gospel according to St. Matthew*, S.N.T.S. Monographs 6, Cambridge, Univ. Press, 1967.

HAR-EL, M.
- 'The Zealot Fortresses in Galilee', IEJ 22(1972) 123-30.

HARNACK, A.
- *The Mission and Expansion of Christianity in the First Three Centuries*, English trans. New York, Harper Torchback, 1961.

HEICHELHEIM, F.
- 'Roman Syria' in T. Frank, ed. *An Economic Survey of Ancient Rome*, IV, 121-257.

HENGEL, M.
- *Die Zeloten*, AGSU 1, Leiden, Brill, 1961, 2nd ed. 1976.
- *Judentum und Hellenismus. Studien zu ihrer Begegnung unter besonderer Berücksichtigung Palästinas bis zur Mitte des 2.Jh.s v. Chr.*, WUNT 10, Tübingen, 1969, 2nd ed. 1973.
- 'Die Synagogeninschrift von Stobi', ZNW 57(1966) 145-83.
- *Nachfolge und Charisma. Eine Exegetisch-religionsgeschichtliche Studie zu Mt 8,21f und Jesu Ruf in der Nachfolge*, Beih. ZNW Berlin, Töpelmann, 1968.
- 'Das Gleichnis von den Weingärtnern, Mc 12:1-12, im Lichte der Zenonpapyri und der rabbinischen Gleichnisse', ZNW 59(1968) 1-39.
- *War Jesus Revolutionär?*, Calwer Hefte 110, Stuttgart 1969.
- Review of S.F.G. Brandon, *Jesus and the Zealots*, in JSS 14(1969) 231-40.
- 'Proseuche und Synagoge. Jüdische Gemeinde, Gotteshaus und Gottesdienst in Diaspora und in Palästina, in *Tradition und Glaube, Festgabe für K.G. Kuhn*, Göttingen 1971, 157-84.
- 'Die Ursprung der Christlichen Mission', NTS 18(1971) 15-38.
- *Gewalt und Gewaltlosigkeit. Zur Politschen Theologie in Neutestamentlicher Zeit*, Calwer Hefte, 118, Stuttgart, 1971.
- *Eigentum und Reichtum*, Stuttgart 1973.

- 'Zeloten und Sikarier', in *Josephus-studien. Festschrift für Otto Michel*, edts. O. Betz, M. Hengel, K. Haacker, Göttingen, Vandenhoek and Ruprecht, 1974.
- 'Zwischen Jesus und Paulus. Die 'Hellenisten', die 'Sieben' und Stephanus', ZTK 72(1975) 151-206.

HERFORD, R.T.
- *Christianity in Talmud and Midrash*, Reprint, Clifton, New Jersey, 1966.

HERZ, D.J.
- 'Grossgrundbesitz in Palästina im Zeitalter Jesu', PJB 24(1928) 98-113.

HILL, D.
- 'On the Evidence for the Creative Role of Christian Prophets' NTS 29(1974) 262-74.

HILL, G.
- *Catalogue of Greek Coins of Palestine in the British Museum*, London, 1910.

HILGENFELDT, A.
- *Judentum und Judenchristentum*, Reprint Hildesheim, Olms, 1966.

HOBSBAWM, E.
- 'Peasants and Politics', JPS 1(1974) 3-23.

HOEHNER, H.
- *Herod Antipas*, S.N.T.S. Monographs 17, Cambridge, Univ. Press, 1972.

HOENIG, S.
- 'Oil and Pagan Defilement', JQR 61(1970/1) 63-75.

HOFFMANN, P.
- *Studien zur Theologie der Logienquelle*, Münster, Aschendoff, 1972.

HUMMEL, R.
- *Die Auseinandersetzung zwischen Kirche und Judentum im Matthäusevangelium*, Beih. Ev. Th. 33, Munich, Kaiser, 1963.

HUNZINGER, C.F.
- 'Spüren Pharisäischer Institutionen in der frühen rabbinischen Überlieferung', in *Tradition und Glaube*, Festgabe für K.G. Kuhn, Göttingen, Vandenhoek and Ruprecht, 1971.

JACKSON, J. FOAKES
- *Josephus and the Jews*, New York, 1930.
JACKSON, J. FOAKES and LAKE, K.
- *The Beginnings of Christianity*, 5 vols., London, 1920-30.
JAKOBY, F.
- 'Justus(von Tiberias) in PW 10/2 (1919) 1341-6.
JEREMIAS, J.
- *The Parables of Jesus*, 3rd ed. English trans., London, S.C.M., 1966.
- *Jerusalem at the Time of Jesus*, English trans., London, S.C.M., 1969.
JOHNSON, S.E.
- 'Jesus and First Century Galilee' in *In Memoriam E. Lohmeyer*, Stuttgart, 1951, 73-88.
JONES, A.M.H.
- *The Cities of the Eastern Roman Provinces*, 2nd ed. Oxford, 1971.
- *The Herods of Judaea*, 2nd ed. Oxford, Clarendon Press, 1967.
- 'The Urbanisation of Palestine', JRS 21(1931) 79-85.
- 'The Urbanisation of the Ituraean Principality', JRS 21(1933) 265-75.
JUSTER, J.
- *Les Juifs dans L'Empire Romain, Leur Condition Juridique, Economique et Sociale*. 2 vols, Paris 1914.

KADMAN, L.
- *The Coins of the Jewish War*, Jerusalem, 1960.
KAHRSTEDT, U.
- *Syrische Territorien in Hellenistischer Zeit*, Berlin, 1926.
KALLMER, D.H. and E. ROSENAU
- 'Regions of Palestine', Geographical Review, 29(1939) 61-80.
KAMINKA, A.
- *Studien zur Geschichte Galiläas*, Berlin 1889.
KANAEL, B.
- 'The Partition of Judaea by Gabinius', IEJ 7(1957) 98-106.
KARMON, Y.
- 'Geographical Aspects of the Coastal Plain of Israel', IEJ 6(1956) 33-50.

KASTING, H.
- *Die Anfänge Christlichen Mission*, Munich, Kaiser, 1969.
KECK, L.
- 'Mk 3:7-12 and Markan Christology', JBL 84(1965) 341-58.
- 'On the Ethos of Early Christians', JAAR 42(1974) 435-52.
KEDAR, J. and GOLAMB, B.
- 'Ancient Agriculture in the Galilean Mountains', IEJ 21(1971) 136-40.
KEE, H. CLARK
- *Community of the New Age. Studies in Mark's Gospel*, Philadelphia, Westminster Press, 1977.
KELLY, J.N.D.
Jerome, New York, Harper and Row, 1975.
KENNARD, J.
- 'Judas of Galilee and his Clan', JQR 36(1945/6) 281-6.
KILPATRICK, G.
- *The Origins of the Gospel according to St. Matthew*, Oxford, Clarendon, 1946.
KINDLER, A.
- *The Coins of Tiberias*, Tiberias 1961.
KINGDON, H.P.
- 'Who were the Zealots and their Leaders in A.D. 66?' NTS 17(1970) 68-72.

KIPPENBERG, H.
- *Gerizim und Synagoge. Traditionsgeschichtliche Untersuchngen zur Samaritanischen Religion der Aramäischen Periode*, Religionsgeschichtliche Versuche und Vorarbeiten 30, Berlin 1970.
KLAUSNER, J.
- *Jesus von Nazareth*, Berlin, 1930.
- 'The Economy of Judaea in the Period of the Second Temple' in *The World History of the Jewish People. The Herodian Period*.

KLEIN, G.
- *Die Zwölf Apostel. Ursprung und Gehalt einer Idee*, FRLANT 77, Göttingen 1961.
KLEIN, S.
- *Galilee: Geography and History of Galilee from the Return from Babylonia to the Conclusion of the Talmud by S. Klein. Completed from the Literary Remains of the Author*

and ed. by Y. Eltizur (Hebr.) (Trans. & Colls. in Jew. Studs. 20), Jerusalem, 1967.

- *Beiträge zur Geschichte und Geographie Galiläas*, Leipzig, 1909.
- *Neue Beiträge zur Geschichte und Geographie Galiläas*, Vienna, 1923.
- *Galiläa vor der Makkabaerzeit bis 67*, Berlin 1928.
- 'Hebräische Ortsnamen bei Josephus', MGWJ 59(1915) 163f.
- 'Zur Geographie Palastinas in der Zeit der Mischna' MGWJ 61(1917) 139-141.

KLIJN, A.F.J.
- 'The Study of Jewish Christianity', NTS 20(1974/5) 419-31.
- 'Jerome's Quotations from a Nazoraean Interpretation of Isaiah' in *Judéo-Christianisme. Recherches historiques et théologiques offertes en homage au Cardinal Jean Daniélou* (= RSR 1972), 241-55.

KLIJN, A.F.J. and REININK, G.J.
- *Patristic Evidence for Jewish-Christian Sects*, Leiden, Brill, 1973.

KLINZING, G.
- *Die Umdeutung des Kultus in der Qumrangemeinde und im Neuen Testament*, Göttingen, 1967.

KOHL, H. and WATZINGER, C.
- *Antike Synagogen in Galiläa*, Leipzig, 1919.

KOPP, C.
- *The Holy Places of the Gospels*, English trans. London, 1964.

KRAUSS, S.
- *Talmudische Archäologie*, 3 vols., Reprint Hildesheim, Olms, 1966.
- *Synagogale Altertümer*, Reprint Hildesheim, Olms, 1966.

KREISSIG, H.
- *Die Sozialen Zusammenhänge des Judäischen Krieges*, Berlin, 1970.

KÜMMEL, W.
- *Introduction to the New Testament*, English trans. London, S.C.M. 1966.

KUNDSIN, K.
- *Topologische Überlieferungsstoffe im Johannes-Evangelium: Eine Untersuchung*, FRLANT 22, Göttingen 1925.

KUTSCHER, E.Y.
- *Studies in Galilean Aramaic*, English trans. Bar Ilan Univ. Jerusalem, 1976.
KUHN, K.G.
- *Achtzehngebet, Vaterunser und der Reim*, Tübingen, Mohr, 1950.
- 'Gilgonim und Sifre Minim' in *Judentum, Urchristentum, Kirche, Festschrift J. Jeremias*, Beih. ZNW 26, Berlin Töpelmann, 1964, 24-61.

LAGRANGE, M.J.
- *L'Évangile selon Marc*, Paris 1926.
LAKE, K.
- 'The Zealots' in *The Beginnings of Christianity*, vol. 1, 1920, Appendix 1, 421-5.
LANDAU, Y.H.
- 'A Greek Inscription found near Hefzibah', IEJ 16(1966) 56-70.
LAPP, P.W.
- 'The Second and Third Campaigns at 'Araq el 'Emir', BASOR 171(1963) 8-38.
LAQUEUR, R.
- *Der Jüdische Historiker, Flavius Josephus*, Giessen 1920.
LAUNEY, M.
- *Recherches sur les Armées hellénistiques*. Bibliothèque des Écoles francaises d'Athènes et de Rome, 169, 2 vols., Paris 1949/50.
LeMOYNE, J.
- *Les Sadducées*, Paris, Gabalda, 1972.
LEVICK, B.
- *Roman Colonies in Southern Asia Minor*, Oxford, Univ. Press, 1967.
LIEBERMAN, S.
- *Greek in Jewish Palestine*, New York, 1940.
- *Hellenism in Jewish Palestine*, New York, 1950.
- 'Roman Legal Institutions in early Rabbinics and the Acta Martyrum', JQR 35(1944) 1-57.

LIEBESNY, II.
- 'Ein Erlass des Königs Ptolemaios II, Philadelphus über die Deklaration von Vieh und Sklaven in Syrien und Phönikien', Aegyptus 16(1936) 257-88.

LIFSHITZ, B.
- 'Der Kult des Zeus Akraios und des Zeus Bakchos in Beisan (Skythopolis)' ZDPV 77(1961) 186-90.
- 'Papyrus Grecs du Desert de Juda', Aegyptus 42(1962) 240-56.
- 'L'Hellénisation des Juifs de Palestine À propos des inscriptions de Besara (Beth Shearim)', RB 72(1965) 520-38.
- *Donateurs et Fundateurs dans les Synagogues Juives*, Cahier de la RB 7, Paris, Gabala, 1967.

LIFSHITZ, B., MAISLER, B., AVIGAD, N.
- *Beth Shearim. Report on the Excavations.* 3 vols. Jerusalem, 1957-71.

LIGHTFOOT, R.H.
- *Locality and Doctrine in the Gospels*, London, 1938.
- *The Gospel Message of St. Mark*, Oxford, Paperbacks, 1962.

LIMBECK, M.
- 'Jesus und die Wirklichkeit des Bösen', in H. Haag, *Teufelsglaube*, Tübingen, 1974, 273-318.

LINDNER, H.
- *Die Geschichtsaufassung des Flavius Josephus im Bellum Judaicum*, AGSU 12, Leiden, Brill, 1972.

LINNEMANN, E.
- *The Parables of Jesus. Introduction and Exposition.* English trans., London, S.P.C.K. 1966.

LIVER, J.
- 'The Half Shekel Offering in Biblical and post-Biblical Literature', HTR 56(1963) 173-98.

LOFFREDA, S.
- *Cafarnao II. La Ceramica*, Jerusalem 1974.

LOFTUS, F.
- 'A Note on SYNTAGMA TWN GALILAIWN, B.J. iv, 558', JQR 65(1975) 182-3.
- 'The Martyrdom of the Galilean Troglodytes (B.J. 1,312-13)', JQR 66(1976) 212-23.

LOHMEYER, E.
- *Galiläa und Jerusalem*, FRLANT 34, Göttingen 1936.
LUTHER, H.
- *Josephus und Justus von Tiberias. Ein Beitrag zur Geschichte des jüdischen Aufstandes*, Halle, 1910.

MADDEN, F.W.
- *A History of Jewish Coinage*, London 1864, Reprint Ktav, New York, 1967.
MAISLER, B.
- 'Beth Shearim, Gaba, Harosheth of the Peoples', HUCA 24(1952) 75-84.
- 'The Excavations at Beth Yerach (Khirbet Kerak)', IEJ 2(1952) 165-73 and 218-29.
MALINOWSKI, F.
- *Galilee in Josephus*, Unpublished Duke Univ. Doctoral Dissertation, 1074 Ann Arbor, Univ. Microfilms.
MANTEL, H.
- *Studies in the History of the Sanhedrin*, Cambridge, Mass. 1961.
- 'The High Priesthood and the Sanhedrin in the Time of the Second Temple', in *World History of the Jewish People, Herodian Period*, 264-73.
- 'The Causes of the Bar Coqba Revolt', JQR 58(1968) 224-42, 274-96.
MARTYN, J.L.
- *History and Theology in the Fourth Gospel*, New York, Harper and Row, 1963.
- 'We have Found Elijah', in *Jews, Greeks and Christians. Religious Culture in Late Antiquity. Essays in Honour of W.D. Davies*, Leiden, Brill, 1976, 186-219.
- 'Glimpses into the History of the Johannine Community', in *L'Évangile de Jean.Sources,Rédaction, Théologie*, M. de Jonge ed. Gembloux Ducolot, 1977, 149-75.
- 'Clementine Recognitions, 1,33-71, Jewish Christianity and The Fourth Gospel', in *God's Christ and His People. Studies in Honour of Nils Alstrup Dahl*, Bergen, Universitetsvorlaget, 1977, 233-47.

MARXSEN, W.
- *Der Evangelist Markus. Studien zur Redaktionsgeschichte des Evangeliums*, FRLANT 67, Göttingen, 1956.
- *The New Testament. An Introduction.* English trans. Oxford, Blackwell, 1968.

MASTERMANN, E.W.
- *Studies in Galilee*, Chicago, 1909.

MAYES, A.M.H.
- *Israel in the Period of the Judges*, SBT 2nd series, 29, London, S.C.M., 1974.

McMULLEN, R.
- *Roman Social Relations*, New Haven, Yale Univ. Press, 1974.

McLEAN HARPER, G.
- 'A Study in the Commercial Relations between Egypt and Syria in the Third Century B.C.' AJPh 49(1928) 1-35.
- 'Village Administration in the Roman Province of Syria', Yale Cl. St. 1(1928) 105-68.

MEEKS, W.A.
- *The Prophet-King. Moses Traditions and the Fourth Gospel*, Suppl. Nov. Test. XIV, Leiden, Brill, 1967.
- 'Galilee and Jerusalem in the Fourth Gospel', JBL 85(1966) 159-69.
- 'The Man from Heaven in Johannine Sectarianism', JBL 91(1972) 44-72.

MEEKS, W.A. and JERVELL, J., eds.
- *God's Christ and His People. Studies in Honor of Nils Alstrup Dahl*, Bergen, Universitetsvorlaget, 1977.

MENDENHALL, G.
- 'The Hebrew Conquest of Palestine', BA 25(1962) 66-87.

MERKEL, H.
- 'Jesus und die Pharisäer', NTS 14(1968) 194-208.

MERRILL, T.
- *Galilee in the Time of Christ*, London, 1885.

MESHEL, Z.
- 'Was there a Via Maris?' IEJ 23(1973) 162-6.

MESHORER, Y.
- *Jewish Coins of the Second Temple Period*, English trans., I.H. Levine, Tel Aviv, 1967.

MEYER, E.
- *Ursprung und Anfänge des Christentums*, 3 vols. Reprint, Hildesheim, Olms, 1962.

MEYER, R.
- *Der Prophet aus Galiläa*, Reprint, Darmstadt, 1970.
- 'Die Angebliche Demaj-Gesetz Hyrkans I', ZNW 38(1939) 124-31.
- 'Der Am ha-Ares. Ein Beitrag zur Religionssoziologie Palästinas im ersten und zweiten Jahrhundert', Judaica 3(1947) 169-99.
- 'Die Figurendarstellung in der Kunst der späthellenistischen Zeit', Judaica 5(1949) 1-40.
- *Tradition und Neuschöpfung im Antiken Judentum. Dargestellt an der Geschichte des Pharisäismus*, Berlin, 1965.

MEYERS, E.
- 'Galilean Regionalism as a Factor in Historical Reconstruction', BASOR 21(1976) 93-101.
- 'Synagogue Architecture' *Interpreters Dictionary of the Bible*, Supplementary Vol., 842-4.

MEYERS, E., KRAABEL, A.T., STRANGE, J.F.
- *Ancient Synagogue Excavations at Khirbet Shema', Upper Galilee, Israel, 1970-72*, AASOR vol XLII, Duke Univ. Press, 1976.

MEYSHAN, J.
- 'A New Cointype of Herod Agrippa II and its Meaning', IEJ 11(1961) 181-3.

MICHEL, O.
- 'Studien zu Josephus. Simon Bar Giora', NTS 14(1967/8) 402-8.

MICHEL, O., BAUERENFEIND, O., BETZ, O.
- 'Der Tempel der goldenen Kuh. Bemerkungen zur Polemik im Spätjudentum', ZNW 48(1957) 197-212.

MILIK, J.
- 'Une lettre de Siméon Bar Kokeba', RB 60(1953) 276-94.

MILLER, J.M.
- 'The Israelite Conquest of Canaan', in *Israelite and Judaean History*, Philadelphia, Westminster, 1976.

MINEAR, P.
- 'Audience Criticism and Markan Ecclesiology', in *Neues Testament und Geschichte, Festschrift Oscar Cullmann,* Tübingen, Mohr, 1972.

MINTZ, S.W.
- 'Rural Proletariat and the Problem of Rural Proletarian Consciousness', JPS 1(1974) 291-325.

MITTWOCH, A.
- 'Tribute and Land-tax in Seleucid Judaea', Biblica 36(1955) 352-61.

MONTEFIORE, C.
- 'Revolt in the Desert', NTS 8(1961) 135-41.

MOORE, G.F.
- *Judaism in the First Centuries of the Christian Era. The Age of the Tannaim,* 3 vols., Cambridge, Harvard Univ. Press, 1927-30.
- 'Nazoreans and Nazareth' in *The Beginnings of Christianity,* 1, Appendix B, 426-32.

MOMIGLIANO, A.
- *Giudea Romano. Richerche sull' Organizazione della Guidea sotto il Dominio Romano (63 a.C. - 70 d.C.),* Reprint Amsterdam, 1967.

MUNCK, J.
- 'Jewish Christianity in post-Apostolic Times', NTS 6(1959) 103-16.

NEUBAUER, A.
- *La Géographie du Talmud,* Paris, 1868.

NEUSNER, J.
- 'The Fellowship in the Second Jewish Commonwealth', HTR 53(1960) 125-42.
- *A Life of Rabban Yohanan ben Zakkai,* Leiden, Brill, 1962.
- 'Jewish Use of Pagan Symbols after 70 C.E.', JR 43(1970) 285-94.
- *Development of a Legend. Studies in the Traditions Concerning Yohanan ben Zakkai,* Leiden, Brill, 1970.
- 'Studies in the *Taqqanôth* of Yavneh', HTR 63(1970) 183-98.

- *Rabbinic Traditions about the Pharisees before 70*, 3 vols. Leiden, Brill, 1971.
- *Eliezer ben Hyrcanus. The Traditions and the Man*. 2 vols. Leiden, Brill, 1973.
- '"Pharisaic-Rabbinic Judaism". A Clarification', HR 12(1973) 250-70.
- *From Politics to Piety. The Emergence of Pharisaic Judaism*, Englewood Cliffs, Prentice Hall, 1973.
- *First Century Judaism in Crisis. Yohanan ben Zakkai and the Renaissance of Torah*, Nashville, Abingdon 1975.
- *The Idea of Purity in Ancient Judaism: The Haskell Lectures 1972-73*. Brill, Leiden, 1975.

NOTH, M.
- 'Studien zu den historisch-geographischen Dokumenten des Josuabuches', ZDPV 58(1935) 188-255.
- *The History of Israel*, 2nd English ed., London, A. and C. Black, 1959.

ODEN, R.A.
- 'Ba'al Shamem and 'El'', CBQ 34(1977) 457-73.

OEHLER, W.
- 'Die Ortschaften und Grenzen Galiläas nach Josephus', ZDPV 28(1905) 1-26 and 49-74.

OEPKE, A.
- 'Die Bevolkerungsproblem Galiläas', ThLB 69(1941) 201-5.

OPPENHEIMER, A.
- *The 'Am Ha-Aretz. A Study in the Social History of the Jewish People in the Hellenistic-Roman Period*. English trans. Leiden, Brill, 1977.

ORNI, and EFRAT, E.
- *Geography of Israel*, 3rd rev. ed. New York, 1971.

OVADYA, A.
- 'Greek Religion in Beth Shean/Scythopolis in the Greco-Roman Period', (Hebrew), Eretz Israel 12(1975) 116-24.

PERRIN, N.
- *The Kingdom of God in the Preaching of Jesus*, London, S.C.M., 1963.
- *Rediscovering the Teaching of Jesus*, London, S.C.M. 1967.

- *The New Testament. An Introduction*, Harcourt, Brace, Jovanovich, 1972.
- *Jesus and the Language of the Kingdom. Symbol and Metaphor in New Testament Interpretation*, Philadelphia, Fortress, 1976.

de la POTTERIE, I.
- 'Jésus Roi et Juge d'après *Jn* 19:13', Biblica 41(1960) 217-47.

PRAUSNITZ, W.
- 'The First Agricultural Settlements in Galilee', IEJ 9(1959) 166-74.

PRÉAUX, C.
- *L-Économie Royale des Lagides*, Brussels, 1939.
- 'Les Villes hellénistiques, pricipalment en Orient: Leur Institutions Administratif et Judiciaries' in *La Ville. Receuils de la Societé Jean Bodin*, 3 vols., Brussels, 1954-7. vol. 1, 67-134.

RABBINOWITZ, J.J.
- 'Note sur le lettre de Bar Kokbha', RB 61(1954) 191f.

RABIN, C.
- 'Hebrew and Aramaic in the First Century' in *Compendia Rerum Judaicarum*, 2, 1007-39.

RAJAK, T.
- 'Justus of Tiberias', CQ 23(1973) 345-68.

REDFIELD, R.
- *The Little Community and Peasant Society and Culture.* Chicago, Univ. Press, 1960.

REDFIELD, R. and M. SINGER.
- 'The Cultural Role of Cities' in *Economic Development and Social Change*, 3(1954) 57-73.

REICKE, B.
- *The New Testament Era*, English trans. London, A. and C. Black, 1968.

REIFENBERG, A.
- *Ancient Jewish Coins*, London, 1948.

REISENFELD, H.
- *The Gospel Tradition and its Beginnings. A Study in the Limits of Formgeschichte*, London 1957.

RHOADS, D.M.
- *Israel in Revoluton, 6-74 C.E. A Political History based on the Writings of Josephus*, Philadelphia, Fortress, 1976.
RICHTER, G.
- 'Präesentische und futurische Eschatologie im 4 Evangelium', in *Gegenwart und Kommendes Reich. Schülergabe Anton Vögtle zum 65 Geburtstag*, ed. P. Fiedler and D. Zeller, Stuttgart, Katholisches Bibelwerk, 1975, 117-52.
RIVKIN, E.
- 'The Internal City: Judaism and Urbanisation', JSSR 5(1966) 225-40.
- 'Defining the Pharisees: The Tannaitic Sources', HUCA 40/1(1969/70) 205-49.
- 'Pharisees' in *Interpreters Dictionary of the Bible*, Suppl. vol. 657-63.
ROBINSON, J.A.T.
- *Twelve New Testament Essays*, SBT 34, London, S.C.M., 1962.
ROBINSON, J.M.
- *The Problem of History in Mark*, SBT 21, London, S.C.M., 1957.
ROSTOVTZEFF, M.
- *Social and Economic History of the Hellenistic World*, 3 vols., Reprint Oxford Univ. Press, 1959.
- *Social and Economic History of the Roman Empire*, 2 vols. 2nd rev. ed. Oxford, Clarendon Press, 1957.
ROTH, C.
- 'An Ordinance against Images in Jerusalem', HTR 49(1956) 151-64.
- 'The Debate on the Loyal Sacrifices', HTR 53(1960) 93-7.
- 'The Historical Implications of the Jewish Coinage of the First Revolt', IEJ 12(1961) 33-46.
- 'The Pharisees and the Jewish Revolution of 66-73', JSS 7(1962) 63-80.
ROWLEY, H.H.
- 'The Herodians in the Gospels', JTS 41(1940) 14-27.

SAFRAI, S.
- *Pilgrimage at the Time of the Second Temple*, Hebrew, Tel Aviv 1965.

- 'The Teaching of Pietists in Mishnaic Literature', JSS 16(1965) 15-33.
- 'Pilgrimage to Jerusalem at the End of the Second Temple Period', in *Studies in the Jewish Background of the New Testament*, O. Michel et al., Assen, van Gorcum, 1969, 12-21.
- 'The Holy Congregation of Jerusalem', St. Hier. 23(1972) 62-78.
- 'Jewish Self-Government' in *Compendia Rerum Judaicarum*, 1, 377-419.
- 'Education and the Study of the Torah', in *Compendia Rerum Judaicarum*, 2, 945-70.

SALDERINI, A.
- *The Fathers according to Rabbi Nathan*, Leiden, Brill, 1975.

SALOMONSEN, B.
- 'Some Remarks on the Zealots with Special Regard to the Term *qannaîm* in Rabbinic Literature', NTS 12(1966) 164-76.

SANDERS, E.P.
- *Paul and Palestinian Judaism*, Philadelphia, Fortress, 1977.

SAUNDERS, T.
- *An Introduction to the Survey of Western Palestine*, London, 1881.

SCHALIT, A.
- 'Josephus und Justus. Studien zur *Vita* des Josephus', Klio 26(1933) 67-95.
- *König Herodes*, Berlin, 1969.
- ed. *World History of the Jewish People. First Series, vol. 7, The Hellenistic Age*. Jerusalem, Masada Publishing House, 1972.
- 'The End of the Hasmonaean Dynasty and the Rise of Herod', *World History of the Jewish People, Herodian Age*, 44-70.
- 'Domestic Politics and Political Institutions', *ib.*, 255-97.

SCHALLER, B.
- 'Hekataios von Abdera über, die Juden, zur Frage der Echtheit und der Datierung, ZNW 54(1963) 15-31.

SCHATTNER, I.
- *Israel Pocket Library. Geography*, Jerusalem, Keter Books 1973.

SCHILLE, G.
- 'Tie Topographie des Markusevangeliums, ihre Hinter-
grund und ihre Einordnung', ZDPV 73(1957) 133-66.
SCHLATTER, A.
- *Geschichte Israels von Alexander dem Grossen bis Hadrian*,
Reprint, Darmstadt, 1972.
SCHMIDKE, A.
- *Neue Fragmente zu den Judenchristlichen Evangelien*,
Leipzig, 1911.
SCHMITHALS, W.
- *Paul and James*, SBT 47, English trans. London, S.C.M.
1965.
SCHNACKENBURG, R.
- *Gottes Herrschaft und Reich*, Freiburg, Herder, 1959.
- 'Das Evangelium in Verständnis des altesten Evangelisten',
in *Orientierung an Jesus. Zur Theologie der Synoptiker,
Festschrift Josef Schmid*, ed. P. Hoffman, Freiburg, Herder,
1973.
SCHOEPS, H.J.
- *Theologie und Geschichte des Judenchristentums*, Tübin-
gen, Mohr, 1949.
SCHOLEM, G.
- *The Messianic Idea in Judaism and Other Essays on Jewish
Spirituality*, New York, Schocken, 1971.
SCHÜRMANN, H.
- 'Die vorösterlichen Anfänge der Logientradition' in *Der
historische Jesus und der kerygmatische Christus*, Berlin
1961, ed. H. Ristow and K. Matthiae, 342-70.
SCHULZ, S.
- *Q. Die Spruchquelle der Evangelisten*, Zürich, Theolo-
gischer Verlag, 1972.
SCHÜRER, E.
- *Geschichte des Jüdischen Volkes im Zeitalter Jesus Christi*,
3 vols., reprint Hildesheim, Olms, 1971.
- Review of A. Büchler, *Der Galiläische Am ha'Arez*, in Theol.
Lit. Zeit. 23(1906) 619f.
SCHWÖBEL, V.
- 'Galiläa: Die Verkehrswege und Ansiedlungen in ihrer
Abhängigkeit von den natürlichen Bedingungen', ZDPV
27(1904) 1-151.

SCOBIE, C.
- 'The Origins and Development of Samaritan Christianity',
  NTS 19(1973) 390-414.
SEITZ, O.J.F.
- 'Love Your Enemies', NTS 16(1969) 39-54.
SEVENSTER, J.N.
- *Do You Know Greek? How Much Greek could the First
  Century Jewish Christians have Known?*, Suppl. to Nov.
  Test. 19, Leiden, Brill, 1969.
SEYRING, H.
- 'Les Éres d'Agrippa II', Revue Numismatique, 6th ser.
  1964, 55-65.
SHANIN, T.
- 'The Nature and Logic of Peasant Economics', JPS 1(1974)
  186-204.
SHERWIN-WHITE, A.N.
- *Roman Society and Roman Law in the New Testament*,
  Oxford, Univ. Press, 1963.
SIMON, M.
- 'La migration a Pella: Legénde ou realité?', in *Judéo-
  Christianisme. Recherches historiques et théologiques
  offertes en homage au Cardinal Jean Daniélou*, 37-74.
SMALLWOOD, E.M.
- 'High Priests and Politics in Roman Palestine', JTS
  13(1962) 17-37.
SMITH, G.A.
- *The Historical Geography of the Holy Land*, 25 ed. London,
  1931.
SMITH, J.Z.
- 'The Temple and the Magician', in *God's Christ and his
  People. Studies in Honour of Nils Alstrup Dahl*, 233-47.
- 'The Social Description of Early Christianity', Rel. Std.
  Rev. 1(1975) 19-25.
SMITH, M.
- 'Zealots and Sicarii. Their Origin and Relation', HTR
  64(1971) 1-19.
- 'Palestinian Judaism in the First Century' in *Israel its Role
  in Civilisation*, ed. M. Davis, New York, Harper and Row,
  1956.
- *Jesus the Magician*, New York, Harper and Row, 1978.

STEMBERGER, G.
- 'Galilee - Land of Salvation?', Appendix IV, of W.D. Davies, *The Gospel and the Land*, 409-38.

STENDAHL, K.
- *The School of St. Matthew*, 2nd ed. Philadelphia, Fortress, 1968.
- 'Quis et Unde. An Analysis of Mt 1-2', in *Judentum, Urchristentum, Kirche. Festschrift J. Jeremias*, 94-105.

STERN, M.
- *Greek and Latin Authors on Jews and Judaism*, vol. 1, Jerusalem Masada Publishing House, 1976.
- 'The Reign of Herod and the Herodian Dynasty' in *Compendia Rerum Judaicarum ad Novum Testamentum*, I, 216-307.

STOCK, K.
- *Boten aus dem Mit-Ihm Sein*. Analecta Biblica 70, Rome, P.I.B. Press, 1975.

STRACK, H. and BILLERBECK, P.
- *Kommentar zum Neuen Testament aus Talmud und Midrasch*, 5 vols. Munich, Beck, 1922-56.

STRECKER, G.
- *Das Judenchristentum in den Pseudoclementinen*, Berlin, 1958.
- *Der Weg der Gerechtigkeit. Untersuchung zur Theologie des Mätthaus*. FRLANT 82, Göttingen, Vandenhoeck and Ruprecht, 1962.
- 'The Concept of History in Matthew', JAAR 25(1967) 220-30.

SINGER, M. and REDFIELD, R.
- 'The Cultural Role of Cities' im *Economic Development and Social Change*, 3(1954) 57-73.

TANNEHILL, R.
- *The Sword of His Mouth*, Semeia Suppl. 1, Philadelphia, Fortress, 1975.

TARN, W.W.
- 'The New Hellenistic Kingdoms', in *The Cambridge Ancient History*, vol. 7, Cambridge Univ. Press, 1928, 75-109.

TARN, W.W. and GRIFFITH, G.
- *Hellenistic Civilization*, 3rd. rev. ed. London, Arnold, 1959.

TAYLOR, V.
- *The Gospel according to St. Mark*, London, S.P.C.K., 1962.

TCHERIKOVER, V.
- *Palestine Under the Ptolemies. A Contribution to the Study of the Zenon Papyri, Mizraim IV-V*, New York, 1937.
- *Die Hellenistischen Städtegründungen von Alexander dem Grossem bis auf die Römerzeit*, Philologus, Suppl. 19, 1, Leipzig, 1927.
- *Hellenistic Civilzation and the Jews*, Philadelphia, Jewish Publication Company of America, 1959.
- 'Was Jerusalem a Polis?', IEJ 14(1964) 61-78.
- 'The Hellenistic Environment', and 'Hellenistic Palestine', in A. Schalit, ed. *The World History of the Jewish People, The Hellenistic Age*, Parts one and two.

TEIXIDOR, J.
- *The Pagan God, Popular Religion in the Greco-Roman Near East*, Princeton Univ. Press, N. Jersey, 1977.

THEISSEN, G.
- 'Wanderradikalismus: Literatursoziologische Aspekte der Uberlieferung von Worten Jesu im Urchristentum', ZTK 70(1973) 245-71.
- 'Die Tempelweissagung, Jesu. Prophetie im Spannungsfeld von Stadt und Land', TZ 32(1967) 144-58.
- '"Wir haben Alles verlassen" (Mk 10:28). Nachfolge und soziale Entwurtzelung in der jüdisch-palästinischen Gesellschaft des 1 Jahrhunderts' n. Ch.', Nov. Test 19(1977) 161-96.
- *Sociology of Early Palestinian Christianity*, English trans. Philadelphia, Fortress, 1977.

THOMAS, J.
- *La Mouvment Baptiste en Palestine et Syrie, (150 a.J.-C. - 300 apr. J.-C.)*, Gembloux, Ducolet, 1935.

TORREY, C.C.
- 'The Name Iscariot', HTR 36(1943) 51-62.

TRILLING, W.
- *Das Wahre Israel. Studien zur Theologie des Matthäusevangeliums*, 3 ed., SANT 10, Munich, 1964.

TROCMÉ, E.
- *La Formation de l'Évangile selon Marc*, Paris, Presses Universitaires de France, 1963.

VAN CANGH, J.M.
- 'La Galilée dans l'Évangile de Marc: un Lieu Theologique?' RB 79(1972) 59-76.
VERMES, G.
- *Scripture and Tradition in Judaism*, Leiden, Brill, 1961.
- 'Hanina ben Dosa. A Controversial Galilean Saint from the First Century of the Christian Era', JSS 23(1972) 28-50 and 24(1973) 51-64.
- *Jesus the Jew*, London, Collins, 1975.
VIELHAUER, P.
- 'The Jewish Christian Gospels' in Hennecke and Schnee-melcher, *The New Testament Apocrypha*, I, 117-65.
VINCENT, L.H.
- 'La Palestine dans les Papyrus Ptolémaiques', RB 29(1920) 161-202.
VOLZ, P.
- *Die Eschatologie der Jüdischen Gemeinde im Neutesta-mentlichen Zeitalter*, 2 ed. Tübingen, 1934.
VON CAMPENHAUSEN, H.
- 'The Authority of Jesus' Relatives in the Early Church' in *Jerusalem and Rome*, Facet Books, Philadelphia Fortress, 1966, 1-19.
VON RAD, G.
- *Theology of the Old Testament*, 2 vols., English trans., London, Oliver and Boyd, 1965.
VON SCHROETTER, E.
- *Wörterbuch der Münzkunde*, Berlin-Leipzig, 1930.

WACHOLDER, B.
- 'Pseudo-Eupolemus. Two Greek Fragments on the Life of Abraham', HUCA 34(1963) 83-113.
WALBANK, F.W.
- *An Historical Commentary on Polybius*, 2 vols. Oxford Univ. Press, 1957, 1961.

WEEDEN, T.
- 'The Heresy that Necessitated Mark's Gospel', ZNW 59(1968) 145-68.

WEINBURG, G. DAVIDSON.
- 'Hellenistic Glass from Tel Anafa in Upper Galilee', Journal of Glass Studies, 12(1970) 17-27.

WEINBERG, S.S.
- 'Tel Anafa', IEJ 19(1969) 250-2.
- 'Tel Anafa. The Hellenistic Town', IEJ 21(1971) 87-109.

WEIPPERT, M.
- *The Settlement of the Israelite Tribes in Palestine*, SBT 2nd ser. 21, London, S.C.M., 1971.

WEISS, H.
- 'Der Pharisäismus im Lichte der Überlieferung des Neuen Testaments', in R. Meyer, *Tradition und Neuschöpfung im Antiken Judentum.*

WELCH, A.C.
- 'The Death of Josiah', JBL 92(1973) 11-22.

WELLES, C.B.
- *Royal Correspondence in the Hellenistic Age*, New Haven, Yale Univ. Press, 1934.

WIEDER, N.
- *The Judaean Scrolls and Karaism*, London, 1962.

WINTER, P.
- *The Trial of Jesus*, Berlin, de Gruyter 1961.

WIRGEN, A.
- 'A Note on the Reed of Tiberias', IEJ 18(1968) 248f.

WORSLEY, P.
- *The Trumpet Shall Sound. A Study of 'Cargo Cults' in Melanasia*, New York, Schocken, 1968.

WRIGHT, G.E.
- 'The Samaritans at Schechem', HTR 55(1962) 357-66.

WRIGHT, G.E. and BULL, R.J.
- 'Newly Discovered Temples on Mt. Gerizim in Jordan', HTR 58(1965) 234-7.

YADIN, Y.
- *Hazor. The Rediscovery of a Biblical Citadel*, New York, Random Books, 1975.
- *Bar-Kokhba*, New York, Random House, 1971.

YEIVIN, S.
- 'Historical Notes', in *Preliminary Report of the University of Michigan Excavations at Sepphoris, Palestine*, 1931, Ann Arbor, 1937, 23-31.

YODER, J.H.
- *The Politics of Jesus*, Grand Rapids, Eerdmans, 1972.

ZEITLIN, S.
- 'A Survey of Jewish Historiography: From the Biblical Books to the Sefer ha-Kabbalah, with special Emphasis on Josephus', JQR 59(1968) 171-214 and 60(1969) 37-68.
- 'Who were the Galileans? New Light on Josephus' Activities in Galilee', JQR 64(1973/4) 189-203.

INDEX OF ANCIENT AUTHORS

I. OLD TESTAMENT

---

*Denotes reference is to be found in notes.

II. PSEUDEPIGRAPHA

Letter of Aristeas		*Psalms of Solomon*		*Syrian Baruch*	
15f	298*	8:5-14	213	62:5	253*
115	104	17:1-11	48	68:3	275
121	151*	17:23	213	77:19	253*
		17:32f	213	77:25	343*
		17:33	187	78:1	253*
Jubilees					
13:8	283			*Testament of*	
13:26f	283	*Assumption of*		*Benjamin*	
30:5	275	*Moses*		9:2	253*
30:7	275	9:1-7	249*		
31:11-12	249*			*Testament of*	
				Levi	
32:15	283	*IV Ezra*		8:11-17	249*
50:12	337*	13:39ff	253*	17:11-18:14	249*

III. QUMRAN

Damascus		8:1-10	302*	*Florilegium*	
Document (CD)		8:4-7	295	*(4QFlor)*	
1:16	295	9:3ff	295	1:1-13	302*
6:11-14	302*	9:3-6	302*		
6:20	302*				
8:1	295			*Ordinances*	
12:15-17	338*	*Habakkuk Pesher*		*(4Q Ord)*	
		(1QpHab)		6f	280
War Scroll (1 QM)		8:8-13	302*		
2:1-3	253*	9:3-7	302*		
Community Rule		9:9-12	302*	*Testimonia*	
(1 QS)		11:4-8	302*	*(4QTest)*	
5:5-7	302*	12:7-9	302*	28:30	302*

IV. NEW TESTAMENT

Matthew		2:14	385*	2:22f	360,361,
2:3	382*	2:20	386*		385*
2:12	385*	2:21	386*	4:12	385*
2:13	385*	2:22	385*	4:12-16	385*

V. JEWISH HELLENISTIC WRITINGS

448

VI. RABBINIC LITERATURE

5. OTHER
RABBINIC
WRITINGS

Aboth de R.
Nathan, A
6:8   252*
27   339*
28a   307

Midrash Rabah
Gn 7:9   21*
Nm 18:22   21*
Ru 1:8   153*

Cant 2:5   327
Qoh 1:1   97*,342*,
         343*
    1:8   361

Midrash Tannaim
(ed. Hoffman)
Dt 26:13(p176) 303*
    32:13(p198)   167

Mekilta de R.
Ishmael
Ex 19:1   280

Mekhilta de R.
Simeon ben Yohai
Ex 18:21   331

Sifre
Lv 26:17   167

Semahoth
3:6   317
10:15   317

Targum Ps.-
Jonathan
Dt 33:11   275

VII. GRAECO-ROMAN AUTHORS

Arrian
Dissertationes
   4,7.6   248*
Cicero
Ad Atticum
   VI,2.4   92*
De Provinciis
   Consularibus
   V,10   206*
Dio Cassius
History
   LV,27.6   94*
Diodorus
   XVIII,6   27
   XVIII,37.3-4   147*
Herodotus
Histories
   I,105   109
   IV.79-80.108   270
Juvenal
Satires
   XIV,97   299*

Macrobius
Saturnalia
   I,23.10   300*
Martial
Epigrams
   XVIII,85   204*
Pliny
Natural History
   V,15.70-72   15
   V,17.75   147*
   V,18.74   112
   V,68   387*
   V,70   381*
   XXXVI,191   174
Plutarch
Quaestiones
   Conviviales
   VI,1f   270
Polybius
Histories
   V,45.10-46.6   30
   V.62.2   31,34,53*

V,65.2f   30
V,66.1   30
V,67   30
V,67.6-10   52*
V,70   269
V,70.1f   53*
V,70f   30,106
V,71.11   31
V,86.10   31,160
V,87.1-7   31
V,87.6   32
XVI,18   136,271
XVI,18-19.39   53*
XXVIII,1   136
XXVIII,20   52*
Strabo
Geographica
   XII,2.9   161
   XVI,2.16   204*
   XVI,2.21   52*
   XVI,2.25   175
   XVI,2.34   299*

VIII. CHRISTIANS WRITERS

IX. PAPYRI

PCZ		59093	147*,151*,	PSI	
59003	29,147*,		204*,205*	324	204*
	201*	59094	205*	325	204*
59004	105,151*,	59341	53*	406	151*,177,204*
	201*,204*,207*	P Col Zen		554	171,201*,
59006	204*	2	51*,204*		204*
59011	201*	P Lond.		594	201*
59018	29,157,	1948	204*	624	204*
	158,171				
59075	151*	P Mich Zen		PTeb	
59076	151*,301*	3	53*	701	174

INDEX OF MODERN AUTHORS

KEDAR,J. Ch. 1, n. 19
KEE,H.C. Ch. 9, n. 51
KELLY.J.N.D. Ch. 9, n. 23
KENNARD,J. Ch. 6, nn. 27, 29
KILPATRICK,G. Ch. 9, n. 60
KINDLER,A. Ch. 4, nn. 68, 111
KINGDON,H.P. p. 238; Ch. 6, n. 95
KIPPENBERG,H. Ch. 7, nn. 24, 54, 56
KLAUSNER,J. p. 170; Ch. 1, 29; Ch. 5, n. 56
KLEIN,G. Ch. 9, n. 75
KLEIN,S. pp. 49, 167, 325; Ch. 2, nn. 37, 47, 52, 59; Ch. 3, n. 64; Ch. 4, n. 60; Ch. 5, nn. 51, 52; Ch. 6, n. 27; Ch. 7, n. 81; Ch. 8, n. 79; Ch. 9, n. 15
KLIJN,A.F.J. Ch. 9, nn. 22, 24, 25, 31, 32, 33, 42
KLINZING,G. Ch. 7, n. 59
KOHL,H. Ch. 4, n. 109
KOPP,C. Ch. 7, n. 37
KRAABEL,A.T. Ch. 4, n. 39
KRAUSS,S. p. 170; Ch. 5, nn. 16, 60, 78, 138; Ch. 8, n. 80
KREISSIG,H. pp. 221, 226; Ch. 5, nn. 91, 93, 130; Ch. 6, nn. 8, 21, 79
KUHN,K.G. Ch. 9, nn. 14, 18
KUMMEL,W. Ch. 9, n. 66
KUNDSIN,K. Ch. 9, nn. 78, 90
KUTSCHER,E.Y. p. 145; Ch. 4, n. 115

LAGRANGE,M.J. Ch. 5, n. 143
LAMARCHE,P. Ch. 9, n. 46
LANDAU,Y.H. Ch. 2, nn. 15, 31; Ch. 4, nn. 24, 95; Ch. 5, nn. 26, 27
LAPP,P.W. Ch. 7, n. 50
LAQUEUR,R. Ch. 3, n. 55; Ch. 6, n. 99
LAUNEY,M. Ch. 4, nn. 6, 87; Ch. 5, nn. 5, 94
LAUTERBACH,J.Z. (ed.) Ch. 7, n. 71; Ch. 8, n. 70
LeMOYNE,J. Ch. 7, n. 68
LEVICK,B. Ch. 5, n. 9
LICHTENSTEIN,H. Ch. 2, n. 45; Ch. 4, n. 28; Ch. 7, n. 68
LIEBERMAN,S. p. 348; Ch. 4, n. 97; Ch. 9, n. 17
LIEBESNY,H. Ch. 4, n. 94
LIFSHITZ,B. Ch. 4, nn. 97, 100, 102; Ch. 7, n. 21
LIGHTFOOT,R.H. Ch. 9, n. 39
LIMBECK,M. Ch. 8, n. 103
LINDNER,H. Ch. 7, n. 95
LINNEMANN,E. Ch. 8, n. 61
LIVER,J. p. 279; Ch. 7, nn. 65, 67, 69
LOFFREDA,S. Ch. 4, n. 112
LOFTUS,F. Ch. 6, nn. 13, 98
LOHMEYER,E. pp. 349, 352, 354, 357; Ch. 9, nn. 3, 8, 9, 13, 29, 43

SUBJECT INDEX

472

INDEX OF PEOPLE AND PLACES

490